ANYTHING YOU CAN IMAGINE

Also by Ian Nathan

Alien Vault: The Definitive Story Behind the Film

Ethan and Joel Coen (Masters of Cinema)

Terminator Vault: The Complete Story Behind the Making of
The Terminator and Terminator 2: Judgment Day

Assassin's Creed – Into the Animus

Inside the Magic: The Making of Fantastic Beasts
and Where to Find Them

Tim Burton: The Iconic Filmmaker and his Work

The Coen Brothers: The Iconic Filmmakers and their Work

ANYTHING YOU CAN IMAGINE

Peter Jackson and the Making of Middle-earth

IAN NATHAN

HarperCollins*Publishers*

For Kat, who can't abide hobbits.

HarperCollins*Publishers* Ltd
1 London Bridge Street,
London SE1 9GF

www.harpercollins.co.uk

First published by HarperCollins*Publishers* 2018

1

A catalogue record for this book is available
from the British Library

ISBN: 978-0-00-819247-1

Set in Celeste with Gill Sans display

Printed and bound in the UK by
CPI Group (UK) Ltd, Croydon CR0 4YY

Contents

'The artist-initiated epic is an obsessive testing of possibilities. . . It comes, too, from a conviction, or a hope, that if you give popular audiences the greatest you have in you they will respond.'

Pauline Kael

'It would be easier to film The Odyssey. Much less happens in it.'

J.R.R. Tolkien

Foreword

It feels like there was life before and life after.

I can remember the first time I saw Gollum. A finished Gollum. It was the sequence by the Forbidden Pool where he turns around to see Frodo, and he knows that something's going on. It's almost like an animal instinct; he can sense it. It was absolutely extraordinary.

You don't know, you could never know. Here, finally, was the first proof that a level of psychological and emotional detail could be conveyed through ones and noughts. That thought could be conveyed through the combination of my performance and what they were doing at Weta Digital. I could sense that thought. I could feel that was exactly as I played it. That was incredibly gratifying.

Then I remember seeing *The Two Towers* for the first time. It was in New York, I was with Miranda Otto, Bernard Hill and Karl Urban. It was mind blowing. I knew every single frame.

I sensed that my life was never going to be the same again.

I supposed that was true for everyone who shared in *The Lord of the Rings*. The actors, the crew, everyone. None of us really knew what we were letting ourselves in for. And we went through so much together. Filmmaking is life. Every day you're making a film is as important as the end result, because it feeds into the fabric of that film. That counts tenfold for *The Lord of the Rings*. That's what attracted me to go back and do so many projects with Peter, Fran and Philippa, and all those guys down there, because it is a way of life. You don't go to work; you're living and breathing it.

Nevertheless, it certainly wasn't the journey I was expecting for a second. Not for a second. Adding together both *The Lord of the Rings* and *The Hobbit,* I have celebrated seven different birthdays in New Zealand. The first one was literally only days after I arrived. We were up at Ruapehu, shooting Mount Doom. That was pretty cool. We were staying at the Powderhorn, which looked like an alpine chalet. It was lovely. They made me a cake. The most memorable one was when Pete gave me the Ring for my birthday and on the same day asked me to be in *King Kong*. That was on an Easter Sunday. Other ones came and went, in so many beautiful places.

I still feel deeply connected to New Zealand. The beauty there is almost overwhelming. I was very into the outdoor life, walking, hiking and kayaking whenever I could. The whole experience was very spiritual. That country, root and branch, mountain and valley, is the soul of the films.

Moreover, I also can't express how honest and open the people are. How much they made us part of their community and gave us such a good time. I made so many great friends.

So many people migrated there to take up jobs on *The Lord of the Rings*, it created a film industry there.

In the end, though, all roads lead back to Pete. And Fran and Philippa, of course. Pete is the most fearless director I've ever met. He has shared so much with me, taught me so much. I have said it often, but there is something truly maverick about him, an indie filmmaker working on the biggest scale possible. That's what it always felt like. We were shooting these personal little indie films. These extraordinary films are an expression of who a person is. Pete is also such a visionary, just breaking barriers all the time with this marriage of technology and artistry.

I remember the glint in his eye when I first met him, so many years ago, in London. I could sense, even then, his vision for Gollum; neither of us really knew what we were letting ourselves in for but it was definitely going to be an unexpected journey. After principal photography on *The Lord of the Rings* ended, Pete signed a poster for me, which said "Many thanks for all the fun... and the fun to come." It was then, and for the next decade, and hopefully always will be just that...

Andy Serkis

Journey's End

Monday, 1 December, 2003 was a typical summer's day in Wellington. The sun was doing its level best, but the eternal, maddening winds were already scuffling over the bay and muscling their way inshore to ruffle pennants and hairdos but never spirits. Not on this day.

The red carpet was less familiar but not unexpected. Over 500 feet of imitation velvet swerved up Courtenay Place to the doors of the Embassy Cinema, recently refurbished at a cost of $5 million to a fetching cream and caramel Art Deco scheme. One of the myriad cinematic gifts Peter Jackson had bestowed upon his hometown. Fittingly, fifteen years earlier, his debut film, *Bad Taste*, had premiered at the Embassy, albeit with less salubrious décor and a smaller turnout.

Less in keeping with the old movie-palace aesthetic was the cowled Nazgûl astride a fell beast that had landed on top of the cinema virtually overnight to take up silent watch over the day's festivities.

That full-size model, or maquette, with its great-scooped neck and outspread wings, sculpted by the imperious talents of Weta Workshop, still exists. Like so many Middle-earthian relics, it has been squirrelled away for posterity in one of Jackson's dusty warehouses, the Mines of Moria of the Upper Hutt Valley.

Jackson might have to still undertake the mandatory global press tour on behalf of his new film, with its procession of glad-handing and crowd waving, but he had been adamant that the official world premiere for *The Return of the King* was to be in Wellington, the city at the heart of the production. This was the victory lap for a filmmaking triumph that, even in his innermost fantasies, he could never have imagined, and he wanted to share the moment with the people who had contributed so much.

Naturally, it was to be a party of special magnificence.

The good folk of Wellington were beginning to line the streets, bringing picnics and an unusual air of excitement for such an imperturbable race. Some had even camped out overnight. It felt like a public holiday, or a homecoming parade. And in some senses that is exactly what it was. By the afternoon, over 125,000 locals were crammed ten rows deep on either side of the streets — quite something for a city with a population of 164,000 — their ranks swelled by out-of-towners (decreed honorary Wellingtonians for such an occasion), many wearing homespun wizard hats and Elf-ears, who had crammed themselves onto long-haul flights from every corner of the world just to be here on this day. You could hear the noise halfway to Wanganui.

Soon enough the stars and filmmakers would glide through the city, setting off from Parliament House on Lambton Quay in a fleet of Ford Mustang convertibles, soaking up the adoration of the crowd with a royal wave, flanked by Gondorian cavalry, enshrouded Nazgûl on stoic horses, pug-ugly Orcs hefting Weta-made swords, beefcake Uruk-hai, supermodel Elves, and dancing hobbits trying not to trip over their outsized feet. At their head, in deference to the country that had become Middle-earth, was an outlier of Māori warriors with florid tā moko tattoos and waggling tongues. They might as well have been another extraordinary tribe dreamed up in leafy Oxford, a million miles away, in the mind of a pipe-smoking don.

When Orlando Bloom wafted past accompanied by Liv Tyler, there was screaming of a kind that was once the preserve of Beatlemania. There exists a framed photo of the four young actors who played the heroic hobbits — Elijah Wood, Sean Astin, Billy Boyd and Dominic Monaghan — that they had made for Jackson's birthday. They are in their hobbit wigs, Shire garments and prosthetic feet, but playing instruments and posed exactly like John, Paul, George and Ringo. 'The Hobbits' is emblazoned on the bass drum. The Beatles are Jackson's favourite band, and had themselves once pondered making their own version of Tolkien's epic as a musical extravaganza.

New Line had reputedly spent millions on the last official world premiere of the film trilogy they had staked their future on. What an inspired decision that seemed now. Had any film in history received a welcome like this? Bob Shaye, the tall, graceful, slightly bohemian CEO of New Line, would sit alongside Jackson in the lead car, the man who had taken the chance on this young director. It hadn't been the easiest relationship. Hollywood's risk-averse mentality was not an ideal mix with the natural Kiwi courage to take on the odds. There would be further tensions to come. For now, Shaye and his partner Michael Lynne's gamble on the impossible book, which had seemed so foolhardy if not outright suicidal to their peers, had that shimmer of Hollywood history about it. That sense of divine obsession on which the movie industry was built, where for every *Gone with the Wind* there was a *Heaven's Gate*.

Figurative tickertape was raining down on Wellington; it was the stuff of dreams with the city's favourite son capturing it all on his video camera. He knew he would never remember it all, it would pass in a blur.

They had made it to the Moon and back again in filmmaking terms. *The Return of the King*, a fantasy epic, that laughably unsophisticated genre, would soon pick up eleven Oscar nominations. This was the culminating chapter in a staggering, and staggeringly successful, adaptation of J.R.R. Tolkien's *The Lord of the Rings*, considered for so long as impossible to capture on film.

Helen Clark, New Zealand's prime minister, the day's host, would give her thanks for all the films had brought to this country. Not only Hollywood dollars and employment — when the accounting was done the films would have utilised the talents of 23,000 Kiwis — but the tourism boom his trilogy of marvels had launched. With the help of a different world Jackson had put New Zealand onto the map.

How proud his country was of him, she said. How much she hoped his success would continue on into the future.

Jackson too would address the crowd, giving his thanks and saying how humble he felt that so many of them would turn out. He wasn't even an All Black.

Everyone would give speeches. Each roared on by the crowd. It was like a wedding or a coronation, with 2,500 specially invited guests. Only this time Viggo Mortensen wasn't expected to sing.

*

Earlier that day, amid the bustle of party business, with various planners and executives clamouring into walky-talkies and lumpen Nokias, Jackson had dutifully arrived on time at his allotted meeting point. Then, he hadn't had to travel far. His home in Seatoun was barely ten minutes away, twenty if you caught Wellington at rush hour when the tailbacks can stretch to as many as ten cars long.

Seatoun lies on the seaward side of the quiet Wellington suburb of the Miramar Peninsula that plays home to Jackson's filmmaking empire — studio, offices, post-production facilities, Weta Workshop, Weta Digital. Hollywood visitors still had trouble seeing past the corrugated iron roofs, brick warehouses, and general disrepair of the former paint factory on Stone Street. Outwardly, barring the immediate beauty of the landscape, everything here seemed so. . . Well, so *unlikely.*

How unlikely too that, in all their planning, no one had thought what to do with their director, the man who had made all this happen, while the final arrangements for the premiere were being made. So it was that Jackson had been guided to a perfectly nice hotel suite to wait in a celebrity holding pattern while the more rigorous demands of readying film stars for a public appearance took place elsewhere.

The memory still strikes Jackson as strange. 'I thought, well, that sounds nice. I thought there would be the actors, but it was just me, and they shut the door. And I was sitting in this hotel room for at least an hour and a half. I was lying there thinking, this is pretty weird. Why aren't we having a drink down in the bar?'

He was as nervous as anyone would be about to speak in front of hundreds of thousands of people. A drink, a laugh, simply passing the time with someone would have helped.

What might have struck him as strangest of all, however, was that he had been left to his own devices. As long as he stayed put, New Line's army of wedding planners weren't going to let their prize catch wriggle free. They virtually put him under lock and key. Gandalf imprisoned on the roof of Orthanc.

Only hours before, with the eleventh hour disappearing in the rear-view mirror, had he completed his adaptation of *The Lord of the Rings* trilogy. With a running time of three hours twenty-one minutes, long even by his own extended standards — and even then he knew that fans would bemoan the loss of lovely sequences that wouldn't be retrieved until the *Extended Edition* a year from now — *The Return of the King* was ready for its heroic debut. For the first time in five years, maybe longer, Jackson didn't need to worry about his films.

There was no need to approve any fresh artwork from the peerless and tireless pencils of John Howe or Alan Lee; or clear an effects shot, a music cue, a sound edit, a costume alteration, a set that had sprung up overnight, a mooted location or schedule, a poster design, or indeed head to the edit suite, because when all else was done he always needed to head to the edit. No actors would need to call upon his wisdom; no lighting set-up or shot trajectory was open for discussion. No stunt team needed marshalling. No new script pages needed to be wrestled into submission; as he no longer needed to fine-tune the sometimes-cumbersome complexities of Tolkien's world toward the dynamic world of cinema — to choose this path or that, often depending on which one smelled the better. Even those public relations folk, who had called upon him to speak to the press when he could least afford the time, were now busy elsewhere.

The constant background noise inherent in this awesome undertaking had finally been silenced — all he could hear was the crowd a few blocks away, cheering even the carpet sweepers.

Jackson was left alone with his thoughts.

He turned on the television and found a telemovie, whatever was playing. He can't remember what it was about let alone what it was called; he doubts it was any good.

Lying there on the bed, some cheesy, low-budget melodrama in the background, his mind must surely have wandered back through the forest of days, the miraculous events and unaccountable toil that had brought him here to this moment of triumph and farewell.

CHAPTER I

Sillification

In June 1958, John Ronald Reuel Tolkien put pen to paper. Without letting his scrupulous English manners slip, he still made his feelings quite clear. The story, he claimed, swelling in his indignation as the letter wound on, had been 'murdered'.

The year before, three American producers sounding not unlike a law firm from a film noir movie — Forrest J. Ackerman, Morton Grady Zimmerman and Al Brodax — had approached Tolkien's publishers, Allen & Unwin, proposing a feature film of *The Lord of the Rings*. Having decried the 'sillification achieved' by the BBC in a 1955, twelve-part radio serial based upon his epic, written and produced by the poet Terrence Tiller (a close friend of Tolkien admirer W.H. Auden) — since lost to the mists of BBC deletion — he couldn't see that dealing with a film version would be any less painful.

However, if not won over, he had begun to be persuaded that these filmmakers were at least responsive to the needs of the book. In the box of notes sent to the author's house in the Oxford suburb of Headington, the trio outlined an ambitious mix of live action and animation running to three hours, including two intermissions, with the aim of shooting among the untamed expanses of the American landscape. Tolkien had been especially impressed at the quality of the concept art. How unlike Walt Disney it was, he noted appreciatively.

A few weeks later, as he had begun to read the story treatment, his heart had sunk. He simply couldn't detect 'any appreciation for what it was about'. Gandalf does not 'splutter', he contended, the Balrog does not speak and Lothlórien does not have shiny minarets. All moral import had been lost. The entire tone was childish, more of a fairy tale. And his book was most certainly not a fairy tale. The treatment did, incidentally, include Tom Bombadil.

His response goes on for several pages. Each documenting a significant narrative failing in the laissez-faire approach Zimmerman, the nominal screenwriter, had taken with the original text.

Wizards can be quick to anger.

Such a maladroit effort, if not rank trivialisation of Tolkien's great adventure, is disappointing for fans of the genre. Not that the book wouldn't suffer an arduous journey through a litany of scrambled attempts before it would be done justice. It was more that one of the prospective producers was meant to have had a keen respect for fantasy fiction.

Ackerman is known as the godfather of geek. He had helped fashion the concept of the fan convention; arriving at the First World Science Fiction Convention in New York in 1939 clad in a 'futuristicostume', he effectively invented cosplay to boot. On a business footing, he served as agent for many of the great Fifties horror and science fiction writers whose imaginations were running rife beneath the shadow of the nuclear age (and the influence of Tolkien). Writers like Ray Bradbury, Marion Zimmer Bradley and Isaac Asimov, the latter of who would create the star-spanning *Foundation* trilogy.

In 1958, Ackerman began his lifelong tenure as editor of *Famous Monsters of Filmland*, a lavish, bustling monthly devoted to genre movies. Within its awe-struck pages were features celebrating *King Kong*, the 1933 classic, including the discovery of a fabled shot of a spider lurking on the cavern roof that fans had thought to be the stuff of myth. It also curated the kind of pun-heavy vernacular that saw the letters page christened 'Fang Mail'.

For Tolkien, used to the unhurried discussion of philological esoterica among collegiate friends and the woody scent of pipe smoke at *The Eagle and Child*, he may as well have been from Mars.

For Peter Jackson and those filmmaking peers who shared a taste for the fantastic and the macabre, kindred visionaries like Guillermo del Toro, *Fantastic Monsters of Filmland* would become a friend in the dark. Here was proof that there were likeminded, monster-mad souls everywhere. Without it they may never have discovered their calling. In his old office, the secret one behind the bookcase that contained his most prized memorabilia, Jackson had his collection of back issues proudly on display.

With a rakish, pencil-thin moustache, high forehead and large horn-rimmed glasses, Ackerman suggested Vincent Price playing an insurance salesman, and he would appear in many of his beloved B-movies. He also dabbled a little in film production. And, together with his partners, was the first recorded prospector to engage with Tolkien about a film version of his great work.

We should respect the fact that Ackerman was ahead of the curve. In 1958, *The Lord of the Rings* was only four years old. While selling respectably, it was a long way from the cult prominence that made it a fixture of late-1960s campuses across America. An unauthorised ACE paperback edition had wriggled through America's insubstantial copyright rules in 1965 and sold in phenomenal quantities. Indeed, by 1966 it was out-selling *The Catcher in the Rye* at Harvard. Students formed Tolkien societies, dressing up as their favourite characters and feasting on mushrooms. A scholarly lapel was naked without badges exclaiming 'Frodo Lives' or 'Gandalf for President'.

Once official editions were issued (through the paperback

imprint Ballantine Books) Tolkien would taste remarkable success. This in turn led to conspicuous quarters of the literary establishment scoffing at something they saw as childish. Among academics, to express affection for Tolkien was deemed as 'professional suicide'.

In 1956, in his sarcastic essay, '*Oo, Those Awful Orcs!*' Marxist critic Edmund Wilson called it 'balderdash'.

Decades on, Germaine Greer claimed that the book's popularity was like a 'bad dream'.

Tolkien had never expected to start, as he put it, a 'tide'. He only wrote the book for those who might like it.

Nevertheless, Frodo's quest to rid the world of a magical ring by tossing it back into the volcanic fires from which it was forged had touched readers around the world. By 1968, three million copies of *The Lord of the Rings* had been sold worldwide. A 1999 poll conducted by Amazon judged it to be the Book of the Millennium. By 2003, once again much to the chagrin of the literary establishment, and perhaps catching a tailwind from Jackson's films, a poll on behalf of the BBC's Big Read named it Britain's Favourite Read. According to recent calculations the book has sold upwards of 100 million copies.

Let us not tarry too long on the history of Tolkien and his literary genius. Reams have been written on the provenance of hobbits and the entirety of Middle-earth. Reams more will come. Born in Bloemfontein, South Africa in 1892, where his father died when he was three, he was raised by his mother in the bucolic Worcestershire village of Sarehole (since consumed by greater Birmingham). She would die when he was only twelve, leaving him and his brother, Hilary, orphans. An early fascination with ancient languages and their mythological roots would lead to his creating his own, and eventually to an Oxford professorship in English Language and Literature, a journey interrupted by enlistment and the First World War.

In the dreadful lulls between fighting on the Somme (where Jackson's grandfather also fought), and while recuperating from trench fever in Staffordshire, Tolkien began to conceive of the vastness of his fictional world, a world that would have its origins in the languages he had devised. He never felt he was writing fantasy but a form of history, a record that would reveal who might have spoken such words and where they might have lived. He saw his book as an attempt to recover a mythology for Britain, which lacked the equivalent lore to that of the Germanic, Nordic and Icelandic sagas he loved. Through a process he called 'sub-creation' grew a backdrop for his later books, a world of intricate construction: races, languages, myriad tales of wars and upheaval and a vast, vital geography against which it all played out.

'I always had the sense of recording what was already "there", somewhere, not of "inventing",' recalled Tolkien.

Philippa Boyens, who would work so closely with Jackson and Fran Walsh on the writing of the adaptation to come, always valued the 'wholeness' of Middle-earth. 'That you can escape into something that feels utterly real,' she says. 'I like that obsession. I like all the detail.'

Laughing, she recalls that whenever any questions from the cast or crew became too entangled in the brambles of Tolkien's mythos they were always fielded to Boyens as the trio's Tolkien nerd. She always impressed upon her fellow filmmakers how much underpinned the books.

'It's such an immersive thing, because as much as he delved into and loved those languages, he loved them because of their connection with who the British are as a people. And that profoundly affected him, and that probably has a lot to do with his childhood.'

Watching the encroachment of industry and the concomitant loss of a tradition; the stark impressions of the battlefront that stripped bare notions of class; the devotion to nature (especially trees); learning; fine company; a dignified, if antiquated properness in his relationship with women: all were ingredients in the wholeness of the book. But deeper still, in Tolkien's early loss of his parents, Boyens sees the loneliness of Frodo expelled from the childlike idyll of the Shire to venture into the adulthood of Middle-earth.

Composed first for his children, Tolkien would publish *The Hobbit* in 1937, a lighter, charming prelude to *The Lord of the Rings*, which would eventually follow in 1954. He never intended his second novel to be divided into three books, or considered a trilogy. This was a necessity brought on by soaring paper costs following the Second World War (another global conflict that overshadowed his writing). It was a single, epic story, over 1,000 pages in length, made up of more than half a million words.

His response to Ackerman and co. provides an insight into how the author generally perceived the idea of transforming his work into film entertainment.

Tolkien had visual sense. In among the treatment's atrocities, he could appreciate, 'A scene of gloom lit by a small red fire with the wraiths approaching as darker shadows.'

He revealed actorly qualities too. In the 1950s, disappointed by that 1955 BBC version, he recorded his own radio play *The Homecoming of Beorhtnoth, Beorhthelm's Son*, in the poem's full alliterative Anglo-Saxon metre. There is a little existing footage of him from a BBC documentary from 1968. He plays well to the camera: warm, curious and knowingly dotty, throwing in an occasional faraway look in his eye as he gazes off into the distance, perhaps to Middle-earth.

Even so, Tolkien didn't regard movies, or drama in general, as legitimate art. We are left to wonder if Sir Ian McKellen's wry Gandalf or Viggo Mortensen's robust Aragorn might have swayed him, but he considered the idea of acting to be a 'bogus magic'. It was pretending.

Nevertheless, as early as 1957 he had written to his publisher Stanley Unwin that he wasn't opposed to the idea of an animated version of the book — evidently having no faith that live action would stand up to the exotic creatures and fantastical locations therein. In another oft-quoted letter to his publisher, in his qualified way he even welcomed the idea.

'And that quite apart from the glint of money,' he added, 'though on the brink of retirement that is not an unpleasant possibility.'

He was no fool about the business.

Tolkien reasoned, with a foresight that would have made him more adept at dealing with Hollywood than his quiet, donnish persona would suggest, that he could either strike a deal through which he would lose control but be correspondingly compensated financially, or retain a degree of control but not the fiscal win.

'Cash or kudos,' he explained to his biographer Humphrey Carpenter.

With few signs of either cash *or* kudos emerging out of granting a six-month option to Ackerman and his associates, as the biography succinctly puts it, 'negotiations were not continued'.

*

From that enshrined afternoon when, bored by marking uninspired English papers in his Northmoor Road drawing room, Tolkien had turned over a sheet and quite from nowhere written the line 'In a hole in the ground there lived a hobbit' a river of events will flow and churn over the years toward a quiet backwater in New Zealand. Those of a mystical bent might call it fate.

But there was a long way to go yet.

Nigh on a decade had passed when, in 1967, Tolkien was approached for a second time about the film rights, this time for both *The Hobbit* and *The Lord of the Rings*.

While he welcomed the financial security the popularity of the novel had granted him, Tolkien had grown guarded if not threatened by the side effects of his success. He had no interest in fame and its attendant adulation. Especially wearisome were those fans who arrived on his doorstep uninvited with all their infernal questions, which he patiently endeavoured to answer. He took to setting an alarm clock in another room. When it rang, he politely claimed this signalled another appointment. Unwisely still to be found in the Oxford telephone directory, he would get calls deep into the night from faraway readers with a poor grasp of time-zone differences.

When United Artists came to him with this new offer, he may have seen it as a chance to deflect attention. Now seventy-five, and lacking the energy to deal with another adaptation he was always going to find fault with, he most likely wanted to wash his hands of the whole business. He could use the money to establish a trust fund for his grandchildren's education. So he agreed to part with the filmmaking rights *in perpetuity* to both books for what now looks like a parsimonious £104,000.

It was a remarkably generous contract. To paraphrase the pertinent details: 'Filmmakers had the right to add to or subtract from the work or any part thereof. They had the right to make sequels to, new versions, and adaptations of the work or any part thereof. To use any part or parts of the work or the theme thereof, or any instance, character, characteristics, scenes, sequences or characters therein. . .'

In other words, the studio was legally entitled to do just about anything it wanted with the books. It remains entirely permissible for the current rights holder to devise a sequel to Frodo's journey.

Six years later, in 1973, Tolkien would pass away without having seen a single frame of his work on screen.

UA, as it was known, certainly in Hollywood, seemed a suitable berth for Tolkien's books. Proudly founded in 1919 by the collective of actors Charlie Chaplin, Mary Pickford, Douglas Fairbanks and, granddaddy of the movie epic, director D.W. Griffith, it was an attempt by the artists to control the means of production. To resolve, they hoped, the eternal 'art versus business' conflict that had dogged, and goes on dogging, the film business from its very inception. A similar philosophy would later underpin Jackson's filmmaking collective.

UA stutteringly lived up to its billing. While the great dream of artists at the wheel would falter — they were too busy acting and directing to find time to steer a film company — and the company would gradually be run along more traditional Hollywood models, it nevertheless endeavoured to maintain a veneer of artistic intent.

Among its library of adaptations are definitive versions of *Wuthering Heights*, *Of Mice and Men*, *Around the World in 80 Days*, *West Side Story*, the *James Bond* movies (cherished by Jackson), *Midnight Cowboy*, *Fiddler on the Roof* and *One Flew Over The Cuckoo's Nest*. The latter produced by Saul Zaentz, who will prove significant.

Former head of production at UA, Steven Bach, who tells his fateful tale of Hollywood hubris and artistic ambition run amok during the making of *Heaven's Gate* in the book *Final Cut*, reports that from the time they made the deal with Tolkien those rights languished for a further decade. They just couldn't find a way, or at least a way they considered commercially viable.

Eminent playwright Peter Shaffer (who wrote the stage play of *Amadeus*) had written what Bach considered an elegant script for a single film version, but it never gained momentum.

In 1969, the English director John Boorman was a hot property. Born in London's studio suburb of Shepperton, the debonair former documentary maker had made an instant impact with the gritty, modernist Lee Marvin thriller *Point Blank*, and a brutish tale of duelling Second World War veterans in *Hell in the Pacific*. His films, thus far, were steely and masculine, but with a touch of the metaphysical at their fringes.

Filled with the zest and fearlessness of youth, and considerable talent with which to wield it, he had approached UA with the ambition of creating an epic out of the Grail legend and King Arthur.

'Well, we have *The Lord of the Rings*, why don't you do that?' they replied.

Boorman embraced the challenge put before him and over six months, squirrelled away at his tumbledown rectory in County Wicklow, he and co-writer Rospo Pallenberg conjured up something dizzyingly strange and knowingly sacrilegious. The finished 176 pages[*] shatter much of the book's grandiosity.

Boorman had a taste for the lusty and pagan, and while Tolkien may have admired his evocation of nature (Boorman would go on to make *The Emerald Forest*) he would have been appalled by all the sex. Before he is ready to look into her mirror, Galadriel seduces Frodo, informing him, 'I am that knowledge.' Boorman is dragging chaste Tolkien towards puberty, but completely over-compensates: Aragorn revives Éowyn with a magical orgasm, and even plants a hearty kiss upon Boromir's lips at one point. The director also gets carried away with the book's reputation as a hippy totem. Wild flowers are a chronic leitmotif, and the Council of Elrond turns into a Felliniesque circus performance with dancers, jugglers and a lively dog that symbolizes fate. To read it all is to be mildly disturbed yet mesmerized. . .

Gone are hobbit holes, Bree and Helm's Deep. Gimli opens the doors to Moria with a jig, while Merry and Pippin are played as a Halfling Laurel and Hardy. There is much cavorting and way too much singing. Sillification lies perilously close. But there are some striking inventions, such as the Fellowship discovering they are walking across the bodies of slumbering Orcs in Moria. And Boorman goes some way toward taming the book's gigantic architecture into a single, three-hour film.

UA didn't understand a word of it.

During his seclusion, there had been a major reshuffle at the studio. The script, which had cost $3 million to develop, was tossed out. Boorman later claimed such shortsightedness mainly came from the fact that, 'No one else had read the book.'

Boorman is too rich a filmmaker to dismiss outright what might have been, however provocative and untamed. After briefly attempting to keep his live-action vision alive at Disney, he would channel much of the effort he put into *The Lord of*

---

[*] It is generally held that one page of script equates to one minute of screen time.

the Rings back into the Arthurian legend with the altogether splendid — and altogether grown-up — *Excalibur*. Bursting with Boorman's visual exuberance, it is earthy, witty, fantastical (at times surreally so) and highly libidinous. It is also an 'absolute favourite' of Jackson's — he has Mordred's golden armour (made from aluminium) in his collection. Visually, it would have a huge influence on him as director and, coming full circle, on the sensibility he would give to *The Lord of the Rings*: the exotic contours of the armour; the scabrous weaponry; the mossy, lyrical Irish landscapes. It has the heft of the real.

Nicol Williamson's whimsical, meddling Merlin has more than a touch of Gandalf about him.

Jackson has never had the opportunity to meet Boorman, who at 84 still lives in rural Ireland, but his manager Ken Kamins once represented the English director and has stayed in contact.

'John sent a nice note through Ken once,' recalls Jackson, 'saying that he loved *The Lord of the Rings*, and he was very happy that I got to make it.'

Boorman has gone on record saying how grateful he is that he *didn't* get to make his film. That may have prevented the project from ever passing to Jackson, whose trilogy he thought was a marvel akin to the construction of the great cathedrals of medieval Europe. There was something secret and vast about the films, a work of almost divine providence.

Then there was the tale of the Beatles. How the Fab Four, at the height of their own impossible fame, had sought out the great Stanley Kubrick at his St. Albans estate to help create a multimedia musical of *The Lord of the Rings* in which they would star and, naturally, provide a backbeat.

Testament to Jackson's lifelong passion for the Beatles can be found in the vision of a homemade cut out of the Sergeant Pepper-era foursome found in the sky blue, wheelchair-enabled Ford Anglia in *Bad Taste*. Jackson had wanted to spot Beatles songs throughout the score, but the rights were far beyond his debut film's paltry budget.

One of the unforeseen spoils of his success would be a chance to meet a genuine hero. When Jackson encountered Paul McCartney at the Oscars following *The Return of the King*'s glorious haul of trophies there must have been a thousand questions stored away in his head, but he 'pinned him down' about that story of a Tolkien adaptation.

Like Boorman, McCartney had praised Jackson's interpretation of Tolkien's book. He was a huge fan of the films. Each Christmas, as was the habit of many families, he would make a ritual outing with his kids to catch the next instalment. Quite how McCartney, one of the most famous faces on the planet, managed to frequent what sounded like his local multiplex so casually raises a sceptical Jackson eyebrow. The director suspects the pop icon probably found other means of seeing the films, but the compliments were sincere. And now he had McCartney's undivided attention, he decided to see if there was any truth to the Beatles' attempt to bring their youthful brio to Middle-earth?

It was true, said McCartney. The band had been on the third film of a three-picture deal with UA. The deal had thus far proved fruitful with the success of *A Hard Day's Night* and *Help!*. Considering where to go next, and having collectively read the book, *The Lord of the Rings* seemed a perfectly sensible avenue for the band. It was John Lennon who was spearheading the concept.

'Paul was going to play Frodo, George was going to play Gandalf, John was Gollum, and Ringo was Sam, I think,' Jackson can't help but chuckle. 'And he said that they all showed up at Stanley Kubrick's house to try and persuade him to be the director. I would love to have been a fly on the wall for that.'

During his lengthier dalliance with a potential adaptation, Boorman had wondered if he might cast the Beatles as the hobbits.

Kubrick, with four Liverpudlian superstars standing on his doorstop uninvited, did the decent thing and asked them in for tea. He listened to their offer, was very polite, but admitted it wasn't for him. He was in the middle of planning a colossal life of Napoleon, which would eventually be scuppered when MGM decided that epics were no longer commercial.

'Did you try another director?' Jackson asked. There was also talk that Lennon was going to approach David Lean next.

'No, Tolkien killed it,' McCartney replied. The author's mis-givings were never given, but can perhaps be assumed.

According to UA, it was Yoko Ono. The Beatles split a year later.

*

So it wasn't Kubrick or Boorman or the Beatles, or even Walt Disney — rumoured to have craved the rights in the sixties, only to be met with Tolkien's disdain for his pretty fairy-tales — who first brought the book to the big screen. Instead, it was a maver-ick animator named Ralph Bakshi, an artist determined to rattle convention. That is except when it came to *The Lord of the Rings*, which he treated almost as Holy Writ. However, the flawed results still spoke more about the titanic complexity involved in both bringing the book under control and getting Hollywood to grasp its potential.

While he had loved Disney, the grown-up Jewish street kid who once fished comic books out of dumpsters, set himself the task of tearing down the fairy-tale edifice of *Snow White and the Seven Dwarves* and the parade of pearly classics that followed. He had learned his trade on children's cartoons like *Deputy Dawg, Mighty Mouse* and the 1967 *Spider-Man* TV series, but he hungered to take animation into adult realms. Offbeat, darkly funny and controversy courting films of the 1970s like *Heavy Traffic, Coonskin* and America's first X-rated cartoon, the cult favourite *Fritz the Cat*. When it came to fantasy, he showed pedigree. The impressive *Wizards* is set in a post-apocalyptic future where the powers of magic and technology battle for supremacy — it's elves versus tanks — which Bakshi insisted was an allegory for the creation of the state of Israel. It is a film Jackson much admires.

An avid science-fiction reader, the curly-haired, Slavic-featured Bakshi had cherished the idea of transforming *The Lord of the Rings* into an animated epic since the fifties. He was convinced he had an understanding of Tolkien that outweighed any other suitor. Learning that Boorman and UA were attempting to condense its three books into a single film, he declared it to be madness.

'Or certainly a lack of character on Boorman's part,' he added sniffily. 'Why would you tamper with anything Tolkien did?'

With Boorman's version slain, he approached UA with his own offer to adapt what the studio was beginning to suspect was unadaptable. It should be an animated film made in three parts, he informed them. They had offered him Boorman's script to read, but he wasn't interested. Bakshi would begin again from scratch and, aside from a few necessary nips and tucks, remain faithful to Tolkien's quest.

In a vivid picture of Hollywood dealing at its most wilfully entangled, with UA unconvinced by his overtures the head-strong Bakshi decided MGM would be a much better fit for both him and Tolkien. A fact that occurred to him in part because they were literally down the hallway. Since its heyday, UA's West Coast operations had occupied a wing of MGM's Irving Thalberg Building in Culver City. Dan Melnick, head of production at MGM, was a man he knew had actually read *The Lord of the Rings*. Melnick would surely have a grasp on the potential of his project. He was right. Melnick paid back UA's $3 million outlay on Boorman's script, and the deal was struck. MGM would make the film, UA distribute it.

UA were evidently relieved to wash their hands of Middle-earth making. Bakshi and MGM were welcome to the meadows of the Shire, Rivendell, Rohan, enchanted Lothlórien, sulphur-ous Mordor and all those other bafflingly named locations that poured incessantly out of that accursed book.

Except Hollywood is more than a match for Middle-earth when it comes to internecine warfare and figuratively hurling heads over the battlements. Within weeks, MGM had gone through a violent takeover, changing ownership, firing Melnick and delivering the news that 'they weren't going to make that fucking picture' to Bakshi.

Here the tale takes a significant turn. The unflagging animator turned to another friend, onetime music mogul turned movie producer Saul Zaentz, whose relatively small investment into *Fritz the Cat* had paid off nicely. The titillating tale of a tomcatting tomcat had made $90 million around the world.

Fiercely independent, and like Bakshi of East Coast Jewish immigrant stock, Zaentz had come from a music industry background and held no truck with the rigmarole of studio politics. What he did have a taste for was the grandeur of the 'important' literary adaption. Through his company Fantasy Films (named for the jazz label Fantasy Records he joined in 1955 rather than anything heroic), Zaentz had invested some of his *Fritz the Cat* rewards into *One Flew Over the Cuckoo's Nest*, which was nominated for nine Oscars (including one for Brad Dourif, Wormtongue to come, as Best Supporting Actor), winning five, including Best Picture. Something he would repeat with an adaption of Peter Shaffer's *Amadeus* and, pertinently, *The English Patient*.

Stout and bearded, with a high domed forehead and glasses like window panes, Zaentz came with ironclad convictions, especially about art, and could spin from charm to confrontation mid-sentence. Once described as a 'buccaneer', he was a deft and deadly dealmaker.

In 1976, spying an opportunity, Zaentz readily agreed to back Bakshi's film.

With their hands full with the ensuing calamity of *Heaven's Gate* (currently grinding through its monumental production in Montana, overschedule, overbudget and by 1981 a flop of such epic proportions it effectively destroyed the studio — a warning to any who dared let the inmates run the asylum), UA relinquished the rights to Zaentz for $3 million. Through his newly fashioned Middle-earth Enterprises, Zaentz now retained the film, stage and game rights to *The Lord of the Rings* and *The Hobbit* as per Tolkien's original agreement *in perpetuity*. The Tolkien Estate retained all literary rights.

In an absurd hangover from the project's brief tenancy at MGM, which would have a huge bearing in the future, the rights to *make* a filmed version of *The Hobbit* remained with the studio. The rights to *distribute* such a film were now the preserve of Saul Zaentz.

Reconsidering his version as two films — Zaentz's financial largesse went only so far — Bakshi still intended to embrace the volume of Tolkien's book, capturing the scope and violence of Middle-earth. He felt children would want to be scared, and adults appreciate the sophistication of Tolkien as seen through his eyes.

As was his wont, Bakshi's approach was far from traditional. For the heft of the world, the ranks of Orcs and men, he pursued a technique known as rotoscoping. In simple terms the animator traced over live footage for added realism. Live-action scenes of extras made up with animal horns, teeth and dressed in furs as Orcs and Nordic-looking riders were shot on the plains of La Mancha in Spain before animation began (Belmonte Castle stands in for Helm's Deep). While static, the heavy, inky backgrounds have the gothic imprimateur of Gustave Doré woodcuts. Slashed with brushstrokes, the intensity of Bakshi's apocalyptic imagery can be hard to shake.

In the portrayal of evil he revealed his grasp of Tolkien. The Nazgûl snuffle like bloodhounds, their limbs convulsing in their drug-like craving for the Ring. The interpretation of an alien-looking Gollum, voiced with an unforgettable toddler's wail by the English actor Peter Woodthorpe was, until Andy Serkis coughed up his hairball performance, definitive.

But Bakshi would later wail that he had been under intense pressure over time and budget (estimated at $8 million). He was forced to cut corners, compromise his vision. The clichéd foreground figures are often no better than Hanna-Barbera cartoons:

Frodo, Merry and Pippin are virtually identical; Sam looks like a melted gnome; and the Balrog is a laughable bat-lion hybrid. The script by Chris Conkling and fantasy author Peter S. Beagle (who had written an introduction to an American edition of the book) is faithful but abbreviated. Frodo sets forth with the Ring with barely a summary of what is before him, the film chalking off the major pieces at an unseemly gallop before it all grinds to a confusing halt after The Battle of Helm's Deep, awaiting a sequel that would never come.

Perhaps Bakshi should have been forewarned of growing indifference when the studio removed any mention that this was *Part One* of two films, which only contributed to the general confusion. The $30 million his film made around the world was deemed insufficient reward by Zaentz and UA and the sequel was postponed forever.[*]

'I was screaming, and it was like screaming into the wind,' lamented Bakshi. 'It's only because nobody ever understood the material. It was a very sad thing for me. I was very proud to have done *Part One*.'

Was the book impossible to adapt? The sheer size of it could have filled out a mini-series. This was *War and Peace* set in a mythological universe. Scale was an issue on many levels for a live-action version. The lead characters, though fully grown, stood four foot tall at most. There was a host of exotic creatures: Orcs, trolls, mûmakil — elephants on growth hormone — giant eagles, Ringwraiths, grouchy arboreal shepherds called Ents, and fell beasts like winged dinosaurs. Then there was Gollum, who was less part of the peregrine biosphere than a fully rounded

---

[*] Unabashed, American animation partners Rankin & Bass would pick over the corpse of Bakshi's dreams and continue their quest to render Tolkien as fearsome as *The Care Bears Movie* with a 1980 television version of *The Return of the King* made to the same twee recipe as their misbegotten version of *The Hobbit* (see Chapter 17). The lack of preceding films is covered by a framing device that has Frodo recall the events of book three at Bilbo's 129th birthday celebrations in Rivendell.

character, arguably Tolkien's most vivid creation. And what of those battles, swarming with untold armies? Sergei Bondarchuk's 100,000-strong 1966 adaptation of *War and Peace* had the Red Army at its disposal.

If animation was the only realistic approach, it almost inevitably reduced Tolkien's grandeur to something childish.

Bakshi would have his part to play. In 1978, the seventeen-year-old Jackson raced into Wellington after school to catch the New Yorker's animated vision. Spectacled, permanently wrapped in a duffle coast and movie mad, he wasn't any kind of serious Tolkien fan but he was obsessed with fantasy. Like so many who saw it, parts impressed him but he left baffled. Was there to be another film?

'My memory of the movie is that it was good until about halfway through then it got kind of incoherent,' he says. 'I hadn't read the book at that stage so I didn't know what the hell was going on. But it did inspire me to read the book.'

Weeks later, due to attend a training course in Auckland before commencing his apprenticeship as a photoengraver, Jackson paused at the concourse bookshop to pick up some reading matter to fill the twelve-hour train journey. There he spotted a movie tie-in edition of *The Lord of the Rings*.

'It was the paperback with the Bakshi Ringwraiths on the front. That was my first copy of the book.'

He still has it somewhere.

'In some respects if I hadn't seen his movie I might not have read the book, and may or may not have made the film. . .'

*

In 1996, Jackson's career was going places. Quite literally: he had made it to the Sitges Film Festival, thirty-five miles southwest of Barcelona. In a satisfying sign that his reputation as a filmmaker was reaching beyond the shores of New Zealand, the annual jamboree devoted to fantasy cinema had invited him to screen his new film, a zombie comedy (or zomcom) called *Braindead*. Back home, after three peculiar horror films, he was still regarded warily by the establishment.

'You've got to understand that, until *Heavenly Creatures*, he was an embarrassment in New Zealand. He wasn't someone to celebrate,' says Costa Botes, a friend and frequent collaborator through the early days. 'Because of the films he was making there were certain factions of the industry actively gunning for him.'

Not a natural explorer, Jackson had been reluctant to go. He was persuaded when he saw the guest list. Here was an opportunity to meet some of his heroes in the flesh. Talents who had helped shape him as a filmmaker like Rick Baker, the genius make-up effects specialist feted for the still-extraordinary werewolf transformation in *An American Werewolf in London*. Or Freddie Francis, the cinematographer who had created the ghoulish, sweet-wrapper hues of the Hammer Horror movies (that cherry red blood that ran down Christopher Lee's chin). Or Stuart Freeborn, the English make-up artist who had helped design Yoda. Or Tobe Hooper, the young director who had shocked the establishment with his debut horror movie *The Texas Chain Saw Massacre*.

'At that time Tobe Hooper and I looked quite similar,' recalls Jackson. 'Dark, shaggy hair and beards. And Stuart Freeborn couldn't figure out who was who. I would go down to breakfast, and Stuart would go, "Hello Tobe." And I would just go, "Hi Stuart." I didn't even bother to correct him. It was kind of fun, there was all these interesting characters. That was the only time I ever met Wes Craven.'

Craven was the horror maven who began the Freddy Krueger phenomenon with *A Nightmare on Elm Street* at New Line.

Grouped in the same hotel, guests would congregate for breakfast and dinner, guaranteed to find an available seat alongside a fellow traveller. Jackson and Fran Walsh instantly bonded with Rick and Silvia Baker. They would head out for walks along the cliff-top where the views of the Mediterranean were stunning.

'But there was this really pushy American guy who would tag

along with us,' says Jackson. 'We'd be literally heading out the
door and he would be there: "Do you mind if I come too?"'

Naturally, there were a lot of fans around, begging signatures
and photos, proof that they had met their heroes (or heroes
to come).

'We got to the point where we wanted to sneak out of the
hotel and not have this guy follow us. I didn't know who the hell
he was.'

Then one afternoon he asked if they were coming to see
his film.

'Oh, you've got a film?' said Jackson, taken aback. 'You're not
a fan?'

'Yeah, yeah, yeah,' he replied, the words rattling out of his
mouth like winning coins from a slot machine. 'I've got a film!
It's called *Reservoir Dogs*.'

Twenty-five years later, Jackson howls with laughter. 'It was
Quentin Tarantino. . . I remember that when it got to the ear-
cutting scene, Wes Craven stood up and walked out because he
couldn't handle it. And Quentin was saying, "This is the greatest
thing in the world, Wes Craven walked out of *my* movie."'

Reservoir Dogs would be picked up for distribution by a small
American indie, Miramax, named after the owners' mother and
father, where this Angelino video-store clerk turned frenetic,
inspired, outrageously brilliant filmmaker would be nursed
toward greatness. That same company would swoop for Jackson
as well in the not-too-distant future.

Also on the list of that year's festival was Bakshi.

They didn't socialise. Bakshi showed no interest in that side of
things, remaining aloof from the gaggle of eager filmmakers, his
career in the doldrums by the early 1990s. Maybe it was because
he was more distant than the others that Jackson requested a
picture with the director of *The Lord of the Rings*. It wasn't something he asked of anyone else — he was a peer now not a fan.

'He didn't have a clue who I was.'

Years later, he would. However, unlike Boorman and

McCartney's gracious approval, Bakshi responded to Jackson's success with indignation. Why hadn't he been sought out for the benefit of his wisdom? Asked to be involved? He turned bitter in interview whenever Jackson's films were brought up. Some wounds never heal.

'I heard reports that they were screening it every single day at Fine Line,' he smarted, erroneously citing New Line's arthouse division as having been voraciously cribbing from his film. Which wasn't true anywhere in New Line.

Jackson remains perplexed that there should be any ill will between them. 'I've read those interviews with him and he is incredibly angry. These really bizarre interviews where he said, "I'm insulted that Peter Jackson never consulted me, because I am the only other guy that had done *The Lord of the Rings* and he didn't give me the courtesy of talking to me." Why would I do that? What was there to gain from it? It was odd. I can't even understand it from his point of view. Why would I need to speak to the guy who made a cartoon version of it? And conversely why would he expect me to?'

Maybe it was simply envy: he got to finish the story.

'I know,' says Jackson not unkindly.

It was also while in Sitges that he and Walsh heard that the New Zealand film commission had finally agreed to finance *Heavenly Creatures*. And *Heavenly Creatures* is where everything changed.

*

New Zealand first heard the infant cries of Sir Peter Robert Jackson on 31 October 1961 — Halloween, no less — in Pukerua Bay, a sleepy coastal town frozen in the 1950s some twenty miles north of Wellington. His doting parents, Joan and William 'Bill' Jackson, by every account delightfully forbearing towards the whimsical pursuits of aspirant filmmakers, were first-generation New Zealanders, emigrating from England in 1950.

Pukerua Bay offered an embryonic Oscar-winning filmmaker

few outlets for his furtive, restless imagination. He forwent uni-versity, film school was unimaginable, and after some aborted attempts to involve himself in the New Zealand film community, he began his professional career working as a photoengraver for the *Evening Post* in Wellington.

According to legend, the biggest inspiration to Jackson and on his determination to become a filmmaker (if not yet a director) was encountering Merian C. Cooper's and Ernest B. Schoedsack's 1933 *King Kong* at the tender age of nine on the household's humble black and white television. It was late to be up, nine o'clock, but he was enraptured by the wonder of it all: this tale of a giant ape on a lost island that also happened to be populated by dinosaurs, who was then captured and brought to New York — Eighth Wonder of the World! And how he perishes, plunging from the Empire State Building. For Jackson, changed forever, it was everything an adventure story should be.

To gain a measure of how much *King Kong* means to Peter Jackson, leap forward to December 1976, about the time Bakshi began half-making *The Lord of the Rings*. At seven o'clock on a sleepy Friday morning, the fifteen-year-old Jackson had caught the first train into Wellington worrying over the length of the queue that would be forming outside the King's Theatre cinema on Courtney Place.

He was there for the first showing of the remake of *King Kong*, a production he'd been following for months in the pages of *Famous Monsters of Filmland*. But the cinema was still locked up and Courtney Place was as deserted as it would one day throng with delighted thousands as Jackson made his lap of honour in an unforeseeable future.

'I kind of bought into the hype,' he laughs — that boy was such a dreamer. 'I convinced myself there would be crowds and crowds of people. There weren't. And, like most people, I was disappointed by it.'

The film is a wreck. Big-talking mini-mogul Dino De Laurentiis, cut from similar cloth to Saul Zaentz, had boasted of using a

forty-foot robotic gorilla that could scale buildings, but the technology had failed him and its motion was never captured. In the
finished film it is Rick Baker in a suit. The modern setting, the
absence of dinosaurs, the flat, un-wonderful ambience generated
by journeyman director John Guillermin (*The Towering Inferno*)
bespoke of all that could fail in a film.

The disappointment of the *King Kong* remake would teach
Jackson a valuable lesson, and he saw it six times. You must
never forget that fifteen-year-old, too early, waiting in the cold.

The presence of Kong would cast a huge shadow over Jackson's
career, but even having finally made his own spectacular remake
in 2005 (another long, wending, troubled journey to the screen),
it is to *The Lord of the Rings* the fifteen-year-olds of all ages and
sexes came back again and again, breathless in anticipation.

It was actually the year before he first saw *King Kong* that
an eight-year-old Jackson began shooting films. With a growing
interest in special effects already stirred by a steady diet of
Thunderbirds, television's *Batman* and the epochal moment
his neighbour Jean Watson, who worked at Kodak, gave him
a Super-8 camera, he also looked upon *King Kong* as much as
a technical triumph as an emotional journey.

'A year after we met, he showed me a Bond parody called
Coldfinger that he'd made when he was fifteen or sixteen,'
remembers Botes. 'He'd copied the editing of *On Her Majesty's
Secret Service.* And he played James Bond himself. I thought,
"This is uncanny — he actually looks like Sean Connery."'

Jackson built a filmmaking career with his own hands. A fleet
of homemade shorts, inspired by his love of *King Kong*, Ray
Harryhausen and James Bond, would grow (or perhaps the word
is mutate) into his first feature film — *Bad Taste.*

Made in fits and starts over four years, and because of day jobs,
only on Sundays, *Bad Taste* began life as the short, *Roast of the
Day* (the powerful tale of an aid worker encountering cannibal
psychos in deepest Pukerua), and slowly sprouted into a feature
film. Doffing a windblown forelock toward Sam Raimi's *The*

Evil Dead, Jackson's unhinged tale of a group of aliens plotting to turn humanity into fast food, would be a test of his native ingenuity and fortitude to rival that of *The Lord of the Rings*.

Roping in friends and colleagues from *The Evening Post*, cast and crew came and went over the ensuing years, written out then written back in again, Jackson more or less making it up as he went along. His parents provided the $2,500 to buy a 16mm Bolex camera. Everything else — prosthetics, special effects, Steadicam rig, props, alien vomit, stunts, acting — was homemade.

At one stage, Jackson, in the prominent role of the nitwit alien investigator Derek, would dangle himself upside down over a local cliff, a rope tied around his ankle the other end attached to a wooden post. Health and safety were for those who could afford them. He only hoped his friends would pull him back up again. If that post hadn't held, *The Lord of the Rings* may linger to this day unmade.

'It crushed all the nerves in my foot,' he laughs; 'it took about six months for the sensitivity to come back.' Which might account for his nonchalance toward going barefoot on the roughest terrain.

Halfway through, they all went to see Robert Zemeckis' thriller *Romancing the Stone*, then almost killed themselves replicating the sequence where Michael Douglas plunges downslope through the bushes.

Eight years later Jackson would be working with Zemeckis.

There were also times it tested Jackson's emotional reserves. One Sunday, dropped off on location by his parents with all the props and costumes, no one else showed up. He just sat there all day. When his parents came to collect him at 5 p.m., he was close to tears. It was a lonely lesson in always working with people you could depend on.

Bad Taste would be his film school. And a film would emerge, half-crazed but hilarious, gurgling with its own outrageous pleasure at the raw act of creation. Following another arduous test of his patience, it would find distribution and stir up a cult following that exists to this day, hanging on to the hope that Jackson will eventually make good on his promise to make a sequel or two.

Significant to this tale were two key friendships that Jackson formed because of his *Bad Taste*. Richard Taylor, who along with his wife Tania was making puppets for a satirical *Spitting Image*-style New Zealand television show called *Public Eye*, had heard about this guy out in Pukerua Bay who was making a sci-fi splatter movie in his basement. 'We really wanted to meet him. It turned out that his sci-fi movie was called *Bad Taste*. He was baking foam latex in his mum's oven.'

Taylor would join forces with Jackson on his very next film, and begin his own journey toward *The Lord of the Rings*.

And this was when Jackson first met Fran Walsh. To be exact, he first saw Walsh on the set of the series *Worzel Gummidge Down Under*, the television offshoot about a talking scarecrow, for which he had been hired to do a few little special effects. She was one of the writers, but they hadn't spoken. Then out of the blue Botes asked if he could show the unfinished *Bad Taste* to a couple of his screenwriter friends, he thought would appreciate it. They happened to be Walsh and her then boyfriend Stephen Sinclair. Walsh remembered being bowled over by how uninhibited the film was, and on zero budget.

She would volunteer her services to help complete the film, and would become not only the most important creative partner in Jackson's life but the story of this book.

Completing *Bad Taste*, says Taylor, 'Peter was bitten by the bug.' Up until then he had thought he might get by in special effects. In New Zealand the thought that you could follow a career as a director was preposterous. But the response to *Bad Taste* was so powerful that it convinced Jackson this was his calling.

Jackson also committed himself to gore, and ruffling the strait-laced New Zealand film community. In 1989 came depraved puppet musical *Meet The Feebles* (shot in a rat-infested ware-house) followed in 1992, after a salutary false start, by *Braindead*, his blood-bolstered, period zomcom. The film that would take him to America — if only for a visit.

A career had been born in a deluge of sheep brains, farting hippos and a zombie baby named Selwyn. Middle-earth was another world.

'When he finally made enough money to move into town,' remembers Taylor, 'it was into the tiniest house in Wellington. He bought the biggest television I have ever seen and we'd sit in his front room, dwarfed by this gigantic thing. When you stood up to make a cup of tea, there'd be half a dozen people out on the pavement, standing there watching the movie!'

*

There is one other adaption of *The Lord of the Rings* we have yet to mention. Indeed, it was the most comprehensive and meaningful adaption to date, one that is still held in the highest esteem by fans. It was also the only version of the book to provide any objective lessons — apart from what *not* to do — in how to successfully dramatize Tolkien, even though there was not a single frame to be seen.

This was, of course, the 1981 BBC radio serialization. Adapted by Brian Sibley and Michael Bakewell with a fine-edged scalpel, trimming great swathes of the book without any discernible loss of the central story (it still runs to a considerable eighteen hours). They also retained a good deal of Tolkien's dialogue, while carefully negotiating the demands of radio dramatization. Events that are reported in the book are transformed into first-hand scenes (a trick Jackson and his writers would apply). Even the battle scenes, inevitably reduced by the medium, have a dense, breathy, clanging atmosphere. All of it eased onward through the addition of a narrator (Gerard Murphy).

Above all, the vocal performances set an enviable standard: Michael Horden swings appreciably between avuncular and steely as Gandalf; Robert Stephens' smoky basso makes Aragorn seem older, wiser and immediately kingly. Jackson would seek a deliberate resonance between the serial and his own films in the casting of Ian Holm as his Bilbo; Holm having made an impassioned Frodo back in 1981.

Having made his mark in Bakshi's adaptation, Peter Woodthorpe would again provide the disturbingly funny duality of his Gollum. Disembodied, that needling, pathetic, hissing voice carries a note of pure heartbreak.

The seminal serial was responsible for bringing another generation to the book. But Hollywood had lost interest or grown weary of its numerous challenges. And for fifteen years the Ring lay forgotton, until it was finally picked up by the most unlikely director imaginable.

CHAPTER 2

An Unexpected Director

*T*he *English Patient* was dying. Saul Zaentz had pleaded with the studio that they were in the process of forging art. He had protested at their shortsightedness. And he had resorted to good old-fashioned brinkmanship. They were only weeks from shooting, but 20th Century Fox were not backing down. Fox had bought the English language rights to this expensive adaptation of Michael Ondaatje's Booker prize-winning novel for a not inconsiderable $20 million (the full budget was $31 million, including $5 million of Zaentz's own money) and were insisting it have a marquee female lead.

Accepting Ralph Fiennes as the hero — if such a straightforward term could be applied to the emotionally fraught and morally elusive weft of Ondaatje's novel — already spoke of a due deference to artistic over commercial merit. This was, they knew, a prestige project. Fiennes was so very English — although his character turns out to be Hungarian.

The Second World War romantic epic came endowed with a tricky structure. It told a story within a story, gradually regaled to Juliet Binoche's free-spirited nurse, and us, by a burn-ravaged Fiennes languishing within the gorgeous grounds of a Franciscan monastery somewhere in the Tuscany countryside. His tale will sweep us all back to a Sahara on the brink of war where spies and cartographers muster and a great love affair ensues, all simmering in a grand manner not seen since the imperial heyday of David Lean. The kind of film, everyone kept saying, no one made anymore.

When it came to Fiennes' romantic opposite – the fragile, conflicted, swan-like Katharine Clifton – Fox were thinking of Demi Moore, in the spring of 1995 box office gold following *Indecent Proposal* and *Disclosure*. Zaentz and his so very English director, Anthony Minghella, whose determination to steer his own artistic choices mirrored that of Peter Jackson's, had set their heart upon Kristin Scott Thomas — more traditionally beautiful, more icy and layered.

Bill Mechanic, who was then president of Fox, later promised on his life that the Moore rumours were untrue. Minghella maintained that 'Demi's name was always mentioned'.

Whatever the case, the fractious production had reached an impasse. Actually, that was no longer true.

Fox had pulled the plug.

Rallying round the desperate project, already encamped in the desert, two of Minghella's closest allies, director Sydney Pollack and producer Scott Rudin, put in a call to Harvey Weinstein, the influential co-founder and co-chairman, with his brother Bob, of the independent film powerhouse Miramax.

'Harvey just stepped in and financed it one hundred per cent,' confirms Jackson, who has been recounting the story as a matter of significant background.

Cynical Hollywood commentators, of which there are many, suspected that Miramax was already well aware the project was faltering, with Harvey ready and waiting for it to collapse so he could swoop in and save the day.

Akin to Zaentz, this was exactly the kind of project that fitted Harvey's view of himself as both Hollywood player and indie king, as well as the philosophy of Miramax as a film company: sophisticated, literary, but with mainstream potential, and

Oscar-worthy, always Oscar-worthy. Spinning gold on behalf of the inevitable awards campaign for *The English Patient*, Miramax's gifted publicists spread a tale of the White Knight who saved great art from studio defilement.

Nominated for twelve Oscars (including one for Kristin Scott Thomas), winner of nine, and making $231 million around the world, *The English Patient* cemented Harvey's reputation. By the mid-1990s, he was the new Selznick, but operating from New York headquarters beyond the borders of Hollywood. He wasn't the kind of studio boss who would demand Demi Moore. He understood the needs of filmmakers. He could manage big, important films outside of the studio system. He also understood the marketplace and how to reach an audience. He could finesse, and he could bully. His methods, often cutting and re-cutting problem films — landing him the nickname 'Harvey Scissorhands' — he insisted were always at the service of the film. This was how, alongside Bob, he maintained Miramax's great duality: cash and kudos.

Not that it was all about literary adaptations. If Minghella was his longing, romantic Sméagol side, then Quentin Tarantino, who wanted to storm the barricades of such strait-laced tradition as *The English Patient*, let alone *The Lord of the Rings*, was his expletive-spitting Gollum.

Between Miramax's multiple personalities, you can also trace Harvey's attraction to Jackson: the young Kiwi embodied that very schism. He was the director of *Bad Taste*, *Meet The Feebles* and *Braindead*, giddy gore hound and natural wit, predisposed never to abide by the Hollywood playbook. But then he would produce something as finely tuned as *Heavenly Creatures*.

It is often claimed that the two poles of Jackson's filmmaking pedigree are what made him so ideal for adapting Tolkien.

The English Patient had finally wrapped production in 1996 when Jackson called his long-standing manager Ken Kamins and casually asked him to find out who might own the rights to *The Lord of the Rings*. For a certain fee, databases can be consulted.

In the litigious universe of Hollywood, it is essential to cover your back. Jackson had assumed they must be with Disney or Spielberg or Lucas. 'They would all be locked up, as they say,' he admits. 'And we wouldn't have a chance. So we really went into this with no expectations at all.'

Kamins didn't take long to discover that thirty years after buying them from UA, the rights to both *The Hobbit* and *The Lord of the Rings* still resided with Zaentz. He might not be a Spielberg or a Lucas, but this wasn't necessarily good news. Having had his fingers burned so badly with the Ralph Bakshi debacle, Zaentz had closely guarded the rights ever since.

It wasn't as if since Bakshi no one had returned to the idea of adapting one of the most popular books of the twentieth century in the intervening years; they had simply come up against the Black Gates of Zaentz's resistance.

If by some miraculous chance he was to agree, says Jackson, word came back that he would want to be attached to it. 'That is just the way he was. He was a producer himself. But he tended to say no. He had done his Tolkien thing, it was a huge disaster for him, and he had lost a lot of money by the sound of it. He just didn't want to know about it.'

They needed a backstairs route to the rights — a secret way into Zaentz, a chance to try and persuade him. And although he didn't know it yet, Jackson already had the perfect guide. In fact, that guide was impatiently waiting for the director to call.

Within the parameters of a first-look deal he had recently struck with Miramax, Jackson was contractually bound to first test the waters on any new idea with Harvey Weinstein. And this was a staggeringly ambitious plan.

'The idea was to do *The Hobbit* as one movie, then two movies of *The Lord of the Rings*,' says Jackson. 'Still as a package: you make *The Hobbit* by itself, if it is successful you then get to do *The Lord of the Rings* films back-to-back. A three-film thing.'

So the initial desire had been to adapt Tolkien's books in chronological order, beginning with his first, younger-orientated

Middle-earth novel: Bilbo, the Dwarves, and dislodging a fire-breathing squatter.

'I could tell on the phone he was really excited right away,' recalls Jackson, not yet knowing that this conversation would change his life.

The English Patient may not have yet been released but Minghella had wrought classical wonders with the strange book. Another attention-grabbing, epic production based on a tricky literary source, as directed by another of his self-styled discoveries, played right into Harvey's view of himself as a promethean, David O. Selznick type for a modern Hollywood.

'Who's got the rights?' he asked.

'Well, it's not going to be easy, Harvey,' Jackson warned him, 'because it is this guy called Saul Zaentz.'

Jackson laughs. 'Harvey was the man who had saved *The English Patient*. We were talking to the right guy.'

If you put it in a script it would sound corny and contrived. No one would believe a word of it, but then so much of Jackson's career has been decreed by what you would call fate.

Says Kamins, 'It's the big theme for him. He has always believed that fate was going to point him in the right direction.'

Jackson's manager cannot think of a single conversation in all the time he has represented him where they have sat down and discussed what he should or shouldn't do with his career. 'Peter sort of functions by his own compass — that fate will deal him the right set of cards. And in this particular instance maybe more than any other, he was proven completely right.'

There are things that can be seen with the naked eye when you're trying to achieve something in the motion picture marketplace and there are the things that lie hidden. You can't ever see what's going on behind the boardroom doors. The business decisions, the politics and agendas, the history, or the simple expediency that can come with good timing: all those invisible but significant factors that allow you to be able to do the unexpected. Otherwise known as fate.

'Saul?!' Weinstein boomed, his thick New York vowels reverberating down the transpacific line, more excited still by the chance to demonstrate the extent of his magical largesse: the beneficent Harvey, fulfiller of wishes. 'I'll call him straightaway. He owes me a *huge* favour.'

*

Print the legend, and the inception of Jackson's great adventure occurred on an unspecified morning while *The Frighteners* was in post-production. He and Fran Walsh had got chatting about how to follow up their spectral comedy-horror. In spring 1996 things were moving for Jackson: he was now working on a Hollywood stage, with Hollywood budgets at his disposal, and to a large extent still on his own terms and staying put in New Zealand. More than ever, they needed to maintain their momentum.

'So how about a fantasy film?' proposed Jackson. Something like Ray Harryhausen once made, the spectaculars he had been whelped on: no irony, but a cornucopia of fantastic beasts. Only they would use the growing digital capabilities of their own visual effects company, Weta, to conjure them up rather than the chronically slow minutiae of stop-motion. Perhaps, Jackson suggested, something more classically swords and sorcery than the Arabian Nights or Greek myth that had been Harryhausen's metier. He searched the air for an equivalent. . .

'Something like *The Lord of the Rings*.'

At that point, he had still only read it the once, when he was eighteen. It was simply what sprang to mind.

'Well,' Walsh replied, 'in that case why *not* do *The Lord of the Rings*?'

Except it didn't go like that. Not exactly. The reality behind the decision to attempt Tolkien was a lot more complicated and painful. The river of fate had many twists and turns to negotiate.

*

In the 1950s, Kamins, eldest of four New Yorker brothers, always played the dutiful son and did whatever he was told. This was the reason Jackson's manager so loved the Marx Brothers of *Duck Soup* and *Horse Feathers*. He longed for their utter sense of anarchy, their disrespect for authority.

'They managed to play by their own set of rules, which I never could,' he says wistfully.

Short-haired and snappily attired (the opposite of his client), with a calm, observant, thorough manner, Kamins is a Hollywood man without the pretension. He sees the world keenly through his rimless spectacles. From his hardwood-floored, glass-walled, art-adorned eyrie that gazes down upon Sunset Boulevard, he has been Jackson's eyes and ears in the movie-town since 1992. It is also easy to see why the Kiwi director has remained loyal to his Hollywood minder. Kamins is no mere facilitator or dealmaker; he is a great storyteller, who parses the madness of the film industry with wisdom and wry humour, and stood in the eye of the hurricane of the trilogy's storm-tossed beginnings. There were times when the future of the project depended on Kamins' gift for talking down dragons.

He openly admits the books had meant very little to him. 'They were not, like, seared on my soul. I mean, I knew of them. But I was in no manner, shape or form an aficionado, or a hard-core fantasy fan for that matter.'

Rather than *King Kong*, Kamins is a '*Godfather*-fanatic'. Film class at college had introduced him to films like *The Grand Illusion*, *Klute* and *Rio Bravo*. That is where his tastes lay. He believed in his client's project without it having to be a religious experience.

Out of college, Kamins had climbed onto the lower rungs of the film industry, reaching the nascent home entertainment business at RCA Columbia at exactly the time his mentor Larry Estes began backing low-budget film productions, laying off theatrical and television rights while retaining the video rights.

Under that paradigm they backed Steven Soderbergh's *sex,*

lies and videotape, which had caused a stir at the Sundance Film Festival. Every independent theatrical distributor had come running in. They ended up making a deal with Harvey Weinstein.

Using this business model, home video specialist LIVE Entertainment would back *Reservoir Dogs* and begin Tarantino's journey toward the sun. Another promising indie named New Line Cinema also began to see significant profits care of its home entertainment investments.

It was while at the now defunct talent agency InterTalent, a few rungs higher in his career, that Kamins' boss, Bill Block, couldn't get a ticket to the *Batman Returns* premiere. Tim Burton's shadowy superhero sequel was the seen-to-be-seen-at golden ticket of the week. In his frustration Block had glanced over the many invites, requests and pleas for representation yet to be cleared from his desk and a letter caught his eye. It came from an attorney. 'Hey, I have this client. He's going to be in LA. He's holding a screening of his new movie.'

Block walked down the corridor and into Kamins' office. 'I'm going to this screening and you're coming with me.'

It was called *Braindead*.

Jackson was stopping in Los Angeles on his way back from Cannes, where he had been endeavouring to sell the distribution rights to his great ode to the flinging of viscera. The film that a mesmerized Guillermo del Toro once claimed made 'Sam Raimi look like Yasujiro Ozu'. While in town, Jackson was hosting a screening at the Fine Arts Theatre on Wilshire Boulevard. Despite clashing with the big-budget antics of The Penguin and Catwoman, every agency in town was sending someone.

Kamins was impressed at the inventive use of effects in what was clearly a 'modestly budgeted' horror film. He certainly had never seen a hero lawnmower his way through a zombie horde. Indeed, it was the film's sense of humour that spoke to him. The director was winking at the audience, egging them on. 'Can you believe this level of madness?'

Kamins was reminded of the Marx Brothers.

'I think that Peter unwittingly tapped into that same sense of anarchy,' he says. '"I'm going to do things my own way. I'm going to challenge norms." And I don't know that I even understood it that clearly at the time. But it resonated for me.'

There was a spate of lunches for Jackson that week. Held at jazzy, star-spotted joints like Spagos or Chasens where the would-be agents reeled off a blur of inane advice. Oh, you should do a *Friday the 13th*. Oh, you should do a *Tales from the Crypt*. Oh, you should do a Freddy movie. All they could see was *Braindead* the horror movie, Jackson the New Zealand Sam Raimi.

Theirs was the last lunch of the week. And Kamins took a revolutionary approach. 'I remember asking him, "Well, what do you want to do?" And he said, "Well, Fran and I are working on this project about matricide. About these two girls growing up in New Zealand, a true story. . ."'

It was called *Heavenly Creatures*.

The next week, Kamins' phone rang. Jackson's chirpy voice came on the line: 'Fran and I have had a chat. We would like you to represent us.'

Kamins wasn't the first agent-manager of Jackson's career. Shortly after finishing *Meet the Feebles*, he had ventured to Los Angeles and found representation with a good-sized agency and a very good lawyer in Peter Nelson, who has stayed the course to this day (and would be another important figure in the many, many negotiations to come). Nelson had sent out the invitations to the *Braindead* screening with the objective of landing Jackson fresh representation. As he put it, the previous agency had 'fallen asleep'.

Speaking to Jackson over lunch, Kamins was impressed by how purposeful and business-like was this young director. 'For somebody who did not grow up here, but who clearly was a fan of movies and had aspirations to be a filmmaker, I was struck by how *not*-awed he was by the town. He had a fearlessness or a blindness to the reality of what he was walking into. All of which seemed to serve him really well.'

*

Heavenly Creatures changed everything. *Heavenly Creatures* got Jackson out of the horror ghetto where Hollywood would be happy to confine him. 'Oh, he makes those low budget splatter movies that have some humour in them.' Typecasting, Kamins could see, that didn't project 'a vision that he could do bigger films'.

Disney had offered him a supernatural rom-com called *Johnny Zombie*, which he wisely turned down. It was made by Bob Balaban as *My Boyfriend's Back* in 1993, and swiftly forgotten thereafter.

He had so much more to him than *Bad Taste*.

Jackson followed *Braindead* by winning the Silver Lion for Best Direction at the Venice Film Festival. Head of the jury David Lynch had quickened to a queasy portrait of small-town murder where schoolgirls turned out to be the perpetrators not the victims. There were further festival awards to follow at Toronto and Chicago, and nine New Zealand Film and Television Awards.

'There was a sophistication to *Heavenly Creatures*,' says Kamins proudly. 'This was not a horror film in the traditional sense.'

Tellingly, in terms of the influence Walsh has had on the trajectory of both their careers, it had begun as her passion project. Jackson hadn't even heard of the real-life murder case, and worried at first that the story was too grim to make a satisfying film.

In 1952, two New Zealand schoolgirls, more than a little emotionally maladjusted, fell into an intense friendship that spilled into a mania for one another. Their relationship was like an addiction. Threatened with separation, they conspired to literally dash the brains out of one of their mothers with a brick. For all the bloody mayhem of his career, this remains the most disturbing sequence Jackson has ever filmed. The shift in mood and moral accountability from *Braindead* is astonishing. They had shot in the footsteps of the actual scene of the crime in Christchurch's Victoria Park. In truth, a few hundred feet further along the wooded path after Jackson had become unnerved by a lack of birdsong at the exact murder scene.

The Pauline Parker-Juliet Hulme case shook the stiff veil of propriety that 1950s New Zealand had inherited from Britain. In fact, it tore it down. This was the scandal of its day, portrayed in lurid, tabloid details by the excited papers and true crime accounts; there was even a novel. Author Angela Carter had written a screenplay inspired by the events called *The Christchurch Murder*, which Walsh had read. When she and Jackson were developing the idea, two rival film projects were already underway: one produced by Dustin Hoffman, the other to be directed by fellow New Zealander Niki Caro (*Whale Rider*).

What makes the Jackson-Walsh script so evocative is the decision to concentrate on the friendship rather than the sensationalist furore of the court case. They were two schoolgirls, barely sixteen, with hints of lesbianism to their unnatural bond — until 1973 homosexuality was still considered a mental malady in New Zealand. However, Hulme (who as an adult was later revealed to be crime author Anne Perry) flatly denied this was so.

Jackson and Walsh strove to interpret what lay behind this dangerous dependency. Individually, Parker and Hulme may have grown into functioning members of society. Together some moral constraint went missing, as if they were spurring each other on, waiting for one or the other to say no.

Scrupulous in their research, Jackson and Walsh burrowed like detectives into the cuttings and court transcripts; dialogue was lifted verbatim from Pauline's florid diary entries.

'The way they worked together was an incredible thing to see,' said Melanie Lynskey, who as dumpy, brooding Pauline witnessed the Jackson-Walsh double act at first hand. It was a true creative partnership, the distinctions of writer and director far less defined than the credits suggest.

Here was a clear signal of the maturity they would bring to Tolkien: the concentration on character, the unhurried but intent building of story and the way in which the camera became a participant in their fantasies. The Parker-Hulme friendship also crossed class boundaries, a theme explored to a more positive outcome with Frodo and Sam.

Here too was Jackson and Walsh's growing felicity for casting. Neither had done any significant acting, and this would be an astonishing exercise in sustained hysteria. Walsh discovered Lynskey at a Christchurch high school near to where the real girls first met. She was looking for someone who in any way resembled Pauline.

'This girl really loves acting,' her teacher had said, pointing out Lynskey. 'She puts on plays that nobody wants to see.'

For the superior, pretty fantasist, Juliet — who had lately arrived from England — Jackson had plucked an unknown British girl from Reading from 600 hopefuls. Kate Winslet had been working in a delicatessen when the call came.

'I'll never forget it as long as I live . . . I actually fell on my knees,' she admitted. Within four years Winslet would be one of the most famous faces on the planet, star of James Cameron's *Titanic*.

Here too is the promise of a cinematic New Zealand being unveiled: the unique light; the vast, primordial landscape; and the confidence with which the local crew rose to the challenges set before them by their ambitious director.

Perhaps most significantly, Jackson would inaugurate a new digital division of his and Richard Taylor's special effects house, Weta (named after a local cricket-like bug[*]), in order to create the

---

[*] The 'Weta' is a Māori name for the large species of spiky-legged insect endemic in New Zealand. As the story goes, Taylor first named the special effects company Weta in 1987 as he awoke one night to find that one of these 'prehistoric crickets' had crawled into his mouth. A giant version of the yellowy-brown insect appeared in *King Kong* (2005), and there were plans for an intergalactic Weta to consume and evacuate Jackson's Derek in an early concept for 'Bad Taste 2'.

abstract world of the girls' flowering imaginations. Key to under-standing Hulme and Parker's descent into murder is the film's ability to slip inside the sickly dreamspace of their conjoined imaginations. A similar sympathy for the devil would be applied to the depiction of Gollum (over which Walsh would have a significant influence).

Between them, the girls invented their own fantasy world. Borovnia would become more meaningful than reality: they traced royal lineages back over the centuries and wrote melodra-matic adventure stories set within its colourful bounds, thirteen novels' worth. They dreamed of having them adapted into big Hollywood movies starring tacky 1950s heartthrob Mario Lanza. Movie mad, we catch them watching Orson Welles in *The Third Man*, and Jackson does a brief rendition of noir in its honour. The resonances — and ironies — are there for all to see.

It was a film about the dangers of losing yourself inside a fantasy world.

Weta was still a single unit at this time. Taylor's workshop would make the rubber suits for the actors playing the 'living' ver-sions of the Plasticene Borovnians the remarkable girls sculpted. Led by George Port, who had worked with Jackson since *Meet the Feebles*, Weta also ambitiously pursued a series of digital effects shots inspired by the groundbreaking work of Cameron's *Terminator 2: Judgment Day*. 'What the Hell,' was Jackson's atti-tude, 'let's try.' Their computer graphics department boasted a solitary Silicon Graphics SGI computer and a scanner. Which thankfully came with an instruction manual. By post-production on *The Two Towers*, Weta Digital would boast the largest amount of processing power in the Southern Hemisphere.

There are fewer CGI shots in *Heavenly Creatures* than is generally recognized. Taylor takes it as a compliment that his prosthetics are mistaken for CGI. The true digital shots were localized to Christchurch's Port Levy morphing into a too-colourful, too-exquisite ornamental garden, complete with giant butterflies.

Extraordinary for 1994, these digital effects now appear charmingly antiquated, but that somehow makes them more fitting for the strange climate of the film. Jackson was using visual effects to express emotions.

'And all for a three-and-a-half-million dollar budget,' announces Kamins proudly. Behind him on his office wall there is a framed poster of *Heavenly Creatures*, with the girls leaping into a pristine lake, a film that remains not only an early marker of Jackson's prowess, but a minor classic in its own right.

New Zealand might be a long way from Hollywood, and leagues further from New York, where Miramax resided in the hip Lower Manhattan neighbourhood of Tribeca. However, word soon reached Harvey that this was a significant film. There was a scramble to pick up the American rights, and Miramax's bullyboy sprang into action, elbowing aside competitors and making entreaties to Jackson. Miramax's Vice President of Acquisitions, David Linde, was despatched to Wellington to see an early cut. Blown away both by the film and the young director, he reported back to Harvey that something major was growing in New Zealand. Linde has remained a good friend to Jackson ever since.

Harvey, wielding his considerable clout, swiftly acquired *Heavenly Creatures* for distribution and negotiated a prestigious berth for its world premiere — opening The Venice Film Festival.

Being picked up by Miramax had distinct advantages. Founded in 1979 by the two brothers from Buffalo, brash in manner but brilliantly acute in business, it had risen to prominence through films as diverse as *My Left Foot*; *sex, lies and videotape*; and *Reservoir Dogs*. It would rise yet further on the glories of *Pulp Fiction* and *The English Patient* to come. Bob Weinstein handled the genre side of the business through the Dimension label, but both brothers always had their say.

The disadvantage was the Weinstein temperament. When things were sunny, all was well. Cross them, particularly Harvey, often over things that ordinarily appear reasonable or, at least, professional, and he would rain down his righteous (or not) fury. It was also a prime negotiating tactic. This was, of course, long before multiple accusations of sexual harassment and worse would bring about an ignominious downfall for the mightly Harvey, sending shockwaves across Hollywood. At this time, he was merely viewed as an industry bully boy.

In 1993, flushed with success, the brothers sold Miramax to Disney for $75 million. They would remain at the helm, with the power to greenlight a film up to the significant figure of $15 million. Any higher and they would require the consent of Disney's hierarchy. Inevitably, the brothers would come to chafe against such restrictions.

After a lauded run at the box office, and with the assistance of Harvey's golden touch at the Academy, *Heavenly Creatures* was nominated for Best Original Screenplay.

'Boom!' declares Kamins. 'The whole perception changed the second the film got nominated. I mean, *everything* changed — perceptually. Now I got my calls returned and the speed with which I got them returned changed; the kinds of conversations that we were having. Everything shifted. Not even in ways that sort of guided a specific path, but just atmospherically it all felt different.'

Smartly, as well as agreeing a deal to distribute *Heavenly Creatures* in America, Harvey had insisted on pinning down Jackson to a first-look deal with Miramax. While offering an avenue for any new film idea he might have, it would soon feel like he was tied to Weinstein's often inflexible apron strings, who now had a prize, Oscar-nominated asset.

Jackson would never bind himself to a studio again. 'It was sort of a strange thing where they would pay some overheads: an office and some people we could hire. In exchange for that they get first refusal on any script we wanted to do. If they say no that's fine, you can take it somewhere else. Also if you get offered something you are allowed to go and take it. It is not like an old studio contract where you are locked into MGM.'

He would ultimately never make a film with Miramax.

*

First Jackson met Robert Zemeckis, and together they made *The Frighteners*, a warped comedy-horror about a spiritual conman (played by *Back to the Future*'s Michael J. Fox) who can actually behold ghosts. It was to be Jacksons' first studio picture. Universal were attracted to a commercial-sounding mash-up of *Ghostbusters*, the *Elm Street* movies and this New Zealand hotshot revealing a knack for visual effects.

Fox's Frank Bannister begins to realize the Northern Californian coastal town of Fairwater (actually Lyttleton in New Zealand) where he plies his supernatural scams is also being terrorized by an undead serial killer in the guise of the Grim Reaper — a killer only he can see. The visual effects requirements were bold: Bannister would interact with a trio of quirky, translucent ghosts, as pliable as cartoons, as well as the Reaper figure, which flits across town like a runaway kite (and not dissimilar in appearance to Ringwraiths). It would take six months to complete, with scenes being shot in duplicate to insert the ribald ghosts. Jackson's Sitges friend Rick Baker would provide the rotting-corpse make-up for the dread departed.

Sprawling and tonally uncertain, yet still underappreciated, *The Frighteners* tends to be forgotten in the journey between the early splatters to the coming of age with *Heavenly Creatures*, which is seen to segue straight into Middle-earth. If anything, it is viewed as a backwards step in the direction of the rabble-rousing days of those early horror movies.

To Jackson's mind, here lies the true point of transition to *The Lord of the Rings*. Without it spans a different career, one that might have made him less global, but no less valuable; making films with more of a New Zealand spirit like Jane Campion. But Jackson's instincts were always toward the commercial.

The project had begun life out of desperation. With *Heavenly*

Creatures still awaiting the go-ahead, Jackson and Walsh were badly in need of some work. 'They needed to make some money,' clarifies Kamins.

Jackson had sounded urgent on the phone. 'We need a writing job. What's out there?'

Fortuitously, Kamins had been in a staff meeting where he had heard about Zemeckis' involvement in Joel Silver's portmanteau *Tales from the Crypt* movie. Different directors would provide their own segments of horror, and Zemeckis, he was told, was still in need of a screenplay. Springing into action, Jackson and Walsh worked up a two-page outline based on an idea they'd had while walking to the shops for milk, the story of a conman who is in cahoots with ghosts. Zemeckis was intrigued. At that stage, he hadn't even realized Jackson was a director; he just figured they were these quirky writers from New Zealand.

'I tell you what,' said Zemeckis, 'you go write the screenplay, I've got to make this movie called *Forrest Gump.*'

'Well, that's fine,' replied Jackson, 'because we have this movie we're going to make called *Heavenly Creatures.*' They would work on *The Frighteners* script while shooting their matricidal drama – the two being closer in theme than is immediately apparent.

Then fate got involved: *Forrest Gump* became an Oscar-winning phenomenon and Zemeckis lost his taste for a *Tales from the Crypt* movie. Now very much aware of Jackson as a director, Zemeckis suggested he direct it as a standalone film, which he would produce for a budget of $26 million.

'*The Frighteners* matters for two key reasons,' says Kamins. 'Number one: it allowed for the build-up of Weta Digital conceptually, which had been a very small unit on *Heavenly Creatures. The Frighteners* would require over 500 visual effects shots, even at that budget, and Peter had the vision to say, "We can create a bigger visual effects company."'

Jackson's plan was typically practical, typically New Zealand: they would lease more computers from Silicon Graphics, then hire out-of-work animators from all over the world, people who were just sitting at home, and double their weekly salaries to come to New Zealand. The only overheads would be space. They would still be able to create visual effects shots much cheaper than ILM. And, sure enough, that's what happened.

The Frighteners also matters, adds Kamins, because Zemeckis and his partner Steve Starkey would give Jackson and Walsh invaluable tuition on how to navigate the political waters that come with a studio project: 'What they need to know and when; how to manage their expectations; when to get them excited about things; and when to hold back on information; how to keep them confident, but not in your hair.'

So coming full circle, as Weta were revealing their potential on the visual effects on *The Frighteners*, Jackson and Walsh's thoughts turned to the future and the potential of making a fantasy film. However, one morning's casual discussion was actually several weeks of brainstorming fantasy concepts. 'It had been a long time since I had read *The Lord of the Rings*,' admits Jackson. Fifteen years had now passed since he had waded through the Bakshi tie-in edition, and he really couldn't remember it at all well.

Whatever ideas he came up with, Walsh and her watertight memory would shoot down: 'No, no, no. You can't do that — that's just *The Lord of the Rings*.'

Jackson sighs. 'You don't want to be seen to be stealing stuff.'

His thought had been to do an original fantasy film, but at every proposal he made Walsh kept on repeating it like a mantra: '*The Lord of the Rings. . . The Lord of the Rings. . . The Lord of the Rings.*'

'It was getting frustrating.'

When he was a teen, no more than sixteen, already displaying a rapacious hunger for filmmaking, Jackson set out to make a Super-8 *Sinbad* film. There was to be a scene of him fighting a stop-motion skeleton in the surf. He shot himself hip deep in Pukerua Bay swinging a homemade sword, but he never got round to putting in the skeleton. Which was down to the fact that, with the tide heading out, Jackson had dived straight onto an exposed rock. Severe bruising led to a pilonidal cyst which led to surgery. He also hadn't quite yet figured out how to do stop-motion.

During the *Bad Taste* era, he had considered shooting a *Conan*-type film on 16mm at the weekends. 'I never got any further than swords and monster masks,' he admits. 'I had never actually sat down and written a script.'

Truth be told, there was no specific, original sword 'n' sorcery concept he'd been yearning to make. It was simply that the genre appealed to his sensibility and offered the chance for Weta to keep expanding. So, why not *The Lord of the Rings*? Frodo's enduring tale was the *ne plus ultra* of the genre. It was fantasy operating on an equivalent dramatic level to *Heavenly Creatures*.

According to prevailing Hollywood wisdom, fantasy, as a genre, was a joke. Jackson agrees. 'I used to watch all the fantasy films. Things like *Krull* and *Conan*. . . Fantasy was one of those B-grade genres. No quality movies were ever made in the fantasy genre. Right from the outset *The Lord of the Rings* was always something different. You can't think of *Krull* and *The Lord of the Rings* in the same sentence. While it was fantasy, in our minds it was always something quite different to that.'

And that was when they had put in the call to Kamins to find out who had the rights, and made their approach to Harvey. And even then things only grew more complicated.

The possibility of adapting Tolkien was soon to be one of three potential fantasy projects for Jackson.

For all of Harvey's confidence in calling in a favour with Zaentz, it would take eight perilous months of negotiation for a deal to be struck. Zaentz had held the rights tight to his chest for three decades; whatever Harvey had done for him on *The English Patient* he wasn't going to part with them lightly. Tribes of rival lawyers were making proposal and counterproposal, putting in calls, arranging meetings, filing memos, coming up with offers, rebuffing counteroffers, and charging by the hour. And Harvey showed zero inclination toward allowing Zaentz any active participation in his project.

Another problem was the weird, bifurcated rights situation surrounding *The Hobbit*. Harvey had endeavoured to go direct to MGM, which had purchased the crippled UA in the wake of *Heaven's Gate*. Ironically, MGM was itself a studio in decline and in one of its many cycles of bankruptcy, reorganization and sale, nobody was about to give away one of its chief assets — even if they were only partial rights to *The Hobbit*.

'The hell with it,' cried Harvey, 'let's forget *The Hobbit*. *The Lord of the Rings* is a better-known title anyway. Let's just go right to *The Lord of the Rings*. Two movies shot back-to-back.'

Still, with no sign of an agreement with Zaentz being reached, Jackson was growing increasingly nervous. The clock was ticking on his Weta project, even his career. It was becoming increasingly clear they were going to have to make something else in the meantime.

'I will never forget it,' recalls Kamins, and true to his word he can remember the exact day: 'Monday, April first, nineteen ninety-six, I went to a premiere of *Primal Fear* at Paramount. I come home and there's a message from Peter on my answering machine. This is like eleven p.m. at night. And he never calls me at home that late.'

Jackson's recorded voice carried a seriousness Kamins had heard only rarely. 'I need to know what my next movie is by the end of the week, otherwise all these great people that I put together to do the visual effects for *The Frighteners* are going to leave. . .'

As is standard practice, six weeks before the end of any movie the freelance visual effects team — and any other department employed on a film-by-film basis — is entitled to start looking for their next job. The buzz had gotten around about the visual effects work on *The Frighteners*, and the more established effects houses were reaching out to the Weta team, trying to entice them back to LA.

Meanwhile, Kamins was maintaining a constant vigil for any opportunities for his client, as he puts it, playing 'backstop' on Jackson's career. Given the mercurial nature of the film business, any director would be foolhardy not to have more than one plate spinning at a time. He swiftly engaged a strategy to push forward on any one of the projects he and Jackson had in various stages of development.

Besides *The Lord of the Rings*, two other noticeably non-Miramax movies were to emerge. Confirming that this was a defining period in Jackson's life and career, each would have a significant influence on his future. That first-look deal with Miramax notwithstanding, Jackson headed to LA to begin discussing the alternatives. He didn't see himself as acting in bad faith. *The Lord of the Rings* had been his priority, but despite Kamins urgent pressing of Miramax it showed little sign of being resolved.

'So we spoke to Universal about *King Kong*,' says Jackson, 'and I did a lot of meetings with Fox about *Planet of the Apes*.'

A *Planet of the Apes* reboot had been jostling about in development for a number of years. Spreading its allegorical net to include the fear of atomic destruction and the civil rights movement, Franklin J. Schaffner's biting, apocalyptic, 1968 *Planet of the Apes*, starring Charlton Heston, could fairly be considered a classic (if not its diminishing sequels). Jackson certainly thought so — he has some original John Chambers' prosthetics in his collection and once designed his own set of ape masks for another of his novice ventures into filmmaking, *The Valley*, which paid homage to the first film's devastating ending.

By the early 1990s, 20th Century Fox were keen to revive the idea of a future where the evolutionary order has been upended and apes have subjugated humanity. Some big directors had toyed with the hair-brained mythology, with all its juicy metaphorical potential, amongst them Oliver Stone, Sam Raimi, Chris Columbus, Roland Emmerich and Philip Noyce.

Jackson and Walsh had initially become involved as screenwriters in 1992, before *Heavenly Creatures*, only for their concept to fall out of favour with a regime change at Fox. But in 1996, following another bloody succession at the helm of the studio, the project was back on the table with Jackson potentially directing.

Ever the traditionalist, central to Jackson's enchanting simian vision was the return of actor Roddy McDowell, who had played the pro-human chimp Cornelius in the original. He'd even gone to lunch with the actor and producer Harry J. Ufland to pitch his concept. McDowell had been resistant to doing another *Apes* film: decades might have passed but he could still remember itching beneath those prosthetics. Unbowed, Jackson pitched him *Renaissance of the Planet of the Apes*. It was to be a continuation of the first line of movies, and the apes have had a flowering of their artistic ability. 'Like Florence or Venice, the Ape World has gained artistic beauty,' he explains. McDowell would play an aged Cornelius-type character, sort of a primate Leonardo da Vinci. McDowell was enthralled. 'Count me in,' he told them.

Amid this renaissance of ape culture, the gorillas would cover the police patrols, the chimps were the artists, and, Jackson laughs, 'I was going to have a big, fat orangutan with all the jowls as the Pope. It was a satirical look at religion.' Everywhere the camera turned we would see statues of apes; then in one twist a statue gets knocked over and beneath the marble, which turns out to be plaster, we glimpse a human face.

'It is all a façade!' enthuses Jackson, the old excitement returning. 'And we were actually going to have a half-human, half-ape character too that Roddy's ape character had in hiding, because he would be killed if the ape society found out that there was this hybrid. It was quite interesting. . .'

Re-pitching his idea (for which, working on spec, he and Walsh had never earned a cent) to Fox's new studio heads, Peter Chernin and Tom Rothman, he was informed the studio were also in talks with James Cameron to produce and Arnold Schwarzenegger to star.

'We got an offer from *Planet of the Apes*, aggressive up front,' says Kamins. 'Not on the back end, because they couldn't afford it because of Jim and Arnold.'

Jackson and Walsh had their qualms: this would be a big studio film and prey to big studio interference. Their natural independence, the very way they worked, would come under intense pressure.

Still the mind boggles a little at the notion: Peter Jackson directing Arnold Schwarzenegger in a *Planet of the Apes* movie produced by James Cameron, set in a crumbling ape Renaissance shot in New Zealand. . .

Jackson wouldn't meet Cameron until 2005. Getting along straightaway, the Kiwi found himself wondering what might have happened if they had said yes. Tim Burton would eventually step into the project in 2001 for a tepid reverse-engineered spin on the original 1968 film with Mark Wahlberg; although the prosthetics masks, created by Rick Baker, were fabulous.

Many moons later, the legacy of the *Apes* would return to Jackson's faraway kingdom. Following Weta's industry-transforming breakthroughs not only with motion-capture but the filigree textures of digital fur through Gollum and then Kong, when Fox rolled the dice on the *Apes* saga once more with *Rise of the Planet of the Apes* in 2011, it was Weta who created the now stunningly lifelike digital simians, with Andy Serkis starring as the sentient chimp, Caesar.

*

Since the 1976 debacle, *King Kong* had remained in the keeping of Universal, the very studio where *The Frighteners* was about to be released sooner rather than later.

The plan had been to lean toward its horror credentials and release the undead comedy around Halloween in 1996. Despite Jackson's best intentions to make a family film, *The Frighteners* had been landed with an adult R-rating (15 in the UK). In the meantime, however, *Daylight* was running late. Universal's tunnel-bound Sylvester Stallone disaster movie, featuring a young Viggo Mortensen, had gone overschedule and was going to miss its 17 July release date.

Seizing the opportunity, Zemeckis called Jackson: 'I want you to put together a short effects reel for me so I can take it into the studio.' He intended to make a move to put *The Frighteners* into the more lucrative summer slot in place of the delayed *Daylight*.

When Weta's visual effects proved to be on a par with ILM, Universal got excited and agreed to the July slot, and set about repositioning *The Frighteners* as a new visual effects extravaganza featuring Marty McFly!

Hollywood was becoming greatly intrigued. This wunderkind from over the ocean kept changing hats. First, he was the horror bandit, gorier even than Sam Raimi. Then he was the Weinsteins' arthouse darling who brought such dark sensitivity to *Heavenly Creatures*. And now he was the new George Lucas, nurturing his own visual effects company.

'So now the narrative's starting to unfold very differently,' says Kamins intently. Fox are making their overtures about *Renaissance of the Planet of the Apes*, *The Frighteners* is all of a sudden a summer movie and whispers of Jackson's devotion to the great 1933 stop-motion marvel have reached Universal's vice-president Lenny Kornburg. It was Kornburg who slyly tempted Jackson with his heart's desire: 'Would you have an interest in doing *King Kong*?'

What a moment of infinite possibility this must have seemed. And it would prove too good to be true. Yet, for a few weeks, Jackson had in front of him the chance of adapting Tolkien's beloved bestseller, reviving Charlton Heston's dystopian talking ape thriller, or remaking the film that had, in many ways, charted the course for his life. Which would, in fact, count as his second attempt to remake *King Kong*.

A twelve-year-old Jackson had constructed the Empire State Building out of cardboard boxes and turned a bed sheet into a cyclorama of New York that featured the Chrysler Building,

Hudson River and assorted bridges for an aborted version of the classic. He still has the jointed model of Kong built from wire, foam rubber and a fox stole his mother no longer wore (at least, she didn't now). When he finally came to remake *King Kong* in 2005, Jackson flew out the original 1933 eighteen-inch armature of Kong designed by Willis O'Brien and sculptor Marcel Delgado, along with its collector Bob Burns, to set in an act of quasi-holy symbolism.

Jackson was fired up by the possibility of any remake of *King Kong*, but his own? Astonishingly, given the company she kept, Walsh had never seen the original. An oversight that was swiftly put to rights, and she was convinced enough for the talks to intensify with Universal.

While the projects circled like 747s awaiting permission to land, Jackson's long-time lawyer Peter Nelson drew up a pro-forma contract that could apply to any one of them. Together Nelson, Kamins and Jackson were determined to set the terms of engagement. There were two significant stipulations. Firstly, that a 'considerable sum' be guaranteed by the studio for research and development into special effects. Secondly, that Jackson become a 'first dollar gross participant' meaning he would receive a percentage of the gross earnings of the film — not the net profit, which according to the elusive magic of studio accounting seldom seemed to materialize. He would also get final cut.

By autumn 1996, still undecided over which pathway smelled fairest, Jackson and Walsh took a holiday, driving around the South Island, taking in the stunning scenery that would so readily lend itself to Middle-earth. 'We decided that during this trip we would figure out which film we were going to make,' he says, and, essentially at this stage, it was a choice of two. Waiting for *The Lord of the Rings* to be 'absolutely nailed' by Harvey was too risky, too frustrating. Unless there was a radical breakthrough in the Middle-earth standoff, it was a case of which ape movie?

'Both Fox and Universal were happy for us to jump into one of their films.' And for Jackson it was the personal connection that finally told. 'We decided to do *Kong*.'

First, though, he had to let Harvey know.

Making the connection across the thousands of miles that lay between New York and the South Island, Jackson got straight to the point. 'Harvey, we are not going to wait any longer, we are doing *Kong*.'

Harvey went straight to force ten, the betrayed producer: 'THIS IS NOT HAPPENING! I AM NOT HEARING THIS! YOU'RE NOT TELLING ME THIS! YOU ARE *NOT* TELLING ME THIS!'

It was Jackson's first taste of the Miramax head's notorious spleen. But he knew well enough the stories of screaming fits that had reduced both M. Night Shyamalan and Uma Thurman to public tears and narrowly missed causing a fistfight with Quentin Tarantino.

Shaken, Jackson managed to remain calm.

'Well, I *am* telling you this, Harvey. We'll do it. Get the rights and after *Kong* we'll come back and do *Rings*.'

The phone went dead.

Kamins, aware they were gambling with an important relationship, admits that Harvey was in his rights to be angry. And, with Harvey, angry always meant apoplectic. 'He had already agreed, in fairness to him, to suspend and extend the period of our first-look deal so that Peter could go and make *The Frighteners*. We didn't have a movie in development with Harvey when *The Frighteners* was proposed. And Harvey understood it was an opportunity for Peter. So we sort of stopped the clock on the deal and then added whatever time he spent on *The Frighteners* to the end of the deal. Now we're coming to Harvey and we're putting him in a situation where he effectively has to bid for Peter's services on his next film. The only thing we wanted to do was *The Lord of the Rings*. And Harvey didn't yet have the rights.'

Feeling guilty that the first-look deal with Miramax was proving fruitless, and conscious *The Lord of the Rings* was still dependant on Harvey, it was Jackson who devised a solution that might placate the Miramax chieftain's ego. It would be a plan that would turn out to benefit Miramax in another, unexpected fashion. Jackson was on the ferry back to Wellington, crossing the often-turbulent waters of Cook Strait, when it occurred to him to see if he could convince Universal to allow Miramax to co-finance *King Kong*. Indeed, Universal were interested in striking a deal.

Miramax would come on as a fifty per cent partner on *King Kong* and Universal would take a fifty per cent stake in *The Lord of the Rings*. That would surely keep Harvey calm, Jackson reasoned. But Harvey, wheeler-dealer extraordinaire, pouted that Universal was getting two films out of the deal while poor Miramax was getting only one. He had his eye on another treasure; there was a property he coveted that had been languishing at Universal. It was a script by Tom Stoppard called *Shakespeare in Love*.

Three years hence, *Shakespeare in Love* would be nominated for thirteen Oscars, winning seven, including stealing Best Picture from under the nose of the favourite, Steven Spielberg's *Saving Private Ryan* (which would have a major influence on Jackson's battle scenes in *The Lord of the Rings*).

Jackson shakes his head. 'To balance this deal up, so it was two for two as it were, he got Universal to give him, without any investment or involvement, the film that would win all these Oscars.'

He lets the irony slip into his voice. 'We were tangentially responsible for getting *Shakespeare in Love* made.'

*

In the foyer of Weta Workshop, still located where Park Road swerves decisively to the right and becomes Camperdown Road, sits a stunning bronze maquette of King Kong wrestling a T-Rex. The two creatures are so tightly entwined you have to get up close to trace where gigantic gorilla ends and struggling dinosaur begins. It sits there as both a monument to the talents of those who work within these bountiful halls, greatly expanded over years of profitable world building, and a salutary symbol of what it is to wrestle with Hollywood.

Through the latter half of 1996, as Jackson and Walsh got to grips with the script for *King Kong*, months of research and development went into the visual effects that were going to bring Skull Island to fetid and thrilling life. Yet more artists and technicians had been brought in from all around the world to this far-off island to bolster the ranks of the sister divisions of Weta Workshop and Weta Digital. They were over six months into manufacturing.

The Workshop's famously loquacious head Richard Taylor takes up the tale. 'We already had some animatronic creatures sculpted, and it started to get wobbly. We could feel this under-tow of uncertainty.' He suggested to Jackson he make a sculpture of Kong fighting a Tyrannosaur (and Jackson was not skimping on dinosaurs), which they could use as a presentation piece to Universal to try and 'invest in them how exciting the moment could be'. Over the following two weeks he sculpted the very piece that now sits outside his office. Five weeks later it arrived at Universal.

'They were excited by it, and, needless to say, they actually put it in their front foyer,' he reports.

Four weeks after that the film fell apart.

Taylor doesn't hide the amusement in his voice. 'And Peter, in true Kiwi form, asked for it back. And we got it back.' And there it sits, a warning to all-comers: you need to be resilient in this game.

Looking back from the vantage of having finally made his version of *King Kong* in the wake of *The Lord of the Rings*, the undoing of their first attempt is viewed by Jackson and Taylor as a lucky escape; the river of fate taking another turn. Beginning again from scratch in 2004, Jackson dusted down the 1996 script. He didn't like what he read. It was the tone. It was too flippant, too jokey.

'We were desperately trying to write an *Indiana Jones* type of film. It was lightweight, a silly kind of Hollywood script.' *The Lord of the Rings* had taught him that fantasy must be treated as if it was reality not a movie.

'I think ultimately we weren't prepared to do justice to such an incredible story,' concludes Taylor.

But it was impossible to be philosophical at the time. It was heartbreaking.

Things had started to fragment with the release of *The Frighteners*. Zemeckis' instincts hadn't served him well. The reviews were uncertain, and the film felt too autumnal and spooky to sit comfortably in a summer wiped out by Roland Emmerich's defiantly inane mega-B-movie *Independence Day*. The fact their opening weekend coincided with the start of the Atlanta Olympic Games hardly helped.

Jackson and Walsh learned a great lesson not only about marketing campaigns but how crucial was a film's release date. Thereafter, they would maintain an influence on a film right through to the promotional popcorn bucket.

The Frighteners flopped, eventually taking a little under $30 million worldwide. According to the ruthless cause-and-effect of Hollywood physics, you're only ever as good as your last film, and Jackson's lustre was instantly tarnished. Virtually overnight, the conversation changed once more. Who was this guy again?

Still devotedly banging the drum for *The Frighteners*, Jackson had flown non-stop to London in early 1997 to do some promotional interviews— the international release date had been delayed to regroup after the film's failure in America, not that it did any good — from there he would fly to Rome and proceed on a European tour.

When he reached his hotel room the phone was already ringing. It was Kamins.

'They're pulling the plug on *King Kong*.'

Universal's change of heart wasn't only due to the failure of *The Frighteners*. Disney were putting out a (as it turns out ghastly) remake of *Mighty Joe Young*, the *King Kong* copycat from 1949, and now the all-conquering Emmerich had announced that for his next trick he was planning to remake *Godzilla*. 'And Universal didn't want to do another monster movie,' laments Jackson.

How could he stay where he was, promoting a film for the very studio that put his next film so abruptly into turnaround? Moreover, he now had twenty or thirty staff working on *King Kong* and no salary to pay them. He had to figure out how the hell they were going to survive. Weta was back on a knife-edge.

He booked himself on literally the next plane home.

'It is the only time in my life I have ever done that,' he laughs ruefully; although, nothing about it at the time felt funny. 'I did not sleep at all as I was dealing with all of this. So I went there and back.' Again.

Before leaving he called Walsh. 'Don't tell the guys. I will tell them when I get off the plane.'

Touching down at Wellington, the sleepless Jackson drove straight to Weta Workshop. He gathered the staff together and told them the film was no more. As always with the death of King Kong, tears were shed.

Harvey, true to form, was spitting mad. Only this time it was on Jackson's behalf. Universal hadn't told him — he heard the news via Kamins — and he was supposed to have a fifty per cent stake in the film. He let it be known to Jackson that, in his humble opinion, *The Frighteners* deserved a better fate, and had Universal and Zemeckis stuck to the Halloween release date he was sure it would have done far better.

Then he got into fighting mode. 'We are going to do *Rings*. We are going to do *Rings*,' he bellowed. 'And *they* are not going to be involved.'

The whole half-and-half deal between Universal and Miramax was split asunder with the end of *King Kong*, but, says Kamins, 'Harvey was just excited now to have Peter all to himself.'

CHAPTER 3

Many Meetings

Of course, nothing is ever new to Hollywood. In 1928, the great Erich von Stroheim filmed *The Wedding March* back-to-back with its sequel, *The Honeymoon*. In 1966, Hammer Films shot *Dracula: Prince of Darkness* in concert with the unrelated *Rasputin: The Mad Monk* so they could make profitable use of the cast and crew, led by the redoubtable Christopher Lee. In 1973, *The Three Musketeers* simply carried on swashbuckling into *The Four Musketeers*. And, in 1978, from behind a veil of secrecy, Warner Bros. brought back *Superman*, knowing they already had *Superman II* ready for take-off. During the double-production, they even managed to dispense with director Richard Donner and replace him with Richard Lester.

While the rights to *The Lord of the Rings* were stagnating at UA, David Lean tried to get the studio to bail out his two-part, single-schedule version of *The Bounty*, which had got as far as building a three-mast replica merchant ship before backer Dino De Laurentiis swam for shore. Attempting to edit down great swathes of *Cleopatra* in 1963, director Joseph L. Mankiewicz recommended releasing a five-hour version in two halves, but 20th Century Fox vetoed the idea.

Perhaps the most publicized of all hybrid productions was

Robert Zemeckis' back-to-*Back to the Futures,* two intertwined sequels filmed in one gallop between 1989 and 1990, impressively spinning from a dystopian future to the Wild West.

Less celebrated by the chronicles of Hollywood was Peter Jackson's avowed intention to make *Bad Taste* 2 and 3 in one go. This extension to his interplanetary saga of man-eating alien fast food operators, while considerably bigger in scope, was still scheduled to take considerably less than the four years it took to complete *Bad Taste.* The sequels have yet to come to pass, but here was proof that Jackson had already given serious consideration to the idea of juggling two films at once.

For all the risks involved — you would be doubling down (in gambling terminology, the doubling of an original bet in Blackjack; or, in more general terms, the doubling of one's commitment to a risky strategy) on a sequel to a film that could stumble out of the gates — Jackson knew back-to-back filmmaking was the only conceivable way to do justice to *The Lord of the Rings.* To wait on the sequel would result in spiralling costs and a loss in the richness and flow of storytelling. Throughout his early discussions with Harvey Weinstein, he was clear they were telling one long, baroque story artfully sliced in twain.

And despite the best efforts of their lawyers to prevaricate until kingdom come, Harvey had called to say that he had finally struck a deal with Saul Zaentz. Miramax were officially making *The Lord of the Rings.* Or would be once they had agreed upon the script.

Throughout the endless legal quibbling, Jackson hadn't even touched a copy of the book. The uncertainty had played on his superstitious nature. He was terrified of re-reading it, getting excited imagining the movie he could make, only for it all to fall apart.

In short, he was not in the business of tempting fate.

So it wasn't until the spring of 1997, on the day they received the news, that Jackson and Fran Walsh took a momentous shopping trip into downtown Wellington to buy what would be his second copy of *The Lord of the Rings*. Until that time, as he admitted, it had 'been a bit foggy'. Years later, interviewers would be staggered to find that Jackson had not spent his puberty pining over Middle-earth. Neither he nor Walsh had ever been Tolkien fanatics. It had been an abstract possibility. Which they now needed to make a reality.

Symbolically, the very copy they bought was the one Jackson would keep to hand throughout the entire production, the margins graffitied with notes. He still has it somewhere: three large paperbacks packaged in a box and adorned inside and on the covers with fifty beautiful watercolours by Alan Lee. The beauty of those pictures the deciding factor in the purchase.

What a pleasure, almost innocent, that moment must have been. Opening it up, flexing the cover back and letting the pages flow past, sensing the film that he might make. Only now realizing the full magnitude of what he was attempting. Only now gauging the thrilling possibility of what lay before him.

However, between the dying breath of *King Kong* and the dawning of *The Lord of the Rings* there had been a lull of six weeks where Jackson had been faced with his persistent Weta Digital problem. Their thirty-five Silicon Graphics machines were sitting idle and growing obsolete. Licence payments were due on the software packages, as well as the wages of the operators who were likely to up sticks for an increasingly bountiful digital revolution in Los Angeles. During development on *King Kong* they had doubled their staff. Mothballing Weta Digital until Middle-earth was ready wasn't an option.

Again it was Zemeckis who arrived in the nick of time. He was in post-production on an expensive, hard-science fiction adaptation of Carl Sagan's *Contact* and offered Weta Digital the opportunity to create the sequence of Jodie Foster plunging through a wormhole.

'That was the first thing we ever did for an outside vendor,' reports Jackson. While only a stopgap, this was enormously significant in industry terms. Here was the first, faint signal that

Weta Digital would one day operate outside of Jackson's projects and rival the likes of ILM and Digital Domain as a visual effects house for all-comers. For now, it was a matter of necessity. And Jackson was still serving as go-between with Zemeckis.

'I supervised it a bit from my end,' he laughs, amused by his credit as Additional Visual Effects. 'He wanted me to help visualize it, and sort of supervise. So, I did act like a visual effects supervisor for that scene, you could say.'

While still wary of jinxing the deal by even touching a copy of *The Lord of the Rings*,* Jackson and Walsh had risked taking one step in the direction of a screenplay. They asked erstwhile collaborator Costa Botes to break the book down scene-by-scene into a working précis. Loading it up onto their computer they could then experiment with different road maps from Hobbiton to the Crack of Doom.

Once they began to re-assimilate the book, the issue of structure became more serious. What of Tolkien's vast story would they keep? What would they excise? What would they dare add to the precious story? How *faithful* would they be to the book? It was the biggest question of all. Could they radically alter Tolkien and still be authentic? Ironically, given what eventually transpired at Miramax, at this stage they briefly explored the idea of 'one long, epic film'. Jackson also wondered whether it really ought to be three films, but Harvey swiftly disabused him of that notion.

Out of these first sessions emerged a ninety-two-page treatment, made up of 266 sequences: the embryo of an Oscar-winning trilogy.

Already mindful of how much interest the adaptation would engender, even in sleepy Wellington, Jackson codenamed the treatment *Jamboree: The Life of Lord Baden Powell.* You suspect more to amuse themselves, this also involved the adoption of

---

* To be fair, Jackson had re-read *The Hobbit* when they originally proposed starting with Bilbo's adventure. He also had a fairly clear memory of the 1981 BBC radio drama, while Walsh's memory from first reading the book remained impeccable.

grand but hardly uncrackable nom-de-plumes: Fran Walsh was Fredericka Wharburton; Peter Jackson became Percy J. Judkins.

Says 'Judkins', by way of explanation, '*Jamboree* was the code-name for the 1933 film *The Son of Kong*, and we gave it the scouting theme on the cover.' The caution to 'be prepared' would gain unwelcome prescience.

Not long afterwards came a stroke of phenomenally good fortune. Unable to gauge whether what they were writing was any good, Walsh decided they needed another voice in the mix. So they contacted Stephen Sinclair, a Kiwi playwright who had worked with them on *Meet the Feebles* and *Braindead.* Sinclair, who knew little of Tolkien, would in turn seek out the advice of his girlfriend, who knew her stuff. In this understated way, Philippa Boyens became pivotally involved in the project.

Parallel to wrestling the book's great girth into two palatable films was an extraordinary period of quasi-scientific research into how the two sides of Weta were going to solve a problem like Middle-earth without sillification. Pint-sized hobbits, out-sized creatures, epic battles, the magnificent variety of place and people that made the book so popular: Jackson needed to prove that not only filmmaking technology was ready for Tolkien, but Kiwi aptitude as well.

By August 1997, they were storyboarding and generating animatics (a rudimentary computer-based pre-visualization, or pre-viz, of key action). The influential artists Alan Lee and John Howe were installed in Wellington, already turning their intuition for Tolkien into reams of concept art. Locations were being scouted, logistics fathomed and the Gordian knot of scheduling loosened.

The journey of writing and visualizing the films will be tackled in the next chapter, but across Miramar the great beast of pre-production was stirring into motion: eighteen months of great hope and greater strife. Jackson and Walsh were slowly, respectfully and fretfully forming a relationship with a strait-laced

Oxford don who had never suffered film people gladly. They were also developing a markedly different kind of relationship with Harvey Weinstein, a film person who didn't suffer anyone gladly.

*

'Fran remembers this stuff much better than I do,' says Jackson stoically. 'It's like a car crash, I tend to sort of wipe out all the bad memories. Fran hangs on to every detail.' However much he may wish to forget, their dealings with the brothers grim are sewn into the fabric of this story. . .

With their initial treatment completed, Jackson and Walsh flew to New York to begin their script meetings at Miramax, and get their first taste of the Weinstein way. There would be three script meetings in all, principally with the two executives Cary Granat (inevitably dubbed 'Cary Grant'), the head of production at Dimension, and John Gordon, a Miramax production executive who had survived as Harvey's assistant, who were managing the project. Harvey and Bob were, as Jackson ominously puts it, 'floating around'. It had been decreed that this was to be the first Dimension-Miramax co-production and both brothers would make their presence felt.

Meetings at Miramax's Tribeca office were conducted in a small, unventilated room walled in frosted glass, known among browbeaten indie filmmakers as the 'sweatbox'. From the very first it was clear the Weinsteins were going to subject the project to the full glare of their nervous scrutiny. The honeymoon of getting the deal sealed was over; this was now about how their money was going to be spent. Jackson had a genuine feeling that it was only now that the brothers were truly rationalizing what was involved.

While Harvey had read the book in college, it became clear many of the executives, including Bob, had not. They were faced with the same frustration that confronted John Boorman and

Ralph Bakshi — how could you drill down into the fine print of Tolkien's world when everything you talked about was met with various degrees of bafflement?

Bob took almost malicious pride in playing the incredulous audience member who had never heard of Mr. J.R.R. Whoever. Any script was going to have to pass the Bob test. Indeed, having submitted an early draft, Jackson remembers Bob slamming his hand down on the table in triumph.

'I know what this is!' he declared. 'The Fellowship of the Ring, these nine characters, are all expert saboteurs. They all have their specialties. It's the fucking *Guns of Navarone!*'

'Really? *The Lord of the Rings*?' laughs Jackson, recalling his own incredulous reaction — and he couldn't be a bigger fan of the fucking *Guns of Navarone.* 'He had figured it all out. He now had a filter by which he could understand this thing.'

Harvey would generally give good notes, nothing too crazy. Bob was big on the fact they had to kill a hobbit. 'Pick one,' he kept telling them. All they could do was keep deflecting this stuff: 'Well, we will certainly think about that. . .' It soon became a slog. They were rewriting and rewriting, then flying to New York to play Tolkien tennis with the Weinsteins. Jackson started to suspect that the brothers might be stalling.

The budget, Harvey insisted, was not to exceed $75 million, which based on the $26 million *The Frighteners* had cost with all its CGI, Jackson naively thought was achievable. Then the whole process was like a whirlpool of elusive possibility in which they were increasingly likely to drown.

Amusingly, if only in hindsight, the Weinsteins revealed a good Harvey-bad Bob routine. Whenever Bob was out of the room, Harvey would tell them to ignore his brother, who was just crazy. Stick with his ideas.

'But you know that is not really the truth,' sighs Jackson. 'You're lulled into thinking Harvey is the one you can talk honestly with. But the *real* truth is he is really tight with Bob. It's an illusion.'

On occasion this Abbott and Costello routine would explode

into full theatrics. For instance, after another of Bob's ill-informed ideas, it was Harvey who slammed his meaty fist onto the table before storming out of the sweatbox. They watched his silhouette retreat down the corridor while Bob carried on regardless. Within moments Harvey's silhouette, as unmistakable as Hitchcock, came back down the corridor clutching an Oscar. The one his half of Miramax had received for *The English Patient*. He burst back into the room and thrust it in front of Bob.

'I've got one of these; you haven't got one of these. So who the hell do you think is the smarter one? Shut up, Bob!'

Looking back with a less jaundiced eye, Jackson likens Harvey's tricks to Tony Soprano or what it must have been like to work for one of the old, bullying Hollywood moguls, a Louis B. Mayer, Samuel Goldwyn or Harry Kohn, who would rage or weep to get their way. Everything had shifted into a different register, one of emotional extremes utterly alien to a New Zealand temperament. It was all so bipolar: tantrums followed by largesse.

During the darkest hours, as relationships fragmented, Harvey had called Ken Kamins and began to rant down the cell phone. Eventually Kamins got a word in edgewise, 'Harvey, I just don't want to hear this. I am with my wife giving birth.'

The next day a huge gift basket arrives care of Miramax.

Beneath all of Harvey's volatility was a stealthy manipulation. As the mists began to clear on a workable structure for the two films, it became starkly apparent that $75 million was vastly short of what was required. Experienced Australian producer Tim Sanders, who had worked on *The Frighteners*, had come on board at Jackson's behest expressly to draw up a budget. Realistically, he estimated the two films would cost $130 to $135 million. The news didn't go down well with Harvey, who had already invested in the region of $12 million toward serious development costs. A fact, Jackson says, 'that was driving him nuts'.

What Harvey wasn't telling Jackson was that he couldn't get Disney to let him greenlight anything beyond $75 million. He later claimed he had tried to entice them onboard as partners, but they turned him down flat.

Kamins isn't so sure that Disney had been so dismissive. 'I have since talked to [then Disney CEO] Michael Eisner and he tells me that he wanted to engage, but Harvey wouldn't show him anything. Wouldn't show him scripts. Wouldn't show him artwork. Wouldn't let him talk to Peter. I don't know if this is history being rewritten by the different participants, but he claims that he had asked Harvey for the ability to talk to Peter and the answer was no. And so when the answer was no, it was kind of like well, "Okay, no to you too."'

Harvey had even ventured to other studios in an attempt to offset the swelling costs. Whether it was the uncertainty of getting into the Miramax business, the pervasive scepticism over the viability of the project, or good old-fashioned *schadenfreude*, no one was buying.

In desperation, Harvey dispatched the 'executive from hell' to New Zealand charged with rationalizing Sanders' estimates back to $75 million. Jackson had looked up Russ Markovitz's credits and 'it was all a bit bloody dodgy'. With loose ties to Dimension through risible straight-to-video horror sequels for *The Prophecy* and *From Dusk Till Dawn*, Markovitz aggravated one and all by showing scant interest in the movie but a great obsession with Jackson having a medical in order to be properly insured. His increasingly paranoid imagination concocting nefarious plots to bump off the director for the insurance money, Jackson kept coming up with excuses to get out of it, before flatly refusing. 'It was a screwy time,' he admits. After two months, the mysterious Markovitz returned to from whence he came and was never heard from again.

With better judgment, Harvey then sent down Marty Katz, a more genial, square-jawed old-Hollywood type fresh from trouble shooting on *Titanic*, who expended a lot of energy trying to get his Porsche shipped over from Los Angeles. Katz, who was an old friend of Zemeckis, got along well with Jackson. He was impressed by what they were achieving in Wellington and reported back to Miramax both his enthusiasm and the confirmation that, 'If you've only got seventy-five million you can only do one film.'

In the end, his Porsche would never get to Wellington. Jackson, Walsh and Katz were summoned to the looming Orthancs of New York for a crisis meeting

'That is when it all sort of went pear-shaped,' says Jackson.

They were sat in the sweatbox. But there were no theatrics, no double-act. In fact, there was no Bob. Which was a very bad sign. Harvey was about to give them the benefit of his feelings and this time the fury wasn't an act. Jackson had betrayed them. He had broken their agreement. He had wasted $12 million of their money. Wasted his time, squandered his good will. Now the director had to do what was right and make a single film of *The Lord of the Rings* of no more than two hours in length for $75 million otherwise he was going to get John Madden to direct it.

Courtly and intelligent, a similar man in some respects to John Boorman, Madden was the very English director currently finishing up *Shakespeare In Love* to Harvey's satisfaction. The featherlight period rom-com concerning the famous playwright's romantic distractions would soon give Harvey another Oscar with which to berate his brother.

Kamins recalls a more radical threat. 'Harvey was like, "You're either doing this or you're not. You're out. And I got Quentin ready to direct it."'

Mad as that sounded, there was no way to know if it was a bluff. At the time he took it as gospel: Quentin Tarantino's fucking Middle-earth.

Harvey had already sent Jackson's two-film draft to British screenwriter Hossein Amini, another talent in good standing at Miramax having adapted Henry James' *The Wings of the Dove*. Amini remembers being baffled by the peculiar cover: '*Jamboree, The Life of Lord Baden Powell.*' Turning the page, it evidently had little to do with the Scout Movement.

Amini was a huge Tolkien fan and had been following the rumours about an adaptation. Now, here in his hands, was the secret script for *The Lord of the Rings*. He knew nothing of Harvey's ultimatum to Jackson that either Madden or Tarantino was waiting in the wings. 'They mentioned it might need some work, but I couldn't really see why. I read it and loved it,' he recalls.

When Miramax suggested converting it into one film, Amini's mind shot back to Bakshi's animated effort. A single film version would do nothing but alienate the massive fan base. 'I believe at the time budget was the biggest stumbling block,' he says, remaining convinced he was a bluff to get Jackson to rethink his approach toward the single film option.

In the sweatbox, with New York indifferently getting on with life somewhere outside, Jackson had reached the same conclusion. His face taking on a Gollum-like pallor, his hands trembling, he refused to crack. He just couldn't see how you could make a single film and still do justice to the book.

Harvey engaged the full orchestra of his fury, threatening lawsuits to get his money back once he had kicked them off the project and back to New Zealand.*

Says Kamins, 'Harvey really didn't want to let go. He didn't want to be embarrassed. And I think Peter was putting him in an awkward place. There was a mix of a lot of different feelings.' Indeed, it remains a tricky situation to parse. Jackson had agreed to a $75 million budget, and his plans had vastly outstripped that. Channels of communication had broken down. But he was on a road that would lead to over three billion dollars and Oscars galore. While no one could have quite predicted that, Miramax's voluble supremo had neither the foresight nor the means to back Jackson's vision, and in his frustration was

---

* In a strange marker of this time, Harvey appears as a talking head in Jackson and Botes' brilliant 1995 co-directed mock documentary about the discovery of a lost silent-era New Zealand filmmaker, *Forgotten Silver*.

pursuing something inevitably inferior. Did he really believe in the single film option?

To Jackson here was irony as bitter as burnt coffee (and he is assuredly a tea man). When they had first come to Miramax, Harvey had actually screened the Bakshi debacle proudly announcing, 'This is something we are never going to do.'

Jackson had been forewarned. Katz had got wind of the single-film scenario, although Jackson had thought he meant a first part with a potential sequel to follow. Even this thin hope was shredded, however, when a memo arrived at his hotel emblazoned 'ultra-confidential'. It turned out to be a litany of suggestions on how to crush Tolkien's novel into a tidy two hours, written without Jackson's knowledge.

Dated 17 June 1998 and written by Miramax development head Jack Lechner, it began, 'We've been thinking long and hard. . .' Despite Jackson's yeomen's efforts, the two-film structure was too dense — code for too expensive — and they had a more radical, streamlined approach utilizing 'key elements' but still dispensing with many. Among its manifest sins, Helm's Deep was cut, Théoden and Denethor combined (QED: so were Rohan and Gondor) and Éowyn replaced Faramir to be Boromir's sister, while the memo vacillated over whether the problematic Saruman should be cut or present at the Battle of the Pelennor Fields. The great, subterranean drama of Moria was to be 'drastically' shortened: Balin's Tomb, Orc attack, Balrog and out.

'It was literally guaranteed to disappoint every single person that has read that book,' concludes Jackson, still smarting.

Scribbled on the copy of the memo now archived in Miramar, was a note from Jackson to distribute it to all the department heads, 'so they can see why the project is coming to a sticky end.'

Harvey had cornered him. He understood the producer was doing what he felt was best for Miramax, that was his job, but Jackson and Walsh were shattered. They couldn't even think straight.

'We just said to Harvey, "We can't give you an answer. Please will you just give us time to fly back to New Zealand to think about it?"'

That was when Harvey's mood got worse.

The filmmakers left Miramax's office as if escaping Mount Doom, dashing across Tribeca to find a haven with their friend David Linde, the executive who had first gone to New Zealand to see *Heavenly Creatures* and since left Miramax to start his own production company, Good Machine. Linde could tell at a glance they were in a bad way. He retrieved a bottle of Scotch from a cabinet, stored for such an emergency.

Jackson smiles. 'It was the first time in my life I had ever drunk scotch.'

Catching the next flight home, Jackson and Walsh headed down the coast for a few days with the intention of celebrating Walsh's birthday. But on 8 July 1998, the trip was more about decompression; a chance to breathe blessed New Zealand air after all that American humidity.

Reflecting on their situation, it must have felt like they were cursed. They had spent nine arduous months on their remake of *King Kong* with Universal only for it to come to nothing. Now their even longer quest to bring *The Lord of the Rings* to the screen was heading the same way, or arguably somewhere worse. Being forced to make a hugely compromised version of the book they knew in their bones, no matter how hard they worked, would only be met with the scorn of fans; who would place the blame squarely upon Jackson's shoulders. This was no longer about making the best version of the book under the circumstance. This threatened their credibility as filmmakers.

Walking along the beach, you like to think with the sun setting, they accepted that there were forces you could not conquer. Skull Island or Mordor had nothing on Hollywood.

'I'd been hit too many times,' says Jackson.

He called Kamins. 'Just tell Harvey we can't do it. We'd rather have our lives and do our films and not deal with all this crap anymore. Tell Harvey to go ahead and make his film and good luck.'

Kamins being Kamins, he didn't actually do that.

Undaunted, resolute, the voice of reason: Kamins allowed fevers to cool down then went back to Harvey with a request. 'At the end of the day, what was the worst that was going to happen?' he laughs. If Weinstein still said no, the disappointment would remain the same.

These guys have killed themselves for you, he insisted. They have a vision that they had all signed up for. Would he give them an opportunity to make the movie the way they envisioned it somewhere else? You're not obligated, but I'm asking.

Harvey agreed, but his terms were draconian.

The most aggressive studio turnaround period, in which a filmmaker can attempt to find a new home for their project, might be six months. Traditionally, it's a year.

'You have four weeks,' Harvey told Kamins. 'If you set it up someplace else, I get all my money back immediately on signature. Not on the first day of photography. I get it all on signature. And I get five per cent of first dollar gross across the board.'

'Okay,' said Kamins, icy calm, 'let me give it a shot.'

*

So the phone would ring again, the shrill, insistent call of fate. Hope was back on the agenda. A fool's hope maybe — Kamins had been frank: relocating a project in four weeks was unheard of — but for now they were back in the Tolkien business. And that was enough.

'Exactly four weeks as the clock ticks,' echoes Jackson ruefully. Twenty-eight days later, if no deal had been struck, Harvey would take back control and offer it to Madden or Tarantino or whoever. You sense Weinstein really didn't believe it would happen, not under his impossible conditions. That ultimately he was hoping Jackson would learn the error of his ambitions and agree to make one film with Miramax.

Miramax had done a fine job distributing *Heavenly Creatures*, raising the New Zealand director's status immeasurably as a commercial filmmaker. They had invested in Jackson and wanted a return on that investment.

'Harvey didn't want to give up the movie,' says Kamins. 'Harvey had really wanted these films and he wanted them with Peter. But I think Bob didn't. They weren't on the same page. Bob was second-guessing the economic investment and was worried that they could really be putting themselves on a bad financial footing.'

Right now, what Jackson needed was a presentation. One that, as Kamins explains, quickly answered the questions, 'Why these movies? Why now? And why us?'

Of course, they were sitting on a hoard of concept art, test footage, storyboards, animatics, and even props and prosthetics. Richard Taylor admits that even as the mood had worsened with Miramax he and his team had refused to stop working. Frankly, they were in denial. The thought of abandoning the project was too painful to recognize. 'We were like addicts,' he says. 'We couldn't stop ourselves.' They went on designing, sculpting maquettes, and forging weapons and armour for a hypothetical Middle-earth. Lee and Howe, at least, would return to England and Switzerland respectively, their brief, wonderful sojourn in the moving picture business over with.

This was far too much material to play show-and-tell with the limited patience of a prospective studio. They would be out of the room before they'd finished setting up their slide show. There was also scant chance of encouraging anyone down to New Zealand to see their nascent operation. Half of Hollywood still couldn't find it on a map. Jackson's solution was to shoot a short film, a presentation piece that told their story. Kamins dubs it 'the making of the making of'.

Jackson still considers it the most important film he has ever made.

Cutting short Walsh's chaotic birthday trip, they were a good three-hour drive from their Wellington base. And so a story, already fraught, once again gathers the patina of movie melodrama as a storm bowled in off the Cook Strait and two filmmakers thinking of nothing else but the ticking clock persuaded a helicopter pilot to brave the tempest.

Jackson sounds rueful. A bad flier, he was known to turn his knuckles transparent gripping the armrests as 747s drooped into LAX. 'We had the worst helicopter ride in the world around the coast,' he remembers. To a Weinsteinian chorus of thunder, pummelled by winds, lashed with rain and plunging between pockets of air it felt as if King Kong had plucked them out of the sky. When they touched down in Wellington, Jackson's legs almost gave out, but it never occurred to either of them they were now risking their lives for the sake of these films.

So while Kamins began a preliminary round of the studios, armed only with the scripts and a basic animatic of the story, Jackson enlisted Allun 'Bolie' Bollinger, cinematographer on *Heavenly Creatures*, and roused his team to help create a forceful 'documentary'.

What immediately impresses is how confidently the thirty-five-minute pitch answered Kamins' questions. It demonstrates an affinity with the material and the certainty that technology had not only caught up with Tolkien's imagination but this New Zealand operation was more than capable of wielding those advances. With a youthful Jackson in the starring role (bearing no ill effects from his recent dalliance with death), the film makes explicit how this vast world would be brought to life.

Talking heads extoll the need for realism. A mythical reality that is 'lived in, sweated in' says Howe. Using the power of the Lee-Howe artwork and behind-the-scenes footage from Weta Workshop, they describe how hobbit stature would be achieved using forced perspective, motion-controlled cameras and body doubles with digital face replacement. There are beautifully lit maquettes by the sculptural magician Jamie Beswarick: powerful, redolent versions of Orcs, Ringwraiths and the Balrog exactly as they would appear in the finished film.

At Weta Digital they talk up the Cave-troll as their test case for digital biology, modelled on a real human skeleton and musculature then distorted into a troll's frame. Motion capture is discussed but not yet in relation to, at this stage, a more alien-looking Gollum. Software magician Stephen Regelous reveals prototype footage of the MASSIVE software program that would allow them to mount battles with thousands of computer-generated 'thinking' soldiers.

There is also a slender tally of things later abandoned or used limitedly: large puppets to scale up humans alongside hobbits, demonic horses for the Ringwraiths and the idea of giving all the Orcs digitally enlarged eyes like Gollum.

Local actors including the steadfast Jed Brophy (whose involvement with Jackson goes back to *Braindead*), Craig Parker (who would play the elf Haldir, as Frodo) and Peter Vere Jones (from *Bad Taste*, as a touching Gandalf), perform choice segments from an animatic of the entire film — something else that had displeased Miramax. Familiar passages from The Council of Elrond, Moria and Mount Doom relayed over cycling storyboards. The scores of *Braveheart* and *The Last of the Mohicans* are used throughout.

The footage is so thorough and ardently mounted it became the prototype for Jackson's vaults of DVD extras. This wasn't a desperate plea it was a fully strategized battle plan.

To complement the video, Taylor's team provided a set of their finest maquettes to accompany Jackson. Something meaningfully tactile that would hopefully serve a better purpose than the sculpture of King Kong sent and then retrieved from Universal.

The idea was that when they got to LA there would be a slew of meetings with their dog-and-pony show raring to go. However, they landed to the news only two meetings had actually been confirmed.

On the other side of the Pacific, Kamins had been burning a hole in his contact book trying to get Jackson through the door. To give the studios a taste of how serious a proposition this was, how good. But he was drawing blank after blank; it was terrifying.

Notoriously, Decca turned down the Beatles, nearly every publisher in London passed on *Harry Potter* and Western Union spurned the chance to spend $100,000 on the patent for an 'interesting novelty' called a telephone. History is littered with bad calls. But in Hollywood commercial misjudgements are an inevitable side effect of the business where every movie is a swing at a curving ball; you can only hope to hit more often than you miss. In Hollywood, as screenwriter William Goldman immortally pronounced, 'Nobody knows anything.' However popular the book might be, *The Lord of the Rings* held no guarantees. It was too long, too tricky and — cue: siren — too expensive. Add in Harvey's prohibitive conditions and Kamins knew he had a hard sell on his hands.

But he hadn't counted on the politics. The obvious objections weren't even raised. That Jackson didn't have the track record to support this kind of venture. That fantasy struggled at the box office. That this sounded like *Willow* or *Labyrinth*. 'It wasn't any of those things,' says Kamins. This was an industry-wide jeremiad against the viability of Tolkien.

Paramount was developing *The Lion, the Witch and the Wardrobe*, the bestselling children's fantasy by Tolkien's friend and peer C.S. Lewis. They felt they were tonally too close (a nonsense). Lewis' book would eventually be adapted by Walton Media and released by Disney to capitalize on Jackson's triumph.

Disney was already in the middle of things with Harvey and had spurned, or been denied, the chance to be involved.

'Regency was interested.' Kamins is referring to independent production house Regency Enterprises, run by the billionaire and former Israeli spy Arnon Milchan — another colourful character in the echelons of Hollywood. With distribution deals at Warner and 20th Century Fox, they can boast hits as varied as *JFK*, *Pretty Woman*, and *LA Confidential*. Milchan had gotten as far as approaching his partners at Fox to say he was keen.

'What's Saul Zaentz's involvement?' Fox had shot back.

'Well, he gets a fee,' Milchan responded carefully. 'He doesn't get a credit, but he gets a fee and a participation on the back end.' Wherever they went the basic terms of Zaentz's deal with Miramax would still stand.

Kamins shakes his head philosophically. Where once *The English Patient* had opened doors, now it was slamming them shut.

'Fox had fumed, "If he gets one nickel, we're out."'

The year Fox walked away from *The English Patient*, Zaentz had given the keynote address at the American Film Market. Even though the film had been revived with Miramax, this turned into a twenty-minute denunciation of the evil empire, Fox. How they hated movies, hated filmmakers and were anti-artists.

'It was a rant,' says Kamins, 'a very public rant.'

So Fox was out. And Regency.

Amy Pascal, the head of Sony, openly told Kamins she didn't care for the scripts. 'I don't know if there was more to it, but that's what we were told.'

After *The Frighteners* and *King Kong*, there was baggage with Universal. They were better to hedge their bets by going back through their old friend Zemeckis. He could surely relate: every studio in town had turned down his pitch about a teenager who accidentally travels back to the 1950s, before Universal agreed to make *Back to the Future*. Sadly, they weren't buying now. Recent history couldn't be rewritten.

Kamins goes on. They tried Roland Emmerich, who had used his newfound clout to set up a production company called Centropolis, but he claimed not to like the scripts either.

'So that left us with New Line, because Peter had a longstanding friendship with Mark Ordesky, who worked for Fine Line, their arthouse division.' It was tenuous, but they were desperate. 'And we went to PolyGram and Working Title.'

Both agreed to listen to Jackson's pitch.

They flew to Los Angeles troubled less by turbulence than a growing sense of dread, and landed to the news that a baggage handler at LAX had dropped one of their flight boxes and a precious maquette of Treebeard had smashed on the tarmac.

'We just felt like fate was against us,' recalls Taylor.

First came PolyGram (who had distributed *Braindead* in the UK) represented by their British production arm, Working Title. 'I believe it was Eric Fellner and Liza Chasin from Working Title,' says Kamins. Stewart Till, the CEO of PolyGram, the man with the power to greenlight the films, wasn't at the meeting but had read the screenplays. Kamins had them delivered to his hotel room and Till had given his corporate blessing to Working Title to pursue the project if they were as keen as him.

Led by the charming, savvy producer Fellner, they couldn't have been more enthusiastic; but he had no idea they were one of only two last-ditch possibilities. 'Really? We got no sense of that,' he says, remembering a very impressive pitch. Being able to handle those beautiful maquettes left a real impression. 'God, if we'd only done it,' he laughs. 'But we were never going to be able to. At the time, it was two films, and I think Jackson wanted $180 million. We just weren't in a place to do that. PolyGram just didn't have $180 million dollars to put into a project.'

In fact, PolyGram was in the process of being sold (it finally folded in 1999) and couldn't make any commitments until the sale was done, let alone one of this magnitude. Realistically, it was going to be two to three months before they could properly talk.

'We have seven days,' replied Jackson.

The yo-yoing of hopes kindled then dashed was taking its toll. Dread was sliding into despair. Why keep subjecting themselves to such disappointment?

'New Line was the only other meeting we had,' he says. 'At that point I really was like, "Let's just do our New Line meeting tomorrow and go home."'

*

In 1986, Mark Ordesky was in the direct-to-video business, sourcing lucrative shockers for B-movie distributor Republic Pictures: ghoulish Z-grade stuff like *Witchboard* and *Scared Stiff*. But even they thought he was nuts for suggesting *Bad Taste*. Ordesky had been gobsmacked after the New Zealand Film Commission had sent him a copy of Jackson's splatter-happy debut and, undaunted, took the tape with him when he moved to New Line.

'I became this kind of Peter Jackson partisan,' he enthuses. 'Whatever was happening, that was my solution to it.'

Slight, with tightly cropped hair and an unwavering gaze, Ordesky is a likably upbeat soul who doesn't see the worth in hiding his insecurities. He is like a recovering Hollywood addict. He openly frets and fusses, always the butt of his own stories, but nothing can disguise his quick, deprecating wit and, especially, his passion. You could bottle the stuff. He would deny it, always crediting Jackson, but that passion truly counted when it came to adapting *The Lord of the Rings*, a book he revered. When Jackson was introduced to Ordesky's mother, she told him about the Alan Lee posters her son had on his wall.

Sure enough, Ordesky had been a *Dungeons and Dragons* addict as a kid and his dungeon master, who he held in great esteem, had presented him with a box of required reading: *The Hobbit, The Lord of the Rings* and a 'bunch' of Michael Moorcock, Robert E. Howard, C.S. Lewis and Jack Vance. He ended up reading *The Lord of The Rings* before *The Hobbit*. And it took hold of him deeply.

'The idea of a small person, which I was and remain, taking on this great journey appealed to me in a very profound manner.'

Ordesky got into the film business by fittingly circuitous means. As a student, he had written a novella called *Lines* that had been picked up by TriStar. Not, he insists, for any great literary merit but because of its double-act of a grizzled old hack teaming up with a callow student journalist to solve the murder of the campus drug dealer. They had Gene Hackman and Matthew Broderick in mind. It never got made, but it did get

Ordesky a job as a script reader at TriStar, which convinced him writing was not his calling.

'My true skill was recognizing great talent in others and being able to articulate and advocate,' he says. That, and the balls to stroll into New Line, past the receptionist and ask round for a job. To get him back out of the building he was offered the chance to provide notes on a script called *The Hidden*. Fortunately, he liked the alien invasion movie as much as CEO Bob Shaye and was hired. This was before his brief spell at Republic, and he would return to New Line, his tape of *Bad Taste* to hand, as a story editor and began to frantically push this guy named Jackson.

In light of his inability to get *Bad Taste* on the map, Ordesky had actually written Jackson a fan letter. Something along the lines of, 'Hello, you don't know me, but I have failed you. I loved your film, although I failed to convince my bosses. But someday I'm going to be a big player in the film business and I will not fail you then.'

The director may have been blissfully unaware, but at New Line Ordesky was championing him for *Texas Chainsaw Massacre 3* and pushing *Braindead 2* (Jackson's zombie comedy had eventually been released via Trimark in America under the braindead title *Dead Alive*). Finally, when they were looking for a suitably bloodthirsty talent to revive the flagging *Nightmare On Elm Street* franchise, Jackson was commissioned to write a script with his *Meet The Feebles* co-screenwriter Danny Mulheron.

'They were friends more than anything else,' observes Kamins. Jackson would stay on Ordesky's 'ratty-arsed sofa' on his earliest visits to LA, and they would sit up all night playing Risk. Even if it eventually landed in turnaround purgatory, Ordesky still adores Jackson's 'meta' take on Freddy Krueger.

'The film was set several years in the future,' he explains eagerly, launching into a description of *A Nightmare On Elm Street 6: The Dream Lover*, the Freddy movie that never was. When the film begins, no one takes Freddy seriously anymore, therefore he's no threat. Springfield teens now go to sleep on purpose, mainlining sleeping pills to enter the dream world and beat up on him '*Clockwork Orange*-style'. The heart of the movie was a cop who gets put in a coma in an accident and must contend with a resurgent serial killer.

'What was really great was that the whole movie took place in Freddy's world,' says Ordesky. In other words, it would entail the creation of an elaborate fantasy universe... New Line were impressed enough with the Jackson-Mulheron script to subsequently ask Jackson if he would be interested in working on their *Freddy Versus Jason* concept, but he declined.

When it came to his Tolkien pitch, Jackson didn't need to dance around Ordesky. He gave to him straight. 'We've got a four-week window before *The Lord of the Rings* goes ahead without us,' he informed his friend by phone. Could Ordesky lay the foundation at New Line before they rolled into town with their presentation? Could he get them a meeting?

Ordesky could hardly breathe when he replaced the receiver. 'Literally when the call came, I knew what pure faith was. I felt that with my love of Peter and my love of *The Lord of the Rings* that this is why you get into things.'

Not that Ordesky's enthusiasm prevented Kamins from cooking up some Hollywood gamesmanship. He kept delaying the meeting, implying Jackson was busy meeting other studios. In reality, with little to do, he and Walsh would head off to the movies, catching *The Mask of Zorro* and *Saving Private Ryan*. The process was becoming surreal, they were so primed, so aware of how little time they had, only now they were drinking Big Gulps in Santa Monica matinees as if they hadn't a care in the world.

Not for the first or last time, their New Zealand pragmatism marvelled at the strangeness of Hollywood. So much of it depended on the pretence of something. It was a fantasy world.

After what Kamins considered a suitable lapse of time to fool their prospective producers, the meeting was scheduled.

'So it was Peter, Fran and me, and it was Marty Katz, who was still the producer of record at the time,' reports Kamins, listing the attendees of their fateful meeting. 'And then it was going to be Mark Ordesky and Bob Shaye from New Line.' Despite Ordesky's fervour and Kamins' games, they still weren't being taken too seriously. New Line's influential Head of Production, Michael De Luca, was in London visiting the set of *Lost in Space*, a clunky attempt by New Line to warm up a science-fiction franchise.

Finally, it was Shaye, sleek and coiffured like an ageing prince, upon whom their tattered hopes were hanging. Co-chairman of New Line (with Michael Lynne, who was based in New York), only he remained with the power to greenlight their two-film adaptation of *The Lord of the Rings*.

In many, less conspicuous ways, New Line was a more influential and versatile indie than Miramax. They courted audience approval not headlines. They had found cash in kudos, bringing foreign masters to American audiences, such as Robert Bresson's *Au Hassard Balthazar* and Eric Rohmer's *The Marquise of O*. But it was the company's pioneering line in low-budget horror that set it apart, and made it so successful. Shaye and Lynne were behind such seminal gore as Sam Raimi's *Evil Dead*, Tobe Hooper's *Texas Chainsaw Massacre* and Wes Craven's *A Nightmare on Elm Street*. They were known as the 'house that Freddy built'. In more recent times, they had lined the coffers by diversifying into action, comedy and action-comedy hits like *The Mask, Dumb and Dumber, Rush Hour* and the *Austin Powers* trilogy. Upholding their kudos with Oscar nominations for Paul Thomas Anderson's *Boogie Nights* and critical appreciation of David Fincher's serial killer hit *Seven*.

Charismatic and prickly, mercurial and driven, in his late fifties Shaye was a complex soul. Unlike Harvey, there was no subterfuge, no games; he told it like he saw it, wearing his heart on his sleeve. He could be moved to public tears. But he wasn't predictable or tame. This former New York hipster and art collector was a filmmaker at heart who once shared a prize with Martin Scorsese from the Society of Cinematologists for a surreal 1964 short entitled *Image*. Started in 1967 with $300 of his own money, working out of his New York apartment with a piece of plinth for a desk, there was something homemade about New Line.

Says Ordesky, 'He had a true artistic streak.' But it could be a double-edged sword. He was quite prepared to slay dreams if he felt they had no reality.

To his chosen 'sons', like De Luca and Ordesky, the paternal Shaye preached a gospel of experimentation and escaping claustrophobic studio thinking. Or as he put it, with his knack for a telling aphorism, 'Not smoking from the Hollywood crack pipe.' In fostering talent, could they 'spot someone one or two stops before the station'?

'In my own small way with Peter Jackson, I did,' claims Ordesky. Indeed, the Kiwi had barely found his seat on the train.

Picture the conference room of New Line's headquarters at 116 N. Robertson Blvd, since vacated when they were subsumed into parent company Time Warner. Well appointed but unremarkable by Hollywood norms: boardroom table, designer chairs, state-of-the-art VCR, television, water and coffee. Did they offer tea?

'The first thing that happens is Bob Shaye is not there,' recounts Jackson.

Ordesky came into the room, his face ashen, to announce that, 'Bob would like a private word with Peter first, then he'll come look at the video.'

Putting on his game face, Jackson got up to go, a lead bar in his stomach. Ordesky could feel everyone looking at him for some kind of response. This wasn't supposed to be happening. Had the bad news arrived before they had even started?

'Mark had warned us Bob Shaye was a plainspoken guy,' notes Kamins. 'We could be six minutes into this thing and he might just say, "Stop the tape, we're done. It's over."'

All they could do was wait for Jackson to return.

Jackson remembers feeling sick as he entered Shaye's office. He knew New Line's kingpin a little from his Freddy Krueger days, but hardly well enough to second-guess his motives.

Shaye looked at him kindly. 'Listen, I'm happy to spend an hour with you looking at this film that you've got for us,' he said, 'but you've got to realize that it's probably something that we're not going to want to do.'

Jackson had no idea how to respond.

Walsh only had to look her partner in the eye to know what had happened. The jig was finally up. All Jackson could do was go through the motions. Like an out of body experience, he watched this version of himself calmly return to his seat and his artwork and his maquettes, only pride and forward momentum keeping him afloat.

It was Ordesky who loaded the tape and pressed play.

He knew this was only more pretending. Yet even now, as those thirty-five minutes of endeavour unspooled, Jackson couldn't yet jettison all hope. He too was an addict of the Ring, lost in denial, and every now and then he would glance at Shaye, just to see. 'But there was no expression, no comment, nothing. . .'

He remained as inscrutable as a cat.

Well aware the odds were stacked against *The Lord of the Rings*, Kamins had not been idle. He knew they needed a backup. While struggling to hawk their Tolkien opus around town, he had actively been looking into other projects for Jackson. Projects that could keep the Weta dream alive.

While balancing on his *Lord of the Rings* high wire, Jackson had taken other calls. 'There was a lot of enthusiasm for me directing the next Bond movie,' he grins, a lifelong Bond enthusiast contemplating 007's alternative universe. Kamins tells the story of an early initiation watching *Thunderball* while his new client talked him through nuances of SPECTRE set decoration. 'It was the Pierce Brosnan one,' recalls Jackson, '*The World Is Not Enough*.' Barbara Broccoli had loved *Heavenly Creatures* and asked to see *The Frighteners*.

He sent over a tape and never heard from her again.

Joel Silver, the ebullient producer behind the *Die Hard* and *Lethal Weapon* films, pitched him *Lobo*, a comic-book series about an intergalactic bounty hunter. Closer to his tastes, Tom Rothman at 20th Century Fox, who he knew from their *Planet of the Apes* discussions, tempted him with *Twenty One*, the tale of a First World War hotshot who shot down twenty-one enemy planes in twenty-one days. Jackson was keen enough to show Rothman the biplane tests he had done for *King Kong*.

Jackson jokes that he could have been David Fincher before David Fincher. He was sent *Fight Club* first. He had read *The Curious Case of Benjamin Button* before Fincher got his hands on it. 'If someone is going to pick up my rejects I am very glad it was him.'

He met with Kathleen Kennedy to talk about *The BFG*, the Roald Dahl adaptation full of big folk rather than little, since fulfilled by his friend and collaborator Steven Spielberg. He was certainly interested, but he had to be honest. Within three or four weeks he might be doing this other film. 'We just don't know yet.'

Kamins suspected that if *The Lord of the Rings* didn't work out, especially after *King Kong*, Jackson and Walsh would have likely 'taken their ball and gone home' to New Zealand to pick up on that smaller, local career. Maybe Jackson would have revived those back-to-back *Bad Taste* sequels featuring Derek in space.

The video ended with a deafening *click*, and silence congealed around them. Ordesky was visibly squirming; if Shaye said no he'd already planned to chase after him to try and talk him round, risking his own standing at New Line. 'I probably contributed to the sense of drama,' he confesses. But Shaye didn't get up. Instead he turned to Jackson and looked him in the eye. There is a sense of events switching into slow motion as a series of checks and balances are determined invisibly in the air — a recalibration of destiny.

'Why would anyone want movie-goers to pay eighteen dollars when they might pay twenty-seven dollars?' he finally asked, his face still betraying nothing.

Everyone tried to process what he was saying. Why were they talking about ticket prices? Had they started their own game of riddles?

'So I don't get this at all,' Shaye continued, 'why would you make two films when there are *three* books?'

Jackson was only becoming more perplexed. Did he mean they should only be doing one film? Were they back at the gates of Harvey's ultimatum? 'I'm like, what does this mean?'

Shaye still wasn't finished. 'Tolkien has done your job for you, Tolkien wrote *three* books,' he pressed. 'If you're going to do it justice, it should be *three* movies.'

You could have heard a Mithril pin drop.

Ordesky can still picture Jackson's face, seeing the wheels begin to turn. An incredible, unforeseen recalculation was underway. The director's voice came out hesitantly, still not quite daring to believe, 'Yes. . . It could be three films.'

*

While it's a pleasure to remain here, basking in the glow of a dream-come-true now enshrined in Hollywood folklore, there was of course much more to it than that. Most immediately, the films certainly hadn't been greenlit yet. According to Jackson, such are the thorny tracts of Hollywood business that it was hardly unusual that the fully ratified, ink-on-paper go-ahead wasn't actually signed until about two weeks out from shooting. Elijah Wood was already trying his feet on.

Back then Shaye did at least switch onto a business footing. His voice a perfected blend of beneficence and caution, he began inching a trilogy forward. 'This is very impressive, something that I wasn't expecting it to be. I can see this. I want to show it to Michael [Lynne]. Can we keep the tape?'

They hadn't wanted to leave the tape anywhere, but how could they say no?

'I don't know where you are in the process; I don't care,'

Shaye went on, 'but I can't do anything until my partner sees it.'

It is strange to report that there was not a trace of euphoria as they filed out of the room. Jackson was too gun-shy for any kind of celebration. 'You don't emotionally invest in anything until you know it was a hundred per cent certain,' he admits. 'So it wasn't euphoric, it was more like *really*?'

As excited as Shaye was by the pitch, there was more to his interest in *The Lord of the Rings* than the thoroughness of Jackson's proposition. The meeting couldn't have been more perfectly timed. New Line was deep into a dry spell. Vacillating talent and spiralling costs had combined to scuttle sequels to their big franchises: *A Nightmare on Elm Street, Dumb and Dumber* and *The Mask*. They were hungry for a branded property with built-in sequels.

Indeed, Shaye's energies had been focussed on an adaptation of Isaac Asimov's *Foundation* books. But in a not unfamiliar turn of events he had come to loggerheads with the rights holders. After a year and a half of development a lot of money had, as Kamins says, 'walked out of the door'. Frustrated, Shaye had let the option lapse. This was no more than a month before Jackson walked in the door.

New Line's chief had a more measured take on the meeting. He knew the proposed budget. He knew the financial structure of the company could handle it. Yes, they needed sequels. And here was an opportunity to have three years of 'potential security and good business'.

Twenty-four hours later, Kamins' phone rang. It was Shaye — Lynne had seen the tape. 'We're ready to start negotiating,' he said and that was that.

The prosaic reality of Hollywood spoils the poetry of the occasion. Deal-making at its most mechanical would continue for months. Yet there is no doubt that it still took a mad flutter from a maverick studio like a PolyGram or a Miramax or a New Line to back the films. Shaye wasn't a corporate soul. He viewed himself in a romantic, old Hollywood mould: David O Selznick stoking the flames of *Gone with the Wind*. Says Kamins, 'Bob Shaye would look for ways to buck the system.'

Shaye felt his calling in Hollywood was to find a balance between art and commerce, cash and kudos. He was a frustrated film director trapped running the company. Whereas Lynne, with his well-tended beard, shining pate and tailored suits, began as New Line's general council before becoming COO in 1990 and CEO in 2001. He was the sense to Shaye's sensibility. He shored up the bottom line, steadying the boat if Shaye's more mercurial style ever set it rocking.

If Bob was 'dad', the gag went; then Michael was 'mom'.

'Bob is an artist and intensely creative,' says Ordesky. 'The reason why he and Michael made such great partners is that Michael is incredibly sharp and business-like. They had known each other from college days. They could see through situations to the heart of an opportunity and find a way to structure that opportunity in a really compelling way. But Bob, even though he had a thoughtful process, was also a gut player.'

Like Miramax, New Line was an indie minnow swallowed by a bigger fish. Shaye and Lynne had offloaded ownership of the company to media mogul (and then husband of Jane Fonda) Ted Turner, who was subsequently swallowed by a whale. Time Warner, the media conglomerate that also operated Warner Bros., merged with Turner, sending a shiver down the New Line spine. Yet within the corporate hierarchy that emerged, Shaye and Lynne were granted far more autonomy than the Weinsteins. They could, within reason, steer New Line's destiny.

Whatever the ultimate driving force behind Shaye's great gamble on Jackson and Frodo, you suspect that an element of it was an opportunity to show up Miramax. Proof that he was operating on a studio scale.

In response, Hollywood thought that Bob Shaye was going to sink the company. New Line was risking north of $200 million on three films made back-to-back by the guy who had directed *The Frighteners*. If the first film flopped, you were left with, as

Jackson put it, 'the *two* most expensive straight-to-DVD films in history'.

Behind his natural Hollywood sangfroid, Kamins' voice becomes intense: 'If you watched Peter and Fran go through the entire process; if you looked at those maquettes; if you looked at the designs and the artwork; if you looked at this documentary. There was a level of seriousness and purpose of responsible filmmakers honouring the investment being made. But also that risk married perfectly with the cultural DNA of New Zealand, which is: we're going to show the world that we can do what they can do.'

It was a sensibility that tallied with New Line's underdog persona. The enterprise was so big and so daring that the risk involved almost felt hopeful. It said something about what was possible in this business. 'I think we all sort of lived in that for the first couple of years,' says Kamins.

Ordesky was more than aware that this was his company, his family, his job security, betting the farm on a mad venture. Yet not for a single second did he harbour a doubt that they had made the right choice.

'I had known Peter as a human being for a long time. I had a conviction about him on a human level, about his stamina, about his brilliance. Not just his creative brilliance, his strategic and intellectual capacities to manage something so huge and with so many parts. And that gave me a certainty.'

CHAPTER 4

Words and Pictures

When Philippa Boyens was twelve years old her mother presented her with a copy of the book that would change her life. She was partial to a vein of old-school, romantic fantasy, inspired by her time spent at school in England. Between terms, her family would tour the country locating the fabled seats of Arthurian history. Myths and legends fired her imagination.

Nevertheless, moons would wax and wane while *The Lord of the Rings* stared at her from the shelf, untouched. She had enjoyed *The Hobbit*, but she was wary of the sheer volume of its grown-up brother. Venture within those pages and she might never come out. Which, you could say, is exactly what happened.

'I've got this memory of my sister having swimming lessons,' she says, 'and me sitting in the car and deciding, "Okay, I'm going to start reading this thing."'

It was like taking a deep breath then diving in.

'Then I read it every year. I'm not joking, *every* year. It was my rainy day book.' There were many wet afternoons in the New Zealand she returned to as a teen.

Boyens had loved C.S. Lewis' Narnia novels, fleet and quixotic, with evacuees finding snow-dusted enchantment at the back of a wardrobe. But Lewis wasn't an obsessive like Tolkien. That is what moved her so deeply. How you could keep delving and there would always be another layer beneath. She lapped up the genealogy, the languages, how every person or place or antique artefact was reinforced in the appendices, and this great legend-arium linked together like history.* Only Ursula K. Le Guin's *Earthsea* novels came close.

She might refute the label of Tolkien expert that is regularly foisted upon her — often by a director swerving a tricky question. 'I'm not an expert. I've *met* Tolkien experts. I can't speak Elvish.' Even so, while a teen, Boyens read Humphrey Carpenter's eloquent biography of Tolkien, high-minded appreciation by David Day and Tom Shippey and the low-minded parody of The Harvard Lampoon's 1969 *Bored of the Rings*, featuring Frito Bugger and Gimlet son of Groin. She would bring to the films an invaluable depth of knowledge and near-photographic recall of the professor's sub-creation. She also had a real thing for the art of Alan Lee.

Her mother, that singular influence, had given her a copy of Lee's seminal collection *Faeries*, a gift she passed on to Jackson. There was an illustration of a 'Gandalf-like character' that, she says, 'really lit Pete's radar'.

What she had resolutely *not* done was watch Ralph Bakshi's half-grown adaptation. On this she was adamant, no one could possibly do justice to the book on film.

In early 1997, Stephen Sinclair was helping Jackson and Walsh fathom how to do just that. While a fine dramatist, who had read the books as a kid, Sinclair was no expert and had no intention of changing that fact. He took what Jackson called a 'cavalier' attitude toward the text. However, Sinclair's girl-friend, a playwright, teacher, editor and director of the New

---

* 'I'm the one who read the footnotes,' Boyens laughs. 'I love a footnote.' As far as she is concerned, they are the height of sophistication. It is something she adored about Susannah Clarke's sprawling fantasy of Napoleonic-era wizards, *Jonathan Strange and Mr Norrell*, which New Line would toy with adapting to fill the fantasy void left by *The Lord of the Rings*.

Zealand Writer's Guild, definitely knew a thing or two about Tolkien.

Boyens can remember the night Jackson and Fran Walsh first called, wondering if he might join their new project. She was in the kitchen when Sinclair got off the phone.

'Oh my God,' he said. 'You'll never guess what Fran and Pete are working on next.'

'I have no idea.'

'It's *The Lord of the Rings*.'

Boyens was incensed. 'Well, they can't. That's crazy. No one can make that film.'

With her deep red, disobedient locks, often shored-up beneath a hat, Boyens cultivates a bohemian air much like her close friend Walsh. The two women who work so closely with Jackson have an aura of the otherworldly about them, as if they already had one foot in Middle-earth. Cloaked in her softly Gothic selection of floor-length dresses and shawls, you might suspect Boyens of being a modern-day sorceress. That is until you get a taste of her earthy Kiwi humour and logical mind. Like her partners, she has little time for the platitudes of Hollywood. There is an undercurrent of conviction to her mellifluous, Kiwi accent that is ironclad.

When Sinclair showed Boyens the treatment, she came back with notes. 'Just ideas about the story,' she vows. Initially, all Jackson and Walsh knew of Sinclair's bookish partner who would alter the course of their creative lives were the incisive despatches that arrived from Auckland via Sinclair (Boyens also unofficially assisted Sinclair in writing some 'romantic' elements while he was still involved in *The Lord of the Rings*), until, intrigued, they invited her down to Wellington. After ten minutes of effusive icebreaking over how impressed she had been by their treatment, she got on to its shortcomings. Which turned out to be the interesting part. If there were things she felt they had done wrong — and there were more than a few — she had a solution for each one.

Boyens emphasized that it was critical to still recognize this as *The Lord of the Rings* within the landscape of the film. It had been an almost counterintuitive experience, assessing the book as a film, prompting an internal debate with her old self. Knowing in her heart that you can't do *The Lord of the Rings* without Tom Bombadil and the Old Forest, but in her head understanding that you have to. Boyens found that she was able to think ruthlessly in film terms.

Impressed, Jackson and Walsh pushed for her active involvement. Meanwhile Sinclair's interest had begun to wane as he itched to return to his plays and novels. The enormity of the project was too much of a commitment. 'He looked at one draft,' confirms Jackson. 'But he was involved for literally a few weeks.' Sinclair was recognized with a credit on *The Two Towers*, where his contribution was most manifest.

Thus it was Boyens who became the third voice in a screenwriting fellowship. She admits to feeling 'terrified' at first. This was her precious *The Lord of the Rings*; it still felt crazy to be even thinking of turning it into a film. But this was an offer to be at the heart of the craziness. To live and breathe Tolkien in a completely new way. How could she say no?

Before she met them, Boyens had been avidly following Jackson and Walsh's blossoming career. She thought *Braindead* was genius. She was in the audience at the New Zealand Awards when *Heavenly Creatures* won everything only to be denied Best Film. 'I felt like, God, New Zealand film needs to grow up. It felt so small and insular, and Fran and Pete have always looked outwards.'

That sense of adventure was infectious.

'The biggest issue was always how do you get into this story?' Boyens had written plays and dealt with screenwriters, but never attempted a screenplay herself. She was hired first as a script editor on the two-film draft, which was still in need of a prologue. So she volunteered to try and write one. The very first thing she officially set to paper was the opening line, 'The world has changed. . .' Over the arduous months that became years of interminable rewrites and restructuring of ultimately three-intertwined, award-strewn scripts, that line never changed.

*

'The most difficult thing on this project has been the script. The script has been a total nightmare.' Jackson was speaking in Cannes in 2001, where he had unveiled twenty-six minutes of footage to raptures from the world's press. The question of how one successfully adapts Tolkien had come up frequently. Something he had been doing his level best to answer for six years.

He mused that it was about getting the balance right. To have the characters represent both Tolkien's intentions and be accessible for a modern cinema audience who didn't have a clue about hobbits or Elves. 'It's about trying to please as many people as possible,' he explained, which he knew sounded horribly general. 'But to reach people,' he insisted, 'you have to start by pleasing yourself. And that is what I did. I thought simply of the film I dreamed of seeing.'

Costa Botes has a memory of seeing the script for *Bad Taste*. Or the lack of it — it was little more than lines scribbled on increasingly crumpled pieces of paper in biro. Jackson had had no idea how to write a formal script. Walsh at least had some experience writing for television. 'But both of them got religion when Robert McKee made a rare excursion to Wellington and they attended his seminar.'

McKee was the Detroit-born playwright and screenwriter turned hugely influential creative screenwriting guru touring the world with his famous Story Seminar. He preached a gospel that it was narrative structure that made a story compelling rather than any of its component pieces: plot, dialogue, characters, etc. You must *tell a story*.

Enlightened, Jackson and Walsh changed their entire approach to screenwriting. Out of which came *Meet the Feebles, Braindead* — which for all its gore is elegantly structured — and, in time, their *Planet of the Apes* and Freddy Krueger scripts. Says Botes, 'I remember Pete showing me the third draft of *Heavenly Creatures*. It's a masterpiece. That's an unbelievable development in a very short space of time.'

Deep-rooted into Jackson's philosophy of filmmaking was the certainty that he, alongside Walsh, would always generate the screenplay. Writing and shooting were stages on the same journey. This is one of the reasons he could hold three films in his head at one time — the scripts were ingrained.

From the moment he reread *The Lord of the Rings*, however, it was clear McKee's principles would be put to a severe test. Tolkien had taken seventeen years to write the damn thing. It was dauntingly complex. Jackson and Walsh had to go back over and over things — 'assembling it in their heads' — seeing how it all connected, figuring out what made this book they had fought doggedly to adapt so adored? More to the point, what, if anything, made it cinematic?

*

The Book: The debate over the relative literary merits of Tolkien's great opus has raged since its publication. There is no arguing that a vast readership is devoted to the point of religious fervour. Indeed, this intense popularity is partly what inflames the literati. Why can't it just be forgotten? They would surely miss it if it were to pass out of fashion. They make such sport out of mocking the book. The aforementioned Edmund Wilson surmised that 'certain people — especially, perhaps, in Britain — have a lifelong appetite for juvenile trash'. The general tenor of literary disgust aggregates around its supposed childishness and lack of moral depth, irony, theme or allusion.

When it was crowned 'the greatest book of the century' by a public poll in 1997 the journalist Susan Jeffreys led a chorus of snobby intellectuals in a familiar song. Writing in *The Sunday Times*, she feared she might actually catch something from the book. 'I won't keep the thing in the house,' she insisted. For the article, she had borrowed a copy and complained about its 'stale, bedsittish aroma'. Ultimately, she found it depressing to find so many readers 'burrowing an escape into a non-existent world' and its popularity proved 'the folly of teaching people to read'.

There is no doubt of Tolkien's appeal to readers of a certain age. This might in part be about escapism. Neil Gaiman, the celebrated fantasy author, recalled that at fourteen all he wanted to do was write *The Lord of the Rings*. Not the equivalent high fantasy, but the actual book. Which was awkward, he admitted, as Tolkien had already done so.

But Jeffrey's 'non-existent' feels underpowered. Tolkien is far from divorced from the real world.

Yes, the story does transport people. The wonderful, unquench-able invention that sheers off every page is intoxicating. 'It is a really exceptional and remarkable creation, an entire cosmology in itself,' enthused actor John Rhys-Davies, who had long considered the book beneath him. This has led to obsession, if not addiction. Jackson and Walsh were keenly aware that they needed to escape the closed feedback loop of Tolkien fixation. In this, their relative ambivalence toward the text to begin with was an advantage.

Nevertheless, re-reading *The Lord of the Rings* through a cine-matic lens revealed a store of promise for the filmmakers.

In 1938, Tolkien gave a lecture at the University of St. Andrews in Fife, Scotland, in which he highlighted the necessary compo-nents of 'the office of fantasy'. A fantasy world, he insisted, while 'internally consistent' must possess 'strangeness and wonder'. It must have a freedom from observed fact. The laws of physics while largely upheld can be a tiresome constraint on mythical storytelling. Quite how Sauron has uploaded a crucial portion of his malign life force into a golden ring is not worth deliberating. Above all, he declared, the secondary world must be credible, 'commanding belief'.

Tolkien was not shy about the fact he had fashioned Middle-earth from the forges of history. This wasn't an alternative uni-verse but our own. Richard Taylor fixates with great pleasure on the estimation that the story can be located to an interglacial lull in the Pleistocene. Are we to consider the mûmakil relations of mammoths? Are the fell beasts a species of Pterodactyl?

It is a perspective somewhat undone by the Edwardian trappings of Hobbiton, although Jackson describes it as 'a fully developed society and environment the records have since forgotten.'

Within the fabric of the world and the weft of the storytelling came Tolkien's firm instruction to Jackson — *command belief*.

And contrary to critical opinion, the book possesses a rich seam of theme and allusion. This was something the arrival of Boyens really brought home. She educated her partners in what lay behind the book that Jackson admits they 'really hadn't grappled with'. A depth, she felt, that would elevate their films above the gaudy clichés of the barbarian hordes.

Says Jackson, 'We hadn't understood that he cared passionately about the loss of the natural countryside, for example. He was very much this nineteenth century, pre-Industrial Revolution guy against the factories and the enslavement of the workers in factories. Which is what Saruman is all about.'

Tolkien's experiences on the Somme pierce the book. It was something to which Jackson, the First World War scholar, really responded. The Dead Marshes, depicting an ancient battleground swallowed up by the earth, are a striking vision of bodies lurking beneath the characters' feet like no man's land. The book is transfixed by death. While in counterpoint it portrays loyalty and comradeship in extremis. The Fellowship isn't only a mission; it is the philosophy that might save them. And in Frodo and Sam the idea of comradeship crosses boundaries of class much as Tolkien had witnessed in the Great War.

The critic Philip French found it telling that Tolkien 'made the object of Frodo's journey not a search for power but its abnegation'. Ironically, for all its Elves, Dwarves and hobbits, the book's humanity makes it timeless — applicable to any age, any war. It remains relevant.

Tolkien's writing can be archaic (he was creating a mythology;

you can take or leave the songs) but he had an intuitive grasp of a set piece modern studios would die for: the Ringwraiths attacking Weathertop; Gandalf confronting the Balrog; the Ents demolishing Isengard; Shelob's Lair. It was a menu of choice, cinematic dishes.

Jackson appreciated how Tolkien's writing so vividly describes things: 'You can imagine a movie: the camera angles and the cutting, you see it playing itself out.'

Ordesky admired how the story expands in a natural way. From the Shire, the world unfolds, getting larger and larger.

And at heart it was a relatively linear story. The unlikeliest of heroes, knee-high to a wizard, must sneak into the enemy's camp and destroy their most powerful weapon right beneath their nose (or Eye). Keeping the focus on Frodo's quest, aided and abetted by a disparate group of individuals, would give the films forward momentum. Through a very distorted lens, here was Bob Weinstein's fucking *Guns of Navarone*.

So it didn't take long to conclude that Tom Bombadil was surplus to requirements. Tolkien had started writing his sequel to *The Hobbit* without a clear sense of direction. The first few chapters charting the hobbits' flight from The Shire don't really cohere until they get to Bree and Strider. Preserving Bombadil, an ambiguous eco-bumpkin-cum-forest spirit immune to the Ring, would only waylay the drama and diminish the authenticity of the world at a critically early stage, no matter how many fans clamoured for Robin Williams to supply the babbling brook of his rustic banter.

'He was never in the script at any point,' asserts Jackson.

The question of Bombadil, so easily answered, signalled that key debate: how faithful they were going to be. Something they would begin to fathom with a treatment.[*]

*

---

[*] Longer and more detailed than an outline or synopsis, a treatment is the intermediate step between a pitch or proposal and the first draft of the screenplay. It often includes some sense of directorial style.

The Treatment: As their initial canary in the cage sent into the Mines of Moria, Botes' scene-by-scene breakdown provided the basis for a ninety-two-page treatment for the two-film screenplay, clarifying Tolkien's 1,000-page edifice into 266 sequences. A document that reveals how the backbone of the eventual trilogy was established very quickly, and where there was still considerable uncertainty.

While the detail is inevitably sketchy, the shape and tone of book are clearly intact. This was not the lightheaded remix embarked upon by John Boorman. The first film would end shortly after Helm's Deep with the death of Saruman (eventually postponed all the way to the extended edition of *The Return of the King*), the second picking up immediately in the wake of battle. Many of the scenes are already determined, especially for what were eventually the first and third films. There are fewer major omissions than you might imagine: Lothlórien is the biggest absentee, while Edoras gets only a fleeting visit.

What impresses is how much of Jackson's vision already emerges so quickly. The opening scene is a 'breathtaking vista of battle' with 150,000 Orcs, Men and Elves on screen. He is already inventing signature shots. With Radagast eliminated (until *The Hobbit*) the great eagle Gwaihir is sent to rescue Gandalf from Orthanc by the intercession of a moth. An idea which just 'popped' into Jackson's head simultaneously with the image of the camera plummeting over the edge of the tower, down its vertiginous flank and into the quasi-industrial pits of Isengard.

Here is both the train of events and the visual language with which he would depict Middle-earth, giving the camera a panoptic viewpoint, swooping and plunging across the landscape indeed like an eagle. For instance, from the moment he re-read the book the siege of Minas Tirith clanged within his eager imagination: 'Thousands of FLAMING TORCHES light the snarling, slathering ORCS. DRUMMERS are beating the DRUMS OF WAR. . .'

*

The Two-film Version (with Miramax): For all his many gifts, Tolkien presented pitfalls for a future screenwriter. The sheer multitudinousness of his sub-creation would always have to be tamed — a landslide of material artfully removed while remaining tangibly Tolkien — but the story is also awkwardly episodic and repetitious. 'You kind of don't notice it when you fall into the world of the books,' groans Boyens. 'But boy, you notice it when you have to bring it to screen.'

There are dramatic cadences that would have McKee wielding his red pen in fury. As Jackson bewails, the good guys 'need to *lose*' the Battle of the Pelennor Fields. Tolkien has to rustle up a further clash at the Black Gates to maintain tension. And his female characters are memorable but marginal.

To counter the problem, Arwen is sent in from the sidelines as, Boyens admits, more of a 'Hollywood stereotype' at the heart of the action. She arrives to fight at Helm's Deep and joins the Rohirrim's charge on the Pelennor Fields. Purists might wince, but this isn't as entirely unsuccessful as the filmmakers later claimed — on page she hacks at the Orcs with gusto and flashes of ironic humour. Whereas the romance with Aragorn is that bit too broad — the second film opens with Arwen and Aragorn frolicking naked in a pool in the Glittering Caves (which recollects John Boorman's erotic leanings).

Ordesky, for whom Jackson's vision was almost sacrosanct, admits to being uncertain of the tone of the scene revealed in the animatic on the pitch video. 'My life is with you,' Arwen gushes, having danced over stepping stones to surprise her beloved, 'or I have no life!'

'I never had any doubt, but that is the only place where I thought, "Huh, that is probably not what it is ultimately going to be".'

With no Lothlórien, Galadriel's moment is threaded into Rivendell as a dream sequence. As Frodo gazes into her mirror (to still see a burning Shire) the scene descends to an almost David Lynchian intensity of dreams within dreams.

Written between 1997 and 1998, the two Miramax scripts

entitled 'The Fellowship of the Ring' and 'The War of the Ring' (the name Tolkien had preferred for The Return of the King) would, as Marty Katz once claimed, still have made for exciting if shallower films. Here is the urgency of a Hollywood thriller — and the bluntness of Hollywood logic. Motivation is spelled out explicitly: 'Those who resist Sauron are doomed. . .' announces a scheming Saruman, 'but for those that aid him there will be rich rewards.'

The biggest challenge Tolkien presented was the absence of a physical villain. 'If you were doing an original screenplay, having your chief bad guy as a big eyeball would be a no-no,' laughs Jackson. 'You also wouldn't have Saruman never leave his tower.'

His and Walsh's first answer to the problem was to stir up some monster-movie action: poor Barliman Butterbur is skewered by a Ringwraith, and Sauron's agents provide a constant airborne terror, attacking Gandalf on the battlements of Helm's Deep where Gimli cleaves one with a battle axe. Sauron returns from the prologue in his super-sized, humanoid manifestation to duel with Aragorn: '. . . he stands at least 14 FEET TALL . . . is CLAD in sinister BLACK ARMOUR!'. A concept that would persist long enough to be filmed.

Ultimately, says Jackson, the issue of villainy would be addressed by making the Ring a character. 'It speaks, it sings, and fills the frame — we were deliberately trying to give it presence.'

Evil is already in their midst, preying on weaker minds.

The two-film version cuts corners and concertinas events. Not illogically, Théoden mismanages his kingdom straight from Helm's Deep, while Gandalf scours Middle-earth on the back of a giant eagle, Aragorn takes the Paths of Dead as a short cut, and to keep the clock ticking Arwen, mortally wounded by the Witch King, will perish if Sauron is not defeated.

Some details have already been filleted out of the treatment: Glorfindel rescuing Frodo on the flight to the ford; Sam looking into Galadriel's mirror; Saruman's dying redemption; the arrival of Elrond's sons, Elladin and Elrohir; and the Ringwraiths trying to intercept Frodo at the Cracks of Doom.

There is, however, still a conscious attempt to keep tabs with the book: there is a Farmer Maggot, a Fatty Bolger, Bilbo attending the Council of Elrond and characters as obscure as Prince Imrahil and Forlong the Fat make cameo appearances.

Aside from a feisty Arwen, Gandalf is more frail and emotional, less in control; Gimli swears like a stevedore; and Faramir is described as a 'fresh-faced seventeen-year-old', making sense of why Orlando Bloom first auditioned for that part.

Ordesky wonders if he might be the only person at New Line to ever have read the original 280-page two-film script. He admired the coherent grasp of the material and the lovely, piquant details that would remain to elevate the films three years hence: a blazing Denethor casting himself off the rocky prow above Minas Tirith like a falling star; Sam's impassioned speech on the slopes of Mount Doom, 'I can't carry it for you, but I can carry you. . .' Ordesky also knew that three films could offer so much more.

*

The Three-film Version (with New Line): 'I will go to my grave saying that the crafting of those three screenplays was one of the most underappreciated screenwriting efforts ever undertaken,' declares Ken Kamins proudly. 'You are writing what is essentially a single ten-hour script, which you have to divide into three movies. You have to set up things in movie one that may not play out till movie three. And you're burdened with having to explain the world to the neophyte.'

As soon as New Line came on board, they became impatient for Jackson, Walsh and Boyens to turn the two scripts into workable drafts of three. Jackson says this meant starting again with a page-one rewrite (essentially beginning afresh), but it is closer to what Boyens describes as a serious 'rethinking'. Each draft would still be codenamed *Jamboree*, still 'an affectionate coming-of-age drama set in the New Zealand Boy Scout Movement'. Only now it wasn't simply the work of Fredericka Wharburton and Percy

J. Judkins, but also Faye Crutchley (Philippa Boyens) and, for his contribution, Kennedy Landenburger (Stephen Sinclair).

Whole passages of dialogue and the structure and rhythm of specific scenes would be retained from the two-film draft, but restructuring to three films brought about a re-evaluation of what these films could be. Renewed emphasis was placed on what was emotionally satisfying. Posing the fundamental question: what were they fighting for? Action scenes needed to be *earned* on an emotional level. Characters needed to make sense. Legolas may be as nimble as Fred Astaire as he releases unerring arrows at blighted Orcs but this wasn't a superhero film.

'The script I'm most proud of is *The Two Towers*, because it was so frickin' hard,' says Boyens. 'It was like, how do you break the story into three and then follow these different threads? *And* make people care. Also you've got no end — how do you create an end?'

Points of transition became a real issue with New Line. Concluding the first film especially would be a real bone of contention during post-production. Shaye was a huge fan of the books, but he was also a canny businessman in search of profit. He understood the screenplays would have to be representative of Tolkien's work as a trilogy, but insisted that they also had to work as individual films.

If you missed the first movie, *The Two Towers* had to be a compelling piece of cinema. And if you missed the first two and still decided to see *The Return of the King*, it would have to work all by itself. Once *The Fellowship of the Ring* was a big hit, the editing of the 'sequels' re-orientated back toward a single saga.

Expanding into three films, says Boyens, allowed them the luxury 'to try and do scenes to the fullest of their capacity.' Within the exigent drive of plot they could explore character and build mood, even stillness. The priceless moment of Bilbo and Gandalf, two very old friends, contentedly blowing smoke rings and galleons upon the doorstep of Bag End; the camera gazing in awe upon the pillared immensity of Dwarrowdelf as

Howard Shore's score swells up through the ancient columns. Such poise was totally contrary to the hyper-kinetic dogma of millennial blockbustermaking.

Obviously they also had room for plenty more Tolkien, and some painful excisions were immediately remedied. 'It was such a relief to have Lothlórien back,' says Boyens, and the Elven forest was the first thing she returned to its designated place.

The book was full of renewed possibility.

Says Jackson, 'Unlike most movies where the pressure comes and you literally take twenty pages out, our scripts actually grew by thirty to forty pages, because we would keep finding stuff in the books. We were constantly thinking, "God, we really should be filming this, this is great, and we'd then write a page, show it to the actors, and they'd go "this is good" and I'd say, "You know, on Friday, I think we can squeeze this new scene in pretty simply." It was very organic.'

The problem was it never ended. They couldn't stop writing, editing, re-writing, trimming, extending, delving into the mines of the text, working with the actors, twisting and turning the mythology into cinema. This went on literally in tandem with the shoot. A honing of story in the same way a special effect can be bettered with care and attention. Such that there was never a definitive finished screenplay, not on page.

An early draft of the three-film version, dated 20 November 1998, reads like an alternative universe to an alternative universe, with many of these scenes shot and abandoned. Opening with Frodo and Sam surveying the limits of the Shire from a hilltop, Farmer Maggot clings on and the hobbit heroes encounter the first Ringwraith without Merry and Pippin. Rivendell, as we shall see, awaits a major overhaul. There is an Orc assault on the borders of Lothlórien, where Aragorn has a flashback to the days he spent there with Arwen and Frodo glimpses Gandalf in Galadriel's mirror.

In this version, the second and third films radically depart from the book, with Arwen's participation expanded even from the two-film draft. She follows the Fellowship to Lothlórien and then on to Edoras rescuing the refugee children from an Orc attack along the way. The love triangle is revived from the treatment, with a semi-comic rivalry established between Arwen and Éowyn. Arwen still battles at Helm's Deep, still skinny-dips with Aragorn, still helps fight off a Ringwraith that swoops for Pippin, and still rides with the Rohirrim, but now alongside Éowyn disguised as a man (diluting the whole effect). Arwen will be left for dead by the Witch-king before Éowyn dispatches him. And Sauron still confronts Aragorn at the Black Gates.

They were constantly trying to insert the structural lessons gleaned from McKee to the glacial magnificence of Tolkien: climaxes, twists, foreshadowings, turning points and delayed reveals. Balanced with wilfully obscure references to his deep mythology. His archaic language could have enormous power when delivered by an Ian McKellen or Christopher Lee. But for clarity they would trim and edit from the book, moving passages around in the chronology or between speakers like a slider puzzle.

Boyens' ancient prologue was still being reworked in post.

'I first wrote it as Gandalf narrating,' she says, running back through the manifold revisions in her head — there had been a Frodo-narrated version at one stage. 'And then I wrote it in the voice of Galadriel. That was Fran's idea, and it was a good one. Then when we were recording the ADR in London, I said to Fran, "Can we overlay it in Elvish?" You want that sense of strangeness of history.'

The trilogy's overture carries the quality of a dream as Blanchett's yearning voice pulls us across the frontier into Tolkien's imagination.

*

The creative dynamic that evolved between Jackson, Walsh and Boyens would define the trilogy: the visualist devising heart-stopping scenes; the realist seeking emotional truths; and the Tolkien authority mindful of the Elvish provenance of

Gandalf's sword. As an unwritten rule, Jackson was responsible for what they categorized as the 'Big Print' set-piece stuff such as the battle with the Cave-troll (which elaborates on Tolkien to great effect). Something, Boyens soon noticed, he did with an extraordinary immediacy and originality. As if in response to that strangeness in Tolkien's world no sequence was allowed to bear the formulaic imprint of a Hollywood blockbuster. Jackson, writing in those caps in which you can feel the camera's hungry eye: 'The dark WATER BOILS as the HIDEOUS BEAST lashes out at the FELLOWSHIP!'

'Philippa and I were very invested in the emotional content of the story,' Walsh explained in a rare interview. 'It's easy for those things to be obscured by spectacle and the sheer sort of exhaustion of that final ascent to Mount Doom. But we wanted to touch the audience in a meaningful way. Maybe that's an easier thing for us to do because we are women.'

Boyens did the bulk of the physical typing sitting up in bed with her laptop or at her desk. 'We got into this rhythm. I was the faster typist and better speller. Fran's great because she can see the scene in her head. When I write, the words don't come unless I actually physically type them.'

They were known to spend a whole day in their pyjamas, writing, writing, writing. 'Then Fran would have time with the kids,' recalls Boyens. Jackson and Walsh's children, Billy and Katie, were still only infants. 'So it was nuts,' she laughs. But nothing could beat that moment of breakthrough. When, as Boyens puts it, 'the landscape held'.

Walsh was the driving force. Jackson's partner would be the first to admit she wouldn't naturally have chosen to adapt *The Lord of the Rings*. She had been seduced by Jackson's passion for the possibility of something epic. As much as she was caught in the slipstreams off the Misty Mountains, addicted to Middle-earth, she could remain more academic about the material: how does it work as entertainment?

'I learned how to write from her and from Pete, but mostly

from Fran,' says Boyens. 'There's so many holes and missteps with a film. There are so many different ways you can go and so many things that you have to break. I'm someone who would paper over the cracks. She couldn't. The other thing that I learned from her is that it's the ideas which are informing the story that are important. Why would anyone care? And understanding how you take what is interior, especially for a character such as Frodo, and translate it to film. She was masterful at the Gollum-Sméagol dynamic.'

Kamins can see that they were a unique producing-directing-writing unit. 'You understood that they were close. They were willing to argue with each other to make something better. To push each other to prove why their point was right.'

And the clear distinction of roles could be deceptive. Walsh and Boyens could be good on the Big Print action scenes and Jackson excellent on the fine print of Tolkien.

Still, freed up by the obsessive dedication of his co-writers, Jackson utilized his energies across preproduction, finding the visual texture with which to clothe the bones of the words. As shooting bore down on him like a mûmak, the director took more of an 'overarching eye', says Boyens. Generally, after a team discussion, she and Walsh would do a draft of a scene and then Jackson would do his pass.

'I was literally almost doing a shot list,' recalls Jackson. 'A lot of screenwriters say don't tell the director what to do, but I guess as I'm the director I don't mind. It helps when I am sitting there reading the script a year later and knowing that I had a thought to do a close-up.'

The original three 150-page scripts presented to each actor were always available for consultation, but they were only blueprints. Rhys-Davies laughed about the dreaded brown envelope that would be slipped under their door each morning with that day's revisions.

Sean Astin describes the scripts as 'fluid'. But if an actor wanted to adjust a line on set, try it in a different way, they would be met with resistance. Jackson would joke that he dare not cross the 'script Nazis'. Given what Boyens and Walsh were going through, he may have been genuinely fearful. They were constructing a monumental house of cards where one minor adjustment could bring the whole edifice crashing down.

Yet the cast did contribute. Both in preproduction and production they would meet with Walsh and Boyens to talk through upcoming scenes. Viggo Mortensen, who always had the books about his person, was relentless when it came to his character. Astin likes to think of it as keeping the filmmakers' 'feet to the fire'. And that drive brought Aragorn to life.

Astin remembers coming up with the idea that Sam had been secretly spying on the Council of Elrond throughout. How else would he be aware of what had been decided? 'Sam belonged there,' he had argued to a sceptical Walsh. It was, he insists, 'a legitimate desire to act as an audience surrogate'.

A compromise was reached where Sam is seen hiding in the shrubbery. Astin wasn't wholly mollified, but nothing was as emblematic of the brinkmanship of writing — and indeed shooting — as mounting the Council of Elrond. 'Just don't make me go back to Rivendell,' Boyens would remonstrate whenever things got complicated.

A great gulp of exposition that often defeats casual readers of the book, here we are introduced to the members of the Fellowship and get a lesson in the complexities of the 'big picture' via a succession of stories within the story, told at exorbitant length by individual characters. Moreover, Jackson has an allergy to any form of reportage. Show-don't-tell is the heartbeat of cinema. You have to picture things, not have actors describe them — even actors as persuasive as McKellen. But this would necessitate a frenzy of flashbacks.

In the book, the Council is where Gandalf finally tells the tale of his capture by Saruman. As early as the two-film draft the writers had decided cleverly to cut away from the hobbits' journey through the Shire to portray Gandalf's excursion to Isengard in real time. This both exploited the potential of two ancient wizards duelling with shockwaves of magic and teased the possibility that the Bombadil episode could have occurred in the meantime. 'We chose to leave some things untold, rather than left out,' is Boyens' escape clause. Only Gandalf's eagle-spirited getaway is suspensefully withheld until Rivendell.

To avoid the scourge of reportage the script syncopates a variety of flashbacks and reveries throughout the story without stalling momentum. A feat doubly impressive given Tolkien's epic mode didn't provide much inner life for his characters — Gollum expresses his internal narrative aloud.

'Backstory was incredibly difficult to do,' confesses Boyens. It had to be character driven, or action driven. Nevertheless, as written, the Council scenes were yawning to a stifling forty minutes while everyone sat in a circle talking politics. There was no way they could effectively put the story on hold for so long. Figuring out the scale issues and eyelines alone was headache inducing.

Ordesky remembers joining Walsh and Boyens at the shoot's hotel HQ while on location in Queenstown as the dreaded Council loomed in the next block of filming. They were in one of the most beautiful places in New Zealand unable to leave the hotel as they wrestled the scene into submission. 'It was such an education,' he says, 'seeing their process of laying tracks in front of the moving train, as Fran liked to say.'

Says Boyens, 'One of the things that I learned in particular and, I think, Fran and Pete did too — and actually the studio did too — is that you didn't have to explain the history of Dwarves. You just needed John Rhys-Davies to turn up and be a Dwarf.'

They needed to trust the actors.

As Boromir, Sean Bean immortalizes the finished scene with his portentous, half-whispered line reading: 'One does not simply *walk into Mordor. . .*' A passage of dialogue scribbled on a piece of paper and literally balanced on his knee (you can spot him subtly glancing down).

'He was so good,' says Boyens, savouring the victory. 'That tension between him and Viggo. . . Man, it was great casting:

those two opposite each other... And I'm very proud of my Pippin line: "Where are we going?" You kind of needed it.'

The humour in the scripts often goes uncelebrated. Enriched by the fine cast, the comic elements help puncture any drift toward pomposity. Merry and Pippin's chittering banter, Gandalf's crabby exasperation, Gimli (surely Jackson's avatar in the films) and his rivalry with Legolas, Sam and Gollum, the slowpoke Ents and the quarrelsome Orcs all contribute a flavour that is consciously Jacksonesque.

'It's taking the piss,' says a delighted Boyens. 'And that is Pete's sense of humour definitely. He always says that you don't earn the pathos if you don't make people laugh.'

Away from the wellspring of Harryhausen and Kong, Jackson adored the sublimely engineered slapstick and anguish of Buster Keaton and Charlie Chaplin, and the gonzo follies of Monty Python. Comedic forces welcome amid the serious business of saving the world.

*

In early 1997, Michael Palin was in Wellington for a one-man show, and Jackson wasn't about to pass up the opportunity to go backstage and meet a hero. They shared the usual pleasantries. Jackson telling the erstwhile Python how much he appreciated his work. Palin enquiring after what the director was currently working on. They got talking about *The Lord of the Rings*. Then it occurred to Jackson to ask a pertinent question.

'Do you know where Alan Lee lives?'

Jackson was desperately trying to get hold of the seemingly reclusive artist's expertise, but so far in vain. It had occurred to him that Palin had worked with Lee on an illustrated children's book called *The Mirrorstone* — he may have even got hold of a copy — about a boy travelling to a wizardly realm via his bathroom mirror.

'Ah, he's a funny chap, isn't he?' Palin recalled. 'I'll find out for you.'

A few weeks later an email arrived bearing Lee's Devon address. 'It's true,' laughs Jackson. 'Michael Palin came to the rescue. No one could figure out how to contact him.'

While re-reading *The Lord of the Rings*, Jackson found himself eagerly anticipating the next of Lee's wonderful illustrations. He was struck by how utterly removed the pictures were from that juvenile vogue for muscle-bound Conan-clones draped in a buxom wench that adorned heavy metal albums and Dungeons & Dragons boxes. 'They were sort of pastoral, with these elegant pastels. Sort of historical, I suppose,' he says. 'We fell in love with those pictures.'

As he surveyed Middle-earth with his internal camera it was Lee's version of the world he would likely see. So he began to gather together as many of the artist's calendars, book covers, posters and compendiums of Tolkien artwork as he could lay his hands on. This was pre-internet, pre-eBay, so it was a matter of trawling second-hand bookshops, collectors' fairs, jumble sales and nagging friends to scour their attics.

'I was tracking down calendars going back to the seventies, trying to see who the other artists were. That was how we saw John Howe's work — in calendars.' Howe had contrasting strengths. Lee was good at the gentle whimsical, hobbit stuff — it was very beautiful. The more dynamic Howe, in Jackson's opinion, 'did really great Nazgûl'. His paintings were 'like freeze frames of a movie'.

Jackson wallpapered an entire room with the two visions of Middle-earth, hoping to absorb the poetry and drama of the images. Then it occurred to him that osmosis was unnecessary. Why not put your inspirations on the payroll? And the decision to involve Lee and Howe as guiding lights was another piece of applied Kiwi logic that bled into the visionary. In a stroke, the films became a continuum of what for many was the definitive Tolkien aesthetic.

However, despite the best efforts of Miramax, Lee had proved elusive. All they could ascertain was that he lived in the middle of Dartmoor — the insinuation being he was some kind of mad hermit. They were also rather suspicious he was a minion of the Tolkien Estate.

Fusing Bruegel with Arthur Rackham, Lee is arguably the greatest of the Tolkien school. Howe is exalted too, and the likes of Pauline Baynes, Ted Nasmith, Ian Miller and Michael Foreman. But Lee, certainly in recent years, is largely responsible for shaping our perception of what Middle-earth looks like.

'I get that, I get people saying my work is exactly as they imagined it,' he says. 'But it's interesting because often it is not exactly as I imagined it when I read the book. But that is the way it turned out through the process of drawing. I would say it is in the right ballpark.'

In conversation Lee speaks in hushed, careful tones as if you've surprised him in a library. Silver-haired and bearded with an intense, indecipherable gaze, he is well cast in a silent cameo as one of the nine kings (second from the right) in the prologue. The immediate impression is someone both reassuringly adult and somewhat mysterious.

Lee had moved into illustrating paperbacks from art school in the late 1960s, gravitating toward anything 'slightly weird or ancient'. He was responsible for the first fourteen covers of that young reader's rite-of-passage *The Fontana Book of Great Ghost Stories*. Through renowned publisher Ian Ballantine* he contributed pictures to two best-selling anthologies: *Faeries* and *Castles*. Lee had first read *The Lord of the Rings* when he was seventeen and working in a graveyard, but it wasn't until *Castles* he first attempted Tolkien with versions of Barad-dûr, Cirith Ungol, and Minas Tirith. These drew the approval of the Tolkien Estate who agreed to his being commissioned to paint fifty watercolours for

---

* Ballantine launched the authorized editions of *The Lord of the Rings* in America in 1965, although the initial paperbacks covers by Barbara Remington, who hadn't read the book beforehand, infuriated Tolkien with their surreal depiction of what resembled ostriches and a pumpkin tree.

the 1992 centenary edition of *The Lord of the Rings.* In 1996, he was asked to illustrate *The Hobbit.*

Like a portent, in 1997 a producer from Granada television approached him about providing concept art for a proposed twelve-part television adaptation of *The Lord of the Rings.* 'The script actually read quite well,' he remembers. 'But in the end he couldn't get the approval for it.'

Then one morning a package arrived by courier all the way from New Zealand containing two videos, two scripts, and a letter of introduction from a fellow named Peter Jackson. He helpfully included a number to call. The videos were *Heavenly Creatures* and *Forgotten Silver.* 'He had neglected to put in *Bad Taste,*' notes Lee. He watched the brilliant *Heavenly Creatures* first. Then he read the letter, in which Jackson explained that the scripts were for another potential adaptation of *The Lord of the Rings* and would Lee like to be involved?

Jackson, meanwhile, had been following the package via his courier and knew it had been delivered, satisfying himself that he wouldn't hear back for weeks. Hours later his fateful phone rang. It was Lee's quiet, gracious tones announcing that he would love to be involved. As luck would have it, he was finishing up a project. With no pressing family ties, he was 'kind of free'.

The artist laughs at the memory. 'I went down to New Zealand for six months. I ended up staying for six years.'

Howe had heard the odd rumour about a potential adaptation of the book, but knew little else. Born in Vancouver, Canada, he had since settled among the chocolate box lakes and mountains of Neuchâtel in Switzerland, no less removed from Hollywood than deepest Devon. Growing up in a rural outpost he had known 'ever since he could remember' that he wanted to live off his artistic talents, but never dreamed it was possible. He should finish high school — get himself a normal job.

His life changed when Tolkien-themed calendars started appearing in the town bookstore in the mid-1970s. It wasn't that he was an avid fan. He read *The Lord of the Rings* during high school, having visited *The Hobbit* as a child. 'They didn't really strike me as anything,' he admits, enjoying the irony. An opinion that might have been shaped by the fact he read the trilogy in the wrong order. Someone had always beaten him to *The Fellowship of the Ring* in the local library. So he ended up reading *The Two Towers* and *Return of the King* before the first part. 'I was a bit confused,' he laughs.

The calendars showed that it was possible to have a career painting pictures based on fantasy novels. Suddenly Middle-earth came alive as a world of infinite possibility; he still remembers his first attempt: 'It was from the Pelennor Fields and had a Frank Frazetta-like touch — a reptilian creature and Nazgûl rising up to tackle Éowyn.' Howe would pick up the latest calendar and each month do his version of the picture.

Over the years, as he established himself as an illustrator, Howe diligently sent samples into HarperCollins for their Tolkien calendars. Until, in 1987, he finally had three pieces published.

Rather than a package, Howe received a phone call in the middle of the night. Jackson had tracked down the artist's number with relative ease but in his excitement had forgotten about the time differences. Ten days later Howe was on a plane to New Zealand.

'The commitment was extremely light at that stage. The project had yet to be confirmed, and if things didn't work out, you have your ticket home.' While his wife and son would follow him, Howe never relocated with any permanence to Wellington. Conscious of his son's education he would exit the project when production finally got underway in 1999. 'We were back home once sets were being built.'

Howe shares the same meditative delivery of his colleague but is more eccentric. Where Lee is almost serenely composed, Howe has an undercurrent of energy that can't be stilled. With his thin frame, flowing brown hair and beard he cultivates a little wizard-liness, that or a mad professor. He too is one of the nine kings (second from the left), but harder to recognize beneath his wig and frown.

Jackson laughs. 'We did Alan first and then we did John. Then we figured out that they had never met each other, and I thought, "God, I hope there's no rivalry here." They literally met each other on the aeroplane.'

They knew of one another's work, of course, and had vaguely corresponded. But it was on the middle leg of their journey from Singapore into New Zealand in 1997 that they became acquainted. Howe had been sitting downstairs when one of the stewards approached him.

'A Mister Lee wants to meet you.'

'I didn't even make the connection,' he says. So it was midway over the Indian Ocean the two artists were introduced, and found they got on very well. Which was a relief.

Although, while changing planes at Auckland, Lee — and the airport ground staff — was startled to discover Howe had packed a suit of armour. As a serious medieval re-enactor he was keen to bestow his historical expertise in forging suits of amour on Weta Workshop, sceptical they were up to the task.

Howe still has a 'laser-sharp image' of arriving into Wellington for the first time, following the coastline as it snaked along the southern hem of the North Island. 'It was an extraordinary feeling.'

From the airport they were driven straight to Jackson's house at Karaka Bay and over the kitchen table, adrenaline keeping overwound body clocks ticking, began to understand how the director saw them working with the production. They would, Jackson informed them, design everything, with the division of labour laid out as per his appreciation of their respective gifts: Lee the light side, Howe the dark. Naturally, lines were blurred. Howe would design the vestibule of Bag End and Lee created Orthanc. Still, it was a place to start and this way they could cover more ground.

'It was also pretty clear Pete wanted to get going on the bigger environments,' notes Lee, who spent his first two weeks in Helm's Deep.

For Howe it was all entirely new, Lee at least had some experience creating concept art for another Python, Terry Jones' *Erik the Viking*, and Ridley Scott's *Legend*. There was only one strict instruction: don't curb your instincts in any way for a film. 'They told us quite quickly that if you can draw it we can make it,' says Howe.

Everything from Minas Tirith to door hinges fell into their remit. There would be no hand-me-downs from old epics. Stationed amid the inspiring bustle of the Workshop, they were going to design this ancient world inch by inch. Recalls Howe, 'We weren't working on computers at that time. That sort of kicked in later. All you needed was enough good paper and enough pencils.'

On a workaday level nearly all of their design work was pencil, colour was too time consuming and too prescribed. They soon understood they were cogs in a giant mechanism that would have to churn out Middle-earth on an industrial scale.

Says Jackson, 'Usually in design meetings you'd been talking about some location: "Maybe there is a bridge here and a building here." Then everyone would go off and come up with stuff. But Alan or John would have their pads and as I was talking they would sketch up something. By the time I had finished describing it they could show me a sketch. It was like instantaneous design.'

'Peter's also somebody who likes looking at artwork,' appreciates Howe. 'He enjoys artwork. He's art literate in that sense.'

The one exception to the no-colour rule was when Howe, whose work would be more legibly dynamic to a studio, was asked to paint a dozen 'great moments' for the pitch meetings in Los Angeles. Lee added large pencil drawings and sketchbook material. They mounted them into a slideshow using Photoshop, something they were only beginning to figure out. 'It was all a bit naff really at that stage,' admits Lee.

It was a strange time. As Miramax wound things up in Wellington, Lee and Howe simply went home. That was that. But they had barely had time to unpack their HBs and plate armour when news came that the presentation had worked, a deal had provisionally been struck with New Line and the artists were back on a plane to New Zealand. 'Peter's no slouch,' notes Howe, approvingly. 'He's a clever man and managed to pull it out of the fire.'

*

Why, when, where and with whose money Jackson was going to direct the films was decided. The question now confronting him was how was he, personally, going to direct so much story? What would his *Lord of the Rings* look and feel like? What would it sound like? What style would he bring to Middle-earth?

While *Heavenly Creatures* and *The Frighteners* had shown there was more to the director's repertoire than splatter satires, *The Lord of the Rings* was a leap of faith. Would he have to curtail his natural excesses to be epic? Was there a nascent Cecil B. DeMille or John Ford or David Lean beneath the crash zooms and wacky angles?

Perhaps the better question to ask is what was there in the flare and versatility of Jackson that so befitted *The Lord of the Rings*? As the pitch documentary proclaimed, he couldn't have been more thorough in his development of the films. The labour of screenwriting was providing him a narrative roadmap — quite literally in terms of location — as well as inspiring camera moves. But Jackson's instincts split between groundwork and natural daring. He was a thrilling stylist who had seen as many slasher movies as *Lawrence of Arabia*s. He was a technically brilliant storyteller guided by an inner Einstein with no space or time for formulaic thinking.

Nevertheless, his governing principle possessed a Kiwi-like directness: 'I was trying to make it feel real. It wasn't so much thinking about what can I do differently, rather than what can

I do for the story? We really approached it like it was real; this is authentic, it is not fantasy, it is a piece of the past.'

Jackson is the artist who once cooked special effects in his mum's oven. Who made 'realistic' alien vomit out of yogurt, pea green food colouring and baked beans. When he found the consistency too runny he added handfuls of soil before his *Bad Taste* actors dug in. Back in those early days he even made puke by hand. He loves the tactile — the texture of the world. *Braindead* is an orgy of sensation. The sheer blood-drenched chaos pours off the screen until you feel sticky just watching it. Inches out of shot you sense the gleeful filmmaker caked in his own stage blood laughing till his lungs burst. When he watched Harryhausen it was as if he could reach out and touch those strange creatures.

'That's what I loved about Pete's approach,' says Boyens, 'and made me feel this was the right person. This guy who did *Braindead* and *Meet the Feebles* — no matter what he did he wanted it to feel real and earthy, and there's a lot of earthiness in Tolkien's work.'

It was Lee and Howe who revealed the dizzying scale of Middle-earth, and warned him not to giggle.

'Everything was always bigger than I thought, and better,' he says. The artists, rooted in Tolkien's grandeur, would always go way beyond what was in his head. Design meetings became thrilling symposiums where the world expanded before his eyes. Not to be outdone, he soon started pushing them for even bigger and better.

He had become fascinated by Lee's cover painting of a flooded Orthanc on his well-thumbed copy of *The Two Towers*: the black, angular walls ascended out of frame, carved with vertical crenulations like the scratches of a blade and wreathed in moody smoke. But the picture only covered the lower four stories. Like many readers, Jackson longed to know what the top of the tower looked like. Only he got to ask. 'I was able to show Alan the picture, which I had lived with for years, and say, "Just create the rest of the tower."'

Lee unveiled an awe-inspiring Gothic skyscraper whose riven sides tapered to a flat summit with blades jutting from each corner like the peaks of an iron crown. Orthanc was fixed in our minds for ever more.

This search for the real in the unreal was a universal obsession. No individual in the swelling ranks of the production was prepared to let their corner of Middle-earth go by unverified by a form of collective integrity. Lee would go through a sequence of sketches that gradually 'crystallized' into the ideal image by 'natural selection'. In other words, he would keep drawing until it made sense, imagining himself inside the picture examining every possible angle for the scene to come.

'Each image was a virtual place that had to be completely consistent.'

They could exaggerate, but Lee and Howe would know intuitively if the credibility of the story was threatened. 'You wanted people to suspend disbelief for the time that they're there,' says Howe — there were points you could assume magic was at work. 'In the case of Barad-dûr, you can't build stone that high. It falls down. So I assumed Sauron has put some dark power into the foundations.'

Indeed, when Sauron is destroyed with the Ring, the tower disintegrates like pie-crust.

The two artists would design every facet of a building inside and out far beyond the bounds of what we see on screen, satisfying their own insistent logic. Imagining Orthanc's summit, Lee provided the outline of a doorway in one of the fins to explain how Saruman gained access to the roof. 'There are stairways leading all the way up,' he maintains. 'You don't see it because it is so dark.'

Like the writing and the designing of the film, how it would be made on the levels of lighting and planning shots, practical and computer-generated effects, editing, music and sound design, would be answered by varying degrees of near scientific research and making it up as they went along. The belief they would find a way to work wonders. But it was a practical magic.

Jackson was to an extent letting Middle-earth guide him. Storyboarding and pre-visualization had the same aura of experimentation. As the scripts were being written — and rewritten — he and a young protégé named Christian Rivers began to storyboard the film. The affable, multitalented Rivers had become a permanent fixture in Jackson's inner circle after his fan letter led to an invitation to lend a hand on *Braindead* (Rivers insists that he called). A gifted artist, he has storyboarded every Jackson film since, as well as branching out in both divisions of Weta (he was a digital artist on the *Contact* effects sequence).

In layman's terms, 'pre-viz' denotes the mapping out of camera moves ahead of time on a computer, usually concentrated on the more complicated sequences. Today, pre-viz is done within virtual environments — as it would be on *The Hobbit* films — but in 1999 the only sequence planned with animated pre-viz was the fight with the Cave-troll (they would later digitally pre-viz the mûmakil attack for *The Return of the King*). Otherwise, their unofficial, analogue variation of pre-viz amounted to Jackson crouched over Weta's growing portfolio of miniatures holding a tiny 'lipstick' camera.

'You always have a perception of what it could be in your head when you write a script. But it gives you a chance to play around with it. I am always looking for other angles. It gives you an ability to actually explore and experiment.'

With the thirty-foot miniature of Helm's Deep, complete with the Hornburg keep, Deeping Wall and polystyrene cliffsides recently constructed with Lee's assistance, Jackson went out and bought 5,000 1/32nd scale plastic soldiers. 'Sort of Medieval guys with pikes,' he reports happily, having cleaned out Wellington's toyshops. A poor soul spent two weeks laboriously gluing them down in groups of twelve to blocks of wood so the director could move formations of Uruk-hai around like Napoleon.

*

Meanwhile back in Hollywood, following the fateful meeting with Bob Shaye, lawyers' phones began to sing. Three separate deals had to be struck: one with Miramax, a new one with Saul Zaentz and one with Peter Jackson. Most pressingly, Miramax were due to be reimbursed their development costs. Kamins had been clear about Harvey's terms when setting up the meeting. He wasn't going to be accused of 'buffaloing' anyone; getting everyone excited then springing the exorbitant catch on them, which included executive producer credits for the Weinsteins. Shaye admitted the terms of the deal had almost dissuaded him from the meeting, but forty-eight hours afterwards he was on the phone to Harvey.

Says Kamins, 'Harvey must have dropped the receiver, I don't think he believed for five minutes this would happen.'

He came around quickly enough. Scenting he could both reclaim his investment and land five percent of the gross with no further risk on his part, he switched back into street-dealer mode. And saw the wisdom in allowing an extension to his initial four-week stipulation for a signature.

Room to breathe.

The reality of New Line's commitment to the project becomes stark when you consider that, according to Ordesky, they spent in 'the low twenty millions for the rights' not only to pay back the Weinsteins but to fund Jackson, Walsh and Boyens to redo the scripts and begin preproduction. This was to even *get to a place* where they could say yes to backing three films.

The first in the trilogy of deals was the trickiest. The production had to be extracted from Miramax and then employed by New Line, who first needed to instigate a process of vetting Jackson's filmmaking outpost. Thankfully, the vibrant and intelligent Carla Fry, head of physical production at New Line, arrived to tour the facilities, get a sense of his capability and to come up with a credible budget.

Ordesky's double-edged reward for bringing Jackson and his ambition through the door was for Shaye to position him as executive producer on the project. After all he knew the book and the director. 'Bob and Michael both believed in the pride of authorship, that if you were an advocate of something then you'd work harder and smarter for it because you were invested in it. So I was surprised and pleased when Bob said, 'Listen, you're going to work on this. You're the Tolkien fanatic, you're the Peter Jackson advocate, you can be there to steer us through this process.'

What Ordesky didn't yet know was how often he would play messenger, mediator and meddler between an irresistible force and an immovable object. He would have to play Gríma Wormtongue one day, Gandalf the Grey the next.

As sums were done and fine print parsed, Jackson and both divisions of Weta were plunged back into a familiar period of uncertainty. The cheques from Miramax had ceased, and New Line had yet to conclude a deal. Knowing it could easily fall apart again — you could smother LA County with the paperwork from collapsed movie deals — Miramax had their own team of bean counters in Wellington totting up everything from artwork to Orc prosthetics, which they considered bought and paid for — something Jackson disputed.

Taylor is haunted to this day by the memory of Miramax suits, scurrying around like Goblins, discussing how to best package up their assets to be shipped back to America. If a miniature didn't fit the shipping crate — as was the case with Helm's Deep — they concluded it should be chain-sawed up into portions that would fit. 'I felt sick,' he admits.

Lee had surreptitiously been taking photographs of all his pictures in case they disappeared.

By contrast, Fry — who passed away from cancer in April 2002 having only seen a completed *Fellowship of the Ring* — like Marty Katz, became a great advocate of the films. 'Carla was a real unsung hero of the whole process,' says Ordesky. Jackson had been pushing for $180 million to make two films, and Fry would stand up for the fact that three films could be made for $207 million.

It was a bold assertion. There were still so many uncertainties. No studio had ever made three films simultaneously. There was no precedent to fall back on, no one to ask how it could be done. As Ordesky explains, a number of what they call 'critical assumptions' went out the window. 'Assumptions about transportation, about lodging, about all kinds of things involved in making films, because no one had ever shot anything on that scale in New Zealand.'

There had to be a hybridization of the Hollywood way with New Zealand culture. None of this was necessarily cynically driven, they were intent on enabling Jackson to make the films, and it was at this time the very capable Barrie Osborne was hired as producer.

Jackson had been keen for Katz to stay on. They had been in the trenches together and Jackson had come to depend on the wisdom beneath the Hollywood tan. More importantly, Katz had shown his 'loyalty' to the production. But he had family commitments. What would amount to five years away in New Zealand was too big an ask. So he never did get to roast his chocolate-coloured Porsche around the leafy avenues of Miramar.

Roughly four weeks after their first meeting with Shaye, $12 million was wired through to Miramax and *The Lord of the Rings* was officially the property of New Line Cinema.

In the interim, a deal was swiftly reached with Zaentz. This was now a simpler process both because it retained much the same legal framework as had been agreed with Miramax and the fact Shaye and Zaentz, in another impossible stroke of fortune, were old friends.

Zaentz later mentioned that Miramax had been facing a large payment to renew their option on the book, which was undoubtedly another motivating factor in Harvey's willingness to cut a quick deal. The vocal impresario, who came to know Jackson and Walsh at various press events following the films' release, would maintain that it was only because of 'their intelligence and enthusiasm' he ever parted with the rights. His view (in hindsight) on the Miramax situation was ardently pro-Jackson. The thought of a single film of the book was 'absurdity'. When Shaye called him with the proposal of New Line replacing Miramax on the project, Zaentz had one stipulation: 'Only with Peter Jackson.'

Ironically, New Line still had to close a deal with the director who had been desperately knocking on their door, which also meant closing a deal with Jackson's fleet of production subsidiaries: Wingnut Films, Stone Street Studios, Weta Workshop, Weta Digital and his post-production facilities. Positive, businesslike relations tensed when New Line cottoned on to the fact they had been the only players in town. Shaye felt duped, and the pro-forma contract shaped by Jackson's team would be subject to some compromise. Jackson lost his pay or play deal (which had meant he would be paid even if the films weren't greenlit). He would effectively only be compensated upfront for one and a half films with backend bonuses. He and Shaye would have to reach an agreement on final cut.

On 24 August 1998, in lieu of any official announcement, the story was leaked to the *Los Angeles Times*. 'New Line Gambles on Becoming Lord of the Rings' ran the headline. Written by film reporter and genre geek Patrick Goldstein, it is curiously off the mark: setting the budget at a conservative $130 million, and claiming that Jackson hoped to have the first film ready for Christmas 2000 (he would still be shooting!) with the next two instalments slated for summer and winter of 2001.

It is a quoted Shaye who proves the most prescient. 'Having seen Peter's script and demonstration reel we believe he has the ideas and the technology to make this a quantum leap over the fantasy tales of ten or fifteen years ago.'

Goldstein also noted that on the internet fans were 'already casting Sean Connery' as Gandalf.

Between the lines, it was clear that sceptisim still reigned in Hollywood. This was commercial suicide.

Ordesky was actually sent a copy of *Final Cut*, that book about the catastrophic money-pit of *Heaven's Gate*. 'It was not given in a kindly way. I thought that if anything is going to throw me off my game it is that book; but this was not *Heaven's Gate*.'

And Peter Jackson wasn't Michael Cimino. He was an ambitious and often obsessive artist, true, but he was also a very practical, diligent, open-minded New Zealander. A quality displayed not least in his burgeoning relationship with fans. Then a similar kind of devotion ran in his veins.

In an extraordinarily smart move, the kind of gesture that comes naturally to Jackson, on 26 August 1998 (two days after the *Los Angeles Times* story) he agreed to take part in an online interview with the website *Ain't It Cool News*. He would answer the twenty most pressing readers' questions, addressing any concerns.

Says Kamins, Jackson wanted to communicate as early as possible that he was up to the task. '*Ain't It Cool News* was a very vogue site at the time, and Peter's hope was that he would show people that he understood the world and if people disagreed with decisions he was making at least they would disagree thinking, "Okay, this guy understands the universe".'

The site's mailbox was besieged with over 14,000 questions, not just from fanboys but fantasy authors and literature professors. Jackson ended up responding to forty questions covering the budget, special effects, how to create hobbits and mount battles, and how with the help of New Zealand's glorious landscapes he was going take moviegoers into Middle-earth.

'I do not intend to make a fantasy film or a fairy tale,' he declared. 'I will be telling a true story.'

'Peter wasn't a dreamer,' affirms Ordesky, 'he had pragmatic plans for how to make dreams come true.'

CHAPTER 5

Concerning Hobbits

During the summer of 1998, Samwise Gamgee was conducting Hollywood business from behind the wheel of his air-conditioned BMW. In this town it was advisable to squeeze in a meeting between meetings, and somewhere along an overheated Burbank Boulevard, Sean Astin's phone had jarred him out of autopilot. It was his agent, whose calls were becoming rare enough to collect. She went by the name of Nikki Mirisch, and like most of her kind Mirisch possessed a crippling allergy to general pleasantries, small talk and complete sentences.

'Listen. . . Peter Jackson is doing *The Lord of the Rings* trilogy for New Line. You'll need a flawless British accent by Thursday.'

All that shot through Astin's brain were the words 'Peter Jackson', 'New Line' and '*trilogy*'. Which was enough to make him pull over.

'You know. . . *Tolkien,*' Mirisch reiterated as if explaining to a senior aunt. You wonder if this was an approach she often found necessary with her clients. '*The Lord of the Rings,*' she stressed again.

Astin remonstrated that there was no way he could be ready by Thursday. It was already Tuesday. Come on, could she push it back a couple of days? He would be so much better prepared.

He was met with a barbed silence.

'Nikki?'

'Thursday, Sean. Be ready.'

You have to admire Astin's honesty. He completes the tale with a chastening visit to a nearby Barnes & Noble where he walked up to the counter and asked if they had anything by J.R. Tolkien?

'Yes sir,' the assistant replied from behind his impregnable Californian sangfroid. 'It's J.R.*R.* Tolkien.'

Faced with the cacophony of editions occupying an entire wing of the fantasy section, deep in Astin's brain synapses began to flare like beacons on distant mountaintops. This was something far more than a big, plump fantasy trilogy or fleshed out comic book. This was *literature.*

Purely on aesthetics he opted for an Alan Lee version.

A year earlier, Harry Knowles, the Austin-based internet pioneer and zealous Jackson advocate at the helm of *Ain't It Cool News*, dropped by the set of Robert Rodriguez's alien-parasite-loose-in-a-high-school B-movie pastiche *The Faculty*. Wherein Frodo Baggins was playing the school newspaper's klutzy photographer Casey Connor. On a break, Knowles wandered over to Elijah Wood.

He and Wood had become fast friends. On the actor's days off he often headed over to Knowles' house to eat barbecue and geek out over movies.

'I just heard that Peter Jackson's going to make *The Lord of the Rings* into a feature film,' announced Knowles, whose own allergy was to not giving the world the benefit of his opinion. 'You should play Frodo.'

Knowles emailed Jackson shortly afterwards to tell him so as well.

Wood had seen *Braindead, Heavenly Creatures* and *The Frighteners.* He'd loved the boundless energy and raucous sense of humour, but there was drama too. Having read *The Hobbit* as a kid, he was tangentially aware of what *The Lord of the Rings* was about and the idea of Jackson directing an adaption made perfect sense to him. With its showcase of human drama with fantasy, *Heavenly Creatures* was a perfect template for what Tolkien required, albeit on a much lower budget. Jackson, he could see, liked to play in that sandbox. The notion of him being attached himself to such a famous series of books was exciting.

Beyond that he had no sense of who Frodo might be or why he was so right to portray him. At that stage, he admits, 'It was an abstract thought.' One he paid no more heed to until almost twelve months later when he read that Jackson was travelling to London, New York and Los Angeles in search of hobbits, and it turned out that seed Knowles had planted in his head had taken root.

Wood's agent made the appropriate introductions for him and he met with the casting director, Victoria Burrows, who was running the Los Angeles end of the operation. He read an early draft of *The Fellowship of the Ring* (which was not to leave the room). Burrows suggested he come back in a day or two to put something on tape.

But the idea of Frodo was now too important to chance on some identikit audition against the featureless wall of a casting office. 'I wanted to do something that would showcase my enthusiasm and passion, something that would push me in a different direction and be more visible. Something I would have more control over.'

Wood had never been bold enough to shoot his own audition tape before — not an unheard-of tactic for zealous actors — but that is what he was going to do, using the three audition scenes he had been given for Frodo. One was a prototype scene between Gandalf and Frodo that never made it to the movie and two were scenes from film three where Frodo has to varying degrees succumbed to the Ring's psychic tentacles. The idea was to show the actor's range across the gamut of Frodo's decline. As two of the scenes were exteriors he headed out the pine-strewn slopes of Griffith Park for a quasi-Tolkien backdrop.

But not before heading to the bookstore and grabbing a pile of illustrated editions of Tolkien's thick tome, Alan Lee's among them. Equipped with a general idea of what constituted hobbit attire, he hired a waistcoat, knee high pants, braces, that kind of thing. Then with his friends George Huang, who had directed *Swimming with Sharks*, behind the camera and Mike Lutz reading the parts of Gandalf and Sam out of shot, he filmed the first ever live-action scenes of Frodo in *The Lord of the Rings*. Edited into shape, the tape was Fed-exed to Jackson, who was in London becoming increasingly despondent that he may never find his ideal Frodo and Sam.

*

Martin Scorsese once said that ninety per cent of any film is casting. And who are we to doubt the master? He is one of Jackson's chief inspirations as a director. But Scorsese has never been burdened with finding a hobbit. One of the keenest pleasures in contemplating a live-action adaption of *The Lord of the Rings* was that game of mentally casting the Fellowship and the host of other named parts.[*] Who was best for Frodo or Sam or Gandalf or Ted Sandyman? In practice, locating the perfect Fellowship and beyond became a quest littered with false starts, frequent despair and pure fluke.

In his prologue (paraphrased by Bilbo in the extended edition of *The Fellowship of the Ring*) Tolkien alludes to hobbits' 'love of peace and quiet' and 'good tilled earth'. They were clearly a romanticized version of the country folk the writer had known from his rural childhood. The twist of course being they grew 'not taller' than four feet and had extremely large feet 'clad in thick and curly hair'.

In the pitch documentary, Jackson is determined his hobbits were to be, as Tolkien said, 'little people'. They were not children,

---

[*] The total of named parts across the trilogy has been calculated to be 86. This is something of a retrospective tally with fans divining nomenclature for unclassified actors based on relating scene to book, such as Michael Elsworth as Círdan the Shipwright and Cameron Rhodes as Farmer Maggot.

or any of the grotesque garden gnomes fancied by less faithful artists. Bakshi had fallen headfirst into that trap. Jackson wanted his audience to relate to them, and be equally as unsettled by big folk.

The director also explained in his pitch how the problematic issue of scale would be achieved via a variety of cunning visual tricks: forced perspective, slaved cameras, crosscutting between differently scaled sets, digital face replacement, distinctively tall and small stand-ins and the (in the end limited) use of giant puppets.

Ian Holm noted the 'great satisfaction' Jackson derived from mastering what the actor called this 'Brobdingnagian event'.

Once shooting, Jackson became increasingly willing to trust the audience to assume the distinction naturally. They could shoot a hobbit actor from over a human's shoulder and we would unconsciously rescale the scene. The sequence where Boromir tries to claim the Ring from Frodo features no trickery at all (excepting the Ring's). Jackson uses the slope of the hill to fool our eyes.

Each hobbit they cast still had to match the others as being of the same species. Within a certain range they were to be uniform in size, features and an elusive hobbit sensibility. Through the bulk of the writing process, this was as far as Jackson's thinking had gone. He had methodically resisted the temptation to indulge in premature casting.

'I would never have guessed at that point that we would have Elijah Wood as Frodo or Sean Astin as Sam. It wouldn't have even crossed my mind. I was seeing fantasy characters. Hobbits that were *this* tall.'

The worldwide search for hobbits along with all the species of the cast began in the summer of 1998.* A process, Ordesky

---

* There had been some minor discussions about casting during the Miramax era, certainly from the studio side, which included a debate over Morgan Freeman as Gandalf.

insists, that was filmmaker driven. 'It was exactly what you would hope it would be. New Line waited until Peter had between five or half a dozen finalists for any give role. Then I would get sent a videotape of the options.' Jackson would always hint which of the five or six he liked the most. It was an effective way of clarifying his thoughts.

Ordesky sighs. 'I should have realized then that this was going to be my task through the whole thing — to run around New Line showing them all the options and basically getting approval for Peter's choices.'

Not that the studio was always going to be entirely accommodating either.

While faceless, Jackson convinced himself that the four lead hobbits at the very least would be actors who 'corresponded' with Tolkien's description of little English gentlemen.* The Shire's general population of Baggins, Boffins, Tooks, Brandybucks, Grubbs, Chubbs, Hornblowers, Bolgers, Bracegirdles and Proudfoots would, in the case of the party sequence, be filled with a gaggle of up to 100 eccentric New Zealand extras.

Producer Barrie Osborne remembers that, on the day he met Jackson in Wellington, the director invited him along to watch *Lock, Stock and Two Smoking Barrels*. He was considering the English actor Nick Moran as one of either Merry or Pippin. Not that he was wedded to established actors. If anything, unknowns would help sustain the reality of the world, and Merry and Pippin would emerge from hundreds who tried their luck on the audition tapes stacking up at Stone Street.

Away from the trials of the Ringbearer and his faithful servant, Frodo's lighthearted hobbit cousins provide a comic reminder of what the little folk are all about. This will ultimately give way to a stark depiction of shattered innocence.

---

* The quota of four hobbits in the Fellowship is noteworthy. When Tolkien headed off to war, three of his closest friends also enlisted. Only two of the four would survive the war.

Dominic Monaghan was by chance the first member of the cast I ever interviewed. He was in London in the summer of 2001, keen to press ahead with publicity, consciously hip in leather wristbands and torn jeans, a threadbare band t-shirt. He told mystical, 'living a dream' stories of a shoot that had changed his life, quite different from Merry in person.

He had been born in Berlin to English parents, a peripatetic infancy that ended in Stockport, an outer farthing of Greater Manchester. That was his vibe: salt-of-the-streets Mancunian, pretentiously unpretentious and a stalwart United fan. A desire to act had guided him to local theatre and a local agent. The twenty-three-year-old Monaghan was by no means green when he auditioned: he had spent four years as the trusty sidekick on amateur sleuth show *Hetty Wainthropp Investigates.*

When the canny London casting director John Hubbard spoke to him about *The Lord of the Rings,* he was playing a skinhead on the London stage. Hubbard was managing the London end of casting with his wife Ros, and Monaghan went in to read for Frodo. It was a common feature of Jackson's casting odyssey that he would discover someone he liked reading the wrong lines. Ordesky remembers Orlando Bloom trying out for Frodo, but everyone else, including Bloom, is certain he had first been up for Faramir.

'It was a very relaxed process and I thought it went rather well,' recalled Monaghan during our interview. He had been in France working on Second World War drama *Monsignor Renard* when he got his fateful call. 'My agent told me they were interested in me for Merry and that I might have to go to Los Angeles or New Zealand in a couple of days to meet with Peter Jackson.'

That was just sinking in when his agent called back. There was no need to worry — he had already been cast. It was a late decision. Monaghan had a week back in England before getting on a plane to New Zealand.

'It was one of those few moments when you're acutely aware of your life turning on a right angle.'

He viewed Merry as a kind of exasperated older brother to the prattling Pippin: smarter, less carefree, but with no suspicion of what lay ahead. There was a satisfying transformation in the role. Merry ends up going to war. 'No hobbit had ever been to war,' declared Monaghan as we parted.

At thirty-one, Billy Boyd was the eldest of the quartet of hobbit actors, even though Pippin was supposedly the youngest. It didn't show: Boyd caught his naïf qualities — how he totters unaware into peril, strained concentration etched onto his face. Pippin became a hero to those in the audience struggling to assemble all the threads of Tolkien's epic tapestry. But, by film three, Pippin's naiveté has been put out like a light.

Born in Easterhouse, Glasgow, Boyd's soft regional brogue was echoed in a fine singing voice that Jackson would put to use. The actor even wrote 'The Steward of Gondor', the song he mournfully sings in *The Return of the King*. He came to acting via bookbinding (he actually bound copies of *The Lord of the Rings*) and a period, he jokes, of finding himself in the Florida Keys, before returning to attend The Royal Scottish Academy of Music and Drama, a *conservatoire* no less, in Glasgow.

With only a hatful of TV appearances and low-budget films, he read for both Merry and Pippin at the Hubbards' behest, and a tape duly wended its way back to New Zealand. A month later, Jackson and Walsh were in London and asked to meet Boyd specifically about Pippin. There Jackson directed him through a makeshift scene: 'Merry and Pippin sneaking up to Frodo's window and seeing him with the Ring, that sort of idea.'

The first of the four hobbits to be cast, Jackson liked the contrast Boyd's accent might offer. He also sensed audiences would like him. Boyd was a class clown, but sensitive too. He was grounded in person. Not only was Jackson looking for actors and actresses capable of filling the roles, he had to judge their temperament. Were they going to disrupt his way of working?

The Scots and Kiwis share that innate suspicion that acting and filmmaking might all be a bit daft.

Boyd had been busy with a theatre workshop in Edinburgh when he got a message to call his agent back. During a break he found a phone box. Then he heard the familiar voice of his agent saying unfamiliar words.

'Guess who's playing Pippin in *The Lord of the Rings*?'

He spent the rest of the afternoon calling her back to see if it was still true. Eventually she advised him to go and lie down.

As if preordained by the script, Monaghan and Boyd would become great friends. Yet it came naturally: they liked the same things, laughed at the same things, already teasing one another. Art and life were happily sharing. On the day they met, Boyd and Monaghan had drifted into Wellington for a coffee. Even then, the town had more coffee shops per capita than anywhere else in the world.

'We asked each other for our stories,' recalled Monaghan, 'and what we'd been up to.' They were just sitting there, Merry and Pippin, like a couple of regular fellas.

Frodo and Sam, however, remained a challenge.

As written, Frodo doesn't actually do much of what might be classified as movie-type heroism. More often than not he ends up on the wrong end of something pointy. There was an air of martyrdom about him. He carried this unimaginable burden to which he was slowly surrendering like a vampire. He was completely unironic, and there was a danger of making him holier than thou. 'He is also very hard to visualize,' stresses Jackson, who spent a lot of time stressing over the conundrum. 'Even more complex when you think that Tolkien made him the narrator of the book.'

In the two-film script, in an effort to invigorate Frodo, Jackson and Walsh introduced an extended sequence on the Seeing Seat relocated from Amon Hen to the Emyn Muil. Here Frodo gains a vision of Gandalf confronting Saruman, before a Ringwraith mounted on a fell beast swoops up behind the evil wizard and swipes him from the summit of Orthanc with a giant mace. With Gandalf set to follow a similar fate, Frodo puts on the Ring and enters its Twilight World, revealing himself to Sauron. The fell beast then tears to the Seeing Seat and battles with Frodo and Sam. Frodo finally thrusts Sting into its heart.

While exciting, like many bold modifications the scene was abandoned as too much of a stretch from Tolkien. They were going to have to rely on the actor to convey the courage of Frodo in more psychological terms. Which made the casting of Frodo that much harder.

Meanwhile, Jackson found it was almost impossible to picture Sam without knowing his Mister Frodo.

He was insistent something of that ineffable, heroic quality in each of them — their 'Frodoness' and 'Samness' — would be obvious when the actor walked in the door. And they still had to be British; he wouldn't bend on that. Audition tape after audition tape, meeting after meeting, and neither Frodo nor Sam had met his gaze. He began to worry he was too fixed in his thinking, too precious about the most important roles in the films.

'We auditioned probably two hundred odd people: people in England, Los Angeles, Australia, New Zealand, everywhere. We personally auditioned about two hundred people all around the world, who couldn't do it.'

But there was some good news. Hobbiton, Frodo's home, the heart of the film, had been found. It was on a sheep farm two hours outside of Auckland.

*

On a Sunday afternoon in September 1998, Waikato Rugby Union was playing Auckland in the Ranfurly Shield. 'Not the All Blacks!' grumbles Ian Alexander. 'They always say the All Blacks.' He shakes his head, as if this simple error repeated ad infinitum by journalists summed up the craziness that had upended his quiet life as a farmer in the green paddocks region of the Waikato, near Matamata at the north of the North Island. Alexander was engrossed in the game, a tight regional play-off, when the doorbell rang. With his wife otherwise occupied, he grudgingly went to the door to find a complete stranger standing on the threshold.

'Hi, my name is David Comer,' the fellow said. 'I'm a location scout for a proposed production of J.R.R. Tolkien's *The Lord of the Rings*. Your farm might be ideal for one of the key settings in the film.'

He might as well have been speaking in tongues.

Exasperated at the interruption, and worried this Mr Comer might be selling something, Alexander was on the verge of slamming the door in his face. He grins guiltily, things could have easily been so different, if his wife, overhearing the words '*The Lord of the Rings*', had not intervened. She knew and loved the book, and having banished her bewildered husband back to his television, listened to what Comer had to say. Mrs. Alexander is another of those emissaries of fate who lurk at the margins of this story. Left alone, Alexander would have shut the door on Hobbiton, which would inevitably have had to find a compromise and something would be lost from the films.

Alexander cackles delightedly, sipping Southfarthing ale in the *Green Dragon*. 'Still haven't read it.'

I have met the splendidly earthbound Alexander and his worldlier eldest son Russell, who now runs a permanently preserved Hobbiton as one of the leading tourist attractions in New Zealand. I have, bizarre as it sounds, lunched with them both in the *Green Dragon*. In truth, a sumptuously rendered, human-sized replica of Hobbiton's renowned tavern with handcrafted leather chairs and crackling fires. They served specially brewed Southfarthing beers (there is a stack of barrels outside).

It hadn't taken much prompting from Russell or the ale for his father to launch into his favourite story.

I also had the privilege of spending a day exploring the South Island by helicopter in the good company of the late Mr Comer as he pinpointed a multitude of hilltops, crags, rock strewn plains and glacial terraces unreachable to anyone but intrepid climbers or a swarm of filmmaking whirlybirds. He could recount the exact moment in which they intersected with Middle-earth. Every one still etched in his memory. He also directed my attention to the rounded summit of the Waiorau Snow Farm near Otago, which Roland Emmerich had co-opted as the prehistoric location for *10,000 BC*, one of the many feature films that came hungrily in search of this landscape in the wake of Middle-earth. An engaging but inscrutable South Islander from Dunedin, as well as a location scout, he had served as a wilderness guide and photographer among the scarps and glens of the Fiordland region. There was a flicker of the lonely ranger about him in his easy reading of the land and uneasiness with company.

Comer knew the book well. When the thrilling commission came to track down the gamut of locations, as one of a team of scouts orchestrated by supervising location manager Richard Sharkey, he had 'a whole array of locations' waiting for this moment. Remote, untouched, otherworldly pockets of majesty he'd dreamed of as Dimrill Dale, Amon Hen or the River Anduin. Comer knew where Middle-earth was to be found.

'What,' he wondered aloud as Queenstown spread out below us like a quilt, 'could be a finer pleasure than that?'

There was an exception. In all his wanderings Comer had never seen Hobbiton. It was too prescribed and idealized by Tolkien. The gentle hill crowned in an oak, the millpond and the enclosed field with a party tree: a bucolic reflection of Tolkien's Worcestershire childhood. This was the idyll for which Frodo endured his burden. The author had even provided a helpful watercolour. But to fake Hobbiton with CGI was unthinkable. This is where their film began, where they needed to establish the 'wholeness' of Tolkien's world.

'Frodo is not trying to save the world,' chimes Ordesky, 'he is trying to save the Shire. And the Shire was in the world.'

Comer thought he had found something 'workable' elsewhere on the North Island, but an instinct took him for one more plane trip across the green paddocks near Matamata. The glacially rounded hills are the nearest New Zealand has to an English landscape. In among the grassy downs his eye was drawn to a small, egg-shaped hill covered in gleaming green grass that flowed down to a small lake. How had he missed it before? Beckoning the pilot to take them closer, his heart stopped. At the lakeside a lordly if misshapen pine tree held court over a small, hedged enclosure. The Party Tree. And because of the lie of the valley among surrounding hills, with the exception of a single hay barn in the middle distance there wasn't a single manmade object in any direction. No roads, no buildings, no electricity lines, nothing. It was a miracle.

After landing, he drove straight out to the farm and knocked on the door, and the next thing Alexander knew a convoy of SUVs like a presidential motorcade was bouncing across the 1,250 acres of his farm in search of the Promised Land. Inside were Jackson and his design team. The director can remember how everyone was struck dumb when they climbed out. All they needed to do was add front doors and chimney pots, a lowering oak, and here was John Howe's lush and evocative depiction of Bag End that Jackson so loved.

Alan Lee and Howe were both on that recce. They were as staggered as everyone else. Perhaps more so: they had never seen their own paintings in the flesh. Had they crossed through some kind of portal, stumbled through the back of a wardrobe?

'We flew up to Hamilton,' recalls Howe. 'We met this farmer, drove through a number of gates and pulled up on the hill above Bag End. So perfect. We immediately sat down and started sketching. We could put this *here* and that could go *there*. . . It was one of those magic moments where you know that's the place.'

Much has been made of the marriage of New Zealand's unblemished scenery and the great sward of Tolkien's evocative world, and rightly so. But only lonely Edoras on the South Island ever rivalled this pouch of sheep-grazed farmland in matching the imagination of a long-dead Oxford Don to such glass-slippered perfection. For the team who sat in the sunshine gazing upon their prize this was their first taste of a strange reality.

Middle-earth was no longer hypothetical.

Says Howe, 'That's when we started to feel that by a completely haphazard set of circumstances this movie was taking place in the best country possible.'

Now of course they had to get down to work. Not least in cutting a deal with the increasingly curious Alexander for the temporary loan of his land. Not for the last time, Jackson convinced the government to lend a hand. The versatile New Zealand army would build a 1.5 km road so they could transport materials, cameras and hobbits to what would become a working set. They also helped with some initial landscaping.

Under the guiding eye of production designer Dan Hennah, work on Hobbiton began a year out from shooting with the planting of cornfields, barberry hedgerows, fields of sunflowers and small allotments of living hobbit agronomy. Then they built the different frontages of the hobbit holes, the mill at Bywater, the stone bridge and the Green Dragon Inn. By the time they planned to shoot here in autumn 1999 (or, as it would turn out, early 2000) the location would, as Jackson insisted, 'have the feel of an established, lived-in community'. Here was the director's *de rigueur* authenticity down to the stalks of corn and weathered gateposts. Though the old oak above Bag End was assembled from numbered pieces of a twenty-six-ton real oak and plastic leaves made in Taiwan. All for nine days of principal photography and a few weeks of second-unit work.

Arriving for the first time at a sun-washed Hobbiton, Wood had never seen anything so immersive in his life. Honeybees were darting between flowers oblivious to their part in movie history. The gentle valley had evolved its own ecosystem. 'It was real. It was there. Smoke was coming out of the chimneys. And there really was no end to it. All you could see was rolling hills. It was the way it was described in the books and the illustrations. Bag End with a giant tree coming out of the top. I mean, it gave us all chills. We were kind of in awe of the reality of the world that we were creating.'

Wood would celebrate his nineteenth birthday in Hobbiton.

When they returned in 2009 to rebuild Hobbiton for *The Hobbit*, Russell Alexander, an entrepreneurial gleam in his eye, negotiated with Jackson to use permanent materials so the heart of the Shire could live on as a tourist attraction. Today, you can take a stroll along Bagshot Row where Sam lives and stare intently at the green front door of Bag End or any of the thirty-seven hobbit holes at either 'Gandalf scale' (human-sized, so small) or 'Bilbo scale' (hobbit-sized, so big). While a team of permanent Sam Gamgees administer to the pot plants and vegetable gardens.

Behind the door of Bag End is nothing more than musty wooden struts and some gardening equipment stowed out of sight. The variously scaled interiors were built on soundstages in Wellington.

Fans, Russell told me, are often reduced to tears as they pass through Gandalf's cutting, where once Frodo engaged the old wizard in conversation, and they behold Hobbiton for the first time.

*

For Bilbo Baggins, much the bachelor squire of Hobbiton who by luck or design has become the current proprietor of the One Ring, Jackson had only one actor in mind. Indeed, the first two names on his wish list had been Sir Ian Holm as Bilbo and Cate Blanchett as Galadriel, and he would get them both.

Holm was of course a veteran of stage and screen. Jackson had loved him in *Alien* and *Brazil*. He was also a little on the smaller side, as Blanchett was rather elfin. Holm's 5'6" squarish frame lent itself to hobbitness. Not coincidentally, all the hobbit actors were relatively compact: Wood is 5'6", Astin 5'7", Boyd 5'6", and Monaghan 5'7". Pertinently, Holm had memorably portrayed Frodo's descent into madness in the 1981 radio serialization.

He may have been born and brought up in the Essex mental asylum where his father worked as a doctor, but Holm insists this had no bearing on his decision to become an actor. Like fellow knight Sir Ian McKellen, he was classically trained. He'd paid his dues to Shakespeare, and gained a reputation for often darkly whimsical supporting turns in films like *Chariots of Fire*, *Big Night*, *The Fifth Element* and *From Hell*. Holm was always his own man as an actor. As boisterous as a cannonball, you can see why he has played Napoleon on three occasions.

His 'kaleidoscope' approach to his craft played right into Jackson's loosey-goosey film schooling. Holm could offer a different line reading and facial expression with virtually every take. 'Just let me know what you are looking for,' he would say before bounding into a scene, often perplexing his fellow actors.

The director loves to retell the story of the British great beginning the big party speech — 'My dear Baggineses and Boffins. . .' — when the polystyrene birthday cake behind him burdened with eleventy-one candles caught light. Holm noticed that the hobbit extras were becoming distracted if not alarmed by the rising flames. Following their glances, he caught sight of what was happening but never broke character. He simply gestured at the burning cake, raised his eyebrows and kept on going. An unusable take, but brilliant nevertheless.

Nothing had prepared Holm for the ambition and pleasure of creating Middle-earth on film — although he would never get to Hobbiton, his two-month tenure on the film was entirely occupied on soundstages. Or the 'quirky nonconformism' of his director. He always seemed to Holm to be itching to join in.

When frequently asked which character he identifies with, Jackson claims it is Bilbo, even if Gimli displays more of his tenacity and humour. 'He's the one sitting at home with his feet up and a nice pint of ale. I certainly identify more with Bilbo than Frodo. Frodo goes through so much and becomes so alienated, I couldn't begin to think what he experienced.'

The morning a strange tape arrived at his London hotel from the '*Flipper* kid' — '*Flipper* was the only thing I knew Elijah for,' he admits — Jackson changed his stance on Americans. 'And as soon as he walked in the room, I faced facts: I had in front of me the perfect Frodo.'

'I thought they were insane with Elijah,' admits Boyens. 'I was like *what*? But then I saw the tape. I was like, "Okay, yup, got it. Understood."'

'Those remarkable, God-given eyes!' sang Holm when asked to share some thoughts on his co-star. 'That glorious, good-natured personality! Elijah's Frodo is a dazzling light in the doom and gloom of war and despair.'

Wood's God-given blue eyes, geometric cheekbones and sweet nature were the perfect template for a child star. He exuded a photogenic innocence, but was in touch with strange energies. Stretch his smile a little wider, hold his stare a little longer and what was angelic becomes darker and edgier. Born in Cedar Rapids, Iowa, his destiny was set when his mother took her striking looking son to a modelling convention out of which came small television roles. Before he was even sixteen he had racked up a substantial résumé: a cameo in the first of those *Back to the Future* sequels seguing into significant roles in *Avalon, Paradise* and *The Good Son* before being top-billed in *North*. In the same year he made *The Faculty* he featured in Ang Lee's acclaimed adaptation *The Ice Storm* starting to escape the pigeonhole of his infancy. And, yes, he had starred in the remake of *Flipper* in 1996.

When at last he met Jackson, Wood had no idea he was one of his last hopes. Jackson would also interview Jake Gyllenhaal, but the *Zodiac* star confessed it was a disaster. He hadn't received the note about a British accent and his Frodo came out a Californian native. 'Fire your agent,' was Jackson's one piece of advice.

Reading through the same Frodo moments in a collected British accent, Wood knew he could do no better. Still, the statutory agonizing months would pass before his agent called and told him to wait by the phone, there was a call coming. Jackson had needed to consult with New Line (who were more than positive, given Wood was an established name) and maybe run over his options one more time (this was *Frodo*).

Wood slammed down the phone and didn't move, his stomach churning like a washing machine. He still managed to be startled when the phone rang again.

Jackson's long-standing assistant Jan Blenkin spoke in a soft Kiwi accent that betrayed no sign that this was anything more than a routine business call. 'Please hold the line for Peter Jackson.'

There came a pause in which thousands of miles of static whispered doubts into his ear before Jackson's friendly voice came on the line.

'Hello Elijah, I was wondering if you wanted to come down and play Frodo.'

'And that was that.'

On 8 July 1999, New Line officially announced that Elijah Wood had been cast as Frodo Baggins. And it seemed so obvious.

With hindsight, Wood can reflect on the momentousness of that brief phone call from across the Pacific being drowned out by the excitement of the moment (there was squealing). He would never be the same again. Here was this kid, eighteen years old, facing not only the role of a lifetime, this iconic beast he would have to carry across three films, but leaving home for the first time to go and live in New Zealand for twenty months. This was only the second movie set he would have been on without his mother.

'It's not lost on me that I was at the age that one goes to college or university and it would occupy a similar amount of time in my life. The profundity of that certainly hit me more once we were filming. What formative years those are. Living an independent life for the first time. There were so many firsts and so much growth associated with the experience that when I think about the films I think about them in life terms. I changed from boy to man in Middle-earth.'

There is an old argument that the true hero of *The Lord of the Rings* is not Frodo but Sam, his faithful friend, companion, valet, bodyguard, Sherpa, cook and erstwhile gardener. That ultimately, this is Sam's story. He more than any other character is the audience's eyes and ears, their hairy feet as well. He is the ordinary hobbit in extraordinary circumstances.

Frodo's tortured experience is beyond us.

As Sam, Astin has published an account of his experiences. His biography is surprisingly candid, painting a picture of a journey both extraordinary and, Astin admits, one hedged by his own insecurity. He says he is a 'compulsive worrier'. Jackson laughs that on set 'Sean' tended to be very conscious about health and safety.

This being a perverse universe, it is always those wariest of accidents who get clonked on the head by an Elven loom. As happened to Astin during the Rivendell shoot when a gust of wind sent the instrument toppling. The actor would insist on going for a CAT scan. All turned out to be fine, and as Jackson notes, 'on one level it was really funny'. Astin had been most alarmed when during the scenes of Frodo, Sam and Gollum making their way through the ghostly woods of Ithilien, the crew were advised to wear hard hats in case of falling pinecones. The actors had no such protection (such additional risks are written into their contracts). As was colourfully documented among the DVD extras, poor Astin gouged open his foot while charging out of the water filming the scenes where Sam and Frodo take flight at the end of *The Fellowship of the Ring*. Some forgotten object in the riverbed had spiked through his prosthetic foot and into his real one and he had to be helicoptered to hospital.

Astin always marvelled at Wood's indefatigable good humour. And that he was apparently indestructible. During the shooting of The Watcher in the Water sequence, Wood was tied by a bungee cord to a rig and whipped around in the air to simulate being swung by a monstrous tentacle. 'He was like a cat – he couldn't get hurt.'

Wood even looked a little like Buster Keaton.

He might have been a bit of a fussbudget but Astin had a huge, caring heart, which was a perfect corollary of Sam's diligent spirit. One would feed the other.

First, though, he had to get the part.

Never having read the books, Astin felt none of the reverence that the other actors might have brought into the room. Wise to the mythos of Hollywood, he was more impressed that a project on this scale was being backed by New Line, 'who didn't throw money around casually'. He was smart enough to realize this was a big deal, possibly the biggest of his career. It was also a ready-made trilogy. That meant a sustained amount of work. Furthermore, excepting the Kiwi cast, Astin was the one actor who had met Jackson before. His stepfather, John Astin, had played The Judge, liveliest of the decomposing ghosts in *The Frighteners*, and had introduced his stepson at the American premiere. It was Astin Snr. who had got him the audition.

Astin had been experiencing a midcareer slump. 'I had reached a point in the auditioning cycle where I had lost faith,' he admits. He had been born into Hollywood. His mother was the actress Patty Duke and he took the surname of the actor-stepfather who had raised him — his biological father was music promoter Michael Tell. Attending the Crossroads High School for the Arts, he had classes with the celebrated coach Stella Adler, no less. If not exactly Method, on set Astin had a way of refocusing himself into the role as if drawing Sam in like a breath. Like Wood he had been a child star. At the age of nine he was starring alongside his mother on television, by twelve he was one of *The Goonies*. After that there was a steady flow of memorable roles: *Where the Day Takes You, Memphis Belle, Toy Soldiers, Courage Under Fire*, but it had never panned out into a regular place at the table.

He is aware he is too short and naturally stocky to fit the bill of a leading man (but perfect for a leading hobbit). He admits he has none of the movie-star magnetism of Wood. Additionally, he had married young and retreated from the graft of maintaining a presence in Hollywood to help raise his daughter. He also harboured a desire to step up into filmmaking.

When they had first met him, at *The Frighteners* premiere, Walsh and Jackson had both praised his performance in *Rudy*, the well-reviewed against-the-odds story about 'the last guy on the bench' who makes it as an American football star.

Before his first audition, Astin had been faxed four or five pages about the language of Tolkien and a handful of Sam's speeches, including being caught eavesdropping by Gandalf and a powerful speech when he believes Frodo is dead, stung by Shelob the spider. 'Please don't leave me here alone. . .'

Emboldened by what he perceived to be the workingman side of Sam's character, he landed on a cockney accent, he hoped more Michael Caine than Dick Van Dyke. Burrows had an assistant tape the session to go over to Jackson.

The unbearable wait that followed what he thought was a decent audition — Burrows had assured him it had gone well — was made worse when the unsparing Mirisch informed him that Jackson was also considering an English actor who was, as Astin carefully worded it, 'more naturally stout' than he was. A name that has emerged from the British auditions is that of Lancashire comedian Johnny Vegas, who got as far as meeting Jackson, but it was as calamitous an introduction as Gyllenhaal's. He arrived hoarse from a stand-up gig the night before, where his mic had broken, and croaked his way through a confrontation with Shelob, and remembers Jackson rubbing his eyes in despair.

Still Sam was described as much fatter than his fellow hobbits, and in a flurry of nerves Astin put together a montage of scenes from his films in which he considered himself out of shape — career suicide under Hollywood circumstances.

Before the shoot Astin had been fit enough to run the Los Angeles Marathon, and the required 30lbs weight gain — through eating 'whatever the hell I wanted' — would become a physical and psychological burden to carry. He talked about how uncomfortable he felt in his skin.

Jackson never mentioned the unfitness video, but he wanted to meet Astin. This was in the same Los Angeles round of auditions in which they discovered that Frodo was an American (who could do an English accent), and likewise the director was joined by Walsh and Burrows. They asked after his stepfather, the atmosphere was convivial and chatty. 'The wall' between actor and prospective employer, says Astin, never went up.

Jackson related how Tolkien had seen action in the First World War and those experiences had forever shaped his worldview and his art. The bond between Frodo and Sam was the most important relationship in the book. It was, he said, 'a specifically English relationship'. That idea of a connection across class boundaries, and how Sam, a common man, embodied a nobility and courage that Tolkien had witnessed on the battlefield. 'My Sam Gamgee is indeed a reflexion of the English soldier,' he once wrote, 'of the privates and batmen I knew in the 1914 war, and recognized as far superior to myself.'

All of this was music to Astin; the character and the trilogy took on a new seriousness, and he came away feeling like he had done his best. But Peter, he told his stepfather afterwards, 'is hard to read'.

The good news came via New Line.

Astin too is the only cast member who has been open about how much he was paid for the films. One of the reasons the studio could invest heavily in visual effects was the absence of a costly star name, not that they didn't try, as we shall see. Nevertheless, Astin was shocked at the offer of $250,000 for all three films (we can assume there was a sliding scale dependent on time and relative fame: the likes of Wood, McKellen and later Mortensen would have been paid more). This would amount to two years' work. There were times, exhausted and weather-beaten, when his mind would wrestle again with the fee. But Mirisch wasn't about to let him dither or whine. This was the chance of a lifetime, take it or leave it.

When he got off the phone he sank to his knees and cried.

*

Wood landed in Wellington for the first time at the end of August 1999, as the Southern Hemisphere's back-to-front seasons bade farewell to winter. He remembers being picked up and taken for a driving tour of the city, marvelling at how small it was, before being dropped off at his hotel. As he sat alone in his room, Wood found himself split between the adrenaline rush of excitement and a nagging anxiety. It was as if only then did the concept that he would be the one playing Frodo become a reality. For the first time he felt pressure.

He had at least already met Astin when they went for a wig fitting at a Los Angeles hotel. A process that necessitated having a cast made of their entire head. In today's Weta Workshop Richard Taylor had devoted an entire room to deathly white casts of celebrity heads, their eyes tightly shut: not only the likes of Wood, McKellen and Blanchett's surprisingly tiny face, but ghostly visages he has collected from the past like Vincent Price, Boris Karloff, James Cagney and Cary Grant. It has the aura of a mausoleum.

Every member of the cast would feature a wig. It was a practical thing both to highlight species-specific hairstyles and enable continuity with scale doubles. Jackson once mentioned to Astin that most of the hair came from female donors in Russia.

So Sam and Frodo would first meet in the foyer of the Ma Maison Sofitel Hotel in Beverly Hills, where they hugged like long lost brothers and pulled apart to examine one another. It was a knowing appraisal on both their parts. Are you ready for this? They wouldn't see each other again until New Zealand.

The two months of preparation for the four principal hobbits was like a rite of passage. Wood is certain none of them could have jumped right in with any confidence. An informal straw poll of friends and acquaintances had quickly instilled in them the weight of responsibility that came with these characters. This was quite apart from the commentary that was beginning to bubble on internet forums. And that way a new kind of madness lay. In fact, the expected backlash to the casting of Americans as Frodo and Sam never fully materialized. Those dissenting voices bellyaching about how Wood was too cute and lacked the gravity to pull off Frodo were drowned out by the digital roar of Knowles, who claimed he was 'jazzed beyond belief' that Wood had been cast.

'The first number of days there was just the four of us and there was a real comfort in that,' says Wood. It diminished the pressure to live up to those expectations.

Wood can remember first meeting Monaghan. He was midway through a costume fitting, a porcupine of dressmakers' pins, when Merry walked in. Nothing was said. They simply grinned at one another and hugged. Loosely.

'There was just some kind of linking force between all of us.

We had left our lives and were going to be in it together for more than a year. There was an immediate sense of needing one another.'

'It was intense,' agrees Monaghan. 'I met Billy and Elijah at the same sort of time, and I met Sean in the hotel foyer with the girls.' Astin was heading out for a stroll with his wife Christine and baby daughter Alexandra (who, grown into a toddler, would play Sam's daughter, Elanor).

The proudly unimpressable Mancunian was surprised to find himself intimidated. '*The Goonies* was a huge thing for me,' he laughs. Astin's fellow hobbits would soon enough become 'uncles' to his daughter.

For those first, disorientating weeks they were put up in the Intercontinental, Wellington's swishiest joint. But after a month of good hotel living they itched to find their own apartments and houses closer to the studio in Miramar. Boyd and Monaghan instinctually found places around the corner from each other.

Chemistry, rapport, camaraderie — whatever name you want to give it — is an elusive property. It calls to something deeper than professionalism and talent. There is an instinct within good casting, the intuition that Scorsese speaks of, which can pay rich rewards in the finished film. Jackson was instinctually drawn to like-minded human beings. Over eighteen months of principal photography nerves were going be frayed. They all had their quirks — the characters were enriched by those quirks. Besides, there was something in the New Zealand air that clarified what was important.

In the name of good research, Astin spent some of those early weeks delving into Jackson's back catalogue and had landed upon *Meet the Feebles*. He was shocked and awed by the depravity of Jackson's dissolute puppet show made in a freezing cold warehouse a stone's throw from the actor's comfortable hotel room. A film pulled together with the same blind determination and willpower that would soon be applied to Tolkien. But it was less the knockabout mayhem his director had achieved on little more than the lint in his pocket than his satirical intent that spoke loudest to Astin. This was a parody of artistic ego. 'They absolutely understood the vanity of actors,' he realized. And they were going to have none of it.

The ranks of the halfling club would soon swell with the boundless energy of Orlando Bloom, who was facing intensive preparations to become the effortless Legolas, and the handsome Irish actor Stuart Townsend who had been cast as Aragorn. 'They were very much a part of the family,' says Woods. 'We had all accepted that we were together on this journey.' The fab four became a secret six throughout boot camp and acclimatizing to Middle-earth.

Physical training took place in a military base a short, lively drive outside of town. Each morning they would be picked up in one of the 'magical mystery minivans', one of which was driven by an endlessly patient local named Paul Randall, who at 7'1" also resolved many of their scale issues. And who was inevitably christened Tall Paul.

Depending on your species there were faculties of horseback riding, canoeing, archery, axe-tossing and sword-fighting. The later class was taken by legendary swordsman Bob Anderson who had taught Errol Flynn to swashbuckle, and more to a hobbit's taste, Darth Vader.

There was individual fitness training for each of them. Which was about building up stamina for the coming shoot as well as physically transforming their bodies into new races. Each character established an individual gait.

Astin had added dance lessons as he was due to whisk Rosie Cotton around the Party Field.

For the hobbits there was also the not so small matter of having their prosthetic feet modelled. 'Those things were like boats with toes,' Holm grumbled. The shoot accounted for 1,600 pairs of them during production. They took getting used to, flexing at the toes like normal feet with what Boyd unscientifically described as a 'strange, spongy, squishy feeling'. They would hope to wear one pair a day, unless there was 'running'. Weta Workshop's menu ran to wigs, noses, pointy ears and for poor John Rhys-Davies as Gimli the Dwarf a full facial prosthetic.

And there were the all-important meetings with Jackson, Walsh and Boyens to get into the meat of their characters and relationships. Soon to be followed by rehearsals and the mechanics of forced perspective.

Inevitably, Astin was the most concerned hobbit. He had looked and listened to other versions of his character. The bumbling Sam in Bakshi's cartoon voiced by the British actor Michael Scholes and Billy Nighy's timorous, yokel sounding Sam in the BBC radio drama. Even the way he had been voiced in the animatic version Jackson showed Astin on a visit to the director's home. None of them felt 'heroic' enough. He was determined Sam wouldn't be a punchline.

Sam's place in the book, Astin reasoned, is 'to be a kind of barometer against which all of the adventure and evil is measured'.

It wasn't compulsory to have read the books. Astin admitted to have struggled to get into it. He was held up 160 pages in when he touched down on Kiwi soil but would arrive at the Grey Havens as the shoot got underway. Wood abandoned it entirely. 'It's a little embarrassing,' he reflects, noting that you could drive yourself crazy reading the book, referencing the book, trying to determine all the elements that made Frodo Frodo. 'At a certain point you just simply have to play the part.'

It was hardly as if he could forget. Tolkien was manifest everywhere you turned: in the environments, the wardrobe and the script. Plus, the book was always in someone's hands.

For Astin and Wood in particular the dialect training was intense. The various accents of Middle-earth would be policed by a punctilious duo of British voice coaches, Roisin Carty and Andrew Jack, and lessons were a morning pleasure in one of the insalubrious Portakabins at Stone Street. An entire science reinforced how and why each character spoke as they did. Language, after all, had been Tolkien's field. With the assistance of recordings from a Tolkien expert, Carty and Jack developed dialects for liquid Elvish, craggy Dwarvish and the spittle-launching Black Speech of Mordor. Their job, Carty explained, was 'to bring the language to life'. They would hover at the sidelines through production, sometimes only inches out of frame. Tact and empathy were essential.

For the hobbits, the idea was that the Shire was substantial enough to have developed regional accents. 'There was a reason behind everything,' appreciates Wood. Being the nephew of Bilbo Baggins, Frodo was from a slightly higher class than Sam, his gardener. Therefore Wood was given Received Pronunciation — the measured accent from the south of England that in movie circles is the national norm.

Those early days, says Wood, were about establishing a 'solid foundation'. Finding the important 'internal vibe for the character'.

Jack and Carty endeavoured to rid Astin of his cockney accent and coax out Gloucestershire's elastic vowels, the agricultural region neighbouring Tolkien's childhood Worcestershire. Sam had a farming background. Astin described the process as 'emotional warfare' as they cajoled him to stretch out his instinctual 'thats' into alien-sounding 'thaaaaaaats'.

There had also been initial concerns that Boyd's natural sing-songy Glaswegian might be too strong. But softening his delivery tended to lessen the humour, so that is basically Boyd's own accent we hear.

While the days were about preparing the group for the long journey ahead, the nights were spent reassuring each other they weren't in it alone. As New Zealand eased toward summer, there was a dinner virtually every night. New members of the cast arrived like the montage of pilgrims to Rivendell, and each occasion needed celebrating. The hobbits half suspected that the production was endeavouring to promote local restaurants. Everything in those weeks felt momentous, but there was one dinner in particular that stays in the collective mind. This was their introduction to Ian McKellen, who had at last been announced as Gandalf and flown over for a few days' familiarization before jetting back to *X-Men*. All the department heads and principal cast already in New Zealand were around the table; it was the closest approximation they yet had to a gathering of the Fellowship.

It was a lovely night. McKellen's presence seemed to reassure everyone. Except Jackson remembers how Townsend refused to be cheered and spent the evening complaining. Indeed, to the point where McKellen lent across the table.

'You do want to be in this film, don't you?' he asked.

'It was strange,' says Jackson, 'Ian picked up on this thing straightaway.'

At an earlier dinner, as his baby daughter fell asleep, Astin and his wife had to make their excuses and head off. He could hear the other hobbits plotting which pub they would head to, the evening far from done with. Producer Tim Sanders could see the conflict on his face.

'You're the married one,' he said sympathetically.

Astin would never be an outsider in the group, but he had to accept there would be a distance from the collegiate freedoms of his co-stars.

Perhaps the most important lesson that was imparted over those giddy, hectic weeks was not so much an indoctrination into the ways of Middle-earth but those of New Zealand. They were 'going native'. Everything in the fledgling production was open to them. They could drop in on Weta Workshop unannounced and be welcomed with glue-splattered arms and Taylor's vociferous updates. Disturb Lee and Howe from their quiet work. Watch the sets take shape at Stone Street.

The phrase almost became a mantra during interviews, but it was true. It felt like the world's largest independent film; this disparate group of people who became a community. 'And it doesn't feel like that can be replicated,' says Wood. 'That wouldn't be the way that something was done now. I mean I was on *The Hobbit*. It was different. It was bigger. There was still that familial vibe for sure, but on *The Lord of the Rings* we were kind of making it up as we went along. It was homemade.'

He reaches for a favourite phrase. 'One of the things that I cherish the most is that it felt like a small town making something for the big city.'

CHAPTER 6

Heavenly Creatures

New Line had suggested Sean Connery. Although, it could be classified as an ultimatum: 'You're not going to get a greenlight unless we can get Connery to be Gandalf.' Peter Jackson had to take a breath. He still hadn't got used to the studio's more abrupt communiqués. Hadn't yet learned to decipher whether they were simply reminding him who was footing the bill for his great venture or genuinely looking to usurp his artistic choices. In this case, you could say it was a bit of both.

The studio was conscious that having a star name don the robes of the famous wizard might strengthen the film's chances among those filmgoers, especially abroad, immune to Tolkien's charms. A marquee name might also quieten down the snide commentary in their backyard. Star power was often the most visible way of shoring up an investment. Star power equated to studio power. It was Hollywood currency. They had airily also proposed Brad Pitt for Aragorn.

But Jackson has never built a film around a name unless you count King Kong or J.R.R. Tolkien. Casting, from his perspective, serves the story. Still, he wasn't *against* the idea of Connery. He was a James Bond fanatic, remember? There were original Connery-era one-sheets decorating the walls of the young director's office. A small corner of Jackson's brain still speculates over what he might have done with *The World is Not Enough*.

'A big part of me was, like, well Sean Connery would be cool. Then it was like, is he really going to come to New Zealand for eighteen months and shoot three movies?'

At sixty-nine, Connery was a hard man to please. The talk in casting circles was that he was losing his appetite for acting.

The rumour that the iconic, former 007 was being feted to bring his so-very identifiable gravitas to the wizard had certainly done the rounds in the early days of the project. But no one ever quite believed it to be true. They were after Connery for Gandalf? *Really*? It felt double-edged, sounding so fantastic and so wrong at the same time. He was brilliant and charismatic, and the likes of *The Name of the Rose* and *The Russia House* suggested he now had a more cerebral, grandee side to his game. And he was Sean Connery! But would we ever see past Sean Connery to Gandalf? And exactly how Caledonian was the old wizard? 'You *sshhhall* not *passsch*!?'

When nothing ever came of it, the story was filed away as fanciful internet speculation like the rumours about Daniel Day-Lewis as Aragorn. But it was true. They did attempt to entice a legend to Middle-earth.

Jackson had got straight back to New Line. 'Do you guys think we have a serious chance?' Bob Shaye smoothly responded that they were going in with a very good offer. But he couldn't shake his nerves. They were so close to filming, and had planned to shoot the Bag End interiors in the first phase of filming, Gandalf arriving for tea with Bilbo. Two identical sets were nearing completion; only one was thirty-three per cent smaller than the other. Did they even have the time to get into a negotiation with the notoriously hard-bargaining Scotsman? Increasingly, his thoughts had turned to the charming English actor Ian McKellen for Gandalf.

Casting was becoming a wearisome business. As with the elusive hobbits, it was as if nearly every named role would be frustratingly hard to pin down. It was a tribute to Tolkien, Jackson reflected: the distinctiveness of each role. Furthermore, each actor needed to define the traits of their race as well as their individual role. To embody what it was to be a Dwarf or an Elf or a wizard without the need for clumsy exposition describing otherworldly grooming habits. There was also the weight of adding human faces to a set of iconic characters that dwelled in the mind's eye of millions of readers. If the films were successful there was the likelihood that for generations to come Frodo would look like Elijah Wood.

In the early years of publication, the Tolkien Estate deterred artists from depicting characters. 'Tolkien himself was reticent about putting imagery on his stories,' says John Howe. 'I do recall the occasional note from the publisher that it's better to focus on wider landscapes.'

Then there were all those other considerations for both director and studio. How marketable was the prospective Arwen or Aragorn? How well did their Legolas or Gimli fit alongside the other actors? Would their Gandalf or Saruman be willing to work in New Zealand, often in the remotest corners of New Zealand, for up to eighteen months? There was nowhere to flounce when halfway up Mount Ruapehu. All of which meant casting was a tall order, even when it came to Dwarves.

So it was, suspecting he was on a fool's errand, that Jackson couriered copies of the scripts to Connery, who they had ascertained was currently residing in his beach house in the Bahamas. As with the parcel that winged its way to Alan Lee's cottage in Devon, Jackson was monitoring its progress SPECTRE-like from his headquarters: the scripts are arriving in the Bahamas. . . The scripts are being driven to his house. . . It should take no more than an hour and half. . . The scripts have been delivered to his house. . .

'Now we were thinking, "How long is it going to take him to read them?"'

New Line was dangling quite a deal. According to Jackson, there was little upfront (leastways, it was estimated at $6-10 million a film), but fifteen or twenty per cent of the gross. Vapours at the time, he accepts, but potentially the payday was staggering. They also put the elite golf courses of Wellington on notice — Connery could be coming to town.

And so they waited, and waited, and waited. . . Days turned into weeks, and even Connery's agent was none the wiser. Like Smaug slumbering in the Lonely Mountain, all that emanated from his millionaire Bahamas redoubt was silence. Jackson simply shrugged his shoulders and turned in the direction of McKellen. There are few now who would contest that fate was once again working in his favour.

It wasn't until a few years later at a Cannes press conference when Connery finally broke his silence. A journalist asked the star if the rumours were true that he had been offered the role of Gandalf. Connery frowned and admitted it was true — the scripts had arrived at his door.

His words were reported all the way back to Wellington. He had never understood it. He read the book. He read the scripts. He had seen the first movie. 'I still don't understand it,' he said. 'Ian McKellen, I believe, is marvellous in it.'

'That's how we heard,' laughs Jackson.

Outside of what was earned via home entertainment, the trilogy made in the region of $3 billion dollars at the box office. At only fifteen per cent of the gross of the films, Connery would have earned $450 million had he understood Gandalf.

*

Visiting *The Grapes*, a public house in Limehouse in the Docklands of East London, you will find Gandalf's staff proudly displayed behind the bar. This fine drinking establishment overlooking the Thames once boasted Charles Dickens among its clientele, who featured this 'tavern of dropsical appearance' in *Our Mutual Friend*. Today, Ian McKellen proudly co-leases the inn, and has embellished the now less dropsical than warmly antique interior with a memento of his days in Middle-earth. He lives only a short walk away on the Isle of Dogs, which is where Jackson and Walsh came for tea.

Boyens had first planted the idea of McKellen as Gandalf into the heads of her partners. She recalled watching videotapes at university of the *Acting Shakespeare* course run by the Royal Shakespeare Company and theatre director Sir Peter Hall. She had the tape where they covered *Troilus and Cressida*. There were so many great actors performing famous scenes. Alan Howard, who would supply the voice both of Sauron and the murmuring Ring, played Achilles. Boyens remembers wondering if Patrick Stewart might make a good Gandalf. That thought went out of her head when she saw McKellen. She took the tape to show Jackson and Walsh the specific scene 'where Hector meets the older generals', one of who was played by the prospective wizard. They were impressed.

By chance, Jackson had recently seen and appreciated McKellen's layered performance as the troubled horror maestro James Whale in the terrific *Gods and Monsters*.

Gandalf is surely the easiest character to picture from the book: tatty grey robes, blue pointy hat, rough-cut staff and a waist-length beard as grey as his cloak. Tolkien may have borrowed facets from Merlin, but Gandalf set the template for the iconography of wizards. He is one of the most immediately recognizable characters in literature. There was no countermanding Tolkien's vision of Gandalf.

A painting of Howe's that pre-dated the project had made a particular impression on Jackson. Gandalf striding purposefully through a rain-swept Shire, his face like thunder, the famous robes blown open by the intemperate weather, revealing his sword Glamdring. 'That was quite a help in eventually getting Sir Ian McKellen kitted up,' notes Howe. Many moons before, while on a walking holiday in Switzerland, Tolkien had been taken with a postcard of a painting by the German artist J. Madlener called *Der Berggeist* — the mountain spirit. It depicted an old man with a white beard, round hat and long cloak. The writer carefully stored away that postcard in a paper bag on which he wrote, 'Origin of Gandalf'.

Jackson never had any doubts his costume and make-up departments could transform a suitably mature actor into the definitive likeness of the wizard. The challenge was capturing what went on inside the riddling shaman.

Ask what drew him to the role of Gandalf and McKellen confesses that it had nothing to do with the books. 'Because I hadn't read them,' he says, unperturbed by such heresies. What excited him was 'Peter and Fran's enthusiasm'.

They had travelled to London seeking, seeking, always seeking their perfect cast and contacted McKellen's agent to enquire if he was interested in meeting them. Aptly enough, McKellen suggested they come for tea. Having got completely lost in the maze of streets east of Limehouse, Jackson and Walsh were quite late by the time they ended up at his front door, which sprang open to the sight of a smiling McKellen.

'Hello, hello, do come in.'

They were laden with designs and artwork and talked passionately about the incredible world they intended to create and this shabby wizard who is such a focal point of the story. He found them wonderfully eccentric, so unlike any other filmmakers he had ever met. In terms of their work, he had only had *Heavenly Creatures* to go on. Which was a good start.

Jackson kept emphasizing the wizard had to feel real.

'I knew nothing else about them: Peter Jackson or Tolkien,' admits McKellen, amused at recalling this impossible time when Middle-earth was still a mystery to him. 'So it was an act of faith: you like somebody, the script seems okay and I was intrigued about New Zealand. Clearly it was a massive project.'

As they got up to leave, Jackson handed McKellen three heavy scripts from his bottomless bag.

It may have taken its time in arriving at his door, but McKellen found stardom quite to his taste. During the shoot he published an online diary he called The Grey Book, charting his progress as Gandalf for the avaricious fans pawing and kneading at the production for any kind of news. He enjoyed the interaction. 'The whole venture across three movies and across the magical landscape of New Zealand is as invigorating as the opportunity to embody a legend,' he reported on 20 August 1999 on his decision to take the role.

Born in Burnley in 1939, McKellen found great solace in theatre, away from his early, troubled years contending with his homosexuality in a strict Protestant household (his father was a lay preacher). He studied English at Cambridge, where he pursued acting in earnest. There he met the young Trevor Nunn, the great theatre director who would have a big influence on his early career.

McKellen developed a wonderfully versatile and melodious voice, and with the Royal Shakespeare Company explored great roles: Macbeth, Iago, Hamlet and Richard III (his King Lear would come later). These were the foundations on which Gandalf was built. It wasn't until the 1990s, in his fifties, that the television and film roles finally came, and with them fame. He featured in *Tales from the City, Six Degrees of Separation* and played Death in *The Last Action Hero*. The breakthrough was bringing his remarkable Richard III, draped in a bold Nazi aesthetic, to the big screen. The film was hailed, and *Apt Pupil* and *Gods and Monsters* swiftly followed. Throughout a forty-year career he remained true to both his Lancashire and theatrical roots — he has cultivated a no-nonsense grandeur — and been an outspoken advocate of gay rights (having come out in 1988).

And so having read the scripts and been encouraged by the deftness with which the fantasy was presented, McKellen called Jackson personally to say he would love to play Gandalf. . . However, he was going to have to decline his kind offer. While Connery was failing to pay them the courtesy of rejecting the role, McKellen had signed on as the metal-contorting villain Magneto in Bryan Singer's first *X-Men* movie. Which in itself wasn't a problem. The problem was *X-Men* had been delayed because their indomitable Wolverine, Dougray Scott, was stuck on an over-schedule *Mission: Impossible 2*. Hence *X-Men* wasn't due to finish until February 2000, and Jackson planned on having Gandalf on set in October.

Jackson called Ordesky. They were still trying to wrap their heads around the Gandalf problem, he warned him. McKellen was out. But they really weren't talking to anyone else. They had discussed Paul Schofield, but he was better suited for Saruman and they had cast that part. Early on, Richard Harris' name had come up in discussions only to be informed by New Line that Harris would *not* be in the movie. There was some kind of history there. The other actors they had considered for the role — Nigel Hawthorne, Christopher Plummer, Tom Wilkinson, Tom Baker, Sam Neill — had fallen away for reasons of ill health or disinterest or they simply didn't click. Bernard Hill, who first read for Gandalf, they now preferred in the role of King Théoden, due to arrive in the second film.

John Astin from *The Frighteners* is mentioned by his stepson as also having auditioned for the role. 'I think I was more innately right for Sam than my dad was for Gandalf,' claims Sean Astin, but he didn't let on until years later.

What happened next falls under the heading of Mutant Chaos Theory. First Shaye bumped into McKellen. Accepting Connery wasn't going to stir, Shaye had warmed up significantly to the idea of McKellen as Gandalf. Dining out in London he had spotted the actor across the restaurant and wafted over to say hello.

'Why aren't you in our film?' he asked. 'You are supposed to be in our film.'

'I'm sorry, I can't,' the cornered McKellen replied. 'I've explained all this. I'm in *X-Men*.'

Shaye, the master tactician, got thinking. He called Jackson and asked if there was any way they could delay Gandalf's entry until the New Year? Rerouting his schedule, Jackson worked out he had enough to shoot around Gandalf until Christmas (for a wide shot of the Fellowship they could use a stand in), but come the New Year things were going to get sticky with an absentee wizard. And McKellen was contracted until the end of February. They couldn't down tools for a month: priceless momentum would be lost while cast and crew were being paid to visit Wellington Zoo.

Fortunately, *Mission: Impossible 2* then fell even further behind and Scott had to admit he wasn't going to make his date as Wolverine, who had to be hastily recast. McKellen had been locked into the mutant epic until February in order to complete Magneto's confrontations with Wolverine, scheduled for the final weeks of the shoot to accommodate Scott's late arrival due to the initial overruns on *Mission: Impossible 2*, which had been hampered by Tom Cruise's *Eyes Wide Shut* having gone on as long as Stanley Kubrick wanted. To add to this briar patch of Hollywood entanglements, McKellen had been too busy to play Commander Swalbeck in *Mission: Impossible 2*, a part that had gone to Anthony Hopkins, who had turned down Gandalf. Anyway, now that Scott had been replaced by Hugh Jackman, who was entirely unaffected by any delays, Singer called Jackson.

They had met years before at an Academy Awards party and got on well. 'He's fun. He doesn't take stuff too seriously,' says Singer, but he could appreciate he was in a serious predicament.

Singer got straight to the point. 'Listen, I give you my word I will deliver Sir Ian to your set on time. I'll shoot his scenes as fast as we can, we'll make it work for you.'

He would be done with Magneto by Christmas. But it couldn't be contractual. The studio wasn't going to gamble on anything legally binding. It was a gentleman's agreement. Jackson had to trust to fate that nothing would waylay Gandalf. He had no plan B.

He nods appreciatively. 'Bryan delivered him bang on time. On the first day of filming in the New Year Gandalf was banging on the door of Bag End.'

On 22 January 2000, McKellen reports in The Grey Book, 'I felt like the new boy at school as they re-grouped two weeks into the year. Term started with a rough cut of the action so far. . .' Jackson had provided beer and wine but McKellen stuck to the candyfloss and popcorn. There followed a party at Barrie Osborne's house where Billy Boyd persuaded the knight to follow him down the twenty-foot fireman's pole in the hall. 'And I wasn't even drunk.'

Singer is delighted to have made a contribution to the adaption of one of his favourite books. 'Peter wrote me a thank-you note,' he recalls, 'and sent me a copy of his documentary *Forgotten Silver*, which postulates that a New Zealander invented cinema and made film from eggs.'

It was a film about the sheer madness of filmmaking.

Across six films Gandalf has been forever inscribed with McKellen's majestic imprimatur. Fans wept at his magnificence, his grace and humour, the extraordinary range he invested into the role: from the gently folding back of an ungovernable lock to the defeat in his eyes as Frodo offers to carry the Ring — Gandalf's plan all along — to the unveiling of supreme power as he forestalls a Balrog. 'YOUUU. . . SHALL. . . NOT. . . PASS!' McKellen brought with him conviction. Through the careful deployment of his delivery, the language sounded rich and true. Sillification was banished. We became instant believers.

'Whenever he walked on set,' says Boyens, 'you got this sense of security. Gandalf's here, it's okay. I'm sure he wasn't thinking that in his head.'

It is unbearable to imagine the films without him, but McKellen will have none of it: 'No, not difficult at all, John Hurt would've done it magnificently. So would've Mike Gambon. I think lots of actors could've done it. I know Sean Connery was asked. But Gandalf of course, is not Scot. . . he was from Oxford.'

Quite. There is that germ of Tolkien in McKellen's interpretation too. W.H. Auden had been a student of Tolkien's at Oxford and heard him perform *Beowulf* aloud to the class. 'That voice,' he said, 'was the voice of Gandalf.'

In Tolkien's mythos, wizards are Istari, a kind of heavenly creature in fogeyish form sent to guide, some might say meddle, in the affairs of Middle-earth. McKellen was keenly aware he was playing someone or something supernatural. 'Gandalf is an angel; he's an undying force rather than a person to be analysed. What he's feeling or thinking is not much relevant, we don't need to know what he had for breakfast, or what his private life is at all. Is he coping? Is he bringing people together? Is he sorting things out? That's what Gandalf's required to do.'

The other Istar we meet is Saruman, friend curdled into nemesis of Gandalf. Saruman's robes are white to Gandalf's grey. His beard and long, straight locks are white, and beneath his skirts his pointed slippers are white. But his heart is as black as his staff, poisoned by ambition, the delusion he could master the Ring. In this, Saruman presents a more modern depiction of evil than the satanic cypher of Sauron: he is the film's test case of virtue corrupted by power. And while Tolkien always denied direct allusions, he hints at the fascism that pervaded the era in which the book was written.

Beneath the white wig was the 6'4" frame of Christopher Lee, a significant presence both in person and in Jackson's childhood film consumption through the London-born actor's tenure, out of a staggering 255 films, as Dracula for Hammer Horror. The fact he had also played Scaramanga, the Bond villain in *The Man with the Golden Gun*, and was Ian Fleming's step-cousin wasn't lost on the director either.

Lee had been filming the BBC adaptation of Mervyn Peake's labyrinthine Gothic fantasy *Gormenghast* (often compared with but of a very different ilk to Tolkien) when he was invited to come and meet with Jackson in London. His agent had warned Lee they might want him to read for a video recording. 'In the case of this story, I am perfectly happy to do that,' he replied. Without fail Lee had read *The Lord of the Rings* annually since its publication.

London auditions took place in the American International Church set back off Tottenham Court Road near Goodge Street. Deconsecrated, it had become a regular rehearsal space. For the unwary it presented a Gormenghastian warren of corridors, and an exasperated Lee had to ask directions to find the small chamber containing a beaming Kiwi fan boy and his placid partner. After Lee's reading, Jackson and Walsh spent forty-five minutes impressing him with photographs of potential locations and artwork of the characters.

'I thought this is unbelievable; this is straight out of Tolkien. This was something I always dreamed about.'

Lee, who died in 2014 at the ripe age of 93, was an enthralling and quite terrifying interview. Nothing that passed his lips was meant in jest. His voice seemed to well up from a subterranean vault within the Earth. And yet, this man who had given cinema a legion of villains never suspected they wanted him for Saruman.

For years Lee had coveted the idea of playing Gandalf, but he recognized he was now far too old. 'I couldn't go wading through the snow like Ian,' he growled, and he had read for Denethor, the insane Steward of Gondor. 'Saruman never occurred to me.'

Jackson maintains he only had eyes for Lee for the corrupted wizard, but he had considered Tim Curry, Jeremy Irons and Malcolm McDowell.

When Lee's agent called a few weeks later bearing the offer of the White Wizard, his mind raced: 'Such a great character, such a great part, I was thrilled.' He could grouch like a bear, but Lee in full flow was fittingly spellbinding.

'Saruman is the Head of the Order, the Head of the Council, he's the most powerful, benevolent, kindest, most brilliant, the greatest. He's almost saintly. That is until Gandalf realizes he's gone over to the other side. So to speak, to the *dark side*.'

*

The spring and summer of 1999 was a tumultuous time, so much was happening on so many fronts: writing, design, storyboarding, pre-viz, scouting, set building, and all the while Jackson and Walsh were dashing round the globe looking for Elves and Dwarves and clandestine kings. Oh my.

There is an alternative universe of stars that could have filled the many roles in the film. As is often the case with the charting of Hollywood history, it depends on whom you ask as to whether they rejected the film or the film rejected them.

Recalls Ordesky, 'In some cases reps made exploratory inquiries on behalf of clients or New Line took the pulse of reps for potential client interest. In such cases a dialogue ensued without an offer necessarily resulting.'

Another myth with a kernel of truth is that they had approached David Bowie to play the Half-elf lord, Elrond. The iconic musician, who had never seemed wholly of this world, had confidently transitioned in and out of films. Jackson had been marginally concerned about reminding people of Bowie's fuzzy-wigged goblin king from *Labyrinth,* a puppeteered reworking of *Alice in Wonderland* that was nothing like *Meet the Feebles*. Dominic Monaghan's widely disseminated recollection of spying The Thin White Duke at an audition is contradicted by the director's claim that he had never actually met or spoken to him.

'The word came back through his people that he was very flattered, but it wasn't something that he would be able to do. But we did try him. . .'

They would instead cast the enjoyably off-kilter Australian actor Hugo Weaving, who had recently dallied contemptuously over his syllables as Mr Anderson in *The Matrix*, the embodiment of anti-virus software.

For Boromir, the sturdy Gondorian warrior with a tragic arc, they met with Russell Crowe (this was before *Gladiator)*, and auditioned Daniel Craig, whose destiny was to become the second 007 not to appear in *The Lord of the Rings*. Bruce Willis, supposedly a fan of the book, was thrown into the mix by New Line but left well alone by Jackson. More conceivably, they got as far as sending the scripts to Liam Neeson before he turned them down.

Boromir was the part that occasioned the most unexpected audition. And not one for which they had exactly asked. 'Word had come through that Simon Tolkien, the barrister, wanted to play Boromir,' says Jackson. Given the distance the family had publicly put between themselves and their 'unsuitable' project, he didn't know quite what to make of Tolkien's grandson volunteering to try out for the films, but he could hardly say no. 'So he came in and read for Boromir in London. It was sort of awkward, but it was nice that he cared. But it wasn't the role for him.'

Breaking ranks with his father Christopher, the literary executor of the Estate, Simon Tolkien remained a firm advocate of the films. Even more so, his nephew, Royd Tolkien, would actually cameo as Golsagil, one of Faramir's band of rangers seen handing out weapons.

The Fellowship's weakest link would ultimately be entrusted to the plainspoken, Sheffield-born actor Sean Bean, who had been television's dashing Napoleonic era hero *Sharpe*. On film he had cornered the market in flawed anti-heroes, even channelling his leading-man looks into another Bond villain in *GoldenEye*. Bean had a clear memory of reading the book at twenty-five, and hearing a new film version was being made had done 'everything possible to be a part of it'. He was speaking in Cannes in 2001 in the afterglow of production, sat alongside Viggo Mortensen, far too polite to mention that as far back as 1 June 1997 newspapers were reporting he was in the running for Aragorn.

In his steady Yorkshire tones he spoke of the delight when Jackson asked to meet him about the possibility of playing Boromir. 'But there was a few months where we weren't sure whether it would happen, or if I'd got the part... And then I finally got it, and I was over the moon. It was fantastic news, that.'

For Faramir, Boromir's younger more enduring brother, New Line expressed an excitement for Stephen Dorff and then, as we shall see, Ethan Hawke. But when it came to the second tier roles their suggestions began to dry up, leaving Jackson to cast as he saw fit. In this case, the Australian David Wenham from *Moulin Rouge!*.

For their deranged father Denethor, whose governorship of

Gondor is spoiling with his sanity, they met the British veteran Patrick McGoohan in Los Angeles, known to Jackson through the surreal 1960s secret agent show *The Prisoner* and the fact that he had once turned down the role of, yes, James Bond. But Jackson was disappointed to find him 'quite grumpy'. They also saw Donald Sutherland, but they would successfully cast John Noble, another relatively unknown Australian. While undoubtedly talented, being Australia-based allowed them to jump in and out of the schedule as required.

Ordesky remembers there being a real struggle to find Gimli. 'You didn't want a caricature.' Gimli more than most threatened to fall into fantasy cliché. The actor would have to embody some form of crotchety, rock-hewn, Wagnerian Dwarvishness without diminishing Jackson's authenticity. He needed to be mightily funny but also plain mighty.

British comedians Bill Bailey and Billy Connolly (who struck some kind of nerve as Jackson would cast him as the cantankerous Dain in the third *Hobbit* film) auditioned, as well as the actors Timothy Spall and Robert Trebor. But John Rhys-Davies had many things going for him: a headstrong personality that correlated with the gruff, tough-as-boots nature of Dwarves; a plangent voice born of his Welsh genes; and, to Sean Astin's glee, he had been in two *Indiana Jones* film as the archaeologist's wry Egyptian assistant Salah. He would, alongside Lee, come to test the director's patience, but as Ordesky says, 'He landed it.'

The unguarded fifty-five-year-old — whose packed CV features the head of the KGB, General Pushkin, in the fifteenth Bond movie, *The Living Daylights* — claimed he had been 'fifty-fifty' about taking the role. 'It occurs to you: "Where is the mileage in playing a Dwarf with prosthetic make-up?" Certainly, the money wasn't attractive.' He hadn't been that wild about the book, having tried but failed to finish as a 'snobbish' student. It would take another outside agent, in this case his Tolkien-zealous eldest son, to persuade him.

Rhys-Davies shaped the entire personality of Gimli while enduring a debilitating allergy to the prosthetics. But it is his valiant stunt-double Brett Beattie we see in anything wider than a mid-shot. This stirred up talk of a shared credit, but Rhys-Davies, who delivered every line of dialogue, swiftly reproved the idea. 'I am not in the habit of sharing credit,' he declared.

Elves were even harder. Tolkien describes them as ageless, almost angelic creatures; but how could anyone relate to their supermodel looks and ballerina's poise? 'When you're casting Elves,' says Jackson, 'you immediately have to cross off eighty-five per cent of the human race. And out of that fifteen per cent there is only a tiny proportion that can actually act.'

Drawing a blank on Legolas, their thoughts returned to an English kid who had read for Faramir. Orlando Bloom, still two days short of finishing at the Guildhall School of Music and Drama in London, had already done some television and had a small role in *Wilde*. Walsh could see there was something heavenly in his features. She rightly suspected that teenage girls, the hardest market to snare, would go crazy for Bloom.

I once had to collect him from a red carpet where he was signing autographs and touching hands with a near feral group of female fans. I have never forgotten the pure hatred in their eyes as I ushered him away from their clutches.

'He never actually auditioned for Legolas at all,' says Jackson, and it would still take a little work. Bloom has a Latin complexion, curly, auburn hair and coffee-dark eyes and according to the book Legolas was as blonde as Abba. They tested him with a series of platinum wigs and bright blue contact lenses (which would scratch his corneas) and he became weirdly beguiling.

The Canterbury-born heartthrob had been in Wellington for two months when Liv Tyler arrived to play Arwen. Each had done their research into the concept of Elves and over a game of pool they compared notes. Bloom talked in interviews about the 'poise' and 'centeredness' he had to acquire. How he watched Kurosawa's *Seven Samurai* for the discipline. Elves he said were 'pretty high status'. It was about toning down his human frailties, although donning the wig helped (each one was worth £15,000).

'Elves have superhuman reflexes and awareness,' he went on. 'It was quite exhausting.' As the film begins they have all but cut themselves off from the world, and are in the process of departing (a slightly ambiguous diaspora into the afterlife). Legolas' journey is one of 'emotional awakening' to the other species.

Arwen is already very much emotionally awakened. She is firmly and riskily in love with Aragorn, a human, even willing to sacrifice her Elven immortality for him. For the writers she offered a solution to the books' marginalization of females, but no other character would lead to as much doubt as the elf maiden.

How do you solve a problem like Arwen Evenstar? Between them Jackson, Walsh and Boyens tore their messy hair out trying to settle on exactly how they wanted to portray their female lead. Arwen should bring romance to the action. Arwen should provide female viewers with a role model as heroic as the men. And Arwen should still be the embodiment of the eternal, dreamlike, wise-beyond-counting nature of Elves so precious to Tolkien, who hardly helped matters be declaring her the fairest creature alive. Little wonder, Arwen would be the last main part to be cast.

'Ashley Judd we met, she was very nice,' remembers Jackson. There were whispers of Helena Bonham Carter being considered, but it was a viewing of the irksomely hip highwayman drama *Plunkett & Macleane* that persuaded him there was something in Tyler. New Line was ecstatic at the idea. Here, unforeseen, was a global star.

Tyler was big in Japan.

As Kamins points out, 'the casting of Liv was very meaningful to New Line. She had been in *Armageddon*, which was a smash hit in Japan. And I think off the back of that that she had gotten a whole bunch of commercials there. So she was kind of a known, that face more so than anybody else was.'

The daughter of Aerosmith rock legend Stephen Tyler (who

like Bowie didn't seem altogether of this world), Tyler had successfully transplanted from modelling into films, gaining great
attention as the heavenly creature at the centre of Bernardo
Bertolucci's lush, romantic drama *Stealing Beauty*.

But settling who would embody Arwen didn't necessarily
resolve how to play the character. On into the shoot they kept
revising the role. Entire sequences were shot of Arwen fighting
at Helm's Deep, having arrived with the legion of Elves from
Lothlórien. An early still revealed her with sword and bloodied
cheek. Fans who have trawled through the films frame-by-frame
claim she can still be spotted at the back of a crowded rampart.
Jackson confesses she had to be digitally erased from the rope
pulling Aragorn and Gimli to safety. Poor Tyler had hours
of combat training. There was, she recalls, a scene of Arwen
mounted on a horse, charging through the Uruk-hai. She was
supposed to be hacking away with her sword, but it never looked
right. 'No matter what I did, I looked weak,' she admits. It was a
failed experiment.

Tyler and the filmmakers came to accept that the essence of
Arwen was not necessarily a fighter; her strength came from her
love and patience. 'The moment we decided to scrap all of that
and focus on their love story, I instantly felt connected. For some
reason that felt better to me, and my interpretation of that character. It was definitely a process.'

Tyler valiantly endured the changes and endlessly explaining
to bemused journalists how her part was canon but stemmed
from the Appendices.* In finally bringing the character back
toward Tolkien's romantic conception, Arwen both gave Aragorn
a dream to cling onto (as the Shire inspires Frodo) and fixed
the relationship between Elves and Men. More subliminally but

---

* *The Tale of Aragorn and Arwen* can be found in Appendix A of *The Lord of the
Rings*, and covers their love story from the moment they first met at Rivendell
and later pledged love to one another in Lothlórien. There exists unused footage
of a beardless Viggo Mortensen and Tyler beneath the enchanted trees of
Lothlórien.

no less powerfully, she reminded us of the sheer strangeness of the book.

'And her Elvish was great,' crows Boyens, 'and that voice she found, it is a voice that does not give into despair.'

They met Milla Jovovich, Danish actress Iben Hjejle (offering a potentially interesting Scandinavian counterpart to Mortensen) and Uma Thurman for Éowyn: beautiful but very human Rohan royalty, erstwhile warrior maiden and romantic third wheel. Thurman was then married to Hawke, a potential Faramir — as a big fan of the book he was keen to take the role. Thurman had her doubts. She had recently given birth to their first child, and the role was in flux, caught up in the debate of how much weight they were giving Arwen. At one stage, Arwen was handed Éowyn's big moment, disguising herself as a man to join the charge of the Rohirrim and slay the Witch-king. She and Hawke would reluctantly decline and Éowyn went to the Australian actress, Miranda Otto.

Years later, appearing with Stephen Colbert, the US late night talk-show host and proud Tolkien nerd, Thurman came clean. 'I do consider it one of the worst decisions I ever made.'

*

There was no greater trial and no greater triumph in the casting of *The Lord of the Rings* than Aragorn. It is a story embedded into the legend of the trilogy's making, emblematic of how fate was truly on the side of hobbits and Kiwis. Look closer, however, and a more interesting tale was being told than the standard heroic hoopla about how Viggo Mortensen saved the day. To begin with, it was a situation of Jackson's own making. He had championed Stuart Townsend knowing full well the studio had their doubts.

Perhaps it was a legacy of his battles with Miramax. Perhaps it was simply the kind of stubbornness needed to get these films made. But he wanted to show New Line that he was willing to fight for his vision.

This was a line in the sand.

Much like Elijah Wood, Vin Diesel had sent in a homemade tape of himself dressed up as Aragorn. Unlike Elijah Wood it went no further. 'He was a big fan,' notes Jackson, 'but at that point we didn't know who he was, and he didn't fit our concept of the character.' Nicolas Cage claimed he turned down the role (Jackson remembers it being Boromir), just as he had turned down Neo in *The Matrix*. 'There were different things going on in my life,' he said, trying not to dwell on the fact he had missed out on two of the biggest franchises of all time. Ordesky has no memory of any offer being put to Cage, but there may have been a 'dialogue'.

Word arrived that Patrick Stewart wanted to meet with them. Having already crossed Boyens' mind as a potential Gandalf, Jackson was encouraged that he might be interested in playing Théoden. 'As the conversation went on we realized he wasn't talking about Théoden, he was talking about Aragorn. It was slightly awkward, because we had a very different perception of him.'

Instead Jackson opted for Townsend, the little known, twenty-seven-year-old Irish actor — a choice that perplexed New Line. Says Ordesky, 'Everyone at New Line figured someone who was a Númenórean* and had been hunting Orcs on the edges of the Shire for sixty years would present older.'

Like Frodo and Arwen, Aragorn presented challenges in the leap from book to film. On the page he came across as an archetype — the stoic warrior with a mysterious past. Walsh thought he lacked depth. During the writing, they wove his psychological journey from Strider, the hardscrabble ranger, into Aragorn, the

---

* According to Tolkien's mythology, in rudimentary terms the Númenóreans were an ancient race of exalted men who gained prolonged life. Theirs was a story of overweening power that led to the fall of their glorious island empire, a fall modelled on the Atlantis myth. Some of their number managed to escape to Middle-earth and founded the line of kings of which Aragorn is a descendant. And while he looked much younger, you were still meant to get a sense of his eighty-seven years.

king in waiting, into a more filmic tradition. As Jackson says, they needed 'to make him a reluctant hero'.

This is what first drew Jackson toward Townsend. Having spotted him in the lightweight comedy *Shooting Fish* and politically minded Northern Irish serial-killer thriller *Resurrection Man*, the duskily handsome Townsend emanated a brooding, stubbled, Eastwoodian presence, countered by a dash of the romantic in his Irish blood. He had also been genuinely enthusiastic about the book.

'We liked him,' insists Jackson. He could see he was young for Aragorn. Both Walsh and Boyens had expressed worries he might be *too* young, but Jackson thought with some grey flecks in his hair his 'natural intensity' could work for Aragorn. Townsend's youth might even play into the role. Give him an unexpected texture away from the book.

New Line pushed for a screen test. So Townsend was flown out to New Zealand to shoot a test in full 35mm. He rehearsed three scenes, one from each film, showcasing different stages of the emerging king: Strider confronting the hobbits in the Prancing Pony; Aragorn on the battlements of Helm's Deep; and later on the Paths of the Dead. None of the other cast had arrived, so they hired local actors to play the other parts, built temporary sets, lit them, and put Townsend in a makeshift costume, adding grey flecks to his temples. They were the only scenes he would ever perform as Aragorn.

'Outside of the studio, no one has ever seen that footage,' confirms Jackson but admits he has kept it. He keeps everything.

The footage was couriered to New Line. The studio hierarchy who viewed that tape found their minds unchanged, doubts lingered on, but they reluctantly accepted the director's decision hoping he would be proved right. He had won the battle, but chosen the wrong fight.

As it was they moved into preproduction with Townsend (ironically the first actor on the production) and the other actors began arriving in Wellington. Spirits were high. They were in touching distance of shooting. Except Townsend was sinking into himself and Jackson's latent misgivings began rising to the surface. The actor's discomfort manifested itself with a lot of obstruction. He wouldn't go to training with everyone else. And this included boat training, safety training and, for Aragorn, the all-important sword training. Jackson was flabbergasted. 'We had Bob Anderson, this guy who'd trained Errol Flynn! But he said, "I know how to do that, I know how to do that. I am not going to go." It was all a bit strange.'

Townsend was liked by his fellow actors; he enjoyed the social life, being part of the growing band of friends. But he was being gnawed by doubts over the character. Having loved the books, he was genuinely excited to have got the part, but at some imperceptible point he had become infected with the idea that he was too young. Maybe he had heard rumours of New Line's concerns. He couldn't seem to get his head into the character.

Not unkindly, Jackson recognizes that it was anxiety. 'Philippa had a long talk with him before he left and she just said he appeared to be very, very frightened and insecure.' Aragorn might be beset by doubts, but the audience had to believe he had it in him to become a king. You need to look into his eyes and feel that strength. That was his arc. Likewise, Jackson had neither the time nor the inclination to mollycoddle an actor through eighteen months of arduous shooting.

That dinner with McKellen was a breaking point. It was such an uplifting night but Townsend sat beneath a storm cloud.

Jackson holds up his hands. 'I don't want to be unfair to him, but his nerves had led him to an attitude of thinking it'll be alright on the day: "I don't want to rehearse, you'll get it on the day." As it was the day never came, we never shot anything with him, apart from the screen test.'

On the second day of shooting, as they shot close-ups of the hobbits hidden from the Ringwraith beneath the roots of a tree,

Barrie Osborne wandered over to his director and, like any good producer, checked in to see how he was doing. He may not have been expecting such a dramatic response. For the Townsend story was also the story of a director able to recognize his own mistakes and respond to the greater needs of the film.

Jackson turned away from the monitor, he can clearly remember it was frozen on the image of a spider on Merry's shoulder, and gave an unexpected answer.

'Barrie, I don't think I can work with Stuart. I don't think it is going to work out.'

They were due to start shooting Strider's introduction in the *Prancing Pony* the following week.

Osborne understood. He said, 'Okay.' And that was that. It was the producer who broke the news to Townsend.

When Jackson gathered the hobbit actors together to tell them of his decision it was a real wake-up call after the goodwill of boot camp and preproduction. Wood, Boyd and Monaghan were visibly shaken by the news. Townsend had spent months with them: he was one of the gang, a friend. What if they didn't shape up? Would they be fired? It was if a tremor had shaken the production.

Says Wood, 'The responsibility suddenly felt that much greater.'

Astin took the news more calmly. He had sensed things weren't right with Townsend. There are times, he says, a studio can give you perceptive notes. As he saw it, the right decision had been made. They needed to move on like professional people. But even he wasn't immune to the suddenness of Townsend's departure.

'When he was gone, he was simply gone.'

'It was my fault. I take responsibility. I made a mistake': Jackson recognizes he had taken a significant step backwards in his relationship with New Line. Fuelled by such doubts they might be having about what the hell he was doing. They were only one day into shooting, literally twenty-four hours, and he was without one of his main characters. But better to react quickly. Weeks down the line and the problem could have festered into something irreversibly damaging.

Attempting to defuse the movie-in-crisis editorials mustering in the Hollywood trades, New Line production president Michael De Luca publicly asserted that Townsend's departure had nothing do with an imperiled production, it was 'just director-actor chemistry'. Which was true. That's all it had been: bad chemistry.

Retreating from the limelight, Townsend's response over the years has graduated from wounded vitriol to a calm acceptance of the slings and arrows of an outrageous business.

'I was there rehearsing and training for two months, then fired the day before filming began,' he fumed in the immediate wake of events, claiming he had been relieved to go and the next night he was sipping cocktails with his friends in Sydney. 'I have no good feelings for those people in charge, I really don't. The director wanted me and then apparently thought better of it because he really wanted someone twenty years older than me.'

Since, he has become philosophical. There is always good to be found in a bad experience. He enjoyed the friendships, and stayed in contact with Bloom. While still smarting a little at the insinuation that he never worked hard enough, he has moved on. 'It was only work, it was only an ego thing. I didn't get my heart broken and no one died on me.'

To this day, he claims never to have seen the films.

Cut back to the *Prancing Pony* where Jackson was shooting what he could, all the coverage of the hobbits entering the forbidding world of humans for the first time. Sam muttering to a worried Frodo: 'That fellow has done nothing but stare at you since we've arrived.' Except he was looking toward an empty corner where 'that fellow' was supposed to be sitting, a cowl obscuring his face, the man of mystery. Indeed, even the director had no idea who he was.

Jackson can laugh now. 'Our Strider was gone, and we didn't have anyone else.'

Ordesky was in London when he got the news. It was late at night, but morning in New Zealand. He knew they were due to be shooting scenes with Strider within a week. They had days to find a replacement. It was like the search for Scarlet O'Hara on fast forward.

'When I hung up the phone, I was so terrified at the enormity of the task I threw up.' Which may have helped clear his head, because he sat down with a piece of hotel stationery and wrote down three names: 'Russell Crowe, Jason Patric and Viggo Mortensen'.

Ordesky flashbacked to an intensely awkward lunch he once had with Mortensen. The introspective Danish-American actor was not what you would call a Hollywood lunch kind of guy. He had, though, described his Danish background at great length. 'He mentioned that the name of the town where a lot of his family lived translated to Ringtown. The only reason that stuck with me is because I was a *Lord of the Rings* geek.'

Not that he mentioned this at the time.

Great ideas can have many authors. New Zealand was on a parallel track. Jackson thought of going back to Crowe and between them Boyens and Walsh brought up Mortensen. They immediately plunged into his back catalogue — *Daylight, The Portrait of a Lady, G.I. Jane, A Perfect Murder* — assured by the intensity of his blue eyes, chiselled cheekbones and the way he commanded your attention with minimal effort.

'Fran's a great believer in fate,' says Boyens. 'The person who needs to play this role will come to us.'

He wasn't in any way British, but both Boyens and Jackson liked that his Scandinavian heritage chimed with the Nordic sagas from which Tolkien had drawn.

Everything about Mortensen seemed to add up. He was an actor for whom the idea of celebrity carried little value. He lived apart from Hollywood — and would place even further distance between them once the films had bequeathed him superstardom. He had romance written into the pages of his life. Born in New York, raised in South America, schooled in the foothills of Argentina, returning to graduate from a New York high school, then off to find a purpose in the Denmark of his father's upbringing. There he took to writing poetry and short stories, odd jobbing as a dockworker and selling flowers. Back then to New York and acting classes, before moving to Los Angeles where a small part in *Witness* began a career in earnest. During which time he never stopped filling his mind and soul with music (he possesses a fine singing voice), photography, painting and publishing books of his own pictures and poetry.

This is before you considered his outdoor side. How he loved to lose himself in the wilderness for days, ride horses, fish, sleep beneath the stars and generally unbuckle himself from civilization. On his mother's side he was related to Buffalo Bill. If he had a credo, then it was 'go see for yourself'. He spoke Danish, Spanish, French and English fluently, travelled the world, read the greats, including the Nordic and Icelandic sagas, and never wasted a word.

To which one can only wonder why had they ever wanted anyone else to play Aragorn?

'He cared, you know?' says Boyens. 'And he was really smart. Yeah, he was gorgeous, but beyond that he's a poet. He's a Renaissance man. All that physicality he did standing on his head. That's who he was. But the other stuff was just a gift. That he had that soul. That he loved language. That he was meticulous, even though sometimes to the point where it drove you crazy. We'd see Viggo coming at you with the book in his hand, and you'd go, "Oh God."'

It fell to Ordesky to make the approaches. While Patric never made it beyond his hotel pad, Crowe was couriered a copy of the script. His agent called back: he appreciated the urgency, he was flattered, but he had 'just done this movie with swords called *Gladiator*'. The epic that would bring superstardom to Crowe was still over eight months from release. 'He's not going to do that again.'

'So it coalesced around Viggo very, very quickly,' confirms Ordesky. 'We had to do phone calls, deal-making and get him on a plane, I think, in two days. He had to be on camera within two days of landing in New Zealand.'

Mortensen's name also calmed the waters with New Line. Shaye was in full agreement. He would be perfect. No one could quite face the idea of not getting him. Ordesky put the call in to Mortensen's agent at CAA, Jane Berliner, who luckily he knew well enough to go direct.

She was receptive to the idea, would get the scripts to him, but warned Ordesky that Mortensen liked to take his time choosing a film.

They would have to wait and see.

Jackson was on set shooting in a Striderless *Prancing Pony*, so it was Walsh and Boyens who took the first call from Mortensen. He was on a payphone somewhere in Iowa. The line wasn't great. Says Boyens, 'He was in the middle of nowhere. And we had to talk him through what we wanted to do with the character, because it really wasn't there on the page. And he referenced *The Volundarkvitha* and I thought, "Holy crap, this is great."'

Boyens was alone in the office when the second call came through. Jan Blenkin, Jackson's assistant, stuck her head around the door and calmly informed her that, 'Viggo Mortensen's on the phone.'

'I was like, "Oh my God." Because we'd said, "Call us back about anything."' This was surely a good sign. She was met by that ruminative voice as slow and steady as an ocean liner.

'How old was I when I was taken to the Elves?'

'You were two,' Boyens coolly replied, but her heart was pounding. 'I was like waving at Jan and doing the thumbs up. That's when I knew.'

There was still one more phone call to come. Mortensen needed to speak with Jackson. Leaving the *Prancing Pony* and heading to his quiet office, Jackson nervously picked up the receiver, having had no experience of Mortensen's glacially paced conversation. He grew worried that he was doing all the talking and the actor barely said a word.

'I would finish and there would be this long, awkward silence. Do I speak now? Do I wait for him to speak? It was all pretty much a one-way thing. I just wanted to set up the idea of where we were on the film. And I thought, "God, this is not going well. He's not enthusiastic." I know now it is just Viggo! Back then, I didn't. I thought, "Oh God, he's not showing any interest."'

As the call wound down, Jackson accepted that they were going to have to keep looking.

'Ah well, that's great,' he said to Mortensen, trying to hide the defeat in his voice. 'Thanks for reading the scripts. I'd better get back to set.'

After another epoch of silence, Mortensen spoke. 'Well, I'll guess I'll see you next Tuesday.'

That was the end of the call, the moment when the film righted its course again and they had found Strider who will become Aragorn and who would elevate both the films and their making in unforeseen and extraordinary ways.

On the other side of the oft-told story Mortensen had been on the verge of saying no, unwilling to be away from his eleven-year-old son Henry for so long. But it was Henry who decided the matter. He had read and adored *The Lord of the Rings* and, discovering what his father had been offered, was adamant.

'You have to do it,' he told him. 'You've got to play Aragorn.'

And that was that.

'We really have Henry to thank,' says Jackson.

True, Henry was the catalyst, another unanticipated agent in the films' eventual success, but this being the deep-dish Mortensen, there was always a bigger picture.

'In the end I obviously decided for myself,' he makes clear. 'When they first asked me, they had already been shooting for two weeks. Which isn't good. I knew that I wouldn't have time to prepare. I didn't feel I could do a good job; I had doubts about it. I didn't want to be away from my son. He knew about the character and said you should do that. But at some point you look at yourself and think is this a situation where I am afraid and do I want to live with that later?'

Ordesky recognizes that Mortensen is an actor who responds to fear. 'Stepping into the breach is something that spoke to his psychology.'

Even though he hadn't yet read the books, Mortensen responded to the scripts. He could see what the role offered and grasped how the archetype of Aragorn had its roots in the sagas he had read as a boy. And how his reluctance mirrored that of the character. 'Aragorn has his doubts whether he can rise to the challenge required of him, and I was stepping into the unknown, not knowing what to expect.'

The deal with Mortensen was done at lightning speed. Ordesky coursed on adrenaline through sleepless nights getting the paperwork signed off. A process that included New Line accepting their initial budget, set at $207 million, would rise to $211 million. 'That pivot from Stuart to Viggo,' as he puts it, 'threw an extra few million onto the budget.'

Because Hollywood can do nothing without neurotically second guessing itself, the powers at New Line then began to worry about Tyler. She had been cast as a match in age for Townsend. And Mortensen was forty-one to the departed Irish actor's twenty-seven. 'There was some discussion about whether this still worked as a match,' says Ordesky. But in an office in Hollywood where hard-hearted suits usually thrashed out million-dollar deals, arguments were made using the technicalities of Middle-earth lore: 'Liv is an ageless Elf and Viggo is a Númenórean who is not ageless but who is very long lived, so it all makes perfect sense.'

On the plane journey to New Zealand, Mortensen read the book. 'I felt like a kid,' he says, but he got a sense of the mythology he was dealing with. Virtually as soon as the wheels squealed

onto tarmac he was into wardrobe fittings — only minor adjustments to Townsend's costume were necessary — sword rehearsal
and finally, within forty-eight hours of arriving, Strider walked
onto set.

It was Day 12 of the production.

Legend gives Mortensen a heroic entrance battling with the
wraiths at Weathertop, but in truth that was still a few days away.
They first had to complete the prolonged *Prancing Pony* scenes.

Recalls Jackson, 'When I saw that first scene he shot at the
premiere I could see he was not yet Aragorn. He is sort of a
Method-type guy who really likes to get into the head of a char-
acter. He was literally off the plane putting on Stuart's outfit.
And he didn't complain, he knew what he was signing up for.
But he hadn't found Aragorn yet. It is the scene where he is in
the *Prancing Pony* bedroom, telling the hobbits about the Nazgûl.
That scene was Day One of Viggo, and I remember thinking he
hasn't got Aragorn yet. Have a look at it again in that context.
Then we shot the stuff of him smoking in the corner.'

Then they moved onto Weathertop, with Mortensen wielding his sword like he was born to it and hurling flaming brands
down the lens of the camera.

Jackson smiles. 'Weathertop was when he got into it completely.'

CHAPTER 7

Jamboree

The four hobbits arrived on set in dressing gowns and moon boots covering their recently applied feet, and with enough excitement to quell the nerves. It was still dark when they were picked up at 5.40 a.m. from their Miramar apartments and taken to make-up at Stone Street for three hours of transformation in earnest. From here on it would be a daily ritual, on some days to the point of distraction: costume, ears, wig and feet. Then Elijah Wood, Sean Astin, Dominic Monaghan and Billy Boyd drove the ten minutes to the unit base — housed in the Mount Victoria Bowling Club on Pine Street — and then, having got their bearings, up the hill to a spooky-looking path on the west side of Mount Victoria near an old quarry, overlooking Wellington.

It is well documented that the very first shot put to film on *The Lord of the Rings* had Frodo, Sam, Merry and Pippin dashing to hide from a Ringwraith. According to the schedule, it was scene 33 (part two of the sequence of shots), six to eight pages in total. The image was a direct reference to a painting by John Howe, but which was also reminiscent of a scene in the Bakshi film. The hobbits hide in a nook beneath the protective embrace of a tree's roots — a physical set brought on location that future fans will search in vain for — foreshadowing Treebeard's arboreal assistance in the future. Merry, revealing a canny streak, then throws a mushroom to distract the Nazgûl.

This was the first thirty seconds of nine hours twenty-eight minutes of finished Middle-earth (eleven hours, thirty-six minutes of extended edition).

They had, in fact, already been up there and paced out the scenes during a couple of days of camera rehearsal. The director didn't want any surprises. At least, not in their first week.

As the gaffers made their final adjustments to the lighting, never fully satisfied — it was cloudier than hoped — Peter Jackson strolled over to greet his hobbits.

'Well, here we go. . .'

For Monaghan, it was a precious moment: 'I had this feeling of, like, we are just about to jump off a cliff. But this guy, our general, has come over and said, "I got you."'

On the morning of 11 October 1999, day 1, Jackson called action and they jumped off the metaphorical cliff. After three years of insisting he and his team were equipped to do the impossible, Jackson had to prove it. The extraordinary, life-changing business of making Middle-earth was underway.

'We'd been in this hermetically sealed preparation zone for six weeks,' says Astin, 'and we show up like the trained bear in the circus. And suddenly we realize there's a good two hundred people we're going to see every day.'

The Ringwraith was played by three different stunt-doubles: Tim McLachland, Sean Thompson (on horseback) and Brent McIntyre as the 'big hand' double. At 6'10" with abnormally large hands, the part-time librarian was a scale-double for the Witch-king in the first two films (although he was too tall to feature as the lead king in the prologue).

The primary unit was divided into two halves, both directed by Jackson. While 1A busied themselves with the main action, 1B would complete the day's work by filming the hobbits scrambling away down the bank, close-ups of the Ringwraith's horse and his armour-clad feet and a Frodo point-of-view of the empty road, on which the director, still feeling out a style, would employ a flamboyant Hitchcockian effect of dollying in on tracks while zooming out, warping the edges of the image as if the presence of evil was contorting the air.

The day's prop requirements matter-of-factly listed 'the Ring'.

'There was a great amount of excitement and nerves,' remembers Wood. 'The idea of not being able to see the end became real for me.'

He'd worked on many films, at eighteen already a veteran, but they had averaged a fleeting three months. You could keep the end in sight; do a mental tally of where you were on any given day. On that spring morning in Wellington, the end was an abstract concept far off in a dimly lit future.

There would be friendships forged, marriages, divorces, births, deaths, tattoos and so many birthdays, along with birthday parties, before the end. Some would falter and depart; others would jump on the train further down the line. And the outside world changed beyond recognition.

'That was a wild feeling,' says Wood. 'It genuinely felt as if this was something that wouldn't have an end. People often ask, "Like, God, did it drive you crazy?" It didn't because it's relative. There was no way to conceive of shooting for eighteen months, and that becomes your perspective. This is what I will always be doing.'

Ultimately, says Jackson, the eighteen months of shooting were 'a psychological hurdle we all had to overcome'.

Their good spirits would falter on the third day. Still shooting on that wooded road, enclosed in a tunnel of trees, they were informed of the departure of Stuart Townsend. Then, says Wood, 'things suddenly became weirdly emotional and confusing'. It was a warning shot, a premonition of the mental toughness that was going to be required. With Gandalf still detained elsewhere the first three months of the shoot had already been heavily reshuffled. Now, without an Aragorn as well, the shuffling began again to push his upcoming entrance back by days, if nothing better.

It was hardly the most auspicious of beginnings, but to be going at all brought with it the rush of possibility. Jackson hadn't walked onto a movie set in four years. In so many different ways, he was home at last, on the side of a hill he had known since he was a boy.

According to Māori legend, New Zealand is the creation of a pantheon of jealous gods not so different from those of Tolkien's mythology. Descended from Io-the-endless, there is Tanu-the-thoughtful, who produced the world and the stars; Tu-of-the-red-face, who brought forth war; and Maui-of-the-topknot, who grasped the kinship between all things and fished up these sacred isles from the Pacific, only to see them scarred with gullies, gorges and mountains by the knives of his jealous brothers. The head of one fish became Wellington.

Not wanting to disturb any local deities, the production would be blessed by Māori elders.

Besides the various, makeshift studio spaces at Stone Street and across the capital city, the shoot would venture out to over 100 different locations, from Matamata to Glenorchy, melding the two islands into a fictional universe that felt real enough to touch.

Location scouting, says Jackson, is much like casting. You have people who take photos. You pick, say, the six places that strike you as interesting from the twenty provided and off you go to see them in the flesh. 'I had no doubt that this was the best country in the world to shoot this thing in.'

'The South Island is rugged and mountainous,' observes Barrie Osborne, 'and at the tip, which points toward Antarctica, there are alpine-like mountains and fjords. Then the further north you go, the more tropical it gets.'

New Zealand covers 103,000 square miles, a land mass not much larger than Great Britain, but one that possesses greater geographical diversity than anywhere else in the world. And with a population of only three million people, there is effectively nobody there. Vast swathes remain as primordial as their day of creation. Which had another benefit, Jackson points out: 'you can shoot in three hundred and sixty degrees and not get a single power line, no buildings, nothing. We also ended up shooting in a lot of places where there were no roads.'

The cast, as they journeyed from one breathtaking landscape to the next, became enclosed in the film, shut off from the outside world. It became less a job, than a task set by the gods. The unspoiled air brokered a merger between life and art. Time grew less meaningful. Yes, it was exhausting to have to put on those feet, or be frozen to your bones, or have to fathom the new-fangled technology incorporated into many shots. There were calamities, weather problems and endless rejigging, along with all the insecurities that come with being an actor trying to find the truth of a character. But that spiritual dimension never dimmed.

'It was kind of an adventure. I mean it really *was* an adventure,' declares Wood, even now struggling to put such an extraordinary period of his life into words. 'So much of what we were experiencing in the making of the thing mirrored that of the experience of the characters.'

They were living out their characters' lives in real time — none more than Viggo Mortensen-the-driven, who liked to sleep in his costume, out beneath the stars with his horse as a pillow in order to see the dawn rise.

'In that place,' he says, 'it felt different.'

*

Apocalypse Now took sixteen months to make, waylaid by typhoons, tropical disease, the Philippine government recalling their helicopters and Marlon Brando not having read the script. *Spartacus* filmed for 167 days, including six weeks of battle scenes and stand-offs between director and leading man. *Heaven's Gate* took 165 days, creeping along like molasses as the director sought perfection from the Montana skyline. *Eyes Wide Shut* shot for 400 days, a Guinness World Record, with an obsessive director who would think nothing of hundreds of takes.

The Lord of the Rings was a monumental undertaking, three films at once, and faced its own crises, but it was also a model of dedication and sound management. The logistical challenge of having up to 2,500 cast and crew across a production with thousands of moving parts was staggering. Then having to move them across the country like a nomadic tribe. Jackson often described it as 'like running a war'. *Jamboree*, still the designated secret identity maintained on all communications, was equal parts artist's studio, factory floor, marching army and travelling circus — and always prepared.

While Jackson created his cosmos, the burden of keeping everyone fed and paid and pointed in the right direction fell to the production managers, led by Osborne. A native of New York, Osborne had begun his career as a runner on *The Godfather Part II* and worked with Francis Coppola again on *Apocalypse Now*, as well as *All The President's Men* and *The Big Chill*, and would bring with him a wealth of knowledge and the slightly testy air of a schoolmaster.

'I was there to shore up the director's vision,' he asserts, 'and stay on track.'

Having produced *The Matrix*, Osborne passed on the sequels in favour of Middle-earth. In fact, when he took the job, he sold his house in Topanga Canyon in Los Angeles and bought a house in Wellington to devote himself solely to Jackson's opus.

'I loved New Zealand,' he says simply. 'I love the attitude of the crews there and the idea that you can do almost anything.'

Tim Sanders, who had been with them as the wheel of fortune turned back and forth, also stayed on as a producer, alongside the multi-hyphenate Jackson and Fran Walsh (who served as writers and producers, and in Jackson's case, of course, director).

However, any of them would tell you that it was Carolynne Cunningham — the formidable 'Caro' — who was the pivot around which everything turned. The Australian-born first assistant director, Jackson's field marshal since *Heavenly Creatures,* ran to an unofficial motto that 'anything is fixable'. Come what may, landslips, gales, floods, freak snow, all the heavy weather of physical production on three massive movies, the imperturbable Caro was determined nothing aside from what was on screen would become a drama.

The 274-day schedule for principal photography was organized around availability of cast, appropriate season (Hobbiton, for instance, had to be shot in the summer), access to locations and the natural economies of movie production (how much of the story could be covered in any one area). And in the immediacy of daily planning there was that weather to think about.

The legend paints a picture of Jackson constantly platespinning seven units beneath a wall of monitors. While it is true that they did get up to a septet of units at certain peak times, it was never for the duration.

'It was always in bursts,' he clarifies. 'There would be a period when we were shooting some battle somewhere and you've got a second-unit director, like Geoff Murphy or John Mahaffie, doing a stint. But it was in fits and starts.'

Mahaffie had been Steadicam operator on *Heavenly Creatures,* while Murphy was an established Kiwi filmmaker who had made some headway in Hollywood on *Young Guns II* and *Freejack.* Both knew the terrain.

Jackson retraces the division of labour in his head. 'Geoff shot six to seven weeks of second unit material of galloping horses for the charge of the Rohirrim. Whereas John did a lot of Arwen on horseback, chased by the Ringwraiths. He also did a lot of Helm's Deep, the nighttime fighting stuff.' Second unit directors would also include Rick Porras (*The Frighteners*), Richard Bluck (*Braindead*) and David Norris (*Jack Brown Genius*), with Osborne and Walsh doing shifts.

As a general rule there was the primary unit, divided into A and B, often in parallel, and when required a second and even third unit, themselves divided in parts A and B, and then two miniature units and a bluescreen unit. Nevertheless, there was also footage from the likes of the 'pocket unit', which quite literally shot the Ring in Bilbo or Frodo's pocket. Ian Holm was amazed that between scenes small beads were loaded into the hip pocket of Bilbo's waistcoat to maintain the bagginess (or maybe that is 'bagginsiness') that has come from endless fiddling with the Ring.

There was often a helicopter unit out capturing aerials, Weta Digital filming 'tiles' of empty sets and landscapes to use digitally and, once Andy Serkis had joined them to play Gollum, you could conceivably include the motion capture unit on the list.

The stacks of monitors, feeding scenes from across both trilogy and country, are also part of the myth. Again, it was a matter of as and when things were happening — particularly when they became geographically stretched.

Says Jackson, 'We had satellites: Geoff would be down on the South Island with a bunch of horses and I would be in the studio able to watch them live, which in those days was pretty radical. We set up a huge, bloody big satellite dish at the location and one here. We had to get the government to help. It was a bit patchy, the picture, but it was enough.'

Things became tricky not so much when he was parsing the myriad monitors, but when he had to direct in two places at once, running two simultaneous units on the backlot complete with two full crews and actors. Yoyoing between sets, he would set up an alternating rhythm where as he finished one shot he would race across the backlot to shoot on the other stage, leaving the first unit to ready the next set-up.

Ian McKellen had days playing both Gandalf the Grey and Gandalf the White, requiring him to dash between stages, changing costume with superheroic speed trailed by a phalanx of out-of-breath hair and make-up artists.

To facilitate the director's passage across Stone Street he was provisioned with an old pushbike on which a skull had been waggishly mounted on the handlebars. Thus there were many days the director of the most ambitious movie project ever mounted could be seen peddling between old factory buildings, on his way to winning eleven Oscars.

*

The Call Sheets: Testament to the stubborn Kiwi foolhardiness, ingenuity, humility, humour and achievement of the production, Jackson has kept on file every single call sheet for *The Lord of the Rings*.* They weave their own fascinating tale of the day-by-day progress of the films: how, where and when the story was strewn over the map of New Zealand. Here follows a very rough overview of the vast, out-of-joint sequence of filming — bear in mind, this doesn't begin to account for the many additional units, reshoots, FX shots and pick-ups that contributed to the heroic mosaic.

'Those call sheets represent all the effort, the agony and the occasional despair,' says Jackson fondly. As well as a schedule of scenes, here is an archive of the physical and emotional trials of the shoot, and also a catalogue of the quirky, quotidian details that come with managing a team of people setting out to scale a mountain.

'No two days,' the director laments, 'were ever the same.'

OCTOBER (THE SHIRE, BREE, THE PRANCING PONY AND WEATHERTOP SUMMIT): On 21 October, Day 9, they returned to Mount Victoria for night scenes of the hobbits fleeing the Ringwraiths through the foggy trees and advice was provided on how to best approach any of the horses on set: 'The trick is to remain calm and let Mr Ed relax.'

---

* Jackson also has in his archive a copy of the 110-day schedule laid out for the two-film version with Miramax that planned to shoot for thirty weeks from 18 April to 25 November 1999, beginning with Rivendell and Orthanc scenes. The films would have been released at Christmas 2000 and on Memorial Day (the last Monday in May) 2001. There even exists a one-film schedule that must have been drawn up at Miramax's behest.

Three days later, Mortensen arrived in the *Prancing Pony*.

Wood recalls the sense of mystery that surrounded this actor arriving to play this mysterious character. 'I just remember being awestruck how quickly it all happened. Thinking like, "Fuck, dude, you're going to be on Weathertop in a week. That is insane." And it was perfect. It was like it was meant to be. And that was the case for the entire cast. It felt sort of predestined that these people would fulfil these roles.'

'He had his own rhythm,' says Monaghan on how best to approach this eccentric semi-Dane. 'Sort of crazy in the best way.'

NOVEMBER (LOTHLÓRIEN, THE PRANCING PONY, FERRY LANE, MIDGEWATER MARSHES, WEATHERTOP, TROLLSHAW FOREST, THE RIVER ANDUIN AND DIMRIL DALE): With Mortensen swiftly established as Strider-Aragorn, and showing signs he may actually *be* Strider-Aragorn, the shoot began to stretch its limbs beyond Wellington.

With an uncanny parallel between plot and production, 16 November, day 26, began a series of unseasonable weather issues, with snow in spring. They had come to Lake Te Anau on the South Island, where Strider will lead the hobbits across the glowering countryside toward Weathertop — our first taste of the heavy going beyond The Shire. The Midgewater Marshes were in fact Henry Creek Marsh.

Old Bill Panto was often on set. Old Bill, the faithful pony who carries supplies as far as Moria, had been in and out of the script. A pony added complications: even the 'livestock' had to have hobbit doubles and there were locations inaccessible to horses such as the pristine flanks of Caradhras. Yet whenever Jackson pictured the signature silhouette of the Fellowship striding forth it always featured Bill. Bill in his own way was iconic.

A 'hobbit scale' Bill was provided by Restus, a chestnut cross between an American quarter-horse and a Shetland, while Weta crafting a 'pantomime' Bill surmounted the issue of bringing Restus to remote locations — something of an irony given Jackson had sworn to McKellen these films 'wouldn't be the stuff of pantomime'. Remarkably lifelike from a distance, 'Old Bill Panto' would be performed according to old-fashioned principles with operators Katrina Talbot and Rebecca Fitzgerald having to decide who would be front and back.

Two and a half years later, *The Fellowship of the Ring* would take home the Oscar for its groundbreaking visual effects.

The marshes happened to be an extremely sensitive conservation site; to gain access had taken months of negotiation— the country may have embraced the production but they certainly didn't have a by-your-leave to waltz into whichever beauty spot they fancied. A darkly worded note from the producers made it clear that various ecological groups 'only too happy to find some breach of the conditions governing our use of these sites' were monitoring them.

To use the national preserves of New Zealand to portray Middle-earth in a very literal sense they had to tread carefully. Later at Mount Ruapehu, the slopes of Mount Doom, it was discovered that the local moss was protected, and to Jackson's great amusement rolls of shagpile carpet were laid down for the crew to walk across.

Sticking to the designated paths wasn't easy when the steady rain thickened into snowfall. As it did when they were far from the main road shooting travelling shots at Bog Pine Paddock where Pippin puts the case for a 'second breakfast'. Deciding the snow added a certain elemental verisimilitude, Jackson kept shooting, but the place was soon blanketed in snow and the actors were getting cold and fed up. Except Mortensen, that is, who couldn't be happier. This was the making of the moment as far as he was concerned, an invigorating blast of Middle-earth. When the police advised them to evacuate the location they had to all but drag Aragorn back to the hotel.

For Wood and co. it was a lovely respite. 'We had to take our feet off in the laundry room. There we were, having our feet removed and drinking wine, marvelling at the fact that it was snowing outside. That was magical.'

Mortensen flatly refused to change out of his costume, and paced around the hotel lobby like a cat, startling the other guests, hoping the snow would relent enough for them to finish the shot.

It was also in November the shoot became multi-limbed, as Liv Tyler departed for Wanaka in the South Island to flee from Ringwraiths with Mahaffie's second unit mounted on trucks. The horseback chase would eventually be assembled from three different locations and bluescreen elements hundreds of miles apart.

But it is the transition of the main unit to Queenstown at the end of 1999 that truly tells a tale within the tale. There are certain films where the insanity of their making becomes imbued into the lifeblood of the drama. Not that Middle-earth ever quite descended into the swamp of *Apocalypse Now* or Werner Herzog's Amazonian nightmare *Fitzcarraldo* — too many softball games and karaoke nights — but it was in the lower reaches of the South Island that New Zealand would throw its worst at Jackson's merry band, only to be met by the invincible Caro and the tightening bonds of cast and crew.

Having finished at last at the *Prancing Pony*, Jackson was informed that a plane had been specially chartered for him to follow the production already setting up to shoot through until Christmas in the impossible beauty around Queenstown. In mid-November, Stone Street would fall eerily quiet as the production was based out of the Coronet Plaza for exterior shooting of the River Anduin, Amon Hen and Dimril Dale.

'Good, good,' thought Jackson, expecting a comfy 737 to soothe his jitters on the brief hop over the Cook Strait. So he headed to the airport along with Osborne, Wood, Monaghan, Boyd, Bloom and assorted crew. The bulk of the production had taken the ferry across to make the stunning drive south in convoys filled with Orc masks and longbows.

The more precious cargo, camera gear and boxes of lenses, would travel down with the director. But in a rarely disturbed corner of the airport, they were confronted with the sight of a DC-3 Douglas Dakota still in its original Second World War livery. Away from the rigours of filmmaking, Jackson is a military aviation buff; with subsequent success he has established a fine collection of antique bi-planes and fighters and came close to remaking *The Dambusters.** It is a passion that doesn't run to actually flying in old planes.

The first person to speak up was Bloom, and not in Sindarin, 'You've got to be *fucking* kidding me.' Thanks to what were pejoratively known as 'budgetary considerations' they were heading to the South Island in the same kind of twin-propped rattletrap that usually brings Indiana Jones to mischief.

What's more, with no ground crew, they had to form a human-Elf-hobbit chain to load their gear. No one, Jackson thought, could accuse them of not putting the money up on screen — the biggest independent film ever mounted.

It was only then that the pilot mentioned the plane was only designed to take 12,000 lb. 'Could be a bit of trouble leaving the ground,' he observed. The prospect seemed to amuse him.

Once they were all strapped in, twenty of them in seats not much better than deck chairs, Jackson asked to see the log book. The Dakota's inaugural flight had taken American troops to Guadalcanal in 1943. 'Oh Christ,' he muttered.

This being Wellington Airport, they would take off over the harbour, and with a cough the plane spluttered into life. In telling the story, Jackson is now providing the sound effects of straining engines and a shuddering frame, revs rising to the screech of a Ringwraith, as God knows what rattled around the cabin.

'And it goes up and comes down, bouncing on the runway. Elijah and Orlando were in front of me waving their arms and

---

* In 2008 Jackson's proposed remake of *The Dambusters* was to be directed by Christian Rivers from a script by Stephen Fry. The financing would eventually fall through, but inside one of his warehouses are the wings and fuselages of five full-sized replica Lancaster bombers like sections of giant model kits.

cheering like it was a rollercoaster. And the end of the runway is coming bloody fast. . .'

The Dakota became airborne at the very second they ran out of runway, gliding perilously low over the water, more Christmas goose than swan, before climbing ponderously into the sky to a cheer from the passengers.

Stopping in Nelson to shoot at Takaka Hill (for Chetwood Forest near Bree) and the bleached marble karst of Mount Owen (for Dimrill Dale on the eastern doorstep of Moria), Jackson reflected that these death-defying flights were becoming a habit. 'I'll drive the rest of the way,' he informed Cunningham, and it was decreed that he and Osborne in one hired car, with Bloom and Bean — who had wisely taken the ferry— in another, would go the rest of the way by road.

This turned out to be a poor decision.

'The problem,' explains Jackson, 'was the weather reports were growing increasingly worrisome and it was imperative we get down to Queenstown pretty quickly and get shooting.'

A storm will soon lash through their southern locations.

After travelling through the night, they realized they were running perilously low on petrol, and Jackson couldn't remember the last time they had seen Bean and Bloom's car. Cell phone reception was patchy in the Southern Alps.

'It was empty as hell. And I'm thinking we're in big trouble.'

Finally, out of nowhere, a lonely petrol station appears at the side of the road. There was no town to speak of, only a few eerily quiet buildings waiting for a horror movie to start filming. At six o'clock on a Sunday morning the place is clearly closed.

Their journey cohering into every kind of metaphor, Osborne spied a house belonging to the gas station. 'That is probably where the guy that owns it lives,' he reasoned. Pulling $500 NZ dollars from the petty cash kept under his jurisdiction, Osborne hammered on the door, getting the poor petrol attendant out of bed in his pyjamas and, having filled up their tank for a cool

$500, he then returned to bed, his part in the history of *The Lord of the Rings* complete.

Bean and Bloom, it turned out, were only an hour behind them. But in that time the ferocious storm had ranged north and half the hillside had collapsed, blocking the road between them and Jackson and Osborne. Turning back, they discovered a further slip had blocked the way they came.

'They are now actually stuck with no cell phones on them,' continues Jackson. 'The whole place is a disaster zone. Helicopters are out rescuing people. There is nothing we can do to help them.'

Fortunately, Legolas and Boromir spot a tiny cottage alone on the rugged moor with an old lady the sole occupant and not a clue as to their identity. Explaining their predicament, they are invited in first for tea and then to stay.

In Queenstown the news wasn't good. The storm had delivered a level of flooding not seen in a century and the town was officially in a state of civil emergency. As John Rhys-Davies laughed later, once laughter was permitted, 'We received a notice that said something along the lines of, "No shooting today, river underwater."' The set they had built for the first of the action sequences they were due to be filming had been swept downriver, with the construction crew stranded.

On page this was to be Jackson in full spate. As the Fellowship negotiate the white water of the Sarn Gebir rapids they are ambushed by a band of Orcs on the shoreline: 'URUK-HAI ARROWS rain down from ABOVE!' There were all sort of thrills and spills planned: one canoe being upturned, dumping Sam into the water; Legolas balancing on the gunwales and dispatching unerring arrows at their foes (making it the first 'Leggy moment') as Gimli desperately tried to keep the bucking craft level; and finally a Ringwraith swooping out of the darkness on a fell beast.

With bitter irony, the river was raging too spectacularly and there was little hope of rebuilding the *ruined* ruined stone jetty for days.

Through the almost hourly rethinks in making *Bad Taste* above all Jackson had learned to adapt. Screaming in the face of your misfortune got you nowhere. Indeed, flexibility could be an artistic virtue. Walsh reminded him that a sandstorm had once torn through the *Star Wars* shoot in Tunisia, so maybe it was a good omen. With an eye on a schedule buckling under time pressures, and the need to maintain to New Line everything was under control, he simply lifted the entire sequence out of the script. It would never be filmed. Years later, Jackson's white water dreams would be channelled into the barrel chase in *The Desolation of Smaug* — in rapids assembled under strict studio conditions.

For now, the three Elven canoes would pass unmolested to the lake of Nen Hithoel, filmed in the ice-cold Lake Mavora, southwest of Queenstown, where Astin would split open his foot wading through the shallows.

There was also the small problem of how to reclaim Bloom and Bean from exile in a magic cottage. With the roads still to be cleared, they had been sleeping on the old lady's tiny couches for four days when, finally, Caro negotiated rescue by helicopter.

Jackson laughs wickedly. 'Sean especially hates helicopters, and they had a horrendous flight to Queenstown. What with the remains of the storm and the buffeting you get over the mountains he was almost unconscious.'

Whatever his conscious state when they touched down, that brief excursion remains scalded onto Bean's memory. 'It was blowing a gale like on the Yorkshire Moors, and this helicopter was swinging around in the wind. I had an iron grip on Orlando's thigh for the entire journey.'

With Caro's hasty revisions to the schedule, they moved to scenes on the lower slopes of Dimrill Dale, located on the edges of Lake Alta high in The Remarkables, a range of peaks with self-explanatory virtues and next to no accessibility. So more helicopters were arranged to ferry crew and equipment up to the location.

Bean paled at the news. 'I can't do it, I can't get back in a chopper.'

'But it's a lovely calm day,' Jackson replied soothingly. The actor was adamant.

'Look,' he said, 'I'll get myself up there.' Even if that meant clambering up the sheer mountainside. So at an ungodly hour wardrobe outfitted him as Boromir complete with shield and sword (to lend him a little Gondorian grit) and he set off.

Says Jackson, 'I remember flying in to land by the lake and there is Sean and his loyal make-up girl. The poor bastard was halfway up this almost vertical cliff like a human fly. He's a pro: he delivered himself on set on time, made up. He didn't hold us up. He just had to do it the hard way.'

Bean had become the embodiment of the entire production. Find a way.

DECEMBER (THE STAIRS OF CIRITH UNGOL, AMON HEN, LOTHLÓRIEN BORDERS, THE FORD OF BRUINEN): With the road to Glenorchy still washed out, they were faced with the spectre of grinding to a halt. They had no McKellen yet, so couldn't shoot anything involving the entire Fellowship. Even with the actors they had available there was no studio space to speak of in Queenstown.

'We were only eight weeks into an eighteen-month shoot and we literally didn't have anything we could film,' reports Jackson.

Kiwi resourcefulness is never thwarted, merely challenged. Looking for some form of wet weather cover, Osborne instigated a search of Queenstown. It turned out the squash court at their hotel had just enough room to accommodate, at extremely short notice, the vertiginous Stairs of Cirith Ungol, or at least a slender ledge near their summit.

'This was film three stuff, but it was the only thing we could do while waiting for the road to be fixed.'

The scene follows Gollum tricking Frodo into believing Sam has betrayed them, and the unreasoning Ringbearer dismissing his heartbroken friend. In other words, this was some real

dramatic meat, challenging the actors to transport their characters to the far side of the trilogy.

Wood can remember how nervous he was. 'For the bulk of the
first two months we primarily shot only *Fellowship*. But here we
were forced to shoot on a cover set, and it was the steps of Cirith
Ungol where Frodo is really not himself. It's a very dark place
he's in. And with Gollum I'm not sure if Andy had even been
cast yet.'

The whole science of how they were even going to portray the
wretch was still in R&D back in Wellington.

'This is classic *Lord of the Rings* lore,' continues Wood, 'but
that was petrifying because we were on safe ground to a certain
degree with *Fellowship*. Frodo's descent really doesn't happen
until the second film. To jump to that so quickly without having
time to prepare was shocking.'

They had to sit down and talk it through. Where these characters were, *who* they were. Being forced into that headspace really
awoke Wood to the path he and Frodo were on. It was a vision
of his own future, this tease of the character's decline he could
begin seeding into his portrayal.

Jackson takes up the tale. 'So we start shooting this scene with
Frodo, Sam and Gollum. After tossing a coin, I shot all of Sam
first from Frodo's perspective.'

The scene cuts back and forth between Wood and Astin.

'This was like one day's shooting. The next day we would come
back and do all the stuff of Frodo. But the next day we woke up
to be told that the road had been fixed.'

'We only shot one side,' laughs Wood. 'We didn't shoot the
remainder of the shot for a year.'

With the road clear they returned to the original schedule, and
Osborne cut a deal with the hotel to mothball the squash court,
now a rocky shelf high above Minas Morgul.

'When that conversation happens between those two,' marvels
Jackson, 'there is a year between the two cuts. But watching the
film you can't tell.'

To reach Paradise, where gangs of fetid Orcs and Uruk-hai would fall upon the scattered Fellowship, they would take the recently cleared road up from the lakeside in Queenstown. They were shooting battle scenes in the beautiful forest by the Dart River for three to four weeks, as well as a skirmish with Moria Orcs on the borders of Lothlórien (a scene involving the hobbits being scooped into the trees by Elves that would never make even the *Extended Edition*). Every day they would pass another movie production: fellow Kiwi director Martin Campbell's mountain climbing thriller *Vertical Limit* was filming up above the snowline and had set up base north of Queenstown.

Jackson can picture it still: 'This fancy looking fleet of helicopters and all these fancy tents on a field, where they were flying their guys up to the shoot. We would think, "God, that is a big budget movie. They can afford six helicopters every day. That is what a real production looks like."'

Without fail they would ceremoniously wave as they went past on their way to their massive little indie, fizzing cameras along zip lines (it is known as a 'flying fox') at a place Tolkien called Amon Hen.

It was in December that they were due to film Boromir's death, at the rending finale to the first film. What with the floods and many delays, however, Jackson was now way behind the eight-ball. He had to shoot fast, flying from take to take as the Fellowship was broken apart in battle. The use of scale stunt doubles came in particularly handy: on a given day Gimli could be marching up the untouched slopes of Caradhras with the second unit (on Mount Aspiring near Otago) and fighting Uruk-hai on the slopes of Amon Hen, where Jackson was going like the clappers. They were scenes invested with urgency.

'Aragorn wielding his sword, Legolas shooting all the arrows, Orcs chasing after them through the woods: we are shooting this stuff as fast as we can, heading for Boromir's death, waiting for it to rain again. Yet every day is absolutely immaculate.'

When it came to the departure of Gondor's stern son, blessed in the beatific light filtering through the trees of Paradise, Jackson took pause and allowed himself the time to capture one of the grace notes of the entire trilogy.

Bean had been travelling down the M1 through an overcast Yorkshire when he heard he was to play Boromir, and in that instant his mind must have flashed forward to this day. This was Boromir's defining moment: 'I've been shot full of arrows and I'm lying in Aragorn's arms.' Years later, Bean can still feel the moment. 'Boromir is granted a peaceful passage into the next world. It's not a painful death, it's more of a self-realization.'

The writing, much of it eleventh-hour revisions, was pitch perfect: 'My captain, my king. . .'

Shooting that scene had a galvanising effect on the production. However tough this was going to be, they were reminded what was at stake. Nevertheless, such were the quirks of scheduling that, despite taking his last breaths, Boromir was still due back in the New Year. He hadn't even got to the Council of Elrond yet.

On Saturday, 11 December, the Christmas party was held at Maggie's Bar in Queenstown, 'from nine-thirty p.m. until you fall over'.

CHRISTMAS BREAK: As they departed for the Christmas holidays, Mortensen was given leave to take his sword with him, although not, one supposes, as part of his carry-on luggage.

On the sporadic days or weeks they weren't due in front of the camera, for those non-natives who stayed in New Zealand, especially among the younger cast, the adventure became extracurricular: surfing, hiking, climbing, rafting, caving, whale-spotting in Marlborough Sounds, bungee jumping and more surfing. Not that they forewent the blasé pleasures of hanging out in bars and coffee shops or Bloom's 'wooden house on the beach'. They took in the heady thrill of the outwardly bound Kiwi mentality and simply drank it up.

'If we had a weekend off we'd all go up to a place called Castlepoint,' recalled Boyd in 2001, 'and we'd hire this kind of beach hut that slept about thirty people. And we'd just go up there and surf all day and have a barbecue at night.'

For others, communing with the wilderness was part of their creative process. Serkis mentions a three-day solo canoeing trip down the remote Wanganui River with his battered copy of the book in order to 'plug into Gollum's isolation'. Soaked and short on food, he had to be rescued by three outwardly bound Wellington councillors who happily shared their supplies.

While many were recharging their batteries and contemplating nature, it was during the Christmas break the production went through a major upheaval, with Tim Sanders and key personnel at Weta Digital leaving, victims of an enforced shake-up by New Line. The studio was growing concerned whether Weta Digital was able to deal with the growing complexity of Jackson's ambitions. There was no list of deliverables, no sense of management and a director who, when it came to the film, already 'refused to be reined in' which would lead to incremental increases (of $5 to $10 million at a time) in the budget. More experienced hands were required to handle Jackson's expanding vision, and visual effects supervisor Mark Stetson was replaced with Jim Rygiel, a Los Angeles-based veteran in computer animation whose CV boasted the likes of *Cliffhanger*, *Starship Troopers* and *The Fast and the Furious*. As he put it, they needed to get into 'production mode'.

'It was a difficult time: people were very hurt; it's a small industry,' notes Jackson, who accepts his own naivety was partly to blame.

January (The Shire, Weathertop exteriors and Hobbiton): Come the New Year, unbitten by the Millennium Bug, the shoot settled into a more even, confident rhythm. Their baptism by fire (and water) had only instilled greater determination for the rest of the journey. They had found an identity.

Cast and crew returned refreshed, and Jackson showed them a reel of rough but impressive footage, including the death of

Boromir, to aid readjustment to Middle-earth. And they were due to shoot, at last, in Hobbiton. The call sheets list some busy livestock requirements: '1 x blackfaced lamb, 1 x goat (normal), 12 x blackfaced sheep, 2 x ducks, geese, songbird (large), 2 x ducks, geese, songbird (normal), and 2 x dogs.

While readers have vouched for the perfection of their Hobbiton, now in full bloom at Matamata, Jackson maintains that it was here they were to an extent making do. 'That was the one feeling we struggled with the most, that sort of classic Shire English countryside. The Paddocks is not like the English rolling countryside particularly, but it was good enough.'

With a sense of relief that flowed through the entire production (not least in Caro's sorely taxed scheduling department) Ian McKellen arrived right on cue as shooting geared up again on 17 January 2000.

Meet McKellen in person and you can see what Jackson means when he describes him as a 'chameleon'. They are quite different, Gandalf and his shadow: the actor is younger, less befuddled, a little more cynical and dry. His self-parody in Ricky Gervais' *Extras* is closer than you think: 'How do I act so well? What I do is I pretend to be the person I'm portraying in the film or play.'

That said, Gandalf's disapproving attitude toward hobbit antics would spill into the real world. Sharing a make-up trailer with the four young actors could be a trial. Wood's collection of cutting edge music did little for McKellen's daily preparations. Asked one morning what he might like to play and he replied, 'How about some silence?' Due to a quirk of the trailer's design a fifth make-up station was divided off from the rest by a wall. The hobbits soon came to understand this was Sir Ian's domain.

McKellen claims to have often asked why he was chosen for Gandalf and never gotten a straight answer. Perhaps such things are hard to put into words — why one actor can be so right for a role. It's in the acting, that *transformation*, which as every good director knows is magic.

For Walsh and Boyens, toiling away on the script — they would generally travel with the production — the reward would so often be arriving on set and having those lines delivered.

'Hearing Ian McKellen do it,' says Boyens, savouring the memory. 'And nail it. Finding the line. Finding the right line. We were dealing with a lot of actors who were all incredibly good and just wanted to get the moment, that chance. It's like let me at it.'

A favourite piece of Walsh wisdom had it that no one cares more about the character than the actor having to play them. And while in every way the cast were on personal journeys, they were there to work. There was a very visible hunger to get deeper and deeper into the characters — to explore their reality.

'It's one of the reasons we did a lot of handheld shooting,' says Jackson, 'because the actors were living in the moment and not being characters. Not being the cliché.'

In counterpoint to the operatic magnitude of the New Zealand locations, there was a constant drawing in close, a search for the intimacy so boldly done in *Heavenly Creatures*. High on a mountainside the actors would find the camera inches from their nose. Jackson filled the screen with unflinching close-ups, studying even Gollum's computer-generated mirror of Serkis' agonies for the dance of emotions.

Says Wood, 'I remember after Gandalf is taken by the Balrog and the Fellowship kind of spills out onto the mountain, and Frodo kind of drifts away. When he turns around you need to see how devastated he is by the death of Gandalf. It was such an important moment.'

Jackson had given Wood a very specific instruction. When Frodo turns around, he told the actor, 'I want the audience to be afraid of what state he's in emotionally. They won't have seen him like this before.'

'It was such a specific, visceral piece of direction that I could really sink my teeth into. I kind of ate it up. He really understood acting, really connected to it.'

This was very much an ensemble, filled with many differ-ent acting styles, from the effortless formalism of a McKellen (just act) to the psychic immersion of a Mortensen or Serkis (just become). But Jackson swiftly came to understand how each of them ticked.

Christopher Lee needed to grumble; Holm to jape; and Astin to fuss and worry until he got there.

'We always listened to what an actor was saying,' insists Boyens.

Wood found his director to be a clear, uncomplicated commu-nicator. He would often use other movies as reference: in Cirith Ungol, jealous for the return of the Ring, Wood should look up from under his eyes like 'Jack Nicholson in *The Shining*'.

Holm always suspected there was a part of Jackson hankering to join them in front of the camera, and the director would reg-ularly enact the moves for his cast to follow. Bean laughs at how Jackson did every thrust and parry of the battle with the Cave-troll — including a fine rendition of a Cave-troll.

'He had it all in his head,' laughs Wood, enjoying the memory. 'But it did depend on the scene. Something that was more emotional, not so much. But something where there was more physicality, he'd sort of play the characters, which was incredibly endearing and also helpful.'

All tales of the eccentricity and passion in the making of *The Lord of the Rings*, however, tend to lead to Mortensen. As Jackson says, he became so synonymous with Aragorn it was hard to see him as Viggo again. 'I have never witnessed an actor enter in the spirit of a role the way he did.'

Fuelled partly by the suddenness of his decision and partly by his quasi-Method approach to acting, Mortensen was consumed by the role. His dedication to the accuracy of his portrayal of the king-in-waiting became borderline pathological. If it were a dawn call, he would demand the unit camp out on set the night before in readiment (which Bernard Hill and Bloom once agreed to). When he broke a tooth midway through a battle scene, he famously asked for superglue (they used chewing gum) to stick it back in so he could finish the scene. He never once touched any of the prop versions of the Ring — it is likely he never has. When his car hit a rabbit, he scooped it up, roasted it, and ate it. And he and that sword were inseparable. In the first weeks, Astin met the great Dane for a burger at The Green Parrot (Mortensen's preferred venue) and his blade was already occupying the seat beside him.

'I don't think I saw him in street clothes during filming,' laughs Bean.

When shooting in Wellington, Mortensen would tend to spend his Sunday mornings at the gym, accompanied by his sword. On one particular morning he was so keyed up about an upcoming fight sequence he started practising his moves, spinning and thrusting with the lengthy blade on the sidewalk outside. Reports flew into the local police station of a wild man swinging a sword around his head. Cars were dispatched, and Aragorn was surrounded by a swarm of flashing lights and shrieking sirens. He was let off with a mild caution as long as he signed a few autographs and posed for some pictures.

'Viggo was our leader; he was a true inspiration,' claims a smitten Bloom. 'He was like a brother to me. Almost more than that.'

'I always try to get a feel for it as much as possible,' says Mortensen, who resists explaining this need to climb inside a character. 'I walked and dressed like Aragorn as Pete always encouraged us to look for the realism in the story. It was a very real performance. At least, I felt like it was true.'

There were times when the practicalities of shooting on location, where the light and weather led them a merry dance, that, Mortensen admits, didn't allow a lot of space for getting too 'thinky' about one's craft.

'I didn't always feel safe, in the sense that you're sometimes diving into a scene, where you are thinking, "I don't know how I am going to pull this off right now." Then, "Here come the clouds, we've got one crack at it."'

And this is where the sense of community among the actors really helped. They could draw strength from one another.

'We had to learn to be flexible or you would perish under the weight of expectation you put on yourself,' says Mortensen.

There was little time for painting, or photographs, or music, but if he couldn't sleep he might write a verse or two of poetry.

One peculiarity of completing Hobbiton in their allotted window was that the schedule had to include the very last scene of the film where Sam returns home to Bagshot Row.

'It was a bit strange to be shooting the end of the third movie,' admits Jackson, who after three months still felt as if he had only just got going.

As he framed the shot, Jackson laughed to Astin. 'You realize the scene we are filming now is not going to be seen for nearly four years.'

FEBRUARY (BAG END INTERIORS, BILBO'S BIRTHDAY PARTY, RIVENDELL, FARMER MAGGOT'S FIELD, HELM'S DEEP EXTERIORS): Bilbo never went to the actual fake Hobbiton. Holm would complete his scenes in a month inside Bag End or on the party field or in Rivendell, all sets constructed at Stone Street. This allowed more control of the scale issue, where the choreography of each scene had to be painstakingly plotted out beforehand. Jackson had commissioned stills of tall and titchy stand-ins beside one another from every conceivable angle. Pouring over them he figured out which trick to use in which shot.

'If we're looking past the shoulder of a big person, down at a small person, that could be an actor standing on a box with a high camera angle. Or this one could be Gandalf in the duplicate set. And here we should shoot Bilbo against bluescreen and then scale him down digitally to be composited in with the other actors. We had this bible of how we would achieve every scale shot.'

Holm noticed that it was only Jackson who showed any enthusiasm for working in the hot, confined duplicates of Bag End.

The homely detail, complete with working fireplaces (which only helped cook theatrical knights), had such a 'profound effect' on Jackson he negotiated with New Line to preserve the set, refitting it as an underground guesthouse for diminutive visitors to the 1930s country estate he built at Masterton.

MARCH (ORTHANC, ISENGARD CAVERNS, RIVENDELL EXTERIORS, THE GREY HAVENS, HELM'S DEEP SECOND UNIT): with Camperdown Studios, the space Jackson had used on his previous films, claimed by Weta Workshop (and hardly capacious all the same), Wellington offered only a handful of television studios barely bigger than squash courts. There was nothing that could encompass the passages of Moria or the Golden Hall of Rohan. They would simply have to build the studio in which to shoot their film, and while still negotiating with Miramax, Jackson and Walsh began looking at what available properties might work for them. One of which turned out to be an abandoned paint factory on Stone Street in Miramar.

Says Jackson, 'If the film happens, we thought, "this is exactly the sort of space we need. There were warehouses that could be turned into stages."'

Even though it had been standing empty for six months it didn't come cheap. There were big risks, they would have to mortgage their house for the down-payment and if the films didn't happen they were left with a disused paint factory on their hands. But they went back for another look, and while touring the mothballed factory, layered in dust like a ghost ship, they came to the old cafeteria. There Jackson spotted a yellowed paperback abandoned on one of the chipped Formica tables.

It was a copy of *The Lord of the Rings*.

According to the call sheet for 15 February, day 74, the central chamber of the corrupted tower of Orthanc could be found in studio A. Apropos of wizardly fixtures and fittings, a month later the summit of Orthanc would be located in the car park at Stone Street Studios adjacent to studios B and C.

Christopher Lee was seventy-seven when he began his first ten-week stint on his dream epic and he couldn't abide the robes. They looked the part, of course, and striding about on the flat was fine, but his skirts would wrap around his long legs whenever he attempted to mount the steps to his throne. He eventually had to hitch them up, like a lady in an evening dress.

'It was quite funny, I suppose,' he admits, sounding like he tended to think otherwise.

Mark Ordesky laughs a little ruefully at the memory of a sly call he once got from Jackson about fingernails. Saruman featured long, brown nails like claws that had to be applied each morning. And Lee wasn't enjoying the process. 'Must they be applied?' he would fuss. 'Are we going to even see his hands? Aren't they going to be hidden in his robe?'

Jackson sounded casual on the phone. 'You should maybe come and have a chat to Christopher about the importance of the nails.'

'How surreal is that?' says Ordesky. 'To show up to have a chat with Christopher Lee about his fingernails.'

For the record, Ordesky, who now treasures the moment, spent a sobering thirty minutes convincing the actor to endure the application of prosthetic talons. Peter, he explained, liked to keep his options open, the camera might pan down to his hands.

Lee also struggled with the number of takes his director pursued in search of perfection — which hardly ran to Kubrickian numbers. According to Astin, having once been asked for fifteen takes of a scene, Lee was irate. 'Why, I've never had a director ask me to do it this many times in my life! This is ridiculous! I've done fewer takes in an entire movie!'

The elder statesman may have required a little more handling — and maybe it was all part of his process — but there was never a second of doubt that it was worth it. Cameras rolling or not, Saruman's stare could cut through stone.

'To be within four feet of a Lee snarl is unsettling,' says McKellen, who knows.

'He would drive you nuts,' agrees Boyens. 'But there were those times when you had to pinch yourself.'

Boyens was on the front lines of ADR* — what with wind-swept hilltops, the clanging of Stone Street's old pipes and the coming and going of jets from Wellington airport, nearly every line had to be rerecorded. She cherishes the days she spent with Lee, who could suddenly start speaking Finnish or break into opera. He had met everyone, she marvels. It became a shared joke where Boyens would try and guess the icons Lee had known: Ian Fleming, of course, Errol Flynn, Hitchcock, *Tolkien*. . .

With little prompting, Lee would regularly regale an audience with his tale of having actually met the great man at an Oxford pub forty-five years before. I too had it at first hand. How he was in town catching up with friends, and they decided to exchange the pompous Randolph Hotel for a good tavern, electing *The Eagle and Child*. As the drinks flowed, one of his friends leaned over and spoke in a hushed voice.

'Look who has just walked in.'

Lee glanced toward the door and there stood a 'benign-looking' gent in tweeds and smoking a pipe he knew instantly to be Professor Tolkien. 'I nearly fell off my chair.'

Miraculously, a member of their party even knew him.

'Oh Professor, Professor,' he called.

Over he came to shake their hands and pass the time of day.

'I knelt, of course,' recalled Lee. 'He was a genius but an English countryman with earth under his feet.'

During the shoot, Lee came to represent a kind of spiritual bridge to Tolkien. No one took the text more seriously. Indeed, it became a challenge among the crew to try and catch him out with arcane questions, researched the night before.

---

* Automatic Dialogue Replacement, or 'looping', is a post-production process whereby the original actor re-records their dialogue under studio conditions. This can be simply to improve the clarity or diction of what we hear, rectify a mistake, or change the dramatic impetus of a line reading.

'They never did,' the actor noted matter-of-factly. 'I don't know everything in the books, but I know a great deal.'

As if channelling some of the dark wizard's furies, the issue of allotted parking spaces, of which there were precious few, at Stone Street became quite contentious: 'If someone is parking in your space,' reads the long-suffering producer's note on the leap day of 29 February 2000, 'don't compound the problem by parking in someone else's.'

One could simply walk into work.

APRIL (EMYN MUIL, RIVENDELL EXTERIORS, THE PLAINS OF GORGOROTH, THE BLACK GATES, ISENGARD CAVERNS, THE VALE OF MORGUL, HELM'S DEEP EXTERIORS): Mordor, if it wasn't located on a Stone Street soundstage, was to be found in the region of Mount Ruapehu, and even up on the slopes of the volcano at the heart of the North Island, which had erupted as recently as 1996.

At its mention, Wood gets a faraway look in his saucer eyes. 'Wow, shooting at Mount Ruapehu, staying at the Powderhorn. . .'

One of a travel brochure's worth of hotels they frequented, The Powderhorn Chateau in Ohakune, the one plucky inhabitation beneath the rim of the volcano, was styled as if it belonged on a Swiss mountainside or the lid of a chocolate box.

It reminded Serkis of the Overlook in *The Shining*. The actor was beginning the process of becoming Gollum 5,000 feet up an active volcano dressed in what he called a 'unitard', much to the merriment of the crew and the director.

'Location shooting's very intimate,' says Wood. 'It's like everyone's on a campout. Everyone's staying at the same hotel and it ends up becoming a lot more communal. There's sort of the novelty of a travelling show.'

For the battle before the Black Gates, as Aragorn draws out the multitudinous forces of Sauron, they were seeking a flat, arid desert-like setting. 'That was how it was described in the book,' confirms Jackson. A landscape which New Zealand does possess, but only in the forty square miles of Rangipo Desert, close to Ruapehu.

'Unfortunately it is this army training area,' chuckles Jackson, 'and littered with unexploded ammo.'

The army had been shooting artillery on one of the few unalluring patches of New Zealand for fifty years, leaving a trail of unexploded shells and the strictest of orders as to where you were and were *not* allowed to tread.

'It was as dangerous as all hell. But it's the only place we could do those scenes.'

Having already helped build roads to Hobbiton, really getting into the Middle-earth spirit the army offered to sweep the area for unexploded shells, designating an area free of potential explosions for Jackson and his filmmaking troops to make camp.

'When we all showed up to shoot, we had a bit of a lecture from the army guys. They had cleared it, but you never knew if some stupid technician was going to trip on something. They had all the types of bombs on the table: "If you see any of these *don't touch them.* Call us."'

Bomb disposal units were put at the ready, and every day Caro had to co-ordinate with them to reconfirm the boundaries of their 'safe area'.

So they come to the scene of a kingly Aragorn riding out to battle. Everyone went over the limits of the safe zone once more. But when Mortensen was in character, and never more so than when he was on horseback, he tended to depart for Middle-earth, where only Saruman had gunpowder. On 'action', he rode up to the camera, turned and then galloped away.

'CUT!' yells Caro at the top of her considerable voice.

Mortensen, his ears filled with the songs of Númenor, doesn't hear her, and to everyone's horror rides clean out of the safe area. Jackson remembers waiting for the explosion. Having found their perfect Aragorn they were going to watch him get blown up by an unexploded New Zealand bomb.

In the end Mortensen pulled up, figuring the shot must be

complete. Turning around he saw the entire crew screaming madly and waving their arms, and he and his guardian angel calmly trotted back to safe ground.

It was during the battle scenes at the Black Gates (themselves a miniature) that Jackson witnessed perhaps the most surreal sight of a surreal shoot. To fill out the forces on both sides, they had dressed up willing New Zealand squaddies as Gondorian soldiers and Orcs, dividing them into platoons under their existing NCOs and officers. Only now mostly covered in Orc prosthetics and rusty armour.

For Jackson it was a perfect solution. 'You just tell them what to do and they tell their men to go and form up. But some guy had obviously done something wrong.'

Finished for the day, he was heading back to the unit base where the extras were queuing outside the Weta Workshop marquee to have their costumes dismantled. His attention was drawn to the unmistakeable sound of a sergeant major — and this was the director who cast R. Lee Ermy as a spectral sergeant major in *The Frighteners* in homage to *Full Metal Jacket* — giving a private a right earful.

'This guy was screaming at him,' laughs Jackson. 'But they were both still Orcs. It was bloody funny.'

MAY (THE BLACK GATES, THE GATE OF MORIA, THE CRACKS OF DOOM, DUNHARROW PLATEAU, THE COUNCIL OF ELROND, HELM'S DEEP EXTERIORS): The magical, western entrance to Moria, known in Dwarvish circles as the Doors of Durin, was constructed on a wet set on the backlot of Avalon Studios in Lower Hutt. The small local studio came with a tank, which would be used for all the 'wet' sets: flooded Isengard, Dead Marshes, Osgiliath, etc. From the foul water would eventually emerge Jackson's Harryhausian upgrade of Tolkien's tentacular Watcher in the Water, once Weta Digital had worked their wonders.

Not that it had been a guarantee.

The Watcher had initiated a stand-off between director and

studio, with New Line reasoning that the creature wasn't a narrative necessity, and with costs steadily rising, could easily make way.

'The Watcher had been on the chopping block even during the scriptwriting,' says Ordesky. Jackson was insistent this was about more than the ABCs of storytelling. If the Fellowship just strolls into Moria you miss a crucial bit of action after a lot of walk and talk. Furthermore, it affected a precise internal rhythm: Moria would be shaped around a beginning, middle and end of monster confrontations.

'Also it talks about the threat of Sauron,' emphasizes Ordesky, but admits it was a hard-won battle. New Line was legitimately conscious of length. If a film was over two hours and forty-five minutes you lost one show per day, per screen, worldwide. Jackson would be granted his Watcher as long as he directed the scene on his own time (i.e. on unbilled hours), leaving the thorny issue of running time to lie in wait for the edit.

As Avalon was an exterior set within view of the street a few blurry pap shots found their way onto the internet featuring the Fellowship encamped by the Doors of Durin, whose glowing outlines were exactly as Tolkien had draw them in the book. It was an early warning of the internet's newfound culture of film sneaks and spoilers, and *The Lord of the Rings* was a prize catch. The issue of set security was pressing. Back on their very first day a photographer was found hiding in the bushes, before being chased away by security guards, and there were growing concerns over the number of crew 'discussing the details' of their jobs online. This was more a matter of naivety than gain, but the unit publicist had to gently remind everyone that their 'confidentiality agreement still applies'.

As well as shooting details and production missives, the call sheets also kept a careful track on lost property: phones, wallets, jackets, even a pair of waders. But surely a rich opportunity for irony was lost when, on 31 May, day 139, while shooting the Council sequence on the stunning studio set of Elrond's balcony, it was noted that 'a ring has been found in Studio A's loading dock area'.

There was no mention of whether it had wanted to be found.

JUNE (THE COUNCIL OF ELROND, SHELOB'S LAIR, LOTHLÓRIEN): On 9 June, day 146, Galadriel came among them. Cate Blanchett arrived for her strict two-week stint of fetching ear-tips, starlit irises and enigmatic smiles, and come what may they were going to get her scenes shot (she had an unavoidable appointment with *Charlotte Grey*). If the exteriors for the gift-giving sequence turned inclement then they were going to become interiors with the banks of the Silverlode bluescreened in later. Thankfully, the weather hovering over the country house at Fernside in Upper Hutt proved cooperative.

When Blanchett got to Stone Street for her entrance in Celeborn's Chamber and the moonlit mirror sequence, as well as dashing to unit 1C to grab the single shot of Galadriel in the prologue, she found herself in a constant state of amazement.

'You're walking past people in Orc costumes, and you go to Weta and you see the extraordinary things they're doing there. . . It really spun me out that there was someone who devoted their time to speaking Elvish. It's like people speaking Klingon.'

As the Australian superstar wafted away again, the first half of the shoot came to an end and they broke for winter.

A week or so earlier, on June 12, day 147, there had been a note attached to the call sheet from the producers, which sounded ominously like a warning: 'the schedule for the second half of the year is daunting, with many sequences to be shot simultaneously in different locations around the country. . .'

WINTER BREAK: Some went home to see loved ones, while others couldn't tear themselves away. For Jackson there were many more meetings, preparations for the remainder of the shoot, more scouting, reviewing footage and updates with Weta Digital. But no rest.

July (Shelob's Lair, Caras Galadhon, River Anduin): The great train of production heaved back into motion again on 24 July, day 158, with Frodo lured into the tunnels of Shelob's Lair by a treacherous Gollum and on the same day mounting the stairs of the Elven tree-city.

With congestion at Stone Street, and the need to cycle sets, studio production had begun to spread across Wellington, converting any available warehouses and former factories into temporary studios. More then ever the city was fusing with Middle-earth. What had been studios A, B and C, now became A, B, C, D, E, F, G, H, I, J, K, L, M, N and O.

The Cracks of Doom ended up in Studio K, a former apple store in Rongotai only feet from the airport runway and over the road from a DHL depot. It was tight, just about fitting in the rock gantry that looms over the river of lava. Jackson would have to make artful use of smoke and dramatic lighting to gain the appropriate geological feel.

August (Moria tunnels, Dwarrowdelf, Balin's Tomb, Khazad-dûm, flooded Isengard, Eregion Hills, Dead Marshes, Dimholt Road, Hobbiton Woods): If anyone had truly rationalised what it would take to get the films shot, recollects Jackson, they would never have begun. Their naivety is what saved them. That and that ineffable need to keep going, but as the schedule both piled up and spread out, it required a dizzying accountancy of units from Osborne and his team to keep track of what still needed to be shot, and where.

The cast and crew were tossed about the story like autumn leaves in a Wellington wind, often unaware of what their fellow actors were up to, and more than ever production started to feel schizophrenic, with all these conflicting personalities in the same body. Wood says he never visited Helm's Deep. He only ever saw it once, driving past in a car. Serkis notes that he never did a single scene with McKellen or Mortensen or Weaving. Working weekends became the norm. There was only Middle-earth.

Take 17 August, day 176, which found 1A shooting Gandalf leaving Frodo in the Hobbiton Woods in Otaki, north of Wellington; 1B was busy with the Anduin scenes at Poet's Corner, Saruman's death on the flooded Isengard set and a bluescreened Lothlórien; 2A was fighting Orcs in Balin's Tomb; while the FX unit were completing the studio insert of Saruman on top of Orthanc and head replacements of Pippin and Merry being carried away by Uruk-hai from Amon Hen. And there were still publicity and merchandising stills to be shot, and 'toy biz' face scans.

It was, says Ken Kamins, like a 'game of three-dimensional chess'.

The only place it cohered was in the mind of the director.

'I don't think being a director is waking up in the morning and putting on a persona and pretending to be something,' ruminates Jackson. 'There is no real magic in being a director. All I do is create this mental image of the film, then I show up for work, we get the camera and the actors and I am simply trying to get to what I imagined in my mind.'

Of course, he says, it is entirely likely an actor will come up with something better than he had imagined. Likewise, a collaborator behind-the-scenes comes up with a better choice of shot, a change of lighting or an adjustment to a visual effect shot or costume. 'You experiment; things come and go. It continually transforms.'

There were two things that drove him through the shooting of *The Lord of the Rings*: fear, the terror that you are making a disaster, and responsibility. People had put their trust in him, and he was sickened by the idea of letting them down.

But there was also that voice in his head. The one that kept telling him he still hadn't got the take, or the shot, or the idea that could transform the film. That voice would not let him rest.

Jackson once described filmmaking as 'a process of constant disappointment'. You only hope that you have set your goals high enough to end up with something that other people enjoy.

'They are not the perfect films I had in my head,' he admits.

It is the compromises and imperfections only he can see that dominate his thoughts. 'You always wished you could shoot something better, direct something better. I felt frustrated that I wasn't capturing something of Tolkien's spirit.'

Before setting out, Jackson had watched Terrence Malick's haunting, elliptical Second World War epic of the Pacific theatre, *The Thin Red Line*, where the camera drifts away from battle to drink in Mother Nature. 'I looked at it and thought, "This is the type of thing we should be doing. This is Tolkien." As it was, we were pressed for time. I couldn't get my shots of the waving grass and the clovers. I had wanted to make the landscape and the weather more of a character in the story.'

He's wrong. The films may not dally over nature quite to the fixated eye of Malick, but Middle-earth bursts out of every frame to the point of delirium. This wasn't merely a postcard from New Zealand; this was New Zealand clothed in a violent, gritty, outlandish and highly varied Lee-Howe alt-naturalism where the camera glides through the mythic air. And much of that has to do with the partnership Jackson developed with Andrew Lesnie.

With Alun Bollinger deciding he couldn't commit to the long haul (he would still shoot second unit), Jackson needed to find himself a cinematographer. This was arguably the key appointment: once in the grip of shooting, the cinematographer is the director's closest collaborator.

Softly spoken and endlessly amused, Lesnie brought the light to the end of the tunnel. The 'shooter' of *Babe* (he also worked on the seminal sci-fi noir *Dark City*), Lesnie came with a temperament and grace under pressure that mirrored the good-naturedness of his director.

The cinematographer had been invited over to Wellington in May 1999 to find himself in a room crammed with people, some of whom he thought might be producers, but Jackson was unmistakable.

'He was barefoot and had his feet up on the desk,' Lesnie recalled, interviewed in 2012. 'I think it was a test.'

Lesnie had considered the book impossible to adapt, but reading the scripts and touring the Workshop he found himself not only swayed but enticed. He asked to meet Jackson on his own, to see if there was that necessary common ground, and a brief meeting turned into hours of talking shots and dreams.

Not that they were always simpatico. Lesnie retained a good cinematographer's sceptisim of his director's choices. It was, he said, a healthy artistic relationship with differences of opinion. There were times, especially under pressure, when some of the director's calls were hard to understand. 'But Peter seeks collaborators. He was interested in my opinion.'

The Lee-Howe paintings maintained an enormous influence on the look of the films. When it came to explaining the 'feel' of any location to his crew, Lesnie often found it easiest to show them a painting. It became a point of pride in how faithful they could stay to the 'tone of their work'.

Such was Jackson's indefatigable calm, says Wood, 'You could never really tell that he was exhausted until sort of the end. Even when there were far too many elements happening at the same time, it never seemed like it affected him. He was always ready for a laugh.'

The demonic, whip-cracking director of Hollywood lore simply wasn't in his psyche. He didn't 'let anxiety flow downhill', as Lesnie put it.

'But there was something about him that was sort of unfathomable,' continues Wood. 'He was not only directing the films but also directing the directors on the other units.'

No one encapsulated the 'rugged, can-do attitude among native New Zealanders' like Jackson, claims Richard Taylor. At any given moment, there may have been thousands of dedicated souls at work on the trilogy, but they were all infused with the spirit of their director. These films are as enriched by his personality as *Apocalypse Now* or *2001: A Space Odyssey* were expressions of their creators. These were films as personal to Jackson as *Bad Taste*, only this time everyone turned up for work.

'Pete got the most fantastical shots and visuals and thought-provoking dialogue,' muses Mortensen, 'but he coupled it with a really grounded vision. It was rough when it needed to be, and it was cold. And it was messy when it needed to be. He shot a lot no matter how extreme the conditions. He shot so many close-ups. There was nowhere to hide. You can see where the characters strengths and weaknesses are. We acted that way and he shot it that way. That's why it's different.'

Even with time running out on a scene, he would always add 'one more for luck'. There was value in overshooting, in having more options in the edit, more brushstrokes with which to paint your masterpiece. Just as the script mixed and matched dialogue, Jackson would be able to slyly repurpose footage to different ends: Orcs on their way to Helm's Deep would find their way into the prologue. There remained acres of footage that didn't even make the extended editions.

Every evening he would watch the dailies. If they were in Wellington, they would be screened at the Camperdown Theatre next to Weta Workshop. Out on location it was a matter of enough space to set up a projector — hotel conference rooms were a favourite. There would be an open invitation for cast and principal crew to join Jackson, with beer and crisps as an incentive.

As he sifted through take after take of the same sequences (he tended to have a mental record of the one he liked, but he needed to be sure) he would often catch the gentle rhythm of snoring. Toward the end of the shoot Jackson was so tired he would take the dailies home on videotape and do his best to stay awake.

When he did sleep, Jackson was haunted by a recurring night-mare where the film crew have snuck into his bedroom and stand around the bed, demanding how to shoot the next scene. But he couldn't remember what the next scene was meant to be. . .

Tiredness was the great enemy. Days when he found himself

struggling to juggle the different elements and come up with inventive shots, falling back on convention like a man toppling from battlements. It was as if his imagination seized up under the pressure.

'On those occasions he could get quite dark,' admits Boyens, not that he burdened her or anyone, apart maybe from Walsh, with his dilemmas. But she could see him sink into himself.

It helped, at weekends, to find time to watch those films and directors who inspired him. 'I am fairly commercial in my tastes,' he admits, but he would gain sustenance from films far off the fantasy track, like Scorsese's psychologically loaded flourishes in *Goodfellas* and *Casino* or the visceral punch of Spielberg's *Saving Private Ryan*. At other times he would load up on the sheer momentum of James Cameron or the frenzy of George Romero.

You can feel all of these contrasting forces nudging into Middle-earth.

But Jackson's closest ally, chief inspiration and frequent saviour was always Walsh. It was almost as if he had cloned himself: they have the same sensibilities, the same attitude, even the same slightly windblown appearance, although Walsh is more slender and serious. The former punk rocker's influence was felt on every level of the production: script, casting, design, effects and music. She ran a frighteningly exacting rule over wardrobe, and became a vital second-unit director.

'My first thought when I saw my name on the call sheet was, "This is a mistake,"' she admitted. But she was a natural.

Whenever Jackson felt that numbing exhaustion begin to creep in at the edges he automatically delegated to Walsh.

'I couldn't have done it without her, no, no, no,' he insists. 'She is the person I trust completely, the only one who knew the project as well as I did.'

'They sort of flow together really,' says Serkis. 'They're an extension of each other in a way. They will not give up until they've explored every single avenue.'

SEPTEMBER (MORIA EXTERIORS, EMYN MUIL, EREGION HILLS, NEN HITHOEL, THE PLAINS OF ROHAN, EDORAS, GONDOR, THE RIVER ANDUIN, ISENGARD GARDENS): On the night of 11 September 2000, day 193, there was a Farewell Boromir party in Te Anau. It was Bean's last day, almost a year after he died.

Just as the producers had warned, the spring months heralded dizzying levels of scheduling complexity. Not only was it physically hard, working fifteen-, sixteen-hour days, but keeping track of your character as you zipped back and forth across the story was a supreme mental challenge. It was as much a case of *when am I* as *where am I*?

Wood's answer was to look about one week ahead, and try to be as prepared as possible. 'Everybody kind of had that same thing. Over the course of three movies, all of the characters go through massive changes.'

At six months, Astin wondered if they were going to make it, but the bonding of those early months stayed true, especially among the hobbits. Between shots they would pile into one another's trailers to nap or play video games, still seeking each other out, never tiring of the company. Even when filming different scenes, recalls Astin, 'We'd be exhausted, but we'd all go out to a bar and drink together until four in the morning, then throw up and be ready to start the week again.'

At the five-month mark, Wood, Monaghan, Boyd and Bloom had taken a trip to Sydney where *Star Wars: Episode II – Attack of the Clones* was filming. They met with Hayden Christensen and Natalie Portman and chatted about their experiences, but Wood remembers a tension between them.

'We felt like the rogue crew. There was a weird sense that, with the two trilogies, there was this odd, undercurrent of rivalry. They all thought that we were quite strange, because we referred to each other as the hobbits.'

There were squabbles between the actors, they became too close for there not to be. Tiredness took its toll, all the early mornings, the endless routine of make-up and wardrobe. Sam's pack, his 'suit of armour' loaded with pots and pans, was cinched into Astin like a corset: 'Okay, breathe in.' He would look on it and despair.

Rhys-Davies, a more conservatively minded member of the Fellowship, was giving much of his performance in close-up and consequently tended to shoot scenes alone (if it was humanly possible Mortensen would be there to read his lines off-camera for his Dwarf companion). He calls it 'the loneliest job I have ever done'. He was also enduring that painfully allergic reaction to the Gimli make-up.

So perhaps one can forgive his patience getting a little testy by Astin's compulsion to do impressions of Rhys-Davies' Sallah from the *Indiana Jones* films within his earshot.

'Indy, they're digging in the wrong place!'

'You know, my boy,' he retorted one day, 'sometimes it borders on the parody.'

OCTOBER (ITHILIEN CAMP, CROSSROADS OF MORGUL, WHITE MOUNTAINS, THE HOUSES OF HEALING, THE GREAT HALL OF THE HORNBURG, PELENNOR FIELDS, CRACK OF DOOM): On the anniversary of beginning, with an end not yet in sight, 1A was in Deer Park Heights shooting Éowyn serving an indifferent stew to Aragorn, discovering he is 87. But there was no time for fanfare, no pause to stop and reflect.

The second unit, led by Geoff Murphy, was shooting Gandalf driving off the Nazgûl on horseback. Through the month and into the next Murphy will gather horsemen to him from all corners of the country and shoot weeks of 'horse stuff' to create the Ride of the Rohirrim.

And Jackson would be behind his monitors conducting New Zealand.

Kamins remembers pausing to watch him, amazed as he landed simultaneous scenes like jumbo jets. 'He'd be filming what he's doing and then he would say, "Unit three, I didn't like that. Can you roll that back? Move the tree back three feet. Unit four, he looked awful in that scene. Move him over five feet to the left. Hey, unit two, can you just play that back for me? I thought I saw something I didn't understand." I don't know how he was doing it.'

NOVEMBER (FANGORN INTERIORS, OSGILIATH RUINS, THE GOLDEN HALL, DUNHARROW ENCAMPMENT, FORBIDDEN POOL, THE PATHS OF THE DEAD, PELENNOR FIELDS): Nature didn't always oblige. Deciduous forests were at a premium in New Zealand. Those very English oaks, birch, cedars and maples so close to Tolkien's heart were rare. Especially given Jackson required them to be 'really gnarly, creepy old trees'.

Fangorn Forest, home of the Ents, would therefore be a set built along the twisted lines that Jackson had imagined when he read the book. Striving to obscure the divide between interior and exterior, Lesnie actually installed the lighting for Fangorn before the set was built. They hung silks beneath large space lights (which replicate daylight) and beneath those ran camouflage nets through which the art department draped foliage so that the light would struggle to reach the set floor.

'The result was a dark, ambient light,' explained Lesnie. Then, he said, they had overexposed 'slivers of sunlight' pierce through the branches like beams. No other department confronted the immediacy of Middle-earth's dual nature — a lived-in strangeness — as the lighting and camera teams.

'You have to intellectualize these things to a certain extent,' Lesnie said. 'For me, Fangorn is one of the oldest places on Middle-earth, and it has a mystique. Just the mention of the name strikes fear into the hearts of the people of Middle-earth, but no one knows why.'

By The Hobbit Mirkwood took the Fangorn aesthetic one stage further with the trees painted in psychedelic hues that emerged as deep greens, browns and purples in Lesnie's brackish illumination.

The lighting team had gone through its own teething problems. Their chief lighting technician, the gaffer, had quit within two weeks, frustrated, he claimed, over the project's lack of professionalism. There were those, Jackson admits, who couldn't shake the idea that this was going to be a 'Mickey Mouse' project. In another frantic rush to fill a vital role, they found Brian Bansgrove, a Kiwi settled in Australia, whose considerable experience was matched by a reputation for hard drinking and language colourful enough to make an Orc blush. He was, according to Jackson, as 'rough as guts' and couldn't even remember the names of the characters, but roaring like a first mate, with a ready supply of salty bon mots, under his tutelage the lighting department became the tightest ship on set.

Jackson remembers offering Bansgrove his thanks for joining at such short notice.

'Well, this job's going to sort the men from the boys,' the unceremonious gaffer replied, 'and I intend to finish like a man!' Everything he said came with an exclamation mark and that soon became an on-set mantra — finish like men!

Bansgrove, that mighty presence, died in 2001, the day before he was due to see *The Fellowship of the Ring*.

Ordesky has a particular memory of Fangorn Forest. 'I was going to the set to ask Peter something very important — it was important to me anyway.'

Only, from between the temperamental trees, Jackson saw him coming. 'Oh, thank God you are here,' he said before Ordesky could say a word. 'I need you to sit here, behind this tree, and read Gimli's off-camera lines while Ian and Orlando and Viggo do their thing.'

'I was stuck behind this tree for two hours reading off lines. One of the only photos of me is on the Fangorn set, and I look fairly sullen because I had been foiled in my attempts to ask him the question. That was Peter, it was all very cheeky and lovely, but he knew how to avoid something.'

He smiles fondly. 'But I did get to play Gimli.'

DECEMBER (OSGILIATH RUINS, HENNETH ANNUIN, DUNHARROW ENCAMPMENT, AMON HEN, MINAS TIRITH INTERIORS AND EXTERIORS, PELENNOR FIELDS): With the end in sight, an inevitable urgency gripped the final weeks. Even by their own intense standards there was a flurry of units and scenes to get them over the finishing line with enough material — if in Jackson's eyes there could ever be enough.

The last official location of principal photography was the ever-versatile Dry Creek Quarry in Upper Hutt, which had played host to Helm's Deep and now provided space for the streets of Minas Tirith for weeks. By early December, the crew was abuzz with the possibility of being an extra at Aragorn's forthcoming coronation on 18 December, day 270 — reward for long months of dedication to the cause.

As Taylor says, 'These weren't movies just made for the sake of a bunch of freelancers getting together to do some business around moviemaking. This was a country coming together to make some extraordinary films.'

The day before he was due to be crowned, Mortensen was planning a lasting memorial.

Nearly everyone in the Fellowship claims it was their idea. But Mortensen was the chief architect of the actual business of getting a tattoo to memorialize their adventure, having settled on the Elvish symbol for nine as designed by Alan Lee.

Aragorn had gone ahead and cleared the morning of Sunday, 17 December at Roger's Tattoo Art, a parlour run by self-styled and formidably tattooed anarchist Roger Ingerton, squeezed in halfway up Cuba Street, Wellington's mildly bohemian fleet of outré shops, bars and alternative lifestyles. There were eight of them who ventured into town that summer morning. Rhys-Davies had opted out, citing an unwillingness to 'mark his body' along with the somewhat far-fetched possibility of contracting Mad Cow Disease (busily making headlines in Europe) from the needle. Perhaps a little pointedly, the other actors extended an invitation to Brett Beattie, Gimli's valiant stunt double, who readily accepted.

Sean Bean (right shoulder blade), who had left New Zealand long before the pact was sealed, would add his own 'nine' during a drunken London night out with Bloom.

They were there for two hours, suffering for their art: Boyd (leg) went first, followed by an eventually persuaded Astin (ankle), a delighted McKellen (shoulder), Monaghan (shoulder), Bloom (right forearm), Wood (hip), Beattie (small of the back) and Mortensen (shoulder). The secret whereabouts of their tattoos was gradually wheedled out of them by talk-show hosts and interviewers.

Astin recalls showing his tattoo to Jackson. The director was visibly moved that they had needed to make real the mark this journey had made on them.

Days later, he, Ordesky and Bernard Hill turned up at Roger's thriving business to each have the Elvish symbol for ten seared onto their skin. On the eve of the Wellington premiere for *The Fellowship of the Ring*, Osborne and Taylor followed suit.

DECEMBER 22, 2000, DAY 274, the final day of production was, according to the weather report, overcast with a fresh wind and the chance of showers. The call sheet, preserved as a historical document, is graffitied in thank you notes and in-jokes. 'We have rewrites for Saturday,' quipped Walsh.

There were two units running. Jackson was with 1A, shooting Gandalf and Aragorn's Council of War in the Great Hall of Minas Tirith. The set had been built in Studio O, another ersatz soundstage to be found in Shed 45 on Waterloo Quay in Wellington docks. Later that evening the wrap party would be held in Shed 21.

That afternoon, Jackson's final shot of principal photography was a sequence of Aragorn donning his armour that ironically never made the cut. 'Viggo, look mean, like you can't wait to go kick Sauron's ass,' came his final piece of direction. The newly returned king was still due to confront a manifested Sauron (the daring deviation from Tolkien later considered unnecessary).

The scenes may have been deadly serious, but there was a last-day-of-term giddiness in the air. No one could quite believe this was ending. A pink feather boa was being handed around, and the guest clapperboard operators — including a visiting Harry Knowles — had to drape it around their shoulders before clapping in the scene.

When the scene was complete to Jackson's satisfaction, champagne flowed like hobbit tears as Wood, Astin and Bloom ran onto the set. Cast and crew held onto one another, trying to hold back time. Jackson was stood to one side, taking it in with a fatherly smile, when his cell phone rang. Walsh, striving for perfection right to the end, was still shooting.

'The *actual* last scene we did, Fran was directing,' he laughs. 'I finished at four or five in the afternoon, it was on a Friday, and across town Fran was directing a unit that was still shooting.'

Walsh's 1B was occupied with a scene of Théoden and Éowyn on the Dunharrow plateau, cheerily discussing the likelihood of that king not returning from battle. Mortensen had been required by both units and, in now a fine tradition, had been seesawing across Middle-earth and Wellington town centre at regular intervals. Second unit director Richard Bluck had also been chalking off outstanding pick-ups from Moria, Fangorn and Orthanc all day.

Jackson grabbed Knowles, leaped into his car and swerved through the Wellington rush hour to reach Walsh before the last frame of film rolled through a camera. When it did, Jackson took a glass of champagne and their great jamboree finally came to an end.

CHAPTER 8

Miramar's Mecca of Merry Souls

As the shoot for *Meet the Feebles* wound down in 1988, with money short and most of the crew gone, Richard Taylor could be found running through the Wellington undergrowth with a deranged beaver on either hand. Beside him, his wife Tania Rodger was doing exactly the same. In front of them, running backwards, was Peter Jackson with a 16mm Bolex camera in one hand and an armed frog puppet on the other.

The young director was determined to finish every page of the script, and they were literally scrabbling to shoot the scenes of Viet Cong beavers chasing the 'frogs of war' through the jungle.

'This is just as good as it gets,' thought Taylor.

Right there, he reflects fondly, is everything you need to know about Jackson's energy, willingness and ingenuity to achieve what he needs — and to draw willing victims into his crazy orbit.

In some senses Taylor has never stopped running through the proverbial undergrowth of Jackson's dreams with puppets on his hands.

Growing up in New Zealand, he says, you pick up a mind-set that you can make anything work. You just have to give it a go. Living at 'the uttermost edge of the world' instils a can-do attitude. With enough effort, resourcefulness and, when it comes down to it, brazenness, anything you can imagine is achievable.

No one credits the influence of this oft-mentioned but mysterious New Zealand elixir on the success of *The Lord of the Rings* quite as much as Taylor, officially costume designer, special make-up, creatures, armour and miniatures supervisor. Unofficially, the brains (and Brains) of the operation.

'People I speak to all over the world, young filmmakers and budding creatives, tell me how inspired they are not only by the films but the manner in which they were realized. If you could somehow evoke that spirit in your book then I guarantee you'll have a bestseller.'

Taylor's oratory goes on, clear as a bell. 'It's an ingenuity born out of necessity. We have a local phrase, "Putting it together with Number Eight Wire."* It comes from our rural culture — if you want to fix something, you twist it together with fencing wire.'

Taylor should know. He grew up on his grandparent's farm to the south of Auckland, a background shared by many of the determined artists and hopefuls he has hired. 'A rural upbringing gives us basic training, motor skills and handicraft. As well as uncluttered thinking.'

Jackson, that shining example of uncluttered Kiwi thinking even if he hadn't been reared on the land, puts it down to problem solving. 'It is what New Zealanders are good at doing. You don't worry about what the rest of the world thinks. You just think, "We can't afford a combine harvester over from America, so we'll just get an old car and bloody build our own."'

'It gives us a unique flavour,' concludes Taylor.

In the moving city of Middle-earth making nowhere better exemplified that unique No. 8 flavour than Weta Workshop, the

---

* No. 8 Wire is British Standard Wire Gauge for the 0.16" high tensile steel wire favoured for sheep fencing, especially in New Zealand, where they put it to many versatile uses. Such is its cultural heritage New Zealand has a No. 8 Wire art prize.

fiefdom ruled over with good judgment, hands-on skill and a ready store of local axioms by Taylor.

Tolkien, he insists, was a perfect fit. Here was a story of the pluck and resolve of an unlikely species faced with a titanic quest. Obviously, when it came to cinematic world-building it was the inventiveness in No. 8 thinking that was put to use. Nothing was actually held together with fencing wire, although they did dice black rubber pipe into twelve and a half million chainmail pieces.

Beneath his John Lennon specs and short, sandy, boyish hair, Taylor is winningly eccentric. Partake of the trilogy's celebrated DVD extras and you will become accustomed to his declarative flourishes, as well as a mind dizzyingly absorbed by the minutiae of his craft and the worlds that surround it. To classify him a geek falls short by leagues: he is an effects archaeologist curating a museum of backstory. No weapon was forged, no necklace fashioned, no model tower raised and no denizen of Tolkien's deeps designed without its history being plotted out in the appendices of Taylor's imagination. With every paintbrush or scalpel or hammer, he trumpets, you are telling a story.

His dedication to his craft, the films and his director was an irresistible force. If the inner circle behind *The Lord of the Rings* took control of the Starship Enterprise, with Jackson issuing commands from the captain's comfy chair, then Taylor would most certainly be Scotty, dispensing doom through the intercom but eking out that last drop of power from the warp drive.

Within the extended family of Middle-earth mountaineers Taylor has cultivated his own folklore. Fans adore him. Even Kate Winslet, remembering happy days working with him on *Heavenly Creatures,* does a fine impression.

Taylor's father was an engineer and his mother a science teacher, bringing an appreciation of function and form. But severely dyslexic as a child, unable to read and write with any confidence until he was twelve, he expressed himself through art. He learned to sculpt using mud dung from the creek at the back of his house, more fascinated by the paintings of Hieronymus Bosch, Giacometti and Rita Angus than the tree climbing or roughhousing that distracted his peers. When it came to Tolkien, he admits he had been stirred more by the artwork than the books, especially the paintings of Alan Lee, who he came to know so well.

After studying graphic design and fine arts at Wellington Polytechnic, Taylor stayed in the city operating a freelance model-building business out of the one-bedroom apartment he shared with his girlfriend and key collaborator Tania Rodger, who had her own crucial part to play in their filmmaking future.

Taylor would throw a sheet of fibreboard across the bed as a not entirely stable worktable. Like Jackson, he and Rodgers would fall sleep to the stench of ammonia. That flat crammed with latex castings and sculptures was the first iteration of Weta Workshop.

He was a firm believer that you set your own destiny. Learning that an advertising producer he knew named Dave Gibson was producing a New Zealand version of the British satirical puppet show *Spitting Image*, he sculpted a puppet of Gibson and left it on his desk with a business card.

Gibson phoned the next day to offer him the job. He was also the only one who had applied.

Taylor and Rodgers worked on *Public Eye* for two series, making sixty-eight puppets out of the surprisingly durable New Zealand margarine, due to Plasticine and other sculpting materials being scarce.

And given you could comfortably fit the Wellington film community onto a bus, word soon reached him about this crazy guy up at Pukerua Bay attempting to make a science fiction splatter movie. Fellow model builder Cameron Chittock — who happened to be working for both of them — offered to bring him to set.

It was a meeting of hearts, minds and lunatic dreams.

Recalls Taylor, 'We became firm friends. Pete had just moved into town and we'd go over to his house to talk movies and all of the things we wanted to make.'

They would play softball on the beach on a warm summer's evening, and flick through Jackson's copies of *Famous Monsters Of Filmland* and *Cinefantastique*. One day, Jackson assured him, he would meet Ray Harryhausen.

So it was inevitable Jackson would invite his friend to join his next project, a zomcom titled *Braindead*. Taylor and Rodgers jettisoned the regular paycheque of *Public Eye*, determined to meet their blood-soaked future head on, only for the funding to collapse and be left with the dreaded possibility of no work. Jackson was back on the phone the next day: how did they feel about drug-addicted puppets?

'Ultimately, Tania and I were thankful *Braindead* fell over, otherwise *Meet the Feebles* would never have happened. And that was a year of the most incredible fun trying to keep up with the inventiveness of Peter. I said to Pete once how much I remember *Meet the Feebles* as being this incredible, joyous time. And he raised his eyebrows and said, "Really? Because I think most people found it pretty tough."'

There is something a little crazy about Taylor. His enthusiasm rises in equal proportion to the demands made on him. When *Braindead* was reanimated, Taylor would embrace the miniatures (including a rendition of a 1930s Courtney Place complete with working trams), speciality props, creature effects and gore. Consulting *Dick Smith Do-It-Yourself Monster Make-up Handbook*, his repertoire of unusual materials expanded to include Chelsea Golden Syrup, which mixed with gravy browning and apple slices gave the blood a lovely, stewy consistency.

'More blood!' became a regular refrain from the director, confounding his effects man, given the set was already coated in a crimson veneer as sticky as tar. Taylor transported the fake blood to set in beer kegs, and every item of clothing he owned was permanently stained red with food colouring.

Some days, he recalls, they just about died laughing.

'I look at the world in a very similar way to how Peter Jackson looks at the world,' he confirms. They share an 'unwritten language'. Jackson would always come back with new ideas, but he trusted his friend's judgement. On *The Lord of the Rings*, through Taylor, the Workshop gained a sixth sense for what their director required.

Joined by the elementary bonds of friendship made in those early, sticky days, Taylor and his team were ready for anything Jackson could imagine.

Taylor lets his mind slip back for a moment to those halcyon days of gore when Jackson educated him in the right kind of movies. 'I saw *The Thing* for the first time sitting at his place. And some of Ray Harryhausen's work that I might otherwise have missed. And various cult splatter movies. There is a misconception about Peter's early career that he was a schlockmeister making splatter movies because that was the limit of what he could make. But *Braindead* is an incredibly sophisticated piece of filmmaking, technically.'

*

In contrast to the marathon productions that would define his career, Jackson spent only one day working on *Worzel Gummidge Down Under*. He'd met the props guy at a party, and shown him a scrapbook of his models. Whereby the props guy, with a mind to an upcoming two-part storyline involving a pair of inflammable voodoo dolls, hired Jackson to make them. For which he would earn a princely NZ$100 dollars and an invitation to the set.

This double episode of the ITV export is significant for a number of reasons, quite apart from the high-wire tension of possessed scarecrows and eerie magic travellers. However humble the circumstances, a foundation stone was laid on a remarkable professional career — this was Jackson's first paid job in filmmaking. During his visit to the set out in the Hutt Valley he would meet Costa Botes, their third AD and also the film reviewer for *The Dominion* newspaper where Jackson worked. Jackson had filled him in on his struggles to finish *Bad Taste*. Here too, of course, is where he first caught a heavenly glimpse of Fran Walsh from afar. Botes would be the one to later introduce them.

As he rigged his latex dolls to ignite, here also was the match to the fuse of Jackson's pursuit of special effects as a means of storytelling. He would instinctually be drawn to stories in which special effects were bound to play an integral role. Even his more personal, 'real-world' pictures, *Heavenly Creatures* and *The Lovely Bones,* offer up a wonderland of teen obsession and a sweeping vision of the afterlife.

Jackson had thought the chance of any kind of filmmaking career lay in practical effects, like that of his heroes Rick Baker and Tom Savini. Between the ages of nine and fifteen, he had set his sights on being a stop-motion animator like Harryhausen. Directing was the stuff of dreams. But *Bad Taste* stirred something inside him, even as he stirred alien vomit in his mother's kitchen. He realized he was a director and would have to live with that fact. Albeit a director with a predilection for special effects.

'We didn't have any film schools in New Zealand, and there was no possibility in my mind that I would ever go to a film school in America. It would have been like going to the Moon. I used to send away for eight-minute Super 8 movies of various Ray Harryhausen scenes advertized on the back of *Famous Monsters of Filmland.* It would literally take six months for these films to arrive. The New Zealand psyche stems from not being able to rely on the rest of the world's infrastructure.'

If you want to create groundbreaking special effects you create a groundbreaking special effects house.

Jackson was a naturally gifted modelmaker. Chittock remembers showing him some of his own handiwork.

'Yeah, that's pretty good,' he said.

'I was like, "Well, let's see what you've done," and he took me down to his basement, and here's four years of special effects work, all these models and creatures, and I was absolutely blown away. This guy had done all this work on his own.'

Jackson also knew how to stretch a budget. With no money to create the requisite gore on *Bad Taste,* he would pop into the butchers on the way to set.

Chittock laughs grimly. 'The butcher would have all this blood, guts and brains — *a lot* of brains — all ready for Peter. At the end of every day I'd stink like hell, because all this stuff would bake in the lights, right? It was hideous!'

But it was the end result that mattered.

Quite honestly, it was the visual potential of Tolkien that had first excited Jackson about the book. The *how* thrilled him as much as the *what.* But the *how* of Tolkien had always been the great stumbling block.

In 1993, Steven Spielberg had found a way to revive dinosaurs in *Jurassic Park,* leaving Jackson's mind reeling with the possibility of what could be achieved. Middle-earth presented a challenge of a different order entirely. To bring Tolkien's sub-creation convincingly to the screen, even greater advances would have to be made. And he had faith that he would find a way.

Says Ken Kamins, 'Peter honestly believed that technology had finally caught up with Tolkien's imagination.'

Weta was officially founded in August 1993 for the making of *Heavenly Creatures,* two months after *Jurassic Park* hit cinemas. Until then Taylor had worked under the mantle of RT Effects, hopscotching around town between nine different workshops, each as dilapidated as the last. 'We were making it up as we went along,' he says. Nevertheless, outside of collaborating with Jackson, they picked up some impressive credentials: animated robots for a GM commercial; toothy, reptilian aliens for a television adaptation of Stephen King's *The Tommyknockers*; four *Teenage Mutant Ninja Turtle* suits for a live performance (for which Taylor lost his eyebrows in a minor conflagration); and a contract to provide the panoply of creatures for the durable sister television series *Hercules: The Legendary Journeys* and *Xena: Warrior Princess.*

This latter gig not only provided life-saving regular work, but foreshadowed the future with early appearances by a young Karl (Éomer) Urban as Cupid, plus Bruce (Gamling) Hopkins, Lawrence (Lurtz and Gothmog) Makoare, Dean (Fili from *The Hobbit*) O'Gorman and a large, bipedal tree bearing the hall-marks of a prototype Ent. Here too was an education in schedul-ing, budgets and fleet turnover. They would be given a week to conjure up two-thousand-year-old Greek myths.

Weta as a concern was co-founded by Taylor, Rodgers, Jackson, Walsh and editor Jamie Selkirk, another who had lent valuable assistance to *Bad Taste*. Faced with the practical demands of *The Frighteners* — and putting on a professional face in front of Hollywood — they agreed it was nigh time to find a perma-nent home for the company. And on a Sunday afternoon bicycle trip around Miramar, ostensibly to pick up a rubber plant from the garden centre on Park Road, Taylor and Rodgers had spied a derelict factory on Camperdown Road and saw the future.

There is a horror movie cliché, naturally originating with Stephen King, wherein supernatural events result from a house being built over an ancient native burial ground or some such desecrated lot. You do wonder whether something of the strangeness that would pour out of Weta Workshop (first known as Camperdown Studios) might have bubbled up from the soil. In 1907, this had been the location of an aquatic theme park, Wonderland: Miramar's Mecca of Merry Souls. It was then a psychiatric hospital, veteran hospital and variously a factory for pills, batteries, talcum powder and Vaseline.

Inside it was as grim as Moria.

The rabbit warren of corridors and shop floors was littered with rusty machine parts, the walls were caked in decades of industrial filth and barely a single window remained intact.

Yet you do not work for Peter Jackson if you cannot envisage what something will become, and when one unsound section of the building was condemned to demolition, Jackson suggested they 'rebuild it as a cinema'. In an impossible future, he would peruse the dailies from *The Lord of the Rings* in the 150-seat Camperdown Cinema.

*

Taylor had been privy to the possibility of a *Hobbit* movie with Jackson's first proposal to Miramax. And when he and his core design team — Christian Rivers, Daniel Falconer, Mike Asquith, Ben Wootten, Sean Bolton and Jamie Beswarick — were summoned to a fish and chip supper at the director's home in Seatoun in spring 1998, he expected to be getting down to specifics on Bilbo Baggins, twelve squabbling Dwarves and the Lonely Mountain.

But this conversation would be delayed for another decade. Jackson began with the news that there wasn't going to be a movie version of *The Hobbit* anymore. Any dismay was short-lived. Instead, he announced that they would be making *The Lord of the Rings*. In that instant, Taylor can remember picturing a deep chasm, and having a choice: he could stay on the safety of the ledge or take a leap and plunge into the dark of Khazad-dûm.

His friend asked what he was prepared to take on. Without hesitation Taylor stepped into the abyss: armour, weapons, creatures, prosthetics and miniatures. 'I chose to take on an insane amount of work,' he says, 'because it was necessary to create a truly integrated, Tolkienesque brushstroke over the films.'

Which is exactly what Jackson had hoped he would say.

As the director handed round his favourite Lee and Howe pictures, the room burst into a thrilling discussion over how they would even begin to tackle Tolkien's vast tapestry. Amid the excitement, Jackson would set forth his credo — they were going to make Middle-earth *real*.

Imagine being there on that evening, the almost electric sense of possibility filling the air as their chips were left to cool, suddenly forgotten.

Sculptor Jamie Beswarick couldn't help himself, and unbidden returned a week later with six maquettes — a Ringwraith,

Balrog, Treebeard, Cave-troll, Uruk-hai and Orc — at least four of which made it into the films almost exactly how he'd first sculpted them.

For all their admirable achievements with *Heavenly Creatures* and *The Frighteners*, Weta had yet to prove itself to the special effects world at large, over which Los Angeles held sway. To the outside world, New Line's willingness to accept that these tenderfeet would be furnishing Middle-earth was another symptom of their delirium. Weta were lacking the manpower, tools, materials, know-how, union control and the resumé even to begin to tackle this famous book. Which through the looking glass of New Zealand was just a red rag to a Balrog.

Beyond native gumption and desire, they had one distinct advantage — they were cheap.

'We were never going to be able to afford American effects houses,' reasons Jackson. 'We had a choice of one.'

The Workshop entered into a furious period of research and development, building up mood boards relating to each realm, species and individual character, experimenting with processes of manufacture and locating the hinterlands where they would give ground to their clean-fingered digital cousins.

'Going into *Lord of the Rings*,' says Taylor, 'you do carry a certain amount of anxiety that you are going to be able to fulfil that expectation.'

The initial budgeting alone was a nightmare. 'Without Tania we'd still be figuring it out today,' he admits.

They also had to channel two different but intertwined forces in Jackson and Tolkien. They were fortunate, says Taylor, to constantly be able to 'go back to the Bible'. And for the first two and a half years Jackson came in every day to scrutinize their sketches and models. Getting a literal feel for things stirred his creativity.

Like a gift from the gods, a year on from that first meeting Lee and Howe set up their drawing boards amid the joyful clamour in the 68,000 square feet of Camperdown Road. 'We were working literally cheek by jowl with all these people,' says Howe. Wandering from room to room, the two artists caught the sense of a brave new world. It was mild chaos, everything was still being set up, thought out, made up as they went along. But the passion and excitement were indeed like a drug. And the closer you looked, says Lee, 'You could see how good the work was becoming'.

The itinerant artists would eventually move into their own office at Stone Street Studios, within proximity of the shoot.

Says Howe, 'We probably spent more time in the same room than any other artists in history. We spent a good year and a half sharing an office on *Rings* and six years on *The Hobbit*. Neither of us wanted separate offices. It's more collaborative and stimulating to work alongside somebody like that — because Alan's very good.'

They weren't the only artists to have an influence on the films. Tolkien's tidy watercolour illustrations were, of course, consulted. And as Harryhausen had based a lot of his work on Gustave Doré's illustrations, so, notes Taylor, '*The Lord of the Rings* is strongly based on a Gustave Doré design aesthetic.'

Doré, sadly, was prevented from coming to New Zealand on account of being a long-dead, nineteenth-century French artist, but his Gothic woodcuts of Dante, Milton and The Bible remain as dynamic as movie stills.

Certain scenes, says Lee, were based on specific paintings. The look of the Grey Havens, for instance, was modelled on Claude Lorrain's *Seaport with the Embarkation of the Queen of Sheba*, and J.M.W. Turner's *Dido Building Carthage*. 'They had the light and atmosphere and sense of antique grandeur that we wanted to capture.'

While Taylor readily recruited local artists and crafts-people untried in film production, Weta was in need of experienced hands. Long before any greenlight was switched on, the Workshop's supervisor travelled abroad on scouting missions to make-up and props trade fairs, offering flyers to quizzical artists that boldly enquired if they were 'sick of living in Los

Angeles?' As he handed them over, Taylor would hint about a 'major project' soon to be underway in New Zealand.

For those who enrolled, *The Lord of the Rings* became that same addiction. Even when the project teetered on collapse, as Miramax drove too hard a bargain, they carried on regardless.

'We knew somehow,' proclaims Taylor, 'that this was our destiny.'

As it would be on set, fighting the elements, the striving, passion and physical dedication within the Workshop became invested into the warp and weft of the world. Every single item was imbued with the obsession of its makers.

Jackson nods in approval. 'I still have all the artwork, right from *Rings* until *The Hobbit*, carefully catalogued and archived. There are a lot of alternative designs, stuff not in the movie. I don't like looking at all that stuff, it drives me crazy, because I always see things that I prefer.'

'It was quite a place,' reflects Howe, 'when you think it was built up from literally nothing. Without Richard Taylor and his sort of wacky, impossible take on all of that stuff, nobody could have mustered the energy to do everything they did when they started out.'

Of particular interest to Howe was the proximity of the armour and weapons department, or smithy. Taylor had surmised that the best way to have your armour and weapons not look as if they were made in the 1990s was to make them in the 1490s. The forges of Miramar were real. 'We set up a blacksmith shop and brought in artisans skilled in old-school trades.'

Howe, being the keen medieval re-enactor, was sceptical. Classical armourers had been thin on the ground for centuries and this, he had fretted, was New Zealand: 'and they hired the armourer quite quickly'.

'I've found a guy making armour,' Taylor had reported to him excitedly. 'He's a panel beater from Karori.'

Howe was instantly won over. 'Pete Lyon turns up with amazing work. He'd done a pair of greaves for the lower leg.

And they are the most impossible piece of armour to actually make because they have to curve around the contours of the leg. I thought, "This is really looking up."' Glance out the Workshop window, and Howe could often be found sword fighting with the weapons department in the parking lot.

Lyons, who worked alongside Stu Johnson and Warren Green, had been servicing the needs of local medieval re-enactors and collectors for years. He even taught fighting techniques to the Wellington Medieval Guild. It was he who forged the sword with which Viggo Mortensen forged the identity of Aragorn. Every signature weapon had beautifully detailed, correctly weighted 'hero' versions for close-ups with five less detailed, safer aluminium and rubberized stunt versions. Mortensen refused to use anything but his 'hero' sword.

Once shooting, Taylor found himself commuting back and forth between the set and the Workshop. Which was a five-minute jaunt when it came to Stone Street. And agreeable enough with the sets and locations scattered across the greater Wellington area. But when the production was out among the hills of greater New Zealand it became exhausting, and the biggest hurdle Taylor faced was always the physical strength required.

'For instance, Mount Ruapehu was four and a half hours away,' he winces. 'I was commuting every day to the mountain, nearly nine hours a day, to be on set and look after everything there, then driving back home, getting a couple of hours sleep, before heading to the bottom of the South Island.'

Even without his near-permanent earpiece and cable coiling beneath his collar to a radio, Taylor would still be hearing voices in his head — mostly concerning foam latex deliveries or fitting a mouthpiece on an Uruk-hai.

'Looking back it had to be like that,' he says, 'because the numbers were staggering.'

He still has them to mind: they created 48,000 props over three films, and 10,000 facial appliances (thirty-two per day), including 2,000 pairs of hobbit feet.

'Just storing the stuff was a bloody nightmare.'

However remote the location, the design team would still have to bring their sketches and maquettes to the director for approval. Lee recalls a visit to Paradise where they flew out in the morning and spent a lovely day sketching beneath the trees, awaiting an audience that never came. They ended up flying all the way back. Getting a moment of Jackson's attention was often the hardest thing of all. At the studio, department heads could be found circling the director's chair like petitioners to a king.

And when granted a meeting, Lee had to learn to decipher the director's gnomic feedback. 'He would never openly criticise. If he didn't like something he would just be less enthusiastic.'

Those 10,000 foam latex prosthetics were made to provision muscly Orc body suits and facial appliances like plates of cold cuts; hobbit feet and ears; delicate Elf ears; and the nose applications that lent differing characteristics to the two wizards. Gandalf would gain a rounded, whimsical nose to compete with his beard, while Saruman's would be hooked like a beak.

Each and every prosthetic was treated as a work of art, seamlessly blended in and painted with the intention of giving even the lowliest Orc a place in the world. When it came to the 'kit' of features used for as many as 200 background Orcs in a shot — as with the weapons there would be 'hero' prosthetics for character Orcs — Taylor's team would devise fictional backstories: the petty quarrel behind this scar, the social standing behind three nose rivets, how a pair of eyes were blood red from patrolling the dark. When the Orcs' motley armour was proudly wheeled out of the Workshop on racks, it looked as if a *Mad Max* movie was holding a yard sale.

On-set make-up application was the province of the good-humoured Gino Acevedo. A 'strange kid' from Phoenix, Arizona, he had grown up addicted to the monster movies that played on local Saturday morning television. 'Classic fiends', he says, like Frankenstein, the Wolfman and Dracula. He was a man after

Jackson's heart. Inheriting his father's gift for art, Acevedo first took up with a local Halloween company specializing in monster masks and vampire fangs, but no one fulfilled their dream of creating the perfect rotting corpse by staying in Phoenix. So he migrated first to Los Angeles, where he would spread his talents for prosthetic painting in creature features like *Wolf* and *Independence Day*, before responding to one of Taylor's flyers and travelling over the rainbow to Oz.

If the stuntmen moaned about how hot and itchy it became beneath a layer of Orc hide, no actor suffered for their art to the extent of John Rhys-Davies. 'Gimli required a comprehensive set of silicone facial appliances,' explains Acevedo, whose job it was to transform actor into Dwarf. Jackson wanted something rugged and weathered about his Dwarves, and Rhys-Davies' entire face was smothered in a sheath of coarse skin that had to be repeated on his scale-double.

The four hours spent in Acevedo's chair, says Rhys-Davies, meant he 'missed out on a lot of the comradeship'. Worse still was that severe allergic reaction. Which, understandably, affected his mood.

'I developed this eczema, and crevices were appearing in my skin. I was this ugly, infected creature,' he explains, unflinching on the graphic details. 'My heart would be quailing now if I had to go back and do it again, and I don't think I could.'

Such was the actor's unsightliness and despondency he even sent his wife away so she wouldn't have to look upon his infected face. 'Everyone was aware of the special nature of the project, and everyone behaved damnably well. The only grumpy person was me; I'm afraid it all got the better of my temper once or twice, looking like shit and being unable to go anywhere.'

Acevedo devoted unsolicited hours to alleviating the actor's suffering. With his fellow technicians, he pioneered Weta's silicone prosthetic system, a piece of pure No. 8 thinking that added a barrier of latex between actor and make-up implanted with 'finely cut cotton flocking' on which the prosthetic could bond. The technique was also put to use on Old Bilbo, Lurtz and Sméagol's decline into Gollum.

The prosthetic artist's talent for painting realistic skin textures and colours — based on a boyhood collection of 'lizards, snakes and amphibians' — would also play a pivotal part in realizing the digital skin textures of Gollum. Indeed, Acevedo's professional journey mirrors that of special effects in general, as he would eventually transfer his very practical skillset to Weta Digital to head up their textures department, swapping his paintbrush for a keyboard, but occupied with the same tasks.

*

The call sheets add their own amusing footnotes on the variety and oddity of the Workshop's daily menu: one order of Shelob's pincers, or Celeborn's ear tips, or the large Uruk-hai leg puppets, if you please. They would have to build an animatronic Treebeard, and a dead mûmak two stories tall. However, the majority of the creatures born in the primordial think tank of the design room were destined to be pixels. And quite contrariwise this only drove the designers toward greater naturalism. Wootten, as well as being a fine sculptor, was a trained zoologist and he challenged his peers to use real-world animal references to anchor the fantastical in nature — they were regulars at Wellington Zoo to examine rhino hide and frog skin.

While vivid in their actions, Tolkien provided relatively little description for the likes of the Watcher, Balrog, Uruk-hai and fell beast, so designs were embellished from their own subconscious and gradually honed through sketches, sculptures and research until it got some way toward that ideal lurking in their director's subconscious.

The sculpting of maquettes was as much a process of characterization. Taylor urged them to find not only the look but also the heart of Tolkien's beasts. To depict them as merely monstrous was short sighted, they should see them as 'victims of circumstance'. Once approved, Acevedo would provide an organic epidermis and the creature would be scanned and sent to Weta Digital, where undoubtedly it would be refined again.

Scanning the maquettes, some of which grew to four and five feet tall, also necessitated a No. 8 brainwave. They simply didn't have any scanners big enough, says Jackson, but someone discovered how the meat industry in New Zealand used a handheld scanner for judging the weight of joints of beef. 'So we got our hands on this bloody meat scanner and used that for the scanning of the trolls and stuff. You just figure it out — it's a problem you've got to solve.'

Beyond his bestiary, the design team went to exorbitant lengths to evoke the depth of Tolkien's mythology in visual terms, defining an 'iconographic look' for each of the cultures that was still accessible to those who knew nothing of his books. The world of the Dwarves, edgy, geometric and labyrinthine; the naturally inclined Elves, spiritual and elusive; the hobbits, rustic and quasi-English; while man came in alternate factions from the ruffians of Bree to the horse-lords of Rohan.

They drew on more artistic sources: Celtic and Anglo-Saxon jewellery and manuscript illumination for Rohan, Art Nouveau for the Elves, Classical and Byzantine architecture for Gondor and Vernacular building styles and folk art for Hobbiton and Bree. This gave an undercurrent of real-world influence, but never enough to be a distraction.

'Even if Tolkien denied that there was ever analogous writing in what he was doing,' adds Taylor, 'we ultimately looked for the analogy in his work because in doing so we were able to enrich his design.'

The themes Boyens had brought to the writers' table would also be explored within the texture of scenes. To encompass, say, Tolkien's lamentation over the loss of pastoral England with the industrial revolution, Taylor pursued a 'progression in the pursuit of material wealth' taking hold of Middle-earth. The cottage industries of the Shire and the serene Elven havens giving way to the industrial clamour of Mordor.

Meanwhile, the faded Byzantine grandeur of Gondor, with its Nero-esque Steward Denethor, spoke of a classical civilization misguided by the lust for power.

To enter into a discussion with Taylor on Middle-earth is to begin a thrilling tutorial on the historiographical basis for Ents or Dwarven mining techniques. How, he implies, could it be otherwise? 'The plausibility of the landscape of Middle-earth was the chessboard on which the characters play out their role,' he observes grandly.

Says Jackson, 'I didn't want the fantasy to create a barrier between the audience and the movie.'

It was an odd sort of business, if anyone had the time or inclination to reflect upon it — realistic fantasy. But every item, often made overnight, had thousands of fictional years of culture invested into its fabric. Every creature belonged to the world.

'It was imperative that we explored design to its ultimate conclusion, and found an aesthetic,' crescendos Taylor. 'It's interesting, because the book was written by a single individual and suddenly two and a half thousand people were trying to realize that vision.'

And they had Jackson as their prism.

Like James Cameron, Jackson knew what it was to shape a film with his own hands. That tactility in the films, the sense of something handcrafted or gouged out of the rock, was an extension of the style that once splattered butcher's offcuts over *Bad Taste*. And it was what drew him to such a daring use of miniatures.

Early birds in Miramar became used to the sight of peculiar-shaped consignments being wheeled down Park Road covered in bin bags, with the odd steeple or branch sticking out. Underneath were miniature versions of Tolkien's architectural wonders — whatever your reaction to the book, the sheer payload of fictional details is inarguable — being transported to the miniature studio down the road.

Directed by another indomitable yet mild-mannered force in Californian special effects, photographer Alex Funke, the miniature studio shot featured sixty-eight individual, meticulous models —works of art — some of which, belying their nature, were as big as houses (hence the in-house coinage 'Bigatures'). 'You're fighting the scaling issues,' notes Taylor.

Jackson wanted the camera to glide in breathlessly close, to 'break away from the rigid shots of model castles and matte paintings' in the fantasy films he watched growing up. This was not only achieved through the staggering finesse of the models, following elaborate but architecturally thorough concept art by Lee and Howe, but also veils of dry ice and cunning lighting. With its dedicated crew, the miniature studio had the consecrated air of a cathedral.

Their remit covered particulars like the pebbles disturbed by Gollum's footfalls and the branches brushed aside by Treebeard. Rivendell was mounted as a series of islands on casters that could be shuffled around for different angles. Recalls Taylor, 'Alan Lee specifically supervised the painting of that model, he wanted to bring in autumnal colours: the Elves were in the autumn of their years, and their world was falling back into nature.'

If Howe had taken a special interest in the welfare of the armour, Lee could be found carving and painting the miniatures, quite literally leaving his mark. 'The model of Orthanc was made in wax; we carved it with penknives.'

The vast Isengard miniature, with Orthanc at its centre like the hub of a great wheel, also revealed the engineering involved. Too big for any soundstage, it had to be assembled from four-foot sections on the backlot at Stone Street along with a large mountain anchored with sandbags to stop it blowing over in the Wellington wind. Taylor then covered the circular expanse with tiny foliage, machine parts and sand, 'like toppings on a pizza'. It was also plumbed so that any rainfall could be pumped out quickly. Isengard survived four months of shooting.

Similarly, the twenty-one-foot-tall, sixty-six-foot-long model of the stairways of Khazad-dûm, leading down to the infamous stone bridge, had to be shot outside to allow room for the camera to crane above it. They worked on that set for a full year, finding birds and insects in the back of shots, and in one set of dailies a real lizard was caught on camera crawling up the stairs. Everyone cheered — it was like watching *The Lost World.*

'And where would we have been without the rock faces?' asks Taylor. Exemplifying an often surreal quest for realism, he would lead field trips to the blustery coastline to take mouldings from rock faces, and create a catalogue of rock moulds, from coarse to fine-grained, regularly topped up with another outing to the beach.

Given an early glimpse of the 'Constantinople Shot', any of Lee's lingering doubts were swept aside by the results from the miniatures studio. This was the grand title given to the early glimpse of Minas Tirith burnished by a low sun seen in *The Fellowship of the Ring.* 'You suddenly saw the potential of these miniatures. Minas Tirith had only been built for long shots, but they could get within an inch of it without it seeming fake.'

This was helped by Jackson's desire to keep his camera moving over his miniature strongholds — plunging from Orthanc and climbing over Minas Morgul — and a signature style evolved (heralded by the shots of the airborne Reaper in *The Frighteners*) to leap across Middle-earth in a breath. They were christened 'flyovers'. Virtuoso shots that hint of another eye watching over the world — a great creator, or the director himself.

'I loved the scale of the world, everything was always bigger than I thought. So you wanted these epic aerials,' explains Jackson, and out in the real world daredevil helicopter pilots were commanded to spin around mountaintops and plummet into valleys. 'It's actually interesting, not to diss anybody, but the first *Harry Potter* movie was made before we came out, before *Fellowship*. The second one was done after *Fellowship*. Look at the difference in the Hogwarts shots from one to two. In the first one they are kind of static. In the second one they are going in through windows. You think, somebody has seen our film.'

It's not a criticism, he maintains, it's flattery. 'After all, I'm the product of films I've seen.'

As *The Lord of the Rings* drew to a close, cabinets laden with Oscars and praised to every beautiful hilt, Jackson and Taylor came up with a unique way to reward the team at Weta Workshop (and fulfil that promise he once made to Taylor) — they invited Ray Harryhausen to Wellington. Having visited the scenic locations by helicopter, the stop-motion maestro came to the Workshop for the statutory tour and a brief Q&A with the crew.

Taylor smiles. 'It ended up lasting five hours.'

*

Once upon a time, Weta Digital was a fellow named George Port sitting at a boxy computer on the dining room table of a house on Tasman Street, between the cricket ground and museum. He had at his command less processing power than your average cell phone, and yet he conjured up fourteen visual effects shots for *Heavenly Creatures*, beginning an avalanche that would give us Middle-earth and *Avatar*'s Pandora.

Though he still adored the models and props of his youth, Jackson had sensed a change on the wind. First with *Terminator 2: Judgment Day* in 1991, then two years later with that first viewing of *Jurassic Park*, he saw into the future. He had only recently completed *Braindead* when he witnessed Spielberg's dinosaurs: he could still smell the film on his clothes, but he recognized that if he wanted to create truly fantastical films he must embrace this new artform.

Eventually, Wellington-born Matt Aitken would join Port. Officially the second member of Weta Digital, Aitken is still with the company today. Port followed romance north to Auckland destined to miss the train to Middle-earth.

With that strain of quiet, Kiwi affability, Aitken has an illu-minating way of talking, more like a patient teacher than a com-puter whizz. 'Matt's the one who can tell you all about those early days,' Jackson had announced.

'Well, I suppose I am,' reflects Aitken, 'it was certainly different.

We were all crammed into the house on Tasman Street, working it out as we went along. We had so little connectivity we could only check emails twice a day.'

The brains trust of Jackson, Walsh, Taylor, Rodger and Selkirk would club together to buy their leased Silicon Graphics Indigo computer outright (it was worth more than the house). This allowed Weta Digital to take further small steps into a gleaming future, adding filigree elements to *Forgotten Silver* and *Jack Brown Genius** before passing their first Hollywood test with *The Frighteners* (which, pro rata, contains more effects shots than *Jurassic Park*). But they were almost flattened when *King Kong* fell apart in 1996. Jackson had gathered them together in a room, spirits wilting, and promised he was going to 'try and get a much more ambitious film off the ground'.

They had no idea what he could be talking about, but Aitken says they always had faith.

Whether New Line knew it or not, Jackson had an ulterior motive. Each new film would help expand his faraway effects house. Middle-earth, he knew, could put them on the map. Venturing to a local technology vendor in search of upgrading to a terabyte of processing power, the salesman was flabbergasted — that was four times what he had sold to the Inland Revenue. By *The Return of the King* they had sixty terabytes of storage with miles of fibre optic cabling running beneath the sleepy streets of Miramar.

For all their ambitions, says Jackson, this was still a matter of necessity. 'We couldn't afford ILM — that was never even a consideration. So, we had to get our guys to be as good as ILM. A lot of the nuts and bolts were actually worked out in the eighteen months of the Miramax period.'

---

* *Jack Brown Genius* is a forgotten film in the Jackson canon. Written and produced by Jackson and Walsh, and directed by their friend Tony Hiles, it follows the exploits of an inventor (*Braindead*'s Timothy Balme) possessed by the spirit of a medieval monk who yearned to fly. File under: interesting curio.

Still, it was on Weta Digital where New Line's chief concerns would be concentrated.

Arguments over the costs of effects shots emerged as early as week two, when the shot of the moth visiting Gandalf at the top of Orthanc was thought too elaborate. Jackson, naturally, wanted to follow the creature flying the 500 feet to the summit of the tower (presupposing some magic agency, given the moth would have to flap at a thousand miles per hour to cover the distance within the sequence). New Line felt you could simply cut to the moth arriving in Gandalf's hands.

Jackson would get his way, with the miraculous animators also conveying a sense that the insect is listening to the wizard.

But as 200 animators gathered in Wellington from far and wide — America, UK, Italy, Spain, Russia, Australia — bringing a cosmopolitan mix of talents and approaches, the department began in disarray. Especially compared to Taylor's well-managed Workshop.

'On *The Frighteners* we did it the old-school way, where everyone kind of got a shot at everything,' admits Stephen Regelous, employee number twelve and pioneer of the extraordinary MASSIVE software developed for the battle sequences. 'It was the least efficient way possible, but it was a great learning curve. What was so successful about ILM is that they were built around a pipeline, so people can specialize. People could get really good at bolting on one thing.'

The demands of Middle-earth were too great for their scatter-shot approach. Making it up as they went along wasn't going to fly in the pressured arena of computer effects; counterintuitively CGI is the *most* time-consuming component of modern filmmaking. New Zealand ingenuity needed an injection of American proficiency, and with New Line applying pressure to get things sorted out, both Tim Sanders and Mark Stetson became casualties (but still credited) of the early blood letting.

As Walsh said, 'Good intentions were not enough.' They needed leadership.

Jim Rygiel landed in Wellington certain he would have to ship all the visual effects work back to Los Angeles. 'However, within the first forty-five minutes, I was swayed with the technical advancements and filmmaking skills that Peter Jackson had built in New Zealand. The task was to get the entire crew moving forward in production mode.'

He swiftly instituted the ILM principal in Miramar, enabling shots to flow efficiently along the pipeline, gaining their digital clothing layer by layer.

Even in 2000, when Rygiel arrived, audiences were becoming habituated to the *sturm und drang* of CGI spectacle and the danger was to reach for excess to keep them sated. Thankfully, says Rygiel, 'Peter absolutely knew what he wanted. And he was always very attentive to our feedback. My job was to help the director tell his story.'

There had never been any debate about how much CGI would be put to use, says Jackson: 'We didn't go into the movie making a CGI film. Lots of movies are made with effects being the primary draw, but this was *The Lord of the Rings*. We were using CGI to show what Tolkien wrote.'

The use of visual effects was to be as intrinsic as a stroke of Boyen's keyboard.

Nevertheless, virtually every frame of the three films contains a digital element, from reshuffling the background scenery (they basically moved mountains) to the fiery maw of the Balrog, extrapolated from a formidable Howe painting. The code to produce the flame and smoke was based on the actual physics of fire.

On occasion, even the Ring needed to be digital. The blood-red flares of magical lettering that appear when it becomes 'heated' could never be satisfactorily overlaid onto the real prop because the surface was too shiny. CGI Rings rather than physical Rings were used in all but one of the shots involving the lettering.

One Ring to fool them all.

Once Rygiel was on board, the advances Weta Digital made

were swift and remarkable. They were pursuing cutting edge techniques the likes of which ILM had only begun talking up: pre-viz, motion capture, key frame animation, particle systems, digital scaling, compositing and so on. But they were doing so in their own style, Jacksonesque to a degree, but something else as well. Weta Digital's house style has Tolkien in its DNA (Lee and Howe had a huge influence): more atmospheric and naturalistic, painterly even, than the crisp, clean lines of ILM. As the two houses came to dominate the field, one would lean toward naturalistic world-building the other to science fiction's polished geometry and the sweetshop frenzy of the superhero genre.

The complexity was dizzying, there was a whole department devoted to the tricky business of ensuring that motion-controlled camera movements aligned. In principle, a camera's movement on set should match that in the miniatures studio and those in the various elements of the digital universe, which would then be composited together as if it was all one shot.* Individual shots could be made up of hundreds of composited elements.

Dwarrowdelf, the forest of stone at the heart of Moria, says Aitken, 'was a real watershed moment'. It was their first entirely digital environment (having scanned in the actors to create digital Gandalfs and Frodos). While made entirely on a computer, the great chamber was still based on a Lee painting of angular, Art Deco columns receding into darkness. Taking the Workshop's unstinting lead, Aitken explains that each column was individually 'hand-tailored for its own chiselled look'. If they had simply cloned the columns, audiences would have picked it up straightaway. Though Aitken admits to a slight 'lighting cheat' that enabled them to behold more than Gandalf's staff would ever illuminate. So be it — the moment is a touch of unforgettable majesty.

---

* Put simply, compositing is the process of combining different elements into the same picture. Usually with the goal of suggesting they are all parts of the same image. Imagine looking through a series of glass panes, each painted with one element of the scene, stacked one after the other.

Such digital environments would have a more prominent part to play in *The Hobbit*.

Weta Digital still had their limitations. Water effects were beyond them. The frothing horseheads in the surge of the Mitheithel river summoned by Arwen, filmed at Skipper's Canyon near Queenstown, was the only shot made in America.

'We didn't have the wherewithal or the knowledge to do the raging water washing the Ringwraiths away,' explains Jackson. 'That was a Digital Domain scene. They had written their own software for doing water. We stumbled our way through the digital effects at the beginning. We had to write a lot of the software ourselves. But as long as you have got the right people, people who won't run away, people who say, "Okay, we can probably work that out." They probably will work it out.'

Even once New Line was appeased, Jackson wasn't going to rest on having proven his Miramar outlaws could rival the American cavalry. There was the impetus to achieve things that had never been done. Tolkien demanded it of him: the looming challenges of Gollum and the author's great battles would require state-of-the-art No. 8 thinking (and their own chapters).

The studio's cash injections notwithstanding, they were still working to a relatively constrained budget compared to, say, the second *Star Wars* prequel gorging itself silly on digital effects across the Tasman Sea. This also contributed to the control and care in the use of effects. Digital wasn't a means to an end, or a safety net.

In counterpoint to the hard bark provided by the Workshop, Weta Digital gave Middle-earth a phantasmagorical glow — its haunting *unreality*. That quality which Boyens felt so important, of crossing into a dream.

Indeed, during post-production, Jackson and Andrew Lesnie digitally colourized the films (along with supervising colourist Peter Doyle). The trilogy would be run through a powerful digital scanner, enabling them to grade the colours of every single frame as if it were a painting, before being run back onto film. The look was subtly altered, softening the 'harsh', clarifying New Zealand light to bring out an atmosphere *unlike* our own. After all the striving for reality Jackson wanted to hint at antiquity and magic, to 'push toward the Alan Lee/John Howe palette'.

We would view Middle-earth though mythical gauze, a veil of storytelling.

Jackson was enthralled by the possibilities the process offered: 'I thought it was one of the greatest tools for filmmakers that I'd seen.' A director could isolate parts of the frame, emphasize foreground or background, lessen or bloom the highlights on a face — as Boromir slips toward death the colour is steadily drawn from the warrior's cheeks. Jackson ended up digitally grading eighty per cent of the film. Though, he hastens to add, the alien blue of Elijah Wood's eyes was always natural.

Together, director and cinematographer produced an overall 'visual arc' for the trilogy that, said Lesnie, entailed a 'slow shift' toward darker and dirtier images. 'For *The Fellowship of the Ring*, I was very conscious of modelling with light, applying a black-and-white philosophy. For *The Two Towers*, I decided that the light should be less controlled.'

The second and third films occur against the backdrop of more aggressive landscapes, so Lesnie and his director 'hardened reality'. As fear mounts, so does the clarity of the image.

Giving a director 'infinite tweakability' did, however, test the patience of compositors struggling to ensure everything matched. A sequence they had been working on for months could be subtly altered at the eleventh hour, and they would have to go through it again frame by frame.

*

For good and ill *The Lord of the Rings* marks a border crossing into a digitally dominated special effects universe. In 2000, Weta was officially sliced in twain: the Workshop and Digital went their separate but still intimately connected ways. Growing exponentially, and not overly partial to the aroma of turpentine,

Weta Digital needed their own digs. They moved into an old panel beater's shop on Manuka Street, a well-aimed paper dart's throw away from the Workshop. Inside, it had been a junkyard of greasy old car parts and oil slicks. To this day, it remains head-quarters for one of the biggest visual effects houses on the globe, as peaceful and dapper as an art gallery.

Both departments remain part of 'the greater Miramar-based creative community of Weta Digital, Weta Workshop, Park Road Post and Stone Street Studios'. Or Wellywood — a sobriquet Taylor, for one, isn't fond of: they never set out to 'ape Hollywood', he insists, but stand on their own two hairy feet.

Six weeks before the end of post-production on *The Fellowship of the Rings*, Joe Letteri first felt the touch of aeroplane wheels on Wellington tarmac. An ILM veteran, a man who had worked on *Jurassic Park* no less, he was drawn by a game-changing challenge surrounding this character Gollum. Inspired by what he found, he would end up taking charge of Weta Digital, helping shape the completion of the trilogy, the future of the company and altering the path of an industry. Not that he knew it then.

Weta Digital now employs 1,500 people across a fleet of plush buildings, working on ground-breaking projects for directors like Spielberg and Cameron, the living emblem of Jackson's faith.

Letteri is astonished by how far they've come. 'We really used to stretch the system back in the early days,' he remembers, 'the software and the hardware. Boy, we had some massive crashes.'

Nothing a little No. 8 Wire couldn't fix.

CHAPTER 9

Proof of Concept

The Cannes Film Festival has always been another world. For ten chaotic days in May the tourist mecca teems with every species of film folk: stars, directors, producers, distributors, marketeers, publicists, journalists, agents, hangers-on, wannabes, hustlers, gazers and the legion of paparazzi. Each and every one of them jostling for attention in the spring sunshine.

Here is where movies and reputations come to be judged. It is the industry at its most joyously paradoxical: great art entwined with crass Hollywood, whose million-dollar yachts bob imperiously in the azure bay. The annual film bash on the Cote D'Azur is the conflict of cash and kudos writ large enough to smother a hotel. All the overpriced, overbooked five-star palaces that line up like wedding cakes along the Promenade de la Croisette — The Grand, The Majestic, The Carlton, The Martinez, The Noga Hilton — renting out their facades to garish billboards of Hollywood's current crop of would-be blockbusters. Back in 2001, the eagle-eyed might have clocked that there was not a single *Lord of the Rings* poster on display anywhere — New Line's big moment was lying in wait.

I was sharing a rented apartment two floors above a bakery on the Rue du Canada, a serviceable clutter of two bedrooms, kitchen, bathroom and sitting room that may have last seen a lick of paint when Hitchcock was in town. The lock was fiddly enough to madden a wizard.

My assignment was due to last five days — quite long enough: journalists who survive the full span of the festival tend to return with the complexion of Ringwraiths. There was the usual merry-go-round of screenings, meetings and drinks receptions wherein studios touted their wares like the sunglasses pedlars on the esplanade, but I had flown into Nice on 9 May and paid a king's ransom to taxi into Cannes with a singular purpose. I was there to view a promised twenty-six minutes of footage from *The Lord of the Rings* and to interview Peter Jackson and assorted members of his cast in the mysterious Chateau de Castelleras, which, according to the map in the front of my guidebook, was situated atop a small hill twenty-five minutes away from the main drag of the festival.

There was also due to be a party of special magnificence in its sprawling grounds. The medallion-shaped invites were the one place you could see an image of Frodo's pensive face — as well as the Black Speech of Mordor — if you were fortunate enough to have one. In Cannes, party tickets equate to social standing, and none was craved as deeply as that that granted entry into *The Lord of the Rings* shindig on Sunday, 13 May. If New Line were less frenzied with preparations, they might even then have detected that their trilogy of films was arousing considerable curiosity.

What was undeniable was that this was a long, long way from New Zealand.

Yet Jackson was no stranger to Cannes. He had first gone under markedly less rarefied circumstances in 1988 with *Bad Taste*, while unemployed and still living at his parents' house. It was to be the outside world's first taste of the director's ener-getic style, and he had also hoped to raise funds for *Braindead*. It would take another four years before he returned with his magnum 'o-puss'. When a suitable berth was not made available for *Heavenly Creatures* in 1994, he had temporarily defected to the Venice Film Festival, held in late August.

It is worth clarifying that the Cannes that had been so beneficial to his early career was not the Film Festival proper, with its red carpets and official selections, but the bustling underbelly of the market where movies of every ilk come to be sold to the distributors of the world.

The screening of *Lord of the Rings* footage would also be unofficial, a sideshow taking advantage of the mustering of distributors and press, and the amplifying power of the annual event. Nevertheless, it would completely overshadow a formal programme which opened that year with Baz Luhrman's modish musical *Moulin Rouge!* and presented the Palme d'Or to Nanni Moretti's moving account of a family dealing with grief, *The Son's Room*.

Readying the footage had been a disruptive business. They had to effectively jump the gun on certain special effects and the recording of Howard Shore's score. But Jackson can now see that New Line wanted to 'announce the films in a way that was undeniable'.

*

Even as the shoot had stretched into its second year, Hollywood maintained a perplexed attitude toward the films. What *was* going on over there on that tiny island deep in the Pacific from which so little was heard? So far, all New Line had seen fit to reveal was a two-minute promo, uploaded onto their website on 7 April 2000. Like a miniaturized version of the pitch documentary, it cut together talking heads and behind-the-scenes footage with bonus flashes of the hobbits surrounded on Weathertop, Arwen on horseback, Mount Doom and glimpses of Boromir, Aragorn, Saruman, Gandalf and gruesome Orcs. While appetizing, this did have the slightly deflating effect of reminding fans that it would still be well over a year before we saw even the first film. Since then not a frame of footage had been seen outside of New Line or New Zealand.

So while the shoot literally toiled up hill and down dale, a Greek Chorus of sceptisim carried on with its Cassandra-like predictions of doom. This was Bob Shaye's swan song, New Line's death knell, another profligate vanity project slipping out of control and into the annals of cinematic folly.

'Until that footage screened in Cannes,' says Ken Kamins, 'most people in this town thought Bob Shaye had lost his mind.'

In an article charting Shaye's fortunes, former Viacom chief executive Tom Freston remembered being with a Hollywood studio head when they heard that Shaye had 'tripled down' on *The Lord of the Rings.* 'The guy looked at me and said, "What an asshole."'

The background radiation of negativity depressed Jackson. 'It was so unfair. No one had any concept of what they might be achieving. Or how any audience might react.' It was all *schadenfreude.* Even the local New Zealand press had joined in, mustering like crows to pick over the scene of his great failure. 'We had been beaten up a lot in the press,' he says ruefully, 'we were a bit of a joke. It was always stories about what would happen if we fail, never the possibility the films might be a success.'

There had been exceptions. *Ain't It Cool News* maintained its position as head cheerleader. And Jackson had been amazed to make the front cover of film magazine *Empire* — which I represented — before they had even finished shooting. The day remains fixed in his mind. They were working on scenes at the fell watchtower of Cirith Ungol where Frodo is held prisoner by a garrison of ill-disciplined Orcs, when the director was handed the new issue of the magazine that had wended its way over to New Zealand from the United Kingdom. On the cover was the image of Frodo gazing upon an unsheathed Sting.

'I brought it on set and we all looked at it and it was like, "Oh my God, oh my God, it's happening." It lifted everyone's spirits.

It was nice to feel there was a bubble of enthusiasm out there, something like that actually makes a bit of a difference.'

Like *Ain't It Cool News*, *Empire* came to be seen as a trusted friend, a modern variation on his beloved *Famous Monsters of Filmland* that was crazy for movies — crazy for *his* movies.

But if the core fans were being partially sated, there was a growing discontent among those with an actual stake in New Line's ambitions. A legacy of the company's early status as a struggling independent was written into its baroque distribution structure. Something its new owners, Time Warner, had trouble swallowing. Especially when the profits began to flow like the Silverlode, and it was estimated that they would miss out on a share of an estimated $1.9 billion gross international profit. Whereas New Line was the de facto owner and producer of their films, and distributor in the USA, the international rights were sold to a network of regular independent distributors. The nature of these long-running deals required that their partners pay up front for the rights, which were offset against the budget. Which also meant there was no backing out even if it appeared as if New Line had lost all sense of proportion and backed 'Howard the Dwarf'. In effect, all of them were risking their futures on Shaye's gamble on *The Lord of the Rings*.

Along with the ameliorating effect of German and New Zealand tax breaks,* the international markets made up sixty-five per cent of the trilogy's total budget (some reports have it as high as seventy-five per cent). This undoubtedly contributed to Shaye's willingness to take the risk in the first place. But it added significant pressure. There were a lot of investors to keep happy,

---

* There were a couple of tax shelters New Line was able to employ. To encourage the agreement to shoot there, the New Zealand government offered to offset local taxes. This was also a time when the German Neuer Markt (secondary stock exchange) was active in film financing and, according to Kamins, 'offered a significant German tax fund that New Line was able to specifically apply against the second and third movies'. On the end credits there's a 'GmbH' logo, which in German denotes a company with limited liability.

and they were growing restless. Companies like Entertainment Pictures in the UK and Metropolitan Filmexport in France, family run businesses, were anxious to know their investment would bear fruit. A collective anxiety was beginning to pollute the production from within New Line's apparatus.

Kamins explains that this was exacerbated by the extended nature of the project. 'We started in 1999, and the first movie wasn't due until December 2001. So you're out of a lot of money, and you have to wait two years or more for a result — and if movie one fails, movies two or three become the biggest made-for-television movies ever. It was hard to relax, is what I guess I am saying.'

The year before at Cannes, Kamins had bumped into Shaye late one night in the operatic lobby of the Majestic. Principal photography hadn't even reached the halfway mark but the reality of the investment was really starting to hit everyone in the gut.

Shaye leaned in close to Kamins. 'You need to make sure that your guy understands that there are a lot of people who have put it all on the line for these movies. These are family owned businesses in many cases. And if it doesn't work, we're all up shit creek.'

Kamins can still picture him: the trembling in his voice, the deadly earnest look in his eyes. 'It wasn't anger. He was really trying to convey something to me on behalf of himself, but also for all those small companies who had invested a lot of money.'

Moreover, New Line was in the grip of a cold streak. Longtime production president Michael De Luca, Shaye's crown prince, had been dismissed after a string of costly flops. The dire $80 million Adam Sandler comedy *Little Nicky* hadn't even fooled his most undemanding fans, and the Kevin Costner thriller *Thirteen Days* was decent but unattended. But the death knell for De Luca was the Warren Beatty vehicle *Town & Country*, this midlife romcom pitching the old lothario into romantic entanglements with Diane Keaton, Andie MacDowell and Nastassja

Kinski had somehow swollen into a runaway production beset by reshoots, rewrites, recasting and rotten press. The film ended up costing a staggering $90 million but made under $7 million.

Behind the scenes, the talk was that Shaye had finally tired of De Luca's behaviour. In the late 1990s, De Luca was known to party hard: tomcatting around Hollywood, arriving to work on a Harley and generally acting more like a rock star than a movie executive, a lifestyle that culminated in a tabloid scandal when he was found enjoying oral sex at an exclusive Hollywood bash. Bitchier rumours hinted that Shaye was jealous.

Even as his precious *Lord of the Rings* had been greenlit, Ordesky had weathered a 'terrible professional experience', having bungled an opportunity to licence the rights to *The Blair Witch Project* at the Sundance Film Festival, only to watch it become one of the most profitable films of all time.

The upshot was that the company's hopes, if not its future, now fully rested with Jackson and Tolkien.

Even after the pressure release of Cannes, Shaye wouldn't let Jackson forget what was at stake. Obliged to attend a party at the New Line chief's Beverly Hills mansion (which boasted an $11.3 million Matisse), while *The Fellowship of the Ring* was still in post-production, Shaye had pulled him into a bathroom to talk. It was the first time he had seen what he calls 'the heart of Bob'. Shaye launched into his sermon about how much was riding on the films — jobs were at risk, livelihoods. He beseeched the director that the films had to be as good as they could possibly be. He was genuinely worried; scared Jackson might let them all down. There were tears in his eyes.

'He was very, very upset about it. He was just trying to say to me do your very best. I said, "Sure, obviously, I'll do my best."'

What else could he say?

Toward the end of 2000, Shaye and New Line were determined, in the vernacular of Hollywood, to change the narrative. It was time to crack open the door and show something more of *The Lord of the Rings* to the world.

The first decision was to fly a handful of their closest partners to New Zealand in December 2000 — at the tail end of the shoot — and like heads of state give them a taste of the country, its enthusiasm and its wine, tour them round Jackson's operation and the wonders of the Workshop, finishing with a screening of select footage that inevitably circumvented incomplete special effects.

For Ordesky and the hierarchy of executives it was a tense occasion. 'All we could show them were talking scenes.' These people who were investing their futures on the promise of spectacle would be confronted with peculiarly dressed actors saying incomprehensible things to one another. 'But they were hugely excited by it,' he reports. It was the first real sense from outside the company of the quality of what they had on their hands.

Months earlier, Michael Lynne had accompanied Shaye down to Wellington for one of their few royal visits. There was the usual programme: a visit to the set and Workshop then, as is standard with visiting studio heads, a viewing of edited material.

For Jackson it was another reminder how far away he was from Hollywood, and not only in miles. 'It was a bit like the *Guns of Navarone* moment with Bob Weinstein: Michael was in the theatre with Bob, and we were screening that sequence where Boromir dies. . .'

Afterwards, there had been an ominous silence before Lynne spoke up.

'My God, it is actually a *drama.*'

'I think he thought it was *Conan the Barbarian* or something. That was when New Line began to get a hold of it. Even though the script was there, and the book, this was the first time they had seen anything cut together and it gave them a perspective on what they had actually made. They finally understood where we were going with it.'

Buoyed by the initial response from the foreign distributors, Shaye, in collusion with his head of marketing and distribution, Rolf Mittweg, made an even bolder decision — one that would completely reshape perception of the project.

Says Ordesky, 'The thought was simply let's do this on a world stage for the same people, but add the press.'

They would give all their clients and a select group of journalists an amuse bouche of Middle-earth footage at the Cannes Film Festival, some seven months ahead of *The Fellowship of the Ring*'s due date. This was still enormously risky: if the scenes went down poorly it would only confirm the rumours of disaster. Yet it was imperative they make a point to the world at large — that they knew what they were doing.

'This was kind of the New Line way,' laughs Ordesky. 'There was always a lot of pressure and a lot of agonizing but ultimately the bold decision was the one that always got embraced.'

There was a precedent for electing Cannes as a litmus test. Faced with a calamitous narrative about a bloated, inchoate, spendthrift production and an unmanageable artist-director — Francis Coppola had even gone as far as putting up the family home as collateral on the film — a jumpy United Artists had given in to Coppola's demands and risked entering a work-in-progress of *Apocalypse Now* in competition at Cannes in 1979.* It paid off handsomely, winning the Palme d'Or, even with Coppola upbraiding an auditorium full of journalists for their 'irresponsible and malicious gossip-mongering'.

In one swoop the film was reborn as a work of groundbreaking cinema.

New Line certainly wasn't going to hazard showing an entire work-in-progress of *The Fellowship of the Ring*. Whole scenes weren't even shot yet. Jackson wasn't due to finish three weeks of supplementary shooting on the first film until late April. In a very real sense, the hood was up with pieces of the engine still scattered across the garage floor.

---

* The lengthier 196-minute cut that was shown in Cannes would eventually be released as an extended cut entitled *Apocalypse Now Redux* including but not necessarily improved by the reinsertion of scenes such as the Playboy Bunnies and French plantation sequences.

Still, he was convinced to down tools and bring a showreel to the Riviera, where he and the principal cast would give an account of themselves amid the gaudy stunts and arthouse snobberies of the biggest film festival on Earth. He was more than aware of the irony: here he was adapting a book notorious for its length, and he had to prove himself with something less than a twentieth of his planned three-film running time. It also involved two of his least favourite aspects of the film business: a very long flight and a very big party. But he could see the benefit.

'New Line really wanted to go out there in May and do something that was going to shut everybody up.'

That auspicious assembly of footage had its own troubled birth — sending an early warning that reaching a consensus on final cut wasn't going to be straightforward. Shaye had originally satisfied himself that an extended trailer would suffice. An emboldened Jackson countered that they should unveil an entire, self-contained sequence that demonstrated the pace and quality of the actual film — rather than the whirligig of marketing. The Cave-troll confrontation in the Mines of Moria, to his mind, fit the bill. Here was the Fellowship showing their mettle, a fine demonstration of the special effects being achieved by Weta Digital — one of the many things being openly questioned in Hollywood — and in the confines of Moria a sense of the concreteness of Middle-earth without giving away the greater wonder of the world outside. Plus, it came early enough in the story to have progressed further along the post-production pipeline.

Shaye, Lynne, Mittweg, and Ordesky flew into Wellington to view the footage. It didn't go well. 'There followed some very stressful discussions about what should and shouldn't be in it,' recalls Ordesky.

Jackson's initial twenty-nine-minute cut was, Shaye reported, 'too dark, too interior; it didn't reflect the full scale and variety of the films'. Feeling like he was already halfway up Everest, Jackson wearily contended he knew nothing about 'making marketing materials' and would bow to Shaye's wisdom. Shaye and his team were welcome to re-edit the footage and they would sign off on the showreel together.

Shaye chose to bookend fourteen minutes of sustained Cave-troll action with Hobbiton and scenes that lead up to Moria on the front, and end with a montage of images from all three films.

'The reel definitely got better,' concedes Jackson.

Yet as they arrived in Cannes they were collectively terrified. However confident you might be that your vision is rich and cinematic and truthful to Tolkien's creation, you can have no idea how people will react.

'Honestly, I'm not sure I've ever myself, let alone on behalf of a client, felt that kind of pressure,' admits Kamins. Half an hour before the first screening, he was standing in a stairwell behind the projection booth alongside Jackson, Shaye and Ordesky, and none of them said a word. 'I don't know whose skin was whiter. Because it was all just going to happen or not happen then and there.'

*

The entrance to the Olympia 2 sits unobtrusively on the Rue de la Pompe, away from the Croisette, which even by midmorning had the genteel ambience of the fall of Saigon. On the overcast Friday morning of 11 May 2001, this is where I was standing quietly awaiting the 10 a.m. screening of footage from New Line's *Lord of the Rings* trilogy with a mild sense of the absurdity of the occasion.

There was little fanfare, no red carpet awaited the small party of journalists who milled outside the locked doors of the cinema, speaking into mobile phones, fussing over getting tickets to the screening of the new Coen brothers film, *The Man Who Wasn't There*, due that evening at the same venue. There was an assumed nonchalance to the members of the media, as we tried to disguise our anticipation. But already this felt like the most meaningful screening at the festival, as if indeed we were venturing into a proving ground. Rather than the expectation of failure, the usual waspish cynicism characteristic of the fourth estate's film department on their annual jaunt to southern France, there was only the unspoken desire to hurry now and get inside to see what the director of *Heavenly Creatures* had done with so famous a book. Some childlike spirit had come among us. We needed it to be good.

So when New Line personnel came to unlock the doors and there was a brief stutter of confusion while a key had to be located, a wave of panic ran through the gang of hardened, pale-faced critics pressed up against the glass. From the inside it probably looked like *Dawn of the Dead*. The problem was swiftly resolved, and those who could speak 'friend' (i.e. you had the correct ID) could enter and take your seat.

Jackson has worshipped in the Church of Cinema since he was a boy, and, like the Embassy in Wellington, the Olympia 2 has had a particularly blessed effect on his career. It was here thirteen years before that *Bad Taste* received a standing ovation from a rowdy screening before selling to ten countries. In 1992 people were almost coming to blows in their efforts to get into the three showings of *Braindead*, after which Jackson and his producers went for celebratory ice creams.

The Olympia 2 is a fine cinema with sumptuous brown leather seating, but New Line weren't willing to take any chances with their prize and had kitted out the French picturehouse for the occasion with a brand-new sound system worth half a million dollars. If they were going to make a statement, they wanted to make sure everyone heard it loud and clear and in Dolby stereo.

Jackson and Shaye stepped out in front of the screen to give their introductions. They made an amusingly apposite couple: one tall, finely dressed and slightly remote, the other small, round and resolutely overcoming the stress of being far from his comfort zone while wearing a pair of weathered shorts. The immediate impression was that he would much rather be sat awaiting a glimpse of Middle-earth in the stalls.

'This footage arrived wet at the airport and our team has been blowing on it to get it dry,' he joked nervously, before iterating that what we were about to see was far from complete, and much of it had a temp score (the same heroic themes borrowed from *Braveheart, Gladiator* and *The Last of The Mohicans* he had used for the pitch documentary), although Howard Shore had completed scoring for the extended scene in the middle. So we would also be getting a first taste of the music.

That patchwork of scenes and clips that followed — barring a couple of shots that ultimately never made the cut — is now so familiar that the birth-of-greatness aura that surrounds the moment appears overwrought. But as we reluctantly stepped back out into the daylight, it honestly felt as if we were the chosen few whose task it now was to spread the word. With the best will in the world, no one had expected it to be *this* good.

*

The Footage: As the New Line logo departed, the screen burst onto the idyllic vision of a wizard's arrival, crossing the stone bridge and climbing the Hill to Bag End. Here was the Alexander farm in all its verdant glory, Tolkien's Hobbiton in uncanny duplicate. The first sensation was the rightness of it all: the colours, the textures, the idling hobbit yokels and the quaint, quasi-Edwardian circular front doors that bore into the hill. As Ian McKellen's Gandalf, unquestionable within seconds, greets Ian Holm's Bilbo — whose giddy hobbit mannerisms took more getting used to — we got our first taste of the challenges of scale. You could sense the digital tricks and editing sleight of hand at work, but quite what was just out of reach, and the urge to fathom the deception soon wore off as the characters took hold. Then came wonderful glimpses as brisk as fireworks: Bilbo's disappearing act at the party, Frodo inheriting the Ring, the hobbits encountering a grim Strider, Saruman's dire predictions, battle scenes, snow, Galadriel, the Council, the forming of the Fellowship and then the fateful decision to take a darker path. 'We don't go over the mountain,' declares Gandalf. 'We go under it.'

The Mines of Moria was the passage in the book to which Jackson most naturally responded. Barring a snowed-up pass, the journey through the subterranean Dwarven city was the first major obstacle confronting the Fellowship. Tolkien's vivid ruin, carved into the heart of a mountain range, was fraught with traps and monsters.

This was the perfect test case for how he was shaping something directly cinematic while keeping faith with the book. Here was the shock and awe of Peter Jackson's Middle-earth: vertiginous thrill; rank, crumbling antiquity cast in silvery-blue light; and the breathtaking, up-closeness of combat with Orcs and worse, without surrendering to fantasy. For those who knew the book, here, unmistakably, was Tolkien, only invested with a new energy.

When it came to CGI, it was soon clear that Jackson would not be fixed by preordained codes. In the fourteen minutes of Cave-troll combat that followed, the camera doesn't sit on the sidelines to admire the handiwork but plunges into the action.

This was Jackson's tribute to Ray Harryhausen, but he was intent on outdoing his hero. The incremental nature of stop-motion animation forced Harryhausen to lock his camera in place. Looking back, Jackson grins, delighted at his heresy. 'I wanted to do a Harryhausen thing, but get far away from what constrained him. The troll wasn't a special effect that we did with beautifully prepared shots. We are in the midst of things with a handheld camera, trying to follow him the best we can as he rampages round.'

The decision to show off such a complex effects shot led to a dramatic redeployment of resources at Weta Digital. For the weeks preceding Cannes, it was basically all hands to the Moria pump. To map out the whirl of documentary-style camera moves, the motion-capture department created a virtual version of Balin's tomb where the Fellowship has halted to discover the fate of Gimli's cousin before being cornered by a Cave-troll and his keepers. Holding a virtual camera (attached to a 'node' they carried), the cameraman viewed the set through virtual reality goggles, venturing around inside and encountering a primitive version of the creature.

Says Jackson, 'That was possibly the first time anyone had done an animated pre-viz sequence. I went onto the stage with a virtual camera and shot the scene like it was handheld. I'd literally run out of the way as the Cave-troll thundered toward me.'

All the moves were then replicated on set and in the key-frame animation used to create the Cave-troll. The creature itself was a stunning representative of how Weta Digital was approaching the creation of life with Frankensteinian obsession, building their digital menagerie in layers, first a skeleton then the corresponding musculature then skin, all working in sympathy with one another, with separate facial animation to communicate inner life.

It was a concept, says Jackson, which dated back to the Miramax era. 'You have a functioning skeleton and build up the muscles that really worked, then put the skin over the top of the muscles. I don't think many other people had approached it like that. They usually just made a digital puppet that they moved around in the computer. We sort of did it organically, like the real thing.'

The look of the creature had been hard to pin down. The fairytale cliché of lumbering semi-giants with big noses and cavemen pelts was everything they stood against. The eventual Weta Workshop maquette scanned into the computer stood five-foot tall and mixed blunt-nosed, apelike features covered with elephant hide and a cloddish, humanoid frame not unlike the Hunchback of Notre Dame.* On screen, the motion-captured creature, its moves choreographed to the precision of a dance,

---

* The Cave-troll's differences to the three relatively more human-looking and conversational trolls in *The Hobbit* — and briefly spotted ossified in *The Fellowship of the Ring* — were post-rationalized as a matter of age, as anything. The poor Moria version was only a baby.

evoked a visceral animal rage. Yet Jackson catches haunting Harryhausen-like grace notes as the beast falls, felled by a (digital) Legolas arrow through the skull, its face softening into dismay and confusion.

The creature's pain touched us.

'We wanted to make the Fellowship's victory somewhat ambiguous,' explained chief animator Randy Cook, interviewed in 2002. He would write out interior dialogue for the troll, and then have his eyes and facial expressions convey these thoughts as closely as possible.

Characteristic of the creative flow between departments, it was Cook who came up with the idea of having the Cave-troll on a leash, 'to make it clear the troll was actually the goblins' flunky.'

Amid the swirl of individual contests that made up the battle, the Fellowship were often replaced with digital doubles — it didn't pay to fling Viggo Mortensen across the room. Or part-digital doubles — Legolas gains magic legs as he sashays onto their hulking foe (in the finished cut). When Frodo is swung by his ankle what we, in fact, see is a convincing puppet version of Elijah Wood. The thrill and the immediacy of the action, splattered with Orc blood as black as tar, crescendoed as the Fellowship dashed across the Bridge of Khazad-dûm, and out of a plume of black smoke leered the Balrog with a molten grin.

Jaws dropped to the Olympia floor. But it hadn't ended.

In another crescendo, the footage bowed out with a montage to remind us that this was merely a foretaste of three films' worth of such spectacle: the night-clad battlements of Helm's Deep; the ruins of Osgiliath; windswept, glorious Edoras; Théoden cursed and revived; the siege of Minas Tirith; Sam at Cirith Ungol; conflicted Faramir; demented Denethor; the charging Rohirrim; and Frodo clutching the Ring at the Cracks of Doom.

Here was both Shaye's desire to boast of the scope of the project and Jackson's determination to show the heft of the dramatic action.

Only Gollum was conspicuous by his absence.

To this day, there is a real distinction in Jackson's memory of before and of after Cannes that pivots around Moria. 'It is inevitable that that sequence symbolizes an important moment of time,' he acknowledges. 'It was the cornerstone of the reel we took to Cannes. That footage was going to make or break us. But it made us.'

There had been a standing ovation from the foreign distributors, born as much from relief as elation.

'Our French distributor, Sammy Hadida [cofounder of Metropolitan Filmexport with his brother Victor], lifted me off the ground and kissed me in his excitement,' laughs Ordesky.

'The press were making their feelings known very openly to New Line and very quickly,' recalls Kamins. 'Word was spreading fast.'

Indeed, you would swear everyone in Cannes had seen the footage and were the first to know that New Line were in possession of the new *Star Wars*. In truth, precious few had.

'You can tell the scope of this film just from twenty-five minutes of the preview — it looks epic and dramatic and remarkably well cast and acted,' said *The New York Times*.

'It captured Middle-earth perfectly,' sang *BBC Radio 1*.

The Sunday Times rhapsodized about technical effects, 'so skillful it is hard to tell where the real actors end and the computerized images begin.'

'OhmygodfuckingcoolWOW!!' swooned *Ain't It Cool News*.

The news sprang from yacht to yacht, restaurant to restaurant, screening to screening: 'The best film at the festival isn't even in the festival.' I got into the Coen brothers that night, which proved a strange, existential noir clothed in velvety black and white, a film I have come to appreciate, but that night it failed to sink in. All I wanted to do was stand in bars and talk about Cave-trolls.

When they had come out of the first screening, Jackson recalls heading to a 'rooftop cocktail thing'. There they simply sat around with drinks in their hands and nobody said a word as the sun set. 'We were all just numb.'

After the first distributor showing, Ordesky had slipped back into the projector booth. He stood there alone for a few moments steadying the intensity of his feelings: relief, validation, pride, the thrill of contemplating what the finished films might be like and the knowledge that this was going to change all their lives.

Back in New Line's frenetic office in The Majestic, the marketing and publicity teams were devising ways to maximise the moment but not let things get out of hand. Following the hullabaloo of Cannes the studio imposed a deliberate six-month publicity blackout in fear of the films being overhyped. Leave them wanting more was Shaye's attitude.

The most immediate effect of Cannes was that it informed the editorial process for the rest of *Fellowship of the Ring* in a positive way. Such a validation of Jackson's approach lightened the load. 'Everyone was feeling really good now,' says Kamins. 'Like, okay, let's put our foot on the gas. Let's ensure this film has everything it possibly needs.'

When the weekend's press responsibilities were over with, Jackson could retreat from the public eye and get on with finishing the films, charged with renewed confidence and more importantly backed by a studio finally alive to the fact this unlikely director was the star of the show.

*

I found Jackson perched on a director's chair beneath a canopy of oaks, which would rain catkins upon us throughout the interview. It was a fitting tableau: Mistral-stroked rustic flamboyance reconceived as Middle-earth cocoon.

The Chateau de Castelleras with its panoramic vistas of Provence and the Mediterranean looked the part. Mixing architectural features borrowed from twelfth-, fifteenth- and sixteenth-century Pyrenees ruins, it was built in 1927 by renowned architect and ecologist Jacques Couëlle with a faux medieval flavour. The name roughly translates to 'Castle of Ruined Castles'.

It had also once housed a film school and served as a backdrop for 1952 French swashbuckling classic *Fan-fan de Tulipe*. The year before, former Serbian double agent and fabled lothario Duško Popov had moved in — and he was reputedly one of Ian Fleming's models for James Bond.

So it was apt that the press conference that kicked off the promotional junket on Saturday, 12 May yielded the inevitable enquiry about Sean Connery having been due to play Gandalf. 'Well, we are very happy with Sir Ian McKellen,' Jackson replied, not wishing to be drawn on the Connery backstory given the notices his Gandalf was already receiving.

Jackson and his creative inner-circle — Philippa Boyens, Richard Taylor, Barrie Osborne and Ordesky — were sat like a row of knights in the castle courtyards with the patient expressions of people aware they are going to be answering these and similar questions for the next three years.

How tightly were they sticking to the book? 'There are going to be people that have different ideas on things,' admitted Jackson, 'but you can't make a film by committee.' He had a soundbite ready: 'It's not a movie made for fans, but it is a movie made by fans.'

Boyens spoke of her initial sceptisim at turning her favourite book into a film. 'At first, I was overwhelmed.'

Osborne described what they had created as having 'a singular Tolkienesque brushstroke'.

While Taylor vouched for the fact that when you strive to keep things real, 'then the audience would be that much more accepting of the fantastical'.

Jackson laughed. 'The heroes generally don't have a bath; once they hit the road there are very few facilities. We have really grubbied them up.'

The press conference done with, I am granted my first private audience with the director, restationed to this quiet corner of the gardens. He was, back then, more guarded than he would be on the many occasions we will speak over the coming years. To be fair, no matter how well his footage had gone down, *The Lord of the Rings* was very much still a work in progress. In hindsight, my questions sound horribly naïve.

Will fans of his early films think he has sold out? 'Possibly,' he mused. 'But I don't have a particular career agenda that says I have necessarily left that behind and become a serious filmmaker. I still feel totally connected with the guy who made *Bad Taste.*'

Did he know he was now a star filmmaker? 'Really,' he replied, genuinely taken aback, 'fame doesn't interest me. The public can consider a director as a star but nothing obliges the director to play that role. No question of going off to Hollywood. I'm very happy in New Zealand, at the end of the world, far away from all that racket.'

He described the assumed rivalry with George Lucas' *Star Wars* prequels as 'complete codswallop'.

We swung back toward the films. He talked of the need for a PG-13 rating, but 'we will push it as far as we can'. Giving Orcs black blood helped disguise his proclivity for gore.

And what of Gollum, I pushed, how have you managed to create such a pivotal yet bizarre-looking character? At that point, the provenance of the wretch was still sheathed in mystery.

Jackson's answer baffled me. 'We're trying to do a CGI character but attempting to have a human actor put his stamp on it in a way that has never been done before. We have this really great British actor, Andy Serkis, in a kind of leotard and we are motion-capturing his movements. He was on set every day.'

I concluded by asking how work was progressing on the second and third films? To which he mentioned that shortly before jetting to Cannes, he had watched a very rough assembly of all three films together. In fact, he could only think of them as one film. 'A long way to go,' he grimaced.

For the sake of time the cast was divided into applicable groups for their interviews with small bands of journalists: the four hobbit actors; the warriors: Sean Bean and Viggo Mortensen; the elder statesmen: McKellen, Christopher Lee and John Rhys-Davies; and the Elves: Orlando Bloom and Liv Tyler.

They were a little drunk on French sunshine and the goodwill that had followed the footage. Jackson had shown them various montages of scenes at different stages of production — to chivvy up flagging spirits, or help actors reconnect with the world following a break. The emotional aftermath to Gandalf plunging into Khazad-dûm in particular had a hugely rejuvenating effect. As Astin says, it felt like something 'permanent'. But nothing they had seen was as wholly complete as the sample they too had witnessed for the first time two days before. There had been a chorus of whistles and hoots, and demands for an encore.

I could sense them mapping out the films to come in light of that promise.

'It has a fascinating look,' Mortensen said, glancing toward Bean for support. 'It feels as if everything is as it is.'

Bean agreed. 'It left me in awe. When filming you cannot see all the special effects and so on, so when you see some finished scenes for the first time, it makes an impression.'

'Inevitably, people will compare *Rings* to movies like *Star Wars*,' Mortensen went on sagely, determined we know that it wasn't only about spectacle, 'but I think that these characters are much more individual, original and fleshed out. Peter went to great lengths to ensure that the relationships included all their unspoken doubts and fears. You really see that being played out: on their faces, in their actions and even in their hesitations.'

John Rhys-Davies's hyperbolizing could probably have been heard all the way to the seafront. 'This is going to be bigger than *Star Wars*!' he boomed. 'In ten years' time, when you look back, and you're composing your list of favourite films, you'll find room for *The Lord of the Rings*.'

In 2011 that certainly was true for millions of fans.

McKellen smiled forbearingly at his co-star's enthusiasm, but preferred a more measured tone. 'Peter has taken this new technology, much of which was invented for this film, and put it at the service, not of something purely fantastic, but of ordinary people in extraordinary situations.'

If Mortensen effused about the emotions of the characters as if he knew them, McKellen talked about acting. There was, he said, dialogue that was really worth speaking. 'You haven't really seen that yet. But there was a lot of acting required in this film that had nought to do with racing up mountains.'

Here was the blurring at the edges of reality and fiction, actor and character, in plain sight. Wood even confessed there were times when he would genuinely think of himself as sharing scenes with Gandalf. Bloom, however, had his head shaved incongruously like a US Marine. It transpired he had flown in from shooting *Black Hawk Down* in Rabat in Morocco, but still spoke about mastering Elven martial arts, bowmanship and the ability to stand still — Elves do not fidget. Tyler, even at twenty-three already an old hand at this publicity game, made the case for the films benefitting from some romance — thus commencing an endless round of explaining to reporters her part of the story came from the appendices, and then having to explain what she meant by appendices. The hobbit actors grinned and laughed and tried being serious while being asked about rubber feet and the dream they had been living in for eighteen months.

Only now they were waking up to the fact these films might live up to their experience of making them.

'That was the first time we were like, "Holy fuck",' remembers Wood, who had been in New Zealand finishing pick-ups for *Fellowship* days before and only made it to Cannes by flying from Wellington to Los Angeles to London to Nice. 'Up until then it was our universe. The notion of it being a real thing, a big thing, was never in our minds. We were in the trenches. We were at home in New Zealand tucked away from the rest of the world making these movies. Cannes was the first time it was like, "Oh shit, this is coming out." It was wild.'

Lee had never had a doubt that the footage would be less than a marvel. He recalled that on set he had sat opposite Shaye at lunch and New Line's uncertain co-chairman drew him in conversation.

'You've been in the industry a long time,' he began. 'You know, I understand, a great deal about Tolkien. You've read the scripts; you've seen some of the material. What do you think?'

'Mr Shaye,' Lee replied as if reading from a stone tablet, 'you, your colleagues and everyone connected with this, the crew, the cast, the director, the producer, *everyone*: you are going to make history.'

Shaye was astonished. 'You really think so?'

'No question about it; one knows, one knows.'

One did know.

The following evening came the party, the biggest soiree in New Line's history. An event, Mittweg boasted to the *Los Angeles Times*, they had been planning since December. There was no arriving except in the designated buses that ferried the lucky few up from town. Gate-crashing was a Cannes sport and New Line was determined to spoil the fun. One did not simply walk into their party.

At dusk, nine dark riders rode sorties up and down the curving driveway that was lit by iron braziers. Orcs roamed the gardens looking for photo opportunities. Art Director Dan Hennah had shipped over entire sections of set, reassembling them in French warehouses — it was like the efforts taken for the pitch meeting but bigger and better, and everybody wanted to come and see.

A hobbit-scale Bag End required you to stoop in sympathy with McKellen and the long-suffering crew; Durin's Gate stood encased in a rock face, resisting all attempts to be opened; and a contorted stone troll looked as if he had been petrified while on the dance floor. Pavilions from Bilbo's birthday bash heralded food and drink, while hired waiters kept a brave face on having to wear Elf-ears.

The cast milled around soaking up the adulation in the warm evening air. Inside the keep could be found a display of props — Glamdring, Gandalf's staff, Sting — and Lee perusing a gallery of lovely, framed black and whites of the principal cast. Nodding appreciatively, he talked his guests through each one: 'Frodo, of course. . . That's Pippin. . . Gimli. . . Legolas the Elf. . . Gandalf. . .' He paused in front of his own image: Saruman in fiercesome pose and lit like a film noir. 'Hmmm, I'll think I'll have that.' And he picked it up and took it with him, leaving a noticeable gap behind.

Tyler was holding her expensive shoes, preferring the grass under her feet. Rhys-Davies was stationed at a bench, instructing all petitioners to sit down so he could tell them tall stories without craning his neck. In the drinks station through the door behind him they had installed the seven-foot 'hobbit scale' bar from the Prancing Pony, forcing you to shout up to the French barman in the hope of getting served.

Billy Boyd and Dominic Monaghan scampered about, laughing, inseparable. Bloom took the opportunity to bounce around the dance floor heedless of admiring female glances.

Hiding among the same trees where we had met the day before, was a bewildered Jackson, no doubt yearning to get away from all this glamour and feel New Zealand again beneath his bare feet. He was currently wearing trainers, and smiled warily in greeting.

'Seen anything good at the Festival?' he asked, talked out on Tolkien and New Line and Cave-trolls.

'I saw the new Coens,' I offered and launched into a clumsy summary of a plot I could barely remember.

'Sounds good,' he responded, perhaps more taken by the idea of a film governed only by the curious whims of its creators and without the future of the studio being at stake. He leaned in furtively and whispered that New Line had spent $2 million on the party.

'It would have been a pretty sad affair if the footage hadn't gone down well.'

Upon leaving there was a goody bag containing a small pipe and tobacco pouch, a commemorative copy of the book and a miniature replica Sting letter opener. Which it would have been wise to stow in my check-in luggage the following day. Deemed unsafe in carry on, it was added to the small pile of miniature Stings behind the stern-faced gatekeeper at Nice Airport.

CHAPTER 10

The Monsters and the Critics

In the early weeks of December 2001, *Ain't It Cool News* heard from an inside source at New Line that Peter Jackson had delivered his finished print of *The Fellowship of the Ring*. And the news was cool.

'I walked into this thinking there was no possible way it could live up to my expectations,' the source had greedily informed the site, who passed it on to the internet. 'When I walked out, all I could think was that there's no way that *The Two Towers* and *The Return of the King* can possibly live up to expectations. Because *The Fellowship of the Ring* is the benchmark by which those movies will be judged. It's perfect!'

If he was reading, Jackson might have savoured the irony.

With all the years that have passed, he still finds it hard to sum up his relationship with New Line: there was so much, good and bad, tied up inside that period and all that came afterwards. The films wouldn't have happened without them, he is well aware of that. And no major studio would have allowed him such freedom. He in turn delivered three excellent films — perfection for some — for all the rising costs, on a budget a studio working with ILM couldn't hope to match. Even Shaye was willing to admit that.

The final production budget of $270 million breaks down to a thrifty $90 million a film.

Nevertheless, admits Jackson, they made for strange bed-fellows. 'New Line was a company used to making much smaller-budget films and very American films. Not arthouse, but fairly commercial films orientated toward the American teen market.'

The trilogy was as much a learning curve for the studio as it was for the director.

Says Ken Kamins, 'I remember when photography started and New Line was excited and their head of marketing at the time. . . I'm not going to say who, because I'm not looking to embarrass anybody. But the head of marketing wanted to put out a congratulatory ad in the trades to everybody in New Zealand starting on this epic journey, blah, blah, blah.'

The ad was due to feature the Fellowship walking across the mountain range. Somehow — given nothing like this had been shot yet — they had managed to come up with a photograph of what looked like the Fellowship, only grown in number to ten or eleven.

Jackson was appalled.

'That's exactly what's going to send me into a death spiral with the fans,' he told Kamins. 'They're going to look at that and say, "He doesn't know what he's doing."'

'So that ad had to get pulled and changed. Peter realized he had to be watchful for those things.'

Still, Jackson did have some sympathy. They had rolled the dice on the biggest films in their history with these 'oddball New Zealand filmmakers' who were trying to give them a 'fairly English sensibility'. From both sides, the marriage was never a particularly comfortable one. Jackson is willing to admit there were times he could have been more politic. He naturally chafed against authority. Whenever the pressure came to bear, he instinctively defended the film, refusing to tame his imagination.

'Whatever our future problems ended up being,' Kamins

makes clear, 'Peter will always credit Bob [Shaye] with making maybe one of the bravest decisions an executive ever made.'

The turbulence began in the early months of production when it became clear that despite Carla Fry's initial projections Weta Digital were in dire need of a further injection of cash to cope with the expanding visual effects.

Once again Shaye felt duped.

'They thought that Weta was screwing them, which wasn't the case at all,' says Jackson. There were, he admits, periods of nasty 'sparring' between lawyers. 'Threats would fly around.'

Michael Lynne claimed that New Line had contemplated pulling the plug even as late as the first break in filming at the end of 1999, during the overhaul at Weta Digital. What had stayed the sword, offered a more generous Shaye, was Jackson's potential. So they had — instinctually — kept on investing. Not that they didn't haggle 'long and hard over things'. And they never failed to let slip to Jackson that the money was being taken away from other directors.

Looking back, he can accept that New Line were to an extent flying blind. They hadn't seen anything of the effects at that stage, and had no idea where their money was being spent. In the absence of proof, worries can bleed into paranoia, constructing a conspiracy where Weta were trying to mislead New Line, and Jackson, as owner of the company, was deliberately pushing the budget in order to cream off more profits.

'The reality is Weta Digital earned no profit at all.'

It was all on the screen, where the effects were expanding to keep pace with Jackson's irrepressible need to constantly better himself. As Tolkien once put it: 'This tale grew in the telling.'

A director feuding with his paymasters is the oldest story in the Hollywood book — cash and kudos duelling over the dark chasm of popular opinion has defined both industry and artform. And it was only New Line's ranking double-act who could crack the surface of Jackson's preternatural calm. Consider the afternoon during the arduous shooting of Helm's Deep, when Jackson was directing a rare daytime set-up of Théoden and Aragorn preparing for war on the parapet of the old fortress. The director looked down across what was ostensibly a construction site framed by the outstretched arm of the Deeping Wall and segments of the mighty Hornburg. What caught his eye was Barrie Osborne parking his car and walking at a furious pace toward the set lugging what appeared to be a suitcase. This was ill news, and he knew it.

Amid the hustle and bustle of crew and stuntmen, getting from the car park to the ramparts could take ten to fifteen minutes, so Jackson turned away and carried on with the scene.

'I would shoot something then watch him get a bit higher up — huffing and puffing with this suitcase — then shoot another take.'

Finally, Osborne, quite out of breath, arrives where they are filming.

'What is *that*, Barrie?' asks Jackson, irritated at the interruption but wary of the expression on Osborne's face. Without a word, Osborne opened the suitcase and began assembling a steampunk contraption with a long aerial like a fishing rod. This turned out to be a satellite phone. There was no hope of cell phone reception within the granite walls of the quarry, and in a better mood the director might have suggested Théoden could try Gandalf on the device. Osborne Stormcrow, meanwhile, was elaborately dialling a number.

'You've got to speak to Michael Lynne,' he says, proffering the receiver. 'They want to sue Weta and sue you if you don't do what they say.'

He may go quiet, sigh, even occasionally sink into depression at the trials the project would bring, but Jackson never lost his cool. But right then, in the midst of a complex scene, exhausted, underappreciated and plain out of tether, that is what he did, and loud enough, he hoped, for his anger to bounce off a satellite and back into Lynne's New York office.

'I am not going to speak to him! If he wants to sue me he

Left A young, beardless Peter Jackson, a Beatles t-shirt beneath his shirt, photographed alongside hero Ray Harryhausen at a German film festival. Harryhausen would have a profound influence on Jackson's career as a whole, but it was the British stop-motion guru's forte for the fantasy idiom that led the young director to even thinking of adapting *The Lord of the Rings*.

Right Jackson pictured with another of his early heroes: Forrest J. Ackerman, editor of influential magazine and Jackson 'bible', *Famous Monsters of Filmland*. Jackson can be seen holding the delicate frame of a Pteranodon puppet seen on the *King Kong (1933)* issue in Ackerman's hands. Ackerman was also the first Hollywood producer to approach Tolkien, in 1958, about adapting *The Lord of the Rings*.

Above left Jackson sat beside Ralph Bakshi, director of the unloved 1978 animated version of *The Lord of Rings*, at the 1992 Sitges Film Festival in Spain. Little could Jackson know then that he too would attempt to adapt the impossible book, or that Bakshi would take offence at not being asked for his advice. *Above right* Jackson and his mother, Joan, during principal photography on *The Lord of the Rings* — a fallen mûmakil marking this as a *Return of the King* day. Joan and Jackson's father Bill were hugely supportive of their son's quirky ambitions, regularly relinquishing the family oven for the cooking of special effects. Sadly, she would die three days before the completion of *The Fellowship of the Ring* (Bill died in 1998).

Above Jackson checks in with chief consultant J.R.R. Tolkien while on location. This is the same symbolic, note-strewn copy of the book — illustrated by Alan Lee — he had bought on the day they landed the rights to the film.

Above Another Grey day: it paid for a wizard to keep a brolly about his person in case of changeable Middle-earth conditions. The incomparable McKellen contemplates the incomparable South Island scenery through the incomparable Kiwi drizzle.

Above Fellowship of the Wing! Producer Barrie Osborne, Dominic Monaghan, Elijah Wood and Orlando Bloom help load the cost-effective if rickety DC-3 Douglas Dakota (in original Second World War livery) that would (just about) get them to the South Island. *Right* The Wizard of Wellington: Jackson tries out Gandalf's pointy hat for size. Sir Ian McKellen was not alone in suspecting there was an eager actor lurking beneath the surface of the magical director. Jackson had, after all, been the star of his first film, *Bad Taste*.

Above The author pictured between Russell Alexander and his father, Ian, on the doorstep of Bag End. It was on the Alexanders' voluminous sheep farm in Matamata that the production discovered a freakishly ideal site for Hobbiton, which is now permanently preserved. NB: all of us are taller in real-life.

Above Cannes 2001: Billy Boyd, Sean Astin, Elijah Wood, New Line CEO Bob Shaye, Peter Jackson, Dominic Monaghan and Shaye's partner Michael Lynne take a well-earned bow at the legendary film festival bash that followed the lauded debut of 25 minutes of footage. Overnight the project had transformed from grand folly into the most anticipated franchise in Hollywood.

Above Held at the lavish Chateau de Castelleras, a bus ride outside of Cannes, and masterminded by art director Dan Hennah, the party recreated Bilbo's birthday celebrations with actual props shipped over from New Zealand. Somewhere amongst the milling guests could be found the author.

Left The hard yards: wrapped in one of a succession of battered 'unitards', Andy Serkis' journey to create Gollum was an astonishing marriage of hands-and-knees acting and technical revolution. One of *The Lord of the Rings'* many triumphs, the motion-captured wretch would transform the industry.

Right Standing in a puddle notwithstanding, a White (and Sky-blue) Wizard holds forth to cast and crew. An ever shorts-clad Peter Jackson, a capped Sir Ian McKellen, and a bandana-sporting Orlando Bloom pose between takes at Edoras, in actuality a rocky outcrop in the Rangiata River valley, another miraculously book-perfect discovery found in the (misty) Southern Alps.

Left A director chairs: principal photography was a monument to Peter Jackson's ability to multi-task on about a thousand levels at any given time. To wit: during a brief respite in the Battle of Helm's Deep, Alan Lee grabs a precious moment of his time to discuss an appropriately forbidding spout for Mount Doom.

Above There was nothing
Peter Jackson enjoyed more
than a day with his beloved Orc
regiments. It was with the foul
ranks of Sauron's army that
Jackson could express his 'bad
taste'. Each Orc was unique, with
the Weta Workshop prosthetics
artists imagining their own tribal
hierarchy based on piercings, and
the scars of infighting.

Right The author clad in
Gondorian helmet with a sword
and shield and non-canon rain
coat, in a Polaroid taken at Weta
Workshop, whose shelves can
be seen in the background.
Cool journalistic composure was
sorely tested by the chance to get
into character.

Above Michael Lynne of New Line with the extravagantly attired producer Barrie Osborne in happier days. Peter can be spotted chatting to Robert Shaye behind them. As the years wore on, relations with New Line's hierarchy were often strained, and Jackson admitted in hindsight they made for strange bedfellows.

Above The films' two knights, Sir Ian Holm and Sir McKellen, pose with Robert Shaye, CEO of New Line. Both theatrical greats had paid their dues to the classics, but came at their craft in different ways. McKellen was a master of the text, easing in and out of character. Holm would offer a different line reading with every take.

Above An extra serving of ham! The author pictured with Alex Funke, Visual Effects Director of Photography: Miniature Unit, helpfully pointing out the smaller of the stunning Minas Tirith miniatures. Requests to 'take it home once they were done with it' were politely declined.

Above The author being interviewed for the DVD extras on the Stone Street backlot, giving a journalist's take on visiting the set, another piece of precious footage that has never seen the light. The lack of a cameraman might be telling.

Left Wave Strider: during an extra-curricular jaunt to catch a few tubes, Viggo Mortensen got himself whacked in the face by a surfboard, leading to a very-much unscripted shiner. Surfing being scarce in the annals of Tolkien, this led to a few days in Balin's Tomb where the hero could only be shot from his left-hand side.

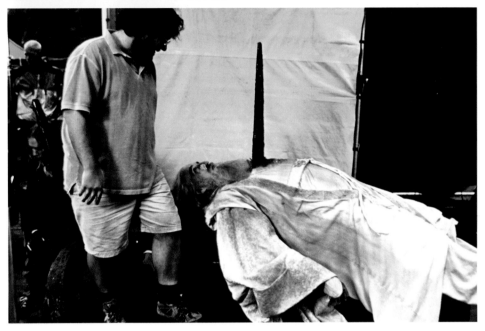

Above A devoted fan of Christopher Lee's vampiric history, Jackson devised an end for Saruman that paid homage to the actor's impalement in *Dracula AD 1979*. Of which Lee was more than aware. Their easy rapport would briefly become tested when the epic death scene was cut from the theatrical version of *The Return of the King*, leading to Lee going public with his wounded feelings.

Right Marked for life: after the Fellowship had commemorated their bond with a tattoo of the Elvish symbol for 'nine', Roger's Tattoo Art on Cuba Street continued its bustling trade when Jackson, Richard Taylor and Barrie Osborne each got a tattoo of the Elvish 'ten'. Billy Boyd and Orlando Bloom were on hand to make sure there were no last-minute rethinks.

Above Return of the kings: in honour of his hometown and country, Peter Jackson insisted the world premiere of the third and final film be held in Wellington, where a red carpet would wend its way up Courtenay Place to the Embassy Cinema (out of shot) and a crowd of 125,000 cheered the homecoming heroes.

Right It is almost impossible to underestimate Fran Walsh's contribution to *The Lord of the Rings*, as writer, producer, erstwhile second unit director, musical consultant and creative rock to her partner. It was, after all, her suggestion to adapt the book. Pictured here with Jackson at the Hollywood Golden Globes awards in 2004.

Above A golden moment: coming off stage, clutching the Oscar for Best Picture, Jackson shares a moment with presenter Steven Spielberg, with Bob Shaye looking on. Up on the stage of the Kodak Pavilion was the first time Jackson had ever met Spielberg. It was the beginning of a beautiful friendship.

Above Fellowship of the Win! Jackson shares his historic victory with manager Ken Kamins and friend and executive producer Mark Ordesky, each of who had played a crucial and unheralded part in getting the films made.

Above A fabulous shot of the brilliant Andy Serkis in his element, sporting some impressive advances on his famous 'unitard'. By *The Hobbit* the motion-capture technology enabled them to capture Serkis' facial expressions as well as body movements in situ. Returning to the character, Serkis had found it hard to 'reclaim' Gollum and make him real again.

Above The late, great cinematographer Andrew Lesnie who died in 2015. During their great adventure in Middle-earth, Jackson and Lesnie were like brothers, full of mischief, but dedicated to capturing majesty in every shot.

Left Philippa Boyens with Richard Armitage (Thorin Oakenshield) during the ADR sessions on *The Hobbit*. Like Lesnie, Boyens' contribution to the films has been priceless. She ensured that Tolkien was always viewed as literature not fantasy.

Left The author takes a stroll on a glacier near Mount Cook on the South Island, care of the helicopter rather than mountaineering. The whirlybirds played an invaluable role on both trilogies, even if they tested the mettle of the films' flight-averse director (not to mention Sean Bean).

Right The author pretending to smoke a pipe in Hobbiton at Matamata. Following the rebuild for *The Hobbit*, much of the lavish filmmaking detail has been made permanent as a hugely successful tourist attraction, with its own army of Samwises to tend to the local ecology.

Left Following in Bilbo's footsteps, a moody shot of the author holding a replica of Sting at Waitomo on the North Island, which served as the exterior for the Trollshaws sequences, including the discovery of the Troll hoard, for *An Unexpected Journey*.

Above and below Visiting *The Return of the King*, the author is treated to elf ear extensions, a surprisingly soothing process, which sadly conferred few elvish graces (and no cameo). In the top picture make-up guru Gino Acevedo can be seen at work in the background.

Above Peter Jackson bestows a special gift on Christopher Lee as Saruman, while shooting at Pinewood, outside of London. With Lee 90 and Ian Holm 81 at the time, and too venerable to travel, Saruman and Bilbo's scenes were the only parts of either trilogy to be shot outside of New Zealand.

Above The Hobbit gang, including a suited Smaug (neé Benedict Cumberbatch) and the director in directorial plaid, pose for a team photo. *The Hobbit*, of course, marked an unexpected reunion for Holmes and Watson from television's *Sherlock*, of which Jackson, unsurprisingly, was a huge fan.

can talk to my lawyers. I am trying to finish this *fucking* film for them.'

Jackson happily utilizes a 'bloody' or a 'bastard' for emphasis, but the F-word signalled a seismic emotional shift.

So Osborne had to slink back down the battlements of Helm's Deep dragging his incongruous case with him.

'Peter can push things to the brink,' acknowledges the producer, 'but he can also compromise.'

'He does change his mind,' notes Boyens. But, she warns, you cannot rush him. '*He* changes his mind, no one changes it for him.'

Jackson was savvy enough to recognize when the studio put in a good note. They had dealt admirably with the transition to Mortensen, and the Cannes unveiling had shown brilliant tactical nous. Moreover, he understood that the distance between Los Angeles and Wellington formed a cultural gap that unnerved the studio as much as it gave the filmmakers security. On the few occasions Shaye and Lynne did visit, Jackson was struck by the almost comic aroma of Hollywood that would waft in with them. In the middle of production, he dutifully toured them around Weta Digital, where Shaye, drifting between monitors, began complaining that it was all far too dark. At which point someone politely suggested he take off his sunglasses.

'That gave us all a laugh,' chuckles Jackson.

On another day, having lunch on set, Shaye ended up in the queue in front of Elijah Wood — there were no airs and graces, even for visiting CEOs. Not having met before, he introduced himself, saying how glad they were to have Wood starring in their film. Then Shaye grinned wickedly.

'You've got a crappy agent,' he told the actor, 'because we would have paid you twice what we did.'

Jackson sighs. 'Don't say that to an actor. Don't tell the guy he would have been paid twice as much. Bob was sort of gloating and he made Elijah aware of that.'

For his part, Shaye was disturbed by the motley interior decoration at Miramar. He wasn't expecting the steel-and-glass,

007 villain futurism that pertained to Hollywood style, but walking down the corridor toward the screening room he was startled to see old Bond posters stuck on the walls with tape. As he and his partner sat down to view the early footage that would so impress Lynne — as well as Boromir's death there were scenes of Gandalf at Bag End and the hobbits on the run — he may have feared that they had put the future of the company in the hands of amateurs. When the lights went up again he had tears in his eyes.

Jackson is frank enough to admit that if it hadn't been for the presence of his old friend Ordesky, absorbing the friction, his relationship with New Line might not have stayed the distance.

After Fry died, Ordesky realized he needed to insert himself between Jackson and the studio. He had to adopt the ultimate split personality: protector of Jackson's vision *and* studio facilitator who was putting both his dreams and his reputation on the line for these films.

Walsh called him their 'guiding light'. Shaye knew him as the 'firewall'. For Jackson he was the 'consummate politician', especially during the travails of post-production.

Ordesky was the perfect double agent.

'New Line encouraged me to be down there and, I think, Peter was happy for me to be there because the more I knew the more helpful I could be. Though, I never thought in a million years I would be down there as long as I was or as often.'

*

Officially, the small matter of final cut rested in a no man's land between Jackson and Shaye. In practice this meant the strong-willed director delivering his 'final cut' having taken on board, or not, any notes New Line had along the way. It was not that they interfered with his cut so much as made their presence felt.

Shaye was not a fool. He had a good eye and a fine brain, he could see the quality of the work, and the response in Cannes had been ecstatic. To fire Jackson would have been suicidal. They had invested millions in this guy, and no one else could hope to navigate the reams of footage. No, these three films represented Jackson's vision, and there was no turning back from that.

'Peter and Bob had a shared final cut,' says Ordesky. 'But with Bob, it never really got invoked. Peter got to direct as if he had final cut. There was vigorous note giving, and often disagreements. But Bob never said in the entire five-year odyssey, or the three years of editorial, "I will not approve this."'

The debates were really about running time. The scripts were so huge and changed so rapidly, even Ordesky is unsure he read everything. 'If you were back in Los Angeles, there was no way you were reading every single revision that came through. So it became very footage driven, very editorially driven.'

He can remember a conversation with his boss about the dailies that had arrived within the first weeks of production.

'Everything is so very serious,' Shaye commented, 'like earnest.'

Reporting Shaye's thoughts back to Jackson, Ordesky was surprised to find the director was gratified by the response.

'If we don't do this straight, it could become funny — funny in a bad way. There is humour and humanity, but it has to be done straight.'

Ordesky, an Olympian of tact, presented the director's response back to Shaye, who was placated. Seeing Wood's Frodo struggle with the Ring on the wooded road — absent of special effects, colour grading, sound editing, music — Ordesky had felt his own belief being rewarded. This was going to work.

Jackson had endeavoured to try editing pieces during production but there was never enough time, or the mental space to concentrate. It was only once they wrapped that he began editing in earnest.

While helping to maintain the idea of three films being one continuous storyline, but, hopefully, also giving them some differentiation in style and feel (and hasten material down the pipeline to Weta Digital), Jackson had the films cut concurrently, with a different editor on each. They were all well versed in the Jackson way: John Gilbert, who edited *The Fellowship of the Ring*, had been associate editor on *The Frighteners*; Michael Horton, who was challenged to sew together *The Two Towers*' many strands, had been on *Forgotten Silver*; while Jamie Selkirk had chosen *The Return of the King* as his focus, while also acting as supervising editor across all three.

Funny, wise, chilled out and Kiwi to his boots, Selkirk went all the way back to *Bad Taste*. With a background in newsreels and documentaries with the New Zealand Broadcasting Corporation — as well as cutting *Worzel Gummidge* through his company, Mr Chopper — he had been a mentor to Jackson in those early days and had worked on every one of his films since. He was also a co-director of Weta Workshop.

'We just got on well,' he explains, 'we're both pretty easy-going and laidback people. I think it was just pure luck, to tell you the truth. We seemed to get on okay, we had the same sense of humour.'

Selkirk's carefree attitude belied another single-minded artist, and he had hoped to edit all three *Lord of the Rings* films, before that proved unfeasible. Across six different Avids,* they were dealing with up to 40,000 feet of footage per day arriving from the plethora of units. Selkirk was also serving as post-production supervisor.

Wisely, Jackson shot precisely with the edit in mind, already splicing things together. Ian McKellen sensed the director waiting for a take to match what was running through his internal projector. Jackson has talked about even having the score playing in his head as he shoots. There were times when he got to the edit when he wished he had shot a scene faster or slower, then among the takes he would always discover he had shot it that way. 'Earlier Pete,' he jokes, 'always knows what later Peter might want.'

---

* In layman's terms, an Avid is the digital editing system that replaced the physical cutting of the negative. Much as purists are loath to admit, it is considered far more versatile. *The English Patient* would be the first film to win an Oscar for editing undertaken on an Avid.

When it came to the cutting room, Jackson would lie spread-eagled on a sofa with a cup of tea within easy reach.

'There was always a cup of tea going,' laughs Selkirk. 'Also lollies — we used to go through huge bags of lollies. These big pick'n'mix bags. New Zealand has a great selection of sweets.'

The hours were gruelling, and they worked long into the night. But Jackson's recall of even individual frames never flagged, as this titanic jigsaw puzzle slowly got assembled and reassembled as he tested different rhythms and pacing for each scene. Just occasionally Selkirk would be cutting away and hear a gentle snoring sound from behind as weariness finally won the battle.

Jackson also made the bold decision of planting Ordesky onto a sofa beside him in the edit suite. To other directors this would be a terrifying, counterintuitive invasion of their inner sanctum. It was like having someone watch you paint. Yet it was a canny move to get ahead of the notes from Los Angeles. New Line would gain what Ordesky classifies as a 'profound insight into what he was intending to do even when he wasn't fully done doing it yet'.

When there were differences, Ordesky would be better able to make the case for Jackson, fully versed in his intentions, but in a language that would land at New Line. Take for instance, the case of 'scary Galadriel'.

A quick recap: while recuperating in Lothlorien, the Elvish forest kingdom locked in a permanent trance, Frodo offers the Ring to the sorceress-queen Galadriel (an imperious, parchment-pale Cate Blanchett beneath a cascade of golden curls). She responds with a lusty blast of visual effects making Galadriel glow with phosphorescent fury. Shaye felt it was over-the-top: if you had an actress of Blanchett's calibre why smother her in CGI?

'Peter felt extremely strongly about it,' says Ordesky. To Jackson the pyrotechnics revealed that Galadriel was far from just a pretty face — she was extremely powerful and more unpredictable than, say, the sagacious Elrond.

The effect was one of the few not done by Weta Digital. Time constraints led to it being farmed out to an Australian company,

GMD, with the instruction from Jackson and Tolkien that Galadriel be as 'beautiful and terrible as the dawn'. They added eighteen colourized layers to bluescreen shots of Blanchett in Kabuki-style make-up with the goal of making it appear as if the light source came from within Galadriel.[*]

A more heated discussion arose with the issue of how to bring the first film to an emotionally satisfying conclusion and yet instil into the filmgoer a hunger for more. In other words, how to imply to those unacquainted with Tolkien this was only part one of a giant three-part story, much of which was in the can. Jackson would wisely insist on putting a rousing trailer for *The Two Towers* — not to be released online — onto the end of *The Fellowship of the Ring*, pre-dating the epidemic of post-credit 'stings' that came with the outbreak of superhero movies. At the end of *The Two Towers* he trusted that people had caught on.

How to actually end the first film was a complex question. 'You needed to leave the viewers with a sense of fulfilment. It can't just be a cliffhanger,' determines Boyens. 'You have to feel that you have been on this journey and something enormous has happened.'

Still nervously trying to prop up Tolkien with movie convention, Jackson admits they had originally filmed and abandoned a 'more Hollywood' ending. Herein Frodo and Sam are at the lakeside scrambling into the boat when a rogue Uruk-hai jumps up like something from *Friday the 13th* and grabs at the Ring yanking Frodo into the water. Following an underwater struggle, Frodo breaks free and is dragged back into the boat by Sam — it was also another attempt to give Frodo a piece of the action.

Whatever the issues between filmmaker and studio, Ordesky

---

[*] I have only minor, personal beefs with the finished films, and this is one occasion where I subjectively side with New Line. I would love to see Blanchett cutting loose without the overlay of effects. But who am I to say, I wasn't directing, and for many this display of supernatural ego is another example of the film's willingness to offset the realism of Middle-earth with the strikingly bonkers.

insists the looser corporate culture at New Line benefitted the films. While he fretted over expenditure and profit, like every studio chieftain since the first flicker of light was beamed onto the wall of a nickelodeon, Shaye responded to Jackson's artistic reasoning.

'Hollywood shows its belief in two ways,' says Ordesky: 'with money and with freedom.'

New Line ultimately allowed Jackson both.

As was so often the case, they ended up going back to the book. After crossing the lake, with Sam nearly drowning, Frodo and his faithful sidekick begin their trek through the alien terrain of Emyn Muil, concluding the first film with what one critic described as an 'arthouse ending'.

Jackson made an eloquent argument that this was a symbolic conclusion to *The Fellowship of the Ring*. During the first film Frodo goes from, 'I'll take the Ring because Gandalf asked me' to, at the Council of Elrond, 'I'll take the Ring because I believe it's right', without really knowing what he is facing. However, by the end of the film he knows and chooses a third time to take the Ring.

'What was interesting,' he reasons, 'was that we were changing what was originally an action-based climax into an emotional climax.'

That was a bold case to make to a studio with hundreds of millions of dollars on the line. By contrast to scary Galadriel, here was an example of the quiet eloquence within Jackson's storytelling. Credit, says Ordesky, must go to the director for conceiving it, to Walsh and Boyens who wrote it and to New Line, who approved it.

Tellingly, when it came to reshooting the scene, Jackson had 'found himself a hundred miles away'. So Walsh was drafted in to direct the finale. This was during supplementary shooting in spring 2001, when they had been granted the funds and the latitude to go back and rethink things, fix them and often transcend them.

Credit should also go to Ordesky who, driven by his own passion and understanding of the book, could frame Jackson's arguments within the studio set-up with eloquence. But he admits this wasn't always the case, on both sides of the Pacific. His own journey was also one of emotional struggle.

'I have only mentioned this once before,' he confesses. 'There were moments where I did not serve the films as well as I could have, even though they, obviously, came out fine. I created a psychodrama in my own mind where Peter and Bob had to be simultaneously happy. No one asked me to do that. I did that.'

Now and again, he radiated a stress that if not quite to Galadriel's radioactive levels was still palpable.

But Jackson only ever had to call him out on it once.

'Listen, you've got to find a way to navigate this emotionally,' he advised his friend, 'because it is challenging to be around.'

He learned to toughen up.

The first cut of the film that Ordesky saw was four hours long. Brilliant, he thought, but obviously too long. 'We were in Hobbiton for an *awful* long time,' he remembers. It was in Hollywood-speak 'quote fat' with a lot of emphasizing and re-emphasizing that the Shire is what Frodo is fighting for. Scenes such as the young hobbit translating the Elvish runes on the boxes of fireworks.

Ordesky laughs. 'Every movie cut you ever watch this question always gets asked: Can't we get to X faster? Can't we get out the Shire faster?'

When Shaye called him, inevitably the first thing he wanted to know was how long it was.

'Well, it's four hours. . .' Ordesky replied uncertainly. Shaye and Lynne were due to be in New Zealand in six to eight weeks to see the first official cut.

The silence on the other end of the line spoke volumes.

'Don't worry, it'll be three hours by the time you get here,' he hastily added, something he really believed when he said it.

But as his bosses were striding across the runway toward

their private jet, he called to warn them that what they would be seeing was, well, *still* four hours long.

'What the Hell?' Shaye was outraged.

'Yes, but it is a *different* four hours now,' his underling offered. Ordesky dared the fury of his superiors in order to give Jackson the space to get the cut right. Jackson had no intention of putting a four-hour cut into cinemas; Ordesky would have had to ring alarm bells if that was the case. The director also wasn't going to be hurried. He was still finding the movie.

A lot of the pressure on what was the 'right good movie' was alleviated by the decision to do extended cuts. 'It was a brilliant solution,' says Ordesky, 'the idea of the theatrical cut being one thing and the extended version being another.' He doubts they would have found a happy solution without it, and New Line might have yet contested the final cut.

That said, Jackson still contends that the theatrical cuts are his preferred versions. 'I did the extended versions for the fans, really. The theatrical versions were very carefully worked out. We spent a whole year trying to get the best possible cut. I did the extended cuts because we had thirty to forty minutes of footage that fans of the books might be interested in. But I was aware that every time I put something in the momentum of the scene was going to be slow. Every time, I thought, "I'm spoiling the film."'

When *The Fellowship of the Ring* came out, a certain amount of tension finally diffused between Jackson and his backers and there was, the director says, enough 'grudging respect' to get them through the next two years of supplementary shooting and post-production. But the scar tissue remained.

Again with hindsight, Jackson can accept that their relation-ship may well have been affected by the tremors of corporate strife that were afflicting New Line in the background. While *The Lord of the Rings* was in production — but after the films had been greenlit — their parent Time Warner had merged with AOL (America Online) in what remains the largest deal of its kind in business history. New Line had been left uncertain of its future.

It was a questionable deal. Time Warner had been blind to the unpredictable nature of the internet and soon found out they were partnered with a dinosaur unable to evolve with the rapidly changing digital landscape.

'I remember Gerald Levine, who was the CEO of AOL-Time Warner, was fired by the board,' says Jackson. 'This is while we were still in post.'

Levine, who had been a driving force behind Time Warner as a media conglomerate, announced his 'retirement' on 5 May 2001, sending further shockwaves through New Line. The great merger would eventually collapse in 2009, one of the most significant failures of corporate activity in modern America. AOL, which had been valued at $200 billion, limped away with a market value of less than $2.5 billion.

Throughout this period, says Jackson, 'There was speculation that Warner Bros. wanted to shut New Line down.'

Shaye's maverick cousin was never a comfortable fit within the Time Warner family. They had arrived as part of the purchase of Turner Communications, and largely because the board was otherwise distracted, had been left alone. Yet the fear remained that eventually the executives would get around to pondering the cost-effectiveness of a second, smaller, de facto film company when they already had a thriving studio in Warner Bros.

'I won't say that we had it factually accurate,' adds Jackson, 'but we certainly got the feeling that Time Warner were invested in the failure of *Lord of the Rings* to some degree, because it would give them a reason to get rid of New Line.'

'AOL definitely had a jaundiced view of the entire investment,' agrees Kamins, a man skilled at deciphering the hieroglyphics of studio politics. He estimates that the success of *The Lord of the Rings* gave New Line another ten years of relative autonomy within the Warner machine. 'I think it saved New Line.'

*

If Time Warner was stumbling into the digital future, almost absurdly New Line was showing signs of grasping the nettle of what the internet could offer. Taking their lead from the director's productive relationship with *Ain't It Cool News*, when it came to marketing *The Fellowship of the Ring* the company pioneered a groundbreaking internet presence. Despite their dusty cloaks and battered shields, *The Lord of the Rings* films revolutionized film promotion in the digital realm.

In addition to the official website, which came in ten languages, New Line sponsored forty fan-created sites. Furthermore, Jackson's progressive attitude toward fans helped ring-fence the production. When it was reported that a spy with a telephoto lens had been driven off from the perimeter of Hobbiton with the threat of lawsuits, Jackson intervened. He and Osborne thought that kind of paranoid Hollywood response was exactly the wrong thing to do, and they invited her back to watch filming.

'I mean she couldn't take photos,' notes Jackson, 'but she could sit and watch and talk about it.'

This was Erica Challis (who went by the Elvish handle 'Tehanu') of theonering.net who, like Harry Knowles, became a powerful ally. theonering.net had been set up by Challis and fellow fan Michael Regina ('Xoanon') in 1999 to publish as much information as they could lay their hands on relating to the production. Now with Jackson's blessing, they were transformed into a hub for discussion of the films for those invested in the books. Meanwhile, Jackson had provided himself with a dedicated conduit direct to the Tolkien fanbase.

This was a way of not only communicating with fans but also controlling the imagery. Naturally, he wanted his films to be judged in the best light. 'Once you start giving out information people don't feel so compelled to steal it. You know what I mean? The best thing that you can do is to release pictures as quickly as possible of actors in costume, innocent photos that don't give anything away, but at least it stops the paparazzi wanting to get glimpses.'

It is a lesson that studios still have a hard time heeding.

'What was also helpful was that New Line had an executive in Gordon Paddison who was their first head of digital marketing and was very forward thinking,' says Kamins. Paddison, who would go on to work for Warner Brothers and Lucasfilm, developed the official website as a portal for those who hadn't read the books to get a palatable dose of Tolkien's history going in.

Says Kamins, 'Gordon being there was a great catalyst for Peter's expressing himself to the fans differently.'

The growing influence of the internet truly struck home when Paddison and New Line 'uploaded' the initial making-of trailer. No one had ever done that before. Jackson can remember the day clearly — they were still shooting up at Ruapehu, scenes of the hobbits in Mordor. He also remembers how bemused he had been.

'Trailers were for the cinema. Plus, we were still a long way from actually having a film. But, I think, within twenty-four hours we had one-point-seven million hits. This is in 2000. New Line couldn't believe it. That was astronomical. That was another time when we realized there was a real expectation for these films.'

By *The Hobbit*, Jackson was boldly releasing online video diaries, giving an appealingly Jacksonesque glimpse behind the scenes like a foretaste of the legendarily exhaustive DVD extras that the director had pursued on the discs for *The Lord of the Rings*.

As Jackson and Walsh had vowed following Universal's garbled release of *The Frighteners*, and being severely overtaxed already notwithstanding, they involved themselves in every aspect of *The Lord of the Rings* release. New Line's marketing department had to get used to the filmmakers taking a very hands-on approach to approving materials for the film.

Andy Serkis remembers being called to a big publicity meeting at Stone Street. Keen for their input, Jackson would often involve his main cast and department heads in all facets of the production. He informed them that the posters were horrible.

'Alan Lee should be designing them,' he insisted.

Recalls Serkis, 'It looked like there were seven hobbits in the Fellowship. It was carelessly done. That was not the way, you know? Everything had to be meticulous and authentic, and we all wanted to carry the torch for it. Everyone agreed that the Alan Lee and John Howe illustrations ought to be part of the heritage of the piece. Any sort of visual representation ought to be derived from them.'

The poster campaign began with two evocative images of Frodo holding the Ring, bathed in moody, golden light. One had him looking directly at the camera with the tagline, 'One Ring To Rule Them All'. In the other he was glancing down at the Ring, beneath which was written, 'Power can be held in the smallest of things'. So began a collection of atmospheric and highly desirable posters across all three films that ranged from individual characters to splendid renditions of Middle-earth's wonders, such as the statues of the Argonath and Lee's grim visage atop Orthanc.

The messaging was crystal clear: this wasn't simply fantasy; this was something bold, serious and epic.

Kamins had worried that the atomized set-up of New Line, where each territory would mount their own campaigns taking a lead from New Line could have a negative effect. It would be the proverbial 'herding cats', he thought. But it was the exact opposite; the book was such a global entity that its adaptation inspired each region to rise to the occasion.

'Individual territorial distributors were tailoring their campaigns to what they believed their territories would respond to. I think, in the end, it worked out better than if a major studio had a single, global, monolithic campaign for the entire world. It was more personal.'

The big worry remained Japan, where the books carried little weight. Rolf Mittweg, as head of international marketing, had put on a real cabaret to land distribution in Japan, personally escorting five potential Japanese distributors to New Zealand to do a nickel tour of the sets and the Workshop, where they would sample Richard Taylor's winning enthusiasm, and even spend time with Jackson.

Says Kamins, 'Thankfully, this was a period when the Japanese theatrical audience was more open-minded toward Western cinema, and Nippon Herald came in for significant money.'

With Liv Tyler's face leading the promotion the films gathered their own serious momentum. *The Return of the King* would make almost $100 million dollars in Japan alone.

*

Kamins was invited to the leather-clad screening room at New Line whenever Ordesky returned from New Zealand bearing segments of footage, still work-in-progress, and he would sit with Shaye and 'the marketing guys' and feel the cool analysis in the room. The first time he saw any kind of cut of the movie was in New Zealand with Shaye and Lynne. It was still extremely long, he admits, 'but you knew right then and there that this was something compelling. It didn't look like every other film. You could see it in the storytelling and Peter's visual style. And New Zealand as a character, which didn't look like anywhere else yet fitted so perfectly into what Middle-earth might conceivably look like to a lot of people.'

Kamins always had faith, but with filmmaking you could never know.

He smiles, sensing how far-fetched it all sounds now. 'I knew it was not going to be an epic failure. It was just like, okay, we have a beautiful piece of marble and now Peter's got to sculpt it into what it can be.'

The narrative had changed again: it was no longer about how good the film might be but how successful.

A few weeks later, at the time *Ain't It Cool News* got wind there was a finished cut, Wood took his seat in that same luxurious screening room and watched a finished version of the first film.

'God, it's often difficult to digest something the first time. So I wasn't sure how I felt about it. Which sounds weird to say now because I think that movie's extraordinary. But there was so much anticipation. . .'

Wood found himself struck by how beautiful it was. How it jumped off the screen in such 'an organic, realistic way'. But to finally see the result of his long labours was overwhelming. He found himself searching for what was and wasn't there, processing variables of his experience versus what it had all been for. This was a screening he had to get out of his system, before he could readily appreciate what had been achieved.

'I don't feel like you can really see something objectively the first time.'

In his blog, McKellen reported that he had seen the film at a private screening put on by Ordesky in New York on 10 November 2001. His carefully chosen words, while copious in their praise, had the opposite effect of sending a ripple of panic through an impatient fanbase who convinced themselves a cover-up was underway and this was *The Phantom Menace* all over again.

To say that 'everything on screen honours Tolkien's imagination' was simply not enough. To suggest that Jackson 'allows the story to be the star' was too vague.

I came to see the finished film at the press screening held the morning of the London premiere at a flagship cinema in Leicester Square. Like Cannes, critics huddled outside beforehand, fearful of displaying too much enthusiasm in front of their peers, but there was the same eagerness.

Critics tend to sport themselves with a practised nonchalance, as if they had been dragged kicking and screaming from their high-minded towers to see the next unholy mess fate and Hollywood had served up. Not today. There was almost a gasp as the lights went down.

So familiar are the images now — and so entangled between theatrical and extended cuts — it is hard to reframe the picture anew. Then it didn't quite feel like a new experience to me. I had seen the footage in Cannes, dined out on my secret knowledge, and I remember a prickle of panic mixed in with the excitement. Could it fail me even now?

Out of the darkness came Cate Blanchett's voice.

Her whispered, liquid Sindarin words were full of anguish and longing. Where does Galadriel recite the prologue from, I often wonder, and from when exactly? Helpfully for mortals, she soon switches to Westron (as in English), but notice has been given — they are taking Tolkien seriously.

'The world has changed,' she declares, 'I can feel it in the water, I can feel it in the air.' It was Boyen's first line, still intact, borrowed and slightly reconfigured from a speech given in the book by Treebeard.

As Wood says, what stood out in the flush of the first viewing was the presence of the world itself, not invented but somehow *discovered*. Less fractured than its sequels, *The Fellowship of the Ring* offers the most traditional quest structure and we are ushered on a relatively linear guided tour of the wonder and variety of Middle-earth: Hobbiton, Bree, Orthanc, Weathertop, Rivendell, Moria, Lothlórien and the Great River Anduin. Cue: Enya.

As with the soupçon in Cannes, the response to the finished film was swift, loud and mostly ecstatic.

Good critics, seldom caught so breathless, were reminded of the joy of first love. 'The most heart-breaking thing about faithful moviegoing is that awe, beauty and excitement, three of the things we go to the movies for, are the very things we're cheated of the most,' extolled Stephanie Zacharek of *Salon*. 'The great wonder of *The Fellowship of the Ring* is that it bathes us in all three, to the point where we remember — in a vague, pleasurably hallucinatory sensation from another lifetime — why we go to the movies in the first place.'

Jackson's sense of scale, she went on to say, was impeccable. The film was vast but not overreaching. There was not a drop of sillification to be found. Furthermore, it wasn't simply the empyreal lustre of New Zealand, it was how it exceeded the natural to become painterly, bizarre and, at times, almost dreamlike. Deep in its roots, we understood that this was not a Hollywood movie.

The first is also comparatively the most fairy-tale of the three: a journey through a dying world cast in the paradigm of hobbits, wizards, the eco-fabulations of the Elves and the Escher-kingdoms of the Dwarves. The bravura shots, sweeping around the miniatures hewn like ancient carvings, showed us a place both familiar and wholly alien.

Here were the contradictions of art: it was strange and heartfelt, huge and intimate, warm-hearted and deadly serious. Jackson's natural visual excesses were held in equipoise by Tolkien's cast-iron mythology. Yet, you could sense the director's gleeful *Bad Taste* still worming away beneath its skin.

'They really achieved a form of immortality in the cinema with this,' asserted Christopher Lee in that unbreakable voice, 'because nobody in the world, to the best of my knowledge, had seen anything like this. I was seeing things and couldn't believe how they had done it.'

'We were dreaming up all this outrageous stuff,' Jackson once said, and here it was: the vertiginous plunges, the operatic archi-tecture, the fantastic beasts and a foretaste of dizzying battles yet to come. Was this the last time CGI was so beholden to story-telling and not its own capacity for numbing proliferation? The level of detail took us right down to Frodo's dirty fingernails.

There were those who praised it to the hilt while still wres-tling with how it contradicted their own vision of Tolkien.

'It is an awesome production in its daring and breadth,' said Roger Ebert of the *Chicago Sun Times*, 'and there are small touches that are just right; the hobbits may not look like my idea of hobbits (may, indeed, look like full-sized humans made to seem smaller through visual trickery), but they have the right combination of twinkle and pluck in their gaze — especially Elijah Wood as Frodo and Ian Holm as the worried Bilbo.'

I can remember fretting over missing details from the book, unable to resist internally nit-picking Jackson's choices. But this

was more about the disappointment of not seeing them envisioned by the director than any religious devotion to the book.
The lack of the gift-giving sequence in Lothlórien jarred, but by
the second or third viewings that feeling was gone.

There were those that praised it to the rafters quite because
participation didn't depend on a love of Tolkien. Here was
'an intelligence and artistry *as a movie* independent of blind
fidelity to the page,' sang Lisa Schwarzbaum of *Entertainment
Weekly*.

The world was complex but the peril was tangible, Jackson
allowed suspense to build gradually to exhilarating heights.
Then taking a breath and building again. Beyond Shore's
splendid score roller-coasting from pastoral Hobbiton flutes to
Wagnerian choirs, the film moved to an intense yet graceful
internal music.

Like Boyens and Walsh, Selkirk talks about how the edit was
'emotion driven' and they treated the effects as almost circum-
stantial. Watch it again for the close-ups, and how often the
camera peers into eyes of the characters. McKellen's face alone
becomes another landscape on which the story unfolds.

I could go on, but this entire book is an attempt to translate
how Middle-earth came so unquestionably to life as it did that
morning.

There were those, of course, who took against it. It is in the
nature of criticism, Tolkien and humankind that someone is
always going to object.

'*The Fellowship of the Ring* resembles from certain angles
nothing so much as a 178-minute electric mandolin solo,' winced
Peter Bradshaw in *The Guardian*. Uncharitably, he also cast his
mind back to *Heavenly Creatures*, where the teenage girls created
a fantasy world as a by-product of emotional dysfunction, and
worried aloud at the stability of the Tolkien fanbase.

David Sterritt of the *Christian Science Monitor* was particularly
put out by Hobbiton. 'It's meant to be charming and gentle,'
he fumed. 'Instead, it's boring, bogus, overflowing with clichés

and largely humourless, despite stabs at quaintly old-fashioned comedy.'

There was no pleasing everyone. Purists bridled at the changes to the sacred text, Tolkienphobes remained uncured of their allergies to Elves and magic rings.

Yet Frodo lived.

'Where we succeeded was to make the films believable,' Jackson is willing to admit despite his natural Kiwi immunity to all forms of pretension. 'I mean, we were dealing with fantastical elements, wizards in pointy hats, Orcs and hobbits, clichéd things. I remember the *French and Saunders* parody of *The Fellowship of the Ring* — you look at that and think, "Jesus, the difference between them and us was so minute." To tip into parody would have been so easy. But you look at Aragorn and you don't look at a guy in a costume. We got people to believe.'

*

The world premiere of *The Fellowship of the Ring* took place in London on 10 December 2001. Lining up on the red carpet, the cast were thrilled to be back in one another's company, jeering good-naturedly at the late arrival of Liv Tyler for a group photo.

'I was just going to the bathroom,' she retorted primly.

'I think this film is a masterpiece,' Ian Holm told reporters.

'It's biblical!' cooed McKellen, who apologized for not having been up front about it being a masterpiece on his blog. 'I was too modest! But it is,' he declared, giddy as a schoolboy.

'This is more scary than making the movies,' observed Jackson, glancing down the gauntlet of journalists and TV crews he would have to negotiate before the safety of the cinema.

The media had wearily concocted a rivalry with the first of the *Harry Potter* films, noting that the screaming hoards in Leicester Square were markedly lower in number than for the premiere of that other fantasy epic. Jackson politely deflected any comparisons. He couldn't wait to see *Harry Potter and the Philosopher's Stone*.

In truth, they were worlds apart.

Even Saul Zaentz had made it to the film's maiden voyage, recounting that he had spent $20 million buying the rights from United Artists in another age. 'It was a hell of a lot of money in those days. That move, made in all innocence, is now looking rather smart.'

Says Kamins, 'The tracking was telling us that we were in a good place. But still no fantasy film had ever come out in December. Yet when the reviews came in everybody was feeling good. At that point, the movie had taken on an aura of The Little Engine That Could. That even though it was a big movie, it was still the largest independent film ever made.'

On 19 December, *The Fellowship of the Ring* opened at cinemas worldwide (although some territories like Japan and Russia would wait until February and March 2002). In the US alone it would end up making $315,544,750 (nearly $100 million more than New Line's previous record holder *Rush Hour 2*).

Adjust that figure for inflation and it made $484,425,600.* In other words, New Line had already recouped their entire investment in one fell swoop. Ultimately, over its four-month theatrical run the first film accumulated $861 million worldwide, outside of what would be made in home entertainment. Adjusted for inflation that translates to an estimated $1,076,000,000.

Then something completely unthinkable happened.

In New Zealand they gathered at Jackson and Walsh's seafront house in Seatoun; it was 1 a.m. and Boyens, Ordesky and Dan Hennah, the art director, were there, as was Serkis, currently deep into his transformation into Gollum. Together they watched the Academy Award nominations being announced, cheering as *The Fellowship of the Ring* was called out, growing silent

---

* The adjusted gross is calculated by dividing the total domestic gross by the average ticket price of that year to estimate the number of tickets sold. These figures were adjusted to the 2017 average ticket price of $8.84. This isn't a wholly accurate science, as certain films have had multiple releases, but it does provide a good estimate.

as they built up to a staggering thirteen in total — a record alongside *Titanic*. They included Best Picture and McKellen as Best Supporting Actor.

'We always hoped there would be a recognition for the technical achievements of the film,' says Ordesky. 'But when *Fellowship* got the Best Picture nomination we truly understood how deeply the films were perceived. Fantasy had been this *verboten* genre to the Academy.'

Not for a single second during the long months of production had anyone even joked about it — winning Oscars. Such talk wasn't in the New Zealand vocabulary, insists Kamins, 'and this was a time when there were only five Best Picture nominees. But the Academy really appreciated the daring of the whole enterprise. They knew that everyone had laughed at it. And laughed at New Line for taking it on.'

We will come onto the journey of *The Lord of the Rings* to Academy Awards recognition in a later chapter, but in 2002 it would prove to be a night of relative disappointment — or better to say delayed gratification.

For Jackson, there was no time to rest or take stock. Landing back into Wellington from the rigours of a global press tour he plunged into post-production on *The Two Towers* — in real terms a process that had carried on seamlessly from the first film. In a matter of months his cast were due to return to New Zealand for supplementary shooting on the second film. To return again to this unending business of Middle-earth, only now equipped with the knowledge that the outside world was equally as addicted to the Ring.

While *The Fellowship of the Ring* held sway in cinemas over that Christmas, Kamins phone rang. It was Mary Parent, the newly installed head of production at Universal.

'Would Peter be open to rekindling *King Kong*?'

To the Edge of the World

On 14 June 2002, banking through the cloud cover and taking some roughhousing from the local airstream — out of the window the wingtips pitch and yaw like a troubled boat — I touched down at Wellington International Airport for the first time. Taxiing to the terminal, all that could be seen of New Zealand's capital city were the quaint clapboard houses clinging to the hillsides. The airport is slotted onto a neck of flatland that joins the alluvial terraces of the Miramar Peninsula to the sandstone mountains that fortify Wellington itself. This made a natural funnel for the north-westerly that skims off the Cook Strait, ensuring a bumpy welcome for travellers.

The short distance to Stone Street Studios, literally over the hill, offered equal parts convenience and exasperation. Famously, during filming, a plane spotter was positioned on the ridge with a walkie-talkie to warn of imminent take-offs and landings, so the business of Middle-earth could avoid the anachronistic boom of jet engines.

A year after Cannes, I had been invited to New Zealand, to Middle-earth, the gold seam of Jackson's great project. I was there as a prospector, a journalist seeking a sense of how the impossible had been achieved. What was this mysterious Kiwi spirit that everyone spoke about? And where was that fabled, magical light?

Outside the terminal it was beginning to drizzle.

Despite having theoretically wrapped on 22 December 2000, cast and crew had returned to Stone Street for six-week blocks of what had been classified as supplementary shooting, or 'pick-ups', on each film. In June 2001, they returned to supplement *The Fellowship of the Ring*. And now it was the turn of *The Two Towers*.

What made this occasion different to the many months they spent here in the past was a sense of accomplishment, laced with a little relief as well. Not only had they come back in the full knowledge the first film of the trilogy has been a huge box office success, *The Fellowship of the Ring* had been strewn with Oscar-nominations — Hollywood's golden validation. And everyone knew it had been a close-run thing for Best Picture.

Their first film had slipped the moorings of its genre. The nay-sayers had been made to swallow their bile. There was a new frame of reference, a new language being used — critics were talking about art, ravishing and elemental. Jackson was now at the helm of a phenomenon, which inevitably meant the beady eye of Hollywood had grown only more intense.

Now the misanthropes, galled at having been proved wrong, were asking a new question. Could he sustain it?

Such debates were not to be heard at *The Green Parrot* or *The Spruce Goose* or *The Prancing Pony*, or any other Wellington spot frequented by filmmaking folk. They were definitely not to be heard on set.

'No one was thinking, "Ah, now we are under this pressure,"' recalls Ordesky. 'Peter did not wear stress poorly, which I think is a testament to him and a testament to the New Zealand culture. He had this expression, "One job at a time, every job a success." He really lived that. That wasn't just some soundbite that he put out there, like propaganda. He really felt that.'

*

DAY ONE: THE GOLDEN HALL. Stone Street Studios, the heart of Jackson's domain, concealed little of its former vocation as a paint factory — there was even a warning over the bathroom taps not to drink the water. A huddle of low, grey, ramshackle buildings, rising no higher than three storeys, the 'complex' looked jerry-rigged and might collapse to the ground if the wind got any stronger. Those Hollywood surveyors dispatched to assess the viability of Jackson's infrastructure must have feared the worst as they pulled up looking for a studio. But, as was so often the case with Jackson's endeavour, outward appearances were deceptive. Don't judge this book by its cover, for inside on cramped but industrious soundstages was a bewildering hub of Tolkien creation.

The economy of space was a marvel. The banners and curvilinear carvings of one half of King Théoden's Golden Hall, the royal palace of Rohan, were to be found on soundstage A, together with an outcrop of Fangorn Forest (being noisily dismantled) and some kind of torture chamber belonging to Christopher Lee. As with most movie sets, the immediate impression was of organized chaos.

And yet, as soon as I glanced into the monitor, there was Théoden's ancient throne room, an extraordinary compendium of Peter Jackson's framing, Andrew Lesnie's lighting, Dan Hennah's art direction, Alan Lee's concept art and J.R.R. Tolkien's imagination, stirred by Saxon history and *Beowulf*.

More incongruous was the large, brown 1960s-retro armchair emblazoned with the White Tree of Minas Tirith unoccupied in front of the bank of monitors. The chair had been provided for the visit of internet guru Harry Knowles during principal photography, and the art department decided that spruced up it might provide a good resting place for their harried director when on set. Jackson's throne had accompanied him as far afield as Waitarere Forest (for the Osgiliath woods) and the Rangitikei River Gorge (for the River Anduin) near Taihape, where they still have the highest bungee jump on the North Island.

Circling the chair was Peter Jackson, mug of tea in hand, wearing a crew body warmer, faded-pink polo shirt, shorts and, reluctantly bowing to the obligations of health and safety, walking boots. He looked like the guy you would ask to point out the director. Jackson would go shoeless at all times if he could. Hugo Weaving, august Elrond, described his director as a 'bare-foot being'. Was the shot of Galadriel strolling unshod over the Lothlórien turf a tribute to the director's habits?

'It's interesting, we've got to the stage now where difficult is easy,' he began unprompted. 'We all know what we are doing. Whereas at the beginning it was all new. We have all been involved in the hardest thing we are ever going to do.'

To this day, Jackson swears by this process of postpartum film-making. It makes practical sense. These weren't that Hollywood pejorative, *reshoots*, the last-ditch attempts to save a sinking ship. These were *supplementary* shoots he purposefully built into the schedule ahead of time. How can you know what needs adjusting until you've seen a cut of your film?

'I don't understand why most movies, with hundreds of millions worth of investment, only go off and do something if it is a total emergency.'

Casting his mind back to those return visits to Middle-earth, Ordesky agrees. 'Supplementary shooting meant whole new content. Because each film had its own editor, even early on Peter got a sense of the shape and rhythm of each one and to see where there were holes. There were literally holes, narrative holes, or there were opportunities to do things better or richer.'

Twenty-five minutes of supplementary footage was created for both the theatrical and extended cuts of *The Two Towers* over these extra weeks.

Jackson likes to call it 'handcrafting a film'.

The same will happen again the following year for *The Return of the King*. Even with the collateral of *The Fellowship of the Ring*'s box office performance, all of this added up to another significant strain on the budget New Line had to swallow. The time and cost involved with additional shooting on *The Lord of the Rings* could easily fund an independent movie.

'I always talk about how the boldest thing that New Line did was not greenlighting the film, which was bold,' declares Ordesky. 'The boldest thing was doubling down on the budget enhancements that took place mostly around visual effects and pick-up shooting down the road with *Two Towers* and *Return of the King*, because a more short-sighted businessman might have said, "Listen, we've got a winner. We've established this thing with *Fellowship*. We don't need to lower our margins by putting more into it." And New Line did put more into it by a meaningful degree.'

Jackson had been more than persuasive about what was needed going forward, he had been *articulate*. 'We have to increase the experience for cinemagoers with these subsequent movies,' he insisted to New Line. 'We can't rest on the laurels of what we developed in *Fellowship*.'

His antennae for audience psychology was, like Spielberg, born out of the fact he had never fully shaken his childhood wonder at movie-going. He remained on the wavelength of his own fourteen-year-old expectations. There was also something of Hitchcock in his blood too, the desire to surprise, even shock an audience, to bring them to life.

There was also a more organic need to push again on the level of visual effects. *The Two Towers* presented three of the biggest challenges of the trilogy. Two of which had been the root cause of much of the tension between Jackson and the studio. The upwardly revised budget was a sure sign of New Line's faith in him and Weta to deliver.

Besides, they weren't fools. Jackson had been elevated by fans, critics and rival studios to the level of a visionary, curbing his vision at this stage would inevitably have New Line painted as penny-pinching suits. Or worse still, as philistines.

Nevertheless, the second film presented challenges the

emboldened team at Weta were only beginning to fathom. They had to bring credibility to the Ents, to non-Tolkienites effectively walking trees with the grouchy demeanour readers tended to attribute to the author. Months of close-quarters combat footage had to be expanded into the clashing of 10,000-strong armies at The Battle of Helm's Deep (a process which would then inform the battle sequences in *The Return of the King*). And there was the greatest test of all, the single element that could yet founder the whole trilogy if they failed to find a way — Gollum.

Ordesky has gone on record that *The Two Towers* is his favourite film of the three. 'Part of the reason, whenever you are participating in the making of films, you are aware of the difficulties and obstacles surmounted. For me, personally, I know how immensely challenging *The Two Towers* was and how nearly it could not have come right.'

Jackson wasn't indulging himself; he was forging a new paradigm for filmmaking. The best way to protect the studio's investment was to make and keep making the best film possible.

But New Line's war chest was being depleted.

'Other resources within the company were limited because of the resources being brought to bear on *Rings*,' admits Ordesky. 'We were essentially increasing the financial risk.'

*

Structurally, *The Two Towers* didn't fit prescribed Hollywood thinking. By cookie-cutter studio practice, if you had a hit movie that called for a sequel you effectively begin again and write a new script. What made the original film so successful would inform the creation of the next one.

Waiting for the Golden Hall scene — a small conference between Gandalf, Théoden and Aragorn — to be readied, Jackson took a thoughtful sip of tea. 'People get worried and get locked into a formula,' he said. 'But in our case, because we have already shot three films at the same time, we are much less able to change anything.'

Their 'sequel' was preordained. Leastways, most of it was already shot.

Obviously, *The Two Towers* had the same sensibilities working for it. The same writers, same director, same cast, same director of photography: everything was a continuation. Yet there were distinct differences both in narrative and tone to *The Fellowship of the Ring*. Differences that all originated in the book. Differences that Jackson saw as ultimately a healthy thing.

This was the middle act of a single saga.

Scanning the elaborately carved pillars, bathed in a cool blue light that mottled fetchingly in the thin veil of dry ice, Jackson explained that the story now centred on the world of Men. 'Which gives it a more realistic, historical feel, a little in the direction of *Braveheart*.'

Bernard Hill, currently pacing out the scene and letting King Théoden's cloak billow regally behind him, later avowed that this would be a better film. 'You're very quickly brought into human frailties, human failure, human emotions like loss, grief, jealousy, all those things that people identify with,' many of them he implies involving his flawed character. 'And there is still the fantasy — grand wizards and all that kind of stuff.'

'This one is the trickiest,' Jackson admitted. Of all three films, their *Two Towers* elaborated upon the book the most, especially in the relationships. There had been more pick-ups required. 'Here we have explored more,' he said.

It was impossible not to marvel at Jackson's capacity to keep these three films in his head. With pick-ups there was the additional challenge of matching camera moves, lighting, the length of Aragorn's fetching stubble from principal photography. Jackson could recall not simply shots, but individual frames over two years old. All the while, footage was piped into his wall of monitors from the other units that were up and running (today three in total) for the director to keep an eye on. And a constant stream of department heads arrived to seek his council.

Watching Jackson on set was to see a man juggling twenty flaming brands without breaking sweat. The fabled calm and good humour of the ringmaster radiated throughout the entire circus.

Recalls Elijah Wood, 'One of the strongest impressions Peter made on my life, in regards to filmmaking, was just the environment he created for the process.'

'I think the most pertinent comment he made was that, "It's just a film,"' says John Howe, 'although it was something he devoted years of his life to, twenty-four hours a day.'

Jackson had been averaging about six to seven takes per scene, more confident now in knowing when he had the shot. During the main shoot it was twice that. Either way, there was always one more for luck.

Beaten-up copies of the book can be spotted everywhere, allowing for quick consultations with Professor Tolkien. Jackson described a process of envisioning things 'off-the-page'.

To describe Peter Jackson as an auteur feels wrong. There is too much baggage to the term, too much self-regard. Yet he has dictated his own terms as a director. This was his kingdom, far from the swaying palms of Hollywood. Even beneath the shadow of Tolkien, he had remained true to himself. The epic was leavened with comedy and a wonderfully visceral sense of horror. He had grounded the fantastic, but still taken an almost childlike delight in all the exuberant possibilities of his medium. The panorama of Middle-earth is worthy of David Lean, the camera swooping like a bird of prey.

'Every movie is a personal movie,' he says as we talk years later. 'Every decision I make is personal. The way I see my job as a director is to be a sponge. Have a plan but be open to everybody else's ideas and just cherry pick the ones that I like.'

Walsh was always nearby, Boyens too, and the close-knit team of loyal department heads for whom working with Jackson had become second nature after so long. Back in the late 1950s, asked at school what her father did for a living, Peter Ustinov's daughter had replied 'Spartacus'. It must have seemed the same for the loved ones of Andrew Lesnie, the quietly spoken cinematographer, or Ngila Dickson, the witty costume designer, or either of the longstanding art maestros: art director Dan Hennah and production designer Grant Major. And Richard Taylor, who appeared at his friend's side whenever armour or Orc prosthetics were to be applied or reapplied, running to his own indefatigable motor, before retreating to Weta Workshop five minutes up the road.

Art and costumes were based in a jumble of outbuildings that dogleg around the soundstages. With Jackson's attention drawn by the scene in hand, I am invited to scuttle through the drizzle and visit these extensions to the central hive of activity.

Numerous sets and props may had been preserved from principal photography (over 30,000 artefacts had been kept in storage), but the art department was still working to a twenty-four-hour cycle, seven days a week, breaking down the wonders of Middle-earth and building new ones in their place overnight. At this moment, they had seven sets and four exteriors at various stages of construction or deconstruction. The softly spoken Hennah, whose frowzy silver hair, beard and welcoming, avuncular manner suggested Peter Jackson's quiet, older brother, could not allow his spirits to flag. He had first worked with Jackson on *The Frighteners,* and even then there was never enough time.

'The space when you finish one set and when you're shooting the next, it gets much smaller,' he grumbled, but good-naturedly, his desk piled with architectural blueprints and the room wallpapered with a gallery of Alan Lee and John Howe artwork. 'My last day off was about forty days ago.'

The Two Towers had presented its own catalogue of architectural challenges. There was the Hornburg, the stone fortress jutting from the rock of the steep-sided valley known as Helm's Deep where battle will unfold. There were the Dead Marshes (outside on the backlot) and Fangorn, the gnarly, ancient forest of the Ents. But it is the hilltop settlement of Edoras, seat of the Golden Hall, which Hennah proudly claimed to be his, and the second film's, magnum opus.

According to the book, Edoras sits on top of an isolated hill strikingly ringed by a mountain range — characteristic of Tolkien's flare for scene setting, but geographically preposterous. And yet, during a location scout on the wilder, more mysterious South Island, Hennah and his team had followed the alluvial fan around the Rangiata River. As the helicopter swooped down the valley, they spotted a lonely outcrop of terminal moraine that seemed to have sprouted both from the valley floor and the pages of Tolkien. While much had been made of New Zealand's facility to represent Middle-earth, this was made-to-measure.

'It was surrounded by the Southern Alps,' said Hennah, who had read *The Lord of the Rings* six times and had his own feeling on how 'things were meant to be'.

This was how Edoras was meant to be.

They took eleven months to create Edoras on top of that rocky outcrop, exterior to the set currently on A Stage. It was an adventure within itself. To even access the location a road had to be built across rivers and marshland. The constant wind varied between gale-force and Biblical — while filming they recorded speeds of 140 km per hour — and this was a twelve-metre-high set with a thatched roof according to the splendid Saxon design by Lee. They constructed the wooden exterior over a steel frame drilled down into the rock — this wasn't a set build, it was structural engineering.

Hannah smiled, as he did often. 'People who lasted the construction period developed very strong characters.'

The shot of Miranda Otto's Éowyn standing on the stone steps of the Golden Hall, the wind catching at her blonde hair and white gown, as the helicopter-shot circles around her drinking in Edoras in the foreground and the unquenchable sweep of the landscape beyond is amongst the trilogy's finest shots.

Her first day on set, this was Otto's introduction to Middle-earth. 'It was like walking into your own fairy tale,' she marvelled. 'Peter had said, "I want people to believe Edoras is a real place."'

'The learning curve on this film was finding out how much vision and how much drive Peter Jackson had,' said Hennah. 'Someone who is obsessive to a degree, who won't compromise. . . You had to go that step further.'

Surrounded by the rag trade bustle of the costume department, with hundreds of photos and yet more artwork pinned to the wall — charting a fascinating evolution for each costume — Dickson possessed a fine disregard for the source material. She was not a Tolkien aficionado. It was likely she never would be. 'This movie is chocka with Tolkien fanatics,' she observed.

Without doubt it helped to have pockets of resistance to the holy word of the don. A counterpoint, Dickson could come at her task from a more dispassionate, perhaps open-minded place.

'Tolkien is much better on location than he is on the dress,' she sighed. There would be conversations with Lee about what Tolkien's vision was for a certain character, where he would immediately do another of his flowing-robe drawings. 'Oh, we need a bit more than *that*, Alan,' she would groan.

'Which character gave you the most trouble?' I enquired.

'I knew you would ask that one,' she pouted, arching an eyebrow like a headmistress suspecting cheek. 'There is always one, and it was Legolas.'

They had begun with something more elaborate and 'Elvish' and kept refining it and refining it. There was a mad flurry the night before Bloom was due on set in his revised costume, working thirty-six hours straight to get it right. Producer Barrie Osborne was feeding them pizzas at four o'clock in the morning.

'It was a complete nightmare,' confessed Dickson.

'That was the first few weeks of filming,' remembers Jackson. They had shot scenes with Bloom in the original costume. One has squeezed its way into the extended cut of *The Fellowship of the Ring*, when the heroes spend the night on a flet in the trees of Lothlórien. Look closely at Legolas and you'll catch a glimpse of a baroque neckline.

'Well, that looks silly,' Walsh had declared watching the dailies. 'He looks like he's got bra straps.'

'In the end simplicity won,' sighed Dickson, who admitted this was the first time she had talked about this. 'Orlando as Legolas has such a lightness. So we threw out all the elaborate details and went to something that allowed him to move.'

Overall, realism was the scariest part for Dickson. Despite all the 'wacky creatures' you had to get into the filthiness of everyone. The weathering of costumes was immense. Her department had made over 15,000 costumes. There were forty-two sets of Frodo travelling clothes alone.

'It's a never-ending story really. Pete always has a new idea, a new approach. We always said, "Whatever Pete wants he gets." There's very much a kind of "get in behind Peter Jackson's philosophy".'

She waved away any complaints. The rewards have vastly outweighed the stresses. Being a costume designer, she said, was like being a drug addict. You get completely off on the moment when you walk onto set and see the actor with his hair and make-up done and costume on and everything has come together. 'I had it with Gandalf and Aragorn, and with Arwen. I stood on set and cried.'

On the last day of principal photography, Jackson presented a specially made book to all the crew. It was an album filled with behind-the-scenes memories.

Dickson laughed. 'There's a photograph of me standing on set with Peter and Ian McKellen behind him and the caption read, "I want it known that I do not dress the director." Actually, I think Peter has a great style. Who else pads about Beverly Hills in bare feet?'

*

Catering was located in a corrugated hut for which the term rudimentary would be bragging. That said, with lunch still a few minutes of hard Middle-earth toil away, it had the tranquil air of the Savoy. A string quartet played in a minor key, a weekly gift of Osborne's to soothe weary Friday brows. Tablecloths were straightened, napkins folded and food prepared, while three Orcs chatted amiably at a corner table.

Gradually, the room filled up to form a perfect tableau of this brilliant, crazy interface between New Zealand hammer-on-nail pragmatism and the mythopoeic grandeur of Tolkien's sub-creation. No one blinks as more Orcs join their brethren, minions of Saruman with platefuls of shepherd's pie. There is no time for the stuntmen to reapply prosthetics so they remain masked throughout the day. A hobbit extra arrives, his prosthetic feet wrapped in bin liners. This turned out to be Thomas Robbins from *Forgotten Silver* who was playing Déagol. Then without fanfare Gandalf the White seated himself at a table with Théoden, Lord of the Riddermark, his beard safely stowed in a hairnet to prevent it drooping into his salad.

A short while later, the din of dinnertime having subsided, Sir Ian McKellen's steel-blue eyes were surveying me with an intensity he reserved for interviewers and Tooks.

'Well, I'm rather relieved, as you can imagine.' The British knight had taken pause to consider the glowing reception he had received for his interpretation of the Grey Wizard.

He went on. 'If you play Hamlet or Macbeth or Richard III,' all of which he had on numerous occasions, 'you're walking on territory hundreds of other actors have done so before. But there haven't been a lot of Gandalfs. But I don't think of it as my part. I've borrowed it. I'm allowed to put on the clothes.'

His humility was well worn, but there will be few Gandalfs to come who won't tremble to follow in McKellen footsteps. He will remain the only actor to be Oscar-nominated for the entire trilogy. Despite all that talk of Sean Connery, it was now impossible to imagine Gandalf without McKellen's cello-rich tones. It was that great voice, edged with weariness and humour, which made Middle-earth so impregnable in the first film. McKellen's conviction made the world real. The wizard's robes fitted him very well indeed. Only now they had changed colour. For *The Two Towers* he had upgraded into a sleek, manicured, more angelic version of the wizard grappling with global politics.

'Well, it is the same person but in a different part of their life.' You sense McKellen couldn't quite see the point, and missed the old, pipe-smoking curmudgeon. 'Gandalf the White has discarded a lot of Gandalf the Grey's age, for example, his decrepitude and ancient bones.'

His work completed for the day, Viggo Mortensen walked in across the concrete floor as shoeless as the day he was born. Like his director, he finds footwear cramps his style. But this was more of a bohemian gesture. He carried with him a silver cup of *maté*, an unappetising herb-infused elixir favoured in Argentina, and was wearing a homemade Denmark football jersey with white chevrons painted inexactly down each sleeve. Half-Danish, Mortensen was declaring his allegiance. Later, England will beat Denmark a healthy three-nil in the World Cup in South Korea. Something Hill will remind his co-star about the next morning.

Sitting down, Mortensen opened a small, battered notebook as if beginning a sermon. 'It really starts happening in the second movie,' he commenced, referring to his notes — thoughts he has put together on the contextual basis for *The Two Towers* — 'especially when it comes to Rohan, which is a proud but isolated people. There is a value of working together, a "commonality".'

While promoting the first film, much was made of Mortensen's full immersion into the role of Aragorn: staying in costume and sleeping rough. In person it was not that which stood out rather his unwillingness to be anybody but himself: wholly serious, philosophical and more than a little out there. He was once beautifully described as Jean-Jacques Rousseau trapped in the body of Rudolph Valentino.

He had a theory he wished to impart, his voice hushed and thoughtful. 'The Ring is not evil in itself,' he proclaimed, still quoting from the Book of Viggo. If I got the gist of his rambling explanation, Mortensen believed the Ring represented the potential for selfish choices in all of us, the potential to try and control the worlds of others. He saw *The Lord of the Rings* as being about uniting to find a way, 'to reject the impulse of the Ring. As led by Aragorn and Gandalf'.

He allowed that this was not a classical reading of the book.

It was the simple questions that tended to stump the star. Asked for a general update on Aragorn's mind-set in the second film, Mortensen looked perplexed. There was a long pause as his internal projector rewound to all those glorious nights spent shooting Helm's Deep in a cold quarry.

'He's more of a soldier in this one,' he said finally. 'He's coming to terms with his destiny to be king.'

On cue, Hill appeared over his co-star's shoulder and pretended to yawn.

Catching sight of him, Mortensen grinned like a lunatic. 'Hey, it's his majesty,' he groaned, and headed for the door and an afternoon's bareback horse riding in the rain.

Hill was one of the new actors *The Two Towers* would introduce. Born in Blackley, Manchester, he rose to fame portraying a destitute, unemployed man hovering over the abyss of mental breakdown in the acclaimed BBC series *The Boys from the Blackstuff*, and has slowly moved up the social ranks ever since. He appeared in *Gandhi*, *The Bounty* and was the captain of James Cameron's *Titanic*. As an actor he had an earthy and unpretentious quality, but with a smooth, musical delivery honed on the Shakespearean boards. And now he was playing the King of Rohan, albeit in the midst of psychic deterioration.

King Théoden, he explained, would experience a kind of 'rebirth'. Rohan had been in serious decline because Théoden had fallen victim to Saruman's scheming as meted out by Gríma

Wormtongue, chief advisor to the king and snake-eyed agent of the corrupted wizard. Théoden had been rendered into a decrepit puppet.

'He has to shake off evil and become pure again,' said Hill. 'It's almost like he grows up.'

Théoden's introduction is one of the ways in which the second film embraces the political. Théoden, like Denethor to come, represents human fallibility at the very top of the chain. He embodies many of the doubts that rattle around inside Aragorn's skull. His struggle to rediscover himself is also a fine example of the script seeking out the human in the epic. Not only Saruman's evil, but old grievances, pride and the contradictions of leadership will muddy the waters of Mortensen's 'commonality'.

Hill might have been a late arrival to New Zealand, but he has enjoyed himself royally. Especially the commonality he has found with his fellow actors. The language that came out of the make-up trailer he shared with Mortensen and Bloom has been described as deplorable.

If there was any downside to all this glorious filmmaking fun, he admitted it was horses. He wasn't a confident rider, and here he was playing king of the horse-lords. Oh, the irony, he gestured. Still, there were plenty of saddle hours to try and acclimatize to riding. He was also given a docile pony.

'He's called Depend, for "dependable",' said Hill. Stoic from his forelock to his fetlocks, nothing could rattle Depend. 'It was Viggo's bloody nag that kept hitting reverse gear and murdering the shot.'

Every Friday afternoon, with tea, there was a raffle. The slight air of madness that flowed around Stone Street had finally taken form. Most of the cast and crew crammed into catering had been working on these films for three years or more. Yet nothing could lessen their enthusiasm at the chance to win a *Lord of the Rings* trading card game or a set of hobbit figurines. There was much whooping and hollering. When Hill, being king, pulled the next name out of a small box, an Orc stood up, pumped his calloused fist in the air and dashed forward to collect his commemorative cap.

*

DAY TWO: ORTHANC. Brad Dourif shuffled out of the inky shadows and into the candlelight of Orthanc, Saruman's 500-foot-tall stronghold, found that morning on B stage. The lingering note of Dracula's Transylvanian château was no doubt in subtle tribute to Jackson's love of Hammer Horror's Gothic melodrama (Christopher Lee was due shortly). Dourif was fully costumed as Gríma Wormtongue, his complexion nauseously pale and short of eyebrows. The idea being that he had been constantly picking away at himself in self-loathing, another example of how the director, along with his fellow screenwriters, had enhanced the character on the page.

Brought to itchy life by Dourif, there is a hint of Igor and Richard III about him. Yet he is never silly or clichéd.

Having presented me with a tilt of the head and an eye as big as a golf ball, Dourif hissed, 'So, you've come to see me fail?'

He preferred to stay in the vicinity of his character.

Meanwhile, the crew buzzed around Jackson as if responding to telepathic instructions. They had long since learned to read their director's mind; it only saved time. Jackson, eager to grab one more shot before lunch, was clutching a crumpled sheet of paper on which something was scribbled in biro. He wanted to insert a line into a scene he had shot years earlier that has Wormtongue inform his master that the people of Rohan are making for Helm's Deep and this might be a good time to launch an attack.

'I'm in make-it-up mode,' the director laughed.

Over a few takes, Dourif felt his way into the dialogue he'd had bare minutes to learn, testing where to lay emphasis. Then like a key slotting into a lock, the West Virginia-born actor found his rhythm and I watched him succeed.

A sure sign of the self-belief that pervaded the production was that nothing appeared to be off-limits. Maybe this was a confidence born of success, but there was none of the paranoia that haunts a Hollywood set — all those troubled smiles of publicists and chaperones, dreading the moment you might talk to someone. Naturally, there was a publicist, the bright and easy-going Claire, but she took a museum guide's enjoyment in showing off her prize exhibits.

It was the ineffable New Zealand spirit again. There was nothing but pride in what they were achieving and they want to share their satisfaction. They were almost giddy to do so. They were serious about what they were doing without taking themselves too seriously.

Which once again was credit to Jackson. The mood of any production tends to be dictated from the top down. A screamer will beget screamers. If your leader is laidback, amused by his own DIY scribblings — though there had been a call to Boyens to give the line the go-ahead — then that counts for everyone.

The day before, McKellen had alighted on an anecdote he felt symbolized the entire spirit of Jackson's adventure. There was a familiar ring to it. A man had been spotted peeping through the railings one day when they were shooting just outside Wellington.

'What's that man doing?' Jackson had demanded.

It turned out he was perfectly innocent. He was only a guy, mad about the films, desperate for a glimpse inside.

'Well, bring him in,' instructed Jackson.

'So he was allowed to stand inside,' said McKellen with an approving nod. 'Three years down the line, he is still working on the film. Plane spotting, I think. Happy as Larry.'

In an alternative universe Jackson knew he might have been standing on the other side of the fence.

Hours earlier, I was left alone to peruse Saruman's chambers. Books, maps, parchments, sooty candelabras and sample bottles, one containing something unpleasantly amphibian: the detail, up close, was breathtaking. Everything had to be authentic.

There had been a parchment written in Elvish on which one line had translated to something like 'Gary was here!' Jackson wasn't impressed, and Gary had to hastily redo it (the publicist had changed the named to protect the guilty). There are people out there who can read Elvish, the director reasoned.

Sitting for a moment on the obsidian throne normally the preserve of Christopher Lee — there is a picture, of course — I paused to ponder the oddity of my surroundings. This was only a movie set: scratch the surface and you would find wood, fibreglass and fine New Zealand workmanship. But it blurs into Middle-earth. Not just the artistry, the way it is perceived. No one calls it a set — they call it Orthanc. There is a sense of willed belief in the air.

Jackson liked to imagine that he and his team had just landed in Middle-earth with their cameras and coffee trolleys and begun shooting.

When we talked later in the day, back out of costume and with some healthy colour back in his cheeks, Dourif proved another ruminative soul. 'I've played a lot of villains, probably too many,' he admitted. 'I have an edge. I just come across as relatively intense. My girlfriend told me this, brave soul that she is: "You do come across as an odd duck." I was ill when I was a child and I have an odd way of focussing. It's either one-dimensionally or I just space out.'

With that distinctive Virginian accent (there's an effective whisper of it still within the Received Pronunciation he gives to Wormtongue), short frame and intense, protruding eyes, Dourif was destined to portray the disturbed and peculiar side of life. His whole career was staked out by the Oscar nomination he received at only twenty-three for the twitchy, stammering Billy Bibbit in *One Flew Over the Cuckoo's Nest*. He was later to voice the psychotic doll Chucky in the *Child's Play* films and play a cowardly, Klan-devoted Southern deputy in *Mississippi Burning*. He was the most established American actor on the film. Having endured the runaway perfectionism of *Heaven's Gate*, he found the comparisons made with the supposed excesses in New Zealand laughable.

'In the morning they would pick us all up and take us riding and we would ride, then we would have lunch, and then the bus would take us roller-skating. Then we would roller-skate until the day was over. I was there for a month and a half before I even shot a scene. That was way over budget and way over time. Peter is on budget and on time. There is nothing extravagant and out of control about it.'

For his part, a relatively small role, Dourif was only required at specific intervals of the initial eighteen-month shoot. Unlike the gulag of *Heaven's Gate*, he was free to depart the production. His experience was more sporadic than most. He did an initial six weeks, then another week, and then four more — all with months between (and returned again for pick-ups). During one hiatus from Wormtongue, he managed to shoot an entire television series called *Ponderosa* (based on the old Western show, *Bonanza*) before returning to New Zealand.

It was a salutary side effect of the extended nature of *The Lord of the Rings* to tally how much else the actors made while still playing their part in the trilogy. Mortensen shot *Hidalgo* and McKellen *X-Men 2* and still returned for more Middle-earth.

With no great appetite for fantasy, Dourif hadn't read *The Lord of the Rings* beforehand. 'Not even in my hippy days when it was required reading for hippies.' But he never thought twice about taking the role.

'Everyone knew it was going to be a big movie. But it's not the kind of role I would turn down, period.'

Wormtongue may be a villain but he is a human villain. It is a literal and figurative distinction. Besides Gollum he is another expression of the tragedy that can fuel evil. 'He did have a value in the kingdom,' said Dourif, 'but he has turned evil under the sway of Saruman.'

Where, in Ralph Bakshi's underfed adaptation, Wormtongue resembled an overweight stage magician, Dourif finds baroque depths in the part. Drawing on the panoply of Dickens eccentrics, Shakespeare and an early liking for Edgar Allan Poe inspired by his 'macabre' father, Wormtongue's unhealthy designs on the king's niece Éowyn (Otto) are laden with a sense of a man wretched in his ugliness. Yet Dourif laces his bewitching voice with a winsome Peter Lorre-like humour.

It was a process shepherded more by Boyens and Walsh than the overburdened Jackson.

'You can't talk to Peter,' noted Dourif without complaint. 'He's got twenty monitors about him. One of the great shames is that I haven't got to sit down and shoot the shit with him.'

His primary sounding board was Boyens. Once they were shooting, she and Walsh had assumed the mantle of building the characters with the actors. Boyens especially was there on the end of the phone, and often in person, to smooth the creases of Tolkien's complexity and help locate human truths where they might be elusive on the page.

Dourif also had the pleasure of sharing many of his scenes with the galvanic figure of Lee as Saruman. He held his hands aloft in admiration.

'That man knows how to talk. He has had this amazing life, and he knows just about everybody on the planet.'

In person, fully garbed as Saruman, with those long, white skirts that have caused him such distress, peering over the hooked, prosthetic nose, Lee cut an intimidating figure. Even with his beard snared in a hairnet. This was during lunch, of course, when we found ourselves on opposing sides of the buffet. The actors happily queue along with everyone else, the idea of slinking back to a trailer unthinkable, and Lee peered at me intently across a bowl of steaming chilli.

'Do you recommend it?'

Saruman the White, corrupted Istari and lord of Orthanc, has evidently mistaken me for a member of the catering staff.

Being English and not wishing to point out his error, I coped as best I could. 'It certainly smells good,' I replied.

There comes an awful pause.

'Hmmm, better not,' he growled, his sidewinding eyebrows folding into a frown and a taloned hand patting his stomach, 'I have to be on set this afternoon.'

He wafted away in search of less volcanic lunch options. To this day, with Lee long gone, I still wonder if that had been humour.

When on set, the boundary between wizard and great doyen of stage, screen, opera and much else besides was barely perceptible. Jackson bobbed and weaved about him with a boyish pleasure, taking the odd ticking off in good stead.

'Yes Christopher, of course,' he repeated, and the image of Baldrick orbiting Blackadder sprang to mind.

Once his scenes were completed — Saruman peering down into the industrialized hell of his battle preparations (currently a blue screen), while a fawning Orc takes instruction — Lee professed he was too tired to talk and then sat down to talk nonetheless. This was part of a ritual. One must recognize the honour it was to have an audience with the eighty-year-old legend. And it was: he made pronouncements rather than gave answers; told grand, well-rehearsed stories, with that tale of meeting Tolkien ever ready; and, in light of *The Fellowship of the Ring*'s reception, to which he had played chief clairvoyant from the very start, proclaimed with equal certainty the greatness of what will follow.

'It's easy to feel confident,' he boomed, and crewmembers scampering around like Orcs in the background stopped in their tracks. 'I don't have any fears as to whether it is going to do less business or whether it's not going to do as well. I think the anticipation is probably greater this time around. The movie is going to be better.'

DAY THREE: WETA WORKSHOP. Richard Taylor's province was so madly cluttered you felt as if you might be squeezed to death by the appurtenances of Middle-earth that he and his team have been fashioning for what must have felt like forever. In real terms, they had not stopped working on some level since the day Jackson first proposed the idea of adapting the book in 1996. The bustling industry was not far off that seen in Saruman's fell pits, albeit with a more upbeat Kiwi aura of endeavour and the hum of local radio stations.

It is all here packed in like a pharaoh's tomb: swords, armour, helmets, jewellery, maquettes, the massive miniatures and Orc skins hanging from a rail like this year's collection: Milan meets Minas Morgul.

'Get a feel of this,' instructed Taylor holding out the handle of Narsil, the broken sword that is Aragorn's heirloom.

Absurd as it sounds, what surprised me was how real it felt in my hands.

The guided tour finally arrived at their largest workshop space where the biggest creations were housed.

In a corner stood Treebeard, or at least the top half of him. The animatronic 'hero' version of the Ent was built for close-ups with Pippin and Merry, played by a bottom-sore Billy Boyd and Dominic Monaghan. Given the rigours of getting strapped into the puppet they used to take lunch while still in the rough grip of his ligneous fingers. Those honey-coloured eyes followed me around the room.

Months later, I caught up with John Rhys-Davies in a New York hotel. He, the hobbit actors and Bloom had completed their filming by the time I was in Wellington. Rhys-Davies was rare (but not unique) among the cast in playing two roles. Aside from stout, comical Dwarf Gimli, after much speculation among fans it was announced he would lend his thoroughbred Welsh baritone to Treebeard. It was a process that had been troubling him.

'How does a tree speak?' he implored.

A question even an actor of Rhys-Davies' varied career seldom gets to ask.

'It's such a risk this one. If I fall on my face it is my fault. You know, we have even tried to add a whale-like communication to his voice.' Then Ents are in a sense the 'whales' of the forest.

Rhys-Davies puffed out his chest and emitted a low, rumbling, mournful facsimile of an ocean giant: '*Wooooommmoomgggh. . .* I trust that PJ has the answer. It's a challenge to be met and conquered.'

I offered a suggestion. Did he sense how much of Tolkien could be found in the character? Tolkien's much documented affection for trees, his whole ecological standing, was channelled into this shepherd of Fangorn as a response to his dismay at the blight of industrialization spreading like a stain across the bucolic England of his dreams.

'I did not,' Rhys-Davies replied, too polite to say if he had. 'I understood there was much of him in Gandalf, but I will take this onboard. I thank you.'

Treebeard and his arboreal brethren were due to be one of the toughest calls made upon Jackson's keep-it-mean approach to Tolkien. In Bakshi's movie Treebeard resembled an ambulatory turnip. In Jackson's *The Two Towers* the Ents are another minor miracle. Their rallying to tackle Saruman's 'mind of metal and wheels' is a surrealist carnival of sumptuous CGI (styled by way of Ray Harryhausen), animatronic design and rich, strange voice acting. The sound editing department, a neglected gang, added layers of rustling leaves and the creaking of ancient boughs to Rhys-Davies' lovely, ponderous delivery.

As the Ents tear Isengard asunder, flooding Saruman's pits by breaching the dam across the River Isen, who doesn't thrill to the exquisite detail of an Ent dipping its flaming branches into the onrushing water? It is a mere touch, but a perfect example of the wit and precision Jackson and his team had given to Middle-earth.

A short walk down Park Road, in another rickety warehouse, history was being made. Not that those involved were aware of it quite yet, they were still at the stage of praying to all the cinematic gods that Gollum would work. Inside, I was met by the fruity aroma of a school gym, although along one side of the space was a procession of heavy computers, each with an operator staring intently at computerized body parts. On another side, with a script open in front of her, sat Fran Walsh, who had taken ownership of the Gollum process.

In the middle of the floor, standing on a wooden box in a blue leotard speckled with black patches and white beads, was the London-born actor Andy Serkis pulling *Matrix* poses to make the crew laugh. An orchard of sensors on steel stands encircled the space, 'capturing' his movements.

Welcome to the 'volume' (the term James Cameron later put into general usage for the 'scanned' area within which motion is recorded) circa 2002, when motion capture was a strange concept indeed. Serkis would act every facet of the role to an extraordinary physical and psychical extent: movement, voice, mind, heart and deviant soul. But what would appear on screen would be a Gollum-shaped CGI simulacrum of his performance. He would be there and not there. If Tolkien had disdained acting as merely dressing up and 'pretending', what, I wonder, would he have made of this?

'I personally think the Frodo-Sam-Gollum relationship is the scariest thing in *The Two Towers*,' Jackson had told me the day before. While taking their lead from the book, he and his screenwriting partners were digging deep into the psychological concept of this emaciated ghoul, cowed by the Ring, who will serve as Frodo's perfidious guide into Mordor.

'He is such an extraordinary character,' agreed Serkis, interviewed later and back in human clothes. 'He's the audience's key to what the Ring does to you.'

We'll return to Serkis and the miraculous origins of Gollum in the next chapter. In the meantime, it turned out that the actor's twisted performance had been temporarily halted by a technical snafu. One of the numerous white 'dots' on his leotard was on the blink and he had been swiftly surrounded by Weta technicians searching for the errant sensor like frustrated fathers tracking down the loose bulb in the Christmas lights.

Whether idling away this momentary downtime or occupied

in some digital multi-tasking, or doing it entirely for my benefit, the terminal operator in front of me hereupon opened up some footage on his screen and gestured for me to look.

He pressed play, and I watched as Gandalf plunged into the abyss of Khazad-dûm tumbling after the fiery glow of the Balrog, the camera nose-diving after them. Even on a computer monitor *The Two Towers* extraordinary opening salvo was a sight to behold. The falling Gandalf clasps his plummeting sword, catches hold of his molten foe and commences an aerial duel, each blow of the sword igniting veins of fire in the Balrog's black skin.

What a gesture of confidence with which to open the second film, commanding our attention with a dazzling overture of Weta magic. Based on a painting John Howe had done for a fantasy card game, it's a purely cinematic interpretation of a moment recounted second-hand in the book, and an instant reminder of who was at the controls.

Says Boyens, 'Jackson was always certain of how he wanted the big things to be done. 'I remember when we were sitting talking about the second film, and he said, "I know how I want it to start." And we were like "Wow!"'

In the finished film the sequence will cut to Frodo starting awake suddenly. Was it a dream? Or a vision sent to him by Gandalf whose death has been greatly exaggerated? If you pay close attention, there are hints of an extra-dimensional connection between wizard and hobbit. Whatever the case, it is the first of a set of inspired transitions that set up a new internal rhythm for the storytelling. One that will syncopate between storylines, but always drawn onward by Frodo's quest.

'*The Two Towers* was the most challenging editorially,' admits Ordesky.

The second film was destined to be the difficult middle-child. It had neither start nor ending, and couldn't, by design, resolve much at all. Tolkien had insisted that the two sides of the second book must be seen through in their entirety to avoid confusion.

Thus he began by charting Aragorn, Gimli and Legolas in pursuit of Merry and Pippin, captured by Orcs — a journey that would reunite them with Gandalf. Then in the second half of *The Two Towers* he charted the tricky path of Frodo, Sam and Gollum toward Mordor.

The defining nature of film, of course, is the facility to juggle time and juxtapose concurrent storylines. Yet Jackson would make sense of the second film by taking a leaf out of Tolkien's book and editing the Frodo-Sam-Gollum story from beginning to end. Only then did he grab the other story strands and figure out where they weave in and out.

Back in the warehouse in Miramar, whatever gremlins were in the works had been chased away and with a whoop Serkis scampered to the middle of the volume and, after a brief conference with Walsh, resumed banging a plastic fish against a wooden box and out of him poured that voice. . .

*

My first journey to New Zealand came with so many rewards. All of them borne out of the production's desire to share in what they saw as their great fortune in being set this incredible task.

I watched the extended cut of *The Fellowship of the Ring* for the first time, only on the big screen in Jackson's Camperdown Road cinema next door to Weta Workshop, lavishly dolled out in an anti-multiplex aesthetic of velveteen and gilt. Seated in the audience were Hill and Mortensen giggling like children. I remember clearly Hill's loud guffaw at the old-school Jackson gag of Pippin farting after gorging on *lembas* bread — a moment of comic relief among the forbidding business of getting to Mount Doom.

I met Mark Ordesky for the first time, although I had seen him in Cannes. His fingernails were painted black. Not some Gothic affection, he hastily pointed out, but the result of a local launch party for Fine Line's *Hedwig and the Angry Inch* that had gone on late the night before.

Here, too, I first got to know Boyens, a different voice amongst the filmmakers and actors: more lyrical, wide-ranging and unrepentently steeped in Tolkien lore.

There was a damp afternoon trip to the pebbly banks of the Hutt River to watch Jackson work on location from his armchair. He sat in a tented enclosure like a sunless sultan, watching as Karl Urban's Éomer and his sodden Rohirrim searched among the bodies of Orc-slain comrades. Absurdly, rain machines were required. Some kind of specific cinematic rain was sought after, picked out by the silvery halogen glow from the lighting rig. Jackson calmly orchestrated the ensemble while glancing to other monitors showing the other units keeping up their end of the bargain back at Stone Street.

I travelled further afield via my first counterintuitive, bubble-in-the-sky helicopter ride to Fernside, a historic country home in the heart of New Zealand wine country. The marvellously named Gertrude Jekyll had designed the lavish gardens and it was on her woman-made lake they had shot Galadriel appearing out of the mist on a swan-shaped boat like a Pre-Raphaelite painting. The same boat had rested in a French swimming pool at the Cannes launch party. More recently, Jekyll's picturesque water feature had provided the exteriors for Sméagol and Déagol fishing in quiet harmony before discovering the Ring, a scene that had been meant for *The Two Towers* before becoming the daringly understated opening to *The Return of the King*.

Then it was a car journey to the sylvan acres of Kaitoke Regional Park where they had shot Rivendell exteriors, and interiors — Elrond's country estate almost an extension of the forest.

And I would go by foot to Victoria Park on a hillside above Wellington. Where in 1999 on a wooded path they had begun shooting with the hobbits hiding from a Ringwraith, unable to even conceive that this would ever end. And it still hadn't.

By *The Return of the King* premiere, fans were following these trails like pilgrims to the Holy Land.

New Zealand was and is vital to the psychology of how Jackson makes films. It is more than simply the primordial scenery and that elusive light, and more than the dogged habits of an unrepentant homebody. If he shot anywhere else he would be a different filmmaker and *The Lord of the Rings* would have been a different set of films. It is the temperament of the place and its indefatigable can-do people who have toughed it out at the edge of the world. Moreover, there was an infectious joy in simply creating that goes back to the giddy days of *Bad Taste*. I'd never been on a set like it. Jackson's homeland feeds him in ways he could probably never articulate. It's almost symbiotic, as if he occasionally plugs his permanently windblown hair into the native trees like the blue aliens of *Avatar* — a film that will one day be shot here too, using all the collective brilliance that this man put in place. He's an auteur with an entire country behind him.

CHAPTER 12

Junkie

In the lee of an ancient ruin somewhere in the boondocks of Ithilien, Gollum balances on his skinny haunches. We never see Tolkien's foremost creation relax: when he's not scuttling about like an insect, he's still twitching, writhing and trembling to the jumping bean urges beneath skin as mottled and veiny as Stilton. Frodo and Sam are asleep, but this doesn't prevent their insomniac guide, bloodshot eyes as big as grapefruits, from engaging in a midnight hour heart-to-heart — with himself.

If we assess the sum and substance of the trilogy with all its astonishment and thrill, solemnity and humour, could this be the defining moment? What follows is a daring, wholly cinematic concentration of Peter Jackson's numinous reach. Shot in a pool of silvery light, Gollum always at his most fetching by moon, here is intimacy, wit and — what's this? — psychological enquiry amid the towering scale.

Cutting between two angles on the wretch — and by now we have all but forgotten he is made of CGI via the dark arts of motion capture — director, actor, writers and a swarm of designers, animators and sundry experts brilliantly externalize an internal struggle. Communicated by Andy Serkis' dancing facial expressions, the shift in angle and the contrasting pitch in the same voice, Gollum and Sméagol are eerily distinct.

'Tolkien doesn't write people's thoughts in his books,' noted Ben Wootten, one of Weta Workshop's elite sculptors, in 2003, 'it's old-saga style, but you get inside Gollum's head because he talks to himself. He is the only character where you see his thought process working.'

Exactly. We *see* this mental pendulum swinging back and forth. The scene is an entrance: that of Sméagol, Gollum's other, possibly true self (such distinctions remain elusive). He had been hovering in the wings as the cruel dominance of Gollum is softened at the hands of Frodo's kindness. But only now is the audience finally allowed into the creepy, double world that Serkis inhabited: Gollum and Sméagol, his infantile, servile and potentially redeemable other half.

In an astonishing *tour de force*, Serkis conveys the turmoil of two characters rooted in the same fractured psyche. A task he had come at with remarkable effort and thought, investing in both the technology and the reality of Gollum.

The look of the computerized creature also elicits a series of fluctuating reactions: uncanny yet sympathetic, scrawny yet threatening, old but childlike, and impossibly real.

Serkis remembers how nervous he was, sat between his wife and friends at *The Two Towers* premiere in New York. A year before, he had been ushered quietly through a side door of the London premiere for *The Fellowship of the Ring*, New Line keeping him out of the reach of the press for now. It had been a strange experience watching the first film, his only contributions the mutterings beneath the shadowy glimpses of Gollum and the voice of the Ringwraith at the Ford of Bruinen.* All the work still going into an upgraded Gollum depended on the first

---

* Serkis' versatile vocal skills were also used to voice the ravenous Orc, Grishnákh, who in *The Two Towers* chases Merry and Pippin into Fangorn Forest only to be squashed by Treebeard.

film being accepted — if it flopped, what then? It didn't bear thinking about.

Like everyone else that night, and nights all over the world, Serkis had been blown away and comforted. 'It set up such a fantastical landscape both psychological and physical. People were really affected.'

The stage was set for his entrance.

New York was the first time an audience had ever witnessed a full-blown Gollum. *His* Gollum. And during this scene, his big moment, Serkis noticed how laughter fell away into an awed hush.

'I tangibly felt that they were getting inside this character's head. Up until then I still wasn't quite sure it was going to work. That is the defining moment, and I suppose the moment of which I am most proud. That scene, which wasn't written until post-production, epitomized everything.'

Directed by Walsh during the first set of supplementary shooting in June 2002, they had approached the three-minute scene as a monologue, only divided into long alternating takes allowing the two characters in one body to bounce off one another.

'It was like being back on stage,' relishes Serkis.

He had been 'buzzing' when the pages had been delivered. This was a journey right into the 'psyche and guts' of Gollum and his counterpart Sméagol. They had found the character's wavelength.

The realization of Gollum is the story within the story of the triumph of *The Lord of the Rings*. The one that arguably says the most about the foresight, talent and courage involved — a revolution in No. 8 thinking and entirely of a piece with Tolkien.

'Gollum was the perfect example of how they were figuring things out as they went along,' says Elijah Wood.

'He was a few steps up from a science experiment,' laughs Joe Letteri.

In 2004, the disagreeable wretch was voted number 10 in the Greatest Movie Characters of All Time by the American movie magazine *Premiere*, in the company of Darth Vader and James Bond. Every comedian and talkshow host was trying out a Gollum gag. '*My Preciousss*,' entered the cultural lexicon. James Cameron claimed the emotion displayed by this digital being told him that *Avatar* was possible. Even so, no purported CGI character has yet come close to the effect of Gollum. Whether we can see through the computer disguise or not (some of the shots are more successful than others), as with the scale issues you forget to look for the joins. The storytelling of him takes over.

'Vitally,' says Jackson, 'Andy ensured that Gollum wasn't perceived as a monster.'

'He hated and loved the Ring, as he hated and loved himself': Tolkien's sublime antihero is a lightning bolt of modernity against that mythical old-saga skyline.

He had his origins in Grendel from *Beowulf* — a game of riddles finds its prototype in Norse and Anglo-Saxon literature — and Caliban from *The Tempest*, while Serkis registered other archetypes: Uriah Heep from Charles Dickens' *David Copperfield*, Victor Hugo's *The Hunchback of Notre Dame* and Cain, the Biblical exile who murdered his brother. Tolkien's staunch Catholic faith never far away.

Nevertheless, his refusal to be drawn in simple moral terms feels contemporary. He's far more psychologically complex than the dilemmas drawn up for, say, Aragorn or Frodo. He may look ghoulish but he toys with the reader's sympathies. We know we cannot trust him, but we are still fascinated and moved by him like no other character. And who is it in the end that saves the world?

Gollum presented the filmmakers with the book's ultimate riddle. How do you fulfil such ghastly promise? The success of the trilogy would be contingent on finding the answer.

*

To begin with they had only wanted an actor's voice. The character would be animated in CGI, his lips synched to the lines. They had experimented with a puppet Gollum, but it was too cumbersome, imposing too many restrictions on filming. Plus, there was always something doll-like about puppets — the spell would be broken. Richard Taylor had suggested make-up on an actor with CGI assistance around the eyes and to elongate the limbs, but Jackson wasn't sold. There was no actor skinny enough, and the director wanted him 'scrambling around on all fours'.

Anyone who had read the book, admits Taylor, 'would have a strong preconceived notion of what Gollum should look like, this was the quintessential fantasy character of the twentieth century.'

So no pressure, then.

You could, in fact, argue that he is the *least* quintessential fantasy character of the twentieth century, but that doesn't make embodying him any easier. That face needed to express an orchestra of deceptions. In a heartbeat he could bawl like a baby and smirk like a master criminal.

Hundreds of sketches and clay sculptures were done exploring variations on Tolkien's sallow, gangly theme. John Howe remembers a time when it seemed like everyone was doing Gollum. Pre-existing art never settled on a look. There was a tendency to veer either to cadaverous and zombie-like or cartoony and cute.

We hardly get more than a hint of Gollum in the first film, six shots in total of him peering out of the gloom in Moria, eyes aglow, and a flashback to his agonized wails and outstretched fingers while being tortured in Barad-dûr (incidentally, the only shot featuring the interior of Sauron's HQ). Still, from behind-the-scenes pictures since released we get an insight into where they were originally headed.

He leaned more to *The Hobbit*'s fairy-tale Gollum: the lank and mysterious, quasi-monstrous cave dweller. The body would remain largely unaltered, but his face began with a more alien cast. He had a pronounced snout like an ape: ironically, a creature in which Weta Digital and Serkis would later specialize. His eyes were bigger and more protruding, his nose stubby. He was certainly weird and certainly pathetic.

The Workshop had carved a super-sized maquette, Gollum posed as Da Vinci's *Proportion of Man*, to provide far greater detail for the surface scans (using the meat scanner). The colouring, says Gino Acevedo, 'was olive green with a pale underbelly like a tree frog'.

What is clear is that this 'froggy' wastrel looked nothing like Andy Serkis.

When his agent called, Serkis had been unimpressed. He had the chance to audition for the voice part of an animated character in a live-action version of T*he Lord of the Rings* shooting in New Zealand. By his agent's estimate, it was three weeks' work, and it wasn't clear that he would even get to go out there. As for the part, well it was Gollum. Serkis had a vague recollection of reading *The Hobbit* on the Number 273 bus to school in North London. He remembered something about a dragon and caves. Hadn't it been for children?

'There must be a dozen parts in that film,' he complained, the enthusiasm draining out of his voice, 'can't you get me one of those?'

When he replaced the receiver, he had half a mind to pass on this strange film. In any case, he was awaiting news on Alan Bleasdale's new adaptation of *Oliver Twist* due to shoot in Prague, for which he had auditioned to play Bill Sykes. Now that was a part: villainous, conflicted and raw with human hungers.

But the Ring *wanted* to be found. In another of fate's significant interventions, as Serkis stewed, being a little actorly and precious he admits, he heard his girlfriend's key slide into the lock of their London home. Lorraine Ashbourne found him perched on the stairs and asked what was up.

Serkis had met fellow actress Ashbourne in 1990, when both were cast in a play at the Royal Exchange in Manchester. With both their characters going through complicated break-ups, they decided to meet in a pub in character to improvise their relationship and ended up in a relationship. They married and had a third child while Serkis was still working on *The Lord of the Rings*.

He mentioned the phone call. How he was up for some character named Gollum, but he wasn't keen. The role didn't sound like it would amount to much.

'But that's brilliant,' she told him. 'You can't say no to this one. This is *Gollum*.'

Ashbourne had loved the book.

Serkis laughs. 'It really was like, "*Duhhh. . .*"'

He cycled to the American Church off Tottenham Court Road to meet the director, muttering and coughing at the London traffic, practicing Gollum's voice. Like his co-stars to come, Wood and Sean Astin, he'd already auditioned a first time on tape and had been called back to audition with the director and his partner, Fran Walsh, who would be so key to Gollum's evolution. With Ashbourne's insistence ringing in his ears, Serkis had begun to get his head into the idea of Gollum, reading the key chapters — there was no time to attempt the whole book. He found himself drawn to this pathetic soul. He sensed the key to his tortured state of mind lay in the gurgling sound that emanated from his throat.

Born in Ruislip Manor in West London, Serkis was an actor destined for unusual things. His father, of Armenian descent, was a doctor in Baghdad and Serkis spent much of his childhood travelling back and forth between Iraq and London. Out of school he had wanted to be an artist and studied visual arts at university. There he conceived of a career in stage design. The mechanics of theatre excited him.

But after a chance role in a student production he became obsessed with acting, spilling out of college straight into theatre, where he thrived. By the mid-nineties he was making a name for himself.

The split in disciplines in his nature would prove significant.

Serkis shares with Mortensen the same level of absorption

into a role. He loves to research, to 'find' a character, drawn to probing the darker, more interesting half of the human psyche. He would make a powerful Bill Sykes in Bleasdale's fine *Oliver Twist,* and in a career of troubled souls would bravely seek out the human behind child-killer Ian Brady in 2006's *Longford.* There is something of the firebrand, social-realist British tradition in him, the unyielding, naturalistic urges of a John Hurt, Alan Bates or Albert Finney. You would never be short changed.

Which belies how quick to smile and generous natured Serkis is in person. With a mane of thick, curly hair; the square, muscular frame of an avid rock climber; and away from all those tormented souls, a more relaxed and handsome face, he laughs at life but there is no missing the intelligence and drive of the man.

Meeting him for the first time, Astin was taken aback by Serkis' intensity. 'I could feel the heat coming off his skin. . . It was an *interaction.*'

So ingrained have the films become, it now feels impossible to recast any of the roles, but remove Serkis and an essential cog in their machinery would be missing.

'Meeting Peter and Fran, as you know, was really cataclysmic in my life,' he says. 'I could sense straightaway that here were some very likeminded people; vintage storytellers who want to try new things. We got on literally from the first time we met at the audition.'

He hadn't held back. When the director pulled out his video camera, Serkis took off his shirt.

Recalls Jackson, 'When we auditioned him, and we auditioned lots of other actors too, it was just for a voice. But Andy got completely into it. He didn't sit in the chair being Gollum — he stripped down to his bare chest and started crawling all over the furniture. It was just great.'

The voice, *that* voice, and movement were inextricably linked. They couldn't be separated. While recording in the ADR studio, they would place the mic on the floor and Serkis would do his lines on all fours.

Once Serkis had retrieved his shirt, said his goodbyes and departed, Jackson and Walsh looked at one another, the potential of something, even if they weren't quite sure what exactly, hanging in the air.

'Wouldn't it be great to have him on set?' said Walsh.

First though they had a familiar hurdle to overcome. New Line, and Bob Shaye in particular, had decided Gollum was too precious to be risked on Jackson's digital start-up. While Weta Digital was beginning to show their quality, a fully rendered CGI character was of a different order entirely. For all their on-going design work, New Line was going to have an American effects house bring him to life. 'ILM or someone,' says Jackson, amused by the irony. ILM's recent attempt at a computer-generated cast member, Jar Jar Binks, had ended up less comic relief than cosmic laughing stock. Doubts remained that a credible synthesis of acting and effects could ever be achieved.

When Shaye made his state visit to New Zealand in early 2000, Jackson would make his case. Being denied the chance to develop something — indeed *someone* — so integral to the story would land a serious blow to his holistic approach. As he saw it, Gollum would draw deeply on both Weta Workshop and Digital, not to say the shoot itself. Outsourcing him would threaten the cohesion of the storytelling in the second and third films.

'It was still early, because he didn't really appear in the first film, apart from a close-up. But we quickly cobbled together a Gollum test and showed it to him.'

Their proof of concept test contained two shots, both created using key-frame animation[*]: Gollum clambering over the rocks, sneaking up on the slumbering Frodo and Sam, and more daringly a headshot of him lip-synching to dialogue.

---

[*] In computer animation, 'key frames' mark the start and end points of a smooth transition in an animated object. The sequence of key frames in a scene chart the movement and timing of an image, with all the other frames then filled in between to create the illusion of uninterrupted movement.

The shots may have still lacked the lifeblood of Serkis, but Shaye walked out of the screening room a convert.

'Okay, okay, you can do Gollum.'

Like so much of Middle-earth, he could have little idea of the heights his climb-down would reach. In truth, that moonlit Gollum to come was beyond anything even Jackson and his team could yet imagine.

The truth was, he admits, they really had no idea if they were going to be able to do Gollum. 'It wasn't until we did that test, with Bob Shaye threatening to take him away from us, that we began to really knuckle down.'

Ordesky laughs. If anything epitomized Jackson's audacious philosophy then it was getting to grips with the book's most enduring and peculiar character. 'Andy Serkis was supposed to do three weeks of voice acting. The character was supposed to be key-frame animation. And that all changed. I remember the debates between the key-frame approach and the more motion capture* approach. Gollum simply became vastly more ambitious.'

The catalyst was always very simple: Jackson would dream up something and his team would figure out how to get it done.

Ordesky puts it in real terms, 'Peter would say something like, "Gollum is going to have close-ups". And everyone would flip out. Not to Peter's face, they would flip out inside. Because if Gollum was going to have close-ups then the level of game that was going to have to be brought was huge.'

*

Joe Letteri had been Jim Rygiel's recommendation. The visual effects supervisor had found himself 'stretched a little thin'

---

* Despite the best efforts of Steven Spielberg and James Cameron to nobly rechristen it 'performance capture', the term motion capture (breezily shortened to 'mo-cap') has stuck for the process of recording a human actor's movements and applying the data to animate a digital character.

finishing *The Fellowship of the Ring*. With the increased ambitions of the following two films, he needed help managing Weta Digital. He and Letteri had worked together in the eighties and stayed in touch as Letteri's reputation grew at ILM. And Rygiel was aware he had a particularly useful set of skills. . .

'I was very fortunate to be at ILM for *Jurassic Park*,' Letteri speaks with the measured pragmatism of a man who has spent much of his career explaining very complicated things to very simple people. 'And one of my specialties was how do you make things appear real? I focused on how we made the dinosaurs look realistic. What does the skin look like? Or how do you create light in a computer that will respond in the way that light does in the real world?'

Hailing from Aliquippa, Pennsylvania and educated at Berkley in California, the visual effects magician's CV was impressive: he had not only worked on Steven Spielberg's seminal dinosaur movie, but used fractals to create a realistic tidal wave in James Cameron's *The Abyss* and inserted a credible Jabba the Hutt into the special edition of *Star Wars: A New Hope*. What drew him to New Zealand was predominantly the lure of Gollum.

'To me the interesting challenge was that he was not a creature, he was a character. He had to hold up side by side with human actors. There was no artifice about him. He wasn't a strange alien creature; he was kind of a malformed human.'

Gollum didn't fall into the category of Cave-troll or Balrog, explains Jackson; Gollum was a Frodo or Gandalf. Which was why it was so imperative to have Serkis on set. To focus the other actors, as well as the animators, on the idea that this was about performance. 'And that was before we even thought of motion capture.'

For Randy Cook, the director of animation at Weta Digital and ostensibly Gollum's midwife, 'it became clear how much Andy was going to drive this role.'

Foremost of Jackson's concerns was that he could end up a Frankenstein's mishmash of forty different animators. Like all artists, animators like to embellish, adding their own stamp. The actor's performance would provide a route map for the CG character to follow.

'Don't stray from the path,' says Serkis. 'Working in CGI the discipline is so often *not* to do things.'

Once they had initiated motion capture, that path would become a blazing trail. For now, at least, the seeds were sown. The ambition for how they were going not only to visualize Gollum but integrate him into the drama as a complete character began to grow.

Serkis arrived in Wellington on 5 April 2000, and having found his feet toured the bustling Workshop and then visited the studious Weta Digital offices. It was there Cook showed him a recent test shot of Gollum on the stairs of Cirith Ungol, using that single day of wet-weather footage from the squash court in Queenstown.[*]

Only then, admits Serkis, did he realize the psychological hurdle he was facing. Contrary to his every instinct as an actor, he wouldn't 'totally own the role'. He would share the creation of a character, that intimate, often indefinable, near magical process at the heart of acting, with a group of other creatives with their own thoughts and talents. What would end up on screen would never be wholly *his* work.

'Still,' comments Astin, 'he was willing to do what was asked of him, so long as everyone understood that he was not just providing the voice of Gollum. He was a real actor. He was an artist.'

Serkis likes to tell the story of his first day on set, an entrance that had been heavily delayed. He had been due to head out for preproduction in September 1999, but that had all been thrown by their scheduling disruptions when anything Gollum-related was postponed until the following spring. Serkis was left for

---

[*] Randy Cook himself had acted out Gollum for the animators, and Andrew Jack, Serkis' voice coach, had provided the voice.

months keeping a lid on his urges, like Doctor Jekyll with Mr Hyde desperate to get loose.

It wasn't until 11 April 2000 he finally could. On the rugged flanks of Mount Ruapehu — Mount Doom, no less: the tumultuous end of Gollum's story — he emerged from wardrobe outfitted in a skin-coloured leotard that covered everything but his eyes. For his own sake, he had shaved his head in preparation for the role to feel 'dehumanized', shorn of identity like concentration camp prisoners, which also meant he was later able to dispense with the hood allowing the other actors to respond to his facial expressions. Taylor admits they had 'made a terrible mistake with the gimp suit' as it hid the performance.

The actor had spent the previous day alone, crawling among the rocks, getting used to the idea that there would be no costume to work with, none of an actor's usual crutches. With the mist rolling in, he had started to feel closer to Gollum.

However, as he took his place on set in what soon became dubbed his 'unitard', Jackson had begun a chorus of schoolboy giggles at the sight of him, which threatened to catch on until Carolynne Cunningham demanded order. Serkis would learn the teasing was the affectionate result of a Kiwi aversion to pretension. After all, he did look kind of funny.

He could also sense the confusion. Wasn't Gollum supposed to be CGI? 'I was in a Lycra bodystocking with Pete laughing his head off at me. And I was in character. Elijah and Sean were kind of like, "Well, are we saving ourselves for the real take, or is this the take, or what is it?"'

Crucially, the director told them, they must never think in terms of a clean pass. There would be times when they animated directly over the take containing Serkis. More to the point, he wanted as much out of Serkis' performance as he could get, to provide ammunition for the animators as well as his co-stars.

'After several takes with Andy,' recalls Jackson, 'it wasn't hard for Elijah and Sean to visualize him still there, while Andy would still do the voice off camera.'

Throughout principal photography, Serkis acted out every beat of Gollum's part in the quest, determined not to allow anyone to undermine his contribution, committed body and soul.

'He hated being called a reference,' says Wood. 'I get that — he was like, "I am the character and I'm doing all this work to be the character."'

Astin was inspired to respond in kind. 'It was a level of intensity that was about 5,000 degrees hotter than anything I'd ever experienced.'

Watching his star, doubts began to grow in Jackson's mind. How could Weta Digital ever match such human intensity, recalibrating Serkis' contortions into Gollum's tiny digital frame? As they moved into post-production on *The Two Towers*, flush with the success of *The Fellowship of the Ring*, he decided to take the process one stage further and try and motion capture the lightning of performance into the bottle of the computer.

'That decision,' Jackson says without any pretence, 'changed the history of cinema.'

Motion capture had been pioneered for videogames as far back as *Virtua Fighter 2* in 1994, and was gradually being adopted as a visual effects gizmo for feature films. Jackson knew that Robert Zemeckis was squirreled away somewhere testing the boundaries between live action and animation. Experiments that had mixed results with *Polar Express* in 2004, and only increased the consternation among actors that it was all a secret ploy to replace them with digital puppets.

Naturally cutting-edge, Weta Digital had begun exploring the possibilities of motion capture as early as the Miramax days, and were pursuing its use in other areas of the films such as on Cave-troll animation, and creating realistic battle moves for the assembled armies and digital doubles of the Fellowship. The principal cast had acted out a range of generic movements to be scanned in and used to animate their doubles into miniature sets or digital environments, or to aid Orlando Bloom in completing Legolas' splendiferous athletics (the Fellowship members dashing across the Bridge of Khazad-dûm are entirely digital). This was most reluctantly in Mortensen's case, another fearful that the soul of his performance might be stolen away.

Indeed, they had already tried it out on Gollum. A set of almost clandestine tests was done during principal photography — and always late at night as if they were dabbling in evil. They were already aware, says Serkis, of 'a lot of fear' in the acting community. At that point, the computers had strained to keep up with him. They would end their sessions frustrated, thinking the world wasn't ready yet.

That had now changed.

'I remember that glint in Pete's eye,' says Serkis, having arrived back in Wellington in early 2002, 'his excitement for something new.'

Like his apprehensive peers, Serkis has been raised on grease-paint and Shakespeare. He understood the concerns, but the epiphany came when the team suited him up and had him stand beside a monitor, asking him to raise his arms. As he did, he saw a basic, grey-shaded version of Gollum follow his every move.

'It was like, "Holy shit, this is extraordinary." It was a real moment.'

Here was a technical solution for dramatic ends. To solve their frustrations over Gollum, not instigate a shift in the paradigm of acting. Not deliberately, anyway. Surely, the actor thought, this extended the possibility of performance?

'This was no longer a science experiment,' asserts Letteri, 'this was an active shooting stage. We brought in everyone that you would have on a shooting stage the same as when Andy and Peter walked on a live shooting stage.'

The only difference was there were no cameras, not exactly.

It brought a new level of madness to Serkis' Method: he would have to recreate every single scene he had acted on set on the motion capture stage, working to rediscover the emotional moment from up to a year before. At times, it felt like he was trapped in 'an Escher drawing' where there was no beginning and no end. Yet here was his performance, *his* Gollum, being channelled directly onto the screen.

'Mo-cap is only as good as the "mo" you "cap",' noted Cook, interviewed in 2002, 'and fortunately Andy provided some terrific "mo".'

A cascade had begun. Once they began feeding the essence of Serkis directly into Gollum, it became clear that the original look of the character couldn't contain the actor's squall of expressions. 'The mechanics of Gollum's face,' says Taylor, 'impeded how far we could push the design.' Gollum needed to become a distorted version of the actor.

Using Photoshop, Christian Rivers juxtaposed a headshot of Serkis between two drawings, one of the old Gollum and a new version where Serkis features had been subtly combined with those of the original look, and showed it to Jackson.

'Peter got it straightaway,' says Taylor.

Confident they had shown little enough of the old concept for audiences to establish a clear picture of him, Jackson decreed that they were going to meld Gollum's physiognomy with those of the young British actor who had auditioned for a voice part.

'The first time I saw the finished maquette it was so spooky,' recalls Serkis, 'he looked just like my father.'

*

Long before Serkis made even his first journey to New Zealand, a package had arrived from Weta Workshop including preliminary sketches of Gollum by Alan Lee, John Howe and a handful of the other designers. What struck him was not how grotesque or fantastical he appeared, it was how human he was. In the emaciated frame, unhealthy complexion, loss of teeth and hair and wide, yellow eyes Serkis saw the ruined body of a homeless drug addict. This, he thought, was what the Ring had done to him.

He was a Ring junkie.

'Basing him on a modern sensibility was crucial, to catch what was ambiguous about him. Not evil, but driven to do evil.

Which is where the whole idea of a heroin or cocaine addiction came from.'

Whatever the potency of the Ring actually represented — whatever its abstruse magic — Serkis would reframe that control in real terms. Gollum harboured no plans for world domination; he coveted the Ring only for himself. He was after the next fix. A craving that makes you sick, physically and emotionally. The paranoid schizophrenia, he thought, was another side effect.

'I'd known people who had gone down that route,' Serkis openly admits. 'You can't wait to taste it, feel it, own it and love it. It was an obsession Gollum loved. . . and hated.'

Whenever he pictured him moving he would always be on all fours like an animal or a cockroach, a crawling wretch — the antithesis of the exuberant hobbits.

'I went through the book and looked at all of Tolkien's descriptions of the way Gollum moved like a cat or a frog or a dog, climbing like a spider: all the different descriptions of his physicality. Then I used a lot of paintings.'

Serkis is another who has written eruditely of his experiences, the aim being to demystify (or, you might say, de-technologize) the creation of Gollum, and he talks extensively about the inspirations from classical art: disturbing painters like Otto Dix, Egon Schiele, Francis Bacon and the broader fantasy pictures of Brom (who specialized in the realms of videogames and *Dungeons & Dragons*). He was looking for how artists evoked psychological pain in a physical way.

'There was one particular painting by Da Vinci — *St. Jerome in the Wilderness*. It was just the particular pose of the character. How physically tortured he was.'

Early on, still under the impression that it would only be his voice on call, Serkis concentrated on how to convey the stricken nature of Gollum's personality through how he spoke. While Tolkien had given him a very specific, darkly humourous syntax, there was the risk of going a little pantomime.

Peter Woodthorpe's vocal interpretation of the slippery villain is one of the few successes in Ralph Bakshi's animated adaptation. If his green-skinned appearance makes him look like a geriatric Martian, the voice acting is by turns hilarious, cruel and winsome. Woodthorpe was a classical stage actor out of Cambridge, much like Ian McKellen, and a Hammer veteran, much like Christopher Lee, and he brewed up a startling mix of serial killer seduction, Carry On camp and bawling toddler. Until Serkis, he was the definitive version of Gollum's neurotic gabbling, and was expressly sought out to replay his whine in the BBC radio dramatization in 1981.

Serkis, however, had never heard it. 'To be honest, I didn't know anything about it. So I wasn't influenced by it. But obviously that was the voice for a generation, one hundred per cent.'

If people have detected similarities in their portrayals then that is likely down to the progenitor. In an early recording, Tolkien can be heard reading the Riddles in the Dark chapter from *The Hobbit* and thoroughly enjoying giving his 'miserable, wicked creature' a Peter Lorre-style falsetto and serpent's hiss, even adding the sore-throated '*Gollum*' sound. Interestingly, as early as *The Hobbit*, the character refers to both the Ring and himself as 'precious', his own identity consumed by that of his magic totem.

Serkis channels all of Tolkien's richness and wit into his interpretation of that voice, or should I say those *voices* (neither Woodthorpe or Tolkien separates the two personas as Serkis does): the exasperation and plotting, the indignant sense of fair play and the babyish entreaties. He is the film's most ironic character, given space to send up Middle-earth, and in his rivalry with Sam showing a joshing, raspberry-blowing, playful side before it curdles into menace. Who else in the films uses sarcasm?

But he goes harder and darker than anyone before. Serkis was famously interrupted from his contemplations by his cat Dix summoning up a furball and later that night in bed he realized this was a gift from the Muses. His version of the *Gollum* sound would be an involuntary convulsion. It was in his throat where Gollum located all his pain and guilt for murdering his cousin long ago, throttling him to death for possession of the Ring.

It was a revelation.

Once settled in Wellington, Serkis would gather together with Walsh and Boyens at Jackson's house to attend to the business of character. The writers were still flat-out untangling *The Fellowship of the Ring*, but he was impressed by the space they allowed to explore ideas within the sturdy framework of the story.

'We started off pulling the two characters apart: Sméagol and Gollum. Trying to bring each of them into existence. We started to think about Sméagol as the younger, on the surface sweeter natured, more innocent and guileless. Whereas Gollum was the survivor and the sort of brutal pragmatist.'

They told him their theory about how the Ring affects a character according to their moral stature. He excited them with his conception of Gollum as a Ring-junkie. Together they began to spin psychological webs.

Playing Gollum body and soul — and effectively twice over — would take its toll. The physical demands alone were bruising as he scrambled over sharp rocks and splashed through icy streams. He drank gallons of 'Gollum juice', which mixed lemon, honey and ginger with hot water to soothe ravaged vocal chords. But no amount of honey and ginger could salve the spiritual demands being made of him.

Serkis was the test pilot of a new technology, wearily having to explain to twitchy peers that this was still acting, something he was still processing. And there was the not inconsiderable issue of a Method actor spending days inside the skin of a creature coming from a very dark place both figuratively and literally.

'I have to tell you, and I don't think I've really talked about this, but it was an incredibly lonely process. Obviously, most of my journey was with Frodo and Sam, and Elijah and Sean were already very close friends. I was very much the outsider. I kind of needed to be. Part of me always kept myself to myself. I would take myself off at weekends when everyone else was partying. I love solitude. I love the wild. So it sort of suited me. I was on this other journey.'

In order to soak himself in Gollum's self-loathing and anger, in the first few weeks he took that three-day trip kayaking down the remote Wanganui River with his battered copy of *The Lord of the Rings*, feeling like Martin Sheen from *Apocalypse Now* drifting beneath the lush vegetation toward a heart of darkness. He climbed mountains, walked remote trails, embracing the isolation that New Zealand offered, only Gollum for company.

'Normally as actors you tend to stick with your own kind. Hang out with other actors. If anyone, the people I got close to were on the other side in visual effects.'

*

When they were informed that Walsh would be making a special visit to Weta Digital, some of the newer artists had sniffed disparagingly about a typical Hollywood wife no doubt in to do some interior decorating. The 120 additional staff employed to meet the demands of the second film were to learn an important lesson about both Walsh and Middle-earth making. Accompanied by Serkis, she began with a strange speech.

'You can't tell the studio this, because it wouldn't sell,' she told them, 'but *The Two Towers* is an addiction film. It is about Frodo's growing addiction to the Ring, his recognizing the same in Gollum and having to believe that Gollum can be saved because *that* is the only hope for himself.'

She then made her point by directing Serkis though a series of intense Gollum moments, scuttling on all fours and clambering onto desks. The animators were left inspired and terrified, faced with doing what could never be done — almost the house motto at both Wetas. Beyond the stream of noughts and ones supplied by the motion capture data, the 'reality' of Gollum was still dependent on how the animators added the detail to Serkis' extraordinary characterization. Walsh kept emphasizing that they needed to trap the spirit of his performance in their main frame and free it again in Middle-earth.

Was that so strange? Hadn't the great painters once aspired to preserve personality in oils? Why not pixels?

Cook saw their mission as 'fighting against the theatrical creepiness' of CGI life. Serkis would often sit beside the animators, imploring them to explore what was going on *inside* the performance. Gollum had to be 'legitimately sympathetic'.

With Jackson's hand always on the tiller, and Serkis' mood swings in view, the animators made their own contributions to the richness of the character, such as the almost coquettish, tactile side of Gollum, a twisted sweetness the actor would feed back into his scenes as the unblemished but still slightly unwholesome young Sméagol.

Serkis 'played the melody' is how Cook succinctly put it, 'while they did the solo riffs off that melody.'

To an extent animation is acting. Animators feed off their own faces and body language using mirrors placed beside their terminals. They are in the business of portraying emotions.

'The camera is a lie detector,' said Cook. 'So we had to think not in poses or in expressions but in terms of thoughts. The animation team wrote out a dialogue track for his thoughts and then posed them out.' They then looked for the key moments when his thoughts changed. It wasn't exact, but it was effective, especially when Gollum wasn't speaking.

The team studied the links between feelings and expressions made by Paul Ekman, a professor of psychology at the University of California who had broken down the face into 'action points' that represented neurological and muscular combinations. Cook extolled the work of Austrian sculptor Franz Messerschmidt, who sculpted facial expressions in lead (and tragically died of lead poisoning). And they uncovered a disturbing archive of old photographs where patients in a French asylum suffered electrodes being jammed into their faces to try and stimulate different emotional states.

An early set of sculptures of Gollum's gamut of expressions had been based on a series of black and white photos of Jackson pulling faces for 'angry', 'hurt', 'confused', and so on. There is a sliver of self-portrait in there somewhere.

When it came to getting the director's approval on the relatively last minute plastic surgery, Taylor would bring a sculpture of Gollum's head into the edit suite on a tray, grabbing a nearby kitchen knife to take on the director's changes then and there.

Over the months of post-production notes from the director and writers often baffled hard-pressed animators. 'Have Gollum be more gothic in frames 22–24. . .' found the team typing 'gothic' into a nascent Google to discover pictures of European cathedrals pimpled with gargoyles. From this they devised a hunched, fiendish posture for Gollum raising his shoulders and dipping his head lower than was humanly possible.

In bare-bones terms, compared to what was later achieved by Weta Digital in *Avatar* and *The Planet of the Apes* films, Gollum is only partly motion captured. There had been experiments with facial capture, with Serkis pulling 'facial gymnastics' into a computer scanner enclosed by angled mirrors, his face covered with dotted lines like one of Tolkien's maps. The results, however, weren't yet subtle enough to be trusted, and Gollum's facial expressions were achieved by an exacting key-frame animation, still stewarded, of course, by Serkis' performance.

There was always some degree of interpretation required, says Letteri. 'Just the fact that his eyes were two and a half times the size of a human eye but set into a face that's about the same size. You have less room for the wrinkles around the eyes and less room for the muscles around the nose to activate.'

Ultimately, the 'digital puppet' (a coinage doing little to pacify discomforted actors) of Gollum came with 675 sculpted expressions and 9,000 sculpted muscle shapes, with the animators able to glissade smoothly from one to the next. To save time, supervised by Walsh, they established a library of pre-set slider settings for frequently used expressions.

Was this so different from an actor's palette of familiar expressions?

They weren't done yet. For Letteri, if they couldn't give him the physical texture of life then all their efforts in performance would be in vain. In any frame it had to appear as if Gollum had wandered onto set from his trailer like all the other actors, a loincloth of Goblin skin his only costume. He needed to belong to the reality of their Middle-earth.

'We started to develop all these new tools and methods, like subsurface scattering for trying to determine what makes human skin look like human skin?'

Insinuating layers beneath the skin was something Letteri had progressed on *Jurassic Park*, but this had to be translucent CGI skin. Subsurface scattering effectively diffused light through the skin to pick up the veins and tissue beneath.

Sean Bean's dead body had been a great help. While on a visit to the Workshop, Boromir's corpse (created for his funeral) caught Letteri's eye. It was so lifelike — or deathlike. This was the work of Acevedo, who had previous experience on the living dead with Zemeckis' Hollywood satire *Death Becomes Her*. Gollum was indeed partly inspired by Meryl Streep. Acevedo devised Gollum's pasty colouring by painting onto a layer of absorbent silicone on a large maquette; Letteri wondered if they could reproduce his methods digitally.

'I crossed over to the dark side,' quips Acevedo. 'They set up a computer in my studio and we started doing tests.' Once he had transferred to Weta Digital's pristine halls and got to grips with a digital airbrush there was no turning back, no matter how much he missed the paint fumes.

Acevedo would also give life to Gollum's distended eyes. No longer were they to have Tolkien's 'lamplike glow' as they did in *The Fellowship of the Ring*, Jackson wanted them bloodshot and faded like an old cue ball, the murky windows on a crooked soul.

Code was created for the moisture on his lips, nostrils and eyelids. The movement of his twenty-five lank hairs was particularly troublesome. While beneath that miraculous skin was a fully articulated set of digital bones and muscles.

As the look evolved so did the character. The director, along with his writers, especially Walsh, devised new scenes to communicate the squabbling halves of his schizophrenic soul. Gollum gave an arc to the schizophrenic second film, and the emotional trajectory of the entire trilogy. The gaunt creature even initiated a readjustment to their entire digital aesthetic. *The Fellowship of the Ring*, says Letteri, had 'hit the fantasy elements a little harder' and in *The Two Towers* they pulled back to make 'everything slightly more naturalistic' so that Gollum sat that much more within the world.

*

Daringly, *The Return of the King* opens not with widescreen spectacle but with a close-up. A wriggling worm is being hooked on a line. We widen to a tranquil scene: two hobbit-like fellows — they are Stoors, distant cousins to Shire folk — languidly fishing on a sun-kissed river as smooth as a mirror. One of them looks a little like Gollum and a lot like Andy Serkis. They are Sméagol and Déagol, and this is Gollum's prologue.

Walsh had floated the idea during principal photography. During *The Two Towers* we would flash back to show Sméagol long before his digital makeover and how he came by the Ring.

'To show that Gollum wasn't always the way he is,' says Jackson, 'and set up what the Ring could potentially do to Frodo.'

Serkis mentions that at one stage they actually hadn't been thinking of using him as the young Sméagol. 'I wrote to Pete, Fran and Philippa and said, "Look, this seems crazy that I'm playing Gollum and that you're going to cast some other actor to play the young Sméagol. To get that transition you're going to want me." I think originally they were going to go for someone much younger.'

Déagol was played by Thomas Robins, something of a lucky

charm for Jackson who had appeared as the fictional film-maker Colin McKenzie at the heart of the mockumentary *Forgotten Silver* (itself a favour, having cut Robins from *Heavenly Creatures*).

There was a risk in showing Serkis' human face, even if only briefly. You could break the spell — remind everyone that Gollum wasn't real, not exactly. The danger is swiftly dispelled by Serkis smoothly implying the same performance, digital skin or not. The opening is worthwhile alone for the rapture on his face as Sméagol sees the Ring for the first time.

Events rapidly descend into a violent struggle over the precious item, discovered by Déagol on the riverbed, and conclude with a montage of Sméagol's degeneration into Gollum. When he couldn't make the sequence fit satisfyingly into *The Two Towers*, Jackson made the brilliant, counterintuitive decision to open the third film inside Gollum's head.

By *The Return of the King*, there was no doubt that they had succeeded, as Cook put it, in 'getting an actor inside the computer'.

The critical reaction to Gollum in *The Two Towers* — and the film as a whole — had been almost ecstatic.

'Amid all the surreal visions, terrifying monsters and overwhelming landscapes,' extolled *Newsweek*'s David Ansen, 'it's the naked, skinny, schizophrenic Gollum who snakes his way most deeply into your memory.'

Gollum, concurred Richard Corlis in *Time*, is wonderfully complex. 'At first a whiny Jar Jar Binks as he might be played by Klaus Kinski, Gollum soon reveals a complex pathos and a facility of expression no human actor could match. He is another example of Jackson's pursuit of a tone both entertaining and serious.'

There were those for whom this masterly delivery of Tolkien's wrung-out Ring victim might be too much of a good thing. While concluding that 'nobody could quibble with the vitality of the result', Anthony Lane in *The New Yorker* feared that Jackson had become enamoured with the writings and hisses of his new baby. 'You don't read Tolkien for the niceties of tangled minds; you read him for pace and wonder, and the virtues of Jackson's trilogy, thus far, have been pace and astonishment.'

Upon the second film's release, Serkis inevitably found himself spokesperson on the ethics of motion capture. And the debate had become heated. Was the result so different, he asked, from what was accepted as acting? An actor is given a costume, a script, wigs and make-up, accents not their own, all manner of tools to help assemble the veil of a character.

'Film is a director's medium at the end of the day,' he argues. 'But the idea of a digital character throws light under what is the essence of acting. You're being moved by an actor's choices, not how it's wrapped up. You're emotionally engaged in the same way that you would be if you were watching any other character have a close-up in a movie.'

There are many actors, he admits, still unable to get their heads around it. They fear somehow the truth of their performance will be garbled by the static of the technology and its button pushing intermediaries. As we shall see, neither of the major Academies in Britain and America could bring themselves to even acknowledge Serkis' achievements.

Fuelled by the spirit of adventure in New Zealand, and a keen sense of the importance Gollum held for the story, his fellow cast members, at least, were excited by the possibilities. McKellen, who you might suspect of being a classicist, 'totally got into it', says Serkis. He understood that it was simply a different way of recording an actor's performance.

Astin felt privileged to be 'part of something so revolutionary that it would change the way movies were made'.

'It was like a new genre of acting,' adds Wood.

The best argument, it seems to me, is simply storytelling. What it boiled down to was that they had found a way to convey the intricacies and oddities — and the freakish look — of this complex character. Or *characters*. Every time I return to the second and third films, the irony blazes like a neon sign — Gollum is the most human character of all.

With the endorsement of both fans and critics ringing in his ears, Jackson's natural response was to see how much further they could delve into the tangled mind and vitality of Gollum.

When Serkis reported for duty for his final set of scenes and motion-captured replays in June 2003, as was now customary, he gathered with Walsh and Boyens for the latest summit on Gollum-Sméagol relations. Only this time he could see there was something in the writers' eyes, an excitement they were unable to conceal.

They had a change of plan, teased Walsh. The pendulum of treachery was to swing once again and the third film would propose that it was Sméagol, driven by the call of the Ring, who was the arch manipulator all along. That was why it was so meaningful to open the film with the sorry tale of Déagol's demise. It was, after all, Sméagol who killed him.

Says Serkis, 'I never thought of Sméagol as evil, just more prone to being corrupted. There are some people who are weaker than others. The fight between Sméagol and Déagol could have gone either way. Déagol was also on the verge of being corrupted. He could have killed Sméagol.'

Yet we would still grasp that the itch was already in him; the Ring only amplified it.

They had attempted to shoot the fight scene on location at Shelly Bay, to be joined with existing footage of the leisurely fishing trip filmed on the lake at Fernside. However, the Kiwi weather had been up to its old tricks, tossing canopies around and uprooting cameras in the gusts of its tantrum. Thus at Barrie Osborne's command they had beat a retreat to Stone Street and overnight the crew recreated the scene on set. The following morning Jackson called Serkis to tell him Walsh had been hit with a migraine. Would he be open to directing the clash between Sméagol and Déagol himself? Richard Bluck, the second unit cinematographer, could handle the camera.

By chance, I was on set that day, and Jackson had casually mentioned that Serkis had been trusted to direct his own flashback scenes. Then it wasn't so great a leap. In many respects, the actor had been directing his own performance throughout, re-choreographing himself back into frames on the mo-cap stage.

Gollum is both an artistic and technical achievement. It wasn't as if any halfway decent actor could have turned up in a blue leotard. Serkis was driven to find the character, respond to him, by embracing the technological process. He was as much a scientist as actor.

'That's so true. It was a reawakening of the marriage of acting and performance and technology for me. And that was one hugely exciting part of the journey.'

So the idea of directing the scene felt 'very natural', he recalls, and he had experience directing short films and theatre. 'That's what I loved and continue to love about New Zealand and the film industry there. People get the chance to express themselves in different ways.'

Another tiny acorn had been planted. Jackson would invite Serkis to shoot second unit on the *Hobbit* films, and he has gone on to direct a major motion capture-assisted production of *The Jungle Book* for Warner Bros., as well as intimate polio drama *Breathe* with Andrew Garfield.

It was also Serkis who, midway through that final lap of production, turned to Letteri and asked a simple question.

'Why can't I do motion capture as we are filming?'

In other words, why can't they sample the motion capture data on set alongside the cameras and co-stars? Good question: why can't they?

'No one had ever done this before,' says Jackson; 'it was always done on a motion capture stage. So Weta set up all the motion capture sensors around the set (turning a live set concurrently into the volume), and it worked. But we only found out towards the end, unfortunately.'

The scenes on Mount Doom of Gollum wrestling with Sam,

rolling around on the rocky slopes (now a set) were all achieved in the moment. The reference was now real.

As Jackson notes, 'Andy was the one who inspired us to figure that out. That is what we do now.'

That is how *Avatar* would be done, as well as Gollum's nostalgic cameo in *The Hobbit*.

Yet Serkis remains content such advances arose as they did: the experiments, the doubts, the redesigns and rewrites, all of the madness of his journey with Gollum fed into the vibrancy of the outcome. As did his sense of humour.

A true indicator of Gollum's near-instantaneous cultural status, as well as Kiwi drollery, came with the MTV Awards on 5 June 2003. Accepting the tub of golden popcorn for the newly minted Best Virtual Performance, Serkis appears in a video, apologizing for not being there in person (oh, the irony). They were, he said, still completing shots for *The Return of the King*.

Of course, as we all know, he is rudely interrupted by a digital Gollum, working himself into a foul-mouthed frenzy.

'I'm not going to thank anyone!' he rants, grabbing the award out of Serkis hands. 'Not you! Not MTV! And not those pixel-pushing pin-dicks at Weta Digital! And Peter Jackson, my precious, who do you think you are, you fucking hack?'

Gollum finishes by claiming that no awards could account for the long hours, low pay, and miserable experience he had, 'making these fucking movies'. On the sly, the video honours Serkis' hardships.

'Weta nearly killed me,' laughs the aforementioned hack, Jackson, 'because we sprung it on them. It was one minute and thirty seconds, and you can imagine how busy Weta were at that point. It took two or three animators about three weeks. Pretty quick.'

Saying goodbye, Serkis had conflicting emotions. It had been a transformative experience beyond flesh into pixels. Not seeing these people, not being with Sméagol and Gollum again (not for ten years, anyway), was a strange wrench.

'It was time, though,' he reflects, 'time to move on and play other characters. Time to act in trousers again.'

In the lengthy gaps between visits to the fouler regions of Middle-earth, Serkis had returned to more traditional roles. And by design or subconsciously, or this is simply where his compass points, they were not so different from his Ring-junkie. In 2001, he gave a scorching rendition of ungovernable but brilliant music producer Martin Hannett in Michael Winterbottom's raucous survey of the Manchester music scene of the eighties, *24-Hour Party People*. Equal parts inspiration and instability, the eccentric Hannett experimented wildly with new technology and class-A drugs, to be felled by heart failure at only forty-two. In 2003, while still recording the ADR for Gollum at weekends, Serkis took on Iago in a production of *Othello* back at the Royal Exchange in Manchester.

He couldn't help but notice how Shakespeare's great manipulator shared Gollum's knack for instigating great wickedness and yet still be sympathetic to an audience. They both amplified a very human thirst for vengeance. Although, he admits, playing both at the same time was 'bad for your mental health'.

Not coincidentally, in thinking about Gollum, Cook had watched footage of Laurence Olivier and John Barrymore playing Richard III.

On 20 April 2003, his final birthday on *The Lord of the Rings*, Serkis was given the perfect present — the Ring. Or, at least, a copy of it: Wood would get his own. It was then that Jackson asked if he was interested in playing a motion capture King Kong.

'I was, like, how the fuck do you do that? But if you can play Gollum at three-and-a-half-foot tall, so why not play a twenty-five-foot gorilla?'

Kong, he mused, was like a lonely, retired, out-of-shape boxer.

CHAPTER 13

MASSIVE

Ten minutes north of Wellington as the 4x4 flies, Dry Creek Quarry bites into the sandstone hillside of the Lower Hutt Valley; its crop of greywacke stone once prized for its dura-bility. From 17 January through to mid-April 2000 this dusty ex-excavation never slept. Like a medieval reimagining of *Close Encounters of the Third Kind*, every night from the former quarry emanated the alien glow of arc lights and the throb of genera-tors. If you got close enough to the security-patrolled gates, as a few intrepid paparazzi managed, you could see crowds of Orcs and humans milling together on the battlements of an old castle built against the rock face. Occasionally, a fight would break out.

The first of the book's three great battle sequences, which are supplemented, of course, by flashbacks to one fought three thousand years previously and a prodigious range of isolated skirmishes, the Battle of Helm's Deep occupies twenty-five brutal minutes of screen time, and attaches *The Two Towers* to an epic tradition. Here was the grandeur of Cecil B. DeMille (or *Forgotten Silver*'s Colin MacKenzie), and a similarly Biblical effort to get it into the camera. Here too was that ever-present duality: the grand and the visceral, informed by a more modern movie sensibility, never owning up to being a fantasy.

'What we did, I guess, is Private Ryanesque,' accepts Jackson: 'we used a lot of handheld cameras for the close-up things. You have to use modern techniques.'

Named within Tolkien's mythos for Helm Hammerhand, an ancient hero of Nordic-timbre, with Saruman's army of Uruk-hai marching on Rohan, it is here Théoden has sequestered his people. More precisely, behind the stout walls of a great fortress that occupies one end of a huge ravine with the monumental aura of a Victorian factory. As Tolkienites will tell you, the name Helm's Deep refers to the steeply-sided valley; the fortress is the Hornburg, and stretching out from this the Deeping Wall, which forms a barrier enclosing the far end of the combe.

For more panoramic shots of Helm's Deep, Weta Workshop would use the twenty-three-foot high 1/35 scale version, their very first miniature, built what now felt like a thousand years ago in 1997 in the hopes of impressing Miramax. The same one on which Jackson had been in 'absolute heaven' marshalling toy soldiers in preparation for this very battle; although the miniature had undergone a few cosmetic updates, since having been shunted between studios on several occasions.

To amass the CGI equivalent of Jackson's plastic divisions, Weta Digital would be faced with another extraordinary visual challenge, one taking them in virtually the opposite direction from Gollum: rather than representing an actor's performance in a singular digital character, this time summoning up an anthill of digital agents that could think like an actor.

First though they had to harvest the live-action footage, involving hundreds of very real actors and stuntmen. This necessitated three-and-a-half gruelling months of night shoots, and the odd wearying day, on the exterior set at Dry Creek Quarry, where as well as full-sized segments of the wall, causeway and front gate, a 1/4 scale model version of the Hornburg had been installed. Still as big as a two-storey house, the model was predominantly there to be blown apart when the Uruk-hai sappers ignite Saruman's bomb.

To give the audience a preview of the valley layout, Jackson devised a bravura crane shot that swooped up from the parking lot at Dry Creek over the Deeping Wall, seamlessly composited together with the 1/35th miniature keep teeming with digital extras, before closing in on Viggo Mortensen and Bernard Hill on the parapet.

While Jackson would be on hand to conduct such signature shots and significant character-based moments, the octopus-like schedule required him in sunny Hobbiton for Gandalf's arrival and back on the soundstages at Stone Street. Helm's Deep was largely the province of John Mahaffie.

Auckland born, the first of the film's platoon of second-unit directors had come up through the ranks of camera departments in New Zealand and Australia: focus puller to cameraman to Steadicam operator to cinematographer. As well as a stint on that baby pool for Middle-earth, the *Hercules* TV series, and Steadicam duties on *Heavenly Creatures*, he had served on fellow Kiwi Roger Donaldson's *The Bounty*, the United Artists production which had begun life as a two-part epic in the hands of David Lean.

Jackson had interviewed Mahaffie for cinematographer, but having lost out to Andrew Lesnie, he accepted the offer of managing the camera team on the second unit, which, he understood, would concentrate on action scenes.

Speaking in 2015, Mahaffie recalled that they were still looking for a second-unit director. Allergic to standing on ceremony, it occurred to Jackson he already had his man. 'Well, why don't you direct the second unit?' he asked him off the cuff. Mahaffie had been amazed. To make, as he put it, such a 'watershed decision' when it came to the specialist position. 'This was a big shift from my history.'

Moreover, what Jackson required was far more than the old-fashioned concept of 'a small additive unit' to pick up incidental pieces of a film that the main unit didn't have time to do or were at distant locations. In terms of footage if *The Lord of The Rings* had been filmed using a single unit (and there are directors determined to shoot everything) it would have taken three times as long.

'This was to be a second unit running for the duration of the main shoot, as big if not bigger at times than the main unit.'

Mahaffie was responsible for the equivalent of a feature film – or two of an indie stripe — albeit action films with little respite.

Exactly what he was apportioned to shoot was a matter of logistics: cast or location availability, weather and the pressure to keep material flowing down the pipe to Weta Digital. As much as he could, Jackson handled the dramatic meat, but often the director would look across the epic schedule and, said Mahaffie, 'determine his priorities'. Which meant sacrificing choice scenes. Mahaffie's first assignment was the horseback chase between Arwen and the posse of Black Riders, with a 'wide-eyed' Liv Tyler regularly sat astride a forty-gallon oil drum mounted to the back of a pick-up truck. His Everest was Helm's Deep.

While frequently working with name cast like Mortensen and Hill, this mainly meant stockpiling often highly complex combat beats with the teams of stuntmen and extras from which Jackson would envisage the fever of battle in the edit.

The second unit would always be in contact with the mothership of the main unit, by satellite link and scratchy phone calls. Mahaffie, meanwhile, followed storyboards and animatics, and spent time watching footage from the first few months of production to 'key into' Jackson's rhythm. Whenever possible they would get together and talk through what was 'quintessential' to the second unit sequences. The template, he said, was set, but once in the grip of shooting, figuring out logistics in the scene, he was left to interpret the scene as he may.

To add to the general discomfort, Helm's Deep not only takes place at night but in a gothic downpour strobed by lightning. In the visceral furore of mud and bodies, critics thought they caught a tribute to Akira Kurosawa's *Seven Samurai*, which was fine by Jackson, only he hadn't seen the Japanese maestro's epics.

You can see their point. Kurosawa coined the phrase 'Immaculate Reality' (as appropriated by George Lucas) to describe how he created the worlds within his films, and the idea could be applied to Jackson's thoroughness. No matter how removed from the commonplace reality of the watcher, through the cumulative effect of production design, costume, locations, stuntwork, the infinitesimal attention given to visual detail and mood, the audience would accept what they watched as real.

Not to say it wasn't stylized.

Alan Lee recalls that in early discussions over the look of the battles Jackson cited a painting by the German artist Albrecht Altdorfer called *The Battle of Alexander at Issus*.*

'What he liked was the enormous scale of the battle, and the way that you can see orderly ranks and masses of cavalry all clearly delineated. He wanted to ensure that whenever we had battles it would never be just a huge confused melee; we would be able to see exactly what was happening at any given moment.'

Peruse the heaving mass of Uruk-hai pouring into Helm's Deep, freeze-frame at your leisure and you can pick out five divisions: swordsmen, pikesmen, crossbowmen, sappers (who blow a hole in the wall in Olympic fashion) and berserkers.

Jackson and editor Michael Horton manage the commotion with extraordinary dexterity and rhythm — as well as intimacy. You might say, one of the core themes of the book is that literally bigger isn't necessarily better (something modern Hollywood has trouble grasping). Against such a visual storm, the minutia of character and storytelling was essential. As a general throughline we follow Aragorn's leadership of the human and Elf forces,

---

* To apply a little art history, Altdorfer was a leading exponent of the school of 'world landscapes' — or *Weltlandschaft* — which had a significant influence over the depiction of the whole of Middle-earth. As the name attests, the gist of the school was the depiction of vast, imaginary and often mountainous panoramas from an elevated viewpoint, drawing upon historical, Biblical or mythological narratives.

focussing on his own heroic deeds, branching off for updates on Legolas and Gimli, preoccupied with accumulating the bigger kill list (Tolkien-sourced gallows levity that Jackson inflates into a gag about movie body counts), a somewhat fatalistic Théoden enclosed in the Hornburg, and the endless Uruk-hai launching gigantic grappling hooks and giant ladders at the walls. Within the overall narrative, we are periodically diverted to the destruction of Isengard by the Ents, and Frodo, Sam and Gollum's capture by Faramir. The final third of *The Two Towers* is a towering lesson in orchestrating tension on multiple fronts.

Altdorfer's painting is also notable for a stone tablet suspended beneath a wreath of storm clouds, on which, inscribed in Latin, the artist provides some historical context (a Renaissance take on a director's commentary). To celebrate the completion of *The Fellowship of the Ring*, Lee presented Jackson with his homage to Altdorfer, blowing up a frame from the prologue — the moment Sauron is struck down issuing a shockwave of light — and adding Altdorfer's tablet, only instead of Latin adding an Elvish inscription: 'A light shone in the darkness, and all who witnessed it were bowled over'.

*

Helm's Deep, a hero's perspective: Above his mirror, Mortensen had pinned a note — 'adapt or overcome'. Every day of production he would steel himself with that advice, and never more so than when striding out across the car park at Dry Creek Quarry to face a night of rain-beaten struggle against stuntmen callused in leathery skin and rusty armour.

'I heard those words from one of the guys who had trained me early on with weapons and it just seemed appropriate.'

Throughout shooting, he explains, you had to adapt to the weather, the location, the technical stratagems of special effects and scenes being rewritten on the day. You had to overcome the exhaustion creeping up on you like a sickness. 'It was like some video game that gets worse with every level.'

Shooting at the Deep felt like being stuck endlessly repeating the same level.

Again, the production and story seemed to offer a mirror of one another. It was a battle in many respects, but without actual bloodshed. Even fictionally, Orc blood was conveniently black as ink, which helped circumvent rating issues.

'You push it as far as you can,' Jackson had told me in Cannes, 'but it should be a PG13: you want kids to see the movie.'

Nothing would greater test Mortensen's mettle and that of the other actors whose passage in the story landed them at Helm's Deep, caked in quarry dust and sweat: Bloom as Legolas, John Rhys-Davies (even more so his scale double Brett Beattie) as Gimli, Bernard Hill as Théoden and Craig Parker as Haldir, as well as bands of stuntmen and indefatigable crew.

Spare a thought for Liv Tyler, who served her time on the battlements only for Arwen to be artfully cut out and digitally erased as her storyline changed. Horse stunts were reputedly a particular discomfort for the actress, but she went uncomplainingly onto the record that it was all for the best.

A 'working day' would begin at 5pm and they would battle through to sun up. Dry Creek Quarry became a world of permanent midnight. Wreathed in fog and soaked through by a combination of both freezing Wellington drizzle (it was autumn after all) and artificial downpours from giant rain bars held aloft by a crane and supplied by 10,000-gallon water trucks, there was no time for the mollycoddled celebrity. Helm's Deep was a great egalitarian effort. Says Mortensen, 'We were all in that same soup.'

In the final weeks, t-shirts circulated among the sun-starved crew emblazoned with 'I survived Helm's Deep'; it had become a rite of passage, a club with a large but selective membership.

No quarter was given anywhere. Weta Workshop would arrive every afternoon with lorry-loads of armour and weapons, which had been exhaustively vetted by John Howe's expertise in matters medieval. There were five different varieties of fletching on the arrows, and Richard Taylor had a rationale for every one. Pneumatic rigs launched volleys of rubber-tipped arrows to crisscross in the air and thump harmlessly into duly armoured and psyched stuntmen, whose efforts never failed to move Mortensen.

'Even in the background they weren't fooling around — we had people fifty or one hundred yards away looking like they were getting killed. If one department even hinted at letting up, the other departments would shame them back into focus.'

He would take a breath, get into character, his muscles primed and ready, and find a stuntman immersed in an intense argument with a Weta designer on the finer points of a thirteenth-century pommel hit: 'Okay, when you're ready.'

The unflagging Dane had strolled off the plane almost fully formed as Aragorn, his Viking genes allowing him to effortlessly jink and jab where others laboured under Bob Anderson's sword-fighting tutelage. All the stunt co-ordinators agreed that he was a natural swordsman.

Yet even Mortensen had to graft when it came to the choreography of battle and an endless list of hand-to-hand routines to learn and execute as if pure reaction. Individual stunts, which could involve up to sixty stuntmen, had to be carefully synchronized and blocked, but still appear frantic and haphazard. Mortensen mentions how hard he had trained beforehand in the gym to fine-tune 'the angles and needs of the scenes', but on set he would have to adjust to the terrain, the skittish nature of even highly trained horses (according to Mahaffie the most unpredictable element) or an improvised flash of brilliance that would send a scene in a new direction.

'We'd have to really trust each other,' he says. Adapt or overcome.

'It can look quite messy,' admits Sean Bean, evaluating his own clatter of fight sequences, a twinge of disappointment in his voice at having missed out on Helm's Deep. 'It was organized precisely, but there were a lot of slashes. At times, you did feel like you were fighting for your life.'

'You had to make it feel like desperation,' says Mortensen: 'biting, kicking, head butts, as well as good sword action.'

Years later, shooting the more diverse — geographically and organically — Battle of the Five Armies in *The Hobbit*, Lee Evans admitted it could get genuinely scary facing his foes suited and booted. 'Sixty of these stuntmen in full Orc costume, with prosthetic teeth, blood, eyes, come charging at you. You've got to remember to stay in character and not run away.'

Staying unshakeably true to his character, Mortensen foreswore the lightweight, urethane stunt weapons and used the heavy version of his blade. He sought what was realistic, not movielike. Aragorn wasn't a superhero.

'I shouldn't be able to just throw my sword around like Errol Flynn did, especially when I'm really tired. It should be hard to fight.'

The physicality is so much a part of Mortensen's performance. He doesn't make things look effortless but effortful.

On a nightly basis, there were cuts, sprains and pulled muscles. Everyone felt the sting of a stray blade; bruises were a badge of honour and an endless frustration for the make-up department. 'I got a tooth knocked out,' the star proudly announced in Cannes, having been caught in the face by a protruding fin of Uruk-hai armour. It swiftly became part of the Mortensen mythology — how he asked for glue, stuck it back in with gum and finished his scene — but, witnessing the moment, make-up artist Jose Perez had feared their leading man had lost half his face. It was blind luck that he had been caught in the mouth.

'I got to say the stunt guys also took some hits,' says Mortensen, the memory making him smile.

Says Bloom, 'He was always taking out stuntmen and buying them a beer because he'd hit them one too many times. He just went for it. . . He knew no limit.'

*

HELM'S DEEP, AN ORC PERSPECTIVE: We are introduced to Saruman's Uruk-hai legions via a grandstanding reverse shot out over the balcony of Orthanc and back and back through the ranks of super-sized Orcs and their leafless forest of banners and pikes. Jackson cuts back to a close-up of a very human Brad Dourif, a tear rolling down his cheek. It's a telling image: shock and awe.

To create the Nuremburg-like roar of the multitude, Jackson had taken his sound recordists to the cricket. On 16 February 2002, New Zealand were playing England in a one-day international at The Basin in Wellington and at lunch, with New Zealand 244 runs to the good, Jackson strolled barefoot onto the field. Armed with a mic, he began conducting the enthusiastic 25,000-crowd in chanting along with the Black Speech scrolling up the video screens. It didn't go unnoticed that England collapsed to a desultory eighty-nine that afternoon.

Taylor admits that finding suitably hulking local stuntmen to fill out the prosthetics of the live-action Uruk-hai was a challenge. 'Stunties' in New Zealand tended to be cast from a pool of Pacific Islanders, Polynesians who were naturally muscular but shorter than what he had in mind. 'We wanted Uruk-hai and ended up with Uruk-lows,' he quips, another prize Taylorism.

They would make up for any short-fallings with their enthusiasm.

Having graduated from Toi Whakaari New Zealand Drama School in Wellington, Shane Rangi had been up for the role of Lurtz, the blade-licking Uruk horror who did for Boromir, but lost out to 'his good mate' Lawrence Makoare. Not one to be disheartened, he went on set as an extra where stunt co-ordinator George Marshall Ruge took one look at his unusual 6'4" frame and enlisted the actor in a three-day Middle-earth stunt workshop.

From there Rangi spread himself thick. He stabbed Frodo on Weathertop in the guise of the Witch-king of Angmar, and was the Haradrim warrior piloting a mûmak who gets skewered by Éomer's spear at The Battle of the Pelennor Fields. Therein he also stunt-doubled for Makoare's Orc general, Gothmog.

Your average Orc, he recalls, was open to all kinds of embellishment. Turning up to the make-up chair, Gino Acevedo, heading up a team of Orc beauticians, would grin and ask, 'Okay, what do you feel like today?'

Says Rangi, 'It's funny, because sometimes you'd be in the make-up chair adding piercings and scarification, going, "Pete'll love this!" But then you turn up on set and he goes, "That's just too much. Take some of it out." And then the next day you go conservative and he'll say, "It would be great if he had a bone sticking out of his nose." You can never tell.'

Jackson knew it paid to be unpredictable.

The Uruk-hai attacking Helm's Deep possessed a more uniform repulsiveness. Rangi jokes that they 'all came out of the same mould': flesh-eating prop forwards with the imprint of a white hand (often Taylor's or Acevedo's) across their faces.

What could be relied upon was that Rangi and his brother stuntmen, clad in foul prosthetics, would end up on the wrong end of a heroic sword, arrow, axe, spear, rock or whatever came to hand. Uruks slain at the top of the forty-foot ladder rigs and falling to the crash mats below, were quickly recycled back up the ladder like the Keystone Cops.

'I died hundreds of times,' he laughs ruefully. 'We were usually cannon fodder in the hero fights for the Aragorns and Gandalfs of Middle-earth. I think I was killed by Faramir a dozen times alone in the attack on Osgiliath.'

Hamilton-based stunt co-ordinator Tim Wong, another who took his first professional post on *The Lord of the Rings*, lost count of how many times Mortensen killed him. 'It would have been at least fifty times in the trilogy, and a couple of dozen in Helm's Deep alone.'

There was a part of the Orc psychosis to which this felt unfair. Tolkien be damned, they wanted to win. And never more so than at Helm's Deep where things got quite Method.

'We Orcs stuck together,' continues Rangi. 'You had your Elves on one side and your Uruk-hai on the other, and at lunch it was exactly like that as well. It was because you'd spend twelve weeks out at the quarry, working five or six days a week, fourteen hours a day. You form a close bond with those people. And you tended to find that the Elves were quite tall and pretty and prissy, and the Uruk-hai were all rugby league players, quite hard. We were all out there suffering, but only the Elves made their misery known, and we didn't want to be associated with the whingeing!'

Wong, whose slenderer 5'5" frame enabled him to also be roughed up as Frodo's stunt double, is slightly more circumspect. 'I've got to be careful here as I've been on both sides of the war so don't want to upset my Orc and Elven brothers and sisters. I've played both, beauty and the beast you could say. But as an Orc or an Elf you would naturally hate the other race.'

Still, he agrees, that while in the employment of the White Wizard they were prepared to go to the dark side. . . 'There was no such thing as too evil when you are an Orc!'

As you may have detected, the close-knit Uruk-hai stuntmen faced the brunt of Helm's Deep with a barracks humour. One night, with the Elves up on the Deeping Wall and a crowd of obstinate Uruks below, Rangi, Wong and their ilk were of the mind, dramatically speaking, that the flash boys weren't as riled up as they ought to be. Their answer was to strike up an impromptu Haka, the Māori ceremonial war dance they, of course, all knew by heart.

Between takes, they enjoyed freaking out their make-up teams by suddenly snapping at them, unwilling to break character.

'You had to make it fun,' says Wong, 'because everyone was suffering.' Though, that does depend on your idea of fun.

The make-up artists would get their own back by adding lipstick and eyeliner unbeknownst to an Orc, or drawing a bullseye on the back of his head.

Watching the Orc teams greet each other with a rousing headbutt, Mortensen colluded with one of his opponents to address Bloom's comely Legolas with a crack of foreheads. All Bloom can remember is a burst of white light and his legs turning to rubber.

The weary make-up department was less than impressed with having to cover up the red welt that had arrived unscripted on an Elvish temple.

Joking aside, the stunt teams were highly organized and highly motivated, rehearsing six-, seven-, eight-point moves, dealing with the weight and sometimes limited sightlines of the prosthetic suits, trying to channel both the brute force of the Uruk-hai and their Samurai-like discipline. This community within the community was never to be found wanting. It was a point of pride.

Taylor is particularly proud of the 'turtle formation' of Uruk-hai shimmying up the stone causeway at Dry Creek to bang on the front door of the Hornburg. The Workshop had built shields the size of coffee tables with two handles on the back. 'They released one handle and grabbed the one next to them,' he says, and the shields locked together like a fluid shell.

When many of the same stuntmen reassembled for *The Hobbit* there was less call for the rigours of prosthetics, with Orcs now encrusted in digital skin. On set they had to get used to grey leotards and strange stalks sprouting from their heads in order to set the eyelines — height no longer a drawback. Nevertheless, Rangi feels the loss of that old-school physical presence that make-up brings.

'You get an in-the-moment reaction. It's like *Star Wars* — the Stormtroopers used to be guys in suits, but then they made them digital. Sure, they look impressive, but they just lose an element of realism.'

The goal for Helm's Deep — apart, that is, from ousting Théoden from his stone bolthole — was to seamlessly join Mahaffie's foreground action to the thousands of Uruk-hai swarming into the valley like angry termites.

However romantic and old-Hollywood it might sound, corralling that number of extras was prohibitively costly and practically untenable. Richard Attenborough had mustered 300,000 extras for the funeral sequence in *Gandhi* in 1981, but that was only for a single day in a densely populated India, and they were required to do little more than patiently stand in place. New Zealand had a population not much less than four million.* 1956 was another era, when De Mille roused 14,000 for *The Ten Commandments*, with no more than tittle-tattle leaking from the set (most of it about De Mille's bullying). Jackson and New Line were ever mindful of maintaining a secure veil across their production. Kubrick might have marshalled 8,500 Californian souls for the chessboard formations of Romans and bushwhacking slaves in *Spartacus*, but none of them needed to be in Orc prosthetics.

As far back as his pitch video, Jackson was convinced the answer was to be found in visual effects.

Yet Weta Digital didn't truly get to grips with Middle-earth warfare until the morning Jackson notified them he required two finished shots of Helm's Deep for the four-minute preview of *The Two Towers* he planned to attach to the end of the first film: a wide establishing shot of 10,000 Uruks clutching flaming brands as they marched on the castle, from a distance not unlike a concert crowd holding aloft mobile phones; and the magnificent image of Uruks swarming up the Deeping Wall on ladders raised in perfect sequence.

Having to figure out those shots was a boon, says Wayne Stables, a Weta Digital veteran who had originally joined to help open up a wormhole for *Contact*, and volunteered as one of the advance party on Helm's Deep. They 'nailed so much' about the battle: lighting (including lightning effects), atmospherics (rain and smoke), environment (incorporating rock textures) and the specific key-frame animation of Uruks clinging to those ladders and leaping onto battlements.

'When we showed Peter a test of the ladder shot,' says Stables, 'he was so impressed he rushed out to grab Fran so she could see it. That was when we knew we were in business.'

---

* 3,858,234 to be exact, and, in fairness to New Zealand, Jackson borrowed divisions of the army for battle scenes at Ruapehu and over 250 volunteer horse-owners made their way to Twizel on the South Island to help stage the spectacular Ride of the Rohirrim.

Underlying the shots, and the real secret to efficiently generating tens of thousands of lifelike Uruks, was another visual effects breakthrough mothered by necessity. The small miracle they knew as MASSIVE.

*

Stephen Regelous was concerned about artificial intelligence. It wasn't the possibility that super-computers might plot the downfall of mankind that was worrying him, he was fascinated in how AI might be used to simulate human behaviour. Ironically, when it came to the fulfilment of the computer graphics software engineer's labours in Middle-earth, his revolutionary programme would in main be used to depict the attempted destruction of mankind.

The glitch of having been born in the British seaside town of Margate notwithstanding, Regelous is a Kiwi in every ingenious and unwavering cell of his body. Having sold stereos in the eighties, determined to do something better with his life he 'bluffed his way into' teaching graphic design and computer animation. Back then, he laughs, all anyone knew about computer animation was the blockheaded warehousemen in the Dire Straits video Money for Nothing, 'but it didn't take a genius to figure out it was moving quickly, and it was going to be viable for movies'.

In the early nineties, Regelous moved into television commercials, 'and pretty much got to know everyone in the VFX industry in New Zealand'. An ocean away from Los Angeles where they decreed the state the art, Regelous taught himself how to write software, working his way through new and improved programmes like boxes of soap powder.

'It snowballed from there. . .'

With his wiry frame, clean Lex Luthor crown and sharp features, Regelous has the intensity of a genuine virtuoso. He mentions tweaking industry standard software as if reordering his sock drawer. He claims to literally dream in code. Even as he snake charms algorithms, he has an artist's restless curiosity, fascinated by the intersection of humans and machines. The meaning behind things. With his blend of native Kiwi honesty and scientific thoroughness, he is touchingly determined to present the truth not the legend of his accomplishments.

Regelous breezed through Wellington's embryonic VFX industry, companies and software systems sounding much like the other: Yeti and Topaz, Pixel Perfect and Prism. He got his hands on a coveted copy of Pixar's RenderMan package — 'which wasn't exactly pirated, but I didn't exactly have a licence' — opened up the hood and slotted in his own code to stream-line his animations, another glorious exponent of the Kiwi DIY genetic code. In the local film and television community, he was like a one-man digital band writing particle systems, facial ani-mation software, key-framing and compositing systems: all tools of the kind that would help sculpt Middle-earth.

When man versus machine epic *Terminator 2: Judgment Day* hit town in 1991 everyone wanted 'something like that', so he wrote morphing software that could rival a face-changing Michael Jackson in the video for Black and White.

'I became the morph king of New Zealand!'

What frustrated Regelous was how computer animation still involved manual labour. He too was nursed on Ray Harryhausen, and knew the painstaking effort that went into stop-motion. The results could be poetic, but it made no sense, decades after *Jason and the Argonauts*, that inside a computer they were still repli-cating life in tiny, maddening incremental moves.

His thoughts kept returning to the concept of artificial intel-ligence. Books like *Artificial Life* by Steven Levy showed how science was capable of mimicking living ecosystems. Evolution, Levy claimed, wasn't confined to nature.

Regelous headed to America to confer with key scientists like Chris Langton, who coined the term 'artificial life', and Craig Reynolds, whose 'flocking and schooling' programmes were making waves in cognitive ornithology (although fell short of psychic communion with Great Eagles). Regelous cites a pres-entation by Carl Sims, in which rudimentary computer creatures, no more than blocks, were supplied with basic brains and left to evolve the best way to achieve simple goals. At one point, fighting each other for resources. It sounds kooky, he admits, but the results were enchanting. 'You could see the effort they were making.'

Returning to Wellington, his complex brain was on fire. Couldn't you have digital agents actually respond to each other using AI? Set up the scenario, fix your parameters and leave them to it. 'There would be no more animation, you would basically be filming stuff that was going on.'

By chance, this was about the time Weta knocked on his door. It was 1995 and they were in the throes of figuring out the artificial afterlife of *The Frighteners*. Even if his research had to be put on hold, Regelous knew this was an opportunity he couldn't turn down.

'You couldn't be in the visual effects in Wellington and not know what Peter Jackson was doing. I saw *Bad Taste* over and over. I think everyone in Wellington had loved that film.'

Everyone, he says, wanted to see what Jackson was going to do next.

Regelous was employee number twelve at Weta Digital, sat upstairs in the little house on Tasman Street with all the musty old furniture that had been stacked out of the way. He even brought along his own SGI computer. With the deal he struck to work on *The Frighteners*, he insisted on retaining the rights to any bespoke code he wrote. Otherwise it would automatically become the property of the studio.

Code is built on pre-existing code. In other words, a framework he had put together beforehand. He would have effectively been handing over his life's work. It was a policy he maintained with MASSIVE.

During the wrap party for *The Frighteners*, Jackson mentioned his plans for a film version of *The Hobbit*. 'One of Peter's greatest skills is knowing what he needs,' says Regelous. 'He could see he needed software to make crowds.' The convention, even at lordly ILM, was to use particle systems and a quota of pre-set animated behaviours, but Regelous had a brainwave. What if he could create the crowds for *The Hobbit* as artificial life?

Jackson remembers his proposal clearly. 'I asked the digital guys how we were going to do these battles, and it was Stephen who had this idea of writing a piece of software that created digital brains. You could put thousands of guys in there and they could all think for themselves. It's one thing to say you needed thousands of CGI things on a screen, but you can't actually animate that number. It will take forever. He came up with the idea that they would animate themselves.'

Impressed, Jackson set him to work. Over a two-year period from 1996 to 1998 Regelous divined his AI system and how to apply it to Tolkien. There was, he says, scepticism at Weta Digital as if he was dabbling in voodoo, but they gave him a desk and kept a beady eye trained on what he was up to.

As earlier chapters of this book have mapped out, *The Hobbit* of course morphed into first a two-film then a three-film version of *The Lord of the Rings*. The crowds only grew bigger. In late 1999, with sets being built at Dry Creek Quarry and the pressure mounting, Regelous put on a pivotal demonstration for Jackson. The legendary Battle of Silver versus Gold.

Essentially, the 'brain' in each MASSIVE agent that Jackson mentioned is made up of a set of variables, or choices, each one a network of 7,000 to 8,000 'logic nodes'. They are then set free in an environment populated with other agents (some with differently ascribed brains) and left to make their own decisions based on their variables. For instance, if you meet an enemy agent you fight to the death.

'This was the test where everyone says one of them was smart enough to run away from battle,' notes Regelous — Jackson especially had enjoyed telling the DVD extras about the inglorious little bastard who had opted to save his own skin. However, says Regelous, 'that's not quite true.'

Something far more interesting was going on. Regelous' software was *storytelling*.

'What was wonderful for me was to watch people's reactions. It is one thing to ascribe what agents are doing, but it is a whole other thing to see what people *think* the agents are doing. People immediately thought those agents were running for the hills. That proved to me the AI approach was valid.'

When things went wrong in the software, they went wrong *naturally*. What Regelous calls viable but entertaining screwups. Happy accidents. Evolution.

Combinations of variables simulated senses like vision and hearing, and the brains of Silver and Gold warriors were such that they would run until they 'saw' an enemy who they would engage in mortal combat. The survivor would then go 'looking' for another enemy. Because Regelous had placed them randomly in the simulation the odd agent was facing away from battle and ran in that direction in search of an enemy they would never find.

They weren't actually running for their lives, it only appeared that way. You could say they were acting. All Regelous needed to do was give them the option of turning around.

If a Gold soldier slew a Silver who had just killed another Gold, the watchers automatically thought of it as revenge for killing his friend. 'They were projecting human emotions into the computer,' marvels Regelous.

The programme had become a metaphor for life.

An extraordinary result undermined by the fact Regelous was still referring to his AI crowd simulator as 'Plod' — his first experiment had simply got an agent strolling around obstacles. Seeking something with a bit more heft, as it were, when someone piped up with 'Massive' a thrilled Regelous even managed to reverse engineer an acronym: Multiple Agent Simulation System in a Virtual Environment. For the life of him, he couldn't come up with an acronym for 'Little Bastards'.

*

Massive was now MASSIVE, another emblem of the uncluttered thinking of this humble island, another challenge set by Tolkien and answered by this peculiar natural resource of, well, resourcefulness.

'There were multiple problems,' says Jackson, 'and you just solve them.'

If you build it, they will come.

Again and again, *The Lord of the Rings* success is put down to pragmatic thinking. But these were solutions that won Oscars and led to seismic changes across an entire industry; Weta was soon to offer a valid alternative to ILM. Whether it was down to the book, the country, Jackson's open-minded leadership, good timing, the powers of fate, or a mix of all these variables, problems weren't solved they were transcended.

Says Mark Ordesky, 'A lot of what happened in *Lord of the Rings* was because we were doing new things. Whenever you are doing new things it is both exciting and challenging. That was part of the stress and pressure as well. But for Peter it was always about overcoming people's expectations.'

Regelous was put in charge of his own MASSIVE department. Having read *The Lord of the Rings*, he calculated they needed over a hundred individually designed types of agent. He hired a team of 'brain builders' who understood animation and motion, designers and programmers, many from the videogame community, who could 'breathe life into the armies'. There followed three fight choreographers, one who had never used a computer before. They borrowed stuntmen from the main unit and established a menu of two hundred different battle moves, stealing onto the motion-capture stage when the Gollum team were unawares to get accurate thrusts and parries onto their hard-drives. Faced with individually animating the cloth dynamics for flags and clothes for up to 300,000 agents (for the Battle of the Pelennor Fields), Regelous wrote his own cloth simulator.

As soon as Joe Letteri had touched down Jackson mentioned that he wanted to give MASSIVE a test drive in *The Fellowship of the Ring*, adding a foretaste of the battles to come into the first film's prologue — a throng of Elves and men in ancient times fighting Sauron's forces on the ashen slopes of Mount Doom.

Letteri had been impressed by Regelous' ingenuity. 'MASSIVE is like directing a crowd of extras,' he says. 'You tell them what you want them to do, and if it doesn't come out quite right, you sort of adjust their behaviours a little bit.'

He loved how it was a human response to the problem. Just add life. The question was whether MASSIVE was ready to take a bow.

Over a single weekend, Jackson and Christian Rivers had built a clay model of this corner of Mordor, blocking out all the action. Weta Digital simply scanned in this tabletop battleground, and finessed it with a few geographical features. Meanwhile, foreground live-action elements were choreographed and shot on a blue-screen stage. And once the MASSIVE performances had been approved, the agents needed to be rendered to match, the digital equivalent of hair and make-up. Given the numbers involved — Jackson had ordered 80,000 warriors for the prologue — this necessitated the invention of another programme able to render armies in 20,000 blocks and christened, with typical Weta waggishness, GRUNT — Guaranteed Rendering of Unlimited Number of Things. Adapt or overcome.

The realism in MASSIVE might not yet be fully realized, but the opening salvo still gives fair warning of what is in store: under a glowering sky as grey and mottled as the Somme we are thrown headfirst into the vastness of Jackson's vision as Sauron smites aside agents as if they were plastic soldiers. Welcome to Middle-earth.

Over the course of three films, working from Jackson's direct input and a roadmap of storyboards, footage and background plates, Regelous refined what MASSIVE could do for the story. The process, he says, became 'very interactive' — they could even build in variables for an agent's level of aggression. To point a unit in the right direction they built a flow field into the terrain, or set up sound sources as if they were responding to orders.

Still the AIs would improvise in ways even Regelous found uncanny. 'Agents fell from cliffs and it would look cool,' he laughs. In a test shot using footage of the Helm's Deep miniature, his team placed agents up on the Deeping Wall and others on the ground behind. Halfway through the shot he found characters had taken it upon themselves to climb up the stairs to get to the higher ground.

By first light on the fifth day, as good as his word, Gandalf arrives with the exiled Rohirrim to charge to the rescue down an almost vertical incline into the ranks of Uruk-hai. Thus, in a fitting echo of pioneering nineteenth-century photographer Eadward Muybridge, who placed split-second shots of a running horse inside a spinning drum he called a zoopraxiscope and effectively invented cinema, Regelous' team rode horses up and down a seventy-foot motion-capture stage while sampling their gait. Within MASSIVE, digital rider and horse would each get its own brain and would occasionally enter into a tussle over direction. The rider also had to decide if he ought to fall off.

Equine variables would reach their apogee with the breathless Ride of the Rohirrim in the third film.

Monitoring footage, Jackson, Letteri and the Weta Digital hierarchy could simply delete any agent caught overacting. More often than not, the hammy Uruk-hai or phony Rohirrim in question was an extra from the live-action shoot. By the third film they were actively replacing miscreant humans with MASSIVE agents, who took direction better.

The software was versatile enough to be put to other uses in Middle-earth. Saruman's flock of evil crows, or Crebain, demonstrated more cognitive ornithology. The scores of Moria Orcs, or goblins, that scuttled down the pillars of Dwarrowdelf in mimicry of swarming cockroaches. For wide-shots of that great Dwarven hall digital doubles of the Fellowship were transmuted into MASSIVE agents, and Regelous found himself fitting logic nodes into the brain of Sir Ian McKellen or Sean Bean, although the rigours of emoting were kept to a minimum as they simply flee the rabbling Orcs. Close-ups were strictly the real life.

Within the widescreen synthesis of Helm's Deep, in order to emphasize Jackson's heroic narratives, Stables points out that they regularly 'turned off MASSIVE' and specifically animated an Orc to lunge at a motion-captured Aragorn or Gimli.

Out of these numerous parts, interlinked like a three-dimensional puzzle, emerged something realistic yet thrilling, a great gothic battle machine, and the critics were bowled over.

'The battles and sieges are conducted with the ferocity of the Crusades, Agincourt and Stalingrad,' extolled Philip French in *The Observer*, who also liked to place things in the context of movie history, '. . . orchestrated in a manner that recalls the great movie epics of Fritz Lang and Sergei Eisenstein.'

In the *Washington Post*, Desson Howe admired the director's capacity to amaze: '. . . you can feel not just the power and sureness of Jackson's direction, but his boyish wonder. In the end, that wonder is the ultimate compass. And he never loses sight of it.'

For *Salon*'s Charles Taylor, the point was that the sense of wonder was always at the service of the material. 'Unlike almost any other director I can think of who dares to work on an epic scale, Jackson doesn't seem to have a whiff of megalomania to him. . .'

Regelous would never get to take a bow. With his restless mind already on applications for MASSIVE far away from Middle-earth — and conscious that imitators would already be at work — once his team was firmly established he departed with *The Two Towers* not yet complete.

'I felt really bad to leave before the end of the trilogy, that I wasn't seeing it through to the end, but I needed to get out there talking to the other studios, preparing a future for the software.'

Based out of Bangkok, today MASSIVE is the industry standard crowd software. Its list of credits is wide and diverse: *iRobot*, *Elektra*, the Narnia films, *Happy Feet*, *2012*, *Hugo* and more recently *The Jungle Book* and the remake of *Ben-Hur*. Remarkably, says Regelous, 'it was used to grow the forests in *Avatar*, because a forest is an ecosystem, making agents for the trees and plants and have them grow and respond and compete with the other agents growing around them.'

There were raised eyebrows at Weta Digital when he left. Loyalty was the unwritten code of *The Lord of the Rings*, and he knows that he left a scent of betrayal behind him. The only thing Regelous regrets, however, is that he didn't get the chance to show Jackson how grateful he was.

'I was still talking to them,' he makes clear, 'implementing extra things. They would get new versions of the software. That was all part of the deal.'

As was the stipulation that Jackson got to say when other studios could use it, and certainly no film before *The Return of the King*.

*

When it came to the third and final film, with the stakes even higher, Jackson's inclination was to go *really* MASSIVE. In terms of scale, he would dwarf Helm's Deep with Sauron unleashing a sea of Orcs to assail the pale walls of Minas Tirith that sits at the prow of the White Mountains. Expanding a meagre 10,000 Uruk-hai to 300,000 Orc grunts — an army hitherto never seen on a cinema screen and a testament to Regelous' achievements.

Overall, Weta Digital would take a different conceptual approach for the Battle of the Pelennor Fields, and its ensuing squabble at the Black Gates. Each film was built on the shoulders of the last, and the possibilities of combining MASSIVE with a virtual landscape opened up the potential of the third book's great siege beyond what they had even conceived of in principal photography.

Following the release of *The Two Towers*, Rivers stole away to a secret room to head up the secret Pelennor Fields pre-viz unit, dreaming up new shots, steepled with ever more vertiginous camera angles. Jackson edited in the new frames of pre-viz and additional live-action footage from supplementary shooting and handed them back to Weta Digital with an apologetic smile.

'There you go, good luck.'

An already burdened team was alarmed to find Pelennor Fields alone had soared to 250 visual effects shots (half of *The Fellowship of the Ring*'s quota of VFX). All of it located in a vast digital environment like a 3D Alan Lee painting — which was largely because Lee had designed it using New Zealand as his palette, sampling landscapes by helicopter like a visit to a country-sized salad bar.

Recalls Lee, 'Joe Letteri thought it would be a good idea to send me down to Queenstown to collect as much material as possible. I'd been on helicopter recces before, but this time I was able to explore more freely.'

A 360-degree environment would involve around one hundred photos or 'tiles'. They shot the Pelennor Fields material and all the mountains behind Minas Tirith in a glacial valley close to New Zealand's most famous (and tallest) peak, Mount Cook; Mordor's forbidding peaks were adapted from the Remarkables range near Queenstown. Says Lee, 'I was up to speed with Photoshop by this time and so was able to use the material for artwork for effects shots and for Weta to be able to build complete environments.'

It was painting with real life.

Lee then sat down at a computer with 3D Sequence Supervisor Eric Saindon and together they laid out the Pelennor Fields: world builders, with Lee pointing out local points of geographical interest that he knew by heart from the book, and adding the plates of the sublime miniature of Minas Tirith.

'It was the ultimate evolution of the matte painting,' he says, amazed at how his journey from his quiet studio in Devon had led to being able to plug himself directly into the visual effects.

Jackson was equally keen to blur the lines between departments in the opposite direction, suggesting Jim Rygiel and his VFX crew shoot the live-action battle footage as Mahaffie had done, only on a vast V-shaped blue screen set attached to shipping containers on the backlot of Stone Street. In front of which was the paddock, an area of turf on which combat was choreographed in less trying conditions than at Helm's Deep. Jackson even had them out on location shooting pick-ups of horses attacking mûmakil.

Meanwhile, Jackson became giddy with the freedom his digital playground presented. 'Let's add a troll here, a Warg there,' he would say as they went over the latest crop of shots that Weta Digital forlornly hoped were finished. Why have only one fell beast strafing the rooftops of Minas Tirith, when you could have five or six?

'It's all optional,' he would tell them. 'You don't have to do it if you don't want to.'

'What does optional mean with Peter Jackson?' Rygiel laughed. It became a joke later into post-production — 'is this an *optional* shot?'

A certain cynicism has attached itself to the use of CGI as a short-cut at the expense of the romance of live-action shooting and model building. And there are valid arguments that it has become a crutch for many filmmakers, pelting us with their marvels, bullying us into awe. But over those fateful years, Weta Digital was a community of artists absolutely committed to the film, pushed to their limits meeting the challenging goals set by their director.

Brief months before the release of *The Return of the King*, I interviewed Jackson for a preview piece in *Empire*. He had sounded tired but upbeat. 'Everything is under control,' he said proudly of the final push. As recorded in those unvarnished DVD extras, when the magazine reached Manuka Street, certain members of the team blew up the quote and stuck it to the wall, to keep reminding themselves, 'Everything is under control. . .'

The future was already upon them, and it would only grow more complex and time consuming — as would the director's delight in his playthings. It would follow that Jackson would shoot swathes of *The Battle of the Five Armies* on the motion-capture stage, stepping in among the clashing quintet of MASSIVE armies with his virtual camera, with nothing to constrain him but his imagination.

As we shall see, I watched him, barefoot in the virtual realm, creating shots of Smaug firebombing a Lake-town that was little more than grey-shaded outlines like a model kit on the monitors. Jackson was like a painter with his brush, able to take his camera anywhere he wished in another corner of Middle-earth.

Actors dressed as Orcs and Dwarves would clash in the volume and against green screens and sets, but I still wondered if the blood, sweat and tears of Dry Creek Quarry was something no computer could simulate.

*

The Two Towers began its worldwide release on 18 December 2002, with the familiar parade of premieres starting in New York. What fears there might have been of a slump in quality or audience interest were swiftly put to rest.

The second part of the trilogy made even more than its predecessor with a worldwide total of $926,495,746 (adjusted for inflation that is at the time of writing a staggering $1,119,984,159). Massive was back to being an adjective used in conjunction with the film's success, and at last it appeared that New Line's nerves were calmed. There was an air almost of swagger to an advert they put out in praise of *The Two Towers*' technological accomplishments.

'Once again you have achieved the extraordinary in the face of the impossible. . .' it read grandly, using a line from the screenplay. 'The defences held.'

How the times had changed. But Jackson was too busy to bother with the irony.

Reinforcing the growing stature of a trilogy, alongside the expected technical nods, *The Two Towers* picked up a Best Picture nomination.[*]

---

[*] In all, *The Two Towers* was nominated for Best Picture, Best Visual Effects, Best Sound, Best Sound Editing, Best Art Direction and Best Film Editing (much deserved).

'That really confirmed the seriousness with which these films were being perceived,' says Ordesky. 'That *Fellowship* wasn't this fluke.'

The more diverse, textured and complex tapestry of the second film was indeed no fluke. Ostensibly a film without beginning or end, Jackson, Walsh and Boyens had done a fine job in establishing the tempo of a standalone movie. Events swell toward the crescendo of Helm's Deep and the cliffhanger of Gollum's conniving.

Even though they were made as one, the middle film offered strange, new currents. Beside Gollum, there was the court of the mad King Théoden, Gandalf's freshly laundered comeback and those tree-hugging Ents. Yet it feels the least like a fantasy. At times, set against arguably even more glorious vistas and using more of natural New Zealand light, *The Two Towers* recalls the horse operas of John Ford; the vision of the four riders' journey to Edoras is magisterial (and encourages a thrilling surge of strings from Howard Shore's score). The film is more emotionally charged, the Fellowship has broken, deepening our relationship with these scattered characters as well as new arrivals: as Éowyn, the underpraised Miranda Otto's fragile nobility and unrequited love for Aragorn feel earthbound and honest.

It is also the funniest of the three. Something I mention to Jackson and he was rather taken aback. 'Is it?' he says wonderingly. The humour came instinctually, to ward off self-importance. Gimli and Legolas' body-count tournament in the midst of battle syncopates a welcome dose of tongue-in-cheek between action beats (Rhys-Davies especially brings a Dwarvish rugger bugger enthusiasm to combat).

Then it speaks to one of the strongest themes of the second film (and the trilogy as a whole) — friendship. These are bonds that endure across boundaries of race, class and adversity. In a thread added to Tolkien, Aragorn makes his way to Helm's Deep late having been left for dead after a Warg attack. Staggering in, he is confronted by Legolas who searches his face intently as if to check he is indeed alive. 'You look terrible,' he says, Bloom edging toward a smirk — hanging out with humans has been rubbing off on the Elf. Mortensen cracks a grin so natural you can feel the off-screen friendship pour into frame.

Bloom tells a story about how, during pick-ups in June 2002, he had flown in to specifically see Mortensen, who was planning a reunion. Only in the protracted time frame of *The Lord of the Rings* could you have a cast reunion with two films still to come out. Bloom, Liv Tyler, McKellen, Henry Mortensen and some of the crew headed by bus into the countryside for an al fresco dinner with their erstwhile leader. Wandering along a river where they made merry, Bloom was struck by how beautifully the moon shone on the water. He dashed back to the fireside, caught in what he admitted was a Mortensen state of mind, to get everyone to 'come and check out the moon'.

Gathering at the riverbank, on a whim Mortensen suggested crossing right to the other side of the full flowing river.

'Fuck off,' laughed Bloom.

'Come on,' Mortensen egged.

So Bloom, never one to shy from a dare, followed his fellow actor into the river. 'We're barefoot, waist-high in water, walking on these little rocks to get to the other side and I'm doing it because I'm an idiot and I'm following his lead. Because *he's an idiot*. And because he's amazing. . . I can't believe how much this is going to make it sound like I'm in love with the guy.'

The Battle of Helm's Deep is, as the critics eulogized, epic cinema both fantastical and vivid. Seeing it for the first time, at no point did I stop to contemplate the fact that much of what was on the screen was the result of technological wizardry. Tolkien had written portions of his mythology while serving as a battalion signal officer at the Somme in 1916 and as is well-documented the memory of the First World War permeated his fiction; imagery that bled into Jackson's gripping depiction of battle and across the second film.

Many miles away, Frodo, Sam and Gollum negotiate the Dead

Marshes — the book's most direct reference to Tolkien's wartime experiences — where apparitions of fallen warriors appear in the water and attempt to lure Frodo to a watery grave. Tellingly, it is Gollum that rescues him.

In 2002, real life would bring a peculiar addendum to the second film's release. In the wake of the 9/11 attacks on the World Trade Center in New York (the release of *The Fellowship of the Ring* in the immediate shadow of those terrible events was written about as a welcome palliative) intrepid but wonky journalists sought to divine a significance in the new film being called *The Two Towers*, inasmuch as it sounded like the Twin Towers (deftly missing the fact that the book had been published nearly fifty years before).

Mortensen was appalled when Richard Corliss, as the actor put it 'a respected movie critic with a long and illustrious career', had written what he viewed 'a letter in support' of the invasion of Iraq and Afghanistan in the guise of a *Time* magazine review of *The Two Towers*.

Moved to write his own letter to the magazine, the outspoken Mortensen pointed out that Corliss' comparison of Christopher Lee's Saruman to Osama bin Laden, and the vastly outnumbered defenders of Helm's Deep to the 'Coalition of the Willing' fighting against Muslim hordes, displayed 'the simplistic, xenophobic, and arrogant worldview that makes the government of the United States feared and mistrusted around the world'.

'The editors claimed they had no space to print my brief letter,' he grumbled later, 'which I felt was dishonest and cowardly.'

Mortensen has a point: this smacks of superimposing an allegorical meaning onto the film where no such theme is on offer. Yet however exaggerated, Corliss was demonstrating how Middle-earth unconsciously held up a mirror to its times, although the suggestion would surely have needled Tolkien no end.

CHAPTER 14

Return to the Edge of the World

Frodo sleeps! Camera technicians rummaged through foam-lined cases. The whine of distant drills filled the air. Fran Walsh and Andy Serkis were deep in discussion, her flurry of black locks threatening to upstage his creamy-something leotard. Samwise Gamgee — although when the camera wasn't rolling his face looked much more like that of Sean Astin — bobbed about on his hairy feet at the point a moonlit corner of the Vale of Morgul became a flat soundstage floor. All the collective hubbub of a working studio exhaling between takes. And yet Elijah Wood was lying by a fake rock pool managing to take a nap.

'It's what Elijah does to pass the time,' reported Astin, following my eye-line to his recumbent partner. 'I swear he can sleep standing up when we are having our feet put on.'

I had returned to the far side of the world, wind-buffeted and jet-lagged, on 12 June 2003 to pay witness to journey's end. Well, at least in terms of the physical production. Even then, stunt teams would keep shooting long after all the actors had departed. The absolute, stone-clad final shot of the trilogy featuring the gang of Orcs and trolls gatecrashing Minas Tirith filmed on the motion capture stage in October 2003 (four years after the hobbits dashed for cover on that forested road) — an unthinkable flexibility compared to where they began.

Making Middle-earth had radically evolved from where they started.

Not that that was wholly apparent amid the bustle of Stone Street Studios, stirred back out of hibernation for supplementary shooting on *The Return of the King.* Borne on the confidence of two smash-hit films, two Best Picture nominations and his special effects division knack for reinventing the wheel, Peter Jackson was doing more than tweaking his third picture, he was refining it. Much more so than with the previous films, major cosmetic changes were underway, with a director determined to outstrip his greatest rival — Peter Jackson.

The media might have been endlessly banging a pan about the heated competition with rival franchises like *Star Wars* and *Harry Potter*, but what concerned Jackson was upping the ante on the marvels of *The Fellowship of the Ring* and *The Two Towers.*

'You know,' he laughed, stopping by to say hello at lunch, not an air or a grace to be seen, 'the first film was entirely exposition, the second film was all exposition, and now we have three hours of pay off.'

No one was disguising the fact that this was anything more than a single story drawing to a close. But you had to go out big. It wasn't as if Tolkien slowed things down.

'I've come to realize that the third film is the reason you make the other two,' said Jackson, slipping away. 'You want to finish it.'

Everywhere there was talk of conclusions, endings, the culmination of a production that had become a way of life. The second day of my visit coincided with Viggo Mortensen's last ever day suited and booted as Aragorn (professionally at least). There was a twinge of tension in the air as they still had a lot to get through and be ready for his farewell party. Actors and crew were in thoughtful, valedictory mood (when awake), trying to assess what had been achieved as they contemplated a universe where they would no longer be Frodo or Sam or Gandalf or Aragorn. *The Hobbit* notwithstanding, this was the point of no return.

Reflects Mark Ordesky, 'It is amazing to me to think that even after all that time, even with the end in sight, the actors were still giving so much of themselves to these films.'

First though was the task of getting back into the heads of characters they had left sleeping a year ago.

'We were working so hard,' protests Wood, reminded years later of his talent for an impromptu siesta. 'And there were big set-ups, a fair amount of downtime. It was a big movie in that regard. It wasn't a quick run and gun. So I would sit in my chair and fall asleep. I would lie down on set and fall asleep. I'm good at sleeping. But Billy Boyd was a fucking sleeper. Better than me. . .'

*

DAY ONE: THE VALE OF ITHILIEN, THE GOLDEN HALL, THE MINIATURES STUDIO. 'You forget how hard it is,' Astin reflected. 'Yesterday was a sixteen-hour day. You put that away when you're not here. Throughout the year you are able to romanticize the painful moments. The patience that is required. But it's amazing: you have this muscle memory of things that happened two years ago. Your body remembers.'

Between sessions in Middle-earth, Astin had shot a TV show (post-apocalyptic drama *Jeremiah*) and an Adam Sandler comedy (*50 First Dates*), and lost thirty pounds. Getting even some way back toward Sam's weight had been painful. 'I'm not where I was,' he winced, 'but I trust it will all work out.'

Sam is the soul of *The Return of the King*. With Frodo increasingly lost to the torment of the Ring, a junkie like Gollum, the argument runs that Sam is now the hero. It is his courage that must save the day. Numerous high-flown essays have posited the theory Sam was the true protagonist all along. This is his story narrated from a distant future (he completes the writing of the history).

Wood talks about Sam's innocence. How he doesn't succumb to temptation. 'It makes total sense to me that he is the hero, certainly of the third film,' he says. 'I don't think that it could have been done without Frodo either. But the ultimate sort of success of Frodo's story is Sam.'

'I certainly feel this is my moment,' said Astin on set, having proudly pointed out the extent of the scar beneath his prosthetic sole he sustained on Gamgee-duty. 'There is a certain darkness now, a rawness I have never gone to before.'

In his biography, Astin admitted wondering if Jackson was tough enough to strike fear into his cast. The director was so stoic and amiable, and showed not a glint of outward panic. But there was never that threat of humiliation to 'trigger a performance' — the great American artistic tradition of being bullied into the truth. The only way they knew that scenes had failed to hit the right note was when Jackson was unable to disguise his disappointment.

Astin came to realize that the thought of letting him down was fear enough. With the hobbits nearing their final destination, sapped and desperate amid the desolation of Mordor, it wasn't disappointment Jackson was unable to disguise.

The scene everyone recalls, the scene that Philippa Boyens says had her in pieces even in the rushes, is of course Sam lifting Frodo onto his shoulders as they clamber up Mount Doom. 'I can't carry it for you. . . but I can carry you!' he cries out, not a dry eye in the house. The accompanying swell of Howard Shore's strings ensures any resistance is broken. Although it had crossed Astin's safety conscious mind that he was literally carrying the whole $270 million franchise at that point.

Something in the blend of Astin's acting, the emotional trajectory of the storytelling and Jackson's native restraint prevents the scene from giving way to the mawkish or manipulative. It is a gesture of defiance, and old-fashioned heart. Moreover, the scene had been *earned*.

Yet for Astin it was in the moment preceding that now classic scene when he knew he was giving the performance of his life. Endeavouring to remind Frodo of the taste of strawberries in the Shire, he felt he could 'quiver and emote' with total control. The tears felt authentic. When Jackson approached between takes, Astin could immediately tell something was different.

'It was the fact that his glasses were fogged and tears were streaming down his cheeks.'

Together with Walsh and Boyens, he and Wood had discussed how Sam and Frodo's relationship crossed boundaries of class — drawing from Tolkien's model of batman and officer in the trenches of the First World War. Wood never thought of Frodo being a higher class, or at least aware of his higher stature. 'That's just where he comes from and the lineage that he's a part of. He certainly doesn't treat Sam any different.'

Nevertheless, the notion of class is there. Less pronounced than in the book, there is still an emphasis on Sam's more humble origins: in his accent, that innocence, and the fact he is lumbered with the victuals. You wonder whether an English actor might have been more attuned to the idea.

They were well aware too of the homoerotic overtones that had been read into their close bond. An entirely valid view, said Astin, but they had never played it with that in mind. Sam cradling Frodo was a 'battlefield death scene', a further echo of Tolkien's experiences. To be fair, sex doesn't figure much in Middle-earth. Even including Aragorn's reveries of longing for Arwen, the only character to express a modicum of lust is Wormtongue for Éowyn.

Today's scene wasn't calling upon either actor's emotional reserves to any great extent — Serkis remained unbowed in his absorption of every second of Gollum's torment — and Astin would trot over to continue conversing between takes as they gradually got the scene done. 'Franly Kubrick', as Boyd nick-named her, always wanted way more takes than Jackson.

Astin mentioned how much he enjoyed Walsh's direction. 'The way she uses language really appeals to me as a performer,' he explained. Walsh tended to drill down into the psychological stuff, whereas Jackson inevitably had to keep the bigger more technical picture in mind. All it took for Astin to retrieve Sam was a moment of concentration, as if rerouting electricity in his brain, before turning on his rubber feet and traversing the few feet back to the Vale of Morgul, his accent relocated to the rolling *rrrr*s and lengthened vowels of Sam's buttery West Country accent. 'Cummin' Mister Frrrrodo!'

According to the call sheet this was the second unit with motion capture data now sampled in situ, but such designations seemed arbitrary in the flurry of getting Jackson's wish-list of updates completed. The director had been back on his bike, ped-alling off to check on other units, but more out of curiosity than concern. His vision now a collective consciousness permeating Stone Street's hectic spaces.

The current scene takes place immediately after that second superlative monologue cleft between the two halves of Serkis' character, with Sméagol peering into the pool and Gollum reflected back (as conceived by Walsh). His interior debate over Frodo and Sam's fate was being violently interrupted by Sam bashing Gollum with a pot.

Astin took up the explanation: 'Plot-wise, we're beginning to run out of bread, and Gollum's playing this trick on us. . . And I'm onto the blighter.'

As they reconfigured the set for the next step up, and not a peep from Wood, Astin gossiped about *Star Wars*. A lifelong fan, he had been thrilled to introduce himself to George Lucas at the MTV Awards (the very event where Gollum had made his potty-mouthed speech). 'He's such a hero of mine.'

But it hadn't gone so well.

'Yeah hi,' Lucas replied, turning a cold shoulder.

'I'm like, "Hey, I'm Sean Astin, you know. . . *Sam*.'

'"Oh," he said, "all you hobbits look the same to me."'

Astin imitated coughing into his fist. 'Yeah, and Jar Jar sucked man.'

Apropos of nothing more than fate or the random patterns served up by this universe, flash-forward two-and-a-half years to Christmas 2005 and the New York premiere party for *King Kong*. It's held in a draughty warehouse on the Hudson where hip DJs drown out conversation with interminable cool and the food is fabulous but is served in portions that would barely have constituted a second breakfast. The warmth and charm of Cannes feel like the hazy dream of the Shire. This is big, soulless studio muscle being flexed. But at least Serkis greets me with a bright smile and a warm hug, asking what I thought of the film. Before I can reply, I am shunted two feet leftwards by a strong hip on a short body. I looked down to see Lucas already thrusting his hand toward mo-cap's patron saint.

'Andy, fantastic, fantastic,' he began, oblivious to my presence.

Serkis shrugged at me apologetically. But I am delighted. Who can say they have been hip-bumped by the creator of *Star Wars*? Plus, it said something about the legacy of *The Lord of the Rings* that by 2005 it was Lucas vying for the attention of a cast member. The Jedi director would surely have recognized Astin after the final film. Sam was the stand-out performance.

Even on set, during pick-ups, Astin was beginning to feel that this was the kind of work that put you into the sightlines of the Academy. Although he never would have admitted it — and potentially jinx things.

For now he was humble enough to shine a light onto his sleeping partner. 'You've got to see where Elijah and Frodo go in the third movie,' he enthused. 'The power of the Ring is almost pulling him apart.'

A little while later, sat in a vacated office, Wood's huge, non-CGI, wide-awake eyes stared at me intently. With the scene completed and the afternoon off, he has had the chance to change out of his costume (a process honed down to a sprightly thirty minutes now). Ears, wig and feet might be gone, but he was still indelibly Frodo.

In the context of the film the question is: *who* is Frodo?

The Return of the King charts the character's full mental and physical breakdown: the psychic rock fall after the gradual erosion of the first two films. Which required from Wood something more akin to what Serkis was doing with Gollum.

'For a while, he holds onto that awareness that the Ring is doing this to him and this is fucked up. And it is changing him. He doesn't mean to be this way. But his defences have gone. Which is really fun. There's so much there to play with.'

During principal photography, he admitted, it had been tough negotiating that psychological transformation from a very innocent, youthful phase to a very dark one. 'Not just having to get to a dark place but having to rock back and forth from one extreme to the other as they shot out of sequence.'

Especially with the second and the third films, where one clump of rocks looks much the same as another, working out literally where you were psychologically was challenging. It became a shared joke: 'Which desolate set of rocks are we in today, Pete?'

It was almost a relief now to be able to concentrate on the true misery of the Ring.

'He's really falling apart on the side of the mountain. He starts to really disassociate and break from reality, which has been scary to have to play and play it well, to play it *real* when I have nothing to draw on. Only how it was written. It's been more than I could possibly have imagined. . . It's been mad.'

Wood's performance is often taken for granted in final assessments of the trilogy. It shouldn't. Fictionally speaking, Frodo has to bear the burden of the Ring. That is true, in a sense, of Wood and the film. He has had to shoulder the burden of Frodo. Which has meant working almost in reverse: creating a character then gradually stripping him away.

'You know what is weird? Coming back each year, we have been lulled into the false sense of security that this will last for the rest of our lives. In actual fact, this is it. But I think a part of me, a part of all of us, will be a little relieved when it is all completed. It will be done, and we can move on with our lives.'

Outside, the winter weather was being more lenient than a year before, and after lunch I stand outside catering — still boasting a corrugated roof — passing the time of day with another hobbit. Having scented that I was a visiting writer, he had sidled up, one more Halfling keen for a chat. It was easy to see why he had found gainful employment at Stone Street. He was short, though not hobbit short. It was more that his features personified the Shire: nose, cheek and dimpled chin like a bag of apples. Attired in his Hobbiton Sunday best, britches hovering over prosthetic feet, he looked like an Alan Lee sketch for a generic hobbit come to life. The effect was completed by the large, curly wig, which looked ready to give its own performance.

'I'm Peter Eastwood,' he said offering a hand. He claimed he had been due to be Sean Astin's stand-in, but wasn't clear on why it hadn't worked out — maybe because he really didn't look like Sean Astin. 'But I've been a hobbit, another hobbit and a Dwarf at the Council of Elrond, and now I'm back to being that first hobbit.'

He was referring to the doltish fellow who prefers an iced bun to kissing his sweetheart in *The Fellowship of the Ring Extended Edition*. That afternoon, he whispered conspiratorially, they were shooting a mysterious party scene. He looked each way, checking the coast was clear — which it wasn't — before blabbing that it was Sam's wedding.

'I'm a tax inspector,' he confided, 'when I'm not a hobbit.'

In a few days' time he would be back among the IR3s and PAYE tables of the New Zealand Inland Revenue.

*

That afternoon, I returned to the glorious interior of the Golden Hall — which had been reconstructed for the third or possibly fourth time, no one can quite remember — as had the victors of Helm's Deep. While absorbed by Legolas and Gimli's drinking game (off camera), Gandalf and Aragorn quietly debated Frodo's chances, a two-shot of Ian McKellen and Viggo Mortensen with some precisely choreographed Rohan revelry behind them. As they did a camera rehearsal, the assistant directors floated between tables advising bearded extras on Middle-earth inebriation.

All seemed to go well on the first take, the camera slowly zooming into a close-up on Gandalf, whereupon McKellen, struck by an irresistible urge, finished the scene by hoisting his thumbs aloft in a non-canon impersonation of the Fonz from *Happy Days*. The party atmosphere was catching.

Jackson's laughter came through the PA. 'Thank you Sir Ian, but maybe we'll go again.'

On the second take the effortless McKellen held his Gandalfian poise for a perfect take.

'Maybe one more for luck?' suggested the director.

Later, in a small anteroom that once housed an office of the old paint firm — the film's production hub was downstairs, as was an office for Jackson, a bolthole to gather his thoughts — McKellen accounted for his day's work.

'Peter wanted to sharpen up the details of the plot. Also attend to the relationship between Gandalf and Frodo — although they don't see each other until the end of the movie, they are constantly thinking about each other [that sense of psychic connection]. These pick-ups are often about inserting emotional beats.'

Once the British actor had dispensed with his white robes and beard, unlike Wood with Frodo, Gandalf was less readily apparent. Talk swiftly turned from returning to the idea of finishing once and for all, which he will in the next week.

'I don't think I am ever going to say goodbye to New Zealand,' he responded. He hinted there was another project he and Jackson want to do together, and he didn't mean *The Hobbit*. 'If you find people you like working with, why spoil it? Peter Jackson is resoundingly one of the few good senior filmmakers out there. I like his outfit here. I like the fact that it is away from the centre. . . It comes from the heart.'

Was he hoping for any particular parting gifts? The bestowing of significant mementoes was now a ritual.

'Oh, I've had my things,' he said: gifts thus far have included a pair of door handles carved as lizards from Orthanc that took his fancy, the keys to Bag End and his staff, which has ended up at his local in Limehouse. 'I don't know whether I am due another present.'

'What about your hat?'

'What would I do with that?' he asked nonplussed.

Since first meeting him in Cannes, McKellen has maintained a healthy but respectful distance between himself and Gandalf. He talked about having 'impersonated' the iconic figure, referring to him as a friend.

'Gandalf knows a lot of things, and he knows more than me about the plot': it's a refrain that has come in handy when questions got a little too Middle-earth orientated. 'Oh, you'd have to ask Gandalf. . .'

Has he never craved to go deeper into his character, beyond the enigmatic figure in the book?

McKellen shrugged his shoulders. 'Yes, well, that's where you have to trust the director. He's got the whole project in his mind, and the last thing you need is some complication in a relationship that might detract from the sweep of the story. So, I just do as I am told.'

Watching them together on set, the rapport was obvious. McKellen may have done as he was told, but the director addressed him as 'Sir Ian', guiding him with an easy deference and ready compliment that saw the actor immediately brighten.

Even amid the monumentality of the third film, McKellen still humanizes the stern wizard with a twinkle of wry amusement in his blue eyes — a hint of the pleasure he is taking in the role. As Gandalf and Pippin approach the halls of Denethor, he lectures the loose-jawed hobbit on what not to reveal to the suspicious Steward (John Noble). There comes an exquisitely timed pause, before he concludes, 'In fact, it's better if you don't speak at all.'

McKellen never lets the brush of humour be lost to the apocalyptic.

Even so, this final film, like never before, will see him as a man of action. 'Age rights!' laughed McKellen at the thrill of crowning Orcs with his staff. Gandalf, he summarized, was running the whole outfit: less a wizard than a general. That said, he had left most of the riding to the stuntmen. He once lost a good friend to a riding accident on a film set — Roy Kinnear had fallen from a horse while filming *The Return of the Musketeers* in 1988, suffering a fatal heart-attack brought on by his injuries. 'They're dangerous animals if you're not used to them. I do the minimum.'

Shadowfax, Gandalf's wind-swift steed, was currently being played by a twelve year-old Andalusian by the stable-name of Blanco. In earlier scenes, however, another Andalusian named Domino had filled out Shadowfax's lustrous reputation. Herein hung a tale.

'Blanco had been Domino's understudy,' explained McKellen, who has experienced his share of theatrical politics down the years. 'Domino was a very proud horse and very sociable. He would not work unless there was another horse watching.'

Blanco's main job had been to come and watch Domino perform. 'Can you imagine being an understudy and having to always watch?' the great thespian shuddered at the idea.

Well, this eventually got too much for poor Blanco, and he gave Domino a good kick. 'So he's now got the part.'

They currently had forty horses on set, said unit horse wrangler Grahame Ware Jr., when I went in search of the stables the next day (literally follow your nose), including fifteen stunt horses who can work in different scenarios: fall, rear, bareback or those who can cope with the saddle falling off; a surprisingly rare skill.

'It is important for the actors to be able to trust the horse,' added Ware Jr., heir of a dynasty of Australian horse trainers, pointing out an unflustered white stallion that turned out to be Blanco. 'He's a real gentleman.'

With humans that is, as opposed to his equine rivals.

Ware also trained the actors, and by the look on his face you suspected this might have been a trickier business. They needed three to four hours a day for a few weeks to come to like and understand a horse.

'Viggo is the best rider,' said Ware with zero surprise.

Talking of whom. Halfway through interviewing Boyd, Mortensen had burst in through the door wielding what looked like a large, green hammer made of sponge (it proved to be some kind of special effects prop that related to a mûmak), soundly wacked his co-star with it, before disappearing back out the door. The incident was made doubly strange by the fact he was fully attired as Aragorn. Having been momentarily dazed, Boyd regained his composure and pouted.

'Fucking Viggo.'

For all his intensity, Wood says there is something of a child in Mortensen. 'Super playful. Super weird. Really funny. Offbeat humour. He has his own rhythm.'

Poor Boyd had soldiered on, recounting his pleasure in the seriousness granted Pippin upon facing war having been spirited to Minas Tirith by Gandalf. 'Working one-on-one with Sir Ian,' he appreciated. 'That's been special.'

Right until the last Mortensen had not flagged. He was the living emblem of the production, his initial daring, all-consuming energy and commitment sum up the inner fire that has driven the trilogy, and its concomitant streak of madness.

'It's hard to think where we would have been without him,' says Jackson in hindsight. 'It's impossible to look at him without thinking about Aragorn, or picture Aragorn and not see Viggo. I have never witnessed an actor embrace the spirit of a role as he did.'

'Viggo had a lot of thoughts about his costume,' said costume designer Ngila Dickson, when I paid her department another visit. 'Right down to how his boots laced up, he imbued that costume with its own life.'

Mortensen had put stock not just in how he looked, but how

he *dressed*. He wanted the audience to see how he donned his gloves, stowed his dagger and laced his boots, to get a feel for how he functioned in the wild. He had, at one point, been fixated on having a tattoo of the Tree of Gondor over his left shoulder and down his arm, and approached Lee for a design. It wasn't entirely clear to the artist whether he intended the tattoo to be permanent. Lee, who had got wind that Jackson and Walsh weren't keen on the idea, had to 'remain very diplomatic and non-committal'.

This, everyone came to understand, was all part of Mortensen's process. And he granted a poet's heart to earthy Kiwi thinking. 'Viggo's just an artist,' cooed Orlando Bloom to me in 2012. Yet when Mortensen's turn to be interviewed came, having dispensed with comedy prop, he winced at the idea he will be remembered as the mythical Viggo, never seen without his sword and rarely out of his costume.

'The way it was written, it sounded like I was doing that all the time, which I wasn't. I wanted to take advantage of being in New Zealand, so sometimes I would go hunting and fishing. I was always in my wardrobe because I was filming all the time. Because I didn't have the rehearsal time everyone else did.'

With an unthinkable single day to go on this great venture into the unknown, nudged by his son's insistence, how did he look back upon his experiences?

Mortensen glanced toward the window in search of an answer in the bright New Zealand sky hanging over Stone Street.

'I can say my conscience is clear. I did my best to study and find as much as I could, which is going to be subjective. I read everything I could that connected to Strider or Aragorn or his environment, to represent that character. It's an obligation to my work, whatever is done with that work is not in my hands anymore. I have done my job and I feel okay about it. I gave them enough to make Aragorn, and it's their choice if they make Aragorn or not.'

This was another window into Mortensen's thinking, his

acting and the creed by which he abided. It's unlikely Jackson was entirely on the same wavelength, but as far as the half-Dane was concerned the movies were the by-product of a deeper experience.

'There was no way of knowing these movies were going to be a hit,' he continued. 'They weren't chockful of movie stars and the subject matter wasn't a proven seller as far as movies go. I'm on the plane reading this gigantic book and thinking, "What the Hell have I done?"'

It's not that he doesn't appreciate the films. 'It's often mind-boggling what is done,' he hastened to add, lest I take it that he doesn't approve of Jackson's choices. 'But no matter how well it is put together, it is something I don't recognize fully.'

He turned to a maxim of Robert Louis Stevenson, whom he happened to be reading: 'To travel hopefully is better than to arrive, and the most important thing is to labour. Something like that.'* The bonds made and the experiences of making the films in this country are what remain real to Mortensen.

He stared unwaveringly at me. 'You know it could have been horrible. But all kinds of people, personalities, ages, nationalities came together in a way they normally wouldn't. Because of the unceasing grind at times, the length of time, we came to know each other's good and bad points. We became entangled in each other's lives. . . in a good way. There was a very easy, unspoken bond.'

He smiled apologetically. 'Sorry, I was not so brief.'

While the third film is named for Aragorn's ordained comeback (the title also carries a more generic sense given he has never been king before) there is less for the actor to get hold of in the final film: he even walks the Paths of the Dead undaunted. He's suitably regal, stirring as a beacon, peerless with a blade,

---

* The full quote from Stevenson's 1881 collection of essays, *Virginibus Puerisque,* reads: 'Little do ye know your own blessedness; for to travel hopefully is a better thing than to arrive, and the true success is to labour.'

but Mortensen had thrived in Aragorn's hesitancy and doubts, the man saddled with melancholy thoughts, the journey not the destination. He would have preferred to stay in the wild.

When it comes to assessing what it is that made these films so much more than blockbusters, if McKellen granted the films a natural conviction lightly salted with humour, Mortensen brought unironic belief — the one thing the part didn't need was the gauze of cool, leave that to Legolas. His distrust of stardom, his multifaceted upbringing, that natural absorption into the truth of a character, all his gifts as painter, poet, traveller and political idealist, his unwavering honesty, his courage and his dense, intellectual presence bound him to Middle-earth.

Mortensen embodied the strange marriage of storytelling with story in the making of these films, where the journey *was* the destination.

When I asked how he imagined it would feel to finally say goodbye, Mortensen finally smiled.

'I will never say goodbye,' he replied. 'It will never end.'

*

In another utilitarian warehouse on Park Road, Alex Funke toured me through his Lilliputian kingdom. Funke went by the windy title of Visual Effects Director of Photography: Miniature Unit; the tall, jovial, grey-haired Californian is still widely considered a master of the fine if waning art of shooting models to appear as if they are gigantic.

As we pass a 1/120th scale overview of the Morgul Pass, Funke recalled the splendid toothy architecture of the 1/72nd scale Minas Morgul, which was coated in a luminescent paint to match Tolkien's description of a 'corpse-like' glow. As was his wont, Richard Taylor theorized that the city, degenerating under Nazgûl administration, had become covered in algae that gave off a 'putrid green glow' in moonlight.

With Mordor and its suburbs having filled their recent schedule, next came the awe-inspiring 1/166th scale, eight-metre tall

Barad-dûr made from hard resin that took four months to construct. 'It's etched in metal, and covered in metallic oxide paint,' Funke declared, grinning like a proud parent and running a hand gently along a buttress. 'The idea is a building that reflects no light.'

For the epic shot of Sauron's citadel in *The Two Towers* as the camera spirals upwards around the twenty-seven-foot miniature, drinking in its brute grandeur, culminating in the flaming, lidless CG Eye of Sauron (a gift of Weta Digital) they had to transport the miniature down to the backlot to give the camera enough room to complete its helter-skelter move.

'Transporting a Dark Tower is not easy!' Funke's habitual chortle brings to mind Doctor Nick Riviera from *The Simpsons*, who delivers dire prognoses through unquenchable giggles.

Born in Santa Barbara, Funke studied biochemistry before transferring to film school — accounting for his scientific pragmatism — with a formative period working for vaunted furniture designers Charles and Ray Eames. Their eye for shape had a great impact on him.

'My first VFX show was *Battlestar Galactica*, with John Dykstra,' he recalled, referring to the old-school special effects titan, who features on Jackson's list of early heroes, 'shooting all the miniatures at different scales'. This included the memorable high-velocity launch sequences where space fighters are propelled into space as if from a peashooter.

Another major American influence, the veteran cinematographer's filmography includes miniatures on *The Abyss*, *Total Recall*, *Waterworld* and *King Kong* wannabe *Mighty Joe Young*.

Commencing production alongside principal photography, the Miniature Unit had carried on without a break getting on for four years. With its dedicated crew of thirty-seven, the librarians of the Weta flock, they run on a different clock to everyone else. Today was day 803, whereas the live-action shoot had barely reached a meagre 312 days, including supplementary shooting.

'We still have over 200 shots to go,' laughed Funke.

Their glacial pace had much to do with the leisureliness of their camera, which moved in tiny incremental stages barely discernible to the eye in order to disguise the scale of the model.

An in-house computer whizz had built all their electronic equipment from scratch. 'It saves money to do it yourself. He built this motion-controlled camera system. . .' Funke pointed to a large contraption, all wires and joints like the limb of a giant robot, which could patiently guide their camera through its ghostly moves. 'It's a wee bit Heath Robinson, but it works perfectly. . . Otherwise we'd be boned.'

Smoke, he continued, was key. To help maintain the deception you need the perfect consistency of smoke. Thus their resident inventor had come up with a machine that read the atmospherics and fed back its findings to the smoke machine to regulate its output. They had to be careful about particles in the air, anything that could distort the illusion of scale. Thus they use a very fine oil to create the misty veil.

'It's called Ondina Oil. . . It's also used to make laxative!'

This was not the only unconventional ingredient. To attain the autumnal hues Jackson desired for a recently conceived cutaway to a fading Rivendell (which had to be hastily patched up), the Workshop dressed miniature trees with spices. 'Chilli, curry powder, dry mustard and paprika,' listed Funke, 'which were perfect for dying leaf colours. The aroma was quite something.'

The miniatures, made with such loving detail and shot with such care, provide the majesty of Middle-earth. They are the wonders of a world already ancient to the Fellowship, and stirred Jackson's imagination, inviting his vaulting camera moves and daring close-ups.

Whatever their limitations, the miniatures lent *The Lord of the Rings* a hefty, handcrafted presence that reflected the discipline and the devotion involved.

For Alan Lee they had been one of the most exciting elements of the production, and he had missed them on *The Hobbit*, where Jackson would switch entirely to digital environments for the flexibility and speed. 'I can see that CGI gives the director an enormous amount of freedom — Pete could get in and play with the camera in that virtual world. But there is something about the physical quality of a miniature, particularly on film, that is hard to match with CG. Also, it was much harder for me to work in CGI; I could put my hands on a model.'

Funke and I moved on with Brobdingnagian strides. In front of us loomed the 'tiny' Minas Tirith, rising in splendid tiers like a seven-foot tall wedding cake, each layer wreathed with streets and houses through which a tiny 'snorkel lens' can prowl. Funke explained that the larger 1/72 scale, twenty-five-foot version of the Gondorian capital so prominent in the final film featured one thousand individual buildings (the Airfix box would be the size of a dance hall). Lee had provided a series of immaculate architectural sketches, which were also used for the live-action set (various streets and courtyards) that replaced Helm's Deep at the versatile Dry Creek Quarry in late 2000.

Funke estimated that the third film will contain about one hundred miniature shots, the same amount as the first two films put together. Further evidence that everything about *The Return of the King* was accumulating, growing, amassing for the big finale, as if Jackson's imagination had finally been let loose.

'Peter recently added what he called "*Star Wars* shots" of the fell beasts dive-bombing Minas Tirith.' Where once the demands of the director might have worried Finke, they have much more confidence now. 'We are at ease with things.'

And after that what was still to be done?

'Well, we've still got to get Mount Doom out of storage.' Funke laughed. 'I hope it's in one piece.'

*

DAY TWO: SHELOB'S LAIR, WETA WORKSHOP. A limb of Shelob's extensive but insalubrious lair extended onto an already crowded soundstage (ten feet away: the culvert where Frodo and Sam take shelter). The tunnel was crisscrossed with webbing sticky to the touch and made, Dan Hennah will tell me, from melting a mix of adhesive and vegetable extract at somewhere between 210 and 230 degrees Centigrade. Any hotter and it would catch fire and be a devil to put out. In the next few days, Wood would be strung up in this demonic silly string.

The floor was littered with Orc bones: Shelob's leftovers. The walls were pockmarked with small indentations, the result of years of her acidic secretions. This was only a fragment of the maze of tunnels where the intrepid hobbits encounter that 'agelong', super-sized, female spider. The net result, as it were, of Gollum's treachery.

Tolkien had very few memories of the South Africa he left behind as an infant. But there were sharp glints of being bitten by a snake and the day he was stung by a tarantula. 'In my garden,' he recollected cheerfully, 'all I can remember is a very hot day, long, dead grass and running. I don't even remember screaming.'

The author was averse to joining the dots between his life and his writing, but you can't help but feel that this sunburst of childhood trauma marks the origin of Shelob, one of his most horrifying creations. One Jackson had artfully delayed until the third film (she appears at the end of the second book), despite Weta Digital craving to get hold of the eight-legged freak.

Having adjourned from set to Weta Workshop, I was back in their boardroom in the company of Taylor whose memory never failed to find a fitting anecdote. Years before, Jackson had invited him and Rodger over for dinner. Well, dinner would be forthcoming, but only once they had helped him clear out his parent's garage.

'He'd just moved into his little cottage by the sea and was seeing what he would take with him,' Taylor explained. Jackson's already extensive collection included his beloved Beatles albums, Bond super-eights and back-issues of *Fantastic Monsters of Filmland*.

Jackson wasn't a shirker by any means. He liked to rip into things. In fact, Taylor was quite surprised to be asked.

'We quickly discovered why.'

It turned out that Joan and Bill Jackson's cluttered garage, part of their seafront house in Pukerua Bay, was experiencing a spider infestation.

'And Pete was a chronic arachnophobe!' The notion was clearly still of great delight to Taylor. 'He was mortified by these huge arachnids in the garage. Tania and I really played up, throwing these big spiders at him.'

Fast forward to designing Shelob, and they had the perfect starting point — Jackson's adult trauma.

'We basically delved into what gave him the heebie-jeebies,' said Taylor.

There was a striking John Howe painting of Sam brandishing Sting at a plump and deadly Shelob that Jackson was partial to, but beyond her bulk Howe's depiction suffered the common problem of making Shelob too alien and bizarre. Jackson wanted a real spider. And the specific arachnid he was most afraid of was *Porrhothele antipodiana*, the New Zealand tunnelweb: hard, shiny, jointed legs with a membrane of spiny hairs, and a big gelatinous sac of a body.

Jackson's particular revulsion of tunnelwebs can be traced back even further to his childhood and mounting *Thunderbirds* rescue missions with his Matchbox cars in the dirt bank of his parents' garden. Just occasionally he would delve too deep and disturb a sleepy tunnelweb. 'That spoiled so many of my adventures,' he said.

To help things along, he persuaded Christian Rivers to trap a tunnelweb in his garden and bring it to the Workshop. From their not-so incy-wincy model they sculpted a five-foot long maquette and made two full-scale pincers, two legs and parts of the abdomen for Astin to grapple with on set. Their pet was then passed along to Weta Digital to examine its morphology and movement; another small but significant part of New Zealand invested into the films.

'We photographed the heck out of it before we let it go again,' recalls Joe Letteri. 'That became our reference. For example, we wanted that scary, translucent look, so we adapted the subsurface scattering technique we had developed for Gollum.'

They also needed to give her a face. A real spider is not an interesting character. Says Letteri, 'Spiders have eight eyes, but when you put that on the screen you didn't know where to look. You're used to looking at two eyes. So we had to feature two main eyes with the other subordinate eyes, which gave her something resembling a face.'

'We actually revisited Shelob a few months ago,' reported Taylor back at the workshop. 'She hadn't reached quite the height of cringe-value that Peter wanted.'

One of the freedoms of working in the digital realm was that adjustments can be made late into the process, allowing them to push and push again on designs. Jackson had reviewed the animation tests of Shelob interacting with actors and felt she needed a greater physical presence. He was a director who knew his monsters.

Jackson was insistent that we also feel her great age. Shelob has lived for centuries, many of them festering away on the outskirts of Mordor, grown fat off hapless Orcs. Drawing upon the rank concoctions of his own movie history, Jackson wanted one side of her face stroke-slumped with a broken tooth, cataracts and numerous tumours. Her hair had to be mangy. She is in a way pitiful.

Shelob's shriek was adapted from a Tasmanian Devil recorded at Sydney's Taronga Zoo, which sounded at its core like an angry old lady. Boyens and Walsh took great delight in a Freudian reading of one of few female characters. 'Are you kidding?' hoots Boyens. 'This hairy female beast at the end of a long dark tunnel into which these boyish hobbits venture at their peril?'

The critic Graham Fuller, in a granular reading of the trilogy in *Film Comment*, really ran with the idea, noting how Sauron's disembodied eye resembled a 'pulsating vagina'. He observed the prevalence of unfortunate males 'entering clefts, crevices, caves and narrow doorways'. All of which, he equated to Tolkien's unconscious 'fear of female sexuality'.

*

Earlier in 2003, Jackson had called a meeting at the Workshop to review every Orc they had so far created. A gallery of grotesques was fixed to the wall with the director sticking Post-it notes on the ones he liked the most. He informed his design team he wanted to 'enhance' the Orcs in the third film.

Now that the battles had grown exponentially, said Taylor, they had to rethink the concept of an Orc. 'They had been a sort of ragtag bunch of schoolyard bullies that sort of hunt in packs and ultimately win by weight of numbers. We came to realize they didn't have a malicious presence.'

The result was an elite fighting force of Orcs. 'To act almost as a "piercing arrow" to penetrate the enemy forces,' enthused Taylor.

'Peter didn't want to have any Orcs with "witchypoo" noses,' recalls Gino Acevedo. 'He also came up with the idea of Orcs with tumours.'

Along similar lines to Shelob's stroke-mangled face, the 'enhancements' included tumours, pustules and blisters, an even purer expression of Jackson's *Bad Taste*. It might be growing exponentially, but *The Return of the King* was also becoming more personal.

After looking over an assembly of Pelennor Fields footage from principal photography, Jackson concluded the Orcs also lacked a bit of battle savvy. They were in need of leadership. With the Nazgûl mounting the aerial attack, an Orc general had been introduced during supplementary shooting. He was named Gothmog, and he was a sight.

Shane Rangi, stunt-doubling as Gothmog, remembers Jackson's delighted reaction as he strolled, fully made-up onto the corner of the backlot subbing as the battlefield. 'He's got that gammy arm, that lumpy face. He was pretty hideous really. Just full of cysts and all those cysts are full of pus. Pete loved it!'

Well he might, the director was largely responsible for this potato-headed Napoleon. He had come to see a more straight-forwardly misshapen Orc at a show-and-tell session at the Workshop, which without fail resulted in the director making hands-on adjustments.* Surveying their proto-Gothmog with a builder's frown, he slapped a lump of wet clay onto the side of his head. 'Make him more like *The Elephant Man*,' he instructed.

Disease, the idea of both physical and mental decay, is a strik-ing motif for the third film. Frodo, for one, is looking increas-ingly peaky thanks to the burden of the Ring. Says Wood, 'The idea was it was physically heavier, dragging him down, rubbing into his skin, causing it to welt and blister.' Adding literal authen-ticity to his deterioration, the make-up department mixed actual dirt from the locations in with their cosmetics to get that sense of the world clinging to them. An equivalent layer of digital grime and bruising was added to Gollum. As would be a digital nosebleed, thanks to Sam walloping him with a pan in the scene filmed the day before. Serkis' appalled reaction springboarding into a priceless session of Gollum slapstick.

'This is the resolution of all these story threads,' declared Taylor, getting to grips with the occasion of their final film. 'And from a design perspective we have to bring a conclusion to things: conclusions to the cultural references that we've been making through the films and more importantly a conclusion to the palette that has unfolded.'

In other words, the design itself had to reach a crescendo.

This meant close-ups of fell beasts, the Witch-king and giant twelve-foot-tall Battle-trolls, the armoured daddy-versions of the Cave-troll. Where there was once one, now there were squads of them. MASSIVE would unfurl hundreds of thousands of Orcs,

---

* During principal photography on *The Hobbit*, I witnessed a show-and-tell session with Sylvester McCoy as an even scruffier version of Radagast the Brown, with a wig crested in a copse of twigs. Between shots Jackson fussed happily over the drape of his brown robes and demonstrated how he might grip his staff.

squared into battalions as symmetrical as Kubrick's Battenberg Romans in *Spartacus*. During principal photography, the Workshop had installed three working catapults at Dry Creek Quarry, which hurled fireballs and the prosthetic heads of fallen warriors over the battlements (a bloody detail not as it happens from Jackson but Tolkien). When Digital reproduced the effect for wider shots they added a few staff faces to the decapitated ammo.

The Workshop built huge new miniatures of the Paths of the Dead where Aragorn ventures to enlist an army of spectral warriors in one of Tolkien's woollier subplots — once you have an unstoppable army of the dead at your command Mordor presents no great obstacle. Hence once his oath is fulfilled, it is made clear the ghostly King (in an early variant of the script identified as Isildur, but dropped in later versions) and his army can finally achieve eternal rest.

A more abstract rerun of Moria's subterranean vaults, I had visited the set of the charnel house of these sleepless warriors that morning, which were in the process of being dismantled by the production crew. Hennah mentioned that the night before shooting Jackson had dropped by to inspect the set.

'We need more skulls,' he had informed them brightly.

An order was put it in to the Workshop and by the next morning crates of hundreds of synthetic human skulls were being forklifted off a lorry. Hennah picked up a skull and passed it over with a grin.

'Poor fellow, to come to this.'

The next day, he said, Taylor was gleefully operating the rig that dumped piles of these skulls onto Bloom.

The Workshop was even called upon to make a full-sized miniature. A dead mûmak the size of a two-storey house and pincushioned with arrows would serve as a visual focus for the close-up battle scenes. Forty-six feet long, it had to be constructed in sections and shipped by lorry to the location or the backlot.

Mûmakil, those mammoth mammoths, are the zoological embodiment of the third film's ambitions. Using pre-viz Jackson and his team had plotted a propulsive confrontation between the surging riders of the Rohirrim (250 shot in person on the plains of Twizel on the South Island, the remaining six thousand generated with MASSIVE) and twenty-one mûmakil.

The sequence remains a glorious argument for CGI; a moment born not only out of the will to astound but the utmost dedication to vivifying the imagination of Tolkien. Surely even the professor would have approved.

Moreover, liberated from budget constraints (if not time constraints), Jackson saw the stampeding mûmakil as the perfect venue for their final 'Leggy Moment'.

There was now an expectation for Legolas to express himself. In another example of how the films had taken on a life of their own, the increasingly balletic displays of the Elf's nimble talents and Terminator sangfroid had become a signature feature — an inspired dash of sillification amid all the heavy weather of Armageddon. Bloom christened them 'Leggy Moments' and audiences went bananas for them.

'For the last film,' recalls Jackson, 'we didn't devise one or two shots, but an entire sequence that was never part of principal photography or even thought of in the original script.'

*

A BRIEF HISTORY OF LEGGY MOMENTS: Necessity being the mother of sexy Elvish acrobatics, the Leggy Moment arose in response to a problem. Elf-appreciators cite Legolas leaping onto the Cave-troll's shoulders in Balin's Tomb or the sewing-machine blur of bowmanship at Amon Hen, but according to the ranks of Weta Digital — who with all due respect to Bloom's athleticism are largely responsible for making him look good — locate the founding Leggy Moment to *The Two Towers* where the fleet Elf mounts a galloping horse by a sort of mad Fosbury Flop via the horse's bridal.

It was pure serendipity. Jackson had intended to shoot Bloom leaping toward the horse and then cut to him landing neatly in front of Gimli. However, after Bloom took an un-Elflike tumble from a horse while on location, leading to two broken ribs, the shot had to be abandoned. Jackson had turned the footage over to Digital asking them to improvise a way to get Legolas up on that horse.

Says Letteri, 'If you look at the photography, Orlando's just standing there as the horse goes by. We painted him out and the digital double does this acrobatic swing up using the neck and you get it all in one shot and it's pretty dramatic. That was our first Leggy Moment.'

Jackson loved it, and they added Legolas shield surfing at Helm's Deep during pick-ups for the second movie, each moment of Elf-prowess designed to out-do the last as the director stepped outside of Middle-earth to sit in the stalls and cheer. By *The Hobbit*, what were grace notes have become lavish, brainstormed set pieces, orchestrated to within a (blond) hair's breadth of self-parody as the featherlight Elf dances on air.

Years later, on set of *The Desolation of Smaug*, Bloom joked to me that he had only one requirement for returning to Middle-earth. 'So long as there's an improvement on the mûmak. Killing that mûmak was *such* a moment.'

Back in 2003, a day was set aside for Jackson to direct Bloom dancing across an elephant torso (built as a set) topped with a wickerwork howdah packed with stuntmen and mounted on a spring-loaded platform that grips could rock back and forth. The high-flying concept was Middle-earth's homage to the old-Hollywood dash of Douglas Fairbanks and Errol Flynn (admittedly with more CGI): Legolas swings up the flank of a moving mûmak, cutting free the battle tower, before tip-toeing to the neck and putting three arrows into the mûmak's brain. As the great elephant collapses the Elf glides down its trunk with a nonchalant shrug, 007 straightening his cuffs.

Cinemas in every land burst into applause.

Truth be told, says Letteri, while the footage was great reference, except for about three close-up shots it is a digital double.

Nevertheless, it's Bloom's serene Elvish expression and John Rhys-Davies' obdurate Dwarf one-liner that crystalize the moment — the (non) human touch.

Supplementary shooting, said Taylor, was simply fate giving them more time. 'A lot of people in this business would see the revisiting of designs and being pushed to the limit as a pain in the arse. But I see it as a wonderful opportunity to revisit. How often do you get the chance to go back into one of your stories? We have been given the benefit of hindsight.'

This had encompassed parsing how the first two films had been received and doubling down on what was embraced by the fans. Contrary to the simplification inherent in Hollywood they learned you could never have enough detail.

Taylor accompanied me to the door.

'Ever held an Oscar?' he asked.

For some absurd reason I had to think about it.

Taylor was already unlocking the trophy cabinet that adorned the Workshop entrance hall, where given the same prominence as the MTV's golden popcorn were the two Oscars he and his team had so far received in recognition of their endeavours in Middle-earth. He lifted one free and handed it over.

They are heavier than you think. And lighter.

I have held two Oscars in my life despite never having won one (so far). The second belonged to Emma Thompson, for her adaptation of *Sense and Sensibility* in 1995, which she kept unapologetically in her loo.

'Oh, you've got to,' she said. Otherwise, you might take it too seriously.

*

Day Three: The Backlot: As the roar finally diminished, Jackson cursed a Wellington sky as blue and flawless as enamel: 'Bloody 737s!' The endless jets swinging in and out of the airport over the ridge were still bugging him. It didn't help that we were stationed outside on the backlot in the unseasonal sunshine.

Away from set, he was less likely to be bugged by passing department heads.

Inside, he was due to shoot a close-up of Gandalf steering the cart back to Hobbiton on his way to the Grey Havens.

The concept of bidding farewell to Middle-earth had little meaning to the director yet, given that once they wrapped in the next couple of weeks he moved straight into the smelting pits of post-production. There were months to go yet.

'But we said goodbye to Viggo yesterday,' he ruminated, 'which was pretty intense.'

Jackson doesn't do sentiment. Not in some therapeutically confessional Hollywood sense anyway. Yes, it was sad to say goodbye to friends, both the actors and the characters, but his head still brimmed with what was done. The third film was more complex on every level, it was more emotional, but behind the camera it was the most relaxed.

'I guess everybody finally knows what they're doing,' he joked. 'We've had two films to practice.'

Looking back, he reflected, no one had any idea how complicated it was going to be. 'We somehow naively went into it thinking we could do it. And naiveté has won out at the end.' If they had known the difficulties they would have to face, they would never have done it. Stumbling along, figuring it out, forgetting the pain and getting enough sleep in order to get up each day to begin again, had somehow seen them through.

What has been so gratifying, of late, was simply the freedom he found to express himself.

'For me personally, my experience on *The Return of the King* this last year has been one where you don't even think about the technical difficulties anymore. You literally have this degree of freedom where anything you can imagine in your head can be accomplished on film. You have to make sure you have the right artists, but basically anything you throw at them can be done.'

The redoubtable computer artists at Weta Digital, who will be sleeping at their terminals by the final weeks, would still have to smile through gritted teeth when Jackson spotted that a shot of Rohirrim hacking at the ankles of a mûmak didn't match his preferred camera angle. The shot had taken weeks to reach its current state, and there was no possibility of shooting new footage or beginning from scratch. Thinking on their feet, Letteri and his team reworked the shot from the preferred angle using a chocolate box selection of digital horses used in other scenes. 'In two days,' recalls Letteri, still amazed at their resourcefulness. Such No. 8 thinking was now common practice.

New Line, basking in the glory of two Best Picture nominees and colossal hits, was now comfortably supportive of Jackson's Kubrick-like obsession with perfection. A potential Oscar victory was hovering in the air.

'There's a good chance we might end up a bit longer than before,' said Jackson. 'On the first movie we had this absolute edict from New Line that we couldn't be longer that two-and-a-half hours, which we kind of ignored. This year we had an edict saying it mustn't be longer than three hours. So we are making progress.'

When he delivered the finished print in early December, it would be three hours twenty-one minutes long.

If there has been any downside lately it has been too much expectation. The world's eyes were now trained on them.

'We've been in a bit of a goldfish bowl,' admitted Jackson. He was never truly going to operate 'beneath the radar' again. He gazed around him at pieces of set being dismantled for the final time, shrugged inside his *Lord of the Rings* body-warmer, wondering quite how it had come to this: recognition, influence and talk of Oscars being due? He had recently found himself on the annual Hollywood power list compiled by *Premiere* magazine.

'I'm not part of the establishment,' he sighed. 'I barely spend more than three days at a time in Hollywood. To see my name there was kind of weird.'

He waves away an imaginary fly.

'Those lists are more flavour of the month than they are about real power. As soon as you have a flop you are going to be straight off again.'

Naturally, it had turned into an on-set joke in New Zealand. Jackson, who had come in at 42, and McKellen, a more than creditable 87, had taken to referring to one another by their chart positions.

'Good morning, Eighty-Seven!'

'The same to you, Forty-Two!'

Jackson's tone remained pragmatic. 'If I am powerful in any Hollywood way,' he concluded, 'then it's not something I can do much with being stuck down here.'

The truth was more complicated. He had become powerful, and it was a gesture of his newfound influence that it was now a given he would remain here in New Zealand and still be able to wield that power.

The attendant absurdity of celebrity had also made it to Miramar. A few weeks ago a Norwegian TV crew had rung on his doorbell hoping he would come out and be interviewed. Their cameras were already rolling.

'It was a bit annoying. I've also had somebody send me scripts for *Lord of the Rings* four and five, and that they should be the next films I make. They had written these complete screenplays.'

Leaving them safely unread, he had no idea how the plot progressed given the McGuffin had melted in a pool of lava — in a mad case of art imitating life, the textures of which were drawn from late-night supplies of pizza — and half the principal cast taken ship to the afterlife.

He was ready to move on. The shadow of *King Kong* already loomed large on the horizon.

As each cast member had finally made their dewy-eyed departure there had been yet another round of ceremonial gift giving: Mortensen got his sword (which they might have had to prise from his grip anyhow), Bloom his bow and Rhys-Davies his axe. A week or so later, at the wrap party, the *final* wrap party, Jackson was presented with all the props from his Hitchcockian assembly of cameos: they had mounted the carrot he crunched into in Bree (a cult character subsequently christened Albert Dreary, and who will make a comeback in *The Hobbit*), the rock he hurled from the battlements of Helm's Deep and the small axe he has while captaining the doomed Corsair vessel with Andrew Lesnie, Taylor, Acevedo and Hennah among his hapless crew — the in-joke wasn't lost on anyone.

And what of those Oscars? The issue of winning Best Picture and Best Director had evolved from laughable to conscious possibility to outright expectation. New Line was already plotting stratagems with which to finally seduce the Academy.

The ironies never ceased.

As he had been throughout this great adventure and endurance test, stirred by the fates and hailed by the fans, Jackson remained unmoved by Hollywood's foibles. Things will be what they may. Why worry?

'It would be nice, of course.'

CHAPTER 15

The Music of Middle-earth

Watford Town Hall Assembly Rooms, the Colosseum no less, sits by the side of a dual carriageway, a brown brick edifice servicing the cultural needs of this London satellite town since 1938. Outside, as I approached, posters advertised an upcoming visit by seventies troubadours The Moody Blues and a weekly disco boasting hits from much the same era.

The setting couldn't have been more unlikely, but this was where my voyage through the creation of Middle-earth had delivered me in October 2003.

Two sets of double-doors opened onto what objectively speaking should have been a glorious sight: an orchestra in all its raiment arranged across the floor of the cavernous concert hall to form a semi-circle, the focal point of which was the conductor's podium equipped with a small screen (for playback) and a red light rather like the beady eye of HAL in *2001: A Space Odyssey* to signal when recording was in progress.

As I was ushered within, however, the London Philharmonic Orchestra was currently finishing up a union-mandated tea break, and I have a striking memory of classical virtuosos eating bags of crisps before furthering the inordinate wonders of Middle-earth. The pulpit from which the composer personally conducted currently stood empty. Howard Shore was travelling at pace between ranks of musicians, a sheaf of papers clutched tightly in one hand, before disappearing through a side door, beyond which a stairway led up to the control booth where Peter Jackson, Fran Walsh and the score's production team were stashed for the latest recording sessions on *The Return of the King*.

I must bide my time on the factory floor. For one night only a member of this august ensemble of musicians, known to me less for their robust renditions of Dvořák's symphonies than over two hundred film scores including *Lawrence of Arabia* and *Star Wars*. Thankfully for all concerned, I am handed nary a cowbell or pennywhistle, my only instruction being to sit very still and double-check my Nokia was switched off. Nor was this the occasion for interviews — the Philharmonic was on the clock. This was an opportunity granted to very few to watch and *listen*.

Shore would inform me when we talked at his London hotel a few days later that he had come to Watford for the acoustics. 'There is a particular resonance to these turn-of-the-century buildings.' He is an avid student of auditory range if not architectural history. 'Town halls have a particular sound to them. But it is also the combination — the sound of the London Philharmonic *in* Watford Town Hall.'

On his quest to score an entire world, Shore has also recorded at Wellington Town Hall, Air Studios in London and the Henry Wood Hall — a retired church adjacent to the River Thames. To Jackson's delight, three years of musical collaboration had been centred at Abbey Road Studios, the north London studio legendary for the many marvels conjured therein by the Beatles.

There was little time for reverie. While in London, the director balanced the slog of such recording sessions with approving visual effects shots brought by messengers on portable harddrives and dealing with the hiccupping connections of 2003 tech-to-video conference with Wellington. Until the film is completed, sleep will remain an afterthought.

Shore returned to the floor. As he stepped up onto his podium, his face intent, the orchestra complete their medley of final tune-ups and the air tightens with anticipation.

'And now back to Middle-earth. . .' he commanded softly, raising his hands — Shore conducts without a baton. From the smiles around me it was clear this was a familiar refrain.

During these lengthy recordings sessions, Shore had never once lost his cool. He was a calm, communicative and thoughtful collaborator, only ever irked by a rebellious note. The only time the orchestra ever saw sadness in their leader was the night they resumed after the terrorist attacks of 11 September 2001. He had lived for years only blocks away from the World Trade Center.

On a large screen mounted on the wall Frodo begins to flail uselessly against the sticky webs of an unrendered but still spectacularly present Shelob looming behind him. The thrill of gaining a sneak preview of one of the most anticipated confrontations of the third film would wear thin as the scene was endlessly rewound and repeated over the session and the timing between music and image divined.

'Shelob has her own compositional work, just for those particular sequences,' Shore later explained to me. 'She is another unique character that has to be represented in the film.'

All her ravenous hunger and rage, her scuttling movement, her vast age and to an extent her femaleness — all the facets of Shelob's festering consciousness — are conveyed by a fusion of Shore's composition and Weta Digital's spider-in-progress.

Quite what informed the quality of each take was lost on me. Misplaced notes went off like klaxons in Shore's pitch perfect ears. Tones were found wanting. Timings awry. To the same degree that Jackson could see the image in his head before he shot it, Shore could hear the music before it was played. 'Can that sound be darker?' he was often heard to ask, mainly of himself.

'We are trying to find an acoustic image,' he said. The physical arrangement of the orchestra, even the position of microphones in the room, was carefully calibrated to the mysterious tenor of Middle-earth. The venue itself was an instrument. Chief music engineer John Kurlander had drawn extensive maps of each venue to keep track of the placements. He had even added a couple of vintage microphones he owned to his Watford chart to lend some lower midrange warmth to the piercing reports of the modern equipment.

A quest for perfection interrupted only by the more prosaic needs of the locals.

'We can never record there on Fridays,' sighed Shore, a flicker of amusement in his Canadian composure, 'this whole huge production has to get out because they have bingo on Friday nights.'

Fifty-four, wizard at the door. . .

*

Months before production got underway in 1999, Jackson and Walsh decided to edit together a series of storyboards (as they had with the pitch video the year before) and get a sense of the timing of incident and character. To enhance the effect Jackson invited the musically minded Walsh to 'lay in' a temp music track that befitted the Middle-earth mood.

Walsh's instinctive reaction was to reach for a set of soundtracks she knew well: *The Fly, The Client, The Silence of the Lambs, Seven* and *Crash*. It was at that point it occurred to her they had something significant in common. They were all by Howard Shore. Seeing (or hearing?) how well the music played beneath their storyboards, music written for contemporary horror movies and thrillers, they realized they may have found their composer.

Likewise with her pursuit of Gollum, Jackson would happily bow to Walsh's talents when it came to the trilogy's musical content. Competent in piano, bass and guitar, and possessed of a good singing voice, in the early eighties Walsh had dropped out of Victoria University to form post-punk outfit The Wallsockets with her brother Martin, based out of her cramped flat above a Chinese restaurant on Courtenay Place (where they would later hatch plans for *Braindead* and later still the parade for *The Return of the King* would pass by).

Walsh generally played bass.

Before the breaking of their avant-garde fellowship, The Wallsockets were trailblazers in Wellington's alternative music scene. Local music magazine *In Touch* described them as 'pop-flavoured punk with a dark edge'. They were known for a capacity for 'ironic shock' as they tackled nuclear annihilation and euthanasia though such songs as the Beatles-influenced Blue Meanie and Snerl ('I'm not a human!') recorded at Wellington's Sausage Studios — the ambiance of which might not have passed muster with Shore.

While Jackson was catching up on George Romero zombie movies and *Q The Winged Serpent* in his parents' basement, Walsh was playing The Terminus and Cuba Mall alongside The Ambitious Vegetables, Life in the Fridge Exists and Blam Blam Blam. Just like her partner's gleefully untethered early horrors (to which she also contributed), Walsh's lively punk noncon-formism would feed its way into the films and their idiosyncratic creation.

When the *New York Times* once referred to Jackson as 'her husband' Walsh had burst into incredulous laughter. 'He's not my husband,' she told them straight. 'He's never asked me, and if he did, I probably wouldn't say yes.'

It is Walsh who provided the Nazgûl scream like a tortured crow. 'I'm a very good screamer,' she said, only half-joking. 'It was a way of letting out all the stress and terror of making these movies.'

Walsh became absorbed with the shape and flavour of the music of Middle-earth. Says Boyens, 'She understood how vital it was to informing the emotions of the film.'

Despite rumours of Danny Elfman, James Horner and Polish composer Wojciech Kilar (who had worked on Francis Coppola's gothic muddle *Bram Stoker's Dracula*) having been approached, Walsh insisted that Shore was their first and only choice to do the score.

'They just described the movie to me,' said Shore, his glassy Canadian accent surprisingly inexpressive. He had been vaguely aware an adaptation of *The Lord of the Rings* was underway in New Zealand through the usual industry gossip, but he didn't know Jackson at all. 'We just had a forty-five-minute conversation on the phone, which was intriguing enough for me to go down and see him.'

Towards the end of 1999, Shore took the flight to Wellington, received the customary tour of sets and Workshop, sampling at first-hand the 'phenomenal' things being done and the collective dedication to this story. New Zealand changed people. Everything was theoretical until you got there. He could see the scale of the undertaking transcended filmmaking.

'I met Alan Lee, the great Tolkien illustrator,' he remembered. 'I met Richard Taylor, Peter, Fran and Philippa. Once you saw that level of commitment I could not *not* do it.'

And having agreed, there was no way he could simply get back on a plane and return to normal life. Cancelling all his plans, he began a short tour of the country, soaking up the landscapes, making notes and feeding his muse.

The actual composing process wouldn't begin until October 2000, 'the culmination', he said, 'of everything I'd learned about films, about drama, about working with other people'. By then it had become all consuming. Whether he was aware of it or not, this was the kind of challenge he had been waiting for: a film score certainly, but one that would take flight across three epics, vast in scope, and out beyond the edges of the celluloid to become a great orchestral work in its own right, potentially his life's work.

As 2000 drew to a close and with it principal photography, Jackson and Walsh had been content they were in a good place with where Shore was heading. By early 2001 that changed, when their court composer played them a section from Journey in the Dark, the passage of music that follows the Fellowship through Moria, the composing of which had been accelerated to go with the Cannes footage — but still took six weeks to record.

There exists a legend about how George Lucas had jubilantly called Steven Spielberg during the scoring sessions for *Star Wars* at Abbey Road and held up the receiver just so his friend could hear John Williams' incredible music.

Likewise, when Jackson and Walsh heard the music written to fill the towering halls of Dwarrowdelf they knew the score wasn't just good, it had the potential to be extraordinary. The French horns and strings swelled toward the vaulted ceiling, but it was a progression of haunting minor chords, a lament for what Shore saw as the 'ruined grandeur' of this once prodigious place. The effect is deeply stirring, magnificent, yet rooted in melancholy and loss: a tide of loneliness filling that imaginary space.

'That piece of music,' Walsh extolled, 'spoke to the darkness.'

Shore enjoyed a close collaboration with Jackson and particularly Walsh; one that differed from how he worked with two other significant artistic allies, David Cronenberg and Martin Scorsese. Cronenberg, a Canadian compatriot, tended to leave him alone to his music eagerly awaiting the results; Scorsese would excitedly play him tracks from his extensive collection of songs, the music in his head already.

Middle-earth required something far deeper from Shore. 'I essentially became one of the writing team. I have approached it the same way they did.' Which likewise began by opening the pages of Tolkien for the first time in decades. He needed to get acquainted with this Oxford Don and his remarkable imagination before he wrote a single note, much as he had done when scoring adaptations of J.G. Ballard's *Crash* and William Burroughs' *The Naked Lunch*.

'The words are very important to me,' he went on: 'the heart of the music always goes back to the invention — the story itself.' Reading, he found, was a way into the music. The printed word, the framework of words and sentences and paragraphs and chapters offered an immediate structure for writing music.

'Music has a linear quality on the page. . . I always start on projects by reading.'

Sitting on a sofa in his London hotel room, dissatisfied with his answers, never fully relaxed in interview, Shore recalled that he had first read *The Lord of the Rings* in the sixties — 'just a kid' — and really hadn't thought about it in thirty years. Meanwhile, his career had flourished.

*

Growing up with Toronto's meteorological counterpoint of blazing summers and treacherous winters, by the age of eight Shore was already proficient in piano, saxophone, organ and flute. By his teens he was committed to a career in music. Which led not only to the Berklee College of Music in Boston, but jazz-rock fusion outfit Lighthouse.

His circuitous route to film scores took in a lengthy sojourn in live television. Just a kid, he had met Lorne Michaels at summer camp, a friendship that led to a five-year stint as musical director for television producer Michael's seminal *Saturday Night Live*. I struggled to picture this small, bespectacled, rather reserved intellectual nervously brushing back his wavy grey hair, dressed as a beekeeper as he accompanied those great buffoons John Belushi and Dan Aykroyd clad as bees as they covered Slim Harpo's *I am a King Bee*.* While they were fun years, and certainly taught him to think on his feet, Shore said he hadn't been overly taxed musically.

When he approached Cronenberg with the offer to score his early shocker *The Brood* (body horror of a less humorous persuasion than Jackson's early films) it was clear that, aside from a handful of straight piano concertos and song cycles, he had

---

* It was Shore who coined the name *The Blues Brothers* for Aykroyd and Belushi's blues-loving double-act on *Saturday Night Live* then parlayed into a hit 1980 movie. *SNL*, cherry picking pop culture, would later make great sport out of *The Lord of the Rings* and *The Hobbit* including Legolas visiting Taco Bell and a Middle-earth reworking of Martin Freeman comedy *The Office*.

found his metier. As a film composer Shore proved unpredict-able. Stylistically, he could switch between big, orchestral stuff (*Gangs of New York, Spotlight*) and electronica (*After Hours*). While he was the go-to guy for the cool, dramatic delineations of those crime thrillers and horror (*Seven, The Game*), he thrilled to the chance to lend playful B-movie pastiches to Tim Burton's *Ed Wood* (amongst his finest work). At the time of writing he has scored seventy-two movies, but you would never describe him as prolific.

Yet when it came to *The Lord of the Rings*, much like Jackson he was seen as an unconventional choice. Another outsider from a country with British roots.

'No one has ever done anything on this scale, the architecture of it,' mused Shore, meaning both the films and his music. 'It's describing the worlds of Lothlórien and Rivendell and the Shire and Rohan in a realistic way. What we think they would sound like. . .'

Holding informal seminars with Boyens — 'a real scholar' — Shore delved deep into Tolkien's capacious mythos, grounding himself in the depth and texture of the professor's universe, aiming to process every facet of the culture and its peoples. What were the essential characteristics of being a hobbit? Where did the Elves come from? He went beyond Tolkien, exploring the origins of ring mythology in Western culture that dated back a thousand years, collecting an extensive library of biographi-cal and analytical texts that have swelled around the author. His New York brownstone, already lined with books, developed a Tolkien wing: biographies, letters, literary studies, source mat-erial and multiple copies of the saga itself, some annotated, some illustrated by Lee.

On his first day with the London Philharmonic in September 2001, Shore had asked for a show of hands: 'Who here has read *The Lord of the Rings*?' A large number of classically trained hands shot up, but it didn't really matter — he distributed brand new copies of the book to everyone. In the early days of recording, tea breaks were often taken up with musicians deeply absorbed in Frodo's travails.

With so many different cultures to portray he spread his own repertoire of inspirations as far afield as Celtic, Middle-Eastern, and African traditions. He experimented with adding anvils, chains and piano wires plucked with gardening gloves to his percussion section. An already encyclopaedic knowledge of rare and unusual instruments led him to tycho drums, bowed lutes and a monochord, a stringed wooden instrument once used for its healing properties.* Archaic instruments were chosen specifically because they sounded so old.

Jackson wanted the music to well up out of the earth as if it already belonged to Middle-earth. Shore referred to it as music that had been lost in a vault somewhere. 'It was music based on thoughts and dreams and feelings, and also trying to give it an antiquity, something five to six thousand years old.'

'He served the needs of the story, not his own musical ego,' said Walsh, marvelling at how Shore could wrap his arms around a large variety of musical forms.

Shore saw the potential of three different expressions of the same story: book, film, and music. He was determined to create music to both serve Jackson's images and transcend them. He scheduled a year for each film, although it would amount to four including his travels and researches. It also speaks volumes of his powers of compartmentalization — and stamina — that between films one and two, he managed to score three other films: *Gangs of New York*, *Panic Room*, and *Spider*.

Everywhere he went he took his battered copy of the book with him, endlessly scribbled with notes and indeed *notes*, a priceless artifact.

---

* On a monochord the strings are positioned underneath and sufferers would lie across its flat upper side in order to absorb the healing vibrations. The use of the instrument might have contributed to the films' often-cited therapeutic properties.

Inevitably, having travelled around the islands, visiting the locations used for the films, writing a lot of the music in the rented house he took in Wellington, the culture of New Zealand became invested into the music. He could see there was a direct Kiwi sensibility endowed into the films quite apart from the book, and he wanted to reflect that.

'It is an English myth, created by an English writer, an Oxford Don, but interpreted by real New Zealanders.'

With the scoring of the Moria sequence having to be expedited ahead of schedule for Cannes, he recorded that section in New Zealand. The sonic descriptions of the subterranean kingdom were created using the Wellington Symphony Orchestra, and the acoustics of Wellington Town Hall served for cavernous Moria. The subsequent use of Watford would partly be motivated in matching that ambiance. The bone-rattling basso rumbles of a choir of Māori and Polynesian singers represented a Dwarven chorus.

Boyens would elaborate upon the six different languages being used within the films, which Shore intended to invest into his score via choral pieces, expressing 'another layer of Tolkien's thinking'. Walsh and Boyens, and Tolkien language expert David Salo, prepared the lyrics, which dialogue coach Róisin Carty then broke down phonetically for the various choristers.

Black Speech was especially tricky to sing.

While Shore is more serious and cerebral, he and Jackson have a lot in common. Both arose in their fields as inspired mavericks. Both have a highly intuitive approach to their craft and both belie a natural shyness as they comfortably command a hundred-piece orchestra or two hundred cast and crew on set.

'He's an excellent guide, a trustworthy companion,' said Shore, slipping into the imagery of the story as so often happens when talking about these films. A composer, he went on, is looking for a leader as well as a common goal.

As Lucas knew all those years before, the addition of music to edited scenes can have a metamorphic effect. Scenes that seem plodding and functional surge to life with the surge of a full orchestra and choir, or the melancholy touch of a lonely violin. But Jackson and Shore were both wise to the fact that music like visual effects is there to complete the story not replace it. Once they entered the scoring sessions it was a careful process.

Moreover, Shore was often working with scenes that weren't fully formed. Creating music for the Balrog required the director to describe what a Balrog looked like, how it moved and what it might even sound like. Which boiled down to Jackson doing his best impression of a Balrog.

'Or you might not see the Nazgûl, or eagles, all sorts of things,' added Shore. 'Peter is constantly describing things to me, telling me things about the story and what he was trying to achieve in scenes and I'd try to help him achieve those things.'

On one afternoon in September 2002, every head of the normally utterly professional London Philharmonic could be seen craning toward the percussion section and the unexpected guest musician. For the arrival of the Fellowship at Edoras it had been decided that Jackson would perform the tam-tam, and the director would be left sweating at the effort it took to get a clean note from this sizeable gong.

The voice of Kurlander burst into everyone's headphones: 'If we could just have about seventeen more takes. . .'

On 31 October 2003, not so long after I had paid my visit to Watford, Shore was seen to rise to his podium, a look of grim determination on his face. He conferred with one of his assistants. 'Well, let's try that, let's try that,' he fussed. It had already been a long session spent on the twisted themes of Mordor. He raised his hands and following an intense downbeat came the unmistakeable ditty of Happy Birthday to You, building up to an elaborate and frankly menacing crescendo.

It was Jackson's birthday.

This time it was his deadpan voice that comes through the headphones: 'We thought it still wasn't spooky enough. . .'

What was it that happened in Shore's head when he composed? Did he simply hear music? Did he picture footage or concept art or his director hamming it up a bit? Shore looked perplexed by the question. I was asking him to express the inexpressible, but he tried nevertheless.

'It's a very intuitive, dreamy process... There is hard work involved... But it's just intuition, just feeling... I write with pen and ink when getting the score on paper... I mean, you watch the movie and you can hear it and feel it... It's just bringing it to life.'

Shore has often claimed he felt a kinship with Frodo. Shouldering the responsibility of this eleven-hour plus score for the 'classic novel of the twentieth century' was like Frodo accepting the burden of the Ring. If that sounded a little cute, he saw something in the fact that when it came to composing, while these great collaborators surrounded him they could never finally understand what it was to write the music. That burden was his alone.

'Even at the end, Frodo climbing Mount Doom feels like finishing *The Return of the King*. It is taking that kind of effort to finish it!'

It was the first time he betrayed how exhausted he felt.

Even now, with not much more than a month to go, he was still actively composing. There was never enough time. Not to compose, conduct, record, mix, produce and put it in the film. 'In the end they drag you away from it,' he laughed, 'they just make you stop.'

But not yet. There was work to be done before the Ring falls finally into the Cracks of Doom, accompanied by the hammering of timpanis and a cacophonous swirl of strings and wind and voices: the many different themes of the Ring blurring together.

'We wanted a constant source of music like Wagner created in the nineteenth century,' Shore concluded. 'We wanted to create something of a really classical nature.'

*

'Both rings were round, and there the resemblance ceased,' grumbled Tolkien whenever the comparison was made between his voluminous saga and nineteenth-century German composer Richard Wagner's hefty operatic cycle *Ring of the Nibelung.*[*] Nevertheless, long before either *The Hobbit* or *The Lord of the Rings*, Tolkien made an informal study of *Die Walküre* — second of the four works that make up the cycle. Some of the parallels are striking: they are both set in worlds of high fantasy featuring different races and both feature highly desirable yet cursed rings that are stolen — there is thematic mention in Wagner of 'the lord of the ring as the slave of the ring'.

This debate has been frothing away since the book's publication. The contention being that consciously or not *The Lord of the Rings* draws deep from the Wagnerian river.

Tolkien's scepticism toward the composer may be in part due to his awareness of how the German nation had launched into two terrible world wars, one of which the writer witnessed first-hand, while waving the operatic mythology like a banner (Wagner's work is deemed anti-Semitic). Wagner falls in and out of fashion with greater alacrity than Tolkien, and was put to ironic use by Francis Coppola in *Apocalypse Now* as the accompaniment to a thrilling yet devastating helicopter attack.

Classical music critic Alex Ross has spoken of Shore's score as being 'echt-Wagnerian'. This was especially so when it came to evoking the power of the Ring itself, where Shore utilizes the spooky chords and brooding harmonies of the old composer to sinister effect (there is a far more complex explanation involving the unconventional coupling of minor chords, but I'll leave that for the musicologists). Ross also believes *The Lord of the Rings* films transcend the book in quality. 'They revive the art of Romantic wonder; they manufacture the sublime,' he sang in *The New Yorker*.

Largely guided in his intentions by both book and film, Shore

---

[*] Wagner based his four-opera Ring Cycle upon the epic High German poem *Nibelungenlied*, incorporating a series of tragic tales of doomed romances, revenge, stolen treasure and dragon slaying. It has been called the German *Iliad*.

proudly worked in a far more traditional vein than the contemporary fashion for prominent yet anonymous scores.

'It is opera-like in its concept and its scope.'

There was also the prevalence of those great choral parts. Shore had taken an operatic approach to his music for *The Fly*, *The Silence of the Lambs* and *Seven*. Operatic meant big gestures, recurring themes and leitmotifs. In other words: the hooks of storytelling. Only film was opera in reverse.

'We wanted to create the same effect,' said Shore, 'but you're writing the music afterwards.'

In musicologist Doug Adams' peerless study *The Music of The Lord of the Rings*, he devotes over 120 pages to an in-depth annotation of over ninety specific themes. Shore's musical approach, he says, 'illuminates Middle-earth from an anthropological viewpoint'. These begin with overarching themes for the main cultural touchstones: Middle-earth itself, the Ring, the Celtic-styled hobbits, the chromatic scales of the Elves, the choruses of the Dwarves, the glorious Fellowship theme, Rohan, Gondor, Mordor, the 'hammered percussion' (anvils!) of Isengard, the monsters, Ents and a two-pronged approach to Gollum.

'He needed the two pieces of music to work against each other,' explained Shore: pitiful and devious.

Beyond the core themes, Shore created particular themes for, say, The Watcher in the Water or Shelob or the imperious Dwarrowdelf, creating a vast selection of individual pieces like herbs to be added to a dish. Yet it was vital that the score remain musically cohesive across the whole trilogy, and the composer adds subtle variations throughout to the narrative.

For instance, the Fellowship theme, which plays in its full brassy majesty as the heroes climb away from Rivendell into the Misty Mountains, re-occurs in various soaring or retreating forms as the key cast unite or splinter. The theme known as Dangerous Passes, which is first heard when the Fellowship make their failed attempt on the Pass of Caradhras, can be heard again very faintly as Frodo, Sam and Gollum ascend the stairs of Cirith Ungol. Listen closely and a tiny fragment of the theme of Gondor can be heard during the Council of Elrond as we are introduced to Boromir.

*

The powerful effect music can have on a film, gluing the drama together, signalling emotion and character, is impossible to satisfyingly set down in words. Music critics and writers have spent centuries trying to convey the ineffable qualities of this most elusive artform.

Still there remains little doubt that Shore's work is monumental.

'I knew or felt it was going to be okay the moment I heard Howard's music,' says Boyens.

Sitting in that concert hall, the music in full spate, it did feel like something washing over and through me. Tears stung my eyes, and I was left a little giddy and disorientated. It was like vertigo. There was a violence to it too, that sense of opera and Wagner. The narrative would unfold in my head even if I shut my eyes to what was on screen.

Even in the habitually elitist circles of classical music appreciation where film scores are often treated as little more than menial labour, what began with the Oscar-winning score for *The Fellowship of the Ring* was deemed an extraordinary accomplishment.

'It was only a matter of weeks before critics and fans realized that Shore's material for the first entry was destined to become a classic of modern film music,' waxed Christian Clemmensen of *Filmtracks.com*, 'and the palpable anticipation of his own two sequel scores was immediate.'

Shore's music is now as synonymous with the world on screen as John Williams' soaring themes with *Star Wars'* faraway galaxy or Vangelis' currents of melancholic synth with *Blade Runner* or Ennio Morricones' twanging, witty operatics with *The Good, The Bad and the Ugly,* or for that matter Max Steiner's sweeping melodrama with *Gone with the Wind.*

In March 2002, Jackson was to be found on the floor of Watford Town Hall trying to hide a sheepish grin. They were recording music for *The Fellowship of the Ring Extended Edition,* and skulking up the podium, he gestured to Shore's brown leather bag. 'I wondered what was in Howard's brown bag, so I took a little peek,' he declared to the room, his hand back inside the bag. 'And I found. . . that!' Out of the bag he brandished an Oscar and the room broke into a clamour of applause and stamping feet.

Shore looked humbled and thanked his players for their part in such recognition. 'We should put it someplace prominent to inspire you for the last couple of hours.' He handed it back to Jackson. 'Just don't drop it!'

The Canadian composer would win the Academy Award for Best Original Score for both *The Fellowship of the Ring* and *The Return of the King,* a clean sweep denied by Elliot Goldenthal's music for *Frida* (*The Two Towers* didn't even warrant a nomination). In 2015, for the sixth year running, the score for *The Lord of the Rings* (now viewed as a single work) was voted the best soundtrack of all time in the Classic FM poll — similar polls have delivered the same result. Shore's score has come to be regarded as the definitive soundtrack of the millennium, the modern benchmark for what a film score can be, although its lessons have gone largely unheeded. Great film music remains an evaporating art.

Also part of the musical equation was the relatively risky decision to have songs play over the end credits of each film, usually the province of romcoms and popcorny blockbusters. Typically, the ambition was bold. Their songs would blend the antiquity of Shore's compositions with a more modern, stand-alone sensibility. The chance, as Jackson saw it, 'to reach beyond the fans'. In other words, they would channel Middle-earth rather than be of Middle-earth.

Walsh would again be at the vanguard of the process, generating lyrics and conferring on the choice of singer. After the first film, appropriate female voices would be sought for each

of the closing songs. Deliberately or not, the three singers represented three of the different Celtic traditions that had once
stirred Tolkien's imagination, hailing from Ireland, Iceland and
Scotland.

With May it Be, which concludes *The Fellowship of the Ring*,
Enya was approached at Shore's behest. He thought her soft,
otherworldly voice, made famous by the hit single Orinoco Flow,
would be a natural extension of Middle-earth. Jackson and Walsh
were amused to discover the singer was a Tolkien obsessive.
Flown down to New Zealand, she was the first 'outsider' to see
the rough cut of the first film, and Jackson hovered outside the
screening room, anxious to she how she reacted. He had nothing
to worry about. She thought it remarkable.

Wary their first song feel like an afterthought or gimmick,
Shore suggested they introduce her voice during the film to soften
the transition. The result was Aniron, which adds a dreamlike
shimmer to the romantic interlude between Aragorn and Arwen
in Rivendell. Enya and her writing team of Nicky and Roma Ryan
(she insisted no one else was attuned to her voice) wrote the two
songs, which Shore then orchestrated 'to grow right out of the
score' and Boyens provided the Elvish lyrics. 'They were close to
Gaelic,' noted Enya.

With an Icelandic father and Italian mother, Emiliana Torrini
brought a brooding, Bjork-like off-centeredness to Gollum's
Song which accompanied *The Two Towers*, arguably the most
subtle and effective of all the songs, with the music now written
directly by Shore, with lyrics by Walsh. Torrini, another fan of
the books, admitted she was 'obsessed' with the first film.

Walsh and Shore often spoke about former Eurythmic Annie
Lennox. When it came to conveying the uplifting yet yearning
Middle-earth spirit of the final song Into the West, they could
think of no one better. Flying home to New York, Shore wrote
Lennox a letter by hand. 'Just to see if she might,' he said.

The three of them would meet in London, where they showed
Lennox a rough cut of the film and she couldn't say no. With

lyrics by Walsh and Boyens, Lennox would coax the song into Oscar-winning splendour at Abbey Road, working directly with Shore and a hundred-piece orchestra.

Shore always felt she resembled Galadriel.

*

Before Shore and Jackson were reunited on *The Hobbit*, there came a rare hiccup in one of Jackson's key collaborations. The director had eagerly come to Shore to compose the score for his remake of *King Kong*. Shore had eagerly accepted and set to work with his usual intense dedication, he even took a cameo as the conductor at the calamitous unveiling of The Eighth Wonder of the World. But something was lost amid the creeping vines of Skull Island and the sparkling modernity of thirties New York. Maybe his operatic style was too synonymous with Middle-earth, maybe the more heightened backdrop of *King Kong* didn't suit his seriousness, but director and composer found they were not on one another's wavelength.

After a number of attempts to try and steer a mutual course, Jackson made the tough decision to go in a completely new direction. The more squarely filmic James Newton Howard (*The Sixth Sense, Batman Begins*) was hired to replace Shore with only a few weeks to go. Suffused with knowing melodrama, Newton Howard's music lovingly pastiches the Max Steiner score for the original *King Kong*.

The official notice from Jackson was respectful but hinted at conflict: 'I have greatly enjoyed my collaborations with Howard Shore, whose musical themes made immeasurable contributions to *The Lord of the Rings* trilogy. During the last few weeks, Howard and I came to realize that we had differing creative aspirations for the score of *King Kong*. Rather than waste time arguing with a friend and trying to unify our points of view, we decided amicably to let another composer score the film.'

It is a horrible thing, he admitted to me in 2005. 'There isn't anything good about a time like that. It either clicks or it doesn't click. And, especially with music, if it doesn't it can be negative for the film. This wasn't a project that was inspiring him to find the music. It became a common consent. These are the real things that are a bummer with being a filmmaker.'

With time, Shore became philosophical about what went wrong. 'You always hope for a great collaboration but people change, things change. It's like a relationship. Sometimes the magic is there and it works, and sometimes it doesn't.'

He couldn't name a particular reason for why it didn't work. Composer and director were just pulling apart and it was a gap that they failed to bridge. Maybe someday his score will see the light of day, a curious footnote to their collaboration.

Whatever the creative differences in the vicinity of Skull Island, there was no hesitation in Jackson asking Shore to return to compose the music for *The Hobbit* trilogy, and no hesitation on Shore's behalf in agreeing. It was a chance to return to a musical journey that would always feel unfinished and explore an entirely new region of Middle-earth and a new set of characters while reacquainting himself with some very old friends.

Interviewed in 2014, Shore mentioned that he had finally written a theme for Gandalf the Grey (surprisingly, there had been a theme for his Whiter self but never the Grey). 'He seemed so elusive,' he explained, 'I didn't want to tie him down with a very strong thematic idea. Hence he only received a motif.' In *The Hobbit*, as he saw it, 'Gandalf the Grey was more of a facilitator, more part of the company, a motif that connected him to wizards.'

As Jackson, Walsh and Boyens went into the appendices to expand the horizons of Tolkien's playful first novel, Shore was keen to locate aural connections between trilogies. For instance, given *The Hobbit* films concerned themselves with Dwarven culture, he brought back fragments of the harmonies he used in Dwarrowdelf. 'I just connected that in a very subtle way,' he said. The idea in his head was that one day they would be watched in chronological order and when the Fellowship arrives in the wonder of Dwarrowdelf it will trigger memories of Thorin and co.

Which accounted for the reason Shore chose to record much of the music for *The Desolation of Smaug* and *The Battle of the Five Armies* with the New Zealand Symphony Orchestra in Wellington Town Hall, where he had once scored the Moria sections of *The Fellowship of the Ring*.

He laughed about his journey coming full circle. 'We started there and we ended there.'

Yet it was a different book, and he strove to distinguish a different palette. *The Hobbit*, he recognized, had been written in the thirties in an episodic, singsong style that reflected its origins as a bedtime story for Tolkien's children. However, as a two-film adaptation expanded into a trilogy and the story was reshaped, portions of his new score were set aside in favour of deliberately repeating old themes from *The Lord of the Rings* and reinforcing the connection between the two sets of films. An echo of the struggles the films would go through in finding an identity.

With appropriate symmetry, as there were three female voices serenading the first trilogy, three male voices would regale the second. Homegrown son Neil Finn, lead singer of New Zealand's most famous band Crowded House, provided the first, having got a 'totally random call' from Boyens inviting him to participate. He was delighted, and in the interests of Middle-earth synergy built upon the moving lament for home, The Song of the Lonely Mountain, sung by the Dwarves in Bag End (written by New Zealand composers Plan 9 and orchestrated by Shore).

'You don't necessarily have to make it sound like the song was made there,' explained Finn in 2011, 'but you have to have your mind on the fact that an R&B mentality wouldn't work in Middle-earth.' Jackson, he laughed, had responded well to his demands for 'more anvil!'

Boyens has a special memory of Ed Sheeran, their second singer, coming to dinner at her house. He had just seen the rough cut of *The Desolation of Smaug* and had really responded to the phrase 'I am fire' uttered by Smaug.

'And I said, "No, you can't do that, because that's the dragon."' Perhaps wryly amused at the particularities of Middle-earth, later that evening Sheeran disappeared clutching her husband's guitar. She found him sitting in her front room, already deep into the song, having adapted the line to 'I see fire'.

The memory begets another, opening a window on the trio's mild creative wrangles. 'Frannie always says to me, "Write it down!" I'll blurt things out. And when I try to say it again, she goes, "No, you ruined it." One of those lines was, "If this is to end in fire, then we shall all burn together." And Pete didn't like it. But Fran said, "Oh no, that is so going in the movie." He wasn't in love with it, put it that way. And then he heard Richard Armitage do it. . .'

Billy Boyd was thrilled to be asked to contribute a song for the final film. In essence the last word on Middle-earth. He had of course provided his own composition, The Edge of Night, to *The Return of the King** and toured extensively with his band Beefcake. While working as a farewell, he hoped The Last Goodbye would also 'feel like it foreshadows what Frodo is going to be going through'. Added to the fact that Pippin is singing, it would bind both trilogies together.

---

* If you tot up the cast members who sing, there is also Elijah Wood, Dominic Monaghan and Billy Boyd combining on a drinking song in *the Green Dragon*; Boyd and Monaghan's duet The Green Dragon Song following Helm's Deep; Viggo Mortensen sings twice (counting *Extended Editions*) both times in Elvish (his own composition for The Song of Lúthien and a Howard Shore arrangement called The Return of the King at his coronation); and Ian McKellen enters humming The Road Goes Ever On and On. In *The Hobbit* films, apart from the Dwarves collectively singing Blunt the Knives and Far Over the Misty Mountains Cold, James Nesbitt would write and sing The Man in the Moon Stayed Up too Late featured in *The Hobbit: The Unexpected Journey Extended Edition*.

CHAPTER 16

King of a Golden Hall

Truthfully, it was on the night of the 74th Academy Awards on 24 March 2002 that *The Lord of the Rings* made its mark. At least, by Hollywood standards. In fact, the pivotal moment came on the morning of 12 February (which meant it was the early hours of the following day in Wellington) when the nominations were announced by Academy president Frank Pierson accompanied, as tradition warranted, by an actress — in this case Marcia Gay Harden.

No one predicted that *The Fellowship of the Ring* would come away with thirteen nominations. This was a fantasy, a family film, a blockbuster far beneath the staid seriousness of the Academy of Motion Picture Arts and Sciences. Yet the various disciplines of the film industry had recognized that something major was being achieved in New Zealand. The clamour of the critics and fans had been hard to ignore.

Not only had the first film picked up technical nods, as might have been expected, but there came shock nominations for adapted screenplay, director, and the film itself. Here too was a nomination for Ian McKellen as Best Supporting Actor for his lovely, oak-smoked rendition of Gandalf.

It's hard now, given the trilogy's accepted place in the

pantheon of greats, to convey how significant a sea change this was. The film had wrapped a knuckle on the glass ceiling of expectation. Sure, there had been glowing reviews, fan adulation, acceptance from all but the most truculent of Tolkien purists and mighty box office gains, but this was the moment — certainly by the lights of Hollywood perception — that Jackson's adaptation truly transcended its own proposition. A genre film — from the *most genre* of sources — made by a gang of unruly outsiders, determined that Hollywood standards could not only be matched, but surpassed. These highly talented barbarians were massing at the gate.

On the night, hosted by Whoopi Goldberg with a more sober, reflective tone than was usual in light of the attacks of 11 September 2001, it was unusually hard to predict which way the Academy might swing. Already, there was a general perception that *The Fellowship of the Ring* marked not only a more populist but artistic success than any of its wildly divergent fellow Best Picture nominees: *A Beautiful Mind, Gosford Park, In the Bedroom* and *Moulin Rouge!* (Jackson would become firm friends with director Baz Luhrman after they met that evening.) In the end, the Academy cowered beneath the blanket of worthiness in *A Beautiful Mind*, Ron Howard's well-meant but trite biopic of maths wizard John Nash (played by Boromir-Aragorn near miss Russell Crowe) who is tormented by a fractured psyche to rival Gollum.

When he reached the stage, *A Beautiful Mind* producer Brian Grazer grabbed the envelope from presenter (and very old friend) Tom Hanks and glanced at what was written. 'It says it was really close,' he smiled, 'which it was. . .'

No one was in any doubt what he was referring to — arguably, the greater accomplishment had been overlooked. *The Fellowship of the Ring* still had a very significant night, but its four wins, Best Original Score, Best Cinematography, Best Make-up and Best Visual Effects, represented the same non-committal acceptance that greeted such genre greats as *2001: A Space Odyssey, Jaws, Star Wars, Raiders of the Lost Ark* and *E.T.: The Extra-Terrestrial.*

A year later *The Two Towers* also gained a Best Picture nomination, and while it again would only receive marginal awards,
a background buzz was now growing such that the Academy
would find it impossible to ignore *The Return of the King*, and
the opportunity to unofficially bless the trilogy as a whole with
its just rewards from its film industry peers. Wouldn't it?

When Richard Taylor landed back at Wellington Airport with
his first Oscar, the airport staff had laid out a red carpet and
had all the folk waiting to catch flights gather on either side.
On the other side of customs the staff of Weta Workshop and
their families were there to greet him cock-a-hoop that their
labours had been given the ultimate accolade. They demanded
to see the Oscar, and from deep within his luggage Taylor pulled
out a Tesco's bag and unveiled the golden statue thirteen and
a half inches tall. The cheering could be heard throughout the
terminal.

Recalls Taylor, 'I had managed to buy one hundred miniature
Oscars and I had them in two big rubbish sacks. I handed out
all these Oscars and everyone drove out the airport with them
mounted on their roof-racks and their bonnets.'

*

In Los Angeles, the Oscars were religion. And the irony of it all
blazed like the sunshine. New Line's reckless, studio-threatening
gamble stood on the threshold of Hollywood's highest honour.
The cosmic joke was that it was now unthinkable that they
might fail to win Best Picture. Could the Academy, the collective
front of the industry, still withhold its approval, leaving the films
tainted with being 'really close' for evermore?

The marketing department was in a state of crisis management.
It is no exaggeration that they felt as if their jobs depended on it.
They had to do everything within the bounds of the rules to sway
the Academy. Building on two years of growing respect, executive vice-president of marketing Christina Kounelias remarked
in 2004 that their job was 'to create this sense of inevitability'.

Thankfully, the news coming from early screenings was exactly what they needed.

Jackson, of course, had needed no reminding of the dangers of complacency at this late stage. He was almost overcompensating in his drive to out-do himself, testing the will of his animators to eke out those last moments of spectacle. Killing them with enthusiasm.

He had passed through his usual psychological torment. It is a malady well known to directors on the completion of photography when on the first look at the rough cut they are filled with despair — what is this appalling mess? 'You really go through this very dark patch,' admits Jackson. 'But then you kind of claw your way out of it and you do the post-production. Eventually the film rebuilds itself and your confidence grows again and then you show it to people and they enjoy it and it's like, "Oh thank heavens. It's okay."'

Like a curse, this happened in triplicate on *The Lord of the Rings*.

'We made *Fellowship of the Ring* and thought it was terrible and then that film did well. Then with *The Two Towers* we thought, "God there's so much expectation. . ." We thought it was so terrible that we worked and worked and worked at it. And then *Return of the King* was terrible and we worked and worked and worked.'

When at last it was shown to critics with only days to spare before release, the curse was lifted.

On review aggregator website Rotten Tomatoes (a contemporaneous internet phenomenon that helpfully quantified reviews for studio executive spreadsheets) the film basked in a 'certified fresh' glow of a ninety-five percent positive reaction. It was as if critics had been set an equivalent challenge to Jackson to out-do all they had written before and reach a crescendo of superlative. Words that were being hurled over the walls of the Academy.

'Was it really only two years ago that Peter Jackson's *The Lord of the Rings* started?' wondered Peter Bradshaw in *The Guardian*.

'This giant movie marathon has dominated everyone's atten-tion and its reputation has grown exponentially while other event-movie franchises have floundered. . .' One of the reasons he cited was the director's contribution to the history of cine-matic warfare: 'His battles are a thing of wonder on their own account. Maybe Kurosawa's battles will one day be described as proto-Jacksonian.'

Maybe.

Chris Cabin, writing for the high-minded cultural site *Slant*, refused to be dragged into picking intellectual holes in what was, for him, 'a rare ascension into the upper echelons of the forceful, intoxicating magic of pop cinema. . . *The Lord of the Rings* trilogy is just as enormous, effective, generous, thrilling, and, yes, exhausting as an adaptation of its magnitude can and should be.'

Andrew O'Hehir in *Salon* reiterated the ironic stakes. 'Expecta-tions for *The Return of the King* are of course outlandish,' he noted. 'If it does not become the highest-grossing film in history *and* win the best-picture Oscar, it may be considered a disappointment — but as unfair as they may be, I expect to see them fulfilled. . .' He saw the film, and the trilogy, as 'a redemp-tion of the spirit of popular spectacle that has seemed so cheap-ened, corrupted and bastardized in recent years.'

It is interesting that for all the vaunted use of special effects, the digital ground broken, Jackson was praised not so much for forging a future than reclaiming the past.

There were, naturally, those that resisted. Almost as a point of pride. 'For the first time in this mammoth undertaking,' said Tom Charity of *Time Out,* 'the director seems overwhelmed by logistics — and if he isn't, we are. *Return of the King* is no less dynamic than the previous chapters, but too much of the dia-logue sounds like an orientation exercise.' There were regular gripes over length, the multiple endings and an increasingly binary moral landscape. Why were all the good guys pretty, and the bad guys so ugly? Faults that were already present in Tolkien.

I saw the film at the UK premiere once again in Leicester Square, watching the cast line up at the side of the cinema, giggling nervously between themselves as they waited to be invited, one by one to the stage to take a final bow. The applause was like thunder, but there was an urgency in the room to get through the preliminaries and surrender to Middle-earth.

Three hours something later, we were done and it felt unreal. The actors illustrated faces (care of Alan Lee) on the closing credits were met with cheers — but it all felt slightly sad. Here was that ability of a film to leave you gloriously exhausted, willingly spent and aglow with something deeper.

Whatever can be levelled against it, *The Return of the King* strives and succeeds in doing much more than astound with spectacle — the intimate is still wrapped up in the epic. Take the electrifying thrill of the lighting of the mountaintop beacons (Jackson, enjoying the threads of his film's absurdity, liked to imagine the poor fellows camped on snowy peaks awaiting the day when they could at last light their bonfires): how it starts with Pippin's stealing beneath the nose of the guards (one of whom is played by Christian Rivers) and finishes leagues away with Aragorn, having danced from mountain to mountain as the helicopter-shot spins heavenly circles. Jackson was now vaulting Middle-earth with a profound confidence.

The Return of the King brings the gift of completion. In this, it feels slightly less its own film. As Jackson said, it is all conclusion, a great swell of momentum and emotion, trusting that the audience had come this far.

Says Ordesky, 'It was marketed as the end of the trilogy. Which doesn't sound like a particularly innovative thought today, but at that time was. Trilogies had never happened over this three-year span, all the marketing was not about just this film but the end of one giant eleven-hour saga. It was about leaning into the triumphant end of this whole adventure. You are basically watching one movie, like serialized cinema.'

The momentum granted by making three films as one stayed

true. After its epic world premiere in Wellington, *The Return of the King* opened on December 17, and began, as was widely expected, the victory lap. The final part of the trilogy smashed the records set by its predecessors and cruised past the billion-dollar mark at the worldwide box office (at the time a feat only achieved previously by *Titanic*). The final figure at the end of the film's theatrical run came to $1,119,507,521 ($1,340,222,465 adjusted for inflation). Rather than the diminishing returns generally expected of sequels, the films had only grown in their popularity with each release. Audiences invested in the trilogy as a single story. Even Tolkien would have approved of that.

'*The Return of the King* did over one hundred million dollars in Japan. *The Hobbit* never got close to those numbers,' remarks Kamins. 'The whole market paradigm shifted between the trilogies. *The Hobbit* movies did more like fourteen to fifteen million dollars in Japan.'

With unprecedented popular success (and for a film well over three hours) all that was left to prove was the Oscars. And New Line was on a mission.

Their first hurdle was overcoming the F-word. The attitude that 'fantasy', no matter how well delivered, was inherently juvenile. Exactly the same attitude had disallowed the book from literary discussion. It was almost a point of pride that no fantasy movie had ever won Best Picture — the subtext being that for all the popcorn Hollywood still knew a slice of carrot cake when it came along. The Oscars was where Hollywood showed its taste.

Says Kamins, 'There were genres that always struggled with the Academy. Fantasy was one. Comedy was another. I remember what a big deal it was when Peter O'Toole was nominated for *My Favourite Year*. Comedy performances were never nominated.'

Russell Schwartz, president of theatrical marketing, knew they had to throw some of their profits at the problem. Where they had spent somewhere between $5 and $10 million on the Oscar campaigns on the first two films, they now had a campaign budget north of $10 million. A still modest sum compared to the excesses of awards season, but for New Line this was unusually aggressive. Outside of Tolkien, the studio's previous campaigns had involved much smaller titles from their Fine Line division. With this in mind, Schwartz hired in a team of veteran publicists who knew how to manoeuvre through the eccentricities of the Academy. Many of the Academy members were seventy-plus and, according to Schwartz, 'had no idea what a fantasy movie was and why they should vote for it'. They needed to talk directly to that group, convince them this was in an epic tradition.

Oscar campaigns have all the hallmarks of political campaigns. There were 6,000 diverse voters to appeal to and a strict set of guidelines (gifts would be seen as bribery). 'You had to reach out to different constituencies,' said Kounelias. From Jackson down, the decision was made to go for broke and push in as many categories as possible. Not only because the film fully deserved credit in all those categories but it also presented the idea of fullness to the Academy — this was a film that had excelled in every department.

At New Line HQ on Robertson Avenue they lined the walls with hundreds of images from *The Return of the King* and spent hours perusing options for their Oscar advertising (which ran in the industry trade magazines and online): 'For your consideration. . .' ads often supplemented with facts and figures: the amount of days shot, the quantity of materials they used, the number of extras; a reminder of the sheer labour it took to get these films made. There was to be no doubt as to the breadth and scope of what had been created.

*

On 26 January 2004, Pierson announced the nominations, this time accompanied by Sigourney Weaver. Amid the celebrations of eleven nominations, including Best Director and Best Picture, there came the worrying news that they had been locked out of the acting nominations entirely. 'Which was bizarre. . .' said Schwartz. 'Everybody was great in the movie.'

Had they been blinded by the spectacle? Put off by the hairy feet and pointy ears? To Jackson's mind, the problem was the ensemble nature of the film made voters reluctant to single anyone out. 'It is such a big cast and they are so good together that no single performance rises above the others. . .' The actors were cancelling one another out. A theory given credence when the film picked up Best Ensemble from the Screen Actors Guild, largely made up of the same community of voters.

Maybe New Line had spread the net too wide. Surely there was a case to be made for concentrating on Sean Astin as Best Supporting Actor. With the same subtle orientations of story-telling, the final film is shaded as Sam's story as the first film is Frodo's and the second Gollum's. Even the natural worrywort Astin felt he was in with a shot.

The lead up to the final film's release had been a complicated time for the actor. He knew he had done his best work in *The Return of the King*, a fact confirmed when he had wept his way through a rough cut during his ADR sessions in London and then into Philippa Boyens' shoulder after it was over.

'You know what?' he informed his agent, tempting fate. 'I think I might get nominated.' Having grown up in Hollywood, the Academy Awards meant that bit more to Astin. Their elixir was in his veins: his mother, Patty Duke, had won Best Supporting Actress in 1963 for *The Miracle Worker*.

However, his confidence had been thrown when he saw the final cut, with many of the scenes he had treasured — scenes such as the march across Gorgoroth with the Orcs that would be reinserted in the *Extended Edition* — had been removed during Jackson's tightening. Absurdly, he was left unsure how he felt about the finished film. He told Wood he had been heartbroken watching the finished film.

'I lost touch,' he admitted. 'I saw it as a slap in the face.'

Even when the reviews came in, singling out his performance — 'Astin is the soul of the movie in a performance,' trumpeted Peter Travers in *Rolling Stone* — he couldn't shake his ennui.

Speaking to *Time* magazine his disappointment spilled over when he claimed that 'only twenty percent of his performance is on the screen'. It was a foolish slip, and not exactly what he meant. Something he regretted instantly. A few days later he got an email from Walsh telling him how hurt Jackson had been by the comment. But it still took a third viewing for him to come around.

Maybe his negativity had hurt his chances.

When the Hollywood Foreign Press Association, the cabal of journalists who vote on the Golden Globes, neglected to nominate his performance, Astin noted that 'the Oscar buzz seemed to diminish'. The Golden Globes are thought to have a significant influence on the Academy voters. He didn't even set his alarm to watch the Oscar nominations live, leaving it to New Line's marketeers to be shocked on his behalf.

Astin can console himself that the great performances that were recognized by the Academy have mostly been forgotten. How well do you recall Djimon Honsou's in *In America*? Benicio Del Toro in *21 Grams*? Ken Watanabe in *The Last Samurai* (an epic partly shot in New Zealand)? Alec Baldwin in *The Cooler*? Or even the winner, Tim Robbins in *Mystic River*? But time has held firm to Astin's humble Samwise, Wood's tormented Frodo, McKellen's sage Gandalf and Mortensen's stirring physicality as Aragorn, or any of the great performances on which the film is founded.

The acting community are often the most conservative. New Line had also made a concerted effort to gain recognition for Andy Serkis' industry-transforming achievements as Gollum. With the release of *The Two Towers*, he had done extensive Q&As with the Screen Actors Guild, aiming to allay fears that the new technology would one day make actors redundant. He impressed on them that he had spent more time acting than any other cast member. They needed to think of motion capture as 'digital make-up'.

Had there been a single supporting performance as profoundly *necessary* to the story as that given by Serkis in both the second and third films? He cracks open the films' moral certainty, deepens their psychology, enriches this world with humour and cunning and channels his director's anarchic sensibility, but to no avail.

'I just don't see the difference,' says Serkis, who feels like he has been repeating himself for fifteen years. 'Authorship of the performance is all that matters. What is at the heart of Gollum is performance.'

The truth was he had opened doors for actors, not closed them.

'On any given day, ninety per cent of the Actors Guild isn't working,' fumes Kamins. 'So if it creates new opportunities for actors, why wouldn't that artform be something that is embraced? I mean, animated films started as hand drawn, then they became Pixar. There are always changes to the media. But we had been pushing for Andy for a long time. People were always excited to talk to him. But we could never get past that threshold to where people look at him as a potential nomination.'

The simple fact of the matter is that Serkis is a great actor doing great work — it is only the camera that is different.

'If they don't award the films this time, I will resign my membership of the Academy,' Christopher Lee had assured me on numerous occasions, and I wasn't the only one. It was a mantra to which there was little doubt he was willing to hold true. That was until he suffered a mortal blow from the final edit of *The Return of the King*. Or you could say he had suffered the lack of a mortal blow: his death scene had been cut.

As everyone who has watched *The Return of the King Extended Edition* will know, Jackson had devised a suitably gothic end for Saruman. Stabbed in the back by Wormtongue, he plummets head over heels from the roof of Orthanc, where once he had imprisoned Gandalf, to be skewered on the spoke of one of his great engines. It was Jackson's sly tribute to Lee's Hammer Horror days, and *Dracula AD 1972* in particular. 'There is something vaguely familiar about this situation,' Lee had chided his director dryly, aware he was being lightly parodied. Aware too it was affectionate.

Late, late in the edit, still wrestling with length, Jackson came to the difficult decision to excise Saruman's death scene. Having already postponed it from *The Two Towers*, he had thought to begin the third film with the wizard's fall, but was nagged by the feeling that they were wrapping up the previous year's film, not beginning the new one.

Even inserting a swift, cut down version didn't work: the film demanded forward motion. He trusted that audiences who had seen *The Two Towers* would take Saruman's defeat as a given (and knew he would reinsert the sequence in the *Extended Edition*). It was a gamble — and remains, to this eye, a crimp in the smooth veneer of the theatrical cut. Amid their swoons, the critics did spare a thought for the absence of the human face of evil in Lee's Saruman. 'Without Saruman,' chafed *The Guardian*'s otherwise upbeat Peter Bradshaw, 'it's not good versus evil. It's good versus. . . a sort of swarming amorphous danger.'

Lee took the news badly, and reacted by phoning everyone he could think of. He called his fellow cast members. He called New Line. He even called me at the *Empire* office. It was an odd conversation. 'Audiences will want to know, "Where is Saruman?"' he told me, his Stentorian tones reverberating down the line. Quite what he hoped to gain was unclear. Did he think I might be able to intercede on his behalf? Maybe he simply needed to vent. I did my best to mollify him, and suggested he should speak with Peter.

Lee and Jackson would mend their differences, with the acting doyen returning to cameo in *The Hobbit* films. Meantime, in support of the disappointments of a passionate man, we at *Empire* fixed a cut-out of Saruman to the top of the office Christmas tree. *There* is Saruman!

The sacrifices of the edit were entirely creative choices. New Line let Jackson know they would love for the film to come in at three hours and made suggestions — including cutting the Grey Havens — but by now deferred to his vision. And length was almost a boon with the Academy — *Lawrence of Arabia* wafted through the desert for over four hours.

Nevertheless, the lack of actor nominations was a real concern. Actors made up the largest constituency of the Academy and if they were fighting shy of the movie, did that mean they would look elsewhere when it came to Best Picture?*

Says Kamins, 'the trick to the Academy Awards for Best Picture is always the actors. We only had one acting nomination for Ian McKellen in Supporting Actor. I remember that first year: as soon as Ian lost, Peter turned to me and said, "We're done." I don't know that we ever really had the full support of the acting branch of the Academy. People admired it for what it was. They admired the craftsmanship of the whole enterprise. But I think the actors' branch had a tough time with it.'

As their eleven nominations acknowledged, every other branch eagerly supported the film's ambition. And the actors might still support the cast in collective terms by voting for Best Picture. In short, they were still the film to beat, and New Line's marketing team pressed on. For having the lead can be a tricky position. It is an axiom of the complex currents that flow through Hollywood's award season that in many cases the early frontrunner loses out. You have to maintain that momentum.

And they were still a fantasy film.

The majority of the cast and principal crew were staying at the Four Seasons Hotel for the ceremony, and as they headed to their fleet of limos, a Haka was performed in honour of New Zealand. 'It was really emotional,' remembers Serkis.

*

On the night of 29 February 2004, at the Kodak Pavilion in the heart of Hollywood, producer Denise Roberts sounded relieved. She had deservedly won Best Film in a Foreign Language with Denys Arcand's French-Canadian campus dramedy *The*

---

* Each award is voted on only by members of that discipline — i.e. actors vote for the acting categories, composer for Best Original Score — with the exception of Best Film, which is voted on by all the members collectively.

Barbarian Invasions, and catching the tenor of the evening began her speech with a joke. 'I'm just thankful that *The Lord of the Rings* did not qualify in this category.'

Given the amount of Elvish and Black Speech spoken it was lucky they hadn't been entered.

The audience laughed knowingly. *The Return of the King* appeared to be winning everything. Host Billy Crystal piled on the gags as the crazy New Zealanders came to the stage to thank more crazy New Zealanders back home, crowded into pubs and bars growing hoarse in their cheering. A faint aura of satire that had begun on the red carpet when Jackson, intercepted by an elfin dope with a microphone, had been asked 'who' he was wearing. 'Who would want to dress me?' he retorted, incredulous.

In fact, he was wearing Versace, not that the Italian designer label was going to make much capital from this model. His tie defiantly askew, Jackson looked as if he was on his way to his first job interview. Over the evening, as he returned to the stage displaying an increasing state of splendid dishevelment, it was as if director and suit were attempting to consciously uncouple. It is almost a shame that Jackson had yielded to the custom of smart shoes. Still, the unlikeliness of his presence in Hollywood's inner sanctum did not deflect from how genuinely he was in awe of the occasion. The mythology that surrounds the Oscars made these awards 'so much more special than anything else'. He had spent the day taming butterflies the size of 'jumbo jets'.

Imagine if he lost. Imagine winning. . .

Jackson remembers the night, as most winners tend to — as a complete blur, as if he had accidently slipped on the Ring. 'When we left the stage, at the end, Steven [Spielberg] had warned me to try and take in as much of it as you can because it all rushes past, but I'm not sure I managed that well.'

As the categories came and went, familiar faces in unfamiliar dress would come to the stage to take their golden statue and give their thanks. Taylor looked like an old hand, collecting his third trophy in a row, thanking a forbearing cast for all 'the rubbery feet and noses'. Alan Lee joined Dan Hennah and Grant Major to accept the award for Art Direction, and praised their director's 'nerve'.

Jackson first came to the stage with Walsh and Boyens to accept Best Adapted Screenplay presented by Francis Coppola and Sofia Coppola — recognition for the trials in taming over one thousand pages. But Boyens was emphatic in her recognition of Professor J.R.R. Tolkien: 'Without him we wouldn't be standing here.' Jackson thanked his children, Billy and Katie, 'for putting up with their mum and dad working on these films all their lives'.

Tom Cruise presented Best Director. There are pictures of Jackson walking off stage arm-in-arm with the beaming superstar, which only compound the oddness of the scene. Jackson squirming inside his Versace disguise; Cruise implacably perfect.

For everyone bar the man himself this was the most important award of the night. The one thing, above all, they wanted to see recognized was Jackson's achievement. 'It felt like that was the whole point of the night,' says Wood. The tears were visible.

'You know,' says Jackson, 'it's weird: just as they open that envelope you hope your name isn't going to be read out.' That New Zealand humility followed him all the way up to the podium to receive the highest accolade of his craft. 'You can't think of anything but hoping you are not going to trip over.'

Looking a little dazed, Jackson thanked Bob Shaye and Michael Lynne. 'God, you did the most risky thing ever done in this industry and I am so happy that it paid off.' He thanked Walsh and Barrie Osborne. But he saved his final thanks for his parents, who hadn't lived to see the films finished, but had encouraged his mad schemes and early explorations in filmmaking. They were the reason *he* was standing there.

Thus far they had won every award for which they had been nominated. All the auguries were set, the drum roll of fate begun. But even then, after ten awards there was still room for doubt. Could it even now be that Hollywood denied these interlopers from the island that time forgot? For a second Astin wondered if the 'perfect game would come to an end'.

Could it be that they still wouldn't win Best Picture?

'Everyone was so exhausted, we were all quite calm,' recalls Ordesky. 'I basically reminded myself of all the great movies that didn't win like *Citizen Kane* or *2001*. I wasn't terribly graspy about winning even though I wanted it to happen. I wouldn't be surprised if Peter felt the same. It is always great to win but the accomplishment was undeniable at that point.'

'At that moment, I did feel strangely calm,' says Jackson. He wasn't so much having an out-of-body experience as an out-of-country one, feeling like he was back home in Wellington watching the night unfurl on television.

Onto the stage came Spielberg, the éminence grise of modern Hollywood. The director who had done more than any living artist to marry the realms of pop-culture and art, whose effortless wizardry had moved Jackson throughout his career. The symbolism was not lost on anyone.

The fellow nominees were *Mystic River*, *Master and Commander: The Far Side of the World*, *Lost in Translation* and *Seabiscuit*. Worthy rivals.

Spielberg tore open the envelope. There came a pause as he took it in, a knowing smile, a trace of relief. 'Well, it's a clean sweep. . . *The Lord of the Rings: The Return of the King*.'

The arrangement of which sent a ripple of heart-stopping confusion through the audience. 'I know, Spielberg said it without saying it,' laughs Ordesky. 'In any case it was great.'

'That was the first time I met Steven,' says Jackson, with an incredulous shake of his head, 'on the stage at the Oscars.'

As they began to make their way back to the stage, beckoned by the orchestra, Walsh stopped at the end of the row in front where the four hobbit actors were sitting in their finest. As they rose for the now customary hugs and backslaps, Walsh gestured for them to follow. 'Let's go, the hobbits have to come with us.'

According to Academy protocol, only the named producers

were supposed to accept Best Picture — in this case Jackson, Walsh and Barrie Osborne — but already buoyed by the hobbits they were joined by Liv Tyler and Ian McKellen. They were the only six cast members who had made it to the actual show.

Mortensen was watching the ceremony with friends and family. It was the first time in years he had tuned in, having long become disenchanted with the competitive nature of prize giving. Such ceremonies, he thought, are little more than a popularity contest.

'There's the sense of competition, fuelled by these mushrooming award shows. Accepting jobs because you might get nominated. Trying to win scenes. They've decided to cry because it's going to get them their nomination, and the other actor doesn't matter a fuck.'

But how could Mortensen not be moved as the awards given to his friends began to pile up? By 2016, he would have to make his peace enough to take part in Hollywood's annual beauty contest when he received a Best Actor nomination for his unconventional patriarch in *Captain Fantastic*.

Orlando Bloom was in Ouarzazate in Morocco shooting Ridley Scott's underrated epic of the Crusades *Kingdom of Heaven* (whose medieval battles were executed with MASSIVE), watching the ceremony on a television set at some crazy hour. 'There was a lot of frantic texting and rejoicing,' he recalled. 'I was with them on some spiritual level.'

Not about to forgo their moment in Hollywood's brightest spotlight, Bob Shaye and Michael Lynne had joined Jackson's fellowship on stage (beginning a new tradition of group hugs). And who is to begrudge them at least this?

Says Ordesky, 'Bob is someone who always felt a bit of an outsider in Hollywood, and I remember being so happy for him. In my full journey, coming to that moment, Peter and Bob, by parallel roads but essentially different roads, meant so much. It was wonderful to watch. Just to see that happen. Once you win it can't be taken away. I can't quite put it properly. In terms of how Bob took it, I think Bob looks at the traditional Hollywood stuff with a bit of a jaundiced eye. But I think that that night he couldn't say no.'

When Shaye and Lynne had taken their seats, Lynne had leant over to the people sitting on their left, their obvious pathway to the stage, and warned that they may have to stand up to let them through. 'That was my optimism at work,' he admitted.

'I was afraid they were going to come up and drag us down,' recalled Shaye, but as Jackson and Walsh had invited the actors to join them he and Lynne were already up on their feet.

'It is hard to talk about it without it sounding like platitudes,' says Ordesky. 'It is hard to put it into words correctly. It was *immensely* satisfying.'

Jackson spoke first, speaking of his relief that the Academy could see past all the trolls, hobbits and wizards. 'Fantasy is an F-word hopefully the five-second delay won't do anything about,' he quipped, noting that '*Bad Taste* and *Meet the Feebles* had been wisely overlooked by the Academy.'

Thanking the 'people of New Zealand', he gently put Crystal back in his place over his patronizing vein of comedy. 'Billy Crystal is welcome to make a film in New Zealand whenever he wants.' But the subtext of the show was to celebrate a brilliant but crazy one-off. A momentary glitch in seventy-six years of comfortable self-congratulation, and the camera cut away, fittingly enough, to Sean Connery not quite laughing. He had never got it.

Coming off stage, Spielberg fell in with Astin and his fellow hobbits. Never one to miss an opportunity, Samwise made a pitch for *The Goonies* 2.

'Let's not talk about *The Goonies* right now,' replied Spielberg, and artfully changed the subject. 'You know how many kids around the world are happy right now, because the Academy finally agrees with them, and has the same sensibilities? They wanted it for *Star Wars*, they wanted it for *Raiders*. . .'

In retrospect, the great sea change that Spielberg hoped for never came about — such high watermarks of genre filmmaking as *Avatar* and *Gravity* lost out to *The Hurt Locker* and *12 Years a Slave* while *The Dark Knight* failed to be nominated for Best Picture at all. The expansion of the Best Picture category to a maximum of ten nominees was an attempt to address this, but the glass ceiling wasn't even cracked.

To some extent, Ordesky feels it was the grand gesture of greenlighting three films simultaneously that was being recognized — the boldness and ambition of that. 'The Academy responds to those kinds of things,' he points out.

The victory of *The Return of the King* — and by extension the trilogy as a whole — was not a victory for genre, it was about a singular piece of filmmaking, a one-off in three parts. Sweeping all eleven awards for which it was nominated, a record total shared only with *Ben-Hur* and *Titanic*, *The Return of the King* had carved its place into Hollywood history. The truth however was that this was the tale of the collective achievement of an idiosyncratic team of New Zealanders (and adopted sons and daughters) working beyond the walls of that tradition, and who stole into Hollywood and took away their precious gold.

'I'll tell you the coolest thing about the Oscars,' says Taylor, eyes agleam, always keen to see the bigger picture. 'People say to you, "How fantastic, it must be so amazing to be at the Oscars." It was, but being from another culture, which isn't totally immersed in the culture of the Oscars, you can sort of rationalize out what they are. It is very hard to pay a New Zealander a compliment. Coming home from the Oscars finally solidified for my team that they could stand up and be proud that we weren't the poor cousins down in New Zealand.'

'I can't believe how that night went,' reflects Jackson. 'It was embarrassing.'

*

With the epic running time of the Academy Awards finally complete, and already starting to feel like a dream, Jackson and his coterie of winners did the unthinkable. They circumvented the rigmarole of the grand Hollywood balls, although McKellen did a turn around the celeb-heavy *Vanity Fair* bash, and headed in the opposite direction. *Theonering.net*, that epicentre of the *Lord of the Rings* fan community, had hired the American Legion on Highland Avenue, within screaming distance of the Kodak for The Return of the One Party, adding a Gondorian beacon to the roof for the occasion.

The dress code was black tie, but with provision for Renaissance gowns and pointy ears. The fans almost crashed the website trying to get hold of the 1,200 $125 tickets (they ended up going for $7,100 on eBay) and had flown in from as far afield as Europe and, yes, New Zealand. Drinks were served at the *Green Dragon*, while a circus troupe entertained guests parodying the musical *Chicago*, which had absurdly beaten *The Two Towers* to Best Picture the year before. They watched the ceremony on a giant video screen, cheering every victory from Best Editing to Best Picture, streamers bursting forth from cannons when Jackson took Best Director.

Several drunken hours later, when the award-winning director, Walsh and Boyens, and all the other winners stepped out onto the stage and hoisted their Oscars it was as if Elvis had entered the building. They didn't linger long, they would have been mobbed, but the gesture was powerful — Jackson had shaken off the Hollywood crowd to greet the fans in person.

He was talked out, but still standing, and thanked the room for the support they had given them over the years. 'And you didn't give us too much shit when we cut Tom Bombadil out,' he said, delivering the perfectly timed in-joke. After which Dominic Monaghan took his chance to do a rendition of Oasis' Supersonic with the house band.

There was still time to do the politic thing and stop in at the New Line gathering at the Pacific Design Centre, where some of the cast had already gathered and Shaye and Lynne toured the room like lords of the manor.

Finally they ended up back at the Four Seasons. Just the inner circle, plus family: those who knew what it was to climb mountains for these films. All the Oscars were laid out on a table like the gold soldiers from those MASSIVE test runs, their human details yet to be rendered. At last they could exhale.

'You know, that felt like the true end of the road,' says Wood. 'There was no going back to New Zealand for pick-ups. The movies were done. They had won Oscars. And that was the last celebration as a group of people who had spent so much time together. It was special to sort of have like one last defining moment together in that context.'

A few weeks later, amid the satisfaction and relief at New Line, Schwartz and his team decided they needed to memorialize the moment. They alighted on the idea of making a dozen commemorative rings, in the style of the chunky, signet-style Super Bowl rings.

Ordesky, at least, could see the irony. 'It was pretty funny that this was a series of films about the dangers of rings, and that is how it was acknowledged.'

CHAPTER 17

Legacy of the Ring

Who knows, maybe deep in the Warner Bros. vault there is a dusty ledger emblazoned with the New Line logo that gives a full account of all the money made from the *Lord of the Rings* films. Such, though, is the elusive nature of Hollywood accounting that it remains impossible to satisfactorily quantify their financial success. Even Peter Jackson would find himself attempting to grasp smoke when he sought to clarify his share of the profits.

And they were vast.

Put it this way. Following the cinema run of *The Fellowship of the Ring* alone, the entire trilogy was already in the black. The two sequels only needed to turn up. Not that the second and third films weren't pursued for every cent they could muster.

Working with ballpark figures, Ken Kamins estimates that the films grossed nearly three billion dollars at the box office. 'At a total cost of, I don't know, four hundred million dollars. . . I mean, just do the math, that's monumental. It was a huge win.'

As accurately as public records allow, the three films made a collective total of $2,917,507,206 at the theatrical box office, based on a production budget which, according to Mark Ordesky, 'ended up somewhere in the mid-threes: three-fifty to three-seventy million'. With the various individual distribution outlets around the globe funding their own campaigns, an overall marketing and publicity spend is also the subject of guesswork. The Hollywood rule-of-thumb is that marketing costs tend to amount to fifty percent of the production budget, which would put it at a total of $175–85 million.

Using this rough estimation, the overall outlay on the trilogy was in the vicinity of $555 million, which gives us a profit margin of $2,362,507,206. Which doesn't begin to account for the home entertainment and television revenues, which were copious, offset only slightly by the fact that the *Extended Editions* had their own budget enhancements for new score and visual effects. 'Nothing was done as a half measure,' says Jackson, and they remain among the most successful DVD releases of all time.

'Look, every part of the enterprise was successful,' reasons Kamins intently. 'They were profitable just off of theatrical. Home entertainment was at its height in terms of the revenue it was generating. And, because of that, Peter also had the freedom to do a whole bunch of behind-the-scenes and extended cuts — things that studios would not spend the money on today. We really were able to take advantage of the salad days of the home entertainment business. Merchandising for film one was not very successful. Because you have to make commitments before anyone knows whether the films were going to be successful. By film two, the merchandising was very successful.'

The array of toys, games and branded products that ulti-mately followed in the wake of the trilogy adhered to a typically blockbuster-like saturation. Suffice to say, such 'merch' ranged from full-sized replicas of swords like Glamdring or Narsil to the action figures *de rigeur* with any science fiction or fantasy franchise. During principal photography, when freed up from acting, cast-members would be sent off in costume for promo-tional shoots and to be digitally scanned for the toy companies. Viggo Mortensen refused to ever set eyes upon his three-inch clone.

'As long as it doesn't look like me,' he had quipped in 2004, 'then there's no voodoo risk.'

Of note is Weta Workshop's successful venture into commercial waters with a range of collectible merchandise. Inspired by Jackson and Richard Taylor's love of movie-related model kits and an appreciation that the talents of their sculptors was worth immortalizing, with the help of New Line's licensing department and an introduction by Gino Acevedo, a joint venture was launched with American company Sideshow Toys Inc. Beginning with a 1/6th scale statue of Saruman communing with the Palantír, a still-expanding range of stunning collectible artworks (statues of characters, creatures, buildings, as well as full-scale replicas of weapons and armour) was launched, designed by the very sculptors who worked on maquettes for the films.

A venture into branded online slot machines (think Frodos and Bag Ends instead of cherries and bars) was less well conceived. Deemed beyond the original contractual bounds of Tolkien's deal with United Artists by the Tolkien Estate, a legal dispute ensued with Warner Bros. (who countersued dizzyingly over a loss of earnings thanks to the Estate's initial suit). This was finally resolved 'amicably' in 2017. The larger significance being the announcement that the parties 'look forward to working together in the future'...

Despite a surge in book sales,* the Estate remained indifferent to the films' success. Agreeing to a rare interview in the French newspaper *Le Monde* in 2012, Christopher Tolkien dismissed the films as belittling his father's work. 'The chasm between the beauty and seriousness of the work and what it has become has overwhelmed me. The commercialisation has reduced the aesthetic and philosophical impact of the creation to nothing. There is only one solution for me: to turn my head away.'

It reads as an opinion formulated solely on the marketing on

---

* Over the course of the three films' release more than two million copies of the film tie-in edition were sold in the USA alone.

the films, but Jackson is philosophical. 'I'm not sure if he has seen the films, which is entirely fair.'

Interviewed that same year, Simon Tolkien, Christopher's son, was upfront about how nothing could prepare his family for the renewed attention that followed the films' release. It was like being 'hit by a juggernaut', he said. He spoke of feeling 'suffocated' at suddenly being seen only as 'J.R.R. Tolkien's grandson'.

Whereas Royd Tolkien, Simon's nephew and J.R.R. Tolkien's great-grandson, embraced the films' success and the attendant fame, even taking a cameo and regularly attending premieres.

The financial legacy for New Line was hugely significant. The revenue stream of the whole trilogy continued to flow for a good two or three years in a meaningful way, enriching their bottom line. 'The gift that kept on giving,' jokes Ordesky. 'And within the Time Warner corporate structure it gave New Line a fresh lease of life for the next five years.'

Internally, all those involved were blessed with the fruits of their success. Following *The Return of the King*, Ordesky and all the senior management were given a five-year contract. 'There was also the assumption that we would be making *The Hobbit* in some short order,' he says. 'It did maintain our ability to perform as an independent company within a larger corporate sphere.'

The sheer longevity of the production had allowed profits from the released films to be ploughed back into the trilogy while they were still being made. This came in the shape of increased special effects, supplementary shooting and most visibly the luxury of the aforementioned *Extended Editions*.

These were not Director's Cuts, the chance to correct the sins of the past. No, these were gifts for the fans that included excised scenes that would bring the films closer to the books. Mortensen for one was very public in his endorsement of these more luxuriant variations. 'It's personal taste,' he says. 'I personally like the extended version of the first movie because it was less computer generated, had more scenes one-on-one and [there were] fewer liberties taken, let's say — that happens to be my preference. It still had the spirit of Tolkien, they had that nailed down all the way — it's just my preference in the way I read him and I feel like the first one was more representative.'

He wasn't alone. The *Extended Editions* have become widely accepted as the definitive versions even though as we've seen Jackson still swears by the relatively pacier theatrical cuts. Once you have indulged in the lengthier cuts, it becomes harder to return to the theatrical versions without feeling something is missing: the gift giving in Lothlórien, the screaming of the fleeing Uruk-hai as the Huorns gather to finish them off after Helm's Deep, the Houses of Healing, all iconic moments from the book.

The reinsertion of Christopher Lee's death scene into *The Return of the King* certainly rounds out the storytelling.

As Ordesky notes, 'If you were to pitch *The Lord of the Rings* today, you might be thinking of a television show. Although, I'm not sure Peter would ever agree to that. He is devoted to cinema.'

More than any other director, Jackson has established a distinction between the experience of watching his epics at the cinema and among the comforts of home. 'Where you can stop to make a cup of tea,' he laughs — tea being an absolute priority. For many, the longer versions feel better paced, deeper and more complete, more at ease with the vastness of Tolkien. *The Two Towers* especially gains a much better rhythm and cohesion. As Mortensen suggested, the performances gain depth and texture.

Open-minded and generous, Jackson packed these special editions full of commentaries and documentaries, peeling open the production far beyond what any DVD usually regards as thorough. It's the geek in him; he simply wanted to create special editions for his fourteen-year-old self.

'Maybe I'll release the ultimate *ultimate* edition for the fiftieth anniversary,' he jokes, but you can tell the idea intrigues him.

There remains unused footage. Scenes that wouldn't necessarily change the narrative (as so much of the Arwen footage would require) but extend yet further what was already there.

Or even simply going back and fixing Gollum in the first film to fit in with the finished guise.

'Perhaps we should have done,' muses Serkis. 'I think Pete's thought about it.'

He has: 'The trouble is, once you start doing that, the CG technology will have advanced and Weta Digital will want to replace every Gollum shot, indeed every FX shot in the entire trilogy.'

*

For Jackson there was simply no stopping. *King Kong* had been officially greenlit on 30 March 2003, and the writing trio were deep into a new script even before *The Return of the King* was finished. The film began production on 10 September 2004.

Says Ordesky, 'Someone once told me there is no convenient time to be pregnant — whenever you do it was going to be challenging. *King Kong* was so precious to Peter that if that was the time to do it, he would do it.'

'It was essentially a fourth *Lord of the Rings* movie in terms of the scale,' says Jackson. But there was no way he could say no. Not only did this represent his childhood dreams. Everyone knows how the 1933 *King Kong* was the film that set his coals burning. But he wanted to make up for the disappointment of that fourteen-year-old who had caught the first train from Pukerua Bay for the 1976 remake.

King Kong was also unfinished business.

Universal's hierarchy had flown down to New Zealand to meet Jackson in 2001, but negotiations hadn't begun until the November just before *The Two Towers* came out. Kamins wanted to wait until Jackson had enough breathing space to even consider a world beyond Middle-earth.

That was hard for the studio to hear. 'They thought this was a kind of game we were playing, but we weren't. I think we started negotiating that deal in November and we finished in, like, February 2002 for it to be the movie that he would do immediately after *Return of the King*.'

Perplexed as to how to approach a director immersed in creating three films back to back, even after the success of *The Fellowship of the Ring*, the studio offers hadn't come flooding in.

Says Kamins, 'There was a lot of "is he interested in books? Is he interested in scripts?" People were trying to kick the tires, trying to get a feel for "how do you engage with him? What's interesting to him? What's not interesting to him?" People were starting to get educated. But no, the phone was not ringing off the hook, because people didn't want to wait two years. Studios are machines, and they have to be fed. The second you start spending money, there's an expectation that within no more than maybe a year, maybe eighteen months, you will start to see a return. They didn't really want to wait. They were like, "We'll call in 2003." But by then it was too late. Universal had planted their flag.'

I visited the set of *King Kong*. The great gates of Skull Island had been erected on the versatile Mount Victoria, and poor Naomi Watts, as Ann Darrow, was dragged along by a tribe of native extras while being soaked by rain machines. Kong, of course, being motion-captured by Andy Serkis elsewhere, was unavailable for comment.

Taylor has no doubt Skull Island benefited from following Middle-earth. 'Peter would have done an astounding job in 1996, but I felt more prepared to do *King Kong* justice. Just as we tackled Tolkien as a piece of British literature worthy of a great amount of investment and focus, we appreciated that this was an American cultural icon.'

If overlong and less tonally consistent, *King Kong* tells its own story of artistic success (Serkis' animalistic Kong is movingly done, the backdrop often breathtaking), box office rewards and the consolidation of Jackson's reputation as the builder of worlds.

Jackson confesses he caught *King Kong* by chance recently on a hotel television. 'We were in LA and I switched the channels and it was on, and I just watched a little bit of it, then I watched a bit more. . . I wanted to recut that film so badly; it should have been half an hour shorter.'

With post-production squeezed to hit the release date it had been hard to be objective.

'I actually sent Universal a note, "If you ever want to do a 20th anniversary version, DVD or blu-ray, then I'll give you a shorter cut." But I actually think the last half-hour — those scenes in New York through the end of the Empire State Building sequence — is probably the piece of filmmaking of which I'm the proudest.'

Where *King Kong* felt like the natural successor to Tolkien, a spectacular itch Jackson needed to scratch, adapting Alice Sebold's *The Lovely Bones,* an unflinching bestseller about a murdered teenage girl who narrates her tale from beyond the grave, harkened to the sensibility of *Heavenly Creatures* and parts of *The Frighteners*. It was also a statement that Jackson, Walsh and Boyens — the creative holy trinity now set in stone — weren't chained to the spectacular. Nor was *The Lovely Bones* exactly a chamber piece.

Particularly challenging was how to depict heaven, or at least the purgatorial 'inbetween' realm to which Suzie (Saoirse Ronan) is confined until her killer is unmasked. Taking their gifts in a new direction (although there are hints of the Grey Havens), with the aid of Alan Lee's designs, Weta Digital spun surreal, sweetshop hued, *Alice in Wonderland* visions of mad topiary, lighthouses, gazebos, cornfields, butterflies (in homage to *Heavenly Creatures*) and vast evocations of girlhood knickknacks. Not unsuccessfully, it was like a caramelized Middle-earth.

On a budget of $65 million it was a smaller film, but a shoot that had its own teething troubles. Ryan Gosling, who ironically felt he was too young for the part, left late on to be replaced by Mark Wahlberg, and Jackson found filming on location in Pennsylvania, where the book is set, frustrating. This remains his only foray outside of his homeland, if you discount the scenes shot with the elderly Ian Holm and Christopher Lee at Pinewood for *The Hobbit*.

The film was delayed by a year, ostensibly to position it in Awards season, and having been given an early glimpse of

Avatar, Jackson had Paramount push the release back a further month, keenly aware the science fiction spectacular was about to suck 'all the oxygen' out of the box office.

Lukewarm reviews wondered at a confused intent. Moving away from the novel's darker textures to maintain a younger female audience, Jackson controversially omitted Suzie's rape and cut her mother, Abigail (Rachel Weisz)'s affair with the detective. Nothing could stop it being smothered by the phenomenon of *Avatar* whose (not altogether dissimilar) heavenly visions had been cooked up under the same roof. It made $93 million worldwide.

On 28 April 2010, Jackson officially joined ranks with Sirs Ian Holm and Ian McKellen. To be exact, he was made a Knight Companion of the New Zealand Order of Merit at a ceremony (if not quite a coronation) in Wellington for services to the arts.

*

Ordesky had got to know Saul Zaentz over the years of *Lord of the Rings* production. They first met in 1999, and he would catch up with the veteran film producer once a year, spending, as he put it, a fair bit of time with him. Something he felt was a privilege, having once sent Zaentz a letter he never answered in 1988.

'*One Flew Over the Cuckoo's Nest* is still one of my top five films of all time.'

Ordesky admired Zaentz's ability to navigate Hollywood on his own terms, how he didn't shy from a fight; another maverick like Bob Shaye. Zaentz would produce one more film, Milos Foreman's biopic *Goya's Ghosts* with Javier Bardem, before passing away on 3 January 2014 at the age of 92 on what would have been Tolkien's 122nd birthday.

Before an ignominious fall from grace, Harvey, along with Bob Weinstein, would have their hits and misses, fighting their fights. Significantly, they would depart Miramax and the clutches of Disney in 2005 to set up The Weinstein Company, maintaining close and productive ties with Quentin Tarantino and returning to Oscar glory in 2010 with *The King's Speech*. With the exception of Terry Gilliam's troubled 2005 fairy-tale remix *The Brothers Grimm*, they gave fantasy a wide berth. Not that they didn't do awfully well out of *The Hobbit*, thanks to the fine print of the deal struck with New Line, much to Warner Bros.' chagrin.

Kamins claims it was the success of the films that inspired him to set up his own management company. 'I'd been in the agency business for eleven years. But I had been affected greatly by watching Peter's spirit of entrepreneurism. You come to understand how big agencies work and you want to break free of that.'

He didn't want an untenable roster of clients and eight-hour staff meetings. He wanted to be immediately available to his chosen few, chief of whom, the Ringbearer if you will, remained of course Peter Jackson. Naturally, Key Creatives L.L.C. also looks after Walsh and Boyens, as well the directors Paul W.S. Anderson and Christopher McQuarrie.

As the world embraced Jackson's interpretation of Tolkien, this fixed the image of Wood as Frodo, Mortensen as Aragorn, et al for evermore. No trilogy had so profound an effect on cinemagoers since the original *Star Wars* films. But as the cast of *Star Wars* could tell their modern counterparts, the lightsaber cuts both ways. Ask Mark Hamill, the erstwhile Luke Skywalker. The actors of the Fellowship will never be able to fully shake their connection to their roles. The imprint of Middle-earth, like their tattoos, was permanent.

'I made my peace with that a long, long time ago,' says Wood. 'It has never irritated me. It would be a shame if I were irritated by it, because it really truly is in reference to one of the greatest gifts of my life. But it will be with me forever.'

Careers have waxed and waned. Wood and Astin found solid work in films and television but nothing to the same level or acclaim, Monaghan landed a role in pioneering television show *Lost* (one of the heralds of the new television age), but out of the younger Fellowship, it was only Bloom who experienced a sudden rush of leading roles in the epics bankrolled in light of the trilogy's achievement: Will Turner in the *Pirates of the Caribbean* films, Paris in *Troy*, which also featured Sean Bean as Odysseus, and Balian in *Kingdom of Heaven*. His celebrity soared, with gossip magazines picking over his love life, but it is an aftereffect that has tapered off as Hollywood's infatuation cooled.

The older members of Fellowship resumed decent careers where they had left off. McKellen settled back contentedly into a rhythm of stage and film work, pausing between Beckett and Shakespeare to return to Magneto and the *X-Men* films, or dip into the mystifying popularity of Dan Brown's art history conspiracies in Ron Howard's wan adaptation of *The Da Vinci Code*.

John Rhys-Davies resumed his mix of voice-work and a belt of a B-movie fantasy films that traded as much as they could in his Gimli credentials (even if he was unrecognizable without the prosthetics).

Instantly bankable, Mortensen had no interest in being categorized as a Hollywood leading man, flatly refusing to capitalize on his status in any way other than that which suited him. Ever since, he has shunned the call of the blockbuster and sought out unusual, often valuable work. He fostered a decent partnership with David Cronenberg for two distinctive, Howard Shore-scored thrillers, *A History of Violence* and *Eastern Promises*, and boldly ventured into deep arthouse — on surreal Argentinian Western *Jauja* he would star, produce, score and correct the subtitles in French, Spanish and English. All of which was an extension of those qualities that he brought with him to New Zealand — the consummate outsider.

'There's no plan to what I do beyond finding movies people might still like in ten years,' he said in 2016.

On the set of post-apocalyptic drama *The Road* in 2008, adapted from the Cormac McCarthy novel, I spent a strange hour chatting to a fully costumed Mortensen by the roadside. It crossed my mind that passing cars must have thought I was deep in conversation with a hobo.

*

Andy Serkis made sure he saved his very first leotard. Stained with the good earth of New Zealand, he didn't want a memento so much as a reminder of the journey of Gollum. That besmirched bodysuit that once set his director giggling like a schoolboy transformed his career. And his career has transformed an industry. No single element of *The Lord of the Rings* has had such a perceptible effect on filmmaking at large than the creation of Gollum through motion capture.

James Cameron may have dreamed of Pandora and its sky-blue feline race of Na'vi years before, but it wasn't until he witnessed Gollum that he saw that *Avatar* was possible.

Speaking in 2009, the director admitted that it was Jackson and Weta creating Gollum that had 'demonstrated to me that, technologically, it could be done'. *Avatar*, he went on to say, would go quite significantly beyond what had been achieved with Gollum, and truly capture the facial performance of the actors, but he went straight to Weta Digital and bought himself a 2,500 acre farm in Wairarapa in order to realize his dreams.

Says Ordesky, 'I suppose someone else could have done the visual effects of *Avatar*, but Cameron came looking for Weta's world-beating legacy.'

Cameron and Jackson have since become close compatriots, two filmmakers determined to be masters of their own destiny.

Avatar, says Letteri, set them on a new course. 'We did a complete refurbishment of all of our software and all of our hardware because that show was so vast. By the time we did *The Hobbit* we had a new foundation laid for world building. . .'

At the time of writing, Weta Digital is the engine room of a fleet of *Avatar* sequels, which Letteri promises will set about 'expanding the language of cinema'.

'Motion capture is a new genre of acting, and will become more and more mainstream,' Serkis predicted to me at the time of *The Return of the King*. He has carried on pursuing the possibilities of motion capture, determined this wasn't simply a technological process but an artform. Little did he know how it would come to dominate his career.

Serkis is now synonymous with the process: King Kong; Caesar, the sentient chimp in the revived *Planet of the Apes* franchise; Captain Haddock in *The Adventures of Tintin*; and Supreme Leader Snoke in the revived *Star Wars* movies *The Force Awakens* and *The Last Jedi*.

In 2011, he founded the Imaginarium at Ealing Studios in London, a state-of-the-art motion capture studio helping to create features and video games, even theatrical productions. At first sight, it is not so different from that old, unventilated warehouse in Miramar, with a bank of desks down one side, burdened with monitors. The picture, however, is deceptive. Fifty mo-cap cameras like the beady red eye of Sauron are rigged around the walls of the gym-sized space and a large HD monitor instantly relays back protean versions of the actors' performances.

Serkis likes to call it a lab. The variety of size and appearance of a character that an actor can play limited only by the imagination. The facility, this child of Gollum, has been used to create the Hulk, and Serkis has worked not only with Weta but ILM and other effects houses.

In 2015, Serkis parlayed his experience shooting second-unit on *The Hobbit* films (another of Jackson's protégés) into directing an adaptation of Rudyard Kipling's *Jungle Book* for Warner Bros., bending the performances of old allies such as Cate Blanchett and Benedict Cumberbatch into the bodies of snakes and wolves.

'I could never have foreseen where that role has taken me,' marvels Serkis, but his relationship with Gollum will always be complicated. 'It was clearly a life-changing and liberating experience, which opened up this whole other avenue of exploration. Pete is such a visionary in just breaking barriers all the time — this marriage of technology and artistry.'

Nevertheless, he has had to make his peace with the fact that every single day of his life people come up to him and want to talk about Gollum, or he will hear the name shouted in the street, or he'll be asked to do the voice. He tries not to give in, unless it's kids or chatshow hosts cajoling him into an impression on live television.

Gollum has become iconic, fixed into the firmament of not only movie history but pop culture at large, parodied and impersonated ad infinitum. He is a gag, a symbol of wheedling evil, ugliness and decline. He has even been blessed with that true signifier of cultural heritage — a cameo on *The Simpsons*.

'I was working on something and a driver said to me, "God, it must be really awful for you because you're never going to be able to escape that." And this is relatively soon after *Lord of the Rings*. I hadn't even considered that. I thought what is he talking about? Not that it's all downhill, but how do you live up to that? I'm going to hopefully do lots of other interesting, exciting things. I have done wonderful things. But the character will follow me to my grave. It will. I'm very proud of the work. It has been such a massive part of my life. And continues to be. I'm sure this is true for most of the cast. But when people go down the street and they see me, there's a sort of mystery, because I don't look anything like the character and yet I do. . . And people are wonderful. They're genuinely appreciative. Which is kind of wonderful really. It doesn't really have downsides, other than it's part of my life every single day. There isn't a day when Louie, my little boy, hasn't had to take a picture of me with someone else. My kids have grown up with that. But Gollum has also transformed my career in ways I could never have imagined.'

*

Jackson's desire to build a full soup-to-nuts filmmaking set-up in Miramar had moved significantly closer to fruition. *The Lord of the Rings* awoke the outside world to their facilities and, furthermore, the calibre of the work. In special and visual effects terms, the two divisions of Weta were now multiple Oscar-winners and represented a viable alternative to ILM and Digital Domain.

'They are getting toward the point where they could stand on their own,' says Jackson. 'I wouldn't have to provide them with work, which is really where we wanted to be.'

Weta Digital worked on *iRobot*, *The Day the Earth Stood Still*, *X-Men: First Class*, *The Planet of the Apes* films and the monumentality of *Avatar*. Like a hive version of Moore's Law, the company has spread all across Miramar, covering eight different sites.

Weta Workshop followed suit, drawing in work from outside the family — practical props for *Avatar*, *District 9*, *Elysium* and *The Great Wall* — expanding into other areas such as the aforementioned collectibles (they even do guided tours of the Workshop), working towards self-sufficiency.

Jackson has ploughed his success back into the facilities in Miramar: not only the Weta brethren, but film equipment hire unit Portsmouth Rentals and Park Road Post with its edit suites and sound editing studios. Films such as *Krampus*, *Pete's Dragon* and *Ghost in the Shell* have made use of the stages at Stone Street.

'It's safe to say people in Hollywood could now find New Zealand on a map,' laughs Ordesky, but he is only half-joking. More than Middle-earth, New Zealand became fashionable. This compact duet of islands offered a highly versatile landscape, excellent facilities and great karma.

Large-scale fantasy productions were inevitably first through the door. Roland Emmerich's flabby caveman epic *10,000 BC*, and the inevitably fast-tracked adaptation of C.S. Lewis' *The Chronicles of Narnia* series (the first two of which were directed by Weta Digital veteran Andrew Adamson) partook of New Zealand loveliness.

Whether he was looking for it or not, Jackson had now become a father figure to his nation's film industry. Another irony the size of Mount Cook, he would reflect, given how many years he had struggled as an outsider of the establishment. In June 2011 a Hollywood-like sign was erected on a hillside by the airport — 'WELLYWOOD'.

In 2012, during principal photography on *The Hobbit*, it was estimated that screen industry in New Zealand was worth NZ$3 billion, supporting 2,700 different businesses.

For the New Zealand Film Commission the challenge has been to capitalize on the sudden influx of attention for the nation as a whole. And importantly not be dependent on Jackson. They are keen to promote the varied landscapes of North and South Islands as capable of far more than representing a pre-industrial northern Europe. Keen to suggest the country's filmmaking potential isn't solely represented by Miramar.

Herein there is also a mission to make sure the self-deprecating Kiwi nature not stand in the way of progress. They needed to move on from the charming talk of homemade movies and No. 8 thinking, and extol the virtues of a state-of-the-art film community, offering favourable tax incentives. In the years since, a steady stream of international productions have arrived: *The Last Samurai*, *30 Days of Night*, *The Light Between the Oceans* and *Mission Impossible 6*, to name but a few.

Tourism soared by as much as fifty per cent. Fans came in search of Middle-earth, and were not disappointed. Air New Zealand famously covered its 777s with hobbit faces and dragon wings. When you land at Wellington, a sign reads 'Welcome to Middle-earth'. There are a multitude of tours that allowed the devoted to follow in the Fellowship's footsteps.

All told, Jackson's determination has led to a hugely significant boost to the New Zealand economy.

The now 4.4 million people of New Zealand have collectively embraced Middle-earth. Some, like the Alexanders at Matamata with their permanent Hobbiton, have directly prospered. Then there are simply those, like the weather reporter on the release of *The Hobbit: An Unexpected Journey*, who gave their forecast entirely in Elvish.

Back in sun-soaked Los Angeles, studio minions were found elbowing nerds aside in the dash for the science fiction and fantasy shelves at bookshops. They also delved deep into their own back catalogues for dormant remake possibilities. Fantasy was promptly flogged to death. Potential franchises withered on the branch, lacking vision, the proper preparation or worthy source material.

Even the briefest of surveys gives you *Clash of the Titans*, *Jack the Giant Slayer* (which utilized Weta), a soggy remake of *Conan the Barbarian, Eragon, Prince of Persia*, the *Percy Jackson* films, and *The Sorcerer's Apprentice*. The *Pirates of the Caribbean* films with Bloom cutting another dash, while *The Last Airbender* utilized Andrew Lesnie as cinematographer.

New Line, as we'll see, strained to uphold a reputation as purveyors of sophisticated fantasy.

There were successes, but a litany of hollow spectacles only served to confirm the exceptionality of Middle-earth (mirroring what happened in publishing with Tolkien's mythological renderings cheapened by a thousand copycat Gandalfs).

The most telling comparison can be made with *Game of Thrones*.

Far lustier, more exuberantly violent and set against an amoral canvas of families feuding over the throne of Westeros, there is still no doubt that *Game of Thrones* stood on the shoulders of *The Lord of the Rings* to become a television phenomenon. In many respects it was the heir apparent.

For all the praise rightfully lavished upon this adaptation of the *A Song of Ice and Fire* saga, for its alt-Tolkien array of street smarts, shagging, political brinkmanship and a postmodern willingness to slaughter name characters, author George R.R. Martin proudly owned up to his chief inspiration. He even modelled his nomenclature upon his hero, and while his story told a wildly different story — Westeros was inspired by the War of the Roses-era England and set about dismantling classical myths — he nevertheless drew deeply upon Tolkien. Martin admitted to actor John Bradley, who plays the good-hearted Samwell Tarly, that his character was 'very influenced by Sam Gamgee'.

Moreover, the showrunners would have been conscious that

Bean's casting as ill-fated patriarch Ned Stark carried with it a bold resonance. Indeed, one season of *Game of Thrones* crystallized Bean's iconic status in the ranks of fantasy, as if Ned Stark was the older, wiser Boromir we never got to see.

Incidentally, Bean's propensity for losing his mortal coil on screen has reached the level of cultural meme. He has perished more than twenty-two times in film and television: shot, impaled, stabbed, throat-slit, strangled by chains, beheaded, blown up, bayonetted, quartered by horses, dropped out of a helicopter (which may account for a lot) and chased off a cliff by sheep. Questioned about his fictional unlucky streak, Bean professed that his favourite demise remains Boromir's redemptive sacrifice.

Sidestepping the copious nudity, stylistically Westeros adopts much of the blueprint set down by Jackson's juxtaposition of grimy realism with architectural splendour. Northern Ireland, where production for the series is based, was soon dubbed the new New Zealand. To my mind, though, *Game of Thrones* lacks the virtuoso touch of *The Lord of the Rings*. It is cinematic but it isn't cinema. It is burdened with television's (and to an extent Martin's) circularity. Stories and characters are trapped, often interminably, in holding patterns like planes waiting to land.

Even after a landmark Oscar victory for a genre film — proof that entertainment and art can mix under one corrugated roof — there was no great sea change the way studios approached blockbuster scale filmmaking.

'I am not sure Hollywood changes much,' mulls Jackson. 'When you talk about how *Jaws* and *Star Wars* created a franchise mentality in Hollywood that still exists, the only thing that *Lord of the Rings* did is promote the idea of backing a filmmaker on that level. Warner Bros. still does with Christopher Nolan on *Batman*, but even that only happens when it happens.'

The comparison with Nolan is interesting. If the likes of Cameron and Spielberg represent an older generation of self-determining filmmaker, Nolan is Jackson's peer. He lent the superhero film a brief jolt of realism with his *Dark Knight* films, and remains solidly his own man.

According to Kamins, the success of these films might have had a more immediate impact in the field of independent, arthouse films. 'In purely economical terms, because the films were funded by and profitable for a whole host of independent distributors, I think it was responsible for the wave of independent film that went through the 2000s, because *Lord of the Rings* was able to pay for a lot of that.' All of the independent distributors who made so much money in their respective territories got to spend that on other independent films. It was a dramatic engine for the independent film business writ large for the 2000s.

An unexpected upshot is a Tolkien biopic. Simply titled *Tolkien* and directed by the Finn, Dome Karukoski, it depicts how both the writer's romance with Edith Bratt and his experiences in World War One led to the creation of Middle-earth.

*

Of course, the most direct legacy of *The Lord of the Rings* triumph was Jackson's trilogy of highly successful and much debated prequels based on *The Hobbit*. Virtually with the opening weekend of *The Return of the King*, to Hollywood minds, Middle-earth now bore all the hallmarks of a franchise, and a readymade prequel lay in wait. If it works, rinse and repeat. Time to get Ian McKellen's beard out of storage.

There certainly had been an immediate keenness on New Line's behalf to start exploring the possibility of a prequel or two in the shape of *The Hobbit*. 'At least as verbally stated,' says Kamins. 'Not to the point of actually moving forward toward a deal or figuring out whether or not they could figure out anything with MGM. But at least at one of the premieres I'm sure Bob Shaye said something like, "Of course, we want to have a conversation about *The Hobbit* at some point."'

Things were far from that simple. Despite the proven success, all the awards and astronomical box office, the journey to *The Hobbit* was more arduously long-winded and booby-trapped than that of *The Lord of the Rings*. This is before you even begin to consider the creative riddle presented by a charming but featherlight book.

Primarily, nothing could be done until the impasse over the rights was resolved.

To recap the legal soup in very basic terms: when Zaentz purchased the rights from United Artists in 1977 to make Ralph Bakshi's animated version of *The Lord of the Rings*, he also gained the rights to make *The Hobbit*. However, as a quirk of the deal UA had retained the rights to *distribute* any film version of *The Hobbit*. When Zaentz sold the rights to make and distribute a version of *The Lord of the Rings* to Miramax, who then gave them up to New Line (which belonged to Warner Bros.), with them went the right to *make The Hobbit*. The rights to distribute *The Hobbit* were now the province of MGM who had bought out the ailing UA in 1981.

In other words, if New Line was going to adapt Bilbo's tale of Dwarves and dragons, they were going to have to cut a deal with MGM.

So Shaye's overtures proved premature. Any negotiations were immediately hampered by MGM's parlous financial state. The studio's fortunes had fluctuated wildly since the late sixties, changing hands and repeatedly asset stripped, leaving them permanently orbiting bankruptcy like a black hole. *The Hobbit* represented a financial Catch 22: MGM were in no position to co-finance such a blockbuster production, but they were also unwilling to let go of one of the few assets currently keeping them from being sucked into that black hole.

Shaye also faced another problem. Jackson needed a break from Middle-earth.

'To some degree it will be a relief to leave these films behind,' he had admitted during pick-ups for *The Return of the King*. 'It will be something to put behind us and just say was done. I am comfortable with the fact my career will in some ways be defined by *The Lord of the Rings* — it will be *The Lord of the Rings* and everything that happens afterwards.'

Even before the final part of the trilogy was released, Jackson began fielding the inevitable question. Did he now want to direct *The Hobbit*? He sounded conflicted. He needed to move on, try other things as a director. He wanted to challenge himself beyond Middle-earth. To find out what kind of director he now was. But he had an emotional ownership of this world to which he had given so much of himself. Middle-earth was now entwined with New Zealand. It was inconceivable *The Hobbit* be shot anywhere else, and without Weta. On some level he would need to be involved. Would he really be content to sit back and watch another filmmaker playing in his own garden?

So in some respects it was a relief that he didn't need to make that decision. Speaking in 2005 with *King Kong*'s release, Jackson's desire to go back remained elusive: 'We haven't been thinking about *The Hobbit* because there's no point getting excited if [New Line and MGM] don't have the rights sorted out.'

Jackson moved on with other projects.

In 2006, he became the linchpin in a huge adaption of the hit Microsoft videogame *Halo*, with he and Walsh producing and the young South African director Neill Blomkamp due to direct on location in New Zealand. Future *Game of Thrones* showrunner D.B. Weiss rewrote a script by author Alex Garland, which had at one stage interested Guillermo del Toro. Weta Workshop had already designed and built armour, weapons and working vehicles for a series of short *Halo* films directed by Blomkamp to promote the latest edition of the game. All was set fair, but Jackson was learning that whatever influence he had gained in Hollywood was relative. Such was the scale of the project, it was to be backed by two studios, Universal and 20th Century Fox. A set-up that ran aground when with production in sight both studios demanded the filmmakers significantly reduce their backend profit participation. And with that, the production fell apart.

Says Kamins, 'That's what sort of forged them all together to create *District 9*.' Based on another Blomkamp short, *Alive in Joburg*, a thinly veiled allegory of his homeland, the hit science-fiction thriller about the brutal oppression of alien visitors was workshopped for a year into a movie. Jackson was clearly interested in mentoring new filmmakers, and it was at this time he began to develop a new version of *The Dambusters* for Christian Rivers to direct, but it failed to secure funding.

For a period, Jackson must have felt cursed. Indeed, any likelihood of *The Hobbit* took a nosedive when his relationship with Shaye and New Line abruptly turned very sour.

The circumstances were not unusual. Jackson and Kamins had sought to do an audit of the New Line accounts for *The Lord of the Rings*. There was nothing accusatory in this, insists Kamins, 'As is the case in most deals, if not all deals where there is a significant backend participant, after a certain period of time the artist has the right to audit the books of the company in question. And we exercised our right to do that.'

There are a handful of significant auditing firms that everybody uses. There is a methodology. They sit across a table. They go over contracts and files and statements, and the auditor brings up how much they might be off and by how much. There's a negotiation. Sometimes it produces no results. Sometimes they meet in the middle. Sometimes there's a discovery of revenue that came in that nobody saw.

'But it's not an assumption of bad will,' iterates Kamins. 'There's just a process.'

However, when their auditor got to New Line's Seventh Avenue offices at his scheduled time in New York they kept him waiting. He sat there all day. The same thing happened the next day.

'He's there almost a week,' says Kamins, 'and they won't show him anything. On the last day they walk in with a box that has maybe four files in it. A movie the size of *The Lord of the Rings* would have many boxes of many files. Every individual territorial distribution agreement, merchandising deals, television deals, storage fees. . . I mean, there would be a litany of agreements.'

The auditing process was inevitably complicated by the cascade of on-going deals that make up New Line's unusual distribution structure. Following the money through so many more entities all over the world added more twists and turns to the labyrinth.

Their auditor remained suspicious. 'They don't want to show you something,' he told them. 'They don't want to show you a *lot* of something.'

As Kamins continues, the story gathering pace, they reached out to find out what was going on, trying to keep their language cordial, respectful of their mutual history. Relations hadn't always been straightforward, but they had come a long way with New Line. 'Essentially the word that got back was "Peter's made enough money". . . We're, like, you don't get to decide whether he's made enough money. Just like we don't get to decide whether you've made enough money. There's no "enough money". He's owed money or he's not owed money. And they got really ornery about it: "If you feel so strongly about it, sue us." At that point, Peter and Fran had never sued anybody in their life. But Peter is a principle guy. It was like, "Look, I'm not saying I'm owed money. Maybe I am, maybe I'm not. But just show me." But they said no.'

In February 2005 they sued, a lawsuit that dragged on for three years.

During this time, Shaye actually returned to directing, and in a fantasy vein. Perhaps he was inspired by the success of *The Lord of the Rings*, or stirred to prove some point to Jackson, or quite possibly himself. Poorly titled, *The Last Mimzy* was a charming if low-key adventure about two children blessed with special powers after discovering a secret box of toys. This will lead them *Alice*-style into a labyrinth to save a poisoned future. Howard Shore provided the score.

Promoting the film's short-lived circuit of the multiplexes (it would make $21 million) in early 2007, Shaye held forth at a press conference as the inevitable question of *The Hobbit* arose. What was the latest?

'I'll tell you what the latest on *The Hobbit* is,' he shot back, his face as unwavering as a gravestone: 'Peter Jackson's not making it. In fact he will never make a movie with New Line while I am working with the company.'

There followed a momentary stunned silence. There had been rumblings of discontent between Jackson and New Line but this was the first time anything had been said publically. Shaye clearly felt slighted.

And he wasn't finished.

'[Jackson's] got a quarter of a billion dollars paid to him so far, justifiably, according to contract, completely right, and this guy turns around without wanting to have a discussion with us and sues us.'

Says Kamins, 'It's clear it's out of a fit of pique over the fact that Peter had the temerity to sue.' And exacerbated by the refusal of several members of *The Lord of the Rings* cast to partake in events to celebrate New Line's 40th anniversary. Evidently, they had sided with Jackson, who had announced that he had 'no choice but to let the idea of a film of *The Hobbit* go and move forward with other projects.' McKellen, for one, expressed how hard it was to imagine returning to Middle-earth without their team-leader.

It was a nightmare for Ordesky personally. For it was to Jackson's old friend New Line management turned to let Jackson's representatives know they were proceeding on *The Hobbit* without him.

'I felt hugely conflicted. I didn't want to make the call. I knew that New Line couldn't be persuaded out of this course of action. The decision had been made. But I knew the call would be hurtful, and I felt disloyal to Peter making it. At the same time,

I was a New Line employee, and my bosses were asking me to do it.'

Reluctantly, he put the call into Kamins, something he describes as unbelievably painful. 'To this day I wish I hadn't, because looking back, that information could have been communicated to Peter another way. I could have said no and kept my integrity. When the news broke the next day, I took a lot of grief.'

Shortly afterwards, Kamins received an invitation to have lunch with the then CEO of MGM, Harry Sloan. 'And Harry's, like, what is all this on *The Hobbit*? Can you walk me through it?'

Sloan revealed that Shaye had contacted him to say he had made a deal with Sam Raimi to direct *The Hobbit*, but things couldn't proceed unless MGM approved the deal. He had heard some bad things about Jackson, and wanted to hear the story from the director's side. With Jackson and Walsh coming to town for the Golden Globes and *King Kong*, they joined Kamins for dinner at Sloan's house where they walked him through the sorry turn of events.

'After that dinner,' reports Kamins, 'Harry calls up Bob and says, "I won't sign off on Sam Raimi. You have a Peter Jackson problem. Fix your Peter Jackson problem."'

The next move came from New Line's head of production, Toby Emmerich, who called Kamins to try and bring about a ceasefire. 'Would Peter be open to a conversation with Bob and Michael?' he asked. 'I think Bob would really like to get on the phone with Peter. I don't think there's anything untoward. I just think this would be a good thing.'

It was vague. But Kamins realized that despite three years of exhausting litigation, Shaye still harboured some feelings for Peter. . . And a desire for a rapprochement. Jackson agreed to the call.

Symbolically, Shaye and New Line were back in Cannes to show twenty-five minutes of their adaptation of *The Golden*

*Compass**. In the intervening years since *The Lord of the Rings* they had attempted to progress from the House that Freddy Built to the House that Frodo Renovated. In other words, they were putting a large portion of their Middle-earth profits toward establishing themselves as Hollywood's fantasy factory.

Says Ordesky, 'My perception was that it was a bit more ad hoc than that. There was definitely the perception that those films both creatively and economically had created this wonderful span of time within the studio, and we were certainly looking to sustain that. *Rings* was at a level you can't expect to replicate, but the idea of sustaining those kinds of global franchises was definitely on the agenda.'

But they couldn't seem to make anything stick.

Having purchased the rights for a seven-figure sum in October 2004, New Line toiled over an adaptation of Susannah Clarke's *Jonathan Strange and Mr Norrell*, the vivid tale of squabbling magicians in a wonderfully soupy alternative nineteenth-century London. They had hired eminent writers, both Christopher Hampton and Julian Fellowes tried to tame the expansive tome, but to no avail.

Jonathan Strange and Mr Norrell was a particular frustration to Ordesky. Following *The Return of the King*, he had negotiated a small discretionary development fund. 'So if there was something I really felt passionate about, I could pursue it at least through the development process,' he explains. When he couldn't get Shaye to share his enthusiasm for the book, he developed it with his discretionary fund.

He sighs. 'That book was a massive undertaking. It needed

---

* Published as *The Northern Lights* in the UK, the first in Philip Pullman's *His Dark Materials* trilogy is set in a parallel version of Tolkien's Oxford, in which human souls exist outside of their bodes as spirit animals known as 'daemons'. When comparisons have been drawn, Pullman has spoken of his books being concerned with 'the death of God' while Tolkien is more trivial: 'Everyone knows where the good is, and what to do about the bad.'

more time to crack than any of us had anticipated, and New Line was already very close to its evolution into New Line 2.0, which was not going to include me.'

The rights would eventually pass to the BBC, where the young British director Toby Haynes turned it into seven episodes of atmospheric television.

The Golden Compass had caught the interest of Ridley Scott and Sam Mendes, but likewise struggled to gain momentum until it was handed to the surprise choice of Chris Weitz, New Line perhaps hoping the juvenile hi-jinks of his *American Pie* franchise might be concealing the same inner David Lean that had been hidden within Jackson's splatter-happy beginnings. The potential was self-evident, here was a story finely balanced between the respective tones of *The Lord of the Rings* and the *Harry Potter* films. However, despite the cast including Daniel Craig and Nicole Kidman and the familiar voice of McKellen as an eloquent polar bear, Ordesky admits many of the more compelling and controversial elements were watered down, and Weitz reveals none of Jackson's command. On a budget of $180 million, its box office of $372 million worldwide was deemed insufficient to warrant a sequel.

'That was predominantly outside the United States,' adds Ordesky, 'which was not particularly helpful in terms of the business side of New Line.

The conference call with Jackson spanned the globe and numerous time zones: Shaye and Michael Lynne were in Cannes, Jackson and Walsh in New Zealand and Kamins was in Los Angeles. Through the static and awkward silence, Jackson's voice came on the line: 'Hey guys, how are you? How's everything going on *The Golden Compass*?'

'And you could almost hear Bob sniffling,' recalls Kamins. 'It was just clear that Bob just needed to hear Peter's voice and the ice started to thaw.'

The tangled webs of Hollywood legal wrangling took another five or six months for a settlement to be reached, during which time Warner Bros. agreed to fully finance the films in return for all distribution rights, with a still-troubled MGM retaining international television rights. Finally, in 2008, came the official announcement that Jackson and Walsh would serve as producers on a two-film version of *The Hobbit*.

Kamins emphasizes the point: 'Not to direct; only to write and be producers.'

*

As *The Hobbit* situation inched toward resolution, the clock had once again begun ticking on the future of New Line. Whatever reprieve *The Lord of the Rings* had granted the unconventional studio, a series of expensive flops and underachievers (including *The Golden Compass*), added to the issues that had metastasized around *The Hobbit,* which put them back under the burning glare of the corporate eye. This time a deal to adapt Tolkien wasn't enough to save them.

On 28 February 2008, four years after that glorious night at the Academy Awards, Shaye got the call from the CEO of Time Warner, Jeff Bewkes, and he knew his time was up. He and Lynne were summoned to an unscheduled meeting at the Time Warner Building; six months of negotiation on how to solve the riddle of New Line's standalone status within Time Warner (itself still stinging from its ill-fated merger with AOL) had come to nothing.

'Coming out of *Lord of the Rings*,' admits Ordesky, 'if you don't have something that is equal scale right there, then it starts to beg questions. So, looking back on it, I think there was a certain degree of inevitability.'

Moreover, at the time, the New Line board was earning more than $20 million a year. They were, by any accounting, top heavy.

Bewkes let them have the bad news: New Line would be subsumed into the company as a production company, releasing films through the traditionally structured distribution network of Warner Bros., with the loss of five hundred staff.

The highs and lows of the film industry couldn't be put in starker contrast. Shaye and Lynne, the great gamblers, were gone. Many of those executives and employees who had worked on *The Lord of the Rings* found themselves out of a job. Gone too was that maverick spirit prepared to back Jackson's crazy ambition. If he made his pitch to New Line as it was now, a thin limb attached to the oak of Warner Bros., it is unlikely he would even have got in the door.

'It was tough to deal with,' admitted Shaye in 2009.

He and Lynne have since formed a new production company, Unique, with an output deal with Warner Bros. and temporarily housed on the floor above the shuttered New Line office on Robertson Avenue — the venue of that famous meeting.

'We got too big,' accepted Shaye, 'and there were too many political dramas going on.' He had allowed himself to become sidelined, more of a cheerleader, unable to implement his 'production desires'. There were those internally who felt his period away making *The Last Mimzy* had left the company without a rudder.

What must have truly galled the former CEO was that Emmerich, another of his protégés, his surrogate sons, had stayed on to run what was left of New Line, and has since been promoted to president at Warner Bros.

Seeking to capture lightning in a bottle once more, Shaye and Unique made another attempt to develop a multi-film adaptation of Isaac Asimov's *Foundation* series, but were outbid for the rights by Sony Pictures and Roland Emmerich.

*

In April 2009, I was once again watching Serkis storming about in a grey leotard inside a warehouse adjacent to the local airport. However, this didn't concern *The Hobbit*. Gollum's alter-ego was ranting and raving in a thick Scottish accent, the warehouse in question was the perfectly soundproofed Giant Studios in Marina del Ray, Los Angeles and Steven Spielberg was hovering at the edge of the soundstage (more accurately 'the volume') holding what looked like a videogame handset but which turned out to be the controller for piloting the virtual camera.

Even for a director of Spielberg's experience this was an unconventional way to make films. *The Adventures of Tintin*, an adaptation of Hergé's cult comic-book hero, was a quasi-animated film hooked on motion-captured performances. Beside Serkis, as belligerent sea-salt Captain Haddock, there was *King Kong*'s Jamie Bell playing the titular intrepid reporter in the full motion capture raiment of sensor-spotted leotard and the new-fangled headgear and dotty fizzog to capture facial expressions. The cast also included incumbent 007 Daniel Craig, as the villainous Sakharine, and Simon Pegg and Nick Frost as the bumbling identikit detectives Thompson and Thomson.

The dormant project had been revived thanks to the friend-ship that had flourished between likeminded directors and mutual Tintin fans Jackson and Spielberg — Spielberg also executive produced *The Lovely Bones* — combined with the ever-increasing capabilities of Weta Digital.*

A direct video link to New Zealand had been set up next to Spielberg's hub of computer terminals, and milling around a sofa-laden office in Miramar like Big Brother contestants were Jackson and Guillermo del Toro. The connection was kept per-manently live for fear of communication disruption (footage is also being piped directly to Weta Digital), and allowed Jackson to simultaneously serve as producer on both *The Adventures of Tintin* and *The Hobbit*, currently deep into preproduction with the Mexican fabulist.

At some point, the pair became aware Los Angeles was watch-ing and commenced goofing around with del Toro peering closer

---

* Spielberg had been developing the adaption since the eighties, and was finally swayed by the proof-of-concept that Jackson had shot to show an ani-mated version of Tintin's quick-witted wire fox terrier, Snowy. Footage in which Jackson played Captain Haddock. If they had taken the live-action route, said Spielberg, he was tempted to cast Jackson in the role.

and closer into the camera until his eyeball filled the entire frame. The effect was quite disconcerting.

Spielberg laughed like a tolerant uncle — those guys.

Any disappointment that Jackson had had his fill of directing Middle-earth and would only write and produce *The Hobbit* had been largely offset with the recruitment of the director of *Pan's Labyrinth* and *Hellboy*.

Even the idlest survey of his career would tell you del Toro was a kindred soul and a fitting replacement. Born in Guadalajara, as a child he had tried his hand at black magic — his mother did Tarot readings — and kept pet snakes, crows and white rats. He described himself as 'morbid', and had picked up English by deciphering the puns in *Famous Monsters of Filmland*.

In high school he made a short film about a monster that clambers out of the toilet. 'An artist unbound by reality,' he wrote in an extended essay on Hitchcock in 1983, 'can create the purest reflection of the world.' By 1985, he had started his own special effects company, Necropia, which made monsters for Mexican B-movies and television, an echo of Weta Workshop.

The comparisons go on. Del Toro is obsessed with myths and folklore. Fittingly, the dragon is his mythological beast of choice. He adores Ray Harryhausen. He has had his struggles with Miramax: on his giant-insects-invade-the-New York Subway horror *Mimic*. According to a *New Yorker* profile in 2012, the studio found him tediously arty. He is an enthusiastic collector, particularly of horror memorabilia, and he once gifted Jackson with a beautiful clockwork automaton featuring the Grim Reaper.

Del Toro is more 'operatic' in style. And much more of a hands-on designer: filling notebooks with marvellous sketches, working his way through a movie by hand.

Says Boyens, 'He's such a masterful filmmaker. And he understands story and film so deeply, so passionately. But he does come at it from a different angle than Peter. He's more of the world of faerie.'

If you ever visit Hobbiton at Matamata, glance over the

left-hand ridge at the top of The Hill (looking outward from Bag End) and you'll spot three isolated hobbit front doors, cut off from the rest. They were specially built for an elaborate shot del Toro had planned for the opening of *The Hobbit* where the camera would zoom in from over a kilometre away, racing across the verdure of the Shire to end up at the front door of Bag End.

Del Toro insisted his *Hobbit* films would exist within the Middle-earth created by Jackson. That was never in question. Boyens remembers del Toro, Jackson, Walsh and herself sitting down in Jackson's Camperdown cinema to watch all three *Lord of the Rings* films when their new director first arrived. 'Fran and I drove them completely crazy. We were sitting at the back like naughty schoolchildren, just talking non-stop, deconstructing them. It must have driven Guillermo completely nuts.'

Did del Toro wonder at how hard it might be for the Three Musketeers to become Four?

He was still determined to make these films his own. Taking on *The Hobbit*, he quipped, was like marrying a widow: 'You have to be respectful of the dead husband but come Saturday night. . . *Bam!*'

His thinking was almost paradoxical. To work within Jackson's world but using his own stylistic tropes. Art director Dan Hennah, who spent months with del Toro, spoke of clockwork as a motif of the Dwarven realm: vast mechanical locks, pipes and engines, the aesthetic of steampunk. Del Toro was going to experiment with sky replacement for a 'painterly effect' — a world more fairy-tale. He wanted to create forests of artificial trees that directly resembled those of Tolkien's illustrations, and keep the Workshop busy making mechanical suits instead of having digital creatures — armour-plated trolls would roll up into balls and skittle into foes. He liked things tactile and present. Thorin would wear a helmet that sprouted thorns.

Without being specific, Jackson had told me there were ideas he retained from his fellow director. He insisted the films still contained 'GDT DNA'.

All was set: once del Toro had begun to direct, and content Middle-earth was in good hands, Jackson could turn his attention onto his own projects. Which at that stage included adapting Philip Reeve's future-set fantasy novel *Mortal Engines* and producing *Halo* for Blomkamp. However, when MGM were forced into yet another financial overhaul to stave off bankruptcy and the start date was put back for a third time, del Toro began to fret he had signed up to a phantom. By December 2010, he had returned to Los Angeles and issued a statement:

'In light of ongoing delays in the setting of a start date for filming *The Hobbit*, I am faced with the hardest decision of my life. After nearly two years of living, breathing and designing a world as rich as Tolkien's Middle-earth, I must, with great regret, take leave from helming these wonderful pictures.'

The Mexican's departure came as a shock. Hollywood was awhirl with rumours: had he and Jackson fallen out? Had his more stylized vision of Middle-earth been a bridge of Khazad-dûm too far? Could it simply be that he had run out of patience?

Whenever pressed on what had gone wrong in New Zealand, del Toro was cagey. 'The visual aspect was under my control,' he insisted. 'There was no interference with that creation.' Nevertheless, he mentioned there had been 'discomfort over his design of Smaug'. Sinewy and snake-like, his dragon had resembled a 'flying axe'. He mourned all the design work he left behind.

Maybe New Zealand didn't suit him. He missed Los Angeles, the balm of surrounding himself with his own collection of esoterica. He admitted he had worried about the physical demands of shooting in remote locations.

Whatever had finally swayed del Toro's heart, Jackson presented the world with the official stance: 'We feel very sad to see Guillermo leave *The Hobbit*, but he has kept us fully in the loop and we understand how the protracted development time on these two films — due to reasons beyond anyone's control — has compromised his commitment to other long-term projects. The bottom line is that Guillermo just didn't feel he could commit six years to living in New Zealand, exclusively making these films, when his original commitment was for three years. Guillermo is one of the most remarkable creative spirits I've ever encountered and it has been a complete joy working with him. . .'

Serkis had met up with del Toro only once. He had been in New Zealand doing pick-ups for *The Adventures of Tintin*. Finished for the day, Jackson had suggested they 'hang out' and he spent an afternoon going over del Toro's designs, gaining an insight into his vision for the two parts of *The Hobbit*. They had discussed about him possibly playing the Great Goblin as well as Gollum.

The actor could see the Mexican's *Hobbit* would have been wildly more operatic. He worried it might have been too big a leap from *The Lord of the Rings*. 'Look, I love Guillermo's films. I think he's a brilliant filmmaker. But to redesign it in such a way that made you feel that there was no continuity? The audience would probably have felt cheated.'

Warner Bros. swiftly announced that this was only a temporary setback and the search for the ideal director had been resumed. No delay in production was anticipated. If any other directors had been sounded out their names have never come to light. For fans it was clear that fate had intervened and the rightful director was right there in front of everyone — he just hadn't accepted the inevitable quite yet.

History was repeating itself. Jackson was again confronted with the agelong issue of both Weta Workshop and Weta Digital being in urgent need of work. Neither strand of Weta had yet become self-sufficient. And they were now bigger and hungrier operations than at the crisis points of the past; in the wake of *Avatar* thousands were now employed in Wellington.

Behind the scenes, Warner Bros. had already spent almost $60 million in development costs on *The Hobbit*, and CEO Alan Horn told Jackson that the only way they could move forward now was if he agreed to direct.

Says Kamins, 'Peter had his reasons not to at that point: he'd done it as well as it could be done. There's no way this was going to generate the same kind of Oscar enthusiasm. He didn't want to see if there was a way to better himself.'

But, out $60 million, Horn was emphatic: he couldn't risk another director coming on and not having it work out, having spent another $5–10 million in development. He would rather eat the $60 million and shut it down unless Jackson considered directing it. It was another ultimatum.

Jackson took three or four weeks to think it over. He really didn't know if he could face it again. He had started orienting himself toward *Mortal Engines* and a set of smaller, homegrown projects he and Walsh were developing. The scripts as they existed were designed as del Toro movies. Did he even have time to go back and retool del Toro's words and pictures to reflect a Peter Jackson film?

'He was really driven by not wanting to let the fans down,' explains Kamins. 'Not wanting to let down all the people in New Zealand working on the films. And not wanting to let Alan and Warner Bros. down for the money they were out of pocket. All of those things contributed to Peter's willingness to step in. And that's how it all ultimately happened.'

'I made my peace with the book,' laughs Jackson.

On 15 October 2010, the *Los Angeles Times* reported that *The Hobbit* films had been greenlit to begin production in January 2011, with Jackson at the helm.

'We're looking forward to re-entering this wondrous world with Gandalf and Bilbo,' read Jackson's official accouncement, 'and our friends at New Line Cinema, Warner Bros. and MGM.'

'There is no human being on the planet as qualified as Peter Jackson to direct these films,' said Warner Bros. President Alan Horn.

New Line Cinema (still the nominal production company) president Toby Emmerich followed up in similar fashion, 'Peter is a filmmaker of incomparable ability; having him return to Middle-earth to produce and direct is a dream come true. A true original, Jackson is a gifted storyteller, visionary director and pioneer in film technology.'

When it was announced that Jackson was going to direct *The Lord of the Rings* trilogy, the news was met with stupefied gasps and general head scratching over who he even was. With the announcement he was to direct *The Hobbit* films it appeared the most obvious thing in the world. He was coming home.

Ordesky couldn't help but have bittersweet feelings at seeing *The Hobbit* finally take shape. He had naturally assumed the day would come when he would work on the Tolkien prequel. However, as New Line was folded into Warner Bros., his contract was expiring and his future, like many of his peers, lay elsewhere. Departing the company, he formed the production house Court Five, whose roster included television show *The Quest*, in which contestants have to negotiate a fantasy world named Everealm. *Variety* called the endearing 'reality' show, 'Quite possibly the nerdiest competition ever televised.'

'I remember thinking to myself: "You are not going to be a part of *The Hobbit*,"' recalls Ordesky. '"Toby Emmerich is going to want to do that." And I was right.'

It was, he admits, heartbreaking to have to email Jackson and Walsh, wishing them the best, knowing he wasn't going to be a part of the adventure this time around. There were no for-old-time's-sake visits to the set. He very consciously maintained his distance. 'So that I didn't create awkwardness for anyone, I decided to keep a low profile.'

Even so, aware of how pivotal he had been to the success of *The Lord of the Rings* and a friendship that stretched back before hobbits and Oscars, Jackson made sure Ordesky and his family were invited to the premieres in Los Angeles and Wellington. In turn, Ordesky lapped up the chance to simply be a Jackson-Tolkien fan again. To arrive not having read the scripts, not having endured the stresses of their creation, was a strange, new pleasure.

He smiles. 'Apart from being glad that the films got made, and

Peter got to make them, I did feel a certain amount of pleasure that it is complete. I have no idea if there will be further Tolkien films, but I don't think so. . . But never say never.'

Funnily enough, for Hobbit Day in 2012, Ordesky was asked to read his favourite section of *The Hobbit* on video.* He went back through the book — an edition gifted to him by Tolkien's great-grandson Royd — and landed upon the chapter, 'A Thief in the Night', where Bilbo betrays Thorin, the head of the company, for his own good and to essentially broker a peace between impossibly conflicted parties.

'I realized that was me: "They say I am the burglar, but I am not sure I am a particularly good one. . ." That is my own metaphor for how I played my role in *The Lord of the Rings*.'

---

* Hobbit Day is celebrated on September 22, the shared fictional birthday of Bilbo and Frodo. The American Tolkien Society first announced its observance in 1978 as part of Tolkien Week, with the celebration often accompanied by costume parties, good food and fireworks.

CHAPTER 18

There and Back Again

K Stage never used to be there. Built for *King Kong*, and dubbed 'Kong Stage', I was reliably informed that the grey, concrete building soaring three, soundproofed storeys into the Miramar sky was state of the art. Only slightly smaller, the conjoined F and G Stages were also new and likewise equipped with catwalks, lighting rigs and rails from which could be hung green curtains the size of sails. Looking northwards towards the rear gate, the backlot had been enclosed in a wall of shipping crates tall enough to give King Kong pause and sheathed in weather-proof, lime green sheeting.

The legacy of *The Lord of the Rings* had transformed Stone Street Studios, but not beyond recognition.

Across the main avenue of the Wellington dream factory circa 2011, A Stage was nestled in the familiar collection of refurbished paint factory buildings that filled out the alphabetical sequence and overflowed with offices and production departments.

Reassuringly, the security guard at the rear gate was still housed in a Portakabin, and in his window had been stuck a handwritten note: 'Ring Lost'.

Some things never change.

Peter Jackson's as-of-yet two-film version of *The Hobbit* had finally begun shooting on 21 February 2011, and a month later I was back in New Zealand, neé Middle-earth: journalist and good-luck charm, there to sample the buoyant beginnings of what would ultimately become a 266-day odyssey to match the endurance test of its predecessor. I returned on three separate occasions to the engine room of *Hobbit* production, observing its own technical evolution and narrative growth spurt. For what began as two films would end up an unexpected trilogy.

Inside on G Stage, Jackson was strolling down memory lane. Quite literally, in fact. We were walking through the cloisters of Rivendell, past the gallery of murals where Boromir and Aragorn first set eyes upon one another (or will do in sixty Middle-earth years). These were the genuine Alan Lee originals, which Jackson had sensibly kept in storage. Proof perhaps that some part of his psyche was keeping the option open on a return to Middle-earth. 'I'm such a hoarder,' he laughed. With a bit of dusting down, they were as good as old.

In 2014, I took a visit to Jackson's two warehouses in the Upper Hutt Valley filled with props and paraphernalia, the spoils of films past. Wandering wide-eyed through these dusty tombs, they were dominated by souvenirs of Middle-earth: swords, armour, candelabra, Bilbo's bureaux, Galadriel's boat (which had been to Cannes and back), even the sad remains of the fell beast that had overlooked the *Return of the King* premiere. They form a slumbering record of film history. The original Bag End interior was transferred to the grounds of Jackson's newly built country pad in Masterton (north of Lothlórien, south of Mount Doom) to be reassembled as a guesthouse.

Australian comedian Barry Humphries, he who plays the hideous, goitrous, vainglorious Great Goblin via motion capture, recalled visiting Jackson's Xanadu and the director absentmind-edly pulling on a bottle in the wine cellar. A panel swung back to reveal a cobwebbed tunnel scattered with skulls and ribcages, at the end of which a bridge crossed a dark, churning river, then up a flight of stairs and through a door in a bookcase they came to Bag End. Both Spielberg and Lucas have been on the guest-list; you picture a pile of A-list directors spilling in through Jackson's front door.

Ten years earlier, the grounds of Elrond's country estate were located among the red and black beeches of the Kaitoke Regional Park. You couldn't ask for a more sylvan setting. But Wellington's capricious winds tested Jackson's patience and for *An Unexpected Journey*'s Elvish pit stop he had brought Rivendell's outdoors indoors. Those vast green curtains would allow Weta Digital to expand the hidden valley to all points of the compass with the latest in waterfall simulation.

'I've learned to trust the studio,' laughed Jackson, enjoying the pun. Whether consciously or not, the digital glow of the scenery would reflect the book's more heightened tone. A reminder also that *The Hobbit* is framed as Bilbo's recollections.

We paused before a painting of Sauron in battle armour, the Ring radiant upon his finger. 'The tone was one of the things that worried me about *The Hobbit*,' he admitted. 'It's not just the dialogue and the characters, it's the actual narrative and the way Tolkien writes it for a much younger age group. So you get a whole sense of *The Hobbit* being a children's book. That was a little bit difficult for us to get our heads around.'

In what would become a sticking point for many critics, Bilbo's adventures with a company of thirteen Dwarves who seek to oust a belligerent fire-breathing squatter from their former home was famously conceived as a bedtime saga: light on its feet, consciously whimsical and far less portentous than its weightier sequel.

Tolkien originally sold the rights to *The Hobbit* and *The Lord of the Rings* as a package, and the very first adaptation made of any of his work came in the shape of American animation partners

Rankin-Bass' generally regrettable 1977 television special of *The Hobbit.** It surely represents everything to which Tolkien might take exception. Bilbo is designed to match the cherubic figures of Disney's dwarfs, more of a garden gnome than Tolkien's sturdy little Englishman. Worse still, Gollum resembles a whingeing, humanoid frog with eyes like a bluebottle. The excruciating sing-songy tone; the horrible, syrupy tunes; the prettified, sanctimonious nature of it all may have followed the framework of the story, but bore none of his wit, or sense of adventure, or the vitality of Tolkien's world.

The best case to be made for the $3 million production is that the use of renowned Japanese animation company Toru Hara — subsequently absorbed into the great Studio Ghibli — gifts a hint of Maurice Sendak and Arthur Rackham to the creature design.

What might also raise an eyebrow is that Gandalf's gravid tones belong to John Huston, legendary director and erstwhile actor (*The Maltese Falcon, Chinatown*), while fellow director Otto Preminger (*Exodus, Anatomy of a Murder*) gave rasping voice to the Elvenking (never clarified as Thranduil). Seeking finance for projects unforthcoming from Hollywood in the twilight of their careers, they would, like Orson Welles with *The Transformers* cartoon, offer their stentorian voices to animation trifles such as this.

So Jackson's hesitancy toward the material hadn't solely been a matter of Middle-earth burn out. In and of itself, *The Hobbit*

---

* Other YouTube discoverable versions of *The Hobbit* do exist. There is an abortive animated short created in 1966 by William L. Snyder, and a Soviet effort made in 1985 called *The Fabulous Journey of Mr Bilbo Baggins* – a *Meet the Feebles*-minded Jackson might have appreciated that in the latter Smaug is played by a glove puppet. In 1993, *The Hobbits*, a Finnish serial, featured the book being read out *Jackanory*-style with specific scenes performed like an atmospheric stage-play. Tellingly, *The Hobbit* is dealt with in one episode and the show gets on with *The Lord of the Rings*, daringly inclusive of Tom Bombadil, who resembles a Native American.

presented a challenge. What kind of film would it make? Was it, you know, for kids? Especially in a universe where a lavishly praised film version of *The Lord of the Rings* had set down what for many was a definitive expectation of Middle-earth. How far from the proven path would the fans or indeed the studio want Jackson to venture while still giving a beloved book with a very different temperament its due?

Slowly, inevitably, *The Hobbit* would aim to emulate the mood of its predecessor, yet there remains a different sensibility in the air, markedly so in *An Unexpected Journey*. At times, Jackson is almost sending himself up. He particularly enjoyed what he calls the Dwarves' 'healthy disregard' for the icons of Middle-earth.

Bilbo too comes with none of the sacrificial heroism of Frodo and Sam. He is a peevish enlistee tumbling headlong through an episodic series of adventures that will bring out the best in him. There is much fish-out-of-water comedy involving the stick-in-the-mud hobbit.

Throughout production the director hosted regular Buster Keaton screenings at his Camperdown Cinema. 'Oh, he's an evangelist for Buster Keaton,' reported Martin Freeman, the bone-dry British actor successfully cast as the titular antsy-hero.

*

Visit One: Rivendell and the Trollshaws. Later that morning, thirteen accentuated Dwarves, a puckish cocktail of heavy metal bassists, Vikings and the quarrelsome Gauls from the *Asterix* comic-books, will pile in through the front gates of Rivendell. Jackson referred to them as his 'little bastards'. They naturally suspect the prissy Elves are up to no good.

The scene proved boisterous and funny.

Ian McKellen was standing on a box. The camera would crane in over Gandalf's shoulder to peer down on his stout companions. Huge advances had been made in the execution of scale differences — including the dreaded slave capture.* After lunch (catering has been relocated to a large pavilion behind the new soundstages), a border patrol of Elf riders mounted on their steeds will sweep in to encircle the scale-doubles impressively within the confines of the soundstage. All the same, there were still occasions when an actor balanced on a box did the job nicely.

Between set-ups, the Dwarves, roasting beneath layers of prosthetic, leather and hipster beard, hunkered down in an air-conditioned tent and plugged themselves into cooling units which pumped cold water through pipes sewn into their undergarments.

'A life saver,' sighed Stephen Hunter, who suffered more than most as the prodigious Bombur. It took three separate costume technicians to load up Bombur. 'Loo breaks are a hassle,' admitted the actor.

I had a rush of sympathy for the screenwriters challenged with making sense of this gang. It was a trial keeping track of which ones I'd interviewed: Fili, Kili, Oin, Gloin, Nori, Dori, Ori, Bifur, Bofur, Bombur. . . Casting them had required both an essential Dwarvishness and enough differentiation to allow them to flourish as characters. There had been another early brush with misfortune when British actor Robert Krasinsky, cast as Fili, made a hasty exit for 'personal reasons' to be replaced with Dean O'Gorman, who was still at the costume fitting stage.

Bored between set-ups, they would tail me with more wit and wisdom at the ready.

------

* Slave Capture involved one scene being simultaneously shot across two stages. One of which is completely green screen. For the Bag End sequences, for instance, McKellen would act his scenes alone in a green simulacrum while the Dwarf and hobbit actors were on the 'proper' set — the two images are then digitally combined at the appropriate scale. An effect that can be immediately fed back to on-the-set monitors. McKellen in particular, however, found the process a trial, bereft of fellow actors to feed off and looking at nothing but green drapes.

'We all have our backstory,' stated Jed Brophy, who has been subject to Jackson's abuses since *Braindead*: 'Nori is a poacher, he's been out in the wild on his own, he likes to steal things.' He pauses to draw a local analogy for me. 'If he was from the UK, I guess he'd be a Cockney.'

All their accents were rooted to the UK, with relatives adopting the same region: Graham McTavish (Dwalin) and Ken Stott (Balin) both use their natural Scottish burrs, as does the riotous Glaswegian comedian Billy Connolly who canters into film three on a war pig as the irrepressibly uncivilized Dain — Jackson was a big fan.

In their downtime — there has been more than expected — they have been bonding. 'Plenty of barbecues,' smiled Brophy. And plenty of fitness training, just to endure.

'We don't feel small,' insisted Irish star Aidan Turner, aka the reckless, dashing Kili, 'I mean they're only four-foot-something and we've been looking at enough tennis balls, but we pack a serious punch.'

'We're not bright like the Elves,' noted William Kircher, who as Bifur has an axe fixed in his noggin (Jackson's idea). 'We're almost like part of the earth, how we sort of move around.' Rock will be a motif; Dwarven architecture, reminiscent of Moria, is angular and Brutalist.

The introspective Armitage sat apart from his brethren studying a small page of script. 'There's a little more comedy, more energy, we're a bit more working class, I suppose,' he mused thoughtfully on how he expected a preponderance of Dwarves to bring a different complexion to *The Hobbit*. 'And there is the singing. We're not going to win any opera awards, but that is how they express sentiment in a way. It's been interesting.'

The loquacious Northern Irish actor James Nesbitt, an affable, chatterbox Bofur, looked askance at the busy set. 'It's just like Cecil B. De Mille,' he announced, but his view begged different as we watched a forklift truck shift a fake tree trunk, part of the fell forested ruin of Dol Guldur being assembled on F Stage. The other day, he marvelled, Jackson had driven onto the lot in the original Chitty Chitty Bang Bang.

During the two years spent developing the script with del Toro, Jackson had been conscious of keeping his distance. He was there to support his director, but he knew his presence might confuse things, even cloud del Toro's authority. He had deliberately avoided seeing what the florid Mexican had come up with alongside Middle-earth veterans like art director Dan Hennah, and artists Alan Lee and John Howe, who had eagerly returned to New Zealand.

Suddenly, he had to ask himself exactly what his *Hobbit* might look like?

'I wanted Guillermo to have the freedom to do whatever he wanted. Then suddenly he wasn't working on the film anymore. That was the most nervous I got. I just thought, "Am I making his movie? Am I having to inherit everything he did?" I hadn't gotten my head into *that* film.'

He needed to go back through everything, all the designs; even those discarded by del Toro. With the clock ticking (there was always too much time or never enough), he needed to try and find *his* version of *The Hobbit*. The right designs for *The Lord of the Rings* already seemed to exist somehow; all they had to do was find them. With *The Hobbit* that certainty eluded them. It was that dreamy fairy-tale tone, it was as if Tolkien was instructing them to fill in the gaps.

'Where we did one thousand sketches of *The Lord of the Rings* we did ten thousand on *The Hobbit*,' says Richard Taylor, speaking in 2016. 'It was exhausting.'

'That was about the time I was rushed into hospital with a stomach ulcer,' said Jackson. With the start date delayed a further four weeks to allow the director time to recover, he laughed grimly that department heads were probably a little relieved to have more time. 'So there was an upside for the film. . . If not me.'

Jackson's hospital bed was soon covered with concepts for a dozen cranky Dwarves, the halls of the Lonely Mountain, Bard the Bowman and Smaug the Magnificent. Whether this aided recovery is a separate matter, but once Jackson was back on his feet and back at Stone Street overseeing imminent production he was hit by his next dilemma — a potential actor's strike.

Seemingly out of nowhere, the New Zealand Actors' Equity, allied with the Australia-based Media, Entertainment and Arts Alliance, advised its members to boycott the production over an obscure contractual issue. Which included just about every Kiwi member of the cast. A standoff ensued, with Jackson defiant his films would not be held to ransom over the larger issue of union contracts. He classified the move as 'very ill-considered and unwise'. Unthinkably, at the time, even going as far as to suggest that Warner Bros. might well transplant the entire production to the UK, lock, stock and Elvish barrels.

To head off a national calamity, Prime Minister John Key offered Warner Bros. (effectively the studio in charge) a solution: additional tax rebates of $7.5 million per picture and a $10 million contribution to marketing. It was dubbed 'a long-term strategic partnership'.

This was about more than filmmaking, this was about New Zealand's economic future. The issue was then quietly resolved.

It was as if having been granted so much good fortune on *The Lord of the Rings*, the universe was balancing things out by sending him bad luck like a flock of crebain.

'Once the stories hit the media they form a reality different to the one we were experiencing. We were making a movie with Guillermo and then he decided to leave, so then we were making it and we had to deal with it. Then we had to deal with a bit of actors' equity stuff, and then I got sick, went into hospital, but we carried on working. . .'

In the decade since they were last in Middle-earth, the camera had undergone a significant overhaul. Right back to his days cooking up his own special effects, Jackson has been fascinated by the boundaries of filmmaking technology. A pioneering spirit that helped elicit wonders for *The Lord of the Rings*. And now

The Hobbit was even pursuing new ways of shooting films. Ask Jackson a technical question and you sample a formidable intelligence as he offhandedly deconstructs slave capture or the concept of convergence in 3D.

The relatively compact Red digital camera was currently being fiddled with by Andrew Lesnie's diligent team, who had the solemn air of keepers of the secret flame of camera tech (once out of earshot, Jackson admitted they were only waiting for the software to update). This box of tricks, an advance funded out of Jackson's own pocket, would provide images not only in 3D, but at 48 frames per second and bring with it a blizzard of criticism.

This basically meant an image twice as sharp, which Jackson boasted would all but eliminate motion blur in action sequences, even as it doubled the workload at Weta Digital with twice as many frames to render and check. By the end of *The Hobbit*, they calculated they had processed 1.5 million frames.

Lesnie smirked. 'We're just testing it out for James Cameron.'

*

On K Stage the full-sized Dwarves were fighting invisible trolls under the direction of Gollum. Andy Serkis was sat (in jeans and t-shirt, no less) beneath an awning surrounded by monitors and directorial doodads, which was itself found to the side of the Trollshaws, the clump of forest on the doorstep of Rivendell where the party falls foul of a trio of talkative trolls with dinner plans (giving formerly savage beasts droll speaking parts was another recent challenge to Middle-earthian logic).

Serkis' promotion to second-unit director was, he said, 'a natural thing'. He had lived and breathed this world for so long on *The Lord of the Rings* (to a much greater extent than any other actor) he had gleaned his director's unwritten 'rulebook'.

'Pete likes lots of choice. It's really working the scene, and working it and working it and eliciting a performance out of the actors. And feeling the freedom to try different things. The writing process for Pete continues into the shoot and the edit and then pick-ups. He loves to rework material until tonally it all fits together. So it was about challenging the actors to try lots of variations.'

However, Serkis leaned more to the Franly Kubrick school of perfectionism. Jackson would later laugh that whereas he might do eight or nine takes of a scene, his second-unit general would deliver up to thirty to the edit.

The actor had still been caught unawares when the email arrived. Jackson had known of his ambitions to move into direction, they had talked about it, but he was thrilled and terrified by the offer to hold all the second-unit reins (the number of units would hover at two, sometimes three). Serkis had directed theatre and a few shorts, and the Imaginarium was up and running, but he was relatively untested in the realm of feature films.

Jackson's natural collaborative instincts were coming to the fore again. Here was valuable continuity with the past. A person he knew and liked. Someone already signed on to the telekinetic wi-fi of his vision. And if Jackson knew anything about the British actor, it was that he tended to rise to a challenge.

'It didn't take too long to persuade me,' laughed Serkis, the addict. 'I knew we could be very honest with each other.'

In the online video diaries, proudly and lightheartedly providing monthly reports of their progress, much ballyhoo was made of the fact the very first scenes filmed on *The Hobbit* belonged to arguably the most iconic moment in all of Tolkien's work: Bilbo's quietly momentous encounter with Gollum over a game of riddles. It was a good place for Jackson to find his feet in Middle-earth again — the familiar sight of Serkis in a leotard.

Nevertheless, Serkis found returning to Gollum for his brief but significant cameo a struggle. He had to shake off the idea that he was doing an impression of Gollum. To reclaim him, as it were, from pop culture.

'It was a tough week and a half. It was just fantastic to play that scene with Martin, and he was on his own journey trying to find Bilbo, but I was equally trying to really find the emotional core of the character. To get right to who is this guy, what's he going through? What is this for *real*?'

His riddling opponent was found holed up in his trailer putting the kettle on. 'You know I'm not a Tolkien freak,' he began apologetically, searching his cupboards for mugs and tea bags. His trailer was nothing excessive, no treadmills or satellite dishes, but he had decorated the walls with classic Motown sleeves — a reminder of a collector's devotion to that soulful brand of music.

'Milk?'

You couldn't find a more dedicated professional than Freeman, and he gives Bilbo a lovely, punctilious, ever-so English sense of exasperation and heart that snugly fits the book's finicky hero. But in terms of personality and approach he was the anti-Viggo. Not for the Hampshire-born actor the melding of man and landscape, the deep breathe of New Zealand. He had barely troubled the local beauty spots let alone the primordial interior, unless called upon to by the script. He preferred working in the studio to location, only five minutes from home. Ask after his relationship with the 'gaffer' — as in Jackson — and he keeps it strictly on set.

'We see each other all day, we're not going to hang out at night, you know? I don't think either of us really feel the need for that.'

Jackson often compared himself to Bilbo — and Freeman suspected in a different universe his director could have played the part — and he has more in common with the character's British alter ego than any of the actors he called upon for *The Lord of the Rings*.

Rising to prominence playing ironic everybody Tim Canterbury in seminal television mockumentary *The Office*, Freeman honed his self-deprecating persona (an extension rather than exact fit of his own modest nature) for movies like *Love, Actually* and the lead in an adaptation of Douglas Adams' treasured science fiction satire *The Hitchhiker's Guide to the Galaxy*. Arthur Dent, thrust unwittingly into a universe brimming with obstinate aliens, has an uncannily similar trajectory to that of Bilbo.

Nevertheless, it was Freeman's performance as a querulous Dr. Watson to Benedict Cumberbatch's contemporized BBC *Sherlock*, which had excited both del Toro and Jackson.

As we chatted, Freeman made it clear he was allergic to all forms of Hollywood psychobabble. Talk of 'emotionalities' and 'personal journeys' made him shudder. He had even found early discussions with Jackson, Walsh and Boyens about the Englishness of Bilbo 'unhelpful'.

'I am English; how do I play English? But I get it, there is a sort of up-tightness to him.'

Freeman recalled his audition in London. He had been filming *Sherlock* at the time and was videoed doing a scene that never made the films: 'Bilbo asking around, "Have you heard of Gandalf?" And this guy goes, "Didn't he play for Long-bottom Rovers?"' I got good. . . not even feedback, I got good pre-feedback.'

Del Toro was still director at the time, although they never met. There were three 'long' phone calls and Freeman was thrilled to be regarded as his first choice. However, as *The Hobbit* drifted into limbo he, like the Mexican director, accepted he had to get on with his career.

This posed the next in Jackson's litany of crises. When it came to Bilbo he remained of one accord with del Toro (Freeman, you could say, is the intersection in the Venn Diagram of their *Hobbits*), but it was too late. Freeman was now commited to another season of *Sherlock* and reluctantly informed Jackson he would have to say no. Crestfallen, Jackson rooted back through tapes of over sixty different auditionees (Matthew Goode, James McAvoy, Eddie Redmayne, Tobey Maguire and Shia LaBeouf have all been mentioned), but he couldn't get Freeman out of his head.

'I was enjoying re-runs of *Sherlock*, but feeling miserable.'

Jolting awake at 3 a.m. one night, he got Kiwi on his problem. Why not use his so-called power for good? If the schedule didn't work, change the schedule. He phoned Freeman's agent himself.

How about he build in two breaks within the shoot to accommodate Freeman's *Sherlock* commitments? Meantime, he could edit
what he had and get some invaluable prep time on excursions
yet to be filmed. Not ideal in terms of establishing a rhythm, but
he would have a leading man.

Bilbo was the only part to be recast from *The Lord of the Rings*.
McKellen was already playing older than his years, and there
was no guide from Tolkien as to whether there had ever been a
young Gandalf. Bringing back Orlando Bloom as Legolas in the
second film was trickier. Critics carped that there was no mention
of the fleet-footed Elf in *The Hobbit*, but Boyens reasoned that
being a prince of the woodland realm where the Dwarves are
held captive and nearly three thousand years of age his presence
made acceptable sense. Though make-up and hair designer Peter
King mentioned that, ironically, it was the handsome British
actor who required the most 'de-ageing' (tape behind the ears
as well as digital softening). Between their twenties and thirties
men undergo a dramatic change of physiognomy. While still a
heartthrob, Bloom had lost his bloom.

Bilbo, however, needed the younger version, with Holm,
now 78, featuring in the framing mechanism (with a virtually
unchanged Elijah Wood as Frodo). Without being a slavish
double, Freeman made a decent match and worked hard to make
subtle connections physically and vocally.

'That is flattering,' he responded when I make the comparison,
'because I think he's fucking brilliant. But hand on heart I don't
feel the pressure of it. As soon as I start trying to live up to being
Bilbo, I'm fucked. And as soon as I start trying to live up to being
Ian Holm being Bilbo then I'm fucked. We can't do it for the
legacy of the last seventy years. It's all over if you start stacking
those odds against yourself. If it's a good story then it should
play as a good story. We don't have to invest it with holiness.'

Not that he or the production weren't treating *The Hobbit* with
the utmost seriousness — he proved one of the great successes
of *The Hobbit* — but there were, Freeman recognized, significant

differences in the DNA of the prequels: 'There was more overt gravitas in *Lord of the Rings*, more overt mythological, quasi-biblical stuff. . .'

Interestingly, within that framework, *The Hobbit* represents a more ambiguous and political story. The Dwarves' motivation isn't saving the world — their actions actually bring about war — but reclaiming their homeland. As well as a pile of gold the size of the Brecon Beacons. Theirs was not the tale of self-less heroism, but a blur of selfishness, identity crisis and racial determination.

'We've talked a lot about what's in it for everybody. Why is everybody doing it?' said Freeman. 'It's about land and it's about just reclaiming what they'd lost.'

Throughout my coverage of three *Hobbit* films, the analogy was frequently made with the real-world situation in Iraq. When you uproot the resident menace — Smaug as Saddam Hussein — you create a power vacuum. To extend the metaphor, Dwarf gold is oil. Tolkien would shudder.

This was less a fellowship than a faction, and Bilbo their hired burglar.

Does that therefore make it easier to play than Frodo?

'He's lighter, I would say. For black and white purposes he's more comic. It's a more comedic. . . journey. God, sorry.'

*

The following day, Jackson invited me to sit alongside him at his widescreen monitor. On the screen and only ten feet away was another newly depicted corner of Rivendell that had sprung up overnight on G Stage. Thorin was being cajoled by Gandalf to hand over the map to Erebor for Elrond's inspection. The scene concluded with Hugo Weaving holding up the parchment to a silver beam of Lesnie's impeccable lighting and cooing in that uniquely Weavingian manner, '*Moon rrrrunes!*'

I watched multiple takes as the actors try different intensities, leaning on the lines for different effects. To this day, I find the process of acting miraculous. Being able to switch on a character the second action is called. Not simply pretending, but instinctually becoming someone else — even a Dwarf or a wizard. Seeing the light harden in Armitage's eyes, hearing the underlying insistence in McKellen's voice. . .

'I never need to worry about Ian and Hugo,' whispered Jackson, 'but it's been wonderful to see how Martin and Richard have found their roles.'

Armitage's decline into dragon sickness — a calamitous genetic gold fever — brings another more ambiguous note to the prequels.

'The good thing about the digital camera,' Jackson noted, 'is you can just keep them rolling and get them to do it over and over again. I don't think it's a waste at all really.'

Is there a limit?

'Well, there's a card here that we are shooting on, I'm not sure how long it is.'

'It's fifteen minutes,' came the teacherly tones of Carolynne Cunningham, the stalwart 'Caro', hovering over Jackson's shoulder protectively.

He looked surpirsed. 'Oh is it? That's quite good, it was always ten minutes with film. . .

'Twelve minutes,' corrected Caro.

Jackson laughed. He was well used to being admonished by Caro, promoted to producer and still the voice of law on set. Our conversation drifted to other challenges presented by the breezier approach *The Hobbit* takes to Middle-earth. The Ring, I pointed out, is depicted as little more than an advantageous trinket. It seems to have no effect on Bilbo.

Jackson pursed his lips; these are debates he, Walsh, Boyens — and presumably del Toro — had been having for the last two years. 'I guess its strength grew over time, so the first few times Bilbo put it on it didn't really have much impact. But because this is not the story of the Ring, but the Dwarves and the Lonely Mountain, we're not making it the bigger end of the story.'

A clever, Boyens-flavoured conceptual parrallel is still made between the empowerment of the Necromancer and the discovery of the Ring.

Freeman, for his part, will gradually inject a growing sense of Bilbo's dependence on it. 'At every turn, I'm trying to put a bit more heaviness into it and I will continue to do that, because it's kind of fun for me to make those decisions. Just those acting decisions when not to be comical.'

Another take completed seemingly without hitch, Jackson bounded up from his chair for a quick word with Armitage. The make-up hornets take the opportunity to descend on their victims, but Jackson was back in a trice.

'I still find it really odd when I have the camera up high looking down on Thorin, and when I give Richard a note and he's suddenly taller than I am. He's a big guy, and I like that about the quality of the character too because he plays Thorin like a big man.'

Much of the balancing act of the new films, between the anarchy and slapstick and the earnest filaments that will connect these films to *The Lord of the Rings*, was held in the performances. And the director enjoyed these more dramatic scenes.

'You think, "Oh yeah, this is just like the old days."'

*

VISIT TWO: LAKE-TOWN AND THE GATES OF MORIA: In June 2013, the furious Wellington sky was pursuing a line in cataclysmic rainfall as I dashed across the backlot to G Stage. Supplementary shooting was well underway on both *The Desolation of Smaug* and *The Battle of the Five Armies* (still known as *There and Back Again*). The actors hadn't been contracted for a third set of pick-ups as it was only supposed to be two films.

Inside, the elements appeared wintry but the air was humid and soapy with dry ice. Leaving only a strip of space on two sides of the soundstage, the fourth set-build of Lake-town was an awe-inspiring piece of Dan Hennah design magic: a vast, rambling warren of rickety wooden walkways, passages and houses that bent beneath heavy roofs toward icy canals. It was as if Dickens had relocated Venice to his socially stricken London. Only a blond Elf was attempting to leap onto the balustrades of a nearby footbridge.

I sat and watched Bloom work at the complicated sequence. In one sweeping Leggy move, he was due to jump ten foot into the air and attempt to land on the rails of the bridge and simultaneously fire off (digital) arrows at a stuntman dressed as an Orc. A stunt 'assisted' by a wire that connected him to a winch that fizzed angrily on each take. Finding the correct angle of entry was tricky.

Amid all the fuss over a CGI takeover, it was gratifying to watch some man-on-wire action on an elaborate set.

'Donning the blond wig and getting suited up, booted up, it's part of a little ritual in terms of getting into it,' said Bloom, having finally 'landed' the scene to his director's satisfaction. 'But honestly it's really hard because you're just thinking, "Fuck, am I going to land this or am I going to twist an ankle?" It's a real psychological thing.'

Bloom had qualms about returning to the role he had left behind twelve years ago, concerned how they could justify his presence considering he wasn't in the book. What impressed him was how Legolas' experiences in *The Hobbit*, as ad-libbed by the writers, would mould how he would come to join the Fellowship in the future. They were sewing in a direct thread.

'It feels authentic and has a continuity, but of course there are some leaps of imagination.'

Before he arrived for his first batch of shooting, he had watched the original trilogy again to reconnect with his character. He hadn't seen the films since the premieres. He had also dug out his old photos from storage. In the intervening years he hadn't stopped working, it was as if his whole life was on hold. 'We all looked like kids,' he smiled. 'It's crazy.'

New Zealand had hardly aged a day.

'The rest of the world is motoring on with technology and all sorts of wonderful mad things and it's stayed the same here. You just have to look at the mobile phone they gave me, it's like the same phone I had when I was here ten years ago with a really shitty little camera on the back of it and no features.'

Next door, Christian Rivers was directing what is now called the splinter unit (Serkis was too busy to return for pick-ups) where Orc stuntmen in regulation leotards and those eyeline tubes sprouting from the heads are taking on a fusillade of chunky Dwarves. This will entrain more of Thorin's flashback to the battle at Moria's East-gate. No longer to be found high in the Remarkables, but on the sward of green flooring on F Stage. Motion capture had come on a notch.

Even the lead Orcs are now digital. The albino menace Azog the Defiler and Bolg, his ghastly offspring, have been motion captured and given hideous digital features; technically astonishing but another hotly debated 'advance' on Weta Workshop's tactile prosthetics. Jackson maintained he would have used CGI in the past if he could have afforded it.

More controversial still, as far as the media was concerned, was the expansion to three films. Two weeks out from Comic-con in July, where Jackson was due to show footage from Bag End and the Riddles in the Dark sequence, he had sat down with Walsh and Boyens to 'talk about the shape of the two films'. They got on to which additional scenes they might shoot in these very pick-ups, and the list just kept on growing. 'What if it was a trilogy?' Jackson had wondered aloud.

'It never structurally had felt quite right as two,' he admitted, and this created the symmetry of two trilogies.

In the prehistoric days with Miramax he had proposed making a single film version of *The Hobbit*. In the del Toro era it had naturally evolved into two. And now it was three — much to the incredulity of a growing pocket of online dissension. The book barely made three hundred pages.

This was never a matter of studio pressure. Warner Bros. were as startled as anyone when Walsh and Boyens flew into Los Angeles and proposed the idea. 'In the end it became about an opportunity to tell part of the story that will never get told if you don't tell it now,' determined Boyens. Unsurprisingly Warner Bros. didn't take much winning over. Any additional costs would be soaked up by a third spin at the box office.

Six months later, the first of three films arrived to great financial success ($1,017,003,568 worldwide) and a mixed critical reception. Critics grumbled that *The Hobbit*'s swelling corpus hadn't done the first film many favours. Fine details do feel stretched and the meandering pace is often at odds with the bawdier tone. The ribald needs to get a move on. 'Such blithe elastication is the root of the movie's fault,' noted Anthony Lane in *The New Yorker* while rightly claiming there was still much to relish.

The Lord of the Rings, however lengthy, was swept along on an air of desperate urgency.

Andrew O'Hehir from *Salon* felt it was more 'inspired by' than 'based on' the book and groaned about Jackson's hubristic ownership of Tolkien (forgetting that these were Jackson's sequels), but it was largely a matter of expectations. 'If you arrive at *The Hobbit* via the flatulent mediocrity of most contemporary fantasy films and fantasy fiction, it looks pretty damn good.'

This was before he launched into an inventory of its shortcomings.

There was an undeniable sense of overreaction in the reviews. Both from those aghast at it falling short of *The Lord of the Rings*, which were exceptional films, and even more so those who bewailed the stretching of the original book's comforting, tucked-up simplicity that had blessed many a film critic's childhood.

'This film is so stuffed with extraneous faff and flummery that it often barely feels like Tolkien at all — more a dire, fan-written internet tribute,' mithered Robbie Collin in the *Telegraph*. 'The book begins with the unimprovable ten-word opening sentence: "In a hole in the ground there lived a Hobbit." Jackson, by contrast, starts with an interminable narrative detour about a mining operation run by a team of Dwarves.'

Inevitably, it was a film burdened by the past.

The experiment with 48 frames per second was another bugbear. Had Jackson leapt too far into the future for his own good? There had been no Cannes presentation — Warner had global distribution rights so there was no longer a scattershot of global partnerships to keep sweet — but Jackson did unveil some early footage in 48 FPS at the Las Vegas exhibitors conference CinemaCon in April 2012, from which the first stirrings of a backlash were heard.

The more snide suggested the unwelcome clarity of image was like watching a daytime soap, or peering though a window onto the set where all the joins were evident, including the seam down the back of Gandalf's hat.

On release, blessed with Lesnie's colour grading, the effect was far less jolting and at times powerfully immediate: Gollum is stunning, and in the sequel Smaug and Bilbo disturbing a trillion slippery coins is a piece of pure cinematic wonder. Yet, like many, I still prefer the painterly warmth and grain of 24 FPS — texture that suggests that movies exist in an alternate reality — were a perfect fit with Tolkien's antique world.

In retrospect, Jackson is reflective but defiant about doubling down on frames. His ambitions, he insists in 2016, were always cinematic. As audiences dwindle, drawn to their iPhones or iPads, wasn't there an onus to 'enhance the cinema-going experience'? He wonders whether at root the criticism came from a simple fear of change.

'Critics went after it mainly because it was so different and it wasn't their perception of what film is. But the overwhelming response from audiences is that it was the best 3D they'd ever seen.' But surprisingly few cinemas were ready, or willing to ready themselves, for the format and its distribution remained limited. Warner Bros. hardly promoted the format at all on the sequels.

The jury is still out. A more recent experiment with higher

frame rates by lauded Taiwanese director Ang Lee, shooting the combat footage for his 2016 Iraq war drama *Billy Lynn's Long Halftime Walk* at 120 FPS for a drastic contrast with the home-spun scenes, was met with equal indifference (Lee's film was a sizeable flop).

Despite the complaints and the muted reviews — and it is worth recording that review aggregator site Rotten Tomatoes calculated a sixty-four percent approval rate — the film had still been a billion-dollar hit. The mood remained buoyant in New Zealand. But there was a sense of relief to have the first film out of the way.

'It would be a very different vibe coming to work every day, shooting these pick-ups, if the first film had been an absolute bomb,' Jackson acknowledged with his usual frankness. 'You would start to think, "Why am I bothering?"'

I had been invited to share lunch with Jackson, Walsh and Boyens, their names now tripping off the tongue like a Wellington law firm, away from the hubbub of catering in the director's Stone Street office. The walls were hung with paintings of World War I trenches, the shelves lined with volumes of Tolkien.

Conversation drifted back to the thinking behind the trilogy. There were, they all insisted, sound storytelling reasons for pursuing a third film. With the second film *The Hobbit* was naturally turning darker, and with more room they could sew more seeds for a future already set.

'At the start of *The Lord of the Rings* the fate of the world is at stake,' said Boyens. 'You begin this story and the fate of a slightly out-of-his-depth, eccentric, respectable hobbit is at stake — only slowly do you understand there's a lot more at stake.'

With *The Lord of the Rings*, she noticed, the geography somehow matched the emotional storytelling: the darkest times for the Fellowship tended to occur in the darkest places: Moria, Emyn Muil, the tunnels of Shelob's Lair. In other words, the geography suggested the emotion. They found that didn't happen with *The Hobbit*.

While still two films, they had drawn the dividing line in a particular geographical location rather than an emotional location — the end of the barrel chase with Lake-town in sight.

'It was a good lesson to learn that it's not about where you end up on the map of Middle-earth,' said Walsh, 'it's about where the characters end up.'

The reasoning behind the creation of Evangeline Lilly's redheaded warrior Elf Tauriel, an entirely non-canon addition, was to address the lack of female characters in the book, which amounts to none at all. 'We had to bear in mind our audience includes young girls,' asserted Boyens.

The Tolkien-mad Lilly is sprightly and engaging, and Tauriel a deadly aim, but the doomed interracial romance with Turner's comely Kili feels less warranted. Romance struggles in Middle-earth, even Aragorn and Arwen's long-distance love affair functioned more as kingly motivation.

What of the dragon? Whichever way you cut it, Smaug remained one of the big selling points of *The Hobbit*. Who wasn't still eager to see Pete's dragon?

'We promise you'll see him this time,' laughed Jackson. Smaug had been a shadowy, flashbacked presence in *An Unexpected Journey* until he awoke in the final scene to reveal a dazzling, feline eye whose flame-gold iris rhymed deliciously with the Eye of Sauron.

A talking dragon, Jackson confessed, had been an issue. Smaug had to be as sinewy in conversation as he was in body. Benedict Cumberbatch delivering a honeyed fusion of George Sanders' Shere Khan, Terence Stamp's Zod, and Jeremy Irons in anything. But the dynamics of speech were complex. Jackson lived in fear of 'doing another *Dragonheart*' — a fantasy folly that predated *The Lord of the Rings* and ironically featured the Gandalf-averse Sean Connery as the voice of a CGI dragon uninspiringly named Draco.

'Like Gollum, he wasn't a creature he was a character,' Jackson insisted of Smaug. 'You almost needed to forget he was a dragon.'

They had tried a telepathic voice echoing in Bilbo's head, but it sapped the character of his power and wit.

The flexibility of motion capture would be put to the ultimate test with Cumberbatch arriving for two weeks of Smaugian conversation. His 747-sized body was left to the cross-Weta committees, where the physics of fire-breathing was hotly debated.

Howe had personally been very concerned about Smaug. 'You know, I like dragons,' he says, looking back to the early days of what became a six-year stint on *The Hobbit*. 'I really wanted to participate. By the end of film one he still had four legs. You can see four legs on Smaug when he flies over [in the prologue]. We were literally six months away from the release of film two when Peter says, "Smaug has two legs rather than four."'

Gollum-style, an urgent redesign was called for from snout to thrashing tail. They never managed to get the T-shirts printed, but an unofficial Team Smaug was formed headed up by Howe and Gino Acevedo, who found so much character and terror in his long, sinewy movements. He felt both real and mythically grand.

Cumberbatch, meanwhile, was doing his utmost to get into character by sky-diving through the New Zealand clouds to see what it felt like to be a dragon. 'They didn't know about that. I kept that quiet. *Star Trek* didn't know about that either — I was in the middle of filming that. I took a sky dive at, I forget how high but higher than 20,000 feet. All that stuff was joyous. I fell so in love with that country.'

The dragon confrontation that closes the second film is a genuine marvel and, despite the callbacks to the Balrog sequence in Moria, manifestly *The Hobbit*. Jackson had always felt the book lacked that necessary collision between Thorin and his old foe, and they expanded the battle of wits between Bilbo and the dragon (a beautifully performed duologue between *Sherlock*'s Holmes and Watson) into an epic, knowingly flamboyant (compared, say, to the gritty sprawl of Helm's Deep) confrontation between the Dwarves and their nemesis. Tearing through the capacious chambers of the Lonely Mountain, Jackson spun many of its elaborate moves in the virtual environment.

*

Visit Three: Post-production and the Motion Capture Stage: The reviews for *The Desolation of Smaug* had warmed up a notch, but the box office had cooled ($958,366,855). Relative distinctions, but the downward trajectory was noted; a knock-on effect, studio prognosticators divined, of an underwhelming first film.

The second film represents the best balance between flighty book and epic scope. It is also Tolkien at his best: not only Smaug's magnificence, but Beorn, a trippy Mirkwood, spiders, stuck-up Elves and the barrel chase. The latter sequence Jackson spent twelve weeks in transforming into an unrepentantly nutty episode of slapstick brio including, in honour of dormant side-projects, a bouncing Bombur. Like the purring grace of the Leggy moments, these expressions of Dwarf mania are pure cartoon. It is a mark of Jackson's capacity for building outwards from the book's brisk, bony plotting that only five chapters of *The Hobbit* are covered by the two hours and forty minutes of the second film. Yet it is fleet and eventful.

In June 2014, I visited this faraway kingdom in Middle-earth post-production mode for my first and their (supposedly) final time. With pick-ups completed the previous year, the various departments effectively had been granted more time. Not that that was evident at Weta Digital. Jackson laughed: no matter how long they are given, they never have enough time. As well as Weta Digital, I would visit sound effects editing (Beorn's roar contained the creaking of an old oven door, Gandalf's magic is heralded by literal thunderclaps) and the edit suite, still to be found along a corridor lined with mint condition but now perfectly framed 007 posters.

Herein, sat on a sofa the size of a barge, Jackson sipped from a Colbert Report commemorative mug (US talkshow host Stephen Colbert had been a very public Tolkien-cum-Jackson advocate) and admitted to being happiest with *The Battle of the Five Armies.*

'Compared to the other two movies, I like a lot of my direction in this movie.' Despite being dominated by the titular five-fold battle, he considered the third film to be a psychological thriller hinging on Thorin's growing madness, before getting down to a MASSIVE set-to. 'I like the fact it wasn't a road movie. I got into my groove more than had happened earlier.'

The lack of initial prep time had required them to shoot in roughly chronological order, and at first Jackson admitted to being thrown off his game.

'I was sort of winging it. I mean, the actors were great the whole way through, but I am more proud of my part of the job in the third movie than the other two.'

Had his initial uncertainty led to a greater dependence on digital environments?

'There's a lot of talk about locations versus digital locations, green screens versus sets,' he replied, maintaining that he wasn't a particular advocate or xenophobe one-way or the other. 'I'm in the position of just doing what you need to do for the movie. It's a lot cheaper to build a set than do like ten CG shots. On the other side, inside Erebor we have these vast Dwarf halls. We didn't have a stage big enough to build them.'

The Hobbit spent nine weeks on location, capturing what Jackson called the 'organic truth' of New Zealand. But it was really a matter of expediency. He could spend ten days camped out on a mountainside waiting for the magic hour or a day and a half in the studio with a digital sunset.

One advantage, of course, to ploughing a digital furrow is that he could keep shooting. 'I'm on the mo-cap stage this afternoon; you must come and watch. . .'

Three hours later, Jackson leaned back in his chair and put his bare feet on the desk. 'Is it a cup of tea level problem?' he enquired.

We were seated to one side of the new, relatively luxuriant

motion capture stage to be found two flights of stairs down from his edit suite. More accurately this was the volume, Jackson's Imaginarium, where any form of virtual shooting was permissible. In a specially designed gallery that overlooked the carpeted space, Weta Digital personnel were sat at terminals like NASA's control centre.

Jackson's stoic AD, Emma Cross, conveyed the question to the gallery through an intercom, and there came a pause as a reply is formulated.

'Shouldn't be long, they've lost the dragon.'

'Well, that's not good.' Jackson sounded amused. He'd long learned that technical snafus, even ones the size of Smaug, can always be remedied.

This might have been my fault. In our discussion of exactly how virtual shooting worked, Jackson had spoken about the 'magic carpet'. This, he explained, was basically a square on which he was 'positioned' with his virtual camera, which could then be moved, within technically obscure parameters, anywhere within the digital environment.

As represented on the monitors, the digital environment was a medium-resolution, grey-scaled version of the pivotal north-eastern constituency of Middle-earth that anchors the third film, including the Lonely Mountain and a Lake-town currently being attacked from the air by a goaded dragon.

Donning VR goggles, Jackson began enacting signature swooping shots down upon the highly flammable town.

He had really enjoyed virtual shooting, which has been scheduled for most afternoons. He had used the system in part for the Goblin-town sequence in the first film, but it had really come into its own when shooting the spectacular battle with Smaug at the end of the second.

The idea of shooting using a virtual camera was pioneered by Cameron on *Avatar*, and utilized by Spielberg on *The Adventures of Tintin*. So it was hardly surprising Jackson would collar the technique for Middle-earth.

'Peter was quite comfortable with it,' recalls Letteri, 'and we brought that into the process of *The Hobbit* both as pre-viz, and scenes we would build around Peter getting on the stage and popping off a few camera angles, especially for the final battle. After everything was shot, he would come back and do passes on that again with the animation, integrating it with a live-action stage.'

This way Jackson could keep shooting until days before he was due to deliver a finished film.

'It's like going back to my Super-8 days,' he enthused. The camera itself could be simply be a piece of wood with a sensor stuck onto it, but in a sweetly personal touch Jackson has inserted the sensor into the shell of an old Super-8 camera. 'The entire crew is just me and my camera.'

He loved the freedom of it, being unfettered from the laws of physics and the gravity of managing cast and crew to come up with any shot he could imagine.

So could we get Smaug's perspective of the attack, I wondered? A dragon POV.

Jackson was intrigued by the notion. 'Can we do that?' he asked Emma, knowing that Weta Digital will find a way.

On the screen the proto-dragon had flickered and then disappeared, which would save Bard the Bowman a good deal of grief but was not exactly as scripted.

A cup of tea later, Smaug has been located, and on the monitors two scaly claws were hanging into frame — it was the view from his vulnerable undercarriage and we were soon plunging toward Bard, a pinprick in the distance.

'You can tell people this is your shot,' announced Jackson from within Middle-earth.

Alas, when I see the final version of *The Battle of the Five Armies*, with a flicker of sympathy for Christopher Lee's long-ago disappointments, I am crushed to discover no trace of 'my shot' amid the devastation of Lake-town.

*

The Hobbit ultimately fell short of the box office made by *The Lord of the Rings* (with the trilogy topping out at $2,935, 490,211), but to judge them anything but huge hits is preposterous. Greeted wearily by the dogged naysayers, who only pined for it all to be over with, *The Battle of the Five Armies* arrived to conjoin six films into a mighty saga and made an individual global tally of $956,019,788. The final film boasted much of what Jackson claimed: a taut psychological structure combined with a thunderous, imaginative concentration on the battle scenes. Whether it was enough to warrant an entire film is a matter of taste.

Still, there was noticeably less fervour surrounding their conclusion than in the past, and a sense of dissatisfaction pervaded.

Maybe it was simply the different cultural landscapes in which they landed. As Ken Kamins had noted since *The Lord of the Rings*, Japan had backed away from Western imports in favour of homegrown films, and the *Hobbits* had fared poorly. 'It's cyclical,' he says. 'Also the dollar's value had fluctuated badly, with an added effect on how much revenue came from abroad.'

Interviewed in 2016, Boyens is frank in her analysis of the films. It had, she iterates, been a stressful process.

'I knew we could only fail in a way. I knew what we were going to have to do to that book. Because it was like it's its own story really. But it was always going to be set against the large backdrop of *Lord of the Rings*. It was a very different adventure. And it was a different adventure for the critics. I kind of knew that was coming. When I say I felt like we could only fail, I mean you had to do it for the right reasons. We did it for the fans.'

For all their differences, you sense that something of New Line's old maverick nature was missed. Working directly with Warner Bros. brought with it a more corporate ethos: they were now directly part of a scheduled strategy aligned to share price fluctuations. There were external pressures from the studio to stick to a winning formula — the one so many studios had rejected a decade before.

I admit I would have liked to see the films dare even more

of Jackson's natural instincts for slapstick and mockery. Paradoxically, they could have done with a bit more sillification, setting the two trilogies apart.

'Trust me, he could have,' says Boyens. 'We got pushed back really. Pete had to watch his sense of humour.'

She pauses to imagine a different set of films.

'Oh my God, we really could have done, but in the end you have to get on with the story. . .'

Was it that *The Hobbit* films were endeavouring to repeat a miracle? A task beset with rights wrangles, panicked directors and an achingly protracted inception that lurched into a last-minute rush. Imagine if Tolkien had published the novels the opposite way around. *The Hobbit* surely would have been perceived as a titanic let down?

They were no longer the unlikeliest blockbuster-makers hidden away in New Zealand, they were now major filmmakers, Oscar winners and, like-it-or-not, Hollywood players. To wildly para-phrase Oscar Wilde, the only thing worse than people expecting you to fail is people expecting you to succeed.

Knowing you already have an audience, Jackson admitted, put 'an edge on the day'.

The climate the films arrived in had radically altered. This was now an era overrun with superhero spectacle with its gabble of self-definition and ironic one-liners. Furthermore, betwixt the trilogies, *Game of Thrones* had shifted the paradigm of popular fantasy toward an even greater and graver realism. If *The Hobbit* was lighthearted compared to *The Lord of the Rings*, it felt light-headed compared to the slaughterhouse of Westeros.

'They weren't perfect, you know?' Boyens isn't defensive, only honest. 'And I don't know that they ever were going to be. I don't necessarily disagree with some of the things critics said, I know we jumped the shark a bit with some of the stuff, but I'm okay with it, because we didn't make them for those people. The fans embraced them, so that was great. And I loved so much of what came out of it.'

They are also better films than the gimlet-eyed reactionaries suggested. For all the trilogy's flaws — rabbit-tugged sleds, waffly White Council meetings, CGI incontinence — watching them later with the pressure off and the storytelling is rich, the visuals often remarkable, and a flavour emerges that is distinctly their own. Armitage, the effortless McKellen, a charismatic Lee Evans as Bard, and the redoubtable if never fully realized little bastards all make their mark. Freeman is now an iconic Bilbo. Smaug magnificent.

Jackson would repeat the trick of *Extended Editions*, only now to arguably even more beneficial effect. Not for more Tolkien, but the extended Jacksonness: skinny-dipping in Rivendell; an even trippier journey through Mirkwood; the rollicking, gore-splattered war wagon chase through *The Battle of the Five Armies* that is part *Ben-Hur*, part Buster Keaton and part *Braindead*.

CHAPTER 19

Augmented Reality

Peter Jackson gratefully accepts a mug of tea. He is seated on a different sofa in a different office, wood-panelled and decluttered (rumours abound of Fran Walsh's profound influence over the interior decoration).

The director's previous inner sanctum at Portsmouth Road Post was concealed behind a bookcase in a perfectly ordinary stationery cupboard that swung open as if by magic. Within was a mini-museum to Jackson's many fascinations: First World War memorabilia, Boer War uniforms, back issues of *Famous Monsters Of Filmland*, and top-of-the-range Apple tech. Everything was in order, apart from the desk, which was a bombsite. 'Oh that desk, it was a wonder he could find anything,' groans Philippa Boyens affectionately. Ent-high shelves were festooned with collectibles beyond the reach of most collectors: *Mars Attacks!* aliens (real), *Corpse Bride* dolls (real), Tracy brothers puppets (replicas, but he has 'extremely fragile' originals), even two maquettes of the holographic chess set from the Millennium Falcon. These are the *actual* Phil Tippett-made maquettes from 1977, which Weta Digital would helpfully scan for J.J. Abrams to use in the *Star Wars* revival *The Force Awakens*. While in the UK, Jackson visited the set, but claims not to be a *Star Wars* obsessive in any great way. He's more of a *Doctor Who* man.

But that was all safely stowed elsewhere when the headquarters of Jackson's filmmaking operation was transplanted up the road to the newly built Park Road Post facility — a lovely, Art Deco building equipped with edit suites, screening rooms and sound effects studios. All earthquake-proofed with the addition of a layer of rubber to the foundations on which the building can safely wobble. The offices of the director of *Bad Taste* are officially shockproof.

It is 23 November 2016, fourteen-and-a-half years since I first ventured to New Zealand, and a familiar spring drizzle dampens the Miramar boulevards outside the windows. Between productions, Park Road Post has the ghostly quiet of an out-of-season resort. The Overlook Hotel springs to mind. The corridors are lavishly carpeted, and vintage travel posters line the walls, encouraging tourists to New Zealand, 'A world in itself!'

The shoeless Jackson, excepting a few new grey hairs flecking his rumpled black hair and no need for glasses since laser surgery, remains unshakeably the same man he was back then. He fixes himself on the sofa, apologizing in advance for his memory. But with only a slight nudge, events and feelings return from the past. To quote another model of unshakeable stoicism, The Dude abides.

Our latest and longest interview is underway, and Jackson admits he hasn't seen *The Lord of the Rings* films for a long time. 'It's funny,' he muses, 'I always get into this strange pattern where once I am through the premieres, where you obviously watch the completed movie, I have no desire to see the film again. I haven't even seen *Meet the Feebles* since it premiered.'

You should, I say: they hold up very well. As, in its own unique way, does *Meet the Feebles*.

He can only wince at the suggestion. 'It would be frustrating; I would just beat myself up. I'd see things that we should have done. I would imagine a scene playing in a totally differently way from the way that I shot it and I would like that new version better than the old one. . .'

All the things he might have done given more time or money, or if fate had played him a different hand; still making the film in his head even now.

Jackson has revisited them once since the original premieres when, in preproduction on *The Hobbit*, he watched them along-side Guillermo del Toro on the big screen, when Walsh and Boyens had joined them and giggled the whole way through.

Boyens shares much the same reluctance to go back as her collaborator. 'It was hard to sit and just receive it, you know?'

She admits the joy of simply reading the book has also been lost to her. She has uprooted every word of those thousand pages and it is impossible to replant them in her imagination.

Jackson is a good friend of the noted British hypnotist Derren Brown. He has often asked him, semi-seriously, if he could hyp-notise him to forget he ever made a movie. Then he could sit down and watch it without any knowledge that he was involved. 'And not know what happens next,' he explains. 'Because when you are shooting the movie, when you are *inside* a movie, you don't know what is good or bad.'

Brown has offered to try, but Jackson fears he may not be 'susceptible' enough for the hypnotism to catch. Still, he reflects, this would surely be the best way for a director to enter post-production — with no memory of production. 'You would just look at your cut and put a bit of common sense into it. That is why I never like looking at my films again. I think, "Why the hell did I do that?" You need a bit of perspective.'

*

Twenty years has passed since that fateful meeting with Bob Shaye at New Line. Two decades in which the films arrived, had their triumphant moment, and passed on into the timeless land where classics never grow old (a general rule of thumb is that it takes at least ten years of perspective for a film to be classifiable as a classic).

In that time there have been sorrows, particularly the untimely death of cinematographer and close friend, Andrew Lesnie, at fifty-nine from a heart attack in April 2015.

'Being an only child, I grew up wondering what it would be like to have a brother,' Jackson wrote in his moving tribute. 'It wasn't until today, in trying to deal with the terrible news of Andrew's passing, that I came to realize how much he had become that person for me. . .'

Lesnie, *Ain't It Cool News* wrote, 'was the Cheshire Cat behind the camera with Peter Jackson'. The obit recalled them giggling together, full of mischief as they wrought impossible magic.

The Lord of the Rings was acclaimed as the most popular novel of the twentieth century, the *Gone with the Wind* of fantasy, which by any reckoning should have made it the most coveted IP (intellectual property: the buzz term of twenty-first-century Hollywood) in the world of film. Yet it was a mountain that had refused to be conquered. At least, that is, to the satisfaction of its legions of fans.

It took this mischievous, unpretentious, determined Kiwi director to achieve the cinematic equivalent of his fellow countryman Sir Edmund Hillary, who was first to the summit of Everest. To the collective awe of the cast, Hilary once dropped by the set for a visit. They spent a lunchtime listening rapt to tales of his real-life exploits. There is something in the veins of this country that reaches for the sky.

To imagine Jackson apart from New Zealand is impossible. 'I don't think there's any other filmmaker in the world who is as specifically identified singularly with his country as Peter is,' says Ken Kamins. 'When you see Peter, the first words that come into your head are New Zealand.'

Jackson could never live in Beverly Hills, keeping an office on a Burbank backlot and power lunching to talk stratagems and scripts. He's smart and savvy about the business, aware of the ties that bind his ambitions to the studio system, but he is happy to remain an outsider.

Kamins continues his homily. 'Apart from the responsibility that he has over a number of employees at Weta Digital, at Park Road Post, at the Stone Street Studios, in many ways he's exactly the same guy that I met almost twenty-five years ago. The only thing that's changed is the height of the wall surrounding his house. And a lot of that is because he opted to stay in New Zealand. He's opted to remain a Kiwi, both culturally and spiritually. That roots him in who he is. There's a piece of Peter that, if you told him that from this point forward and forevermore all he can make are low budget genre movies, he'd be perfectly happy.'

It's not a pose, his manager insists, it's a belief system, a way of life, a state of mind. To travel to far off locations is a good reason to resist a project. As *The Lord of the Rings* gathered up awards from around the world, Jackson perfected the art of sending in zany video acceptance speeches (Gollum's vulgar triumph at MTV had been Jackson's idea). These typified his reluctance to travel and an unwillingness to take such accolades too seriously. For the Empire Awards (on which I worked), he provided a trilogy of Best Film videos: Jackson literally submerged in a sea of tangled celluloid (he was apparently editing *The Two Towers*); Jackson and Richard Taylor suited in Rohan armour, over which the director had balanced his specs; and finally sputtering out his lines while riding a possibly symbolic rollercoaster.

Jackson once told me that the principal advantage of basing *The Lord of the Rings* in Miramar was that it was 'only five minutes from home'. He wasn't kidding. Home is key to everything. It's a theme of both Middle-earth trilogies. The Dwarves' quest is to reclaim a beloved homeland, a devotion that Bilbo comes to recognize that he shares with his companions. Frodo's fundamental motivation to carry the Ring being to protect the Shire. Among the many motivations in undertaking Tolkien, Jackson wanted to show the world that New Zealand was capable of doing so and not going to worry about it apparently being impossible. Mountains are there to be climbed.

Twenty years on from that last-ditch meeting, Jackson sits out the dance of Hollywood. The rituals of power hold no interest; the shifting sands of influence. Kamins admits his client has become a little disillusioned at Hollywood's current modus operandi: superhero films leave him cold, although a studio would leap tall buildings for the chance of having Jackson enter the comic-book fray.

'I think he looks at the studio movie model and thinks it's broken.'

That said, Weta Digital has helped provide valiant pixels for *Man of Steel*, *The Avengers*, and *Justice League*. And Marvel shot *The Avengers* episodes three and four as two films back-to-back. I wonder where they got that idea?

And hasn't Jackson always been this way? Not necessarily disillusioned, but detached from the trains of faceless, terrified, overthinking executives desperate to protect their investments and save their jobs. This distance is what allowed him to invest such personality into his films, so much of himself. Shaye, too, was not some passive-aggressive corporate bully. He was almost an old-school Hollywood type, sulky and defensive, but always engaged with the glorious possibility of filmmaking.

The Oscar victory doesn't play on Jackson's mind. Now he has won one there is no urge to seek out the circumstances and material that might lead directly to another. 'It's almost a relief that I don't have to think about that,' he laughs. Talk like that in Hollywood and they would imprison you on a therapist's rooftop.

'I'm the same person who made the Super 8 movies and *Bad Taste*,' he says. He has achieved everything he ever dreamed of when he turned his mind to filmmaking at the tender age of nine (with the exception of shooting a Bond movie) and it feels liberating not having to worry.

'I have no interest in trying to beat myself, in trying to make every film bigger and better than *The Lord of the Rings*, because it probably never will be.' Jackson seeks only to reinforce the Peter Jacksonness that enabled *The Lord of the Rings* to happen.

In this, it is impossible to downplay Walsh's contribution to Jackson as a filmmaker and Middle-earth. So many of the ironies, the darker emotional shades and complexities of character, branch out from her talents and predilections. There is an argument to be made that she co-directed these films. Beyond her quota of second-unit scenes, she was fundamental to the storytelling. It was, in the end, her suggestion.

But to make that argument is to miss the point: they have found the perfect balance, this instinctual give and take to one another's strengths. Jackson the visualist and figurehead, who can see the film in his head. With Walsh the chief architect of character.

It is a partnership built on absolute trust. I rarely saw Walsh and Jackson together while shooting. There was no need to confer. He notes that Walsh is currently away in Los Angeles casting *Mortal Engines*, their next project. They have handed the directorial reins to Christian Rivers, with that indomitable three-headed writing-producing team providing the script and infrastructure.

'That feels right,' says Kamins. 'And it also feels familial. The entire crew down there is really excited that Christian's getting a shot at something of size and scope and that a studio's going to get behind. It's a rekindling of some very old feelings.'

'I'm happy to be producer,' says Jackson. In 2008, he had been all set to direct the adaptation of Philip Reeve's young adult science-fiction story — depicting a far-flung future in which cities crawl across the ruined Earth on giant wheels — but *The Hobbit* had hoved into view, blocking the horizon. A decade later he is content to play mentor again, and guide a new generation.

Creatively, his attention has been grabbed by the possibilities of augmented reality (AR). This involves a view of the real world that has been supplemented by computer graphics and sound via a smart phone, iPad or, when the technology catches up, adapted glasses. While it has so far been orientated toward game technology (*Pokemon Go* being a big success) through their new division, WingNutAR, Jackson and Walsh have joined forces with Apple to explore the storytelling possibilities of the medium. In other words, Jackson could bring Middle-earth to the middle of your living room.

*

It has also been twenty years since Boyens came down from Auckland with a head full of Tolkien and even more crucially an idea of what the book *meant* to people. It was Boyens who wrote the prologue, that aperitif of Middle-earth's antiquity. Boyens, then, who set the tone: the hugeness and strangeness of Tolkien's vision. She ensured it was treated as a literary adaptation not a fantasy film.

The list goes ever on: Richard Taylor, Andrew Lesnie, Dan Hennah, Carolynne Cunningham, Barrie Osborne, Ken Kamins, Mark Ordesky, Alan Lee, John Howe, Joe Letteri, Andy Serkis, Viggo Mortensen, Sir Ian McKellen, Elijah Wood, and the entire cast and crew who bent their back to Jackson's vision. In retrospect, every one of them an integral piece of the puzzle. Even Shaye and Michael Lynne played their part.

Jackson is a natural collaborator. A 'sponge', picking and choosing the best of what he absorbs. In turn, those same collaborators paint a picture of the many facets of this singular personality that made the films possible.

A convenient comparison is often drawn with Frodo, but on the surface there is something unlikely to Jackson as the all-conquering director. He is reserved and a little shy, away in his own world. He has preserved the best parts of his youthful innocence, dreaming the dreams on behalf of the nine-year-old smitten by *King Kong*.

'I hate to use the word geeky,' Hugo Weaving told me during

The Hobbit, 'but there's always that little boy who's playing with toy soldiers. And there's this brilliant mind.'

'He's the wisest, toughest nine-year-old you've ever met,' said Boyens in 2005.

There is a will of iron beneath the jokes and enthusiasm. Tantrums might not be in his genetic make-up, but Jackson is impossible to bully. 'There is no exterior force that can influence him,' says Neil Blomkamp. He withstood the hurricanes of Harvey, the squabbles with New Line, the mockery of Hollywood and the New Zealand weather and got his films made.

That takes mental toughness.

Shaped by his *Bad Taste* days, when he was responsible for every department on the film and gives the liveliest performance, his technical facility is bewilderingly brilliant. As well as being able to draw and sculpt with a high degree of skill, he can turn his hand to every facet of filmmaking. Barring an ability to write code, he could work for any department.

'It seems to me that there was no problem on *The Lord of the Rings* that couldn't have been solved if we could have cloned Peter,' says Costa Botes. 'He can't be everywhere at once but yet he wants to be. He wants that level of control. I guess any filmmaker that's trying to put their personal stamp on something will.'

Jackson is a geek auteur; an artist raised on Hammer and Harryhausen and a man of healthy contradictions. 'Every film I make is a personal film,' he once told me. 'How can it not be?' *Bad Taste, Braindead, Heavenly Creatures*, and *The Lord of the Rings* are all products of the same sensibility, and the same ability to convince others to embrace his madness.

He brought to these films the meticulousness of a model-builder, the ability to clamp his mind to a task. 'He's a control freak in the best way,' noted Martin Freeman. 'He will shoot the bejazzers out of something until he is happy.'

Says Botes, 'What I noticed in the editing of *Lord of the Rings* is that Peter would look at *everything*. Endless shots of swords being drawn, horses galloping by: there was *so* much footage. It was an unbelievable amount of footage. But the more options he had, the happier he seemed. I was thinking, "This would drive me absolutely batshit crazy." But he has that kind of mind. He's ideally suited to it.'

'He could mix with the best, if you want to start deconstructing theories on filmmaking,' posits Boyens, 'but that is not his approach; he just wants to tell a story.'

Jackson can happily discuss the psychology behind individual Scorsese shots, but he blends intellectualism and artistry with the subversive spirit of one of nature's practical jokers. When asked to attend a Hollywood dinner in tribute to fellow Kiwi Sam Neill, Jackson unsurprisingly sent a film. Shot with the help of Botes, it began with Jackson in a car saying, 'I think we should show all your friends your house in Wellington, because it's lovely.' In a single shot, he drives up to the house where a gang of Hell's Angels have amassed outside. They'd broken into Neill's house. 'And it was really his house,' hoots Botes. 'Peter had managed to get hold of the key — and we drive up to a scene of devastation.'

Jackson tries to stop them stealing all Neill's things but leaves with his tail between his legs, imploring the camera that, 'We're going to put it all right, Sam. We're going to get all those ugly stains out of the carpet. . .' And while he's talking, the house actually catches fire and explodes behind him. It was all shot handheld and he had given it to Weta Digital to put in the effects.

And there was that man-of-steel determination that a way will be found whatever the hurdle. Or if you couldn't find a way, make one. Hennah recalled telling his director they had found the perfect location for Edoras in that remote glacial valley. But he warned his friend it was seriously inaccessible and would require the building of three bridges and a mile of road just for construction access. 'His response was that we were making an epic film that needed epic locations and a few bridges and a bit of road shouldn't get in our way.'

Whenever anything looked daunting, Hennah would be reminded of his director's adage — you can always build a road.

'Peter will push and he will push,' laughs Taylor, 'but it is always pushing to get a better picture from all involved, as opposed to building up his own ego. There is no ego.'

Up on Mount Ruapehu, their sacred Mount Doom, there were several units running. Co-producer Rick Porras, a San Francisco native who had began his career as Robert Zemeckis' assistant, was directing second unit on a side of the mountain away from Peter and the main unit. 'There was a moment where we looked out and the light was changing, the sun was getting near that golden hour and then this incredible cloud formation seemed to appear. It was hard not to feel like there was some magic in it all, as it just seemed to come from nowhere and unfold in front of us. We had a camera so we started shooting, and we couldn't wait for dailies so we could show off our cloud coup. Next day, we're all in dailies and we started seeing that same cloud come up from different angles. . . Everyone had stopped what they were doing to shoot that cloud.'

To be directed by Peter, claims Sean Astin, 'is to feel included in the cosmic game'.

*

To paraphrase another American, we should not only ask what Jackson did for *The Lord of the Rings*, but what *The Lord of the Rings* did for this humble Kiwi. Never let it be forgotten that a quiet Oxford don with a prodigious imagination was the great well from which these films were drawn. In deciding to make a fantasy film, Jackson and Walsh went right to the source. Boyens' precious participation came about because she was devoted foremost to the professor. Lee and Howe were inspired first by the books. Something about this vast yet intimate story filled cast and crew with a supernatural devotion.

'It was a love of *The Lord of the Rings*,' says Taylor, 'the world it depicted, that pushed everyone to go to levels beyond where they ever thought they could go. It set a level for us to attain.'

During the shoot, on the glue-strewn Workshop benches and at the workstations of Weta's weary animators, well-thumbed copies of the book were ever-present for consultation. Tolkien was an invisible presence right across the production.

There is something in the arrangement of archetypes and a quest narrative within the conviction of Tolkien's world building that has spoken to and goes on speaking to millions. Frodo's quest is a universal one — the underdog triumphing because of his very unlikeliness and his wise choice of companions.

Says Howe, 'It can't be denied there's a spirit in Tolkien's writing, he struck a chord with so many people. I've got to know a lot of kids who saw the movies first and then will read the books. Which is interesting because it's backwards for people like me.'

There is a spiritual dimension to our love of Middle-earth. Channelling the ancient traditions of mythology (from Norse to Greek to Biblical) Tolkien served as a prism for that love of dense, historical, quasi-religious arcana that now entwines the comic-book universe. There is clearly a cultural dependency on this form of imaginary archaeology (the necessity of story is itself a theme of the book).

Tolkien's ultimate ambition was to establish a mythology for Britain. He ended up giving one to the world. When he set out to make *Star Wars* in 1977 George Lucas explicitly delved into those mythical archetypes*, and lo, it still has the power to transport generations even as the joins begin to show.

Even then, the books are more than repositories of myth. Tolkien claimed the central theme was death itself and 'the

---

* Specifically, he studied Joseph Campbell's study of comparative mythology *The Hero with a Thousand Faces*, whose findings could be applied to *The Lord of the Rings*. Campbell posits the idea that myths all share the same fundamental structure — the 'monomyth'. Herein a hero leaves the safety of home for a 'region of supernatural wonder' and there encounters 'fabulous forces'.

desire for deathlessness'. In other words, he was preaching about the immortality of story. While largely absent of pre-scribed religion, the book is infused with the author's staunch Catholic faith and critics have noted the subtle daubs of Catholic imagery in Jackson's interpretation — Galadriel as the Madonna, anyone?

Tolkien raises questions we often ask of the real world. Are the heroes of Middle-earth guided by nothing but their own free will or does fate play its part? 'There are other forces at work in this world, Frodo,' Gandalf tells the Ringbearer in a lovely moment of calm before the storm of Moria, and without belabouring events Boyens made sure the script hinted at the various tiers of Tolkien's pantheon. The wizard, whose supernatural supervision of the world is bidden by unseen forces, predicts that Gollum is still fated to play his part. Expiring after his battle with the Balrog, he is 'sent back' to finish his appointed task.

The films certainly hone in on Tolkien's abhorrence at the encroachment of the city upon the countryside of his upbring-ing. The books are viewed as anti-industrialist. Nature is depicted as wise and decent; the rise of machinery — embodied by the pits of Isengard (and the clanking of Howard Shore's anvils) — equated with evil.

Tolkien refuted that his story was in any way an allegory of the Second World War and the Nazi blight, but while writing *The Lord of the Rings* throughout that period admitted he had felt its 'oppression'. But as already noted, it was his personal expe-riences of the First World War and the Somme that are buried deep in the fiction.

The point is Middle-earth is open to many different interpre-tations. I'm partial to an ingenious reading of events that posits Frodo and his fellow hobbits as symbolic teens thrust from the idyll of childhood (the Shire) out into the forbidding world of adulthood (Middle-earth). The Ring, curse it, represents the death of innocence with the perils of adult responsibility. From there it is all committee meetings (Council of Elrond), employment

(Frodo is 'appointed' Ringbearer) and the burdens of growing up (the treacherous world). Even the females are depicted as some-what angelic and out of reach...

Jackson tells me a story about a woman who came to a book signing in New York shortly after *The Fellowship of the Ring* had come out. She had been standing patiently in line to have her book signed (presumably one of the many making-ofs that fol-lowed in the films' wake), and finally found herself in a brief audience with the director.

'I've seen your film twenty-three times,' she informed him, without much ado.

'Which is more than I have,' laughs Jackson, remembering.

A couple of months later he was in Los Angeles at another event that offered the public the chance to mingle, however momentarily (as Jackson's celebrity grew with each film, such public-facing events became untenable), with the makers of the hit epic and there she was, patiently awaiting her turn once more.

'Remember me?' she asked.

Jackson had smiled back. 'Ah, you're the person who has seen *The Fellowship of the Ring* twenty-three times.'

'It's forty-seven now!' she beamed.

Buoyed by the capacious internet coverage and Jackson's instinctive engagement with his potential audience, the films were welcomed into the world by a readymade fanbase. Which was largely an extension of the book's phenomenal following. Naturally, there were purists who sniffed. Those who will find no peace unless they had been treated to every nook, cranny and Goldberry of Tolkien's sprawling mythos, but for many serious devotees of the book the films were an astonishing, kindred experience.

What was on screen matched our own imaginations. I was watching my Hobbiton, my Moria, Lothlórien or Edoras. Jackson believes much of that is down to the art of Lee and Howe having come to dominate our picture of Middle-earth, but there per-sisted that sense that the filmmakers were finding a world that already existed. Tolkien's creation had been downloaded into culture. This was how Minas Tirith looked, simple as that.

Since the trilogy's success, there has been a wonderful blurring of the edges of reality as fans make their way to New Zealand on pilgrimages into both a fictional space and onto a real-life filmmaking trail.

'Once you've gone beyond the business of paying seventy bucks to go to Matamata to get pushed through, that becomes totally unimportant,' says Howe, recalling the fans who come to visit the busy Hobbiton attraction, passing along the road from the gift-shops to see it there, resplendent, a small corner of living myth. 'Not only are you seeing the landscape itself, but you're overlaying all of your memories in a really unique way. I find that quite moving actually, and very much central to the whole human experience.'

There has been surprisingly little scholarly writing on the films. Film academics are seemingly as phobic of Tolkien as their literary counterparts. In one of the few higher-brow pieces, written for *Film Comment*, Graham Fuller thrills to what he calls the 'interior movement' within the film: a network of flashbacks, memories, recollections and dreams that threads through the story. This he sees as 'part of the myth-making process'. Each of the prologues provide visions of the past, be they Galadriel's account of far-flung history, Frodo's psychic encounter with Gandalf's recent fate or, most powerfully, Gollum's memory of his Ring-bound downfall. Memory is a big theme in both book and film. Tolkien saw 'hoarding memory' in the shape of stories as a way of forestalling death.

For all of Jackson's commitment to realism, the trilogy has an otherworldly quality (which separates it from *Game of Thrones*). Aragorn is often caught dreaming of Arwen (much of their romance takes place in his head), while Galadriel (through her liquid mirror) and Elrond provide elusive Elvish prophecies. The influence of art (centred on Lee and Howe) gives Middle-earth a lovely, painterly texture rather than a crisp, digital one, another reason for rejection of 48 FPS on *The Hobbit*.

Fuller calls the films 'a dream of cinema'.

He also asks whether they even reached beyond the 'pseu-do-mythical' trappings of the book and provided greater psychological realism. One of the great joys of the films is how Jackson, his fellow writers and his cast never allow their characters to feel archetypal. They are fully alive.

Did new themes arise fifty years after the books were published? Viggo Mortensen, a tuning fork for the grand interpretation, certainly thought so. Myths are as relevant to the now as to the then.

Frodo's quest is not to find a magical weapon, but to rid the world of one. Tolkien may be dismissed as escapism, but both book and the extraordinary films adapted from them only grow more relevant and more hopeful in the face of darkness.

There is a private joke between the three writers. Whenever one of them brings up a potential project, something they might get down to in five years or so, Jackson will shake his head. 'Then I'll say, "No no no, we'll be too busy. *The Silmarillion* is coming up, and that'll be seven movies." That is our constant joke to each other. . . At least, I hope it is a joke.'

Encompassing all of Middle-earth's ancient history right back to its creation, *The Silmarillion* had been Tolkien's lifelong project, which he never saw into print. His son Christopher edited together his father's mythopoeic writings and poems, including detailed family trees, for posthumous publication in 1977. Therefore the rights were never part of the deal Tolkien struck with United Artists. Which rather rains on the fan dream of Jackson turning his eye to the great tragedies of Elves and men.

He sounds philosophical. 'Christopher Tolkien, who is executor of the estate, as is his right, doesn't want to release the film rights.'

Even then, the book presents sizeable hurdles — admittedly, something once said about *The Lord of the Rings*. Not least is the fact that it is a collection of stories, and most of those are more poetic outlines. It also suffers a lack of hobbits. With work, I suggest it might be better suited to an HBO-style series.

'Or a series of films! You think HBO, Warner think films.' Jackson has clearly given this a modicum of thought. 'You are small-minded. Warner are big-minded! It could never be one film, at all. The stories need a lot of fleshing out.'

Including the tricky business of the book parsing thousands of years of conflict, hence there is no single protagonist, rather generations of them.

'Yes, it is a history,' Jackson muses. 'This would be literally a series of different films where you have new characters. The Elvish ones linger around, but there is no single character. . . Hey, I'm not going to talk about that! You've got me talking about *The Silmarillion!*'

*

Films are just films in the end. Books only books. Nevertheless, there is something greater than the considerable sum of its three-part adaptation at work in Jackson's *The Lord of the Rings*. You might call it the fated moment of these films: a creative journey like no other, unrepeatable and historic, achieved — outwardly at least — against the odds.

'My career will always be divided into before *The Lord of the Rings* and afterwards,' says Jackson. 'I'm fine with that.'

Blessed with awards, critical acclaim and financial rewards, the films were finally a triumph of storytelling, and the need for storytelling. They were also a reinforcement of what cinema could achieve: not simply as groundbreaking spectacle, technical artistry and great acting, but as pure transportive human experience. Of course, Jackson didn't set out to make a masterpiece. He set out to amaze his younger self by simply following his own instincts. Great films tell two stories: that which is written in the script and in the eyes of the director, and the story of their making. The rigours that went into creating *Apocalypse Now* became ingrained in the celluloid. David Lean's obsessions fill up the world of *Lawrence of Arabia*. The unflagging determination and giddy imagination that went into *Bad Taste* declared their own potential.

In the blending of Middle-earth and New Zealand, in the sheer daring and lack of inhibition, with a cast and crew inspired by this mix of director and book to achieve the impossible, the experience of making the films magnified them yet further.

We would do well to leave the last word to Frodo and his erstwhile keeper, Elijah Wood.

'I felt like an adult when I went there, but I think I was more of an adult when I finished. Genuinely. And so much of that was the life experience afforded to me as a result of working on those films. We all went on individual journeys. There were people that died along the way. There were babies born. There were marriages, and there were breakups. Our experience in the years of working on *Lord of the Rings* encapsulated every aspect of life. All the ups and downs and every kind of nuance and element of life: we shared in that. That's an exceptional thing. It's still a part of our lives. And out of it came three pretty good movies. You know?'

We know.

Afterword

As this book passed into its final stages, like a prophecy fulfilled the news broke. On 13 November 2017, Amazon Prime Video, the television and film production arm of the online retailer, announced a multi-season commitment to produce a television show based on *The Lord of the Rings*. The television rights (which had never been included in the original deal with United Artists) had reportedly set them back something in the region of $250 million (the figures were not officially unveiled). That is just to get them to a blank page — the production costs, which are sure to amount to the hundreds of millions, are on top of that. Nearly twenty years after Jackson went cap in hand to New Line, Middle-earth is the most desirable property in town.

Jeff Bezos, the CEO of Amazon, is known to be a big fan of fantasy fiction, and will likely have looked on enviously at the success HBO had with *Game of Thrones*. And with the saga of *Game of Thrones* drawing to a close, the timing looks propitious.

'We are thrilled to be taking *The Lord of the Rings* fans on a new epic journey in Middle Earth,' said Amazon scripted series chief Sharon Tal Yguado in an official press release. What was noticeable about the announcement was that this was specifically a deal for *The Lord of the Rings*, not Middle-earth as a whole. This was not a deal for *The Silmarillion*. Neither was this a deal to remake the book. The press release made clear that the series 'was set in Middle-earth and explores new storylines preceding Tolkien's *The Fellowship of the Ring*.'

Which could mean weeks before Bilbo's party or thousands of years into the past. Tolkien watchers immediately focused their attention on Appendices A and B, which are attached to the end of *The Return of the King*, and therefore technically covered under the provision of having the rights to *The Lord of the Rings*. A and B are not intricate family trees or Dwarvish lexicons, but give a brief account of some of the history leading up to Frodo's mission. Appendix A, in fact, recaps many of the ancient events covered by *The Silmarillion*, including the fall of the Númenórean kings (aka Aragorn's ancestors) and their return to Middle-earth. It also covers the history of Rohan and some of the events that precede *The Hobbit*. Appendix B concerns more wizardly matters, and includes an account of the battles of the north during the War of the Ring (i.e. concurrent to the events of the *Lord of the Rings* films), so seems a less likely source. There is the option, if all goes well, to create a spin-off show as well.

What is so telling is the shift in paradigm to television, as Mark Ordesky predicted, with all the benefits of long-form storytelling. Length will be a boon to encompassing the breadth of the world. Significantly, the series will be made in co-operation with New Line Cinema and Warner Bros. Entertainment, which automatically throws open the possibility for Amazon's Middle-earth to share Peter Jackson's.

As I disappear into print, there is no word on the involvement of Jackson, Weta or New Zealand. Would they transfer to Scotland or Canada, or as Forrest J. Ackerman once proposed, the wild expanses of the USA? Nor, for that matter, is there any news on the involvement of any of the established cast. Would they dare recast a Gandalf or an Elrond? One report, by the film website *Deadline*, contended that Amazon 'has not tried to enlist the help of, or even reached out to Peter Jackson.' Could they ever hope to recapture, or somehow match, the element of Jacksonian magic in the mix?

Whatever the case may be, however fine the Amazon series turns out, the shadow of the past will loom large.

Acknowledgements

Foremost, I owe an immeasurable debt to Peter Jackson for his time, friendship, honesty, humour, wisdom, movie banter and multiple cups of tea. There are so many times he went above and beyond, not least for giving me unprecedented access to his filmmaking world and encouraging me to write this book. If not a biography, as such, this book stands as a tribute to the quality of both man and director.

The full list of cast and crew who have given their time and thoughts over the years can be found in the Bibliography. For the record, the scariest was Christopher Lee, the strangest was Viggo Mortensen, and the maddest was John Rhys-Davies (yet offering never less than wonderful copy). My particular appreciation goes to the on-going generosity of Andy Serkis, Elijah Wood, Alan Lee, John Howe, the mastermind Ken Kamins, and the always delightful Philippa Boyens. With special mention to Mark Ordesky, a prince among geeks and a great resource.

Then there are those, too, behind the scenes who have not only smoothed the path but been very fine company: the rock that is Sebastian Meek, the awesome Melissa Booth, Dominic Sheehan, Matt Dravitski, Jan Blenkin, Claire Raskind, Ri Streeter, Amanda Walker, Vanessa Gray, Louisa Radcliffe, and the late, lovely Tracy Lorie of New Line who made those early trips to New Zealand very special. Tracy was always the consummate professional, even braving a local bar at an ungodly hour to watch the 2002 World Cup football games.

Massive thanks also have to go to my friends and colleagues at *Empire* magazine through the years. Especially to former editors Colin Kennedy and Mark Dinning for indulging my disappearances to New Zealand and my bulging word counts, and also encouraging me to one day write this book. And to my Fellowship of companions: Debi Berry, Kelly Preedy, Ian Freer, Dan Jolin (for prime Tolkien pedantry), Liz Beardsworth, Damon Wise, Chris Lupton, Chris Hewitt, Philip de Semlyen, and the brilliant Nick de Semlyen for his knowledge, assistance, and peerless Richard Taylor impression.

To my editor Chris Smith for his patience, velvet-gloved support and deep-dish Tolkien knowledge, I salute you.

Finally, my thanks go to the understanding of my family and friends, who can't quite fathom what I've been up to or why it has taken me so long, but have supported me nevertheless. And, as ever, my endless appreciation goes to Kat, who I love and adore and who makes all things possible.

Picture Credits

Pierre Vinet (page 2 [top], page 3 [middle], page 6 [top] & page 9 [middle]); Ian Nathan (page 3 [bottom], page 6 [bottom], page 8 & pages 14–15); Getty Images (page 4); New Line Productions, Inc. (page 10, top); Berliner Images (page 10 [bottom] & page 11 [bottom]).

Photos on pages 12, 13 & 16 © Warner Bros. Entertainment Inc. All rights reserved.

All other photographs reproduced courtesy of Peter Jackson from his personal collection.

While every effort has been made to trace the owners of copyright material reproduced herein and secure permissions, the publishers would like to apologise for any omissions and will be pleased to incorporate missing acknowledgements in any future edition of this book.

Bibliography

AUTHOR INTERVIEWS (2002–2017)
Peter Jackson, Fran Walsh, Philippa Boyens, Richard Taylor, Mark Ordesky, Ken Kamins, Andy Serkis, Elijah Wood, Sean Astin, Sir Ian McKellen, Viggo Mortensen, John Rhys-Davis, Sean Bean, Orlando Bloom, Billy Boyd, Dominic Monaghan, Liv Tyler, Cate Blanchett, Hugo Weaving, Christopher Lee, Bernard Hill, Brad Dourif, Miranda Otto Shane Rangi, Tim Wong, Martin Freeman, Richard Armitage, James Nesbitt, William Kirchner, Jed Brophy, Ken Stott, Aidan Turner, Stephen Hunter, Evangeline Lilly, Lee Evans, Barry Humphries, Alan Lee, John Howe, Joe Letteri, Matt Aitken, Gino Acevedo, Wayne Stables, Christian Rivers, Costa Botes, Cameron Chittock, Barrie Osborne, Stephen Regelous, Andrew Lesnie, Peter King, Dan Hennah, Ngila Dickson,

BOOKS AND MAGAZINES

Adams, Doug, *The Music of The Lord of the Rings Films*, Carpentier, 2016
Astin, Sean, *There and Back Again: An Actor's Tale*, Virgin Books, 2004
Bach, Steven, *Final Cut: Dreams and Disaster in the Making of Heaven's Gate*, Faber & Faber, 1985
Biskind, Peter, *Down and Dirty Pictures*, Simon & Schuster, 2004
Brodie, Ian, *The Lord of the Rings: Location Guidebook*, Harper Collins, 2003
Burgess, Clare & Hawker, Luke, *The Art of Film Magic: 20 Years of Weta*, HarperCollins, 2014
Carpenter, Humphrey, *J.R.R. Tolkien: A Biography*, George Allen & Unwin, 1977

Carpenter, Humphrey edited by (with the assistance of Christopher Tolkien), *The Letters of J.R.R. Tolkien*, George Allen & Unwin, 1981

Day, David, *A Tolkien Bestiary*, Gramercy, 1979

Garth, John, *Tolkien and The Great War*, HarperCollins, 2003

Holm, Ian, *Acting My Life: The Autobiography*, Corgi, 2004

Kocher, Paul, *Master of Middle-earth, The Achievement of J.R.R. Tolkien*, Pimlico, 1972

Pearce, Joseph, *Tolkien: Man & Myth: A Literary Life*, HarperCollins, 1998

Serkis, Andy, *Gollum: How We Made Movie Magic*, Andy Serkis, HarperCollins, 2003

Shippey, Tom, *J.R.R. Tolkien, Author of the Century*, HarperCollins, 2001

Sibley, Brian, *Peter Jackson: A Film-maker's Journey*, HarperCollins, 2006

Smith, Jim & Matthews, J. Clive, *The Lord of the Rings: The Films, The Books, The Radio Series*, Virgin Books, 2004

Tolkien, J.R.R., *The Hobbit*, George Allen & Unwin, 1937

Tolkien, J.R.R., *The Lord of the Rings*, George Allen & Unwin, 1954, 1955

Tolkien, J.R.R. (edited by Christopher Tolkien), *The Silmarillion*, George Allen & Unwin (Publishers) Ltd, 1977

Woods, Paul A. edited by, *Peter Jackson: From Gore to Mordor*, Plexus Publishing 2005

ARTICLES

Aftab, Kaleem, *Orlando Bloom Interview, The Independent*, 19 April 2014

Auden, W.H., *The Hero is a Hobbit, The New York Times*, 31 October 1954

Baille, Russell, *Taking on the World One Creature at a Time, The New Zealand Herald*, 24 September 2016

Baker, Bob, *And Frodo Makes Five, Los Angeles Times*, 29 February 2004

Bradley, Bill, *Dominic Monaghan Recalls David Bowie's Audition For Lord Of The Rings, The Huffington Post*, 27 January 2016

Brew, Simon, *Lord of the Rings: Nicolas Cage turned down role of Aragorn, Den of Geek*, 5 October 2015

Cinefex: April 2002, January 2003, January 2004

Cohen, Sandy, *Jackson's Motivation: 'Constant disappointment', The San Diego Union-Tribune*, 13 August 2009

Collin, Robbie, *Cannes: Harvey Weinstein on Tarantino's Western and Gyllenhaal's Oscar chances, Telegraph*, 20 May 2015

Collin, Robbie, *Tolkien's Adventures in Hollywood, Telegraph*, 12 December 2014

Cook, Terri, *The Geology of Middle-earth, Earth*, 15 December 2015

Davidson, Paul, *Sean Bean Talks Lord of the Rings, IGN*, 8 May 2001

Desowitz, Bill, *Immersed in Movies: Peter Jackson Talks 'The Hobbit' and Controversial 48 fps, Indiewire*, 5 December 2012

Digiacomo, Frank, *The Lost Tycoons, Vanity Fair*, 4 February 2009

Empire Magazine: February 2001, January 2002, September 2002, January 2003, October 2003, January 2004, August 2011, September 2012, January 2013, August 2013, January 2014, October 2014, January 2015

Fallon, Jimmy, *Interview with Jake Gyllenhaal, The Tonight Show*, 22 March 2016

Fitzsimons, Craig, *Interview with John Rhys-Davies, Hot Press*, 17 January 2002

French, Lawrence, *Creature Effects for The Two Towers, Peter Jackson: From Gore to Mordor*, 2005

Fuller, Graham, *Kingdom Come, Film Comment*, January/February 2004

Geiger, Angelo M., *Pullman: Trivializing Tolkien, Mary Victrix*, 25 January 2008

Goldstein, Patrick, *Bob Shaye has a Unique New Line, Los Angeles Times*, 10 July 2008

Goldstein, Patrick, *End of an Era at New Line, Beginning of One for De Luca, Los Angeles Times*, 30 January 2001

Goldstein, Patrick, *New Line Gambles on Becoming Lord of the Rings, Los Angeles Times*, 24 August 1998

Granshaw, Lisa, *Weta Workshop at 20: An Interview with Richard Taylor, SyfiWire*, 26 February 2015

Gray, Simon, *A Fellowship in Peril, American Cinematographer*, December 2002

Gray, Tim & Lang, Brett, *The Ringmaster, Variety*, 16 December 2014

Handy, Bruce, *Lord of the Rings Composer Howard Shore Talks Hobbits, His Start on SNL and Working With Martin Scorsese, Billboard*, 11 March 2014

Hogg, Trevor, *Ring Master: Matt Aitken talks about The Hobbit: The Desolation of Smaug, Flickering Myth*, 12 February 2014

Jancelewicz, Chris, *Dominic Monaghan And Billy Boyd: Lord Of The Rings Stars Reunite For Wild Thing Episode, The Huffington Post*, 5 June 2014

Keleman, Adam, *Interview: Guillermo del Toro, Slant Magazine*, 4 May 2009

Kermode, Jennie, *The Hobbit (1966) Film Review, Eye for Film*, 12 December 2014

Kiang, Jessica, *John Boorman Talks Almost Making 'Lord Of The Rings,'*

Working With Marcello Mastroianni, What He's Doing Next & More, *Indiewire,* 17 December 2012

Knowles, Harry, *One Ring, Ain't it Cool News.com/Total Film,* January 2002

Krok, Karol, *Interview: Howard Shore, The Digital Fix,* 10 December 2014

Lane, Anthony, *Full Circle, The New Yorker,* 5 January 2004

Leigh, Danny, *Viggo Mortensen on Actors Behaving Like Babies and Why He won't Vote for Hillary, The Guardian,* 8 September 2016

Levi, Dani, *Uma Thurman: Turning Down Lord of the Rings Was One of the 'Worst Decisions Ever Made', Variety,* 21 February 2017

Malinalda, Myla, *An Exclusive Interview with Doug Adams, Middle-earth News,* 18 December 2014

Malvern, Jack, *Writers Who Fell Under Tolkien's Spell, The Times,* 16 March 2017

McFadden, Robert D., *Saul Zaentz, Producer of Oscar-Winning Movies, Dies at 92, The New York Times,* 4 January 2014

McLean, Craig, *The Evolution of Andy Serkis, The Independent,* 12 July 2014

McLevy, Alex, *What's it like to be a Second-unit Director on Hollywood Blockbusters?, A.V. Club,* 22 June 2015

Mellor, Louisa, *John Rhys-Davies Interview: The Shannara Chronicles, Den of Geek,* 24 February 2016

Newsweek Special Edition, J.R.R. Tolkien – Mind of a Genius, March 2017

Norman, Philip, *The Prevalence of Hobbits, The New York Times,* 15 January 1967

Otto, Jeff, *Interview: Peter Jackson, IGN,* 8 December 2005

Pinchefsky, Carol, *The Impact (Economic and Otherwise) of Lord of the Rings/The Hobbit on New Zealand, Forbes,* 14 December 2012

Plimmer, Charlotte & Denis, *J.R.R. Tolkien: 'Film my books? It's Easier to Film The Odyssey', The Telegraph Magazine,* 22 March 1968

Rampell, Ed, *Viggo Mortensen: Do Something or Get Out of the Question, The Progressive,* 18 October 2016

Rérolle, Raphaëlle, *Tolkien, L'anneau de la Discorde, Le Monde,* 5 July 2012

Ressner, Jeffrey, *Fantastic Voyage, DGA Quarterly,* Summer 2013

Robinson, Tasha, *Interviews: Ralph Bakshi, A.V. Club,* 6 December 2000

Ross, Alex, *The Rings and the Rings, The New Yorker,* 22 December 2003

Roston, Tom, *The Chosen One, Premiere,* September 2001

Roston, Tom, *The Hero Returns, Premiere,* January 2003

Sargent, J.F., *5 Amazing Lord of the Rings Movies We'll Never See, Cracked. com,* 9 December 2014

Sellers, Robert, *The Strained Making of Apocalypse Now, The Independent,* 23 July 2009

Shashwat, D.C., *Interview: Jim Rygiel, Cyber Media News*, January 2006

Suskind, Alex, *11 Oscars to Rule Them All: An Oral History of The Return of the King's Best Picture win, Vanity Fair*, 27 February 2014

Tims, Anna, *How do I become . . . A Dialect Coach: Interview with Roisin Carty, The Guardian*, 15 October 2015

Unattributed, *A Heavenly Trajectory: 20 Years of Weta, The Land of Shadow.com*, 6 October 2014

Unattributed, *An Interview with Billy Boyd, IGN*, 14 April 2003

Unattributed, *Emiliana Torrini Interview, The Tripwire*, 4 December 2008

Unattributed, *Enya interview, The Legendary Musical Collection*, 2 June 2011

Unattributed, *James Cameron talks Avatar, Den of Geek*, 1 September 2009

Unattributed, *Lord of the Rings: Sean Connery Turned Down Role of Gandalf, The Huffington Post*, 19 September 2012

Unattributed, *Model Behaviour, The Economist*, 5 March 2009

Unattributed, *The Tolkien 'Curse': Author's grandson claims Lord of the Rings films were 'like a juggernaut that tore my family apart', MailOnline*, 19 November 2012

Wallace, Amy, *Eats Roadkill, Speaks Danish: The Appealingly Weird World of Viggo Mortensen, Esquire*, 27 February 2006

Weintraub, Stephen 'Frosty', *Exclusive Interview with Weta Workshop's Richard Taylor; Talks Lord of the Rings Blu-ray, The Hobbit, Neill Blomkamp, More, Collider.com*, 15 April 2010

Zalewski, Daniel, *Show the Monster, The New Yorker*, 7 February 2011

Index